GERMAN

A Structural Approach

WALTER F. W. LOHNES

AND F. W. STROTHMANN

Stanford University

GERMAN

A Structural Approach

W · W · Norton & Company · Inc · New York

Copyright © 1967, 1968 by W. W. Norton & Company, Inc.
First Edition

Library of Congress Catalog Card No. 67-11084

Printed in the United States of America
2 3 4 5 6 7 8 9 0

CONTENTS

CONTENTS

ANALYSIS (Sections **58–73**) 120

The Dative Case   Verbs with Only a Dative Object   Verbs Governing the Dative and Accusative   Adjectives Governing the Dative   Prepositions Governing the Accusative   Prepositions Governing the Dative   Word Order within the Inner Field   The German Perfect   Formation of the German Participle   The Use of **sein** and **haben** as Auxiliaries   Position of the Participle   The English and the German Perfect   Stretch-of-Time Phrases   Further Notes on Time Phrases   Replacement of **er, sie, es** by **der, die, das**   **es** and **das** Followed by Plural Verb Forms

EXERCISES 143

VOCABULARY 150

Review 153

Numbers—The Past—The Pluperfect—Verb-Last Position—Open Conditions—um . . . zu—mit—Word Formation

UNIT 5

PATTERNS 157

READING 167

Viel Lärm um nichts? (Fortsetzung) 167

ANALYSIS (Sections **74–96**) 169

Cardinal Numbers   The Past Tense of Weak Verbs   Regular Deviations in the Past of Weak Verbs   Past Tense of Strong Verbs   The Principal Parts of Strong and Irregular German Verbs   The Difference in the Use of the Perfect and the Past   The Use of the Past Tense of **haben, sein,** and the Modals   The Use of the Past in Dependent Clauses   The Formation of the Pluperfect   The Use of the Pluperfect   Dependent Clauses   Verb-Last Position   Position of the Subject in Dependent Clauses   Intonation of Dependent Clauses   Review: The Position of the German Finite Verb   Open Conditions   **um . . . zu,** in order to   **mit** as a Verbal Complement   Word Formation   The Suffixes **-chen** and **-lein**   The Suffix **-er**   Compound Nouns

EXERCISES 191

VOCABULARY 196

LIST OF STRONG AND IRREGULAR VERBS 197

Review 199

VOCABULARY CHECK LIST, UNITS 1–5 201

Review

**UNIT
10**   Adjectives

Predicate Adjectives and Adverbs   Predicate Adjectives and Attributive Adjectives   Strong
Endings   Weak Endings   Attributive Adjectives after **ein**-Words   Attributive Adjectives
without **der**- or **ein**-Words   Series of Attributive Adjectives   Variations   **der**-Words   **so,
solch**   **all, ganz**   Adjectives Used as Nouns   Participles Used as Adjectives   **-d** Adjectives   **derselbe**   **was für**   **viel, wenig**   **ander-**   **mehrere, einige, ein paar**   Word
Formation: Nouns of Action Derived from Weak Verbs   Nouns of Action Derived from Strong
Verbs   The Suffix **-ig**

**UNIT
11**   Infinitive Constructions—**hin** and **her**—Comparison of Adjectives—The Rhetorical
nicht—Numbers

Reflexive Verbs—Imperatives

**UNIT
12**

The Passive—**es** in the Front Field—Pre-Noun Inserts

**UNIT
13**

Dative Objects   Use of the Actional Passive to Express Activity as Such   The Use of **von,**
durch, and **mit** in Passive Sentences   Examples Illustrating the Difference between Action and
State   **sich . . . lassen**   The Impersonal **es** in the Front Field   **jetzt** and **nun**   Pre-Noun
Inserts

PREFACE

This book has been used in mimeographed form at Stanford University since the autumn of 1962. After the first draft, the manuscript was used in four classes of first-year German. The second draft represented an extensive revision, based on the experiences gained in this first trial run. After another round with a limited number of students, we started teaching all our first-year classes from this book in the autumn of 1964. Since then, several thousand students have used the book in mimeographed form, and the results have been most gratifying.

Without the support of our teaching assistants, the book could not have been written. These brave young souls, unhampered by tradition, always skeptical of dogma but always open to argument, very often knew better than their elders what can and what cannot be done in a classroom. Our attempts to explain German syntax have run the gamut of their criticism; they have wrestled with four successive mimeographed editions. Their help has been invaluable, and we thank them all.

Our debt and gratitude are also due to many others, too numerous to list by name, who helped with the preparation of the manuscript, with vocabulary counting, typing, proofreading, and running several million sheets of paper through a mimeograph machine. Our particular thanks go to Professor Jack M. Stein of Harvard University, the Norton advisory editor in German, who was our severest critic. Miss Katherine Stechmann and Mrs. Greta Frankel of W. W. Norton & Company, Inc., took infinite pains in copy-editing the finished manuscript. We also want to express our appreciation to Mrs. Heidi Hopkins who faithfully stenciled thousands of pages, only occasionally bemoaning our almost illegible hands.

The authors are indebted to the Embassy of Lebanon for permission to reproduce the photograph that appears on page 186 and to the German Information Center for use of the photographs on pages 47 and 51. The many photographs of German scenes that appear throughout this book were obtained and reproduced through the courtesy of the Deutsche Zentrale für Fremdenverkehr.

Stanford, California
June 1967

W. F. W. L
F. W. S.

INTRODUCTION

From the very beginning, this book aims at four skills: listening, speaking, reading, and writing. Our initial emphasis is on listening and speaking.

We have not, however, adopted a pure audio-lingual approach. Our aim of teaching students to speak truly idiomatic German has forced us to go beyond the audio-lingual method and to adopt what we would prefer to call "a structural approach."

In learning our native language, we absorb its syntactical principles by osmosis. We have no conceptual knowledge of many of these principles, and we certainly do not think of them every time we utter a sentence. Nevertheless, we know when to say *He thinks not* and when to say *He doesn't think*. By a series of "pattern drills" which stretches from birth into adolescence we learn how to use a linguistic code without necessarily having a conceptual knowledge of that code. An American student may not have heard of the difference between the past tense and the present perfect; nevertheless, he is not tempted to say *Washington has never told a lie*, whereas a German speaking English is likely to say just that, because in German he would say **Washington hat nie gelogen.**

A first-year student must certainly drill the structural patterns of German sentences intensively and over a long period of time before he can approach active control and native fluency. But since college students are linguistic adults who already speak one language, they cannot be exposed to the nonconceptual learning process a German infant is exposed to.

In the first place, our students do not have that much time. It takes a German child years to master the various forms of verbs like **gehen.** In one year of college German, an American student cannot afford to learn such verb forms by trial and error and from context only; he has to resort to the grammatical lullaby of **gehen, ging, ist gegangen** if he wants to master German strong verbs quickly.

In the second place, the linguistic "code" of English which our students have absorbed acts as a perpetual source of interference; it prevents them both from understanding many German sentences they hear and from actively using German sentence patterns correctly. No American student will automatically understand the German sentence **Ich habe lange keinen Kaffee trinken dürfen** to mean *For a long time I was not allowed to drink coffee (but I am allowed to now).* His own ingrained speech habits will incline him to misinterpret the sentence to mean *I haven't been allowed to drink coffee for a long time (and I still am not allowed to).* This is to be expected, for once we have absorbed one linguistic code by osmosis, we cannot learn a totally different code without a contrastive analytical knowledge of that new code.

In the third place, college students who want to learn German have reached an age at which they are both able and eager to grasp the systematic concept behind the individual phenomenon. When they play around with the simple sentence **Ich bleibe heute natürlich zu Hause,** they want to know, and know right away, why it is perfectly acceptable to say **Zu Hause bleibe ich heute natürlich nicht,** but impossible to say **Zu Hause bleibe ich heute natürlich.** A conceptual understanding of German sentence structure is a time-saving short cut, and we see no virtue in postponing the immediate comprehension of German syntax by refusing to tell the student, as he manipulates structural patterns, what the principles underlying these patterns are. We are very much in favor of "keeping grammar out of the classroom"; but since we are also against "teaching grammar behind closed doors," we suggest that structural syntactical analysis be handled in a new way.

PATTERN SENTENCES make up the first large part of each unit. Work with these patterns must occupy the greatest amount of classroom time, for it is here that the student will transform his concept of the language into an instrument of communication. Each pattern group contains a sufficient number of examples to illustrate a grammatical point, and there are cross references in the page margins to relevant discussions in the analysis.

From the very beginnning, we aim at the student's ability to comprehend, speak, read, and write not only the German he will see in formal print, but also the German he will hear in informal speech, and we have not shied away from the colloquial German used by educated people in everyday speech. Colloquial as well as literary German is recognized as socially acceptable, and the students are taught that **Wo kommen Sie denn her?** and **Wo willst du denn hin?** are just as correct as **Woher kommen Sie?** and **Wohin willst du?**

We have attempted not to write typical classroom German, and we have never yielded to the temptation to produce unidiomatic expressions for the sake of making our patterns fit into a preconceived mold. For instance, the use of the attributive genitive must obviously be illustrated, but this is no excuse for introducing sentences like **Die Farbe meines Kugelschreibers is blau** as starting points for pattern drills as long as there is available a wealth of idiomatic phrases such as **ein Freund meines Mannes, gegen Ende des Jahres,** and **der Erfolg der neuen Methode.** We have mitigated the rigidity—and perhaps also the boredom—of many pattern drills by insisting that the student create sentences that could occur in actual speech. It serves no purpose to have a substitution drill end with **Sie werden ihre Tränen getrocknet haben.** On the other hand, we do expect the student to be able to handle complex structures such as **Seine Frau soll sehr aufgeregt gewesen sein** or **Ich hätte natürlich auch zu Hause bleiben können,** for such structures do belong to the living language as it is actually spoken.

Many pattern sections either contain built-in variations or are followed by a separate set of variations. These are designed in such a way that they can be used in class immediately after a group of pattern sentences has been introduced. After the first few units, there are short review sections in which major grammatical points are illustrated again.

ANALYSIS is the intellectual core of each unit. The analysis sections have intentionally been written as detailed and unhurried discussions of grammatical points. Pains have been taken to explain grammar in terms the student will understand. We have shied away from short, terse rules that would force the teacher to spend precious classroom time for elaboration of these rules. The analysis sections should be assigned as outside reading as the new patterns are introduced in class, so that the student, while he works on the patterns, will have the feeling that he knows what he is doing and why he is doing it.

In the analysis, our first and foremost concern is syntax; in addition, we present all the major features of German morphology. After an introductory section on the pronunciation of individual sounds, Unit 1 deals with sentence intonation; in the following units, the basic structure of German sentences is developed. A discussion of the two-part predicate, the most characteristic feature of German syntax, is followed by an analysis of word order in the inner field of a sentence. Negation and time phrases are dealt with at length. Modal auxiliaries and the subjunctive—indispensable in "real" German—are introduced very early. A number of sections deal with "flavoring particles," sentence adverbs like **doch, ja,** or **denn.** Other sections are devoted to principles of word formation.

In order to contrast German structures with corresponding English structures, we have occasionally spent much time analyzing English usage from a German point of view. We wanted to call attention to those features of English that differ from German, and are therefore the primary cause of error.

EXERCISES are provided in addition to the variations in order to reinforce the student's control of each structural element. Their sequence is the same as that of the patterns and the analysis sections. Unlike the variations, however, the exercises should not be done until the student has thoroughly drilled and studied the corresponding patterns. We have intentionally included more exercises than most teachers will want to use, in order to save the teacher the time-consuming effort of writing practice drills of his own. At the back of the book, a separate set of laboratory exercises is also provided; these exercises are keyed to each unit, and full instructions are given to the student. But the texts of these exercises appear only in the Teacher's Manual. Thus their use is not restricted to the language laboratory; they can also be used for further oral drill in the classroom. In addition to the laboratory exercises, the complete set of tapes also contains recordings of pattern sections, and of the conversations and the reading selections.

CONVERSATIONS are included in all but the last few units; they are based upon the contents of the unit in which they appear, and demonstrate to the student how the material he has learned can produce lively, colloquial, and idiomatic talk.

READING, as the book progresses, becomes a major concern. We have used a wide variety of topics in our reading selections. Some of them give brief glimpses of the contemporary German scene; the story by Matthias Koch (Units 10–13) may be used as a starting point for excursions into recent German history.

The reading selections gradually increase in syntactical difficulty; hence they also progress from colloquial to more literary German. In Units 12 and 13, the distinction between the informal, spoken language and the formal, written language becomes quite clear. Some of the last reading selections are meant to introduce the student to literary, expository prose.

Writing should be practiced from the very beginning. At first the student should be encouraged simply to copy from the text. Later on, dictations should be given regularly. A number of the lab exercises are dictations as well. From Unit 7 on, we have provided structured compositions, based on the material of the conversations and the reading.

VOCABULARY study is essential to the successful completion of a German course. In the pattern sentences the vocabulary has purposely been restricted so that the student can concentrate on learning the structures introduced; it is the conversations and reading selections that provide the setting for new words and phrases. All vocabulary is introduced in the context of whole sentences, and vocabulary should be *practiced* in context only. We do, however, recommend very strongly that the student memorize *all* the vocabulary listed at the end of each unit.

ILLUSTRATIONS for the book have been selected either to demonstrate linguistic points or to show the student some of the places where the reading selections take place. We have deliberately not chosen typical "tourist" pictures, devoid of any linguistic message.

A TEACHER'S MANUAL is available which contains a number of detailed suggestions on how to teach individual parts of this book, some outlines for typical lesson plans, and the scripts for all those lab exercises that do not appear in the printed text.

SUGGESTIONS FOR USING THIS BOOK

Each of the 13 Units of this book can be taught in an average of two weeks, thus leaving about two to three weeks of the academic year for review and testing. At Stanford, we have taught Units 1–5 during the first quarter, 6–9 during the second quarter, and 10–13 during the third quarter. For the semester system, we recommend working with Units 1–7 during the first semester, and Units 8–13 during the second semester. We have used the book in a 5-hour course, but it is flexible enough to be easily adapted to a 4-hour or 3-hour course. The Laboratory Exercises should be sufficient to meet any needs. To facilitate the use of the tape program in varying laboratory situations, the recordings are available in a full-length version (approximately 20 hours) and in a shorter version (approximately 12 hours).

We have provided enough text, both in the Patterns and in the Exercises, to eliminate the need of preparing additional practice material. If a teacher wants to cut down, we strongly suggest that, rather than leaving out entire sections, he eliminate only parts of sections; for example, in a Pattern section containing 20 sentences, 10 may suffice to drill the grammatical point in question. The students can then work with the remaining 10 sentences outside the classroom or in the language lab.

Not too much time should be spent at the beginning on the section "The Sounds of German"; one should not expect perfect pronunciation before starting Unit 1. It will be more fruitful, we believe, to review this section periodically throughout the year. The students should be encouraged to listen to the special pronunciation drill tapes as often as possible.

The grammatical material of Unit 1 has to be dealt with as one block: the entire analysis of this Unit is illustrated in each section of the Patterns. From Unit 2 on, however, each group of Patterns should be introduced with the corresponding Analysis section. At the beginning of each Unit, the students should be advised to read, at home, the entire Analysis section to get an idea of the linguistic principles introduced in the Unit. In the classroom, the Patterns should be introduced and drilled with their variations; and while this work is going on, the students often should be asked to keep their books closed. Homework should always consist of further practice with the Patterns as well as of a thorough rereading of the applicable parts of the Analysis. We have found, in five years of teaching this material at Stanford, that it is rarely necessary to discuss any of the Analysis sections in class. Class time should definitely be used for active work with the language.

The Conversations and the Reading selections are best taught at the end of each Unit. They always serve as a review of the grammatical material presented in the Unit, and they introduce new vocabulary which will reappear in the Pattern sections of the following Units.

The Exercises at the end of each Unit are extensive enough to be distributed over the two-week period devoted to each Unit. They should not be done, however, until after the students have thoroughly mastered the corresponding Analysis sections. The English-German translations found at the end of each Unit serve as a review of the material covered. We have found that if the students have mastered the material of a Unit, these English sentences will enable them to generate German equivalents spontaneously. We believe that this kind of exercise serves a very useful purpose: as long as translation is not transliteration, the student is forced to express entire ideas in the target language.

Although all new vocabulary is, of course, introduced and presented in context, we consider it necessary to hold the students responsible for the entire vocabulary of each Unit. The vocabulary lists at the end of each Unit should be thoroughly memorized. We have known for some time that native Germans acquire their basic vocabulary by "osmosis" rather than by memorizing word lists, but this painless process of osmosis takes years and cannot be imitated in a few hours a week in an American classroom.

Further suggestions for using this book and the entire tape script are provided in the separate Teachers' Manual.

THE SOUNDS OF GERMAN

Throughout this book, major emphasis is placed on the intonation of entire utterances, on the characteristic sound of whole German sentences. The pronunciation of the individual sounds that make up those complete sentences is dealt with only in this section. It is imperative that you practice these sounds, with the help of your teacher, and that you listen to the accompanying tapes until you have mastered the sounds. You should review this section frequently as you work your way through the book. After four weeks or four months you will find that this section on pronunciation may be even more useful to you than at the outset.

We have avoided all technical discussion of the German sounds; instead, we have provided a large number of contrastive drills to show the distinction between two or more different German sounds which, to the ear of an American student, very often sound alike when he first hears them. Many German sounds are sufficiently similar to English sounds so as not to cause the beginner great trouble. Our main concern will be those German sounds which either have no equivalent at all in English or tend to cause an American accent if pronounced like their English spelling equivalents. In many cases, an American accent will not make the German sound unintelligible (though you shouldn't take this as an excuse to retain an American accent); in some cases, however, the wrong pronunciation of certain sounds will produce unintended results. If you mispronounce the **ch**-sound in **Nacht,** as many Americans tend to do, you will not produce the German word for *night,* but the word **nackt,** which means *naked.*

Good pronunciation is essential if you want to speak German correctly and naturally. With patience and lots of practice, you should easily be able to overcome your initial difficulties. Don't worry about making mistakes at the beginning; you'll learn more from them than from not speaking at all.

German Vowels

German has long and short vowels, and diphthongs. The distinction between long and short vowels is very important, but unfortunately it is not always indicated by spelling. As a rule of thumb, however, you can assume that a vowel is short if it is followed by a double consonant (for example, **bitte**) or by two or more consonants (**binde**). German vowels are either quite long or very short.

In the following table, all German vowel sounds appear in words. On the tape, this is Pronunciation Drill 1. All the pronunciation drills in this section appear on tape. You should listen to them repeatedly and review them periodically. It is just as important, however, that you listen carefully to your instructor as he drills these exercises with you in class.

PRONUNCI-ATION DRILL 1		LONG	SHORT	UNSTRESSED ONLY
	a	Saat	satt	
	e	Beet	Bett	
	/ə/*			-be (gebe)
	/ʌ/*			-ber (Geber)
	i	ihn	in	
	o	Ofen	offen	
	u	Buhle	Bulle	
	ä	bäte		
	ö	Höhle	Hölle	
	ü	fühle	fülle	DIPHTHONGS
	au			Baum
	ei (ai)			kein (Kain)
	eu (äu)			Heu (Häuser)

NOTE: The two dots over **ä, ö,** and **ü** are called Umlaut. Occasionally, especially in names, these sounds are spelled **ae, oe, ue.**

As the table shows, there are twenty different vowel sounds, of which two occur only in unstressed positions. These two are here represented by the symbols /ə/ and /ʌ/, which are not letters in the German alphabet, but are written as **-e** and **-er.**

All German vowels are "pure"; that is, they are monophthongs and do not have any diphthongal glide at the end as do the English letters *a* and *o*. As you hear the following examples, the difference will become clear.

PRONUNCI-ATION DRILL 2	ENGLISH *a*	GERMAN LONG **e**
	gay	geh
	ray	Reh
	stay	steh
	baited	betet

* We are using phonemic symbols here; in the alphabet /ə/ is **-e** and /ʌ/ is **-er.**

ENGLISH *o*	GERMAN LONG **o**
moan	**Mohn**
tone	**Ton**
tote	**tot**
boat	**Boot**

Long a vs. short a

Many American students have real difficulty in hearing the difference between these two sounds and consequently have trouble pronouncing them. Yet very often the difference between long **a** and short **a** is the difference between two totally unrelated words, as the following examples show.

PRONUNCIATION DRILL 3

LONG **a**	vs.	SHORT **a**
Saat (planting)		**satt** (satisfied)
rate (guess)		**Ratte** (rat)
Rabe (raven)		**Rappe** (black horse)
Wahn (insanity)		**wann** (when)
fahl (pale)		**Fall** (fall)
kam (came)		**Kamm** (comb)
Maße (measures)		**Masse** (mass)
Bahn (track)		**Bann** (ban)

Now say these words again, but stretch the long **a** sound. Instead of **Saat**, say **Saaaat**, etc. You cannot do this with the short **a:** if you stretch the words in the second column, you have to stretch the consonant; for example, **Kamm** will become **Kammmm**.

Long e, long ä, short e and ä, unstressed e /ə/ and er /ʌ/

This group of vowel sounds will need your special attention.

Remember that the long **e,** like all other vowels, does not end in a glide: **geh,** not *gay.*

Some Germans do not really distinguish long **ä** from long **e,** except where there is a difference in meaning, for example, in **Gräte** (fishbone) vs. **Grete** (the girl's name Greta).

Short **e** and short **ä** represent the same sound: the **e** in **Kette** is indistinguishable from the **ä** in **hätte.**

The unstressed /ə/ occurs most frequently in endings and in prefixes; it is quite similar to the unstressed English *a* in *the sofa*. If /ə/ appears in front of final **-n,** it often all but disappears; thus **nennen** sounds like **nenn'n** and **kommen** like **komm'n.** These forms are hard to hear and hard to distinguish from forms without the **-en** ending. Yet very often it is essential to realize the distinction, as in **ihn** vs. **ihn(e)n, den** vs. **den(e)n.**

The unstressed /ʌ/, which is written as **er,** is one of the most difficult sounds for most Americans to produce. At first, you will have difficulty hearing the difference between /ə/ and /ʌ/, but the distinction is there and may be crucial, as in **bitte** (*please*) vs. **bitter** (*bitter*).

The following drills are designed to show you the differences between the various sounds of this group.

PRONUNCI-ATION DRILL 4

LONG e	vs.	SHORT e
Beet		Bett
Wesen		wessen
reden		retten
wen		wenn
den		denn
stehen		stellen

Note again that short **e** and **ä** represent the same sound:

PRONUNCI-ATION DRILL 5

SHORT e	vs.	SHORT ä
Wetter		Blätter
kenne		sänne
hemme		Kämme
Schwemme		Schwämme

PRONUNCI-ATION DRILL 6

LONG ä	vs.	LONG e	vs.	SHORT e OR ä
Gräte		Grete		rette
Ähren		ehren		Herren
bäte		bete		bette
wähne		Vene		Wände

PRONUNCI-ATION DRILL 7

/ə/	vs.	/ʌ/
bete		Beter
Rede		Reeder
nehme		Nehmer

/ə/	vs.	/ʌ/	(cont.)
gebe		Geber	
Esse		Esser	
Messe		Messer	
Summe		Summer	
Hüte		Hüter	
führe		Führer	
Kutte		Kutter	
gute		guter	
Güte		Güter	
Liebe		Lieber	
Spitze		Spitzer	
Pfarre		Pfarrer	
gehören		(erhören)	
gearbeitet		(erarbeitet)	
gegessen		vergessen	
gestört		zerstört	

Long i and ü, short i and ü, long and short u

The two i-sounds are not very difficult to produce. They resemble the English vowel sounds in *bean* and *bin*.

The ü-sound, on the other hand, does not exist in English. To produce it, say i (as in English *key*); then freeze your tongue in that position and round your lips; or, to put it another way, say English *ee* with your lips in the English *oo* position. If you are musical and can get B above C above middle C on a piano, whistle it, and your tongue and lips will be in perfect ü-position. The letter y, which occurs mostly in foreign words, is usually pronounced like ü.

The long u-sound is similar to English *oo* in *noon;* the short u-sound is— to oversimplify matters a bit—just a very short version of the same English *oo*-sound, but again both sounds are much more clearly articulated in German.

LONG i	vs.	SHORT i
Miete		Mitte
biete		Bitte
riete		ritte
ihnen		innen

PRONUNCI-
ATION
DRILL 8

PRONUNCI-ATION DRILL 9	LONG i	vs.	LONG ü (y)				
	Miete		mühte				
	Miete		Mythe				
	Kiel		kühl				
	schiebe		Schübe				
	Stiele		Stühle				

PRONUNCI-ATION DRILL 10	SHORT i	vs.	SHORT ü		SHORT i	vs.	SHORT ü
	Kissen		küssen		Liste		Lüste
	missen		müssen		Gericht		Gerücht
	sticken		Stücken		springe		Sprünge
	Bitte		Bütte		Kiste		Küste

PRONUNCI-ATION DRILL 11	LONG ü	vs.	SHORT ü		LONG ü	vs.	SHORT ü
	Hüte		Hütte		Wüste		wüßte
	rügen		rücken		Düne		dünne
	pflügen		pflücken		Füßen		Füssen
	kühnste		Künste		fühle		Fülle

PRONUNCI-ATION DRILL 12	LONG u	vs.	SHORT u		LONG u	vs.	SHORT u
	Mus		muß		schuf		Schuft
	Ruhm		Rum		spuken		spucken
	sucht		Sucht		Buhle		Bulle
	Fuder		Futter		Buße		Busse

PRONUNCI-ATION DRILL 13	LONG u	vs.	LONG ü		LONG u	vs.	LONG ü
	Mut		Mythe		Schub		Schübe
	Hut		Hüte		tuten		Tüten
	gut		Güte		Huhn		Hühner
	Schwur		Schwüre		Kuhle		Kühle

PRONUNCI-ATION DRILL 14	SHORT u	vs.	SHORT ü		SHORT u	vs.	SHORT ü
	Mutter		Mütter		mußte		müßte
	Kunst		Künste		wußte		wüßte
	durfte		dürfte		Bund		Bünde
	kurze		Kürze		Luft		Lüfte

Long and short **o**, long and short **ö**

Remember that the German **o**-sound does not end in a glide toward **u**: **Mohn**, not *moan*. To produce an **ö**, say a long German **e**, then freeze your tongue and round your lips. Note also the clear distinction between German **a** and German **o**. An American would be likely not to distinguish between **Bann**, **Bahn**, and **Bonn**, but the three sounds are clearly different.

LONG **o**	VS.	SHORT **o**		
wohne		Wonne		
Schote		Schotter		
Ton		Tonne		
Lote		Lotte		

PRONUNCI-ATION DRILL 15

SHORT **o**	VS.	LONG **a**	VS.	SHORT **a**
Bonn		Bahn		Bann
komm		kam		Kamm
Sonne		Sahne		Susanne
hoffen		Hafen		haften
Schollen		Schalen		schallen
locken		Laken		Schlacken
ob		gab		ab

PRONUNCI-ATION DRILL 16

LONG **e**	VS.	LONG **ö**
redlich		rötlich
heben		höben
bete		böte
lege		löge

PRONUNCI-ATION DRILL 17

LONG **o**	VS.	LONG **ö**
Ton		Töne
Lohn		Löhne
Hof		Höfe
Not		Nöte
Bogen		Bögen

PRONUNCI-ATION DRILL 18

SHORT **e**	VS.	SHORT **ö**
stecken		Stöcken
Recke		Röcke
westlich		östlich
helle		Hölle

PRONUNCI-ATION DRILL 19

PRONUNCI-ATION DRILL 20	LONG ö	VS.	SHORT ö
	Goethe		Götter
	Schöße		schösse
	Öfen		öffnen
	Höhle		Hölle

PRONUNCI-ATION DRILL 21	LONG ö	VS.	LONG ü	VS.	LONG i
	Söhne		Sühne		Kusine
	löge		Lüge		liege
	Öl		kühl		Kiel
	schöbe		Schübe		schiebe

PRONUNCI-ATION DRILL 22	SHORT ö	VS.	SHORT ü
	Stöcke		Stücke
	schösse		Schüsse
	Röcken		Rücken
	Hölle		Hülle

PRONUNCI-ATION DRILL 23	SHORT u	VS.	SHORT ü	VS.	SHORT i
	mußte		müßte		mißte
	Stuck		Stück		Stickstoff
	Kummer		Kümmel		Kimme
	Kunde		künde		Kinder

Diphthongs

There are three German diphthongs, two of which can be spelled in two different ways: **ei** (**ai**), **eu** (**äu**), and **au**. They will not present much of a problem. They are similar to *i* in English *light,* *oi* in English *foible,* and *ou* in English *mouse,* but, like all German vowels, they are more precise, more clearly defined, and not as drawn-out as their English counterparts.

PRONUNCI-ATION DRILL 24	ei (ai)	eu (äu)	au
	leiten	läuten	lauten
	freien	freuen	Frauen
	zeigen	zeugen	saugen
	leise	Läuse	Laus
	Meise	Mäuse	Maus

You will be bothered by the fact that the combination **ei** represents a diphthong, but the combination **ie** is simply a long **i**. The following drill should help you overcome this difficulty. To keep the two sounds straight, think of the English phrase *The hEIght of my nIEce* or of the German phrase **wEIn und bIEr.**

PRONUNCI-
ATION
DRILL 25

ei	vs.	ie
meine		Miene
deine		diene
leider		Lieder
reimen		Riemen
Zeit		zieht
bereiten		berieten
keimen		Kiemen
verzeihen		verziehen

Read the following words, distinguishing carefully between **ei** and **ie**:

Viel, Kleid, sieben, Liebe, Leib, leider, Lieder, Seife, siegen, zeigen, liegen, schieben, scheiden, Tier, einheitlich, einseifen, einfrieren, vierseitig, Bierseidel, Zeitspiegel, Spieglein, Meineid, Kleinigkeit.

German Consonants

In presenting the German vowel system, we have, of necessity, had to use almost all German consonant sounds. As you worked through the preceding section, you have doubtless noticed that some German consonants, such as **m** and **n,** differ hardly at all from their English equivalents. Others, such as **z,** have probably surprised you because they are not pronounced the way you expected them to sound. The combination of sounds represented by German **z,** however, does exist in English: if you can say *cats* in English, you should be able to say "Tsoh" in German, even though it is spelled **Zoo.**

There are only two consonant sounds in German which have no equivalent in English; they are both graphically represented by **ch.** The following notes and drills will introduce the German consonants and show you where you will encounter difficulties. We shall start with the two **ch**-sounds.

ch after a, o, u, au

This sound is relatively easy for Americans to produce; it corresponds to the **ch** in the Scottish word *loch*. To produce it, start with the sound **h**, let the air flow freely, and then, without diminishing the air flow, reduce the space between the back of your tongue and the roof of your mouth.

Most Americans tend to substitute a *k* for this **ch**-sound. The following drill will show you the difference. Note that the vowels preceding the **ch** are sometimes long and sometimes short.

PRONUNCI-ATION DRILL 26

LONG VOWEL	SHORT VOWEL	DIPHTHONG
nach	Bach	auch
hoch	noch	Lauch
Buch	Bruch	Bauch

PRONUNCI-ATION DRILL 27

k	vs.	ch
nackt		Nacht
Akt		acht
Laken		lachen
lockt		locht
dockt		Docht
Kokken		kochen
Pocken		pochen
zuckt		Zucht
pauken		brauchen

ch in combination with other letters; chs

For most Americans, this is the most difficult German consonant to produce. There are several ways of learning how to produce it. Say the English word *you* with an extended *y: y-y-y-you*. This *y* is a voiced sound; if you take the voice out of it, you'll produce something very close to this second **ch**-sound. (You can figure out the difference between a voiced and an unvoiced consonant by comparing the *s*-sounds in English *see* and *zee* (the letter *z*) or *Sioux* and *Zoo*.) Another way of getting at this second German **ch** is by starting with a word like *Hubert* or *huge*. Strongly aspirate the *h* and stretch it out: *h-h-huge;* the result will be quite similar to the **ch**-sound. Try the following combinations:

PRONUNCI-ATION DRILL 28

a human
say Hugh
the hue
see Hubert

Again, you must be careful not to substitute *k* for **ch**:

k	vs.	ch
Bäcker		Becher
Leck		Lech
schleckt		schlecht
häkeln		hecheln
siegt		Sicht
nickt		nicht
Brücke		Brüche

PRONUNCI-
ATION
DRILL 29

The following drill contrasts the two **ch**-sounds. The words in the second column are the plurals of the words in the first column.

Dach	Dächer
Bach	Bäche
Loch	Löcher
Buch	Bücher
Bruch	Brüche
Brauch	Bräuche

PRONUNCI-
ATION
DRILL 30

In the following drill, the **ich**-sound occurs after consonants:

München
mancher
welcher
solcher
Milch
Furcht

PRONUNCI-
ATION
DRILL 31

Another difficulty arises when the **ich**-sound appears initially, as in the suffix -**chen**. Note that if the preceding consonant is an **s** or **sch**-sound, the **ch** in -**chen** is pronounced almost like an English *y*.

Männchen
Frauchen
Säckchen
bißchen
Häuschen
Tischchen

PRONUNCI-
ATION
DRILL 32

Finally, the combination **chs** is pronounced like English *x*.

<table>
<tr><td></td><td>

sechs
Luchs
Lachs
Sachsen
wachsen
Büchse

</td></tr>
</table>

b, d, g and p, t, k; pf, ps, ng, kn

You will have no trouble pronouncing these sounds, but there is one area where you must watch out: if **b, d, g** appear at the end of a syllable or in front of **t**, they are pronounced like **p, t, k.** In the following drill, the German words are not translations of the English words.

<table>
<tr><td></td><td>

ENGLISH *b, d, g* vs.	GERMAN b, d, g
glib	gib
glide	Kleid
lied	Leid
lead	Lied
bug	Bug

</td></tr>
</table>

Compare the pronunciation of **b, d, g** in the following two columns:

<table>
<tr><td></td><td>

b, d, g	vs.	p, t, k
lieben		lieb, liebt
heben		hob, hebt
sieben		Sieb, siebt
Abend		ab
loben		Lob, lobt
leiden		Leid
Lieder		Lied
baden		Bad
Süden		Süd
kriegen		Krieg, kriegt
fliegen		flog, fliegt
lügen		log, lügt

</td></tr>
</table>

b, d, g vs.	**p, t, k** (cont.)
beobachten	Obdach
aber	abfahren
radeln	Radfahrer
Tage	täglich
sagen	unsagbar

Now read the following words.

Bad Soden, Abendland, wegheben, abheben, Aberglaube, Staubwedel, Abwege, Feldweg, Waldwege, Laubwald, Laubwälder.

The **p** in the combinations **pf** and initial **ps** is always pronounced; the latter occurs only in foreign words:

Pfeife	Psychologie
Pfarrer	Psychiater
hüpfen	Psalm
Köpfe	Pseudonym
Topf	
Napf	

PRONUNCI-
ATION
DRILL 36

The combination **ng** is pronounced as in English *singer,* not as in *finger.*

Finger
Sänger
Ringe
lange
England

PRONUNCI-
ATION
DRILL 37

The **k** in **kn** must be pronounced.

ENGLISH	GERMAN
knave	Knabe
knack	knacken
knead	kneten
knee	Knie
knight	Knecht
knob	Knopf

PRONUNCI-
ATION
DRILL 38

z

The German letter **z** represents the combination **ts,** which, in English, does not occur at the beginning of words. To learn to produce it in initial position start with the English word *cats;* say it again, but make a break between *ca-* and *-ts.* Then do the same with *Betsy: Be/tsy.* If you only say *tsy,* you almost have the first syllable of the German word **Ziege.**

**PRONUNCI-
ATION
DRILL 39**

INITIAL	MEDIAL	FINAL
ziehen	heizen	Kranz
zog	duzen	Pfalz
gezogen	geizig	Salz
zu	Lanze	Kreuz
Zug	Kanzel	Malz
Züge	Kerze	Pelz
Zahn	Kreuzung	stolz

However, if it occurs in the middle or at the end of a word, the *ts-* sound is usually represented by **tz.**

**PRONUNCI-
ATION
DRILL 40**

Katze
putzen
sitzen
Platz
Fritz

s, ß, sp, st, sch

German **s** does not present much of a problem. It is neither as strongly voiceless as the English *s*-sound as in *see* nor as strongly voiced as the *s*-sound as in *zoo.*

**PRONUNCI-
ATION
DRILL 41**

INITIAL	MEDIAL	FINAL
so	lesen	das
sie	blasen	los
sagen	gewesen	Glas
sicher	Käse	Mus

The *s*-sound may be represented by the symbol **ß** (instead of **ss**). It is called an **s-z** (**ess-zet**) and is used:

(a) between two vowels of which the first is long:

PRONUNCI-
ATION
DRILL 42

LONG VOWEL + ß	SHORT VOWEL + ss
Maße	Masse
Buße	Busse
Straße	Rasse
große	Rosse

(b) after a vowel or a diphthong before a consonant (mostly in verbs whose stem ends in -ss):

> weißt
> mußt
> paßt
> heißt

(c) in final position:

> Fuß
> Roß
> weiß
> daß

Many Germans no longer use the ß symbol, but write ss instead.

The s in German sp and st at the beginning is pronounced like English *sh:*

PRONUNCI-
ATION
DRILL 43

Spaß	Start	Strand
Sport	stehen	Strom
spät	still	streng
Spinne	Stock	streichen
Spule	Stück	streuen

German sch is pronounced like English *sh.*

PRONUNCI-
ATION
DRILL 44

> schön
> waschen
> Busch

sch	vs.	ch
Tisch		dich
mischen		mich
Esche		Echo
Büsche		Bücher

w, v, f

There is no German equivalent of the English *w*-sound as in *water*. German **w** is pronounced like English *v*.

wann

wer

wo

wie

warum

German **v** is usually pronounced like English *f*.

Vater

verliebt

viel

voll

von

In some foreign words, German **v** corresponds to English *v*.

Vase

Villa

German **f** always corresponds to English *f*, as does the *ph*-sound in foreign words.

fallen

Fell

fliegen

fünf

Philosophie

Physik

f	vs.	w
fein		Wein
fand		Wand
finden		winden
fort		Wort
Funde		Wunde

l and r

These two consonants are mispronounced by most Americans. Such mispronunciations will not normally lead to a misunderstanding, but they do in large measure contribute to a "typical American accent." Constant practice with these two consonants is therefore essential.

The English *l* is a "dark," back *l,* and the German **l** s a "clear," front **l.** Listen to the difference:

ENGLISH *l*	vs.	GERMAN **l**
feel		**viel**
stool		**Stuhl**
mall		**Mal**
fall		**Fall**
toll		**toll**
still		**still**
hell		**hell**
lewd		**lud**
light		**Leid**
long		**lang**
bald		**bald**
built		**Bild**

In some parts of Germany, the **r** is trilled, but the preferred sound is a uvular **r.** To produce it, say **Buchen,** with the **ch**-sound as far back as possible. Then add voice to it and you should be saying **Buren.**

ENGLISH *r*	vs.	GERMAN **r**
run		**ran**
rudder		**Ruder**
reef		**rief**
rest		**Rest**
ray		**Reh**
row		**roh**
brown		**braun**
dry		**drei**
fry		**frei**
fresh		**frisch**
creek		**Krieg**
warn		**warnen**
start		**Start**
stork		**Storch**
worst		**Wurst**

We introduced the **er**-sound (ʌ) under the vowels. Many Germans use this same sound for **r** before **t**.

<table>
<tr><td>PRONUNCI-
ATION
DRILL 48</td><td>er fährt
er lehrt
er bohrt
er irrt
er knurrt</td></tr>
</table>

	INITIAL r	r AFTER CONSONANT	MEDIAL r	r BEFORE t	FINAL r (ʌ)
PRONUNCI-ATION DRILL 49	raffen	graben	fahren	fahrt	fahr'
	Rebe	Bregenz	Beeren	fährt	Bär
	riefen	Friesen	vieren	viert	vier
	rot	Thron*	Toren	bohrt	Tor
	Ruhe	Bruder	Uhren	fuhrt	Uhr

	ch	vs.	r
PRONUNCI-ATION DRILL 50	Buchen		Buren
	suchen		Suren
	fachen		fahren
	Acht		Art
	Docht		dort
	Sucht		surrt
	Dach		dar
	Loch		Lohr
	Tuch		Tour

	l	vs.	r
PRONUNCI-ATION DRILL 51	wild		wird
	Geld		Gert
	halt		hart
	hold		Hort
	bald		Bart
	Spalt		spart
	spülen		spüren
	fühlen		führen
	fallen		fahren
	tollen		Toren

* The combination **th**, which occurs in a few German words, is always pronounced as **t**: English *throne,* German **Thron**.

h

At the beginning of a word or syllable, **h** is pronounced as in English *house*. It is never silent as in English *honor*. The symbol **h,** however, is also used to indicate that the preceding vowel is long.

sehen	seht	steh'
fehlen	fehlt	geh'
Lehrer	lehrt	Reh

PRONUNCI-ATION DRILL 52

q

As in English, **q** appears only with a following **u,** but it is pronounced like English *kv*, not *kw*.

ENGLISH	GERMAN
quicksilver	Quecksilber
quadrant	Quadrant
Quaker	Quäker
qualify	qualifizieren
quality	Qualität
quarter	Quartier

PRONUNCI-ATION DRILL 53

j

This letter is pronounced like English *y*.

ENGLISH	GERMAN
yes	ja
year	Jahr
young	jung
youth	Jugend
yacht	Jacht
yoke	Joch

PRONUNCI-ATION DRILL 54

The Glottal Stop

The glottal stop is a phenomenon much more common in German than in English. In certain parts of the eastern United States, the word *bottle* is pronounced *bo-'l* with a very short open *o*, after which the glottis is closed and then suddenly reopened. This sudden release of air occurs in German in front of all initial vowels: **ein alter Affe.** Most Americans tend to run these words together: **[einalteraffe]**; this is another contributory factor in a "typical American accent." If you neglect to use the glottal stop, you may get yourself into embarrassing situations. For instance, if you don't use the stop in front of **-'au,** you will interpret the name of the village of **Himmelsau** as *Celestial Pig* instead of *Heavenly Meadow.*

ein alter Affe

Himmelsau

der erste Akt

ein alter Omnibus

er aber aß Austern

alle anderen Uhren

es erübrigt sich

es ist aber veraltet

eine alte Eule sitzt unter einer alten Ulme

Note the difference in

vereisen (to get covered with ice)	and	**verreisen** (to go on a trip)
verengen (to narrow)		**verrenken** (to sprain)

Sentence Intonation

Since sentence intonation is closely connected with syntax, it is dealt with in various units of this book, as new syntactical patterns are introduced. A few prefatory remarks, however, are in order, to explain the symbols used in the intonation graphs.

Like English, German is spoken on three basic levels of pitch; these levels are indicated by three horiontal lines:

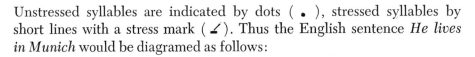

Unstressed syllables are indicated by dots (**.**), stressed syllables by short lines with a stress mark (◢). Thus the English sentence *He lives in Munich* would be diagramed as follows:

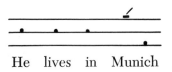

He   lives   in   Munich

If this same sentence is spoken as a question, the last syllable, though unstressed, shows a rise in pitch. This rise is indicated by the symbol (♪). If the last syllable is stressed, rising pitch is indicated by (◢) and falling pitch by (◣).

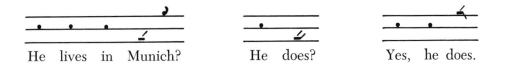

He lives in Munich?   He does?   Yes, he does.

Syllabication

German syllabication is considerably simpler than English syllabication.
A few basic rules will suffice to see you through this book.

German words are divided before single consonants and between double
consonants:

Va - ter	kom - men
Da - me	reg - nen
Te - le - fon	Mün - chen

The only exception to this rule is **st**, which is never separated:

fe - ster
mei - stens
Fen - ster

Unlike English, German does not consider suffixes independent units;
thus it is **Woh - nung**, not [**Wohn - ung**].

Compound words are divided according to their individual parts:

Brief - trä - ger
Glas - au - ge
Sams - tag

Punctuation

Generally speaking, most German punctuation marks are used as in English. Only the use of the comma is different. The comma may be used to
separate main clauses if the second clause contains a new subject, especially in front of coordinating conjunctions. The comma *must* be used to
separate dependent clauses from main clauses. Relative clauses are dependent clauses, and German does not distinguish between restrictive and
nonrestrictive relative clauses. In contrast to English, the comma is not
used in front of **und** in series: **Männer, Frauen und Kinder.**

The first of a pair of quotation marks in German appears below the base
line in writing or printing, the second appears at the top: "Be quiet!"
„Sei ruhig!"

GERMAN

A Structural Approach

UNIT 1: The Present Tense—**sein** and **haben**—Gender— Verb-Second Position—Intonation Patterns—**auch** and **denn**

Practice and read aloud the following sentences until you have mastered the intonation pattern.

[1] Assertions: Basic Intonation Pattern

Intonation sample: Es *reg*net.

Es *reg*net.	It is *raining*.
Du *hast* es.	You *have* it.
Das *sagt* er.	That's what he *says*.
Sie *glaubt* es.	She *believes* it.
Wir *kom*men.	We are *coming*.
Das *braucht* ihr.	You *need* that.
Das *glaubt* er.	He *believes* that.
Er *wohnt* hier.	He *lives* here.
Es *kocht* schon.	It is *boiling* already.

SEE ANALYSIS 1–11 (pp. 10-19)

[2] Assertions: Enlarged Pattern

Intonation sample: Wir brauchen *al*le Geld.

Wir brauchen *al*le Geld.	We *all* need money.
Sie hat *Hun*ger.	She is *hungry*.
Ich bin *hung*rig.	I am *hungry*.

3

Das ist Frau *Mey*er.	That's Mrs. *Mey*er.
Das ist *Herr* Meyer.	That's *Mr.* Meyer.
Wir brauchen *Re*gen.	We need *rain.*
Wir *ar*beiten heute.	We are *working* today.
Wir bleiben heute zu *Hau*se.	We are staying *home* today.
Ich bleibe heute natürlich zu *Hau*se.	I am staying *home* today, of course.
Wir arbeiten *al*le in Köln.	We *all* work in Cologne.

[3] Assertions: Syntactical Stress on Last Syllable

Intonation sample:	Er ist in *Köln.*

SEE
ANALYSIS
1–11
(pp. 10-19)

Er ist in *Köln.*	He is in *Cologne.*
Sie *kommt.*	She is *coming.*
Das sagst *du.*	That's what *you* say.
Er hat *Geld.*	He has *money.*
Sie lernen *Deutsch.*	They are learning *German.*
Er wohnt in Ber*lin.*	He is living in *Berlin.*
Das glaube ich *auch.*	I believe that, *too.*
Ich studiere Medi*zin.*	I am studying *medicine.*
Übrigens wohnt er in Ber*lin.*	By the way, he lives in *Berlin.*
Ich glaube, er wohnt in *Köln.*	I believe he lives in *Cologne.*

[4] Assertions: Syntactical Stress on First Syllable

Intonation sample:	*Fritz* ist schon hier.

SEE
ANALYSIS
1–11
(pp. 10-19)

Fritz ist schon hier!	*Fritz* is already here!
Du bist's!	It is *you!*
Geld hat sie!	She has *money!*
Hunger hab' ich!	I am *hungry!*
Butter brauchen wir!	It is *butter* we need!

[5] Syntactical Stress on More than One Syllable

Intonation sample: Sie geht schon *wie*der nach *Deutsch*land.

Sie geht schon *wie*der nach *Deutsch*land.	She is going to *Germany again*.
Übrigens gehen wir *näch*stes Jahr nach *Deutsch*land.	By the way, we are going to *Germany next* year.
Na*tür*lich gehen wir sonntags in die *Kir*che.	Of *course* we go to *church* on Sundays.
Ich glaube, die *Toch*ter ist intelli*gent*.	I think the *daughter* is *intelligent*.
Erika geht heute abend *wie*der ins *Ki*no.	Erika is *again* going to the *movies* tonight.
Sie geht *näch*stes Jahr wieder nach *Deutsch*land.	She is going to *Germany* again *next* year.

[6] Word Questions

Intonation samples: Wann kommt *ihr* denn nach Köln?

Wo ist Frau *Mann?*

Wann kommt *ihr* denn nach Köln?	When are *you* coming to Cologne?
Wo *bist* du denn?	Where *are* you?
Was *hast* du denn?	What do you *have?*
Wo *wohnt* er denn?	Where does he *live?*
Wann *kommt* er denn?	When is he *coming?*
Wann *kommst* du denn?	When are you *coming?*
Wo *wohnt* ihr denn?	Where do you *live?*
Wo *arbeiten* Sie?	Where do you *work?*
Wann regnet es denn in *Deutsch*land?	When does it rain in *Germany?*
Wann kommst du nach *Hau*se?	When are you coming *home?*
Wo ist denn die *Zei*tung?	Where is the *newspaper?*
Wo ist Frau *Mann?*	Where is Mrs. *Mann?*
Wer ist denn *das?*	Who is *that?*
Wann gehst du wieder nach *Köln?*	When are you going to *Cologne* again?

SEE
ANALYSIS
12–13
(pp. 19-21)

[7] Yes-or-No Questions

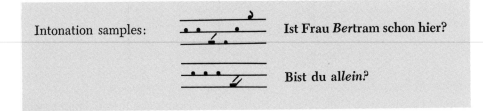

Intonation samples:

Ist Frau *Ber*tram schon hier?

Bist du al*lein?*

SEE
ANALYSIS
1 2–13

(pp. 19-21)

Ist Frau *Ber*tram schon hier?	Is Mrs. *Bertram* already here?
Hast du *Hunger?*	Are you *hungry?*
Arbeitet *ihr* heute?	Are *you* working today?
Ist die *Zei*tung schon hier?	Is the *newspaper* already here?
Lernst du *auch* Deutsch?	Are *you* learning German, *too?*
Lernst du auch *Deutsch?*	Are you learning *German, too?*
*Reg*net es in Köln?	Is it *raining* in Cologne?
Bist du jetzt al*lein?*	Are you *alone* now?
Kommst du *mor*gen abend?	Are you coming *tomorrow* evening?
Geht ihr Sonntag in die *Kir*che?	Are you going to *church* Sunday?
Studieren Sie *auch* Medizin?	Are you *also* studying medicine?

''**Pedestrian crossing**''

[8] Assertions Intonated as Questions

Intonation sample: Du wohnst *auch* in München?

		SEE ANALYSIS 12-13 (pp. 19-21)
Du wohnst *auch* in München?	You live in Munich, *too?*	
Er arbeitet jetzt in *München?*	He works in *Munich* now?	
Du gehst *morgen* abend ins Kino?	You are going to the movies *tomorrow* evening?	
Ihr arbeitet *heute?*	You are working *today?*	
Ihr *arbeitet* heute?	You are *working* today?	
Du *wohnst* auch in München?	You also *live* in Munich?	
Ihr braucht *Geld?*	You need *money?*	
Meyer kommt?	*Meyer* is coming?	
Erika ist hier?	*Erika* is here?	
Erika ist hier in *Köln?*	Erika is here in *Cologne?*	
Nein?—Ja?	*No?—Yes?*	

CONVERSATION

Practice reading these conversations aloud until you have memorized them.

A: Guten *Morgen,* Frau *Schmidt!* Was tun *Sie* denn hier in München?

Good *morning,* Mrs. *Schmidt.* What are *you* doing here in Munich?

B: Ich *wohne* hier! Wohnen Sie *auch* hier?

I *live* here! Do *you* live here, too?

A: *Fritz* sagt, Erika ist intelli*gent.* Was sagst *du?*

Fritz says Erika is *intelligent.* What do *you* say?

B: Sie *ist* intelligent.

She *is* intelligent.

A: Sie kommen al*lein,* Inge? Wo ist denn *Hans?*

You've come *alone,* Inge? Where is *Hans?*

B: *Hans* kommt *auch.* Er kommt *später.*

Hans is coming, *too.* He will come *later.*

A: Hier in *Köln regn*et es. Regnet es in Hamburg *auch?*

Here in *Cologne* it is *raining.* Is it raining in *Hamburg, too?*

B: *Ja,* hier in Hamburg regnet es *auch.*

Yes, here in *Hamburg* it is raining, *too.*

A: Die Frau ist intelli*gent*. Hat sie auch *Geld?*

That lady is *intelligent*. Does she have *money,* too?

B: Ja, *Geld* hat sie *auch*.

Yes, she's got *money, too*.

A: Was tust *du* denn hier in Köln?

What are *you* doing here in Cologne?

B: Ich studiere Medi*zin*. Hans ist übrigens *auch* hier.

I am studying *medicine*. Hans, by the way, is here, *too*.

A: Studiert er *auch* Medizin?

Is he *also* studying medicine?

A: Hm! Sie arbeiten hier in *Köln?* *Woh*nen Sie auch hier?

Well! You are working here in *Cologne?* Do you *live* here, too?

B: Ja, ich *woh*ne auch hier.

Yes, I also *live* here.

READING

Practice reading these sentences until you can read them rapidly and with correct intonation.

Natürlich	**bleibe**	ich morgen abend zu Hause.
Ich	**bleibe**	morgen abend natürlich zu Hause.
Morgen abend	**bleibe**	ich natürlich zu Hause.

Wir	**gehen**	natürlich Sonntag morgen in die Kirche.
Natürlich	**gehen**	wir Sonntag morgen in die Kirche.
Sonntag morgen	**gehen**	wir natürlich in die Kirche.

Übrigens	**gehen**	wir Sonntag abend ins Kino.
Wir	**gehen**	übrigens Sonntag abend ins Kino.
Sonntag abend	**gehen**	wir übrigens ins Kino.

Es	**regnet**	im Winter in Deutschland.
Im Winter	**regnet**	es in Deutschland.
In Deutschland	**regnet**	es im Winter.

Übrigens	**bin**	ich heute abend zu Hause.
Heute abend	**bin**	ich übrigens zu Hause.
Ich	**bin**	übrigens heute abend zu Hause.

Wir	**sind**	übrigens nächstes Jahr in Deutschland.
Übrigens	**sind**	wir nächstes Jahr in Deutschland.
Nächstes Jahr	**sind**	wir übrigens in Deutschland.

Typical street signs: "Straight ahead and right turn only."
"Begin. No parking from 7 p.m. to 7 a.m. and no stopping from 7 a.m. to 7 p.m."

1 The Infinitive

The infinitive is that form of the verb which is used as a dictionary entry. Thus the English forms *am, is,* and *was* are found in the dictionary under *be; bought* is found under *buy;* and *does* is found under *do.*

Most German infinitives end in **-en: arbeiten, bleiben, brauchen.** The infinitives **sein, tun,** and certain others to be introduced later end in **-n.** That part of the verb which precedes the infinitive ending **-en** or **-n** is called the stem. Thus:

STEM	+	INFINITIVE ENDING	=	INFINITIVE
arbeit-		-en		arbeiten
bleib-		-en		bleiben
brauch-		-en		brauchen
tu-		-n		tun

2 Personal Pronouns

SINGULAR			PLURAL	
ich	I		wir	we
du	you		ihr	you
er	he		sie	they
sie	she			
es	it		Sie	you

English "you": du, ihr, Sie

Modern English alone among all the Indo-European languages has just one form (*you*) for the second person. English *you* is both singular and plural, formal and informal. In German, there are three mutually exclusive forms:

1. **du** (corresponding to the archaic English *thou*) is the familiar singular.

It expresses intimacy and is therefore used in the family, with close friends, and in prayer. It is also used with *all* children up to the age of about fourteen.

2. **ihr** is the plural of **du.**

3. **Sie,** on the other hand, implies a certain formality and the recognition of social considerations. It is always used with **Herr, Frau, Fräulein,** or other titles. This polite **Sie,** which is both singular and plural, sounds like the plural **sie** (they) and it takes the same verb form. When written, it is always capitalized.

Brauchst du Geld, Maria?	Do you need money, Mary?
Brauchst du Geld, Karl?	Do you need money, Karl?
Braucht ihr Geld, Kinder?	Do you need money, children?
Du bist mein Gott.	Thou art my God. (Ps. 31:14)
Brauchen Sie Geld, Herr Meyer?	Do you need money, Mr. Meyer?
Wohnen Sie in München, Herr Doktor?	Do you live in Munich, Dr. Meyer?

Beware!	[**Herr Meyer, brauchst du Geld?**]	DO NOT USE!
Americanism!	[**Frau Meyer, brauchst du Geld?**]*	

NOTE: Germans love titles. If **Herr Meyer** has earned any kind of doctorate, he is addressed as **Herr Doktor** (no last name), and he is referred to as **Herr Dr. Meyer** or as **Dr. Meyer.**

The polite **Sie,** which maintains a certain distance between the speaker and the person spoken to, can be used together with the first name under specific social conditions. For instance, among sophisticated people of the upper class who are good acquaintances but not close personal friends, the polite **Sie** is often used with the first name.

Er: Guten Abend, Doris! Sie kommen allein? Wo ist denn Max?
Sie: Max kommt später. Er ist noch zu Hause und arbeitet.

3 Inflected Verb Forms

The predicate verb of a sentence or a clause is always an "inflected" form —that is, a form modified by a personal ending. (With the exception of -*s*, as in *he lives*, all personal endings have been dropped in English.)

The present tense of regular verbs is formed as follows:

---

* Brackets are used in this book to indicate unacceptable forms—either Germanisms in English or Americanisms in German.

PRONOUN	STEM	+	PERSONAL ENDING	=	INFLECTED FORM	
ich	glaub-		e		ich glaube	I believe
du	glaub-		st		du glaubst	you believe
er					er	he
sie	glaub-		t		sie } glaubt	she } believes
es					es	it
wir	glaub-		en		wir glauben	we believe
ihr	glaub-		t		ihr glaubt	you believe
sie	glaub-		en		sie glauben	they believe
Sie	glaub-		en		Sie glauben	you believe

4 Absence of Progressive and Emphatic Forms in German

A native speaker of English will always differentiate between the "simple present" and the "progressive form." The "simple present" usually expresses either a timeless fact:

> Water boils at 100° C.

or some habitual attitude or activity:

> He is usually nasty.
> He smokes only cigars.
> I just love our new house.

Use of the progressive form, on the other hand, expresses the idea of "being in the middle of it." Thus, it would make no sense to say *I am just loving our new house,* but it is possible to say:

> He is being nasty again.
> The water is boiling.
> This week we are reading Emerson.
> Dad is working in the garden.

Standard German does not express the difference between *boils* and *is boiling* by verb forms. Instead, German relies on syntax (**Wasser kocht** = *water boils;* **das Wasser kocht** = *the water is boiling*), and on context. One should not "translate" *he is having, he is being, he is working* into German. Otherwise one will start by saying **er ist . . .** and end up with an Americanism. **Er arbeitet** means both *he works* and *he is working,* and **es regnet** means both *it rains* and *it is raining.*

German also has no emphatic form. It cannot express the difference between *I go* and *I do go* by different verb forms. Instead, German relies on intonation and on certain particles. The unaccented **ja,** for instance, adds the flavor of *indeed,* implied in *we do go.*

Wir gehen *je*den Sonntag in die *Kir*che.	We go to church *every* Sunday.
Aber Vater, wir *ge*hen ja jeden Sonntag in die *Kir*che.	But, Father, we *do* go to church every Sunday.

5 Future Meaning of Present-Tense Forms

Just as the progressive form *I am going* has a future meaning in *I am going to Germany next year,* so the present tense of German verbs frequently assumes a future meaning:

Wir gehen nächstes Jahr nach Deutschland.	We are going to Germany next year.
Morgen abend gehen wir ins Kino.	We are going to the movies tomorrow night.

6 Variations in Personal Endings

In the case of **er glaubt** or **er kommt,** the ending **-t** is easily pronounced and heard. However, in the case of such verbs as **arbeiten** and of all other verbs whose stems end in **-d** or **-t,** the vowel **-e-** is inserted between the stem and the endings **-st** and **-t** to make these endings clearly audible. For similar reasons, it is **es regnet,** not [**es regnt**].

ORDINARY VERBS		VERBS WITH STEMS IN -d OR -t	
du	glaubst	du	arbeitest
er		er	
sie	glaubt	sie	arbeitet
es		es	
ihr	glaubt	ihr	arbeitet

Since the infinitive **tun** ends in **-n** and not in **-en,** the **wir**-form and the **sie**-form also end in **-n: wir tun, sie tun.**

7 sein and haben

A few of the most frequently used German verbs are quite irregular. In this lesson, we introduce **sein** (*to be*) and **haben** (*to have*). In the present tense, they are inflected as follows:

ich	bin	wir	sind
du	bist	ihr	seid
er		sie	sind
sie	ist	Sie	sind
es			

ich	habe		wir	haben
du	hast		ihr	habt
er			sie	haben
sie	}	hat	Sie	haben
es				

8 Gender of Nouns

Indo-European, the ancestor of most modern European languages, including English, distinguished between three classes of nouns, which we call masculines, feminines, and neuters. All Indo-European languages, including Old English, inherited this distinction. Modern English is the only Indo-European language which has given up the difference almost completely. All nouns in French and Spanish are either feminine or masculine. German, Russian, and some other languages have kept all three classes alive. Usually, the German nouns themselves can no longer be recognized as masculine, feminine, or neuter just by looking at their dictionary forms: **Winter** (masculine), **Butter** (feminine), and **Wetter** (neuter) all end in **-er.** However, the articles (and also the pronouns and the adjectives) used with nouns still show the old difference:

masculine	*der* **Winter**	(*the* winter)	*der* **Löffel**	(*the* spoon)
feminine	*die* **Butter**	(*the* butter)	*die* **Gabel**	(*the* fork)
neuter	*das* **Wetter**	(*the* weather)	*das* **Messer**	(*the* knife)

"Gender" is a linguistic, not a biological, term. There is obviously nothing "masculine" about a spoon, nothing "feminine" about a fork, and nothing "neuter" about a knife, though the genders of the German nouns are masculine, feminine, and neuter respectively. To be sure, it is **der Mann** (*the man*), **die Frau** (*the woman*), and **das Kind** (*the infant*), and this is the reason why the term "masculine" came to be applied to *all* nouns used with **der,** the term "feminine" to *all* nouns used with **die,** and the term "neuter" to *all* nouns used with **das.** German children are not conscious of gender, and they never hear the term until they go to school. But they always hear their elders and the other children say **der Löffel, die Gabel**, and **das Messer.** They imitate what they hear and thus learn gender without effort. For the English-speaking student there is only one thing to do: learn the article together with the noun.

9 Position of the Inflected Verb

The "inflected verb form" is that form of a verb which by its ending and by its position belongs to a particular grammatical person. Thus, the forms **bin, habe,** and **gehe** can only belong to **ich,** and the forms **bist, hast,** and

gehst can only belong to **du.** To be sure, the forms **gehen** or **brauchen,** which belong to **wir** and **sie** (they), are identical with the infinitives **gehen** and **brauchen.** However, when a German hears the words

Morgen   gehen . . . . . .

he knows right away that the next syntactical unit will be either **wir, Sie,** or **sie** (or a plural noun, the equivalent of **sie**); *for in every assertion the inflected verb is the second syntactical unit.* In the phrase "**Morgen gehen . . . ,**" **gehen** can therefore not be an infinitive. It must be either the **wir**-form or the **sie**-form.

The place in front of the inflected verb is occupied by only one unit—that is, by the answer to only one possible question:

Er hat Geld.	**Wer hat Geld?—Er!**
Heute bleibe ich zu Hause.	**Wann bleibst du zu Hause?—Heute!**
Fritz und Maria brauchen Geld.	**Wer braucht Geld?—Fritz und Maria!**
Geld hat sie.	**Was hat sie?—Geld!**

The student should therefore never imitate English sentences like

Tomorrow night we're going to the movies,

for the verbal element *are going* is here preceded both by *tomorrow night* and by *we*—that is, by the answer to two possible questions. In German this English sentence is expressed either by

Morgen abend   gehen   wir ins Kino

or by

Wir   gehen   morgen abend ins Kino.

10 Word Stress

Almost all simple (non-compound) German words stress the first syllable: **A'bend** (*evening*), **ar'beiten** (*to work*), **heu'te** (*today*). Words composed of two nouns stress the first noun much more strongly than the second: **Haus'frau** (*housewife*), **Haus'hund** (*house dog*), **Hun'dehaus** (*dog-house*).

Words of non-German origin frequently do not stress the first syllable: **natür'lich, die Natur', studie'ren.** Our vocabulary will indicate which syllable is stressed in these cases.

11   Syntactical Stress and Intonation of Assertions

Word Stress versus Syntactical Stress

If one analyzes the stress situation in a short sentence like

    August wohnt in Berlin.   Gus lives in Berlin.

one can either look at the individual words as words, or one can look at the sentence as a whole.

Looking at the words **Au'gust** and **Berlin'** as words, one can say that **Au'gust** is stressed on the first and **Berlin'** on the second syllable. This is a question of word stress. Word stress is fixed, and it is simply a mistake to say **August'** or **Ber'lin.** In fact, **Au'gust** is a personal name and **August'** is the name of a month.

Looking at the sentence as a whole—that is, as one single unit of thought —we find it ambiguous in its written form. The speaker may want to say:

    1. **Au**gust wohnt in Berlin.   *Gus* lives in Berlin.
    2. **August *wohnt* in Berlin.**   Gus *lives* in Berlin.
    3. **August wohnt in Ber*lin.***   Gus lives in *Berlin.*

The one written sentence turns out to be at least three spoken sentences, which are not interchangeable. Each of them has a specific meaning. Each of them is used in situations where the other two cannot be used:

    1. Question: *Wer* wohnt in Berlin?
       Only possible answer: *August* wohnt in Berlin.
    2. Question: **Was tut August denn in *Berlin?***
       Only possible answer: August *wohnt* in Berlin.
    3. Question: **Wo *wohnt* August?**
       Only possible answer: August wohnt in *Berlin.*

In all three sentences, **August** is stressed on the first, and **Berlin** on the second syllable. But the stress on **Au'gust** in the first sentence above is so strong that, in comparison, the stress on **Berlin'** becomes insignificant. For in each sentence the speaker singles out at least one word into which he packs the major news value and upon which he therefore places such a strong emphasis that, as far as the sentence as a whole is concerned, all other syllables can be regarded as unstressed. Syntactical stress, by which the speaker distinguishes between important and unimportant words, overshadows word stress; and whereas word stress is fixed, syntactical stress can shift from one word to another, depending on which word is chosen by the speaker to be the important one in a certain situation. The stressed syllable of this important word is called the "stress point" of a sentence.

The Basic Intonation Pattern for Assertions

As long as only one syllable of an assertion receives syntactical stress, this one syllable (the stress point) is also the syllable with the highest pitch.

Pitch in German (and English) is usually distributed over three levels, symbolized by the three lines below.* An assertion usually starts on level 2, moves up to level 3 for the stress point, and then falls to level 1. By using dots for the syllables without syntactical stress, and a short line with an accent over it for the stress point, the pitch distribution can be diagramed as follows:

Sie *wohnt* **hier**   She *lives* here

The short assertion **Sie wohnt hier** exemplifies the distribution of pitch for a three-syllable sentence. You will find further examples of this type in Section [1] of the Patterns.

Intonation of Assertions: The Enlarged Pattern

Depending on which syllable is selected by the speaker to assume the role of the stress point, the sentence **Maria wohnt in München,** as pointed out above, can be pronounced with the following three intonations:

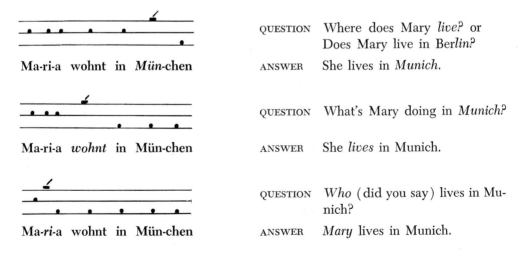

QUESTION Where does Mary *live?* or
          Does Mary live in Ber*lin?*

ANSWER   She lives in *Munich.*

QUESTION What's Mary doing in *Munich?*

ANSWER   She *lives* in Munich.

QUESTION *Who* (did you say) lives in Mu-nich?

ANSWER   *Mary* lives in Munich.

Observe that all the unstressed syllables preceding the stress point may be spoken with even level-2 pitch, and that all the unstressed syllables following the stress point show level-1 pitch.

* For a full explanation of the symbols used in the intonation diagrams, see the introductory section on the sounds of German.

Syntactical Stress on the Last Syllable

The drop from level 3 to level 1 at the end of a sentence functions as a signal. The drop in level means, "This is the end of the sentence." This drop must therefore be maintained, even if the last syllable is the stress point. The last syllable itself must then show a downward glide:

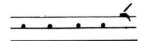

Er wohnt in Ber-*lin*

Compare the difference between *No!* (⌁) as an answer and *No?* (⌁) as a question.

Assertions with More than One Stressed Syllable

Many German sentences contain more than one syllable which carries a strong syntactical stress. The sentence **Wir arbeiten alle in München,** for instance, may be pronounced in the following ways:

ONE STRESSED SYLLABLE

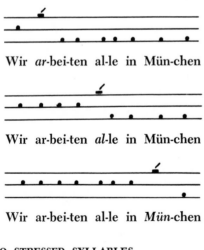

Wir *ar*-bei-ten al-le in Mün-chen

We all *work* in Munich.
(Question: What are you all doing in *Munich?*)

Wir ar-bei-ten *al*-le in Mün-chen

We *all* work in Munich.
(Question: How *many* of you work in Munich?)

Wir ar-bei-ten al-le in *Mün*-chen

We all work in *Munich.*
(Question: Where do you all *work?*)

TWO STRESSED SYLLABLES

Sie ar-bei-ten *al*-le in *Mün*-chen

They *all* work in *Munich.*
(This stress pattern is probably not the answer to any question.)

As the last example shows, if a German sentence contains more than one stressed syllable, the first one has level-3 pitch, and the ones following are lower than the first. The end of the sentence provides the usual signal: the intonation falls to level 1 and thereby indicates the end of the assertion. All stressed syllables express items which have significant news value for the specific situation in which the sentence is spoken.

12   The Grammatical Structure of German Questions

As far as grammatical structure is concerned, German, like English, uses three types of questions.

Yes-or-No Questions

Questions which can be answered by **ja** (*yes*) or **nein** (*no*) may start with an inflected verb in both English and German. However, there is an important difference. The opening verb in English can only be (1) a form of *to be* (*Is Bob in?*), (2) a form of *to have* (*Has he gone?*), (3) a modal (*Can he play?*), or (4) a form of *to do* (*Does he want to play?*). In German, *any* verb can open a yes-or-no question, and the use of **tun** as an auxiliary is impossible. The German questions

> **Regnet es heute?**
> **Arbeitet er in Berlin?**
> **Brauchst du Geld?**

correspond in English to the unacceptable Germanisms

> [Rains it today?]
> [Works he in Berlin?]
> [Need you money?]

Conversely, the English questions

> Does he work?
> Do you need money?

correspond in German to the unacceptable Americanisms

Beware!	[**Tut er arbeiten?**]	
Americanism!	[**Tust du brauchen Geld?**]	DO NOT USE!

Word Questions

Questions which start with interrogatives (question words) such as **wer** (*who*), **wann** (*when*), **wo** (*where*), or **wie** (*how*) we shall call word questions. In word questions, the inflected verb follows immediately after the interrogative:

Wann kommt ihr?	When are you coming?
Wer ist das?	Who is that?
Wo wohnt sie?	Where does she live?

NOTE: Any German verb can follow the interrogative, and the use of **tun** as an auxiliary is again impossible.

Beware!	[**Wann tust du kommen?**]	
Americanism!	[**Wo tut sie wohnen?**]	DO NOT USE!

Questions Structured Like Assertions

German assertions, as we pointed out in **9,** are characterized by the fact that the inflected verb is always the second unit in the sentence. Any such assertion can be changed into a yes-or-no question by changing its intonation (see **13.**)

13   The Intonation of German Questions

Word Questions

Normally, German word questions follow the intonation pattern of assertions:

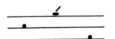

Wo *wohnst* **du?**
Where do you *live?*

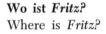

Wo ist *Fritz?*
Where is *Fritz?*

Wann kom-men *Sie* **nach Köln?**
When will *you* come to Cologne?

Yes-or-No Questions

Yes-or-no questions, including assertions changed by intonation into questions, show an upward movement after the last stressed syllable. Although there are several other possibilities, the beginner, after starting as usual on level 2, should place the last stressed syllable on level 1 and then move upward.

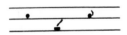

Hast *du* **Geld?**

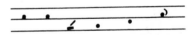

Ist die Zei-tung schon hier?

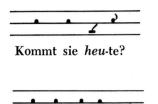

Kommt sie *heu*-te?

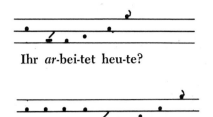

Ihr *ar*-bei-tet heu-te?

Woh-nen Sie in *Köln?*

Ar-bei-tet ihr *al*-le in Mün-chen?

Note that after a stressed syllable on level 1 no other stressed syllables can follow.

14 auch

German **auch,** meaning *also* or *too,* is one of the most frequently used words. The stressed **auch** refers *back* to a preceding unit, regardless of whether this unit is stressed or not. The unstressed **auch** refers forward to a *stressed* unit, except in one case: Since the inflected verb is always the second unit in a German sentence, one cannot imitate the English sentence *He also likes money,* or *He also lives in Munich.* Instead, the stressed verb precedes the unstressed **auch,** as shown on the next page.

,,Er wohnt auch in Köln ''

Er *wohnt* auch in München.	He also *lives* in Munich.
	He *lives* in Munich, too.

Here are some further examples:

Sie ist *auch* intelligent.	*She, too,* is intelligent.
Sie ist auch intelli*gent.*	She is also *intelligent.*
Er hat *auch* ein Büro in Köln.	*He, too,* has an office in Cologne.
Er hat auch ein Bü*ro* in Köln.	He also has an *office* in Cologne.
Er hat auch ein Büro in *Köln.*	He also has an office in *Cologne.*
Er *wohnt* auch in Köln.	He also *lives* in Cologne.

15 denn

Idiomatic German is characterized by the very frequent use of "particles" which, in addition to their definable dictionary meaning, have a psychological meaning sometimes hard to define. English occasionally uses such particles, too. Thus, *there* has a definable dictionary meaning in *She is there.* However, when a mother runs up to her crying baby, pats it on the back, and says, "There, there!" *there* is no longer the same word as in *She is there.*

The particles used most frequently in German will be introduced one by one; use them as often as possible in spoken German. We shall start with **denn.**

The unstressed German **denn** occurs most frequently in questions. It expresses either impatience or interest.

IMPATIENCE A: **Ist Meyer hier?**
            Is Meyer here?

            B: **Nein, Meyer ist noch nicht hier.**
            No, Meyer is not here yet.

            A: **Wo bleibt er denn?**
            Well, where is he?
            (I have been waiting long enough.)

INTEREST   A: **Fritz ist hier!**

            B: **Wo ist er denn?**
            Where is he?
            (I am interested in finding out.)

Similarly:

Wann *kommt* sie denn?
When is she coming?
Wo *wohnt* er denn?
Where *does* he live?

Wann *gehen* wir denn nach Deutschland?
When *are* we going to Germany?

The use of this **denn** is so frequent in spoken German that about half of
all questions contain it. It follows the inflected verb and personal pronouns, and it may even follow nouns.

Hast du denn *Geld?*
Hast *du* denn Geld?
Hat *Meye*r denn Geld?
Wann *brauchst* du es denn?
Wo *ist* das Büro denn?

EXERCISES

A. Using the pattern *I study and you do not study, you study and he does not study,* write out,
and say aloud, the following German sentences. (In Unit 1, **nicht** should be used only in the
patterns of this exercise.) Be prepared to go through these sentences in class without your book.

SEE LAB
EXERCISES
1.1–1.3

(p. 622)

Ich studiere, und du studierst nicht.
Du studierst, und er studiert nicht.
Er studiert, und wir studieren nicht.
Wir studieren, und ihr studiert nicht.
Ihr studiert, und sie studieren nicht.

1. Ich arbeite, und du ARBEITest nicht.
   Du ARBEITest, und er ARBEITet nicht.
   Er ARBEITet, und wir ARBEITEN nicht.
   Wir ARBEITEN, und ihr ARBEITet nicht.
   Ihr ARBEITet, und sie ARBEITEN nicht.

   works

2. Ich wohne in Berlin, und du wohNST nicht in Berlin.
   Du wOHNST in Berlin, und er wohNt nicht in Berlin.
   Er wohnt in Berlin, und wir wohNEN nicht in Berlin.
   Wir wohnen in Berlin, und ihr wohnt nicht in Berlin.
   Ihr wohnt in Berlin, und sie wohNEN nicht in Berlin.

   lives

3. Ich bleibe zu Hause, und du bleibest nicht zu Hause.
   Du bleibest zu Hause, und er bleibt nicht zu Hause.
   Er bleibt zu Hause, und wir bleiben nicht zu Hause.
   Wir bleiben zu Hause, und ihr bleibt nicht zu Hause.
   Ihr bleibt zu Hause, und sie bleiben nicht zu Hause.

   stays

4. Ich tue es nicht, und du _tuest_ es auch nicht.
   Du _tuest_ es nicht, und er _tut_ es auch nicht.
   Er _tut_ es nicht, und wir _tunn_ es auch nicht.
   Wir _tunn_ es nicht, und ihr _tut_ es auch nicht.
   Ihr _tut_ es nicht, und sie _tuen_ es auch nicht.

5. Ich bin hungrig, und du _bist_ nicht hungrig.
   Du _bist_ hungrig, und er _ist_ nicht hungrig.
   Er _ist_ hungrig, und wir _sind_ nicht hungrig.
   Wir _sind_ hungrig, und ihr _seid_ nicht hungrig.
   Ihr _seid_ hungrig, und sie _sind_ nicht hungrig.

**SEE LAB
EXERCISES
1.4, 1.5**

(p. 622)

B. Write down *one* possible answer to the following questions. To answer a yes-or-no question, start your answer with **ja** or **nein** followed by a comma and an affirmative statement. To answer a word question, put the words expressing the information requested at the end of the sentence. Be prepared to answer these questions in class, orally and at normal speed, without looking at your book or paper.

Wohnen Sie in Berlin?	**Ja, ich wohne in Berlin.** **Nein, ich wohne in München.**
Wo ist Fritz?	**Fritz ist zu Hause.** **Er ist in Bonn.**

1. Ist Fritz zu Hause?
2. Wer ist das?
3. Studieren Sie Deutsch?
4. Arbeiten Sie in Köln?
5. Wo arbeiten Sie?
6. Bleibst du heute abend zu Hause?
7. Sind Sie heute abend zu Hause, Herr Meyer?
8. Wo wohnt er?
9. Studiert sie in Heidelberg?
10. Wann kommt ihr denn?
11. Was tut ihr heute abend?
12. Wohnen Schmidts *auch* in Köln?

C. Write down one *yes-or-no* question which could be answered by the assertions printed. Copy the assertions also. Be prepared to ask these questions orally in class.

Haben wir (habt ihr, haben Sie) Geld?   Ja, wir haben Geld.

1.	Ja, wir wohnen in Berlin.
2.	Ja, sie arbeiten heute.
3.	Ja, ich bleibe heute zu Hause.
4.	Ja, das ist Frau Meyer.
5.	Ja, Frau Meyer ist schon hier.
6.	Natürlich ist Meyer intelligent.
7.	Ja, sie (die Zeitung) ist schon hier.
8.	Ja, wir gehen Sonntag in die Kirche.
9.	Ja, ich studiere Medizin.
10.	Ja, sie (Erika) wohnt *auch* in München.
11.	Nein!
12.	Ja!

D. Write down the *word* questions which could be answered by the statements printed. Be prepared to ask these questions in class at normal speed, when you hear the statement.

SEE LAB EXERCISES 1.6–1.11

(pp. 622-623)

Wo arbeitet Herr Meyer?	**Er arbeitet in Berlin.**
1.	Das ist Herr Meyer.
2.	Wir wohnen in Berlin.
3.	Fritz ist in Köln.
4.	Zu Hause!
5.	Ich bin in Köln.
6.	Herr Meyer.
7.	In Berlin.
8.	Er studiert Psychologie.
9.	Herr Meyer kommt heute.
10.	Ich bin Anna Meyer.

E. Express in German. Be prepared to give the German equivalents instantly without using book or paper.

1. I am hungry.
2. We need money.
3. Hans will come later.
4. The newspaper is here.
5. Where does Dr. Meyer live?
6. We are studying psychology.
7. Of course it will rain tomorrow.
8. You're going to Cologne. I'm going to Munich.
9. I believe Erika is intelligent.

10. Hans is here, too.
11. Tomorrow night we are staying home.
12. She, too, is intelligent.
13. Does Meyer *also* live here?
14. Meyer also *lives* here.
15. We are also going to *Munich*.
16. Is it raining in Hamburg?
17. When are you coming to Munich, Mr. Meyer?
18. Sunday we'll go to church.
19. On Sundays we go to church.
20. Sunday night we go to the movies.

VOCABULARY

der Abend evening
  abends evenings
  Guten Abend! Good evening!
alle all, all of us
allein alone
arbeiten to work
auch also, too
bleiben to stay, to remain
brauchen to need
das Büro' office
die Butter butter
das that (*demonstrative*)
denn (*see* 15)
Deutsch German (language)
  Deutschland Germany
der Doktor doctor
die Frau woman, wife
  Frau Meyer Mrs. Meyer
gehen to go, to walk
das Geld money
glauben to think, to believe
der Gott god
  Gott God
gut good
haben to have
das Haus house
  ich gehe nach Hause I go home

ich bin zu Hause I am at home
der Herr gentleman
  Herr Meyer Mr. Meyer
heute today
  heute abend this evening, tonight
  heute morgen this morning
hier here
der Hund dog
der Hunger hunger
  ich habe Hunger I am hungry
  hungrig hungry
in in
intelligent' intelligent
ja yes; indeed
das Jahr year
jetzt now
das Kind child
das Kino moviehouse
  ich gehe ins Kino I go to the movies
die Kirche church
  ich gehe in die Kirche I go to church
kochen to cook, to boil
kommen to come
lernen to learn

der Mann man, husband
die Medizin' medicine
  Medizin' (the science of) medicine
der Morgen morning
  morgen tomorrow
  morgen abend tomorrow evening
  Guten Morgen! Good morning!
nach to, toward; after
nächst next
  nächstes Jahr next year
die Natur' nature
  natür'lich naturally, of course
nein no
nicht not
noch still
  noch nicht not yet
die Psychologie' psychology
regnen to rain
  der Regen rain
sagen to say
schon already
sein to be
der Sonntag Sunday
  Sonntag abend Sunday evening

Note: Articles and pronouns are not included in this list. See **2** and **8** in the Analysis Section.

Sonntag morgen Sunday morning

jeden Sonntag every Sunday

sonntags on Sundays, every Sunday

spät late

später later

studie'ren to study

die Tochter daughter

tun to do

übrigens by the way, incidentally

und and

Wann? When? (*interrogative*)

Was? What?

Wer? Who?

das Wetter weather

wieder again (second or third time); back (to the place of origin)

der Winter winter

im Winter in the winter

Wo? Where?

wohnen to reside, to live (in a place)

die Zeitung newspaper

zu to; at

UNIT 2: Plural of Nouns—Nominative and Accusative of Personal Pronouns and of **ein**-Words and **der**-Words— Adverbs and Predicate Adjectives—Sentence Structure—**doch**

PATTERNS

[1] Accusative of Personal Pronouns

Find out the system by which this exercise is constructed. Then practice the sentences aloud until you can say them rapidly, without having to pause for the correct pronoun.

SEE
ANALYSIS
20–21

(pp. 40-41)

du brauchst *mich,* und *ich* brauche *dich*
er braucht *mich,* und *ich* brauche *ihn*
sie braucht *mich,* und *ich* brauche *sie*
ihr braucht *mich,* und *ich* brauche *euch*
sie brauchen *mich,* und *ich* brauche *sie*
Sie brauchen *mich,* und *ich* brauche *Sie*

ich brauche *dich,* und *du* brauchst *mich*
er braucht *dich,* und *du* brauchst *ihn*
sie braucht *dich,* und *du* brauchst *sie*
wir brauchen *dich,* und *du* brauchst *uns*
sie brauchen *dich,* und *du* brauchst *sie*

ich brauche *ihn,* und *er* braucht *mich*
du brauchst *ihn,* und *er* braucht *dich*
sie braucht *ihn,* und *er* braucht *sie*
wir brauchen *ihn,* und *er* braucht *uns*
ihr braucht *ihn,* und *er* braucht *euch*
sie brauchen *ihn,* und *er* braucht *sie*
Sie brauchen *ihn,* und *er* braucht *Sie*

ich brauche *sie,* und *sie* braucht *mich*
du brauchst *sie,* und *sie* braucht *dich*
er braucht *sie,* und *sie* braucht *ihn*
wir brauchen *sie,* und *sie* braucht *uns*
ihr braucht *sie,* und *sie* braucht *euch*

(Facing) **Policeman in Frankfurt**

29

du brauchst *uns,* und *wir* brauchen *dich*
er braucht *uns,* und *wir* brauchen *ihn*
sie braucht *uns,* und *wir* brauchen *sie*
ihr braucht *uns,* und *wir* brauchen *euch*
sie brauchen *uns,* und *wir* brauchen *sie*
Sie brauchen *uns,* und *wir* brauchen *Sie*

ich brauche *euch,* und *ihr* braucht *mich*
er braucht *euch,* und *ihr* braucht *ihn*
sie braucht *euch,* und *ihr* braucht *sie*
wir brauchen *euch,* und *ihr* braucht *uns*
sie brauchen *euch,* und *ihr* braucht *sie*

ich brauche *sie,* und *sie* brauchen *mich*
du brauchst *sie,* und *sie* brauchen *dich*
er braucht *sie,* und *sie* brauchen *ihn*
wir brauchen *sie,* und *sie* brauchen *uns*
ihr braucht *sie,* und *sie* brauchen *euch*

[2] Accusative of Personal Pronouns in Context

Practice these short conversations until you are ready to assume the role of either of the two speakers. After these conversations have been drilled in class, try to invent some variations of your own.

SEE
ANALYSIS
16–21
(pp. 38-41)

A: Erikas Mann heißt Max.
   Kennst du ihn?

B: Nein, ich kenne ihn nicht.

A: Aber ich weiß, er kennt dich.

B: Nein, er kennt mich nicht. Er weiß nur,
   wer ich bin.

A: Wagners Frau heißt Irene.
   Kennst du sie?

B: Nein, ich kenne sie nicht.

A: Aber sie sagt, sie kennt dich.

B: Nein, sie kennt mich nicht.
   Sie weiß nur, wer ich bin.

A: Irene ist jetzt Frau Wagner.

B: Liebt Wagner sie denn?

A: Ich glaube, ja.

B: Liebt *sie* ihn *auch?*

Erika's husband's name is Max.
Do you know him?

No, I don't know him.

But I know that he knows you.

No, he does not know me. He just knows
who I am.

Wagner's wife's name is Irene.
Do you know her?

No, I don't know her.

But she says she knows you.

No, she does not know me. She only knows
who I am.

Irene is now Mrs. Wagner.

Does Wagner love her?

I think so.

Does *she* love him, *too?*

A: Ich weiß nicht. Ich glaube, sie liebt Wagners Geld.

I don't think so. I think she loves Wagner's money.

A: Irene ist jetzt Frau Wagner.

Irene is now Mrs. Wagner.

B: Liebt sie ihn denn?

Does she love him?

A: Ich glaube, ja.

I think so.

B: Liebt *er* sie *auch?*

Does *he* love her, *too?*

A: Ich weiß nicht; ich glaube, er liebt Irenes Geld.

I don't think so; I think he loves Irene's money.

ER: Liest du *auch* schon wieder? Was liest du denn da?

SIE: Ich lese Faulkner: "Der Bär".

ER: Ist das ein Buch für dich? Das ist doch ein Buch für Männer.

SIE: Natürlich ist es ein Buch für Männer. Aber es ist auch ein Buch für mich. Für uns Frauen sind Männerbücher interessant. Und was liest du?

ER: Ich lese Daphne du Maurier: "Rebekka".

SIE: Also ein Buch für Frauen.

ER: Für uns Männer sind alle Frauenbücher interessant.

[3] Nominative and Accusative of Possessive Adjectives—**wissen**

Find out the system of these exercises. Practice the sentences aloud until you can easily repeat them.

SEE
ANALYSIS
18, 22

(pp. 38,
41-43)

Ich *weiß* nicht, wo meine *Mut*ter ist.   my
Du *weißt* nicht, wo deine *Mut*ter ist?   your
Er *weiß* nicht, wo seine *Mut*ter ist.   his
Sie *weiß* nicht, wo ihre *Mut*ter ist.   her   *fem.*
Wir *wissen* nicht, wo unsere *Mut*ter ist.   ours
Ihr *wißt* nicht, wo eure *Mut*ter ist?   your
Sie *wissen* nicht, wo ihre *Mut*ter ist.   their
Sie *wissen* nicht, wo Ihre *Mut*ter ist?   your

Ich *weiß* nicht, *wo* mein Vater *ar*beitet.   my
Du *weißt* nicht, *wo* dein Vater *ar*beitet?   your
Er *weiß* nicht, *wo* sein Vater *ar*beitet.   his
Sie *weiß* nicht, *wo* ihr Vater *ar*beitet.   her
Wir *wissen* nicht, *wo* unser Vater *ar*beitet.   ours
Ihr *wißt* nicht, *wo* euer Vater *ar*beitet?   your
Sie *wissen* nicht, *wo* ihr Vater *ar*beitet.   their
Sie *wissen* nicht, *wo* Ihr Vater *ar*beitet?   your

Ich zahle für *meinen* Kaffee, und *du* für *deinen* Kaffee.
Du zahlst für *deinen* Kaffee, und *er* für *seinen* Kaffee.
Er zahlt für *seinen* Kaffee, und *sie* für *ihren* Kaffee.
Sie zahlt für *ihren* Kaffee, und *wir* für *unsren* Kaffee.
Wir zahlen für *unsren* Kaffee, und *ihr* für *euren* Kaffee.
Ihr zahlt für *euren* Kaffee, und *sie* für *ihren* Kaffee.
Sie zahlen für *ihren* Kaffee, und *ich* für *meinen* Kaffee.

Ich lese *mein* Buch, und *du* liest *dein* Buch.
Du liest *dein* Buch, und *er* liest *sein* Buch.
Er liest *sein* Buch, und *sie* liest *ihr* Buch.
Sie liest *ihr* Buch, und *wir* lesen *unsere* Bücher.
Wir lesen *unsere* Bücher, und *ihr* lest *eure* Bücher.
Ihr lest *eure* Bücher, und *sie* lesen *ihre* Bücher.

[4] ein-Words and Personal Pronouns in Context

Practice these brief conversations with another student.

SEE
ANALYSIS
22
(pp. 41-43)

A: Hast du einen *Freund* hier in München?

B: Na*tür*lich habe ich einen *Freund* hier in München, und eine *Freun*din habe ich *auch.*

Do you have a friend here in Munich?

Of course, I have a friend here in Munich, and I also have a girl.

A: Frau *Schmidt,* Sie kennen doch Frau *Hoff*mann! Kennen Sie auch ihren *Mann?*

B: Ja, ihr Mann arbeitet für *mei*nen Mann.

Mrs. Smith, you know Mrs. Hoffmann, don't you? Do you also know her husband?

Yes, her husband works for my husband.

A: Gut, daß du *kommst,* Ingrid! Wo sind denn deine *Kinder?*

B: Unsere *Kinder* sind zu *Hause.* Mein *Mann* ist schon wieder zurück.

Nice that you are here, Ingrid! Where are your children?

Our children are at home. My husband is back.

ER: Was liest *du* denn da, Erika?

SIE: Ein Buch!

ER: Ist es interes*sant?*

SIE: Ja! Ein Stu*dent* liebt eine Stu*den*tin.

ER: Und *sie?* Liebt *sie* ihn *auch?*

SIE: Nein, diese Stu*den*tin liebt ihren Pro-*fes*sor.

ER: Und *er,* der Professor?

SIE: Der Pro*fes*sor ist ein Dummkopf und liebt nur *seine Bü*cher!

HE: What are you reading there, Erika?

SHE: A book!

HE: Is it interesting?

SHE: Yes, a student loves a coed.

HE: And does *she* love him *too?*

SHE: No, this coed loves her professor.

HE: And the professor?

SHE: The professor is a fool and loves only his books.

[5] Further Practice with **ein**-Words and Pronouns

Practice and invent your own variations:

Ich *weiß* nicht, liebt meine Frau *mich,* oder liebt sie mein *Geld?*

Ich *weiß* nicht, liebt Erika ihren *Mann,* oder liebt sie sein *Geld?*

Ich *weiß* nicht, liebst du deinen *Mann,* oder liebst du sein *Geld?*

Ich *weiß* nicht, liebt mein Mann *mich,* oder liebt er mein *Geld?*

Ich *weiß* nicht, liebt Erikas Mann *sie,* oder liebt er ihr *Geld?*

Ich *weiß* nicht, liebst du deine *Frau,* oder liebst du ihr *Geld?*

[6] Numbers; Plural of Nouns

Invent your own variations:

Wir haben nur *ein* Haus. Werners haben *drei* Häuser.—Meyers haben jetzt *einen* Sohn und *zwei* Töchter, aber *Schmidts* haben nur einen *Sohn.*—Ich glaube, *Holl*manns haben zwei *Töchter.* Oder haben sie nur *eine* Tochter?—Ich glaube, *Holl*manns haben *zwei* Söhne und *vier* Töchter. Oder haben sie nur *ein*en Sohn und vier Töchter?

We have only one house. The Werners have three houses.—The Meyers now have one son and two daughters, but the Schmidts have only a son.—I think the Hollmanns have two daughters. Or do they have only one daughter?—I think the Hollmanns have two sons and four daughters. Or do they have only one son and four daughters?

SEE ANALYSIS 23 (p. 43)

[7] The Second Prong of the Predicate—The Front Field

Study these sentences carefully. Practice them until you can develop all variations without having to look at your book.

IRREDUCIBLE VERBAL PATTERN: *das Licht anmachen*

Wir	machen	abends um sechs	das Licht an.
Abends	machen	wir um sechs	das Licht an.
Um sechs	machen	wir abends	das Licht an.
Abends um sechs	machen	wir	das Licht an.
Warum	macht	ihr schon um sechs	das Licht an?
	Macht	ihr schon um sechs	das Licht an?

SEE ANALYSIS 26–35 (pp. 45-55)

IRREDUCIBLE VERBAL PATTERN: *das Licht ausmachen*

Anton	macht	leider jeden Morgen um eins	das Licht aus.
Leider	macht	Anton jeden Morgen um eins	das Licht aus.
Jeden Morgen um eins	macht	Anton leider	das Licht aus.
Warum	macht	Anton jeden Morgen um eins	das Licht aus?
	Macht	Anton jeden Morgen um eins	das Licht aus?

,,Sie lernt jetzt hoffentlich fahren''

IRREDUCIBLE VERBAL PATTERN: *fahren lernen*

Sie	lernt	doch jetzt	fahren.
Jetzt	lernt	sie *doch*	fahren.
Wann	lernt	sie denn	fahren?
Hoffentlich	lernt	sie jetzt	fahren.
Sie	lernt	jetzt hoffentlich	fahren.
Jetzt	lernt	sie hoffentlich	fahren.

IRREDUCIBLE VERBAL PATTERN: *abfahren*

Der Zug	fährt	um 6 Uhr 5 (sechs Uhr fünf)	ab.
Um 6 Uhr 5	fahren	wir	ab.
Wo	fährt	denn der Zug nach Köln	ab?
Wann	fährst	du denn	ab?
	Fährt	der Zug jetzt	ab?
Meyers	fahren	schon um sechs Uhr	ab.

IRREDUCIBLE VERBAL PATTERN: *nach Berlin fahren*

Morgen	**fahre**	ich doch	**nach Berlin.**
Leider	**fahre**	ich morgen *doch*	**nach Berlin.**
Ich	**fahre**	morgen leider	**nach Berlin.**

IRREDUCIBLE VERBAL PATTERN: *wieder nach Hause fahren*

Morgen abend	**fährt**	sie gottseidank	**wieder nach Hause.**
Gottseidank	**fährt**	sie morgen abend	**wieder nach Hause.**
Sie	**fährt**	gottseidank morgen abend	**wieder nach Hause.**
Warum	**fährt**	sie denn morgen abend	**wieder nach Hause?**
	Fährt	sie morgen abend *doch*	**wieder nach Hause?**

IRREDUCIBLE VERBAL PATTERN: *ein Dummkopf sein*

Meyer	**ist**	leider	**ein Dummkopf.**
Leider	**ist**	Meyer	**ein Dummkopf.**
Wie du weißt,	**ist**	Meyer leider	**ein Dummkopf.**
Meyer	**ist,**	wie du weißt, leider	**ein Dummkopf.**
Leider	**ist**	Meyer, wie du weißt,	**ein Dummkopf.**

IRREDUCIBLE VERBAL PATTERN: *wieder gesund werden*

Nächstes Jahr	**wird**	Mutter hoffentlich	**wieder gesund.**
Mutter	**wird**	nächstes Jahr hoffentlich	**wieder gesund.**
Mutter	**wird**	hoffentlich nächstes Jahr	**wieder gesund.**
Hoffentlich	**wird**	Mutter nächstes Jahr	**wieder gesund.**

IRREDUCIBLE VERBAL PATTERN: *gut sein*

Das Bier	**ist**	doch	**gut**	in München.
In München	**ist**	das Bier	**gut.**	
	Ist	das Bier	**gut**	in München?
	Ist	das Bier in München	**gut?**	
Warum	**ist**	das Bier in München	**so gut?**	

Memorize this conversation and be ready to recite it in class.

ER: Weißt du *was,* Inge? *Erika* ist hier in Frankfurt!

You know what, Inge? Erika is here in Frankfurt!

SIE: Erika? Was tut denn *Erika* hier in Frankfurt?

Erika? What's Erika doing here in Frankfurt?

ER: Sie sagt, sie braucht einen *Sport*wagen!

She says she needs a sports car!

SIE: Einen *Sport*wagen*! Ei*nen Wagen *hat* sie schon, und *jetzt* braucht sie einen *Sport*wagen! Ja, ja, *sie* hat *al*les, und *wir* haben *nichts!*

A sports car! She already has *one* car, and now she needs a sports car. I tell you, she has everything, and we have nothing.

ER: Aber *Inge! Wer* hat denn *al*les? Du glaubst, Erika hat *al*les. Aber *ich* weiß, Erika ist *un*glücklich. Erika weiß es *auch! Sie* glaubt, sie hat *nichts.*

But Inge! Who does have everything? You think Erika has everything. But I know she is unhappy. Erika knows it too. She thinks she has nothing.

SIE: Aber *Geld* hat sie! Ist *Geld* „*nichts*"?

But she has money! Is money "nothing"?

ER: *Geld* ist *viel.* Aber Geld ist nicht *al*les. *Wir* sind Stu*den*ten. Stu*den*ten haben doch *nie* Geld! Aber ich bin *glück*lich, und *du* bist hoffentlich *auch* glücklich. Na*tür*lich hat Erika *Geld.* Sie ist doch jetzt Frau *Fischer. Frau Dr.* Anton *Fischer!* Warum bist *du* übrigens nicht Frau *Fischer?* Du weißt doch, Anton—

Money is a great deal. But money is not everything. We are students. Students, after all, never have any money. But I am happy, and I hope you are happy too. Of course Erika has money. She is now Mrs. Fischer, the wife of Dr. Anton Fischer. By the way, why aren't you Mrs. Fischer? You know, don't you, Anton . . .

SIE: *Ich?* Frau *Fischer? Antons Frau? Nein! Nie!*

I? Mrs. Fischer? Anton's wife? No! Never!

Eine Frau lügt nicht

Frau Lenz kommt zu Frau Bertram:

FRAU B: Guten Morgen, Frau *Lenz! Gut,* daß Sie *kom*men! Was machen Sie denn heute *a*bend? Ich glaube, *ich* gehe ins *Ki*no.

Good morning, Mrs. Lenz. I'm glad you came! What are you doing tonight? I think I'll go to the movies.

FRAU L: Ins *Ki*no!

To the movies!

FRAU B: *Ja,* ich brauche heute abend nicht zu *arbeiten,* und da bleibe ich natürlich nicht zu *Hause.*

Yes, I don't have to work tonight. And so, of course, I'm not staying home.

FRAU L: *So!* Sie gehen ins *Kino! Ich* gehe *nie* ins Kino.

Well! So you're going to the movies! I never go to the movies.

FRAU B: Warum kommen Sie nicht *mit* ins Kino! Frau *Hoff*mann—*ken*nen Sie Frau *Hoff*mann?—Frau Hoffmann kommt *auch* mit.

Why don't you come along to the movies too! Mrs. Hoffmann—do you know Mrs. Hoffmann?—Mrs. Hoffmann is coming along too.

FRAU L: Ja, Frau *Hoff*mann *ken*ne ich. Aber ins Kino? Ich *weiß* nicht. *Hermann* und *ich,* wir gehen *nie* ins Kino. Er sagt, wir haben kein *Geld.* Aber ich *glau*be, er bleibt lieber zu *Hause* und liest die Zeitung.

Yes, I know Mrs. Hoffmann. But to the movies? I don't know! Hermann and I, we never go to a movie. He says we can't afford it. But I think he'd rather stay home and read the paper.

FRAU B: Wo *ist* er denn heute? Wann kommt er denn heute nach *Hause?*

Where is he today? When is he coming home today?

FRAU L: *Heu*te kommt er *spät* nach Hause. Er arbeitet heute in *Bonn.*

Today he is coming home late. He is working in Bonn today.

FRAU B: In *Bonn! Das* ist doch *gut. Wir* drei, Sie, Frau *Hoff*mann und *ich,* gehen in's *Kino;* und *er* arbeitet in *Bonn*—und *glaubt* natürlich, seine *Frau* ist zu *Hause.*

In Bonn! That's just fine! The three of us, you, Mrs. Hoffmann, and I, will go to a show; and he is working in Bonn —and thinks, of course, that his wife is at home.

FRAU L: Ich *weiß* nicht. *Hermann* sagt—

I don't know. Hermann says—

FRAU B: Aber Frau *Lenz!* Sie sagen doch, Ihr Mann kommt heute *spät* nach Hause.

But Mrs. Lenz! You say your husband will come home late tonight.

FRAU L: *Gut,* Frau Bertram. Wir gehen alle *drei* ins Kino. Und *Hermann* sage ich *nichts.* —Übrigens, Frau Bertram, wie *heißt* denn der Film?

Fine! All three of us will go to the movies. And I shall say nothing to Hermann. By the way, Mrs. Bertram, what's the name of the movie?

FRAU B: Der *Film?* Ach *ja!* Der Film heißt: „Eine *Frau lügt* nicht".

The picture? Oh, yes! The picture is called: "A Woman Does Not Lie."

16 Verbs with Vowel Change

Certain verbs change the stem vowel in the **du**-form and **er**-form. In these cases, the vocabulary at the end of the unit will show in parentheses the correct **du**- and **er**-form. Example: **fahren (du fährst, er fährt)**; **lesen (du liest, er liest)**. Note that if there is a change of vowel, it occurs both with **du** and with **er,** but nowhere else.

ich	fahre	I	go		ich	lese	I	read
du	fährst	you	go		du	liest	you	read
er		he			er		he	
sie	fährt	she	goes		sie	liest	she	reads
es		it			es		it	
wir	fahren	we	go		wir	lesen	we	read
ihr	fahrt	you	go		ihr	lest	you	read
sie	fahren	they	go		sie	lesen	they	read
Sie	fahren	you	go		Sie	lesen	you	read

17 Stems Ending in -s

After a stem which ends in **-s,** like **lesen,** the **du**-form adds **-t,** not **-st,** to the stem. As a result, the **du**-form becomes identical with the **er**-form:

ich lese
du liest
er liest

18 **werden** and **wissen**

Like **sein** and **haben, werden** (*to become*) and **wissen** (*to know facts*) are irregular. In the present tense, they are inflected as follows:

ich	werde		ich	weiß
du	wirst		du	weißt
er			er	
sie	wird		sie	weiß
es			es	
wir	werden		wir	wissen
ihr	werdet		ihr	wißt
sie	werden		sie	wissen
Sie	werden		Sie	wissen

19 Singular and Plural Forms of Nouns

With a few exceptions, English nouns form the plural by adding -s or -es to the singular: *house, houses; glass, glasses;* but *foot, feet.*

In German, the plural form of a noun usually does not end in -s. It may be the same as the singular form, as in the case of English *sheep,* or it may be different from the singular form, as in the case of English *mouse, mice* or *child, children.*

Since there are no rules by which to tell the plural form of a given singular, there is only one safe way to learn the plural: memorize it together with the singular.

From Unit 2 on, the plural forms are indicated in the vocabulary as follows:

der Vater, ÷ means that the plural of	**der Vater** is	**die Väter;**
das Kind, –er	**das Kind**	**die Kinder;**
der Hund, –e	**der Hund**	**die Hunde.**

The articles preceding plural nouns are the same for all three genders.

SINGULAR	PLURAL
der Vater	**die Väter**
die Mutter	**die Mütter**
das Kind	**die Kinder**

The nouns used in Unit 1 have the following plurals:

der Abend	**die Abende**
die Frau	**die Frauen**
der Gott	**die Götter**
das Haus	**die Häuser**
der Herr	**die Herren**
der Hund	**die Hunde**
das Jahr	**die Jahre**
das Kind	**die Kinder**
die Kirche	**die Kirchen**
der Mann	**die Männer**
der Student	**die Studenten**
die Studentin	**die Studentinnen**
die Tochter	**die Töchter**
der Winter	**die Winter**
die Zeitung	**die Zeitungen**

Nouns of non-German origin may end in -s:

das Auto	**die Autos**
das Büro	**die Büros**
das Kino	**die Kinos**

20   The Nominative and Accusative Cases

In English we don't talk much about "cases" of nouns and pronouns, because the function of a noun in a sentence is ordinarily determined by its
position. For instance, how do we know who bites whom in the sentence
The dog bit the cat? Position alone indicates that *dog* is the subject and
that *cat* is the object. By reversing position, the functions of *cat* and *dog*
are *also* reversed.

However, in English sentences such as *I love him* the situation is quite
different. Here, function is indicated by position *and* by form. Form alone
would be sufficient, and, at least in theory, one could say *Him love I* without being misunderstood.

In German, the term "nominative case," or simply "nominative," is used
whenever a noun or a pronoun, *by virtue of either its form or its position,*
is marked as the subject or as the predicate noun. The term "accusative
case," or simply "accusative," is used whenever a word, *by form or position,* is marked as the direct object of a verb or of certain prepositions such
as **für.**

Whenever function is not indicated by form, German, like English, relies
on position. In

> **Meine Mutter kennt diese Frau**   My mother knows this woman

meine Mutter and **diese Frau** can both be either nominative or accusative
as far as form is concerned, but position makes **meine Mutter** the subject.
In

> **Diese Frau kennt meine Mutter**   This woman knows my mother

position makes **diese Frau** the subject and **meine Mutter** the object.

On the other hand, the two German sentences

> **Er liebt seinen Sohn**

and

> **Seinen Sohn liebt er**

both mean *He loves his son.* The **er** indicates by its form that it is the
subject, and **seinen** indicates by its form that **seinen Sohn** must be the object. In this case, therefore, form alone is sufficient to indicate function.

21   The Nominative and Accusative Forms of
         Personal Pronouns

NOMINATIVE	ich	du	er	sie	es	wir	ihr	sie	(Sie)
ACCUSATIVE	mich	dich	ihn	sie	es	uns	euch	sie	(Sie)

There is no difference in form between the nominative and the accusative of **sie, Sie,** and **es.**

Agreement between Nouns and Pronouns

Since **der Kaffee** is a masculine noun, the thing denoted by **dieser Kaffee** (this coffee) is, from a German point of view, a "he" and must be referred to by using the masculine pronouns **er** and **ihn:**

> **Er (dieser Kaffee) ist gut. Wo kaufst du ihn?**

Similarly, **die Zeitung** is a "she" and must be referred to by using the feminine pronoun **sie:**

> **Sie (die Zeitung) ist uninteressant. Ich lese sie nie.**

On the other hand, **das Geld** and **das Kind** are both neuter nouns. If these nouns are replaced by pronouns, one must use **es:**

> **Ich brauche es (das Geld).**
> **Ist es (das Kind) gesund?**

22 The Nominative and Accusative of **der**-Words, **ein**-Words, and Nouns

The term "**der**-words" is used for all words which indicate gender, case, and number in the same way in which the definite article **der,** by changing its form, indicates gender, case, and number. For instance, **dieser, jeder,** and **wer** are **der**-words. The term "**ein**-word" is used for all words which indicate case and number in the same way in which the indefinite article **ein** shows case and number. **Kein** (*no, not a*) and the possessive adjectives are **ein**-words.

The possessive adjectives are:

mein	my		**unser**	our
dein	your		**euer**	your
sein	his		**ihr**	their
ihr	her		**Ihr**	your (polite)
sein	its			

The Nominative and Accusative of **der**-Words

	MASC.	FEM.	NEUTER	MASC.	FEM.	NEUTER
NOM. SING.	der	die	das	dieser	diese	dieses
ACC. SING.	den	die	das	diesen	diese	dieses
NOM. PLUR.		die			diese	
ACC. PLUR.		die			diese	

EXAMPLES:

Der Vater kennt diese Frau.   Father knows this woman.

Diese Frau kennt der Vater.   (Function indicated by form; **der Vater** can only be nominative.)

However:

Die Mutter liebt dieses Kind.   Mother loves this child.

                                      (Function indicated by position only. The nominative and accusative forms of **die Mutter** and **dieses Kind** are identical.)

Die Mutter kennt diese Frau.   Mother knows this woman.

                                      (Function indicated by position only. The nominative and accusative forms of **die Mutter** and **diese Frau** are identical.)

NOTE:

1. Only the masculine singular of the **der**-words distinguishes the nominative from the accusative.

2. In the plural, all three genders have the same forms.

The Nominative and Accusative of **ein**-Words

	MASC.	FEM.	NEUTER	MASC.	FEM.	NEUTER	MASC.	FEM.	NEUTER
NOM. SING.	ein	eine	ein	mein	meine	mein	kein	keine	kein
ACC. SING.	einen	eine	ein	meinen	meine	mein	keinen	keine	kein
NOM. PLUR.	*(no plural)*				meine			keine	
ACC. PLUR.					meine			keine	

EXAMPLES:

Mein Vater kennt diese Frau.   My father knows this woman.

Diese Frau kennt mein Vater.   (Function indicated by form; **mein Vater** can only be nominative.)

However:

Frau Schmitz, meine Freundin versteht Ihre Tochter.   Mrs. Schmitz, my friend understands your daughter.

                                      (Function indicated by position.)

Frau Schmitz, Ihre Tochter versteht meine Freundin.   Mrs. Schmitz, your daughter understands my friend.

                                      (Function indicated by position.)

Note:

1. Only the masculine singular of the **ein**-words distinguishes the nominative from the accusative.

2. Remember: The plural of **ein Kind** is **Kinder.**

3. In the accusative of **unser** and **euer,** the **-e-** before the **-r-** is frequently dropped.

> **unseren** or **unsren** 　　　　**unsere** or **unsre.**

4. In the plural, all three genders have the same forms.

The Accusative of Nouns

Only very few nouns distinguish between nominative and accusative—for example, **der Mensch** and **der Student,** which add **-en** in all cases but the nominative singular. **Der Herr** adds an **-n** in all singular forms and an **-en** in all plural forms.

NOM. SING.	der Mensch	der Student	der Herr
ACC. SING.	den Menschen	den Studenten	den Herrn
NOM. PLUR.	die Menschen	die Studenten	die Herren
ACC. PLUR.	die Menschen	die Studenten	die Herren

23 Cardinal Numbers

The cardinal numbers from 1 to 6 are:

1	eins		4	vier
2	zwei		5	fünf
3	drei		6	sechs

The numeral **eins** is used only for counting, for telephone numbers, in arithmetic, etc; it is never used together with a following noun. In front of a noun, the numeral looks like the indefinite article **ein** and is declined the same way. In the sentence **wir haben eine Tochter, eine** means *one,* if it is stressed, and *a,* if it is not stressed.

NUMERAL	Ich glaube, Meyers haben zwei *Söhne.*—Nein, sie haben nur *einen* Sohn.	I believe the Meyers have two sons. —No, they have only *one* son.
INDEFINITE ARTICLE	Ich glaube, Meyers haben jetzt auch eine *Tochter.*—Nein, sie haben nur einen *Sohn.*	I believe the Meyers now have a *daughter,* too.—No, they have only a *son.*

If the other numbers are followed by a noun, they are not changed:

> **Wir haben drei Kinder, zwei Autos und einen Hund.**

24   Adverbs and Predicate Adjectives

In the English sentences

> He lived happily ever after
> He was happy as long as he lived

the word *happily* is an adverb and characterizes the verbal act, the mode of living. The word *happy* is a predicate adjective. It characterizes the subject, not the verbal act.

German normally makes no distinction in form between a predicate adjective and an adverb.

PREDICATE ADJECTIVE	**Der Mensch ist gut.**	Man is good.
ADVERB	**Er fährt gut.**	He drives well.
PREDICATE ADJECTIVE	**Hildegard ist so natürlich.**	Hildegard is so natural.
ADVERB	**Hildegard lacht so natürlich.**	Hildegard laughs so naturally.

NOTE: For the time being, do not use adjectives attributively—that is, in front of the noun to which they belong.

25   Sentence Adverbs

In most cases, adverbs modify

a verb:	He lived *happily* ever after.
an adjective:	He is *unusually* intelligent.
another adverb:	It happened *very* suddenly.

However, in order to use German adverbs correctly, it should be noted that certain adverbs, called "sentence adverbs," express the attitude of the speaker toward the content of the whole sentence.

Thus, *unfortunately, naturally,* and *obviously* are used as sentence adverbs in

> Unfortunately he died.
> (It is, in my opinion, unfortunate that he died.)

> Naturally, he was not at home.
> (As I had expected, he was not at home.)

> He was obviously not stupid.
> (It was clear to all of us that he wasn't stupid.)

Two German sentence adverbs were used in Unit 1: **natürlich** and **übrigens.** Three more—**leider,** *unfortunately;* **gottseidank,** *thank goodness;* and **hoffentlich,** *I hope*—are introduced in this unit. In both English and German, these sentence adverbs count as *independent syntactical units* as far as word order is concerned.

26 German Word Order

To the native speaker of English, German word order often appears outrageously capricious and illogical. It seems strange that a German, disregarding the "logical" order of the English sentence

During the winter the street lights go on here at four,

will insist on saying

Im Winter gehen hier um vier die Laternen an,

which, literally imitated, would read in English

[During the winter go here at four the street lights on.]

Why is it that what is "unnatural" to the native speaker of English is so "natural" to a German—and vice versa?

The explanation is that position is used as a "signal" to express meaning—as anybody can see who looks at the three sentences:

He looked over the fence.
He overlooked the fence.
He looked the fence over.

Word order—the arrangement of words within a sentence—is comparable to the Morse Code: it is established by convention. Once a specific system has been adopted, and once both speaker and listener are used to the "code," the position of a word becomes a semantic signal conveying to the listener a very specific message. That is why the three English clauses

When I had that trained dog
When I had that dog trained
When I had trained that dog

are not interchangeable, for the meaning and function of *trained* depends just as much on its position as on its form.

If the student is willing to learn a new system "from scratch," German word order ceases to be a major problem, for the German system, though not at all like the English system, is really quite simple and logical.

27 The Over-all Structure of German Assertions

The structure of the simple statement

Das Bier ist übrigens gut hier in München

exemplifies the structure of all German assertions. This unvarying structure can be represented by the following schematic diagram:

FRONT FIELD	First Part of Predicate	INNER FIELD	Second Part of Predicate	END FIELD
Das Bier	ist	übrigens	gut	hier in München

Not all German assertions use this pattern in its entirety, but *no German assertion will disregard it,* and all German assertions have at least a front field and a first part of the predicate. The following statements use the pattern

FRONT FIELD	First Part of Predicate
Ich	lese
Es	regnet
Sie	kommen

The following statements use the pattern

FRONT FIELD	First Part of Predicate	INNER FIELD
Das	weiß	ich
Da	ist	Frau Meyer
Hier in München	wohnt	auch Professor Dübel

The following statements use the pattern

FRONT FIELD	First Part of Predicate	INNER FIELD	Second Part of Predicate
Ich	bleibe	natürlich	zu Hause
Wir	fahren	morgen	nach Berlin
Das Bier	ist	übrigens	gut

The following statement uses the complete pattern

FRONT FIELD	First Part of Predicate	INNER FIELD	Second Part of Predicate	END FIELD
Das Bier	ist	übrigens	gut	hier in München

The structural features most alien to the American student are the two "slots" reserved for the first and the second part of the predicate. We shall discuss this problem in the following two sections.

28 Compound Verbs

If one compares the English sentences

He carried this for half an hour

and

He carried this on for half an hour

,,Das Bier ist übrigens gut hier in München''

it becomes apparent that the addition of *on* in the second sentence influences the meaning of *carried* to such an extent that, while the *this* in the first sentence must be an object, the *this* in the second sentence must be some activity. In a dictionary, one must therefore recognize that *to carry on* is a verb different in meaning from the simple verb *to carry*.

We shall call *to carry on* a "compound verb"—that is, a verb whose full meaning is the compound effect of two parts: of a simple verb such as *to carry*, and of a complement like *on*.

German has literally hundreds of verbs comparable to English *to carry on*. One such verb was used in the sentence

> **Hier gehen um vier die Laternen an**
> Here the street lights go on at four.

The verbs **gehen** and *go* are fused with the prepositions **an** and *on* into a new unit of meaning: **gehen an** and *go on* mean "are turned on."

That **gehen an** and *go on* have become one single semantic unit can also be shown in the following way: By leaving out **hier,** *here* and **um vier,** *at four,* the sentence

> **Hier gehen um vier die Laternen an**
> Here the street lights go on at four

can be reduced to

> **Die Laternen gehen an.**
> The street lights go on.

However, a further reduction is impossible; for leaving out **an** or *on* would result in

> **Die Laternen gehen.**
> The street lights go.

It is easy to see that the result of this further shortening would be not merely a reduction, but a completely different sentence, applicable only in a completely different situation. This proves that **gehen an** and *go on* are *irreducible verbal patterns;* and from the point of view of German sentence structure *all such irreducible verbal patterns are compound verbs.*

The sentence

> **Natürlich bin ich heute abend zu Hause**
> Of course I shall be at home tonight

also contains an irreducible verbal pattern. If a good friend of mine tells me over the phone, "I just heard that Mr. Bigwig is flying in at six, and it is important that you see him right away," I might say to him:

Gut, ich bin heute abend zu Hause.
Fine, I shall be at home tonight.

I might leave out **heute abend** and say

Gut, ich bin zu Hause.
Fine, I shall be at home.

But I cannot make a further reduction and say

Gut, ich bin.
Fine, I am.

That simply would not make any sense. The **bin zu Hause,** in other words, is an "irreducible verbal pattern"—that is, from the German point of view, a compound verb; and **zu Hause** is the complement of **bin.**

For our purposes, then,

Die Laternen | **gehen** | **an**

and

Ich | **bin** | **zu Hause**

are parallel cases: Both statements contain an irreducible verbal pattern consisting of a simple verb and a complement. In one case, the complement is the preposition **an;** in the other case, it is the idiom **zu Hause.** Adjectives, adverbs, infinitives, and other words may also be used as verbal complements.

The feeling of the "togetherness" of **bin** and **zu Hause** is, by the way, so strong in German that the question **Bist du zu Hause?** can be answered by **Ja!** or by **Ja, ich bin zu Hause,** but not by

Beware: [**Bist du zu Hause?—Ja, ich bin.**]   DO NOT USE!
Americanism:

If one wants to use the infinitive of a compound verb—and one frequently has to—the complement is always placed in front of the simple infinitive. Thus the infinitive belonging to the sentence **Ich fahre morgen wieder nach Hause** is **wieder nach Hause fahren,** and the infinitive belonging to **Der Zug fährt jetzt ab** is **ab'fahren.**

The case of **abfahren** shows that if the complement is a preposition like **an** or **aus**, or a one-word adverb like **ab**, **zurück**, or **wieder**, it is always joined to the simple infinitive and carries the main word stress. In dictionaries **abfahren** is listed under **ab**, not under **fahren**.

*an*gehen	to go on	**Die Laternen gehen an.** The street lights go on.
*aus*gehen	to go out	**Die Laternen gehen aus.** The street lights go out.
*an*machen	to turn on	**Wir machen das Licht an.** We turn on the light.
*aus*machen	to turn off	**Wir machen das Licht aus.** We turn off the light.
*ab*fahren	to depart	**Der Zug fährt sofort ab.** The train will depart at once.
*zurück*fahren	to return	**Ich fahre morgen zurück.** I shall return tomorrow.
*wie*derkommen	to come back	**Ich komme nächstes Jahr wieder.** I will come back next year.
*fah*ren lernen	to learn how to drive	**Sie lernt jetzt fahren.** She is now taking driving lessons.
zu *Hause* bleiben	to stay home	**Ich bleibe heute zu Hause.** I am staying home today.
zu *Hause* sein	to be at home	**Ich bin heute zu Hause.** I am at home today.
nach *Hause* kommen	to come home	**Er kommt heute nach Hause.** He is coming home today.
nach *Hause* gehen	to go home	**Ich gehe jetzt nach Hause.** I am going home now.

29 The Two-Pronged Predicate

If one realizes that **angehen** and **zu Hause sein** are compound verbs, one can say that in the sentences

Hier gehen um vier die Laternen an

and

Natürlich bin ich heute abend zu Hause

the inflected verb forms **gehen** and **bin** are the first, and the complements **an** and **zu Hause** the second part of the predicate. Schematically, the patterns used in English and German would look as follows:

Here the street lights go   on at four.

Hier gehen um vier die Laternen an.

Of course I am at home tonight.

Natürlich bin ich heute abend zu Hause.

In the German sentences, the two parts of the predicate are separated by the inner field. *This pulling apart of all compound verbs is the most characteristic feature of German syntax.* Any student set upon acquiring idiomatic habits of speech must, therefore, master this principle from the very beginning. For the sentence

[Hier die Laternen gehen an um vier.]

is just as unacceptable as the Germanism

[Here go the street lights at four on .]

,,Im Winter gehen hier um vier die Laternen an.''

The two parts of the German predicate embrace the inner field like a pair of parentheses, or like the prongs that hold the jewel of a ring in place. And since it is inconvenient to speak of "the first part of the predicate" and "the second part of the predicate," we shall call them "the first prong" and "the second prong."

As was pointed out in **9,** the first prong—that is, the inflected verb—is position-fixed. *The second prong is also position-fixed:* it follows the inner field.

30   The Front Field and Its Function

As was pointed out in **9,** the front field is always occupied by only *one* unit—that is, by the answer to only *one* possible question

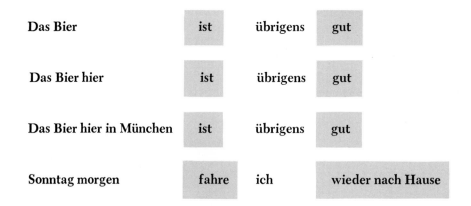

One of the main functions of the front field is to mention an element already known to the listener about which the speaker wants to say something not yet known to the listener. Usually, the element in the front field has, therefore, no news value at all. (It contains the answer to a *possible* question, not the answer to an *actual* question.) Rather, the front field picks up an element already mentioned and thus connects one statement with a preceding statement.

QUESTION   Wann regnet es denn in *Deutsch*land?
ANSWER   Im *Win*ter. or: In Deutschland regnet es im *Win*ter.
NOT   [Im *Win*ter regnet es in Deutschland.]

QUESTION	Wer ist denn *das?*
ANSWER	Frau *Mey*er. or: Das ist Frau *Mey*er.
NOT	[Frau *Mey*er ist das.]

QUESTION	Wo wohnt denn Dr. *Mey*er?
ANSWER	In *Köln.* or: Dr. Meyer wohnt in *Köln.*
NOT	[In *Köln* wohnt Dr. Meyer.]

QUESTION	Wann gehen denn hier die La*ter*nen an?
ANSWER	Um *vier.* or: Die Laternen gehen hier um *vier* an.
NOT	[Um *vier* gehen hier die Laternen an.]

Only after questions of the type *Who did you say lives in Munich?* or *What did you say her name was?* is the answering unit frequently found in the front field.

QUESTION	Wie *heißt* er denn?
ANSWER	*Hans.* or: Er heißt *Hans.*

QUESTION	*Wie* heißt er?
ANSWER	*Hans* heißt er.

If the subject does not occupy the front field—and very often it does not—it is part of the inner field. *Personal pronoun subjects stand at the very beginning of the inner field.* The position of noun subjects varies.

31 Directives as Verbal Complements

The question **Wohin?** (Where to?) is frequently answered by a prepositional phrase:

Wohin fährt er denn?—Er fährt nach Köln.

We shall call such prepositional phrases *directives*. German directives are verbal complements—that is, they form a second prong and are, therefore, just as position-fixed as **zu Hause** in **zu Hause sein.**

Morgen	fahre	ich leider	nach Berlin.
Ich	fahre	leider morgen	nach Berlin.
Leider	fahre	ich morgen	nach Berlin.

Morgen	fahre	ich gottseidank	wieder nach Hause.
Ich	fahre	morgen gottseidank	wieder nach Hause.
Gottseidank	fahre	ich morgen	wieder nach Hause.

32 Predicate Adjectives and Predicate Nouns as
Verbal Complements

German predicate adjectives and predicate nouns are verbal complements;
they form a second prong and follow the inner field:

Erika	ist,	wie du weißt,	intelligent
Wie du weißt,	ist	Erika	intelligent
Meyer	ist,	wie du weißt, leider	ein Dummkopf
Leider	ist	Meyer, wie du weißt,	ein Dummkopf
Wie du weißt,	ist	Meyer leider	ein Dummkopf

33 Shift of Position

It has already been pointed out several times that a speaker does not
necessarily have to start the assertion **Ich bleibe heute abend natürlich
zu Hause** with the subject **ich.** Depending upon the specific situation,
he can choose any of four possible positions.

Ich	bleibe	heute abend natürlich	zu Hause.
Ich	bleibe	natürlich heute abend	zu Hause.
Natürlich	bleibe	ich heute abend	zu Hause.
Heute abend	bleibe	ich natürlich	zu Hause.

These four variations show that any unit in the inner field can be brought
into the front field, thereby forcing the unit already in the front field
into the inner field. The second prong, however, stays in its position. For
the time being, do not change the position of the second prong. In the
sentence [**Zu Hause bleibe ich heute abend natürlich**], **natürlich** would
mean *natural,* not *naturally.*

34 The End Field

Most German assertions end with the second prong and have, therefore,
no end field. The end field *may* be used for afterthoughts—that is, for
syntactical units added *after* the assertion has been completed by the
second prong. If the speaker thinks of these afterthoughts in time, he
places them in the inner field or in the front field. If sentence adverbs
appear in the end field, they are set off by a comma.

Heute	ist	er	zu Hause	, gottseidank.
Heute	ist	er gottseidank	zu Hause	
Er	ist	heute gottseidank	zu Hause	
Er	ist	heute	zu Hause	, gottseidank.
Gottseidank	ist	er heute	zu Hause	

Sometimes the end field is used to clarify, by way of an afterthought, one of the units already mentioned. Thus **hier in München** in the following sentence clarifies **das Bier**:

Das Bier	ist	übrigens	*gut*	hier in München.

Das *Bier* hier in München	ist	übrigens	gut

35 Word Order in German Questions

German questions follow the pattern of word order found in assertions.

In word questions, the front field is *always* occupied by an interrogative, and personal pronoun subjects are always placed at the beginning of the inner field.

FRONT FIELD	1st Prong	INNER FIELD	2nd Prong
Warum	bleibst	du heute abend	zu Hause?
Warum	fahren	Sie morgen	nach Köln?

Yes-or-no questions have no front field, and again pronoun subjects are placed immediately after the opening verb—that is, at the beginning of the inner field.

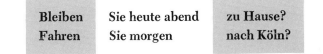

Bleiben	Sie heute abend	zu Hause?
Fahren	Sie morgen	nach Köln?

36 doch

The word **doch** may be stressed or unstressed. The stressed **doch** implies that the fact reported is contrary to expectations. This stressed **doch** is frequently preceded by **also**, which adds the flavor of "so" when used at the beginning of English sentences.

Er kommt *doch!*	He's coming after all!
Es regnet also *doch!*	So it's raining after all. (That's what I was afraid of.)
Sie wird also *doch* **wieder gesund.**	So she is regaining her health after all. (Nobody had expected it.)
Er ist also *doch* **ein Dummkopf.**	So he really *is* a dumbbell. (There is no longer any doubt about it.)

The unstressed **doch** appears with great frequency in questions and assertions. It expresses the hope of the speaker that the opposite is not true or that the statement made cannot be contradicted.

Du bist doch ge*sund!*	You're healthy, aren't you?
Erika hat doch *Geld!*	Erika has money, doesn't she?
Sie *kom*men doch heute abend?	You are coming tonight, I hope?

EXERCISES

A. Complete the following conjugation samples. Be prepared to go through these sentences in class without your book.

SEE LAB
EXERCISE
2.1

(p. 623)

1. Ich bin zu Hause. _____bist_____ du zu Hause?
   Du _bist_____ zu Hause. _____ist_____ er zu Hause?
   Er _ist_____ zu Hause. _____sind_____ wir zu Hause?
   Wir _sind_____ zu Hause. _____seid_____ ihr zu Hause?
   Ihr _seid_____ zu Hause. _____sind_____ sie zu Hause?

2. Ich gehe heute mit. _Gehst_____ du heute nicht mit?
   Du _gehst_____ heute mit. _Geht_____ er heute nicht mit?
   Er _geht_____ heute mit. _____Gehen_____ wir heute nicht mit?
   Wir _gehen_____ heute mit. _Geht_____ ihr heute nicht mit?
   Ihr _geht_____ heute mit. _Gehen_____ sie heute nicht mit?

3. Ich weiß es. _Weißt_____ du es *auch?*
   Du _weißt_____ es. _Weiß_____ er es *auch?*
   Wir _wissen_____ es. _Wißt_____ ihr es *auch?*
   Ihr _wißt_____ es. _Wissen_____ sie es *auch?*

4. Ich fahre morgen nach Berlin. _Fährst_ du morgen *auch* nach Berlin?
   Du _fährst_ morgen nach Berlin. _Fährt_ er morgen *auch* nach Berlin?
   Er _fährt_ morgen nach Berlin. _Fahren_ wir morgen *auch* nach Berlin?
   Wir _fahren_ morgen nach Berlin. _Fahrt_ ihr morgen *auch* nach Berlin?
   Ihr _fahrt_ morgen nach Berlin. _Fahren_ sie morgen *auch* nach Berlin?

5. Ich lese keine Zeitung. _Liest_ du auch keine Zeitung?
   Du _liest_ keine Zeitung. _Liest_ er auch keine Zeitung?
   Er _liest_ keine Zeitung. _Lesen_ wir auch keine Zeitung?
   Wir _lesen_ keine Zeitung. _Lest_ ihr auch keine Zeitung?
   Ihr _lest_ keine Zeitung. _Lesen_ sie auch keine Zeitung?

NOTE: **kein** is an **ein**-word (see **22**); use it only in the pattern of this exercise.

B. Express in German:

SEE LAB EXERCISES 2.3–2.4

(p. 623)

1. We have a dog.
2. Our dog's name is Susi.
3. My mother knows this woman.
4. My father is well again.
5. I need a car.
6. Is that your son, Mrs. Meyer?
7. Is that your daughter, Mrs. Meyer?
8. He loves his son.
9. She loves this student.
10. Our girl-students live here.
11. Does your wife work in Cologne, Mr. Meyer?
12. Do you know my girl friend?
13. Do you know this woman?
14. Do you know this child?
15. That is her father.
16. She loves her father.
17. The Meyers love their children.
18. He loves his daughters.
19. He loves a co-ed.
20. She loves her sons.

C. Count:

Ein Kind,	zwei _____,	drei _____,	vier _____,	fünf _____	sechs _____,	

Ein Abend,
Eine Frau,
Ein Zug,
Ein Wagen,
Ein Sohn,

Eine Tochter,
Eine Kirche,
Eine Zeitung,
Ein Buch,
Ein Mensch,

D. In the following sentences, replace the subject by a pronoun.

1. Erika ist jetzt meine Frau.
2. In Köln hat Meyer drei Häuser.
3. Frau Bertram ist eine Dame.
4. Unser Hund ist eine „sie“.
5. Dieses Buch ist uninteressant.
6. Der Zug fährt nach Frankfurt.
7. Mein Freund hat eine Freundin.
8. Seine Frau hat Geld.
9. Dein Kind hat Hunger.
10. Herr Meyer ist mein Freund.

E. Replace the object by a pronoun.

1. Wir kaufen das Auto in Köln.
2. Ich kenne Herrn Lenz nicht.
3. Er liest diese Zeitung nicht.
4. Wir kaufen den Wagen in Frankfurt.
5. Liebst du Inge?
6. Verstehst du deinen Vater?
7. Ich verstehe Hans und Erika gut.
8. Kennen Sie seine Kinder?
9. Ich brauche das Buch.
10. Wann brauchst du das Geld?

F. Formulate affirmative answers to the following questions, using personal pronouns.

Kennen Sie Frau Bertram?	**Ja, ich kenne sie.**

1. Kennen Sie Fritz Bertram?
2. Kennen Sie mich?
3. Kennst du die drei Frauen da?
4. Hast du das Geld schon?
5. Arbeitet dein Vater da?
6. Verstehst du deine Mutter?
7. Liebst du deine Mutter?

8. Liebt Erika ihren Vater?
9. Brauchst du heute den Wagen?
10. Fährt der Zug sofort ab?
11. Machst du das Licht aus?
12. Ist das Bier gut hier?

G. By shifting position, write down all possible variations of the following sentences. Do not forget the principle of the two-pronged predicate. The number of possibilities is suggested by the empty lines. For your guidance, the units which may shift position are placed in parentheses. If the subject is moved into the inner field, place it right after the first prong. Do not use the end field.

1. (Ich) bleibe (heute) (natürlich) zu Hause.
2.
3.

SEE LAB
EXERCISE
2.6

(p. 623)

1. (Diese Laterne) geht (um sechs Uhr) an.
2.

1. (Morgen abend) ist (er) (natürlich) wieder zu Hause.
2.
3.

1. (Sie) fährt (morgen) (hoffentlich) wieder nach Hause.
2.
3.

1. (Hoffentlich) ist (Mutter) (nächstes Jahr) wieder gesund.
2.
3.

VOCABULARY

aber but; however
ab off
alles everything
also therefore; well; in other words
an on; at
    angehen to go on
aus out
    ausgehen to go out
das Auto, –s car
das Bier, –e beer
das Buch, ̈-er book
da there; then; under these

circumstances
die Dame, –n lady, woman
daß that (*conjunction*)
dieser, diese, dieses this
doch (*see* 36)
drei three
der Dummkopf (*plural:* **die Dummköpfe**) dumbbell, fool
eins one (*cardinal number*)
fahren (**du fährst, er fährt**) to drive, to go (by train, boat, plane, car)

abfahren to depart, to leave
fahren lernen to learn how to drive
der Film, –e movie, film
der Freund, –e friend (*masculine*)
die Freundin, –nen friend (*feminine*)
fünf five
für for (*governs accusative*)
gesund well, healthy
glücklich happy
    un'glücklich unhappy

gottseidank thank heavens, thank goodness
heißen to be called; to mean
hoffen to hope
   hoffentlich I hope (*sentence adverb*)
interessant' interesting
   un'interessant uninteresting
jeder, jede, jedes each, every
der Kaffee coffee
kaufen to buy
kein no (not any)
kennen to know (to be acquainted with)
lachen to laugh
die Laterne, –n street light
leider unfortunately (*sentence adverb*)
lesen (du liest, er liest) to read
das Licht, –er light
lieben to love

lieber rather
lügen to tell a lie
machen to make; to do
   anmachen to turn on
   ausmachen to turn off
der Mensch, –en man, human being
mit with; along
die Mutter, ⁀ mother
nichts nothing
nie never
nur only
oder or
der Profes'sor, die Professo'-ren professor
sechs six
so so
sofort immediately
der Sohn, ⁀e son
der Student', –en student (*masculine*)
   die Studen'tin, –nen student (*feminine*)

die Uhr, –en clock, watch
   um ein Uhr at one o'clock
um around; about; at
der Vater, ⁀ father
verstehen to understand
viel much
   soviel so much, as much
vier four
der Wagen, – car; wagon
warum why
werden to become
wie as; like; how
wissen to know (as a fact)
wohin? where, where to? (asks for a goal, not a location)
zahlen to pay (in a restaurant)
der Zug, ⁀e train
zurück back
   wieder zurück back, back again
zwei two

UNIT 3: aber, oder, denn, und—Negation by **kein** and **nicht**—The Modals—Contrast Intonation—The Imperative

PATTERNS

[1] aber, oder, denn, und

Dieses Jahr bleiben wir zu *Hause*.	*This* year we'll stay at *home*.	SEE ANALYSIS 37
Aber *nächs*tes Jahr fahren wir nach *Deutsch-*land.	But *next* year we are going to *Germany*.	(p. 80)
*Nächs*tes Jahr fahren wir aber nach *Deutsch-*land.		
Kommst du *heu*te, oder kommst du *mor-*gen?	Are you coming *today*, or will you come *tomorrow?*	
Alle Menschen sind egoistisch; denn *jeder* Mensch will *glück*lich werden.	*All* humans are *egoistic*, for every human being wants to be *happy*.	
Meyers fahren nach *Köln*, und *wir* fahren nach *Mün*chen.	The Meyers are going to *Cologne*, and *we* are going to *Munich*.	

[2] nicht, nicht wahr

Wohnen Sie in *Köln?*	Do you live in *Cologne?*	SEE ANALYSIS 38–39
Sie wohnen doch in *Köln*, nicht *wahr?*	You live in *Cologne*, don't you?	(pp. 80-81)
Sie wohnen doch in *Köln*, *nicht?*	You live in *Cologne*, don't you?	
Haben Meyers einen *Sohn?*	Do Meyers have a *son?*	
Meyers haben doch auch einen *Sohn*, *nicht?*	Meyers also have a *son*, don't they?	
Meyers haben doch auch einen *Sohn*. Nicht *wahr?*	Meyers also have a *son*, don't they?	

[3] nicht ein

Ich kenne hier auch nicht *ein*en Menschen.	I really don't know a *single* soul here.	SEE ANALYSIS 40
Meyers haben *fünf* Töchter, aber auch nicht *ein*en Sohn.	The Meyers have *five daughters*, but not *one* son.	(p. 81)

(Facing) **Porter #82**

63

[4] kein

The following sentences demonstrate the use of **kein.** Study these sentences first; then practice until you can say the sentences with **kein** when you hear the sentences without **kein,** and vice versa.

Compare the first two sentences of this group with the two sentences of group 3; observe the difference between **kein** and **nicht ein.**

SEE
ANALYSIS
41–42

(pp. 81-83)

Ich kenne hier *kein*en Menschen.	I don't know *any*body here.
Meyers *ha*ben keinen Sohn.	The Meyers don't *have* a son.
Hildegard hat *Geld.*	Hildegard hat *kein* Geld.
Ich trinke *Wein.*	Ich trinke *kein*en Wein.
Wir haben ein *Haus.*	Wir haben *kein* Haus.
Ich habe eine *Frau.*	Ich habe *kein*e Frau.
Du bist ein *Kind.*	Du bist *kein* Kind.
Das ist doch kein Automo*bil.*	Das ist ein *Kind*erwagen! (baby buggy)
Sie haben einen *Sohn,* Frau Meyer?	Nein, wir *ha*ben keinen Sohn. Wir haben auch keine *Toch*ter.
Trinken Sie *Bier?*	Nein, ich *trin*ke kein Bier.
Von Köln nach Bonn braucht der Zug zwei *Stun*den.	Von Köln nach Bonn braucht der Zug doch keine zwei *Stun*den.
Das Essen kostet drei *Mark.*	Hier kostet das Essen doch keine drei *Mark.*

[5] Negation by **nicht**

Be prepared to produce orally the sentences in one column when you hear the sentences in the other column.

SEE
ANALYSIS
43–44

(pp. 83-85)

Er *braucht* mich.	Er braucht mich *nicht.*
He *needs* me.	He does *not* need me.
Hast du mein *Buch?*	Nein, ich *ha*be dein Buch nicht.
Do you have my *book?*	No, I don't *have* your book.
Das *Was*ser kocht.	Das Wasser kocht *nicht.*
The *water* is boiling.	The water *isn't* boiling.
*V*ater ist gottseidank wieder ge*sund.*	*V*ater ist leider nicht ge*sund.*
Thank goodness, *father* is *well* again.	Unfortunately, *father* is not *well.*
Soviel ich *weiß,* ist *In*ge seine *Toch*ter.	Soviel ich *weiß,* ist *In*ge *nicht* seine Tochter.
As far as I *know,* Inge is his *daughter.*	As far as I *know, Inge* is *not* his daughter.
*Sonn*tags gehen wir ins *Ki*no.	*Sonn*tags gehen wir *nicht* ins Kino.
On *Sundays* we go to the *movies.*	On *Sundays* we do *not* go to the movies.

Natürlich bleibe ich heute abend zu *Hause*.

Of course, I will stay *home* tonight.

Warum gehen denn die Late*rn*en *an?*
Why are the *street lights* going *on?*

Hoffentlich kommt sie morgen *wie*der.
I hope she comes *back* tomorrow.

Natürlich bleibe ich heute abend nicht zu *Hause*.

Of course, I will not stay *home* tonight.

Warum gehen denn die Late*rn*en nicht *an?*
Why aren't the *street lights* going *on?*

Hoffentlich kommt sie morgen nicht *wie*der.
I hope she does not come *back* tomorow.

[6] schon, noch, mehr

Be prepared to produce orally the sentences in one column when you hear the sentences in the other column.

SEE
ANALYSIS
45

(pp. 85-86)

Regnet es *im*mer noch?
Is it *still* raining?

Nein, es *reg*net nicht mehr.
No, it isn't *raining* any more.

Er ist schon zu *Hause*.
He is at *home* already.

Er ist noch *nicht* zu Hause.
He is *not* at home yet.

Er ist noch zu *Hause*.
He is still at *home*.

Er ist nicht mehr zu *Hause*.
He isn't at *home* any more.

Wir wohnen noch *im*mer in München.
We *still* live in Munich.

Wir *woh*nen nicht mehr in München.
We don't *live* in Munich any more.

Ist er *im*mer noch krank?
Is he *still* sick?

Nein, er ist *nicht* mehr krank.
No, he *isn't* sick any more.

Ist er *im*mer noch dein Freund?
Is he *still* your friend?

Nein, er *ist* nicht mehr mein Freund.
No, he *isn't* my friend any more.

Haben wir noch *Bier?*
Do we still have some *beer?*

Nein, wir *ha*ben kein Bier mehr.
Das Bier ist *al*le.

No, we don't *have* any more beer.
We are *out* of beer.

Haben wir kein *Bier* mehr?
Don't we have any *beer* any more?

*Doch, Bier ha*ben wir noch.
Yes, we still *have* some beer.

Sie ist noch ein *Kind.*
She is still a *child.*

Sie ist kein *Kind* mehr.
She is no longer a *child.*

Sie ist *im*mer noch ein Kind.
She is *still* a child.

Sie ist noch *im*mer ein Kind.
She is *still* a *child.*

Du bist doch noch ein *Kind,* Inge.
You are still a *child,* Inge.

Nein, Mutter, ich bin *kein* Kind mehr.
No, mother, I'm *not* a child any more.

Ich bin doch kein *Kind* mehr, Mutter.
But I am not a *child* any more, mother.

Du *bist* noch ein Kind.
You *are* still a child.

Er ist noch Stud*ent*.

    He is still a *student*.

Er ist schon *Arzt*.

    He is already a *doctor*.

Ich habe noch einen *Brud*er.

    I still have a *brother*.

Ich habe *noch* einen Bruder.

    I have *another* brother.

Er ist noch kein *Arzt*.
Er ist noch nicht *Arzt*.

    He is not a *doctor* yet.

Er ist kein Stud*ent* mehr.

    He is no longer a *student*.

Ich *habe* keinen *Brud*er mehr.

    I don't *have* a brother any more.

[7] mehr, mehr als, nicht mehr als

Observe that in the following sentences **mehr** has a quantitative meaning and not a temporal meaning as in [6] above.

SEE
ANALYSIS
45

(pp. 85-86)

Meine Frau sagt, sie braucht mehr Geld.

    My wife says she needs more money.

Meine Frau braucht mehr Geld als ich.

    My wife needs more money than I need.

Meyer braucht viel Geld, aber seine Frau braucht noch mehr Geld als er.

    Meyer needs much money, but his wife needs even more money than he does.

Er arbeitet mehr als ich.

    He works more than I do.

Er weiß mehr, als er sagt.

    He knows more than he says.

Er hat mehr Geld, als er braucht.

    He has more money than he needs.

Ich habe nur zehn Mark; ich habe leider nicht mehr.

    I only have ten marks; unfortunately, I don't have any more.

Das kostet nicht mehr als fünf Mark.

    That doesn't cost more than five marks.

Ich habe nicht mehr Geld als du.

    I don't have more money than you (have).

[8] doch as Answer to a Negative Question

Study these sentences as questions and answers. Be prepared to formulate the answers orally when you hear the questions, and vice versa.

SEE
ANALYSIS
46

(p. 87)

Fahren Sie heute nach *Köln*?
Fahren Sie *nicht* nach Köln?

Trinken Sie *Kaf*fee, Frau Schmidt?
Trinken Sie *kei*nen Kaffee?

Nein, ich fahre erst *mor*gen.
Doch, natürlich fahre ich nach Köln.

Nein, ich *trin*ke keinen Kaffee.
Doch, natürlich trinke ich Kaffee.

Haben Meyers schon *Kin*der?	*Ja,* einen *Sohn* und eine *Toch*ter.
Haben Meyers noch keine *Kin*der?	*Doch,* einen *Sohn* und eine *Toch*ter.
Gehst du heute abend ins *Ki*no?	*Ja,* mit *In*ge.
Gehst du heute abend *nicht* ins Kino?	*Doch,* aber *nicht* wieder mit *In*ge.
Ich höre, Sie fahren dieses Jahr wieder nach *Deutsch*land.	*Ja,* aber erst im Sep*tem*ber.
Ich höre, Sie fahren dieses Jahr *nicht* nach Deutschland.	*Doch,* aber erst im Sep*tem*ber.

[9] können

Study the following sentences, which contain all the present tense forms of **können.** Then practice these forms by following the instruction under "Variations."

Ich kann heute *kom*men.	I can *come* today.	SEE ANALYSIS 48–54 (pp. 87-91)
Ich kann heute *nicht* kommen.	I *cannot* come today.	
Kannst du heute *kom*men?	Can you *come* today?	
Kannst du heute nicht *kom*men?	Can't you *come* today?	
Kann Herr Bauer heute *ar*beiten?	Will Mr. Bauer be able to *work* today?	
Nein, er kann heute *nicht* arbeiten.	No, he will *not* be able to work today.	
Wir können das Haus *kau*fen.	We can *buy* the house.	
Wir können das Haus *nicht* kaufen.	We *cannot* buy the house.	
Ihr könnt das Geld *mor*gen schon haben.	You can have the money *tomorrow.*	
Ihr könnt das Geld morgen noch *nicht* haben.	Tomorrow you *can't* have the money yet.	
Sie können jetzt das *Licht* ausmachen.	You can switch off the *light* now.	
Sie können doch noch nicht das *Licht* ausmachen.	You can't switch off the *light* yet.	

VARIATIONS

Ich kann heute kommen.

Er _____.

Er _____ nicht _____.

Sie _____ nicht _____.

_____ Sie _____?

Warum _____ du denn _____ nicht _____?

Warum _____ ihr denn _____ nicht _____?

Wir _____ leider nicht _____.

Könnt _____ nicht _____?

Doch, ich _____.

Nein, wir _____ nicht _____.

Heute _____ ich noch nicht _____.

Form the same variations using (1) **das Haus kaufen,** and (2) **nach München fahren**

READING PRACTICE

Read the following two paragraphs aloud until you can reproduce them quite fluently.

Sie kann *tanzen,* aber *er* kann leider *nicht* tanzen. Kannst *du auch* nicht tanzen?—Natürlich kann ich tanzen.

She can *dance,* but unfortunately *he cannot* dance. Can't *you* dance *either?*—Of *course* I can dance.

Du fährst heute schon wieder nach *Hause?* Kannst du denn nicht *hier*bleiben?—Ich *kann* natürlich, aber was kann man denn hier *machen,* bei dem *Regen?*—Man kann zum Beispiel *tanzen.*—Aber ich *kann* doch nicht *tanzen.*

You are going *home* today? Can't you *stay?* —I can, of course, but what can you *do* here in this rain?—You can *dance,* for instance.—But I *can't* dance.

[10] müssen

The following sentences contain all present-tense forms of **müssen.** Note that **brauchen zu** (*to need to*) is often used to negate **müssen.** If **müssen** is negated, it is usually strongly stressed.

SEE
ANALYSIS
48–54

(pp. 87-91)

Ich muß *ar*beiten.
Ich *brau*che nicht zu *ar*beiten.

I have to *work.*
I don't *have* to *work.*

Du mußt *kom*men.
Du *brauchst* nicht zu kommen.

You have to *come.*
You don't *have* to come.

Er muß morgen nach Ber*lin* fahren.
Er *muß* morgen nicht nach Ber*lin* fahren.

He has to go to *Berlin* tomorrow.
He does not *have* to go to *Berlin* tomorrow.

Wir müssen morgen leider *ar*beiten.
Wir *brauchen* moregn nicht zu arbeiten.

Unfortunately, we have to *work* tomorow.
We don't *have* to work tomorrow.

Ihr *müßt* Tante A*ma*lie besuchen.
Ihr *müßt* sie nicht be*su*chen.

You have to visit Aunt *Amalie.*
You don't *have* to visit her.

Sie müssen jetzt das *Licht* ausmachen.
Sie brauchen das Licht noch nicht *aus*zumachen.

You have to switch the *light* off now.
You don't have to switch the light *off* yet.

Mein Mann und ich haben *mehr* Geld als wir *brau*chen. Wir *brau*chen nicht mehr zu *ar*beiten.

My husband and I have *more* money than we *need.* We don't *have* to work any longer.

Warum wollen Sie denn bei dem Regen nach *Hamburg* fahren?—Ich *muß!*	Why do you want to drive to *Hamburg* in this rain?—I *have* to!
Sie sagen, Sie arbeiten auch *sonn*tags?—Das *brauchen* Sie aber nicht.	You say you work also on *Sundays?*—You don't *have* to do that.
Sie *ar*beiten heute? *Müssen* Sie das?	You are *working* today? Do you *have* to?

VARIATIONS

Mußt du morgen arbeiten?	Nein, morgen _____ ich nicht zu arbeiten.
Ich hoffe, du brauchst morgen nicht zu arbeiten.	Doch, leider _____ ich auch *morgen* arbeiten.
Braucht er heute nicht zu arbeiten?	Nein, heute _____ .
Müßt ihr heute arbeiten?	Ja, wir _____ .
Muß Erika immer noch arbeiten?	Nein, sie _____ nicht mehr _____ .

Form the same variations with (1) **nach Berlin fahren,** (2) **zu Hause bleiben,** and (3) **mit Tante Amalie ins Museum gehen.**

[11] wollen

Be prepared to produce orally the negative sentences when you hear the affirmative sentences and vice versa.

Ich will *hei*raten.	Ich *will* noch nicht heiraten.	SEE ANALYSIS 48–54
I want to *marry.*	I don't *want* to marry yet.	
Willst du jetzt *schla*fen?	Willst du jetzt *nicht* schlafen?	(pp. 87-91)
You want to *sleep* now?	*Don't* you want to sleep now?	

Sie will *immer Kaf*fee trinken.
  She *always* wants to drink coffee.
Wir wollen heute abend ins *Ki*no gehen.
  We want to go to the *movies* tonight.
Wann wollt ihr denn *hei*raten?
  When do you intend to get married?
Sie wollen *ar*beiten.
  They want to *work.*

Sie *will* keinen Kaffee mehr trinken.
  She doesn't *want* to drink coffee any more.
Wir wollen heute abend *nicht* ins Kino.
  We *don't* want to go to the movies tonight.
Warum *wollt* ihr denn noch nicht heiraten?
  Why don't you *want* to get married yet?
Sie wollen nicht mehr soviel *ar*beiten.
  They no longer want to *work* so much.

VARIATIONS

Hans und Erika wollen heiraten.

Hans _____ heiraten.

Ich _____ noch nicht _____.

Wir _____ erst nächstes Jahr _____.

So, du _____?

Wann _____ ihr denn _____?

Form the same variations with (1) **Hans und Erika wollen nach Hause fahren,** and (2) **Hans und Erika wollen ein Haus kaufen.**

[12] sollen

For each sentence, form a parallel example according to the translation on the right.

SEE ANALYSIS 48–54

(pp. 87-91)

Ich soll heute abend zu *Hau*se bleiben.
_____

I am supposed to stay *home* tonight.
I am supposed to visit Aunt *Amalie* tonight.

Aber *Hans!* Du *sollst* doch keinen Kaffee trinken.
_____

But Hans, you're not *supposed* to drink coffee.
But Hans, you're not *supposed* to work so much.

Sie *soll* sonntags nicht mehr arbeiten.
_____

She's not *supposed* to work on Sundays any more.
She's not *supposed* to go to the movies with Hans any more.

Was sollen wir denn *tun?*
_____

What are we supposed to *do?*
When are we supposed to *visit* them?

Warum sollt ihr ihn denn schon wieder be*su*chen?
_____

Why are you supposed to *visit* him again?

Why aren't you supposed to *read* this book?

Herr Meyer, Sie sollen morgen nach Ber*lin* fahren.	Mr. Meyer, you are supposed to go to *Berlin* tomorrow.
	Mr. Meyer, you are supposed to stay *here* tomorrow.

VARIATIONS WITH MORE THAN ONE MODAL

Hans *kann* heute nicht ins Kino gehen; er soll zu *Hause* bleiben.	Hans *cannot* go to a show tonight; he is supposed to stay at *home*.
Warum soll *ich* denn schon wieder nach *Hamburg* fahren? Kann *Meyer* nicht fahren?—*Nein, Mey*er soll *hier*bleiben.	Why am *I* to go to *Hamburg* again? Can't *Meyer* go?—*No, Meyer* is to stay *here*.
Man *kann*, was man *will;* aber man will nicht immer, was man *soll*.	One *can* (do) what one *wants* to do; however, one does not always want to do what one *ought* to do.

[13] möchte

After studying these sentences, practice the forms of **möchte** as indicated below.

Ich *möch*te jetzt nichts essen; ich möchte *schla*fen.	I don't *want* to eat anything now; I want to *sleep*.	**SEE ANALYSIS 48–54**
Möchtest du Frau *Mey*er kennenlernen?—Er möchte *Arzt* werden.—Sie möchte nächstes Jahr *hei*raten.—Wir möchten nächstes Jahr *hei*raten.—Wann möchtet ihr denn *hei*raten?—*Al*le Menschen möchten *glück*lich werden.	Would you like to meet Mrs. *Meyer?*—He would like to become a *doctor*.—She would like to *marry* next year.—We would like to *marry* next year.—When would you like to get *married?*—All men want to become *happy*.	(pp. 87-91)

Dr.med.Otto Krömer
NERVENARZT
Sprechz.: 10-12 , 16-18 außer Samst.
◄ EINGANG KÖNIGSTRASSE **4**

,,Er möchte Arzt werden''

Ich möchte eine Tasse *Kaf*fee trinken.— Möchten Sie *auch* eine Tasse Kaffee?

I should like to have (drink) a cup of *coffee*.—Would you *also* like to have a cup of coffee?

Möchtest du heute abend *nicht* ins Kino gehen?—*Nein,* ich möchte *wirk*lich zu *Hause* bleiben.

Would you rather *not* go to the movies tonight?—*No,* I *really* want to stay at *home*.

Sie *brauchen* das Buch nicht zu *le*sen, wenn Sie nicht *wollen.*—Aber ich *möch*te es lesen.

You *need* not *read* the book if you don't *want* to.—But I would *like* to read it.

VARIATIONS

Ich schlafe.	Ich möchte schlafen.
Ich fahre nächstes Jahr nach Italien.	_____
Ich werde auch Arzt.	_____
Morgen gehe ich nicht ins Kino.	_____
Wohnst du in München?	_____
Gehst du nach Hause?	_____
Ißt du jetzt?	_____
Meyer kauft unser Haus.	_____
Mein Sohn studiert Medizin.	_____
Wir essen heute abend im "Regina."	_____
Wir trinken noch eine Tasse Kaffee.	_____
Ihr trinkt keinen Wein?	_____
Fahrt ihr jetzt nach Hause?	_____
Kaufen Sie den Wagen, Herr Doktor?	_____
Meyers fahren morgen zurück.	_____
Ich glaube, sie kommen nächstes Jahr wieder.	_____

[14] dürfen

After studying these sentences, go through the variations below.

SEE ANALYSIS 48–54 (pp. 87-91)

Ich darf ihn nicht be*su*chen.—Ich darf ihn noch nicht be*su*chen.—Ich darf ihn nicht mehr be*su*chen.

I am not permitted to *visit* him.—I am not yet permitted to *visit* him.—I am no longer permitted to *visit* him.

Darfst du *Kaf*fee trinken?—Darf er jetzt wieder *Kaf*fee trinken?

Can you drink *coffee*?—Can he drink *coffee* again (now)?

Dürfen wir euch morgen be*su*chen?—Dürft ihr uns be*su*chen?

May we *visit* you tomorrow?—May you *visit* us?

„Darf man hier rauchen?"
„Nein, hier darf man nicht
rauchen."

„Hier darf man rauchen."

Sie dürfen uns nicht besuchen.	They may not *visit* us.
Darf ich meinen Mann morgen besuchen, Herr Doktor?—Natürlich dürfen Sie Ihren Mann morgen besuchen, Frau *Meyer*.	May I *visit* my husband tomorrow, doctor? —Of *course,* you can visit your husband tomorrow, Mrs. Meyer.
Möchtest du heute abend ins Theater gehen, Inge?—Ich *darf* nicht. Ich muß zu *Hause* bleiben.	Would you like to go to the *theater* tonight, Inge?—I am not *allowed* to go. I have to stay *home*.

VARIATIONS

Vary each sentence with the new subjects indicated.

Ich darf morgen meinen Mann besuchen. Du _____
 Frau Meyer _____

Wir dürfen keinen Kaffee mehr trinken. Er _____
 Erika _____

Ich darf sonntags nicht ins Kino gehen. Inge _____
 Wir _____

Wir dürfen hier nicht rauchen. Ihr _____
 Man _____
 Du _____

Ich darf heute zu Hause bleiben. Wir _____
 Er _____
 Ihr _____

[15] Second Prong

SEE
ANALYSIS
52–53
(pp. 89-91)

FRONT FIELD	1ST PRONG	INNER FIELD	NICHT	1ST BOX	2ND BOX
Ich	möchte	das Buch			lesen
Ich	möchte	das Buch	nicht		lesen
Ich	darf	Kaffee			trinken
Ich	darf	keinen Kaffee			trinken
Morgen	kann	sie Ihren Mann	noch nicht		besuchen
Wir	dürfen	sonntags	nicht mehr		arbeiten
Er	scheint	jetzt			zu schlafen
Er	scheint	jetzt	nicht		zu schlafen
Er	kann		nicht mehr		schlafen
Er	scheint		noch nicht		zu schlafen
Warum	brauchst	du morgen	nicht		zu arbeiten?
Seine Frau	scheint	wirklich	nicht	intelligent	zu sein
Das	muß			seine Frau	sein
Das	kann	doch	nicht	seine Frau	sein
Das	scheint			seine Frau	zu sein
Das	scheint		nicht	seine Frau	zu sein
Ich	darf	nächstes Jahr		nach Berlin	fahren
Ich	darf	nächstes Jahr	nicht	nach Berlin	fahren
Morgen	kann	ich	noch nicht	nach Berlin	fahren
Erika	möchte	heute abend		zu Hause	bleiben
Erika	möchte	heute abend	nicht	zu Hause	bleiben
Ich	möchte	sie		wieder-	sehen
Ich	möchte	sie	nicht	wieder-	sehen
Ich	möchte	sie wirklich		kennen-	lernen
Ich	brauche	sie	nicht	kennen-	zu-lernen

[16] Contrast Intonation

Read these sentences aloud until you have thoroughly mastered this intonation pattern.

SEE
ANALYSIS
55–56
(pp. 91-93)

Du fährst morgen nach I*tal*ien? *Ich* kann *nicht* nach Italien fahren.

You are going to *Italy* tomorrow? *I* can*not* go to Italy.

Hast *du Geld?* *Ich* habe *kein* Geld.

Do *you* have *money?* *I don't* have any money.

Trinken Meyers *Kaf*fee?—*Sie ja*, aber *er* nicht.

Do the Meyers drink *coffee*?—She does, but *he* does *not*.

Ist er intelli*gent* oder interes*sant*?—Intelligent *ist* er, aber interes*sant* ist er *nicht*.

Is he *intelligent* or *interesting*?—He is *intelligent* all right. But *interesting*? No!

Wo ist denn *Fritz*?—Ich *weiß* nicht. Zu *Hause* ist er *nicht*.

Where is *Fritz*?—I don't *know*. He is certainly not at *home*.

Möchtest du heute abend ins The*ater*?— Nein, ins The*ater* möchte ich *nicht*. Aber zu *Hause* bleiben will ich *auch* nicht.

Would you like to go to the *theater* tonight? —No, I don't want to go to the *theater*. But I don't want to stay at home *either*.

Du bist ge*sund*, du hast einen *Mann*, du hast *Geld*, du mußt doch *glück*lich sein!— Ja, einen *Mann* habe ich, und *Geld* habe ich *auch*. Aber *glück*lich bin ich *nicht*.

You are *healthy*, you have a *husband*, you have *money*, you must be *happy*.—Yes, I have a *husband*, and I have *money*. But I am *not happy*.

Ich höre, dein Bruder studiert Psycholo*gie*. Was studierst *du*?—*Ich* studiere Medi*zin*.

I hear your brother is majoring in *psychology*. What are *you* majoring in?—*I* am in *Med. School*.

Guten Morgen, Herr *Mey*er! So! Sie sind in *Hamburg*! Hier in *Köln* regnet es. Regnet es in Hamburg *auch*?—Nein, *hier* regnet es *nicht*.

Good morning, Mr. *Meyer*. So you are in *Hamburg*. Here in *Cologne* it's *raining*. Is it raining in Hamburg *too*?—No, it is not raining *here*.

Kennen Sie Fritz *Enders*, Frau *Holl*mann? —Nein, seine *Mutter* kenne ich *gut*, aber *ihn* kenne ich *nicht*.

Do you know Fritz *Enders*, Mrs. *Hollmann*? —No, I know his *mother well*, but I do *not* know *him*.

Warum gehst du nie mit *Inge* ins *Kino*? Sie ist doch *so* intelli*gent*.—*Ja*, intelli*gent ist* sie.

Why don't you ever go to the *movies* with *Inge*? She is *so intelligent*!—*Yes*, she is *intelligent* all right.

Warum gehst du so oft mit *Inge* ins *Kino*? Ist sie intelli*gent*?—*Nein*, intelli*gent* ist sie *nicht*.

Why do you take *Inge* to the *movies* so often? Is she *intelligent*?—*No*, she's not *intelligent*.

[17] Contrast Intonation

Das ist *Wasser*. Das ist *kein* Wasser. *Wasser* ist das *nicht*.

This is *water*. This is *not* water. This is *no* water.

SEE ANALYSIS 56 (p. 93)

Wir trinken *Wein*. Wir trinken *keinen* Wein. *Wein* trinken wir *nicht*.

We drink *wine*. We do *not* drink wine. *Wine* we do *not* drink.

Meyers haben einen *Sohn*. Meyers haben *keinen* Sohn. Einen *Sohn* haben Meyers *nicht*.

The Meyers have a *son*. The Meyers do *not* have a son. The Meyers have *no son*.

Wir brauchen *But*ter. Wir brauchen *keine* Butter. *But*ter brauchen wir *nicht*.

We need *butter*. We do *not* need butter. We need *no* butter.

Vary the following sentences in the same manner as above:

> Sie haben eine Tochter.
> Wir trinken Bier.
> Hans hat eine Freundin.
> Ich kenne hier einen Arzt.

[18] Imperative

SEE
ANALYSIS
57
(p. 94)

Arbeiten Sie nicht soviel!	Don't work so much.
Bleiben Sie doch hier!	Why don't you stay here?
Gehen Sie doch nach Hause!	Why don't you go home?
Kommen Sie doch morgen!	Why don't you come tomorrow?
Lernen Sie Deutsch!	Learn German.
Sagen Sie doch etwas!	Say something.
Seien Sie nicht so egoistisch!	Don't be so selfish.
Tun Sie das doch bitte nicht!	Please don't do that.
Machen Sie bitte das Licht an!	Please turn on the light.
Kaufen Sie doch einen Volkswagen!	Why don't you buy a VW?
Schlafen Sie gut!	Sleep well!
Lassen Sie mich allein!	Leave me alone.

Form further imperatives from the following sentences:

> Er geht nach Hause.   Gehen Sie doch nach Hause.
> Er studiert *auch* Medizin.   _____
> Er fährt mit Meyers nach München.   _____
> Er bleibt noch ein Jahr in Amerika.   _____
> Er ist nicht immer so kalt.   _____

[19] Rapid Reading Practice

Read these sentences aloud at normal speed.

Geht er?
Ja, er *geht*.
Will er *gehen*?
Ja, er will *gehen*.
Geht er nicht?
Nein, er *geht* nicht.
Will er nicht *gehen*?
Nein, er will nicht *gehen*.

Geht er ins *Ki*no?
Ja, er geht ins *Ki*no.
Will er ins *Ki*no *ge*hen?
Ja, er will ins *Ki*no *ge*hen.
Geht er nicht ins *Ki*no?
Nein, er *geht* nicht ins *Ki*no.
Nein, ins *Ki*no *geht* er nicht.
Will er nicht ins *Ki*no gehen?
Nein, er *will* nicht ins *Ki*no gehen.
Nein, ins *Ki*no gehen *will* er nicht.
Geht er heute abend ins *Ki*no?
Ja, er geht heute abend ins *Ki*no.
Ja, heute abend geht er ins *Ki*no.
Will er heute abend ins *Ki*no?
Ja, er will heute abend ins *Ki*no.
Ja, heute abend will er ins *Ki*no.
Geht er heute abend nicht ins *Ki*no?
Nein, er geht heute abend *nicht* ins Kino.
Nein, heute abend geht er *nicht* ins Kino.
Nein, ins *Ki*no geht er heute abend *nicht*.
Will er heute abend nicht ins *Ki*no?
Nein, er will heute abend *nicht* ins Kino.
Nein, ins *Ki*no *will* er heute abend nicht.
Nein, ins *Ki*no will er heute abend *nicht*.

CONVERSATION

I

TANTE AMALIE:	Was willst *du* denn studieren, Erika?	What do *you* intend to study, Erika?
ERIKA:	Ich *will* nicht studieren. Hans und ich wollen *hei*raten.	I don't *intend* to go to a university. Hans and I intend to *marry*.
TANTE AMALIE:	Und Hans will *auch* nicht studieren?	And Hans does not intend to go to the university *either*?
ERIKA:	Nein!	No!

TANTE AMALIE:	Will *er* heiraten, oder willst *du* heiraten?
	Does *he* want to marry, or do *you* want to marry?
ERIKA:	*Hans* will immer, was *ich* will.
	Hans always wants what *I* want.
TANTE AMALIE:	Ach *so!* Er möchte also *doch* studieren!
	Is that *right?* So he wants to go to a university *after* all!
ERIKA:	Na*tür*lich möchte er. Ich möchte *auch*. Aber kann man heiraten *und* studieren?
	Of *course* he would like to. I would like to, *too*. But can one marry *and* be a (university) student?
TANTE AMALIE:	Das *kann* man. Aber dann muß man *Geld* haben, *viel* Geld. Aber man kann auch *erst* studieren und *dann* heiraten, nicht wahr?
	One *can* do that. But then one must have *money*, a good *deal* of money. But one can also *first* go to a university and *then* marry.
ERIKA:	Ich *weiß!* Das *kann* man. Aber das *wol*len wir nicht.
	I *know*. One *can* do that. But we don't *want* to do that.
TANTE AMALIE:	Ich glaube, das willst *du* nicht. Ich kann dich *wirk*lich nicht ver*steh*en, Erika. Ich hoffe nur, *Hans* versteht dich.
	I believe *you* don't want that. *Really*. I can't understand you, Erika. I only hope *Hans* understands you.

II

INGE: Du, Hans, wir haben nicht viel *Zeit*. Sollen wir nicht ein *Taxi* nehmen?

HANS: Nein, ein Taxi nehmen wir heute *nicht*. Aber wir *fah*ren *doch*. Ich habe einen *Wa*gen!

INGE: Einen *Wa*gen? Du hast einen *Wa*gen? Das ist aber *prima*. Ist es *dein* Wagen?

HANS: Nein, nein, es ist nicht *mein* Wagen. Ich habe keinen Wagen. Es ist *Ottos* Wagen, aber er *braucht* ihn heute nicht. Also brauchen wir heute nicht ins Theater zu *geh*en, wir können ins Theater *fah*ren.

INGE: Du, das ist *gut*. Jetzt haben wir noch *so* viel Zeit. Es ist ja erst sechs *Uhr*. Jetzt können wir *erst essen* und *dann* ins Theater fahren.

HANS: *Essen will* ich jetzt nichts; ich habe keinen *Hun*ger. Ich möchte jetzt nur eine Tasse *Kaf*fee. Aber *du* sollst natürlich *essen*, wenn du *willst*.

INGE: *Nein,* du mußt *auch* essen. Weißt du, was die Leute *den*ken, wenn *ich* esse und *du* trinkst nur Kaffee? Das ist ein Stu*dent*, denken sie, er hat also kein *Geld* und sagt, er hat keinen *Hun*ger.

HANS: Aber ich habe *wirk*lich keinen Hunger.

INGE: Also gut, dann *esse* ich etwas und *du* trinkst *Kaf*fee, und die *Leu*te sollen *den*ken, was sie *wol*len.

Der Mensch, das kann man schon bei Aristoteles lesen, ist ein Tier. Aber dieses Tier, sagt Aristoteles, hat Vernunft.

Und was ist Vernunft? Vernunft ist nicht Intelligenz. Vernunft ist mehr als Intelligenz.

Wer nur intelligent ist, glaubt: „Alle Menschen sind egoistisch. Ja, sie müssen egoistisch sein. Denn jeder Mensch will glücklich werden. Das heißt aber, der Emil möchte haben, was Fritz hat; und der Fritz möchte sein, was Emil ist. Aber der Emil kann nicht immer alles haben, was er möchte; und Fritz kann nicht sein, was Emil ist. Und darum haßt der Fritz den Emil, und der Emil den Fritz. Darum haßt ein Sohn seinen Vater, und darum haßt Nation A Nation B. Der Krieg zwischen Fritz und Emil, zwischen Sohn und Vater und zwischen Nation A und Nation B ist also natürlich. So ist es, und so bleibt es. Leider!"

Aber warum „leider"? Was ist, ist, und es kann nur so sein, wie es ist. Warum also „leider"?

Hier spricht nicht unsere Intelligenz. Hier spricht unsere Vernunft. Unsere Intelligenz sieht nur, was ist. Unsere Vernunft sieht mehr. Sie sieht: Das, was ist, soll und darf nicht sein.

Natürlich will jeder Mensch glücklich werden. Er will es instinktiv. Er muß es wollen. Der Hans will *sein* Glück, und ich will *mein* Glück. Er will also nur, was ich auch will. Ich habe ein Haus und bin glücklich. Hans hat kein Haus und ist unglücklich. Aber, so sagt meine Vernunft, ich kann nicht glücklich sein, wenn Hans unglücklich ist. Denn wenn Hans sagt: „Du hast ein Haus und ich habe kein Haus", dann sagt er auch

Man, one can read already in Aristotle, is an animal. But this animal, says Arisotle, has reason.

And what is reason? Reason is not intelligence. Reason is more than intelligence.

Whoever is merely intelligent believes: "All human beings are egoistic. Indeed, they have to be egoistic. For every human being desires to become happy. But this means: Emil would like to have what Fritz has; and Fritz would like to be what Emil is. But Emil cannot always have what he would like (to have); and Fritz cannot be what Emil is. And for this reason Fritz hates Emil, and Emil hates Fritz. Therefore, a son will hate his father, and Nation A will hate Nation B. War between Fritz and Emil, between father and son, and between Nation A and Nation B is therefore natural. That's the way it is, and that's the way it will remain, unfortunately."

But why "unfortunately"? Whatever is, is, and it can only be as it is. Why, therefore, "unfortunately"?

Here (through this "unfortunately") speaks not our intelligence, but our reason. Our intelligence sees only what exists. Our reason sees more. It sees that what is, should not and must not be.

Naturally every human being desires to become happy. He desires it instinctively. He must desire it. Hans wants *his* happiness and I want *my* happiness. Thus he only wants what I want too. I have a house and am happy. Hans does not have a house and is unhappy. But, my reason tells me, I cannot be happy if Hans is unhappy. For if Hans says, "You have a house and I have no house," then he will soon say also, "Why

bald: „Warum sollst du ein Haus haben, und ich habe kein Haus?" Und so beginnen alle Kriege. Aber ich will keinen Krieg; Hans will auch keinen Krieg, er will ein Haus. Ich muß also etwas für ihn tun. Er ⁵ braucht mich und kann ohne mich nicht glücklich werden; und ich brauche ihn und kann ohne ihn nicht glücklich bleiben. Also muß ich für ihn tun, was ich kann.

Das heißt aber: Ich muß ihn lieben. Denn ₁₀ „lieben" heißt ja „für den Mitmenschen das tun, was gut für ihn ist". Der Krieg, so sagt meine Vernunft, ist nicht natürlich. Natürlich ist nur die Liebe.

Aber leider zwingt mich meine Vernunft ₁₅ nicht. Ich weiß jetzt, was ich soll, aber meine Vernunft läßt mich frei, zu tun oder nicht zu tun, was ich soll. Und das ist unsere Tragik. Wir wollen oft nicht, was wir sollen; und wir können, wenn wir wollen, auch tun, ₂₀ was wir nicht sollen.

Aber wir müssen lernen zu wollen, was wir sollen. Ja, der Mensch ist nur dann wirklich frei—frei zu tun, was er will—wenn er will, was er soll.

should (shall) you have a house, and I don't have a house?" And thus begin all wars. But I don't want a war; Hans wants no war either, he wants a house. Therefore I have to do something for him. He needs me and cannot become happy without me; and I need him and cannot remain happy without him. Therefore I must do for him what I can.

But this means: I must love him. For "to love" means, after all, "to do that for a fellow man which is good for him." War, says my reason, is not natural. Only love is natural.

But unfortunately my reason does not force me. I now know what I ought to do, but my reason leaves me free to do or not to do what I ought (to do). And that is our tragic fate. We often do not want to do what we ought to do; and we can, if we want to, also do what we ought not to do.

However, we must learn to want to do what we ought to do. Indeed, man is only then really free—free to do what he wants to do ₂₅ —when he wants to do what he ought to do.

ANALYSIS

37 aber, oder, denn, und

aber, oder, denn, and **und** are coordinating conjunctions—that is, conjunctions that connect two main clauses. They precede the front field and are not counted as syntactical units. Of these four conjunctions, only **aber** can also be placed in the inner field. It then follows pronoun subjects and pronoun objects. If **denn** stands in the inner field, it is not the coordinating conjunction **denn**, *for,* but the particle **denn** discussed in **15.**

38 kein, nicht, and nichts

In English, most negative statements contain either *no* or *not.* The most frequently used German words of negation (besides **Nein!**) are **kein** and

nicht. However, the use of **kein** and **nicht** does not parallel the use of *no* and *not*. To speak socially acceptable German, the student must therefore learn from the very beginning how and when to use **kein,** and how and when to use **nicht.**

German **nichts** means **nothing** or **not anything;** it is the antonym of **etwas,** *something.*

> **Hast du etwas gegen Erika?**
> Do you have anything against Erika?
> **Nein, ich habe nichts gegen Erika.**
> No, I have nothing against Erika.

39 Nicht wahr? and Nicht? as Complete Questions

Nicht wahr? (an abbreviation of **Ist das nicht wahr?**—*Isn't that true?*) corresponds to English *Isn't that so?, don't you?, haven't you?, weren't you?* etc. This **nicht wahr?** is frequently shortened to **nicht?** Since **nicht?** or **nicht wahr?** asks for confirmation, the preceding sentence frequently contains **doch** (see **36**).

> **Sie *kom*men doch heute abend, nicht *wahr?***
> **Sie *kom*men doch heute abend, *nicht?***
> (You are coming tonight, aren't you?)

40 nicht ein

German **nicht ein** does not correspond to English *not a.* The **ein** in **nicht ein** is the numeral *one* and is always stressed. German *nicht ein* therefore means *not one* or *not a single:*

> **Ich habe nicht *ei*ne Frau.**
> I don't have a *single* wife. (Though I am a Mohammedan and could have three or four.)

This **nicht ein** is frequently strengthened by a preceding unstressed **auch** which may be translated by *even:*

> **Ich kenne hier auch nicht *ei*nen Menschen**
> I don't know even *one* person around here.

41 Negation by kein

German **kein** is declined like the indefinite article **ein.** For the time being, the student should not use **kein** without a following noun. When used with a following noun,

$$\textbf{kein} + \text{noun equals} \begin{cases} \textit{no} & + \text{noun} \\ \textit{not any} & + \text{noun} \\ \textit{not a} & + \text{noun} \end{cases}$$

Ich habe kein Geld	I have no money
	I don't have any money
Ich habe keine Frau	I have no wife
	I don't have a wife
Ich habe keinen Wagen	I have no car
	I don't have a car

kein after the Inflected Verb

To make a negative statement, **kein** *must* be used in front of a noun object or in front of a predicate noun, *if* in the corresponding affirmative statement the noun would be used *either* with the indefinite article **ein** *or* all by itself without any article or possessive adjective.

POSITIVE	NEGATIVE
Das ist Wasser	**Das ist kein Wasser**
Meyers haben einen Sohn	**Meyers haben keinen Sohn**
Meyers haben Kinder	**Meyers haben keine Kinder**
Meyers haben Geld	**Meyers haben kein Geld**

NOTE: The plural of **ein Kind** is **Kinder,** the plural of **kein Kind** is **keine Kinder.** The negation of **zwei Kinder** is **keine zwei Kinder**; of **zwei Jahre, keine zwei Jahre.**

kein in the Front Field

Occasionally, **kein** plus noun is found in front of the inflected verb: **Kein Mensch weiß, wo Meyer wohnt**—*Nobody knows where Meyer lives.* However, such usage is very restricted. To be safe, *do not use kein in front of the inflected verb.*

42   Intonation of kein

The difference in stress distribution between **sie ist** *kein* **Kind** and **sie ist kein** *Kind* parallels the difference between *she is not a child* and *she isn't a child:* **kein** is stressed if it strongly contradicts a preceding affirmative statement; if no strong contradiction is intended or if the noun is mentioned for the first time, the noun itself is stressed.

Mutter:	Deine Tochter geht heute abend schon *wie*der mit Fritz ins Kino.	Mother:	Your daughter is going to the *movies* tonight, and *again* with *Fritz*.
Vater:	Na *und?* Sie ist doch noch ein *Kind!*	Father:	So what? She is still a *child*, isn't she?
Mutter:	Sie ist *kein* Kind mehr.	Mother:	She is *not* a child any longer.
Er:	Warum bist *du* übrigens nicht Frau Dr. Anton Meyer? Du weißt doch, Anton . . .	He:	By the way, why aren't *you* Frau Dr. Anton Meyer? You know, Anton . . .
Sie:	*Ich?* Frau *Mey*er? Antons *Frau?* Ich bin doch kein *Dumm*kopf!	She:	*Me?* Mrs. *Mey*er? Anton's *wife?* I'm not stupid, you know.

43   Negation by **nicht**

To form a negative statement, **nicht** is used whenever **kein** does not have to be used. For instance, the sentence

FRONT FIELD	1st Prong	INNER FIELD	2nd Prong
Ich	bin	sehr oft	zu Hause
I	am	very often	at home

does not contain a predicate noun or a noun object and therefore cannot be negated by **kein;** it has to be negated by **nicht.** The problem is where this **nicht** should be placed.

Placed at the end of the inner field, i.e., in front of the second prong, *nicht negates the entire predicate.* The sentence

Ich	bin	sehr oft nicht	zu Hause

therefore means basically: *I am not at home;* and the **sehr oft** expresses the idea that this not-being-at-home happens *very often.*

If **nicht** is placed in the inner field, the validity of the predicate is left untouched. The sentence

Ich	bin	nicht sehr oft	zu Hause

means basically: *I am at home;* however, this being-at-home happens *not very often.*

Usually, the speaker wants to negate the predicate (and thereby the entire sentence); and for the time being we will use **nicht** mainly in this function. *This means that the student must develop the habit of placing **nicht** behind the inner field,—that is, right in front of the second prong, if the sentence has a second prong.*

Sentences without a Second Prong

FRONT FIELD	1st Prong	INNER FIELD	nicht
Meyer	arbeitet		nicht.
Heute	regnet	es	nicht.
Ich	verstehe	Meyer	nicht.
Warum	kommt	er heute	nicht?
	Kennst	du mich	nicht?

Sentences with a Second Prong

nicht PRECEDES A PREDICATE ADJECTIVE

FRONT FIELD	1st Prong	INNER FIELD	nicht	2nd Prong
Er	ist	leider	nicht	gesund.
Leider	ist	er	nicht	gesund.
Warum	ist	er denn	nicht	glücklich?
	Ist	sie wirklich	nicht	glücklich?

nicht PRECEDES A PREDICATE NOUN

FRONT FIELD	1st Prong	INNER FIELD	nicht	2nd Prong
Sie	ist	doch	nicht	meine Mutter.
Soviel ich weiß,	ist	Inge	nicht	seine Tochter.
Warum	werden	Sie	nicht	Arzt?
	Sind	Sie	nicht	Frau Meyer?

nicht PRECEDES A DIRECTIVE—THAT IS, THE ANSWER TO A *wohin*-QUESTION*

FRONT FIELD	1st Prong	INNER FIELD	nicht	2nd Prong
Nächstes Jahr	fahren	wir	nicht	nach Deutschland.
Wir	gehen	sonntags	nicht	ins Kino.
Warum	geht	ihr sonntags	nicht	in die Kirche?

nicht PRECEDES OTHER VERBAL COMPLEMENTS

FRONT FIELD	1st Prong	INNER FIELD	nicht	2nd Prong
Morgen abend	bleibe	ich natürlich	nicht	zu Hause.
Warum	bleibst	du morgen abend	nicht	zu Hause?
Warum	fährt	denn der Zug	nicht	ab?
Warum	lernt	sie denn	nicht	fahren?

44 Intonation of **nicht**

The intonation of **nicht** corresponds to the intonation of English *not:* If the sentence containing **nicht** is an intentional and somewhat curt contradiction to an immediately preceding statement, **nicht** is stressed and functions as the stress point of the sentence:

Sie sind Frau Schmidt, nicht *wahr?*	You are Mrs. Schmidt, *aren't you?*
***Nein,* ich bin *nicht* Frau Schmidt.**	*No,* I am *not* Mrs. Schmidt.

In all other cases, **nicht** is completely unstressed.

Sie sind Frau *Schmidt,* nicht *wahr?*	You are Mrs. *Schmidt, aren't you?*
***Nein,* ich bin nicht Frau *Schmidt,* ich bin Frau *Dö*ring.**	*No,* I am not Mrs. *Schmidt,* I am Mrs. *Döring.*

45 **noch, schon,** and **mehr**

Noch means *still* or *yet* and signifies that a state of affairs continues to exist.

Sie ist noch ein *Kind.*	She is still a *child.*
Er *schläft* noch.	He's still *asleep.*

* Both **wo** and **wohin** correspond to English *where.* **Wo** asks for the place at which an entire action takes place; **wohin** asks for a goal toward which an action is directed and at which it ends.

This **noch** can be emphasized by a preceding or following **immer** (which, when used without **noch**, means *always*).

Sie ist *immer* noch ein Kind.	She is *still* a child.
Sie ist noch *immer* ein Kind.	
Er schläft noch *immer*.	He's *still* asleep.
Er schläft *immer* noch.	

If a negative state continues to exist, **noch** (**noch immer, immer noch**) precedes **nicht** or **kein**:

Er *schläft* noch nicht.	He isn't *asleep* yet.
Er schläft *immer* noch nicht.	He *still* isn't asleep.
Sie *haben* noch keine Kinder.	They don't *have* any children yet.

NOTE: **noch ein** frequently means *another*:

Trinken Sie noch eine Tasse Kaffee?
Would you like another cup of coffee?

Schon signifies that a state of affairs exists already, perhaps earlier than expected. **Schon** is therefore the opposite of **noch nicht** and **noch kein**.

Er schläft schon.	Er schläft noch nicht.
He's already asleep.	He isn't asleep yet.
Er ist schon zu Hause.	Er ist noch nicht zu Hause.
He's already at home.	He isn't home yet.
Sie haben schon zwei Kinder.	Sie haben noch keine Kinder.
They have two children already.	They don't have any children yet.

To express that a state or an action has come to an end, German uses either **kein . . . mehr** (with a noun between **kein** and **mehr**) or **nicht mehr**. In this context, **kein . . . mehr** and **nicht mehr** have the same (temporal!) meaning as *no more* in *He is no more*. The usage of **kein . . . mehr** and **nicht mehr** parallels that of **kein** and **nicht**.

Ich brauche das Geld nicht mehr.	I don't need the money any more.
Sie ist kein Kind mehr.	She is no longer a child.
Wir wohnen nicht mehr in München.	We don't live in Munich any more.

German **mehr** and English *more*, either by themselves or together with an immediately following noun, can also have a *quantitative* meaning, which always involves a comparison. This comparison may be merely implied. English *more than* is expressed by **mehr als**.

Er arbeitet mehr als ich.	He works more than I do.
Ich brauche mehr Geld.	I need more money (than I have).
Er hat mehr Geld als ich.	He has more money than I have.
Er hat nicht mehr Geld als ich.	He doesn't have more money than I have.
Hier sind fünf Mark; mehr (Geld) habe ich nicht.	Here are five marks; I don't have any more.

46 doch to Answer a Negative Question

If a negative question is answered in the affirmative, **doch** with a strong stress is used instead of **ja.**

Fährst du nicht nach Köln?	*Doch,* natürlich fahre ich nach Köln.
Fährst du nicht nach Köln?	*Doch,* aber nicht *heute.*

doch is also used to contradict a negative statement with an affirmative statement.

Ich bin doch kein Kind mehr.	*Doch,* du *bist* noch ein Kind.

47 Professional Status

Certain nouns, such as **Arzt, Student,** and **Studentin** can be used to express legal or professional status, and in this function they are used all by themselves without any article.

It is perfectly normal to say

Wir brauchen einen Arzt.	**We need a doctor.**

However, the question *What is your profession?* can only be answered by:

Ich bin Arzt.
Mein Sohn wird Arzt.

If these sentences are negated, either **kein** or **nicht** may be used.

Ich bin kein Arzt.   or   **Ich bin nicht Arzt.**

48 Infinitives with and without zu

The infinitive of a verb is not merely used as a dictionary entry. Both in English and in German, infinitives are frequently used in connection with other verbs. The infinitive is used sometimes with, and sometimes without, *to* or **zu:**

Infinitive with zu:

Er hat nichts zu tun.	He has nothing to do.
Er scheint zu schlafen.	He seems to be asleep.
Warum brauchst du heute nicht zu arbeiten?	Why don't you have to work today?

Infinitive without zu:

Er kann arbeiten.	He can work.
Du mußt kommen.	You must come.
Soll ich gehen?	Shall I go?

49 Modal Auxiliaries

The most important verbs used with a following infinitive without **zu** are the modal auxiliaries, or simply the modals.

They usually express, by themselves, not a specific action, but an attitude toward the action expressed by the infinitive. Thus English *shalt* and *must* in *Thou shalt not steal* and *I must go home* view the action expressed by *steal* and *go home* as forbidden or necessary.

These modals are conjugated irregularly both in English and in German: *he must,* not *he musts;* **er kann,** not **er kannt.**

The English modals are incomplete: they have, for instance, no infinitive and no compound tenses. The German system, though grammatically complete, has peculiarities of its own. For instance, **müssen** is primarily used in positive statements. In negative statements, **müssen** is usually replaced by **brauchen zu:**

Ich muß arbeiten.	I have to work.
Ich brauche nicht zu arbeiten.	I don't have to work.

50 The Six German Modals and Their Meaning

It is definitely unwise to attempt to equate each form of a modal with a corresponding English modal. Instead, the student should master the basic meaning of each modal.

können	to be able to		*expresses ability*
Ich kann lesen.		I can read.	
müssen	to have to		*expresses necessity*
Ich muß nach Hause gehen.		I have to go home.	
dürfen	to be allowed to		*expresses permission*
Ich darf hierbleiben.		I have permission to stay here.	
Das darfst du nicht tun.		You mustn't do that.	
mögen	would like to		*expresses desire*
Ich möchte hierbleiben.		I would like to stay here.	
wollen	to want to		*expresses intention*
Ich will ins Kino gehen.		I intend to go to the movies.	
sollen	to be (supposed) to		*expresses imposed obligation; in questions it may express a suggestion*
Ich soll nach Bonn fahren.		I am (supposed) to go to Bonn.	
Sollen wir ins Theater gehen?		Shall we go to the theater?	

51 The Forms of the German Modals

	KÖNNEN	WOLLEN	MÜSSEN	MÖGEN*	SOLLEN	DÜRFEN
ich	kann	will	muß	möchte	soll	darf
du	kannst	willst	mußt	möchtest	sollst	darfst
er sie es	kann	will	muß	möchte	soll	darf
wir	können	wollen	müssen	möchten	sollen	dürfen
ihr	könnt	wollt	müßt	möchtet	sollt	dürft
sie	können	wollen	müssen	möchten	sollen	dürfen
Sie	können	wollen	müssen	möchten	sollen	dürfen

52 Position of Dependent Infinitives

When infinitives like **arbeiten** or **zu arbeiten** depend on modals or on verbs like **brauchen,** they form a second prong, follow the inner field, and are preceded by **nicht.**

NO MODAL IN THE FIRST PRONG, SECOND PRONG EMPTY

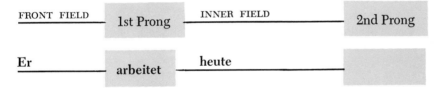

If a modal comes in, it pushes **arbeiten** into the second prong.

MODAL IN FIRST PRONG, INFINITIVE IN SECOND PRONG

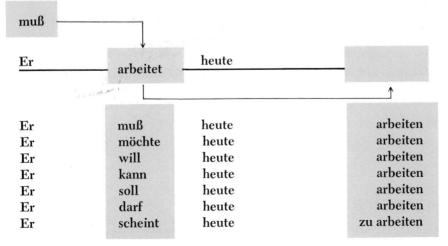

Er	muß	heute	arbeiten
Er	möchte	heute	arbeiten
Er	will	heute	arbeiten
Er	kann	heute	arbeiten
Er	soll	heute	arbeiten
Er	darf	heute	arbeiten
Er	scheint	heute	zu arbeiten

* These forms of **mögen** will be explained in Unit 9.

Questions are treated in the same way:

Warum	**arbeitest**	du heute?	
Warum	**mußt**	du heute	**arbeiten?**
Warum	**willst**	du heute	**arbeiten?**
	Arbeitet	er heute?	
	Muß	er heute	**arbeiten?**
	Kann	er heute	**arbeiten?**

The procedure is the same if **nicht** stands at the end of the inner field:

Er	**möchte**	heute	nicht	**arbeiten**
Er	**kann**	heute	nicht	**arbeiten**
Er	**braucht**	heute	nicht	**zu arbeiten**
Er	**scheint**	heute	nicht	**zu arbeiten**
Warum	**will**	er denn heute	nicht	**arbeiten?**
Warum	**braucht**	er denn heute	nicht	**zu arbeiten?**

53   The Two-Box Second Prong

If a simple verb like **arbeiten** is pushed by a modal out of the slot for the first prong, it moves into the slot for the second prong. But what happens if the verb displaced by the modal or by an auxiliary such as **brauchen** and **scheinen** is a compound verb with some complement already filling the slot for the second prong?—The second prong has two boxes, so to speak, and the infinitive dependent on an auxiliary verb always goes into the second box, whereas all complements go into the first box. The following diagram shows what happens:

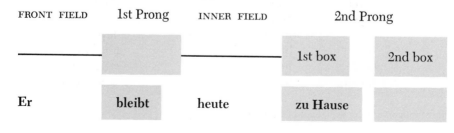

FRONT FIELD	1st Prong	INNER FIELD	2nd Prong	
			1st box	2nd box
——————		——————		
Er	**bleibt**	heute	**zu Hause**	

Modal comes in and pushes **bleiben** into the second box:

FRONT FIELD	1st Prong	INNER FIELD	2nd Prong	
Er	will	heute	zu Hause	bleiben

Further examples are given in the Patterns [15].

This two-box second-prong pattern, in which the verbal complement precedes the infinitive without **zu,** is used so frequently in German that German dictionaries list many compound verbs, especially if the complement is a preposition or an adverb, in the form in which they appear in this two-box sequence (see **28**). Thus the **fahre zurück** in **Ich fahre morgen zurück** is listed under **zurückfahren,** because it occurs so frequently in such sentences as **Ich will morgen zurückfahren.**

If an infinitive with **zu** is required, this **zu** is inserted between complement and infinitive, and the whole thing is written as one word.

> **Er braucht nicht zurückzufahren.**
> **Er braucht das Licht nicht auszumachen.**

54 Replacement or Omission of the Dependent Infinitive

An infinitive can be replaced by **das,** if the verb was mentioned in the sentence immediately preceding:

> **Sie arbeiten heute? Dürfen Sie das?**

The infinitives **gehen, fahren,** and others, if clearly understood, are frequently omitted. Compare English *He wants out.*

Ich muß nach Hause.	(**gehen** omitted)
Ich will heute nach Köln.	(**fahren** omitted)
Du brauchst nicht zu arbeiten, wenn	
du nicht willst.	(**arbeiten** omitted)

55 Contrast Intonation

Imagine the following situation: Mr. and Mrs. Baker have had a serious traffic accident. A friend calls the hospital and asks "How are Mr. and Mrs. Baker?" The doctor answers, "Mrs. Baker is alive." Can this be the answer to the question, "How are Mr. *and* Mrs. Baker?" It can be, but only if the doctor uses the intonation pattern

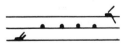

Mrs. Baker is alive

By using this intonation pattern, the doctor clearly implies that Mr. Baker is dead. A German doctor, in the same situation, will answer

Frau Meyer lebt

No German will fail to register the implication that Herr Meyer is dead.

This "contrast-intonation" pattern is not the same pattern as in sentences with two stressed syllables such as

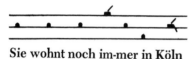

Sie wohnt noch im-mer in Köln

Contrast intonation is characterized by the fact that the first stressed syllable has a rising pitch starting on level 1, and the second stressed syllable has a falling pitch starting on level 3.

CONTRAST INTONATION

In die Kir-che geht er nie

IMPLICATION

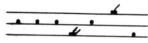

A-ber ins Ki-no geht er
(contrast intonation)

or:

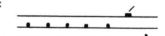

A-ber er geht ins Ki-no
(normal intonation)

CONTRAST INTONATION

Geld hat sie

IMPLICATION

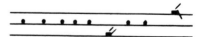

A-ber in-tel-li-gent ist sie nicht
(contrast intonation)

or:

A-ber sie ist nicht in-tel-li-gent
(normal intonation)

56 Word Order under Contrast Intonation

Under contrast intonation, the second prong frequently appears in the front field. The two sentences:

   and

Sie ist in·tel·li·gent   In·tel·li·gent ist sie

are not interchangeable. The first one is a remark of praise, the second is a sophisticated insult. Likewise,

Er ist nicht zu Hau·se   Zu Hau·se ist er nicht

are not interchangeable; for only the second contains some implication like "Let's try to reach him somewhere else!"

Under contrast intonation, **kein** is replaced by (**ein**) . . . **nicht**.

  Meyer ist kein *Dummkopf.*
  Ein *Dummkopf* **ist Meyer** *nicht.*
  Ich habe kein *Geld.*
  Geld **habe ich** *nicht,*   or: *Geld habe* **ich nicht.**

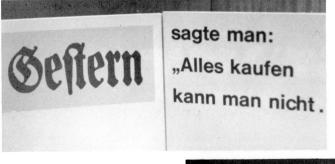

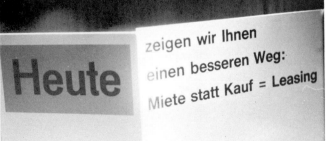

57   The Imperative

The English imperative is identical with the infinitive. One can say *Be my guest* no matter whether one calls the person addressed *Jack* or *Dr. Able*. German distinguishes between the **du**-form, the **ihr**-form, and the **Sie**-form of the imperative. At this point, we introduce only the **Sie**-form, which looks like the infinitive plus an immediately following **Sie: Kommen Sie! Gehen Sie! Sehen Sie!** The imperative of **sein** is **Seien Sie**.

Imperatives, like yes-or-no questions, have verb-first position; they are distinguished by intonation.

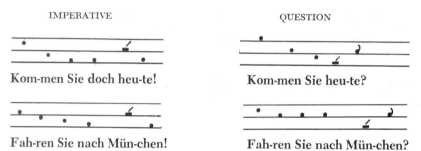

In a polite request, the stress-point of an imperative sentence is placed on level 2, as in the examples above. If **bitte** (*please*) is used, it must be placed either at the very beginning, or after the unstressed elements following the first prong.

> **Bitte besuchen Sie uns doch!**
> **Besuchen Sie uns doch bitte!**

If the stress point is raised to level 3, the request, in spite of the use of **bitte**, is changed into a command:

Kom-men Sie bit-te heu-te!

A. (**Review**): Conjugate the following sentences. Be prepared to go through these sentences in class without your book.

1. *Ich* bin schon zu *Hause*, aber *du* _____ noch *nicht* zu Hause.
   Du _____ schon zu *Hause*, aber *er* _____ noch *nicht* zu Hause.
   Er _____ schon zu *Hause*, aber *wir* _____ noch *nicht* zu Hause.
   Wir _____ schon zu *Hause*, aber *ihr* _____ noch *nicht* zu Hause.
   Ihr _____ schon zu *Hause*, aber *sie* _____ noch *nicht* zu Hause.

2. Ich esse zuviel, und du trinkst zuviel.
   Du _____ zuviel, und er _____ zuviel.
   Er _____ zuviel, und wir _____ zuviel.
   Wir _____ zuviel, und ihr _____ zuviel.
   Ihr _____ zuviel, und sie _____ zuviel.

3. Ich hoffe, du fährst morgen ab.
   Du _____, er _____ morgen ab.
   Er _____, wir _____ morgen ab.
   Wir _____, ihr _____ morgen ab.
   Ihr _____, sie _____ morgen ab.

4. Weißt du, wer ich bin?
   _____ er, wer du _____?
   _____ ihr, wer wir _____?
   _____ sie, wer ihr _____?
   _____ Fritz, wer Inge _____?

5. Ich lasse meine Kinder zu Hause, und du _____ _____ Kinder zu Hause.
   Du _____ _____ Kinder zu Hause, und er _____ _____ Kinder zu Hause.
   Er _____ _____ Kinder zu Hause, und wir _____ _____ Kinder zu Hause.
   Wir _____ _____ Kinder zu Hause, und ihr _____ _____ Kinder zu Hause.
   Ihr _____ _____ Kinder zu Hause, und sie _____ _____ Kinder zu Hause.

6. Glaubst du, ich brauche dich?
   _____ er, du _____ _____?
   _____ ihr, wir _____ _____?
   _____ Inge, ich _____ _____?
   _____ Fritz, wir _____ _____?
   _____ Meyers, wir _____ _____?

7. Du kennst mich, aber meine Mutter kennst du noch nicht.
   Ich _____ ihn, aber _____ Mutter _____ ich noch nicht.
   Ich _____ Inge, aber _____ Mutter _____ ich noch nicht.
   Er _____ dich, aber _____ Mutter _____ er noch nicht.
   Meyers _____ uns, aber _____ Mutter _____ sie noch nicht.
   Wir _____ Fritz, aber _____ Mutter _____ wir noch nicht.

B. (Review): In the following sentences, replace the *subject* by a pronoun.

1. Fritz ist mein Bruder.
2. Frau Bertram ist eine Dame.
3. Unser Hund ist eine "sie".
4. Erika ist meine Freundin.
5. Herr Meyer ist mein Freund.
6. Unsere Vernunft läßt uns frei.
7. Das Bier ist gut.
8. Unser Wasser ist gut.
9. Wann fährt der Zug denn ab?
10. Wann gehen die Laternen denn an?

C. (Review): In the following sentences, replace the *object* by a pronoun.

SEE LAB
EXERCISE
3.1

(p. 624)

1. Liebst du Inge?
2. Verstehst du ihren Vater?
3. Morgen besuche ich seinen Vater.
4. Kennen Sie seine Kinder?
5. Wann brauchst du das Geld?
6. Ich lese deine Bücher nicht.
7. Warum läßt du deinen Hund nicht zu Hause?
8. Ich brauche das Buch noch.
9. Ich liebe aber meine Frau.
10. Sie liebt aber ihren Mann.

D. Express in German:

1. He is intelligent, isn't he?
2. He lives in Munich, doesn't he?
3. She has a house in Cologne, doesn't she?
4. You are a doctor, aren't you?
5. They have a son, don't they?

E. Transform the following sentences by substituting **kein** for **nicht ein.** Say each pair of sentences aloud to practice the shift in intonation.

> Ich kenne hier auch nicht *einen* Menschen.
> Ich *kenne* hier keinen Menschen.

SEE LAB
EXERCISE
3.2

(p. 624)

1. Er hat auch nicht einen Freund.
2. Wir haben hier nicht einen Arzt.
3. Heute abend fährt auch nicht ein Zug nach Köln.
4. Heute trinke ich nicht ein Glas Wein.

F. Negate the following sentences by using **kein**; use **kein . . . mehr,** and **noch kein** only where necessary.

1. Er ist Arzt.
2. Liest er eine Zeitung?
3. Haben Sie einen Wagen?
4. Sie hat eine Tochter.
5. Das ist eine Studentin.
6. Brauchst du Geld?
7. Sie ist eine Dame.
8. Trinken Sie Kaffee, Frau Meyer?
9. Trinken Sie Bier, Herr Meyer?
10. Du bist noch ein Kind.
11. Haben wir noch Butter?
12. Habt ihr noch Geld?
13. Wir haben schon ein Haus.
14. Sie haben schon Kinder.
15. Haben wir noch Bier?
16. Ich habe Hunger.
17. Ich habe noch Hunger.

G. Negate the following sentences by using **nicht**; use **noch nicht** and **nicht mehr** only where necessary.

1. Du bist doch meine Mutter.
2. Er liebt mich aber.
3. Das Wasser kocht schon.
4. Sie wohnen noch in Köln.
5. Ihr seid intelligent.
6. Das glaube ich heute immer noch.
7. Das Bier hier ist gut.
8. Wir gehen sonntags ins Kino.
9. Er ist schon zu Hause.
10. Schläfst du schon?
11. Ich brauche ihn.
12. Meyer ist gesund.
13. Ist das seine Frau?
14. Geld macht glücklich.
15. Er braucht mich noch.

SEE LAB
EXERCISES
3.3–3.5

(p. 624)

H. Complete the following sentences by using **mehr (als)** or **noch mehr (als)**.

Ich weiß, ich rauche zuviel, aber Hans raucht noch mehr (als ich).

SEE LAB
EXERCISE
3.6

(p. 624)

1. Erika hat viel Geld, aber Inge _____.
2. Ich weiß, Meyer trinkt zuviel, aber seine Frau _____.
3. In München regnet es viel, aber in Hamburg _____.
4. Du sagst, meine Frau ißt zuviel? Deine Frau _____.
5. Wir kennen viele Leute hier in München, aber Meyers _____.

I. Write replies to the following negative statements or questions by using **doch.**

> **Wohnt er nicht mehr in München?**
> **Doch, er wohnt immer noch in München.**

SEE LAB
EXERCISE
3.7

(p. 624)

1. Ich bin doch kein Kind mehr.
2. Fährst du heute nicht nach Köln?
3. Sind Sie heute abend nicht allein?
4. Haben wir keine Butter mehr?
5. Lebt denn Tante Amalie nicht mehr?
6. Hast du denn keinen Hunger?
7. Schläft Hans noch nicht?
8. Aber Meyers wohnen doch nicht mehr in Köln.
9. Ich glaube, ich kenne ihn nicht.
10. Das kann ich nicht.

J. Conjugate the following examples.

SEE LAB
EXERCISES
3.8–3.11

(p. 624)

1. Ich muß arbeiten, und du brauchst nicht zu arbeiten
   Du _mußt_ arbeiten, und er _braucht_ nicht zu arbeiten
   Er _muß_ arbeiten, und wir _brauchen_ nicht zu arbeiten
   Wir _müssen_ arbeiten, und ihr _braucht_ nicht zu arbeiten
   Ihr _müßt_ arbeiten, und Meyers _brauchen_ nicht zu arbeiten

2. Ich möchte ins Kino gehen, aber ich darf nicht
   Du _möchtest_ ins Kino gehen, aber du _darfst_ nicht   _allowed_
   Er _möchte_ ins Kino gehen, aber er _darf_ nicht
   Sie _möchten_ ins Kino gehen, aber sie _dürfen_ nicht
   Wir _möchten_ ins Kino gehen, aber wir _dü_ nicht
   Ihr _möchtet_ ins Kino gehen, aber ihr _durft_ nicht
   Sie _möchte_ ins Kino gehen, aber sie _dürfen_ nicht

3. Ich soll nach Bonn fahren, aber ich will nicht
   Du _sollst_ nach Bonn fahren, aber du _willst_ nicht
   Er _soll_ nach Bonn fahren, aber er _will_ nicht
   Sie _sollen_ nach Bonn fahren, aber sie _wollen_ nicht

Wir _sollen_ nach Bonn fahren, aber wir _wollen_ nicht
Ihr _sollt_ nach Bonn fahren, aber ihr _wollt_ nicht
Sie _sollen_ nach Bonn fahren, aber sie _wollen_ nicht

K. For each of the following sentences, invent a preceding sentence with contrast intonation.

_____, und *ich* bleibe zu *Hause.*
Du kannst ins *Kino* gehen, und *ich* bleibe zu *Hause.*

SEE LAB
EXERCISES
3.12–3.16

(pp. 624-625)

1. _____, und *ich* muß *arbeiten.*
2. _____, aber intelli*gent* ist sie *nicht.*
3. _____, aber eine *Tochter* ha*ben* sie nicht.
4. _____, aber ihr *Freund* hat Geld.
5. _____, aber *ich* studiere *Deutsch.*
6. _____, aber *ar*beiten *will* er nicht.
7. _____, aber *kochen kann* sie.
8. _____, aber *kochen* kann sie *nicht.*
9. _____, aber *nächs*tes Jahr bleiben wir zu *Hause.*
10. _____, aber *Herr* Meyer ist ein *Dumm*kopf.

L. Express in German:

1. I do not know one single person (human being) here.
2. It is still winter.
3. Today, I don't believe that any more.
4. I would not like to be Erika, but I would like to have her money.
5. Would you still like to live in Berlin, Erika?
6. I know he is not home yet.
7. Money is not everything, but can one be happy without money?
8. Our reason leaves us free.
9. No, I do not have to go to the museum today.
10. I cannot work at home.
11. We do not intend to buy a house yet.
12. I know she can't be happy.
13. He is not permitted to drink wine.
14. Can't he drink coffee either?
15. We are supposed to go to America next year.
16. This train is going to leave at 5:06.
17. You don't have to switch off the light yet.
18. May I switch off the light now?
19. Does Erika have money?—Yes, she's got money all right. But she *still* has no husband.
20. He doesn't seem to be living in Munich any more.

21. Thank goodness he is not my husband.
22. I don't want to become his wife. Of course, I would like to get married. But I will not marry *him* (contrast position). After all, I am no fool.
23. I hear (the) Meyers have a child now. Do they have a son or a daughter?
24. He eats too much, and he also drinks too much. I, too, am eating too much.
25. You can come tomorrow, can't you?
26. Don't eat so much.
27. Is he home yet?—No, not yet.
28. Is he still at home?
29. I don't have more money than you have.
30. Does she really have to work more than he does?

VOCABULARY

ach so oh, I see
alle all gone
als than
der Arzt, ⸚e physician, doctor
bald soon
bei at, at the home of; near
beginnen to begin, to start
das Beispiel, –e example
   zum Beispiel for example
besuchen to visit
bitte please
der Bruder, ⸚ brother
dann then; in that case
darum for that reason
denken to think
denn for (*conjunction*)
der Dok'tor, die Dokto'ren doctor
dürfen (*see* **49** *ff.*)
egoi'stisch egoistic, selfish
erst first; not until, only
   erst dann not until (*or* only) then
essen (**du ißt, er ißt**) to eat
   das Essen food, meal
etwas something, somewhat
frei free
gegen against

das Glas, ⸚er glass
das Glück happiness; luck
hassen to hate
heiraten to marry, to get married
hören to hear
immer always
   immer noch, noch immer still
die Intelligenz' intelligence, intellect
Ita'lien Italy
   italie'nisch Italian
kalt cold
kennenlernen to meet, to become acquainted with
können (*see* **49** *ff.*)
kosten to cost
krank sick
der Krieg, –e war
lassen (**du läßt, er läßt**) to let, to leave
   die Kinder zu Hause lassen* to leave the children at home
leben to live, to be alive
die Leute people (*plural only*)

die Liebe love
man one (*pronoun*); *accusative:* **einen**
die Mark mark
   zwei Mark two marks
mehr more
   mehr als more than
   nicht mehr no longer
mögen (*see* **49** *ff.*)
das Muse'um (*pl.* **die Muse'en**) the museum
müssen (*see* **49** *ff.*)
na und? so what?
nehmen (**du nimmst, er nimmt**) to take
oft often
ohne without (*with accusative*)
prima wonderful (*colloquial*)
rauchen to smoke
scheinen to seem; to shine
   er scheint zu schlafen he seems to be asleep
schlafen (**du schläfst, er schläft**) to sleep
sehen (**du siehst, er sieht**) to see
der September September

* Do not confuse this with
   abfahren to depart; to leave (intransitive)
   der Zug fährt ab the train is leaving

sollen (*see* **49** *ff.*)

sprechen (**du sprichst, er
     spricht**) to speak, to talk

die Stunde, –n hour

die Tante, –n aunt

tanzen to dance

die Tasse, –n cup

das Taxi, –s, or die Taxe, –n
     taxi

das Theater, – theater

das Tier, –e animal

trinken to drink

die Uhr, –en clock, watch
     sechs Uhr six o'clock
     wieviel Uhr what time

die Vernunft reason (intel-
     lect)

von from

wahr true

das Wasser water

der Wein, –e wine

wenn when; whenever; if

wiedersehen to see again
     auf Wiedersehen good-by

wieviel how much

wirklich really

wollen (*see* **49** *ff.*)

zehn ten

die Zeit, –en time

zu to, too
     zuviel too much

zwingen to force

zwischen between

UNIT 4: The Dative—Prepositions with Dative and Accusative —**lange** versus **schon lange**—The Perfect

PATTERNS

[1] The Dative of the Personal Pronouns

This pattern drill contains all the dative forms of the personal pronouns (with the exception of the polite **Ihnen**). After memorizing these pronouns, follow the system used in this drill and recite these sentences until you can do them automatically.

Heute helfe ich dir, und morgen hilfst du mir.
Heute helfe ich ihm, und morgen hilft er mir.
Heute helfe ich ihr, und morgen hilft sie mir.
Heute helfe ich euch, und morgen helft ihr mir.
Heute helfe ich ihnen, und morgen helfen sie mir.

Heute hilfst du mir, und morgen helfe ich dir.
Heute hilfst du ihm, und morgen hilft er dir.
Heute hilfst du ihr, und morgen hilft sie dir.
Heute hilfst du uns, und morgen helfen wir dir.
Heute hilfst du ihnen, und morgen helfen sie dir.

Heute hilft er mir, und morgen helfe ich ihm.
Heute hilft er dir, und morgen hilfst du ihm.
Heute hilft er ihr, und morgen hilft sie ihm.
Heute hilft er uns, und morgen helfen wir ihm.
Heute hilft er euch, und morgen helft ihr ihm.
Heute hilft er ihnen, und morgen helfen sie ihm.

Heute hilft sie mir, und morgen helfe ich ihr.
Heute hilft sie dir, und morgen hilfst du ihr.
Heute hilft sie ihm, und morgen hilft er ihr.
Heute hilft sie uns, und morgen helfen wir ihr.
Heute hilft sie euch, und morgen helft ihr ihr.
Heute hilft sie ihnen, und morgen helfen sie ihr.

SEE
**ANALYSIS
58–59**

(pp. 120-123)

(*Facing*) **Fahrkartenkontrolle** [ticket checking] **auf dem Bahnhof**

Heute helfen wir dir, und morgen hilfst du uns.
Heute helfen wir ihm, und morgen hilft er uns.
Heute helfen wir ihr, und morgen hilft sie uns.
Heute helfen wir euch, und morgen helft ihr uns.
Heute helfen wir ihnen, und morgen helfen sie uns.

Heute helft ihr mir, und morgen helfe ich euch.
Heute helft ihr ihm, und morgen hilft er euch.
Heute helft ihr ihr, und morgen hilft sie euch.
Heute helft ihr uns, und morgen helfen wir euch.
Heute helft ihr ihnen, und morgen helfen sie euch.

Heute helfen sie mir, und morgen helfe ich ihnen.
Heute helfen sie dir, und morgen hilfst du ihnen.
Heute helfen sie ihm, und morgen hilft er ihnen.
Heute helfen sie ihr, und morgen hilft sie ihnen.
Heute helfen sie uns, und morgen helfen wir ihnen.
Heute helfen sie euch, und morgen helft ihr ihnen.

[2] The Dative with **glauben** and **helfen**

Follow the instructions for [1]. Do not change intonation.

SEE
ANALYSIS
58–59

(pp. 120-123)

Wenn du mir nicht *glaubst,* kann ich dir nicht *hel*fen.
Wenn er mir nicht *glaubt,* kann ich ihm nicht *hel*fen.
Wenn sie mir nicht *glaubt,* kann ich ihr nicht *hel*fen.
Wenn sie mir nicht *glau*ben, kann ich ihnen nicht *hel*fen.

Wenn du uns nicht *glaubst,* können wir dir nicht *hel*fen.
Wenn er uns nicht *glaubt,* können wir ihm nicht *hel*fen.
Wenn sie uns nicht *glaubt,* können wir ihr nicht *hel*fen.
Wenn ihr uns nicht *glaubt,* können wir euch nicht *hel*fen.
Wenn sie uns nicht *glau*ben, können wir ihnen nicht *hel*fen.

[3] The Dative with **danken**

Follow the instructions for [1]. Do not change intonation.

SEE
ANALYSIS
58–59

(pp. 120-123)

Ich *weiß,* du hilfst mir *gern.* Aber wie kann ich dir *dan*ken?
Ich *weiß,* er hilft mir *gern.* Aber wie kann ich ihm *dan*ken?
Ich *weiß,* sie hilft mir *gern.* Aber wie kann ich ihr *dan*ken?
Ich *weiß,* ihr helft mir *gern.* Aber wie kann ich euch *dan*ken?
Ich *weiß,* sie helfen mir *gern.* Aber wie kann ich ihnen *dan*ken?

Wir *wiss*en, du hilfst uns *gern*. Aber wie können wir dir *dan*ken?
Wir *wiss*en, er hilft uns *gern*. Aber wie können wir ihm *dan*ken?
Wir *wiss*en, sie hilft uns *gern*. Aber wie können wir ihr *dan*ken?
Wir *wiss*en, ihr helft uns *gern*. Aber wie können wir euch *dan*ken?
Wir *wiss*en, sie helfen uns *gern*. Aber wie können wir ihnen *dan*ken?

[4] The Dative with **antworten**

Follow the instructions for [1]. Do not change intonation.

Na*tür*lich kannst du mich fragen! Aber ich brauche dir nicht zu *ant*worten!
Na*tür*lich kann er mich fragen! Aber ich brauche ihm nicht zu *ant*worten!
Na*tür*lich kann sie mich fragen! Aber ich brauche ihr nicht zu *ant*worten!
Na*tür*lich könnt ihr mich fragen! Aber ich brauche euch nicht zu *ant*worten!
Na*tür*lich können sie mich fragen! Aber ich brauche ihnen nicht zu *ant*worten!

SEE ANALYSIS 58-59
(pp. 120-123)

[5] The Dative with **gehören**—Replacement of **er, sie, es** by **der, die, das**

Practice these pairs of sentences until you can produce the second sentence orally when you hear the first.

Das ist mein Wagen. Der gehört mir.
Das ist meine Zeitung. Die gehört mir.
Das ist mein Haus. Das gehört mir.

Das ist dein Hund. Der gehört dir.
Das ist deine Uhr. Die gehört dir.
Das ist dein Buch. Das gehört dir.

Das ist sein Hut. Der gehört ihm.
Das ist seine Uhr. Die gehört ihm.
Das ist sein Auto. Das gehört ihm.

Das ist ihr Hut. Der gehört ihr.
Das ist ihre Uhr. Die gehört ihr.
Das ist ihr Auto. Das gehört ihr.

Das ist unser Wagen. Der gehört uns.
Das ist unsere Zeitung. Die gehört uns.
Das ist unser Haus. Das gehört uns.

Das ist euer Hund. Der gehört euch.
Das ist eure Zeitung. Die gehört euch.
Das ist euer Haus. Das gehört euch.

SEE ANALYSIS 58-59, 72
(pp. 120-123, 141-142)

Das ist Ihr Hund. Der gehört Ihnen.

Das ist Ihre Zeitung. Die gehört Ihnen.

Das ist Ihr Haus. Das gehört Ihnen.

Das sind meine Zeitungen. Die gehören mir.

Das sind deine Häuser. Die gehören dir.

Das sind seine Hüte. Die gehören ihm.

Das sind unsere Zeitungen. Die gehören uns.

Das sind eure Häuser? Die gehören euch?

Das sind ihre Hüte. Die gehören ihnen.

After you have mastered the pattern above, be prepared to produce orally **Das ist mein Wagen** when you hear **Der Wagen gehört mir.**

Wo ist denn Ihre Tochter, Frau Bertram?   Die hat geheiratet.
                                                 Sie wohnt jetzt in Berlin.

Maria ist intelligent.   Ich gehe gerne mit ihr ins Kino.
                             Mit der gehe ich gerne ins Kino.

[6] The Dative with **gehören**

Formulate similar questions and answers. Do not place the word containing the answer in the front field. Be prepared to do this orally in class.

SEE
ANALYSIS
58–59, 72

(pp. 120-123,
141-142)

Wem	gehört	das *Haus* da?
Das	gehört	Frau *Schulz.*
Wem	gehören	denn diese *Häus*er hier?
Das da	gehört	*mir.*
So? Das	gehört	*dir?*
Frau *Schmidt* sagt, das Auto	gehört	*ihr.*
Nein, es	gehört	*uns.*
	Gehört	dieses Auto *euch?*
Nein, es	gehört	Frau *Ber*tram.
Was? Dieses Auto	gehört	*Ih*nen, Frau Bertram?
Wem	gehört	denn der *W*agen?
Meinem *V*ater	gehört	er *nicht.*
Meiner *Freun*din	gehört	er *auch* nicht.
	Gehört	er deinem *Freund?*
*Do*ris sagt, der Wagen	gehört	ihrem *V*ater.
Wem	gehört	dieses *Haus?* Euren *Kindern?*
Ja, es	gehört	unseren *Kindern.*

[7] Variations—Plural Verb Forms after **es** and **das**

Practice these sentences until, when hearing one, you can produce the other four.

Das Haus gehört dem *Vater.*—Das Haus gehört meinem *Vater.*—Das Haus gehört *ihm.*— Es ist *sein* Haus.—Das ist *sein* Haus.

Die Zeitungen gehören der *Tante.*—Sie gehören meiner *Tante.*—Sie gehören *ihr.*—Es sind *ihre* Zeitungen.—Das sind *ihre* Zeitungen.

Der Wagen gehört der *Tante.*—Er gehört meiner *Tante.*—Er gehört *ihr.*—Es ist *ihr* Wagen.—Das ist *ihr* Wagen.

Die Bücher gehören den *Kindern.*—Sie gehören unseren *Kindern.*—Sie gehören *ihnen.*— Es sind *ihre* Bücher.—Das sind *ihre* Bücher.

SEE ANALYSIS 58–59, 72–73

(pp. 120-123, 141-142)

[8] Word Order in the Inner Field

Study the following sentences and observe the word order. Note that if you answer with a complete sentence, the element containing the answer always stands at the end of the inner field unless the verb itself is the answer.

Herr Lenz will seinem Freund die *Stadt* zeigen.
Was will Herr Lenz seinem Freund *zei*gen?
Die *Stadt.*
Er will ihm die *Stadt* zeigen.
Wem will Herr Lenz die Stadt zeigen?
Seinem *Freund.*
Er will die Stadt seinem *Freund* zeigen.
Er will sie seinem *Freund* zeigen.
Wann will denn Herr Lenz seinem Freund die *Stadt* zeigen?
Wann will er denn seinem Freund die *Stadt* zeigen?
Wann will er ihm denn die *Stadt* zeigen?
Wann will er sie ihm denn *zei*gen?
Er will ihm die Stadt *mor*gen zeigen.
Er will sie ihm *mor*gen zeigen.

SEE ANALYSIS 58–60, 64

(pp. 120-124, 126-128)

Ich schenke meiner Frau einen *Hut.*
Ich schenke ihr einen *Hut.*
Ich schenke den Hut meiner *Frau.*
Ich schenke ihn meiner *Frau.*
Ich schenke ihr den *Hut.*
Ich *schen*ke ihn ihr.

Ich gebe meiner Frau eine *Uhr.*
Ich gebe ihr eine *Uhr.*
Ich gebe die Uhr meiner *Frau.*
Ich gebe sie meiner *Frau.*
Ich gebe ihr die *Uhr.*
Ich *gebe* sie ihr.

Was willst du denn deiner Mutter *schic*ken?
Ich glaube, ich schicke ihr *Blu*men.
Was willst du denn mit diesen *Blu*men hier machen?
Die schicke ich meiner *Mut*ter.
Ich glaube, ich schicke sie meiner *Mut*ter.
Ich glaube, ich schicke diese Blumen meiner *Mut*ter.

Fritz möchte seiner Freundin ein *Buch* schicken.
Was will Fritz seiner Freundin schicken?
Ein *Buch!*
Er will ihr ein *Buch* schicken!
Wem will Fritz das Buch schicken?
Seiner *Freun*din!
Er will das Buch seiner *Freun*din schicken.
Er will es seiner *Freun*din schicken.
Warum will Fritz seiner Freundin denn ein *Buch* schicken?
Warum will er seiner Freundin denn ein *Buch* schicken?
Warum will er ihr denn ein *Buch* schicken?
Willst du das Buch deiner *Freun*din schicken?
Willst du es deiner *Freun*din schicken?
Willst du es ihr *schic*ken?
Willst du deiner Freundin ein *Buch* schicken?
Willst du ihr ein *Buch* schicken?
Nein, ich will ihr *Geld* schicken.
Wann willst du ihr das Geld denn *schic*ken?
Wann willst du es ihr denn *schic*ken?

[9] Adjectives with the Dative

Form variations by changing the pronouns.

SEE
ANALYSIS
61
(p. 124)

Das ist interessant.	That's interesting.
Das ist mir interessant.	I think that's interesting.
Er ist böse.	He is angry.
Er ist mir böse.	He is angry with me.

Sie ist zu jung.	She is too young.
Sie ist mir zu jung.	She is too young as far as I'm concerned.
Ist Ihnen das recht, Frau Meyer?	Is that all right with you, Mrs. Meyer?
Natürlich ist mir das recht.	Of course that's all right with me.
Ist das Ihrem Mann recht, Frau Meyer?	Is that all right with your husband, Mrs. Meyer?
Natürlich ist ihm das recht.	Of course that's all right with him.

[10] Prepositions with the Accusative

Form variations of your own, but do not replace nouns by pronouns.

Wir müssen		durch	die Stadt fahren.	**SEE ANALYSIS 62**
Ich hoffe, wir kommen gut		durch	den Winter.	
				(pp. 124-125)
Herr Lenz arbeitet		für	meinen Vater.	
Herr Kaiser arbeitet		für	die Stadt Köln.	
Wer (Whoever) nicht		für	mich ist,	
	ist	gegen	mich.	
Hast du etwas		gegen	mich?	
Wir sind		gegen	diesen Krieg.	
Wir sind		gegen	alle Kriege.	
Ich muß		ohne	ihn abfahren.	
Ich fahre nicht		ohne	meinen Mann ab.	
Ich kann		ohne	dich nicht leben.	

[11] Prepositions with the Dative

Woher *kommst* du?—	Aus dem *Kino!*	**SEE ANALYSIS 63**
	Aus dem The*a*ter!	
	Aus der *Stadt!*	(pp. 125-126)
Wir sind *a*lle hier	außer meinem *V*ater.	
	außer *ihm.*	
	außer *Ih*nen, Herr Lenz.	
Hans ist heute	bei seinem *V*ater.	
	bei seiner *Mu*tter.	
	bei *ihr.*	
	bei *uns.*	

Mit wem gehst du ins Kino?   Mit Frau *Hoff*mann!
                                                        Mit *ihr!*
                                                        Mit *der?*
                                                        Mit meinem *Freund!*
                                                        Mit *ihm!*
                                                        Mit *dem?*
                                                        Mit *Hoff*manns!
                                                        Mit *ih*nen!
                                                        Mit *denen?*

Wann dürft *ihr* denn heiraten?—   Nach dem *Kriege!*
                                                        Nach einem *M*onat!
                                                        Nach einem *Jahr!*
                                                        Nach drei *Jah*ren!

Er geht   nach Ber*lin.*
                                                        nach *Ham*burg.
                                                        nach *Hause.*
                                                        nach *Ame*rika.

Ich komme heute sehr spät nach *Hause.*—*Wann?*—Um *neun.*
Wie *spät* ist es jetzt?—*Zehn* nach *sechs.*

Seit wann bist *du* denn hier?—   Seit einer *Stunde!*
                                                        Seit zwei *Tag*en!
                                                        Seit drei *Wo*chen!
                                                        Seit einem *Jahr!*

Von wem hast du das *Buch?*   Von meinem *Bruder!*
                                                        Von meiner *Tan*te!
                                                        Von zwei *Freun*den!
                                                        Von zwei *Freund*innen!
                                                        Ich habe es von meinem *Vater!*
                                                        Ich habe es von *ihm!*

Wohin *gehst* du?   Zu meinem *Vater!*
                                                        Zu *ihm!*
                                                        Zum *Bahn*hof!
                                                        Zur Universi*tät!*
                                                        Zu meiner *Tan*te!
                                                        Zum *Essen!*

„Wohin gehst du?"—„Zum
Postamt"

[12] The Perfect

Read these sentences aloud to get used to this pattern, in which the participle
appears at the end of the sentence.

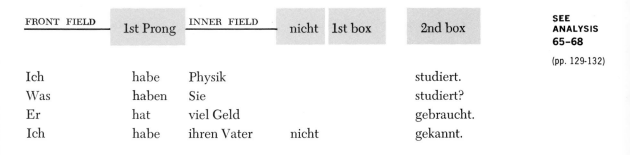

FRONT FIELD	1st Prong	INNER FIELD	nicht	1st box	2nd box
Ich	habe	Physik			studiert.
Was	haben	Sie			studiert?
Er	hat	viel Geld			gebraucht.
Ich	habe	ihren Vater	nicht		gekannt.

SEE
ANALYSIS
65–68

(pp. 129-132)

FRONT FIELD	1st Prong	INNER FIELD	nicht	1st box	2nd box
Er	hat	sie	nie		geliebt.
Sie	hat	ihn	nie		geliebt.
Herr Kurz	hat	ein Haus			gekauft.
Sie	haben	uns gestern			besucht.
Ich	habe	das Buch	nicht		gelesen.
Mein Vater	hat	die Zeitung			gelesen.
Was	hast	du			gelesen?
Wen	habt	ihr in Köln			gesehen?
Wir	haben	Frau Meyer			gesehen.
Wir	haben	Sie	nicht		verstanden.
Warum	haben	Sie mich	nicht		verstanden?
Er	ist	heute morgen			gestorben.
Wir	sind	gestern abend			gekommen.
Der Zug	ist	schon		ab-	gefahren.
Um sieben Uhr	sind	die Laternen		an-	gegangen.
Ich	bin	gestern		in Berlin	gewesen.
Hans	ist	heute		zu Hause	geblieben.
Warum	seid	ihr heute		zu Hause	geblieben?
Du	bist	gestern		nach Berlin	gefahren.
Sie	ist	schon		nach Hause	gegangen.
Meyer	ist	schon immer		ein Idiot	gewesen.
Ich	bin	auch damals	nicht	glücklich	gewesen.
Ich	habe	gestern			arbeiten müssen.
Ich	habe	gestern	nicht		zu arbeiten brauchen.
Er	hat	noch nie			arbeiten wollen.
Ich	habe	ihn leider	nicht		besuchen dürfen.
Ich	habe	bei dem Regen	nicht		arbeiten können.
Ich	habe	bei dem Regen	nicht	nach Köln	fahren können.
Ich	habe	gestern	nicht	zu Hause	bleiben wollen.

[13] The Inner Field—The Perfect

Find substitutions for the elements in the inner field of each group of sentences.
Leave the perfect verb forms unchanged.

Wer hat denn gestern Tante Amalie zum *Bahn*hof gebracht?
Wer hat denn Tante Amalie *gestern* zum Bahnhof gebracht?
Wer hat sie denn gestern zum *Bahn*hof gebracht?
Warum hast *du* sie denn nicht zum Bahnhof gebracht?

Herr Kunz hat seiner Frau in Frankfurt ein *Au*to gekauft.
Er hat seiner Frau das Auto in *Frank*furt gekauft.
Er hat ihr das Auto in *Frank*furt gekauft.
Er hat es ihr in *Frank*furt gekauft.
Nein, in Ber*lin* hat er es ihr *nicht* gekauft.

Fritz hat meinem Sohn gestern eine *Uhr* geschenkt.
Was hat er deinem Sohn gestern geschenkt?
Er hat ihm gestern eine *Uhr* geschenkt?
Wann hat er ihm die Uhr geschenkt?
Er hat sie ihm *ges*tern geschenkt.
Wem hat er die Uhr geschenkt?
Er hat sie meinem *Sohn* geschenkt.
Und wa*rum* hat er sie ihm geschenkt?

Was hast du denn gestern deiner *Frau* gekauft?
Ich habe meiner Frau gestern einen *Hut* gekauft.
Ich habe ihr gestern einen *Hut* gekauft.
Ich habe meiner Frau gestern in Berlin einen *Hut* gekauft.
Ich habe ihr gestern in Berlin einen *Hut* gekauft.
Ich habe den Hut gestern meiner *Frau* geschickt.
Ich habe den Hut meiner Frau *ges*tern geschickt.
Ich habe ihn gestern meiner *Frau* geschickt.
Ich habe ihn meiner Frau *ges*tern geschickt.
Ich habe ihr gestern den *Hut* geschickt.
Ich habe ihn ihr gestern ge*schickt*.

[14] The Meaning of the German Perfect—Time Phrases

The following conversational sentences contain time expressions which denote
a date or a point in time. Observe that English always uses the past tense. Get
used to the "all-past" meaning of the German perfect.

Meyer ist heute morgen nach *Pa*ris gefahren?—*Nein*, er ist schon *ges*tern gefahren.	Did Meyer go to *Paris* this morning?—*No*, he went *yesterday*.

SEE
ANALYSIS
64–68
(pp. 126-132)

SEE
ANALYSIS
69–71
(pp. 133-141)

Wie hast du denn heute nacht ge*schla*fen? —Heute nacht habe ich *gut* geschlafen.

How did you *sleep* last night?—Last night I slept *well.*

Darf ich Ihnen jetzt den *Kaf*fee bringen?— Nein *danke!* Ich habe schon vor einer *Stun*de Kaffee getrunken.

May I bring you your *coffee* now?—No *thank* you. I had my coffee an *hour* ago.

Hier in *Ham*burg hat es gestern ge*reg*net. —Bei *uns* hat es gestern *nicht* geregnet.

Here in *Ham*burg it *rained* yesterday.— Where *we* live it did *not* rain yesterday.

Wann will Hans denn *hei*raten?—Er hat schon vor einer *Wo*che geheiratet.—Wen hat er denn ge*hei*ratet?—Die Erika *Mey*er!

When does Hans want to get *married?*—He got married a *week* ago.—Whom did he *marry?*—Erika Meyer.

Kennen Sie Frau *Leh*mann?—Ja, die habe ich vor einem Jahr in *Mün*chen kennengelernt.

Do you know Mrs. *Lehmann?*—Yes, I met (was introduced to) her a year ago in *Munich.*

Das Haus neben der Kirche hat früher den *Mül*lers gehört, nicht wahr?—*Ja,* aber Herr Müller ist vor zwei Jahren ge*stor*ben. Seine *Frau* hat wieder ge*hei*ratet und wohnt jetzt in Ber*lin.*

Didn't the house next to the church use to belong to the *Müllers?* Yes, but Mr. Müller *died* two years ago. His *wife remarried* and is living in *Berlin.*

Was habt *ihr* denn gestern abend ge*macht?* *Wir* sind gestern abend ins *Ki*no gegangen.

What did *you* do last night? *We* went to the *movies* last night.

Sie wollen nach *Mün*chen fahren? *Da* kommen Sie zu *spät.* Der Zug nach München ist schon vor einer *Stun*de *ab*gefahren.

You want to go to *Munich?* Then you are too *late.* The train to Munich *left* an *hour* ago.

Hast du gut ge*schla*fen, Tante Amalie?— *Nein!* Die Laterne vor eurem Hause ist erst heute *morgen aus*gegangen. Und bei *Licht* kann ich nicht *schla*fen. Außer*dem* habe ich gestern abend zuviel *Kaf*fee getrunken.

Did you *sleep* well, Aunt *Amalie?*—*No!* The street lamp in front of your house didn't go *out* until this *morning.* And I can't sleep when there is a light on. *Besides,* I drank too much *coffee* last evening.

[15] Stretch-of-Time Phrases

The following sentences contain stretch-of-time phrases. Note the difference between "all-past" and "up-to-now" situations.

SEE
ANALYSIS
71
(pp. 140-141)

Kennen Sie *Mün*chen?—Ja, ich habe zwei Jahre lang in München ge*wohnt,* vor dem *Krie*ge.

Do you know *Munich?*—Yes, I *lived* in Munich for two years before the *war.*

Hast du *Erika* schon besucht?—*Ja,* aber erst *ges*tern. Ich habe *lange* nicht gewußt, wo sie *wohnt.*

Have you seen *Erika?*—Yes, but only *yesterday.* I didn't know for a long time where she is *living.*

Ich bin damals Athe*ist* gewesen und habe *lange* nicht an Gott ge*glaubt.* Aber *heute* *weiß* ich: ohne *Gott* kann man nicht *le*ben.

At that time, I was an *atheist,* and for a *long* time I did not *believe* in God. But *now* I *know:* One cannot *live* without *God!*

Wie geht's denn Herrn *Mey*er?—Oh, *jetzt* geht's ihm wieder *gut.* Aber *letz*tes Jahr ist er monatelang *krank* gewesen und hat *lange* nicht *ar*beiten können.—Und wie geht's seinem *Bruder?*—*Dem* geht's noch immer *gut. Der* hat noch *nie* zu arbeiten brauchen.

How is Mr. *Meyer?*—Oh, *now* he's *all right* again. But *last* year he was *sick* for *months,* and for *quite* some time he wasn't able to *work.*—And how is his *brother?*—*He* is still doing *fine. He* has never had to work *yet!*

Ich *weiß,* Erika wohnt seit drei Wochen hier in *Köln,* aber bis *heu*te habe ich sie noch *nicht* be*su*chen können. Ich habe *wirk*lich noch keine *Zeit* gehabt, sie zu be*su*chen.

I *know* Erika has been living here in *Cologne* for three weeks. But up to *now* I have not yet been able to *visit* her. I *really* haven't had the *time* yet to *visit* her.

Warum hat Maria denn noch *im*mer keine Arbeit? Sie hat doch stu*diert!*—Ja, stu*diert hat* sie, fünf *Jah*re lang! Aber leider hat sie Ägyptolo*gie* studiert. Und *was* kann man heute mit Ägyptolo*gie* machen!

Why does Mary *still* have no work? She went to the *University,* didn't she? Yes, she went to the *University* for five *years.* But unfortunately she studied *Egyptology!* And *what* can you do with *Egyptology* today!

Na*tür*lich muß mein Sohn in Tübingen viel arbeiten. Und warum auch *nicht! Ich* habe *auch* vier Jahre in *Tü*bingen studiert, und *ich* habe *auch* viel arbeiten müssen.

Of *course,* my son has to *work* hard in Tübingen. And why *not!* I, *too,* went to the University of *Tübingen* for four years, and *I, too,* had to work hard.

Also, da *seid* ihr ja. Wie *geht's* dir denn, Erika, und wie geht's *dir,* Otto? Und natürlich hast du wieder auf Erika *war*ten müssen, nicht *wahr,* Otto? Fritz und *ich* sind schon *lange* hier.

Well, there you *are!* How *are* you, *Erika,* and how are *you,* Otto? And, of course, you had to *wait* again for Erika, *didn't* you, *Otto?* Fritz and *I* have been here for a *long* time.

Ist Schmidt ge*sund* aus Afrika zu*rück*gekommen?—*Nein,* seine Frau hat *jahre*lang auf ihn ge*war*tet. Aber *letz*tes Jahr hat sie gehört, daß er nicht mehr *lebt.*

Did Schmidt get home *safe* from Africa?—No, his wife *waited* for him for *years,* but *last* year she heard that he is no longer *alive.*

Schmidt ist *krank* nach *Hause* gekommen. Er hat nur noch *drei* Jahre gelebt. Seine *Frau* wohnt jetzt bei ihrer *Toch*ter.

Schmidt came back a *sick man.* He only lived for *three* more years. His *wife* is now living with her *daughter.*

Seit wann wohnt denn seine Frau schon bei ihrer *Toch*ter?—Oh, schon *lange*, schon seit *vier* oder fünf *Jah*ren.

Since when has his wife been living with her *daughter*?—Oh, for *quite* some time, it must be *four* or *five years* by now.

Erika will *hei*raten.—Das weiß ich schon *lange*, aber ge*sagt* hat sie mir noch *nichts*.

Erika wants to get *married*.—I have known that for a *long* time. But she *still* has not said *anything* to me.

Wo ist denn *Ihr* Sohn, Frau Meyer?— *Mein* Sohn ist seit Anfang Mai in Ber*lin*. Er studiert Medi*zin*. Sie *wis*sen ja, er hat schon *im*mer *Arzt* werden wollen.

And where is *your* son, Mrs. Meyer?—*My* son has been in *Berlin* since the beginning of May. He is studying *medicine*. As you *know*, he has *always* wanted to become a *doctor*.

Wie lange sitzt du denn schon hier und *war*test?—Seit einer *Stun*de!

How long have you been sitting here *wait-ing*?—For an *hour*!

Habe ich Sie nicht letztes Jahr in Pa*ris* gesehen?—*Nein!* In Pa*ris* bin ich noch nie ge*we*sen.

Didn't I see you last year in *Paris*?—*No*, I have never *been* in *Paris*.

Nein, hier hat es gestern *nicht* geregnet. Hier hat es schon *wo*chenlang nicht mehr geregnet. Wir warten schon *lange* auf *Re*gen.

No, it did not rain *here* yesterday. It hasn't rained here for *weeks*. We have been waiting for rain for quite some *time*.

CONVERSATION

HERR LORENZ: Jetzt muß ich aber wirklich *gehen*, Herr *Kunz*. Ich muß um *sie*ben zu *Hause* sein. Denn ich will nach dem Essen noch mit meiner Frau ins *Kino*.

HERR KUNZ: Aber es ist ja erst *fünf*, Herr *Lorenz*, und mit dem *Wagen* sind Sie doch in *zehn* Minuten zu *Hause*!

HERR LORENZ: Mit dem *Wagen*, *ja*. Aber ich muß heute mit dem *Zug* nach Hause fahren. Den *Wagen* habe ich zu *Hause* gelassen. Meine Frau geht doch jeden Montag in die *Stadt*, und da hat sie natürlich den *Wagen* haben wollen. Sie *wis*sen ja, wie Frauen *sind*. „Ich kann doch nicht mit dem *Zug* in die Stadt fahren, bei dem *Regen*!" hat sie gesagt. Also bin *ich* mit dem *Zug* in die Stadt gefahren und habe *ihr* den *Wagen* dagelassen.

HERR KUNZ: *Ja*, ich *weiß*. *Mei*ne Frau ist *auch* so.

FRAU KUNZ: Was soll *das* denn heißen: „Meine Frau ist *auch* so"? Ich *darf* doch noch nicht einmal *fah*ren. Bis *jetzt* hat der Wagen *nur dir* gehört.

HERR KUNZ:	Haben Sie das *gehört*, Herr *Lorenz*? Der Wagen *hat* (!), *hat*(!) mir gehört. Meine Frau lernt jetzt *fah*ren, *wis*sen Sie; und wenn sie erst *fah*ren kann, dann gehört der Wagen *ihr*, und es ist *mein* Wagen *gewe*sen.
FRAU KUNZ:	Na *und*? Dann müssen wir natürlich *zwei* Wagen haben, einen für *dich*, den *VW*°, und *einen* für *mich*, einen *Mer*cedes. *Üb*rigens, Herr *Lo*renz! Glauben Sie, Ihre Frau ist schon aus der Stadt zu*rück*?
HERR LORENZ:	Ich *glau*be, *ja*.
HERR KUNZ:	Warum rufen Sie Ihre Frau nicht *an* und *sa*gen ihr, sie soll mit dem Wagen zu *uns* kommen? Dann können Sie noch *hier*bleiben und ein Glas *Bier* trinken, und Sie brauchen nicht mit dem *Zug* zu fahren und sind *doch* um sieben zu Hause.
HERR LORENZ:	Das ist eine I*dee*. Vielen *Dank*! Zu einem Glas *Bier* sage ich *nie* nein.
HERR LORENZ:	(*Wählt eine Nummer*): Be*setzt!* Ich hoffe, sie spricht nicht schon wieder mit ihrer *Freun*din.
FRAU KUNZ:	Warum sagen Sie Ihrer Frau nicht, sie soll zum Abendessen zu *uns* kommen. Dann können wir nach dem Essen *al*le ins Kino gehen. Ist Ihnen das *recht*, Herr *Lo*renz?
HERR LORENZ:	Das ist mir *sehr* recht! Vielen *Dank!*
FRAU KUNZ:	Darf *ich* mit Ihrer *Frau* sprechen, Herr *Lo*renz?
HERR LORENZ:	Aber na*tür*lich! Dann können *Sie* ihr ja sagen, sie soll mit dem Wagen kommen.
FRAU KUNZ:	Ihre Nummer ist doch *drei*-fünf-*drei*-eins-*zwo*†, nicht wahr?
HERR LORENZ:	Nein, *drei*-fünf-*drei*-zwo-*eins*.
FRAU KUNZ:	(*Wählt*): A*ha! Nicht* besetzt! Frau *Lo*renz?—Gertrud *Kunz!* Guten Abend, Frau *Lo*renz.—*Dan*ke, mir geht's *gut*.—*Ja*, meinem Mann *auch*, und *Ih*nen?—Ich *weiß*, Ihr Mann ist noch nicht zu *Hau*se. Er sitzt seit zwei Uhr bei *uns*.—*Ja*, er ist mit meinem Mann aus der Stadt zu *uns* gekommen, und dann hat er bis *jetzt* hier ge*ar*beitet.—*Nein*, er will schon *lan*ge gehen. Aber ich höre, Sie wollen nach dem Essen ins *Ki*no. Möchten Sie nicht zum Essen zu *uns* kommen? Dann können wir *erst* hier *es*sen und dann alle *vier* ins Kino gehen.—*Gut, gut!* Ich habe Sie ja schon *so* lange nicht mehr ge*se*hen!—*Ja*, gut. Hier ist ihr *Mann!*
HERR LORENZ:	*Ot*ti? Guten Abend!—*Ja*, ich habe schon *ja* gesagt. Das ist dir doch *recht*, oder?—Du kannst so*fort* kommen?—*Gut*, wir *war*ten auf dich!

° VW: pronounced **Vau-we**
† To avoid confusion with **drei**, **zwo** is frequently used instead of **zwei**, especially on the telephone.

TAXI-FUNK
Berlin e.G.m.b.H.
66 00 22
Berlin 61
Mehringdamm 107

TAG
UND
NACHT
BEREIT

66 00 22

Vorbestellung
jederzeit

„Willst du mit dem Taxi ins Museum, Tante Amalie?
Die Nummer ist sechs-sechs, null-null, zwo-zwo.''

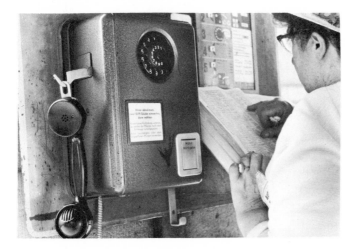

READING

Viel Lärm um nichts?

KAPITEL EINS: A News Item

New York Star. International Edition. Paris, April 30.—According to a report from Konstanz, Germany, the famous German novelist Johannes Schmidt–Ingelheim has been missing since April 8. Schmidt–Ingelheim had gone to Africa to collect material for a new novel which is to deal with the fate of General Rommel, the famous

Viel Lärm um nichts
the German trans-
lation of *Much Ado
about Nothing.*

commander of the German Afrika Korps. In a letter from Cairo, dated April 8, Schmidt–Ingelheim promised to call his wife on April 12, her birthday, from Casablanca. Since then he has not been heard from. Schmidt–Ingelheim's novel *Wie das Gesetz es befahl* (*As the Law Demanded*) is the literary sensation of the year. Even here in Paris, critics praise his objectivity and the penetrating realism of the scenes dealing with the battle on the Normandy beaches. Everybody here feels that this book was written by a man who, "as the law demanded," did his best as a soldier, but who nevertheless remained a human being. Just a few weeks ago Schmidt–Ingelheim was awarded the *Grand Prix Littéraire de l'Europe.*

KAPITEL ZWEI: Frau Schmidt–Ingelheim am Telefon

Hier Frau Schmidt–*I*ngelheim! . . .
*Meh*rens?—*Bit*te, ich kann Sie nicht ver*st*ehen. . . .
Ach *so*, Behrens, B wie *Ber*ta. . . .   15
Und Sie sind ein Freund von meinem *Mann*, Herr Behrens? . . .

Ach *so*, Sie haben den Artikel im *New York Star* gelesen. Und *Sie* sind von der *Bild*-Zeitung? . . .

Nein, nein, ich bin *nicht* mit meinem Mann nach *Kai*ro gefahren. Er hat mir nur aus Kairo ge*schrie*ben! „Ich fahre morgen nach 20 Casa*blan*ca", hat er geschrieben. . . .

Nein, nein, nicht mit einer *Jacht!* Mit der *Luft*hansa! . . .

So, Sie kennen Herrn Thistlethwaite? Ja, Herr Thistlethwaite ist ein *Freund* von meinem Mann. . . .

Und Sie sagen, Herr Thistlethwaite hat am 9. April [am *neun*ten 25 April] auf seiner Jacht in Alexandria von *den I*ngelheims geredet? . . .

„Die Ingelheims sind auf meiner Jacht", hat er gesagt? . . .

Nein, da haben Sie Herrn Thistlethwaite nicht richtig ver*st*anden. Ich *sa*ge Ihnen doch, ich bin *nicht* mit meinem Mann nach *Ä*gypten gefahren. Ich bin zu *Hau*se geblieben. . . .   30

Nein, unsere Tochter ist es *auch* nicht ge*we*sen. Unsere *Toch*ter ist doch erst *acht*. Wir haben ja erst vor *neun* Jahren ge*hei*ratet, in Berlin! . . .

Bin ich *glück*lich mit Johannes? Aber na*tür*lich bin ich *glück*lich! . . .

Warum *Kä*the nicht glücklich mit ihm gewesen ist? Aber wo haben 35 *Sie* denn von *Kä*the gehört? . . .

So, *so*, die *Zei*tung weiß alles! *Ja*, mein Mann hat von seiner ersten Frau eine *Toch*ter. Erika heißt sie. . . .

ersten first (disregard the ending **–en**)

Nein, sie muß jetzt *zwanzig* sein. Ich *kenne* sie nicht. Ich habe sie *nie* gesehen. . . .

Ja, mein Mann redet *viel* von seiner *Tochter*. Aber be*sucht* hat sie uns *nie*. . . .

Na*türlich* möchte ich die Erika *kennenlernen*. Aber sie *darf* uns nicht ₅ be*suchen*, die Mutter *will* das nicht. . . .

Nein, die Tochter ist *nicht* mit ihrem Vater nach Alexandria gefahren. . . .

Was die Tochter *tut?* Ich *glaube*, sie studiert Archä*ologie*.—Aber hier kommt der *Brief*träger. Vielleicht bringt er einen Brief von ₁₀ meinem *Mann*. . . .

Gut, Sie rufen mich später wieder *an*.

Fortsetzung folgt (To be continued)

ANALYSIS

58   The Dative Case

The term "case" was explained in **20.** There are four cases in German: nominative, genitive, dative, and accusative.

In this lesson, the dative case is introduced. The dative is the case of the indirect object, or—to use the German term—of the dative object. This dative object answers the question *To whom*—**Wem?** It is usually a person.

> She gave the money to Charlie.
> She gave the money to him.
> To whom did she give it?—To Charlie, to him.

Note that, whenever you have a genuine dative object in English, you can, by rearranging the sentence, force the form with *to* to appear or to disappear:

> She gave him the book.
> She gave the book to him.

The *him* in *She gave him the book* is therefore syntactically not the same kind of *him* as that in

> She loves him

for only the first *him* can be changed into a *to him*. The *him* which can be replaced by *to him* corresponds to the German dative. Note also that the *to* in

> He took Charlie to the station

cannot be eliminated, since *to the station* is not an object but a directive. It is important that you remember this distinction when dealing with the German dative (indirect) object, which *never* uses the preposition *zu*.

The Forms of the Dative Case

INTERROGATIVE PRONOUNS

NOM.	**wer**	who
DAT.	*wem*	to whom
ACC.	**wen**	whom

NOTE: The interrogative pronouns **wer, wem,** and **wen** have the same endings as the corresponding forms of the masculine definite article **der, dem, den.**

der-WORDS

	MASC.	FEM.	NEUT.	PLURAL
NOM.	der	die	das	die
DAT.	*dem*	*der*	*dem*	*den*
ACC.	den	die	das	die

ein-WORDS

	MASC.	FEM.	NEUT.	PLURAL
NOM.	kein	keine	kein	keine
DAT.	*keinem*	*keiner*	*keinem*	*keinen*
ACC.	keinen	keine	kein	keine

NOTE: There is no difference between the dative endings of the **ein**-words and those of the **der**-words.

PERSONAL PRONOUNS

SINGULAR:	NOM.	ich	du	er	sie	es	Sie
	DAT.	*mir*	*dir*	*ihm*	*ihr*	*ihm*	*Ihnen*
	ACC.	mich	dich	ihn	sie	es	Sie
PLURAL:	NOM.	wir	ihr		sie		Sie
	DAT.	*uns*	*euch*		*ihnen*		*Ihnen*
	ACC.	uns	euch		sie		Sie

NOUNS

In the singular, nouns have no special ending for the dative. Occasionally, masculine and neuter nouns of one syllable use **-e** (**dem Manne**), but this ending is obsolescent and no longer required, except in such idiomatic expressions as **zu Hause** or **nach Hause.**

A number of masculine German nouns have the ending **-en** in all cases except the nominative singular—e.g., **der Student, dem Studenten, den Studenten,** plural **die Studenten; der Mensch, dem Menschen, den Menschen,** plural **die Menschen.**

The noun **Herr** is declined as follows:

SINGULAR	NOM.	der Herr
	DAT.	dem Herrn
	ACC.	den Herrn
PLURAL	NOM.	die Herren
	DAT.	den Herren
	ACC.	die Herren

In the dative plural, all German nouns must end in **-n,** except those foreign words the plural of which ends in **-s.** If the nominative plural already ends in **-n,** no additional **-n** is required.

NOM. SING.	NOM. PLURAL	DATIVE PLURAL
der Mann	die Männer	den Männern
die Frau	die Frauen	den Frauen
die Freundin	die Freundinnen	den Freundinnen
das Auto	die Autos	den Autos

NOTE: Nouns ending in **-in** double the **n** in the plural in order to keep the **i** short: **die Freundin, die Freundinnen.**

59   Verbs with Only a Dative Object

For the English-speaking student, the *him* in

> They helped him

is clearly a direct object. For a native German, the verb **helfen** means *to give help to.* For this reason, **helfen,** and a number of other verbs, take a dative object, *not* an accusative object, in German.

We are introducing five of these verbs in this lesson. They are

| gehören | to belong to (ownership) |
| helfen | to help, give help to |

danken	to thank, give thanks to
glauben	to believe (someone), give credence to
antworten	to answer, give an answer (to someone)

Das Haus gehört ihm.	The house belongs to him.
Kannst du mir helfen?	Can you help me?
Ich danke dir.	I thank you.
Glaubst du ihm?	Do you believe him?
Ich muß ihm antworten.	I must give him an answer.

Note that of the five corresponding English verbs, only *belong* must be used with the preposition *to*. You can only say *The book belongs to me*, not *The book belongs me*. English, unlike German, does not distinguish between ownership and membership. German **gehören zu** expresses membership only:

| Der Hund gehört uns. | The dog belongs to us. |
| Maria gehört zu uns. | Mary is one of us, belongs to our group. |

The indispensable *to* (when *to belong to* expresses ownership) is one important case where an English verb cannot get rid of the *to*, and where German nevertheless cannot use **zu.**

60 Verbs Governing the Dative and Accusative

In English there are a number of verbs that can be used with both an indirect and a direct object:

Mr. Jones gave his wife a hat.

The German sentence

Er schenkt seiner Frau einen Hut

has the same structure.

Er	subject	nominative
seiner Frau	indirect object	dative
einen Hut	direct object	accusative

The most important verbs in this group are

geben	to give
schenken	to give (a present)
bringen	to bring, to take
zeigen	to show
glauben	to believe
sagen	to tell, to say
antworten	to (give an) answer (to)

Er schenkt mir einen Hund.	He will give me a dog.
Er bringt mir eine Tasse Kaffee.	He is bringing me a cup of coffee.
Morgen zeigen wir euch die Stadt.	Tomorrow we will show you the city.
Das kann ich ihm nicht sagen.	I can't tell him that.

NOTE:

1. The English phrases *to take something to somebody* and *to take somebody home* are expressed in German by using **bringen:**

Er bringt ihr eine Tasse Kaffee.	He is taking her a cup of coffee.
Er bringt sie nach Hause.	He is taking her home.

2. **glauben** sometimes takes only a dative object and sometimes only an accusative object:

Ich glaube dir.	I believe you.
Das glaube ich nicht.	I don't believe that.

But, unlike English, German can combine these two sentences into one:

Das glaube ich dir nicht.	I don't believe what you say.

Observe that the dative object represents the person and the accusative object represents the facts.

3. **antworten** can also be used with two objects:

Er antwortet mir.	He gives me an answer.
Was hat er geantwortet?	What did he answer?
Was hat er dir geantwortet?	What answer did he give you?

61 Adjectives Governing the Dative

Certain adjectives like **interessant, böse,** and **recht,** as well as most adjectives preceded by **zu,** can be used with the dative to point out the person for whom the grammatical subject has the quality denoted by the adjective.

Das ist interessant.	That's interesting.
Das ist mir interessant.	I think that's interesting.
Er ist böse.	He is angry.
Er ist mir böse.	He is angry with me.
Sie ist zu jung.	She is too young.
Sie ist mir zu jung.	She is too young as far as I'm concerned.

62 Prepositions Governing the Accusative

A small group of prepositions is *always* used with the accusative. This group includes: **durch** (*through*), **für** (*for*), **gegen** (*against*), and **ohne** (*without*).

Ich fahre durch die Stadt.	I am driving through the town.
Er arbeitet für seinen Vater.	He works for his father.
Wir sind gegen diesen Krieg.	We are against this war.
Ich kann ohne dich nicht leben.	I cannot live without you.

63 Prepositions Governing the Dative

Some prepositions are *always* used with the dative case. All the important prepositions of this group are introduced in this unit: **aus** (*out of*), **außer** (*except*), **bei** (*with*), **mit** (*with*), **nach** (*after*), **seit** (*since*), **von** (*from*), **zu** (*to*).

Er kommt aus dem Haus.	He is coming out of the house.
Wir sind alle hier außer dem Vater.	We are all here except father.
Ich bleibe bei meinem Freund.	I am going to stay with my friend.
Wir gehen mit dir.	We'll go with you.
Er kommt nach dem Abendessen.	He's coming after supper.
Er wohnt seit dieser Zeit in Köln.	He has been living in Cologne since that time.
Er hat das Buch von seinem Vater.	He has (received) that book from his father.
Er geht zu seiner Freundin.	He is going to visit his girl friend.

NOTE:

1. A third group of prepositions, which includes **in** and **vor,** is used with either dative or accusative. These prepositions will be introduced later.

2. **Bei** does not normally correspond to English *by;* it expresses the idea of close proximity, and frequently means *at the house of.*

Er wohnt in Potsdam bei Berlin.
Er wohnt bei seiner Tante.

3. Some prepositions are normally contracted with the following article into a single word, as long as the article is not stressed. (See **72.**)

von dem:	Ich komme vom Bahnhof.	I am coming from the station.
zu dem:	Ich gehe zum Bahnhof.	I am on my way to the station.
zu der:	Ich gehe zur Universität.	I am on my way to the University.
durch das:	Er geht durchs Haus.	He is going through the house.
für das:	Er hat kein Geld fürs Kino.	He has no money for the show.
bei dem:	Meine Frau ist beim Arzt.	My wife is at the doctor's.

But

Bei *dem* Regen kommt er nicht.   He won't come in *this* rain.

4. **Nach** is *usually* used to indicate time:

Nach dem Abendessen gehen wir ins Kino.	After supper, we'll go to the movies.
Er kommt nach acht Uhr.	He will arrive after eight o'clock.

Nach indicates *place*, if a geographical proper name is mentioned:

Er geht nach Amerika.
        nach Deutschland.
        nach Alabama.
        nach Berlin.

and in the idiom:

Er geht nach Hause.

5. If no geographical proper name is used, **zu** is normally used to express direction:

Er geht zum Bahnhof.	He goes to the station.
Er geht zur Universität.	He is walking to the University.

Zu must be used with persons:

Er geht zu Karl.	He goes to Karl.
Ich gehe zu meinem Vater.	I go to my father.

and in the idiom:

Er ist zu Hause.	He is at home.

64 Word Order within the Inner Field

Word order within the inner field is governed by *one* principle: The various elements are arranged in the order of increasing news value. The following rules govern most normal situations and are therefore safe to use.

The Position of the Subject

If a pronoun subject like **er, sie,** or **wir** stands in the inner field, it follows the verb immediately:

Gestern hat er es ihm gesagt.	He told it to him yesterday.

Since nouns generally have more news value than pronouns, noun subjects in the inner field are usually preceded by pronoun objects.

Heute ge*hör*t ihm das Haus.

However,

Heute gehört das Haus *ihm*.

is also possible.

Accusative Pronouns Precede Dative Pronouns

The dative pronouns **mir, ihm, ihr** are longer in sound than most accusative pronouns. The accusative personal pronouns therefore always precede the dative personal pronouns.

Warum will er es ihm nicht sagen?	Why doesn't he want to tell him that?
Leider kann ich es Ihnen nicht schenken.	Unfortunately, I can't give it to you.
Ich habe es ihm geschickt.	I have sent it to him.

Pronoun objects stand at the beginning of the inner field and can be preceded only by a subject.

Nouns and Pronouns

Nouns have more weight and more news value than pronouns. A noun object therefore follows a pronoun object.

Ich habe es meinem Vater schon gesagt.	I've already told it to my father.
Ich kaufe mir morgen einen Hut.	I am going to buy myself a hat tomorrow.

Dative and Accusative Nouns

Nouns preceded by definite articles usually refer to something already known or mentioned before. Nouns preceded by indefinite articles (**ein Buch,** plural **Bücher**), on the other hand, usually introduce something not mentioned before—something, therefore, of news value.

Since the sequence of elements in the inner field is determined by increasing news value, noun objects preceded by definite articles are usually placed before nouns preceded by indefinite articles.

> **Ich habe dem Studenten ein *Buch* gegeben.**
> **Ich habe das Buch einem *Studenten* gegeben.**

If both nouns are preceded by a definite article, the sequence is also determined by news value. In the sentence

> **Hast du dem Kind die Medi*zin* gegeben?**

the topic under discussion is the child; in the sentence

> **Hast du die Medizin dem *Kind* gegeben?**

the question is raised of what has happened to the medicine.

Time Phrases

Time phrases like **gestern, gestern abend** are preceded by pronoun objects:

> **Ich habe es ihm gestern gesagt.**   I told it to him yesterday.

Several time phrases follow each other in the order of greater specificity:

> **Er ist gestern morgen um 10 Uhr 5**   He died at 10:05 yesterday morning.
> **gestorben.**
> **Er ist gestern abend um neun nach**   Last evening at nine he went to Munich.
> **München gefahren.**

Place Phrases

Sentences of the type

> **Ich kaufe mir morgen in Berlin einen Hut.**

are so frequent that one can say: Usually, place follows time.

On the whole, place phrases which are neither directives (which belong in the second prong) nor used in connection with a preceding time phrase are comparatively rare. Their position within the inner field depends on their news value:

> **Ich habe meine Frau in der Sonntags-**   I met my wife in Sunday school. (when the
> **schule kennengelernt.**   topic "wives" is under discussion)
> **Ich habe in der Sonntagsschule meine**   (when the topic "Sunday school" is under
> **Frau kennengelernt.**   discussion)

Quite often place phrases which are not directives occur in "irreducible verbal patterns," and therefore belong in the second prong. Thus

> **Ich wohne**   and   **Er ist**

make no sense unless complemented. This is the reason why one must say:

> **Ich   wohne   nicht   in Berlin.**

> **Er   kann   noch nicht   in Berlin sein.**

Sentence Adverbs

Sentence adverbs, if used in the inner field, are preceded by a pronoun subject or object:

> **Morgen kann ich ihn leider nicht sehen.**
> **Das sage ich natürlich meinem Vater.**

65 The German Perfect

By now you have become accustomed to the fact that German does not have as many verb forms as English. English *I see, I am seeing,* and *I do see* are all expressed in German by **Ich sehe.**

This is also true in regard to the past tenses. While English has the forms

PAST   I did   PRESENT PERFECT   I have done
       I was doing   I have been doing

German must get along with

PAST   **Ich tat**   PERFECT   **Ich habe getan**

As can be seen from these examples, the forms of the German perfect correspond in structure to the English present perfect; that is, the German forms

ich habe . . . gesehen
es hat . . . geregnet
sie ist . . . gegangen

correspond structurally to the English forms

I have seen
it has rained
she is (has) gone

Thus the German perfect, just like the English present perfect, is a "compound" tense: it is formed by combining a form of **haben** (**hat geregnet**) or **sein** (**ist gegangen**) with a participle.

66 Formation of the German Participle

German verbs form their participles in either a "regular" or an "irregular" way.

Regular Verbs

All *regular* verbs place the *unchanged* stem in the frame

    ge_____t

Thus the participle of **lieben** is **ge-lieb-t,** the participle of **glauben** is **ge-glaub-t.**

the ge_____t frame are called "weak" verbs.

	STEM	PARTICIPLE	
	glaub-	geglaubt	*believed*
	hass-	gehaßt	*halted*
	hoff-	gehofft	*hoped*
lachen	lach-	gelacht	*laughed*
lernen	lern-	gelernt	*learn*
lieben	lieb-	geliebt	*love*
machen	mach-	gemacht	*turn make*
regnen	regn-	geregnet	*rain*
sagen	sag-	gesagt	*say*
wohnen	wohn-	gewohnt	*live*
zahlen	zahl-	gezahlt	*pay - restaurant*

The **ge-** prefix is never stressed. Since the **-t** of the frame must be audible, verbs like **heiraten** insert **-e-** before the **-t**.

INFINITIVE	STEM	PARTICIPLE	
arbeiten	arbeit-	gearbeitet	*worked*
heiraten	heirat-	geheiratet	*married*

A participle cannot have more than one unstressed prefix. Therefore all verbs formed with unstressed prefixes such as **er-**, **ent-**, **ge-**, **ver-**, **emp-**, and **be-** form their participle without the **ge-** prefix. Verbs ending in **-ieren** like **studieren,** which always begin with at least one unstressed syllable, also form their participles without **ge-**.

INFINITIVE	PARTICIPLE	
gehören	gehört	*belong*
studieren	studiert	
telefonieren	telefoniert	
telegrafieren	telegrafiert	

Irregular Verbs

Most irregular verbs place either the unchanged stem, or a changed form of the stem, or even an entirely different stem in the frame

     ge_____en

Thus the participle of **bleiben** is **ge-blieb-en,** that of **fahren** is **ge-fahr-en,** and that of **sein** is **ge-wes-en.°** Verbs using the frame **ge_____en** are called "strong" verbs.

° Beginning with Unit 5 the participles of all newly introduced irregular verbs will appear in the list of irregular verbs at the end of each unit.

A few irregular verbs place a changed form of the stem in the frame
ge_____t. Thus the participle of **kennen** is **ge-kann-t.**

Since the irregular verbs are used with great frequency in everyday German, you should memorize the following participles together with their
auxiliaries.

INFINITIVE	PARTICIPLE	INFINITIVE	PARTICIPLE
beginnen	hat begonnen	scheinen	hat geschienen
bleiben	ist geblieben	schlafen	hat geschlafen
denken	hat gedacht	schreiben	hat geschrieben
essen	hat gegessen	sehen	hat gesehen
fahren	ist gefahren	sein	ist gewesen
gehen	ist gegangen	sprechen	hat gesprochen
haben	hat gehabt	trinken	hat getrunken
heißen	hat geheißen	tun	hat getan
kennen	hat gekannt	verstehen	hat verstanden
kommen	ist gekommen	werden	ist geworden
lassen	hat gelassen	wissen	hat gewußt
lesen	hat gelesen	zwingen	hat gezwungen
lügen	hat gelogen		

Modal Auxiliaries

Whenever the modal auxiliaries and **brauchen** are used with a dependent
infinitive, their participles are identical with their infinitives.

Er hat gestern arbeiten müssen.
Er hat gestern nicht zu arbeiten brauchen.

If the modals are used without a dependent infinitive, their participles are
"normal"; that is, **gemußt, gewollt, gekonnt, gesollt, gedurft, gebraucht.**

67 The Use of **sein** and **haben** as Auxiliaries

Certain English verbs used to form their compound tenses with *to be.*
Thus the older versions of the King James version of the Bible, translated
in the seventeenth century, had *Christ is risen.* But now even the Bible
translations have changed from *Christ is risen* to *Christ has risen,* so that
to have is today the only auxiliary still used. In contrast, the use of **sein**
as an auxiliary is still very common in German.

The German verbs using **sein** instead of **haben** are all intransitive; that is,
they do not govern an accusative object. Usually, though not in the case
of **sein** and **bleiben,** they indicate a change in the position or the condition

of the grammatical subject. Since it is most inconvenient to constantly ask oneself, "Should I use **haben** or should I use **sein?**" it is best simply to memorize the participles together with their auxiliaries. See the list in **66.**

68 Position of the Participle

The participle has a reserved "slot": the second box of the second prong. This means that it is preceded by **nicht** and by the verbal complements (if any) in the first box.

FRONT FIELD	1st Prong	INNER FIELD	nicht	1st Box	2nd Box
Er	kommt	heute.			
Er	ist	gestern	nicht		gekommen.
Das	weiß	ich.			
Das	habe	ich	nicht		gewußt.
Der Zug	fährt		noch nicht	ab.	
Der Zug	ist		noch nicht	ab-	gefahren.
Warum	machst	du es	nicht	aus?	
Warum	hast	du es	nicht	aus-	gemacht?
Er	kommt	morgen		wieder.	
Er	ist	leider	nicht	wieder-	gekommen.
Sie	ist	leider	nicht	glücklich.	
Sie	ist	leider	nie	glücklich	gewesen.
Ich	bleibe	natürlich	nicht	zu Hause.	
Ich	bin	natürlich	nicht	zu Hause	geblieben.
Er	fährt	morgen		nach Köln.	
Er	ist	gestern	nicht	nach Köln	gefahren.

NOTE: Verb complements like **aus, ab,** and **wieder** are written with the participle as one word: **abgefahren, ausgemacht, wiedergekommen.**

When a modal is used with an infinitive, the participle of the modal (which looks like an infinitive) goes into the second box behind the dependent infinitive.

FRONT FIELD	1st Prong	INNER FIELD	nicht	1st Box	2nd Box
Ich	will	morgen		zu Hause	bleiben.
Ich	habe	gestern	nicht	zu Hause	bleiben wollen.
Ich	darf	ihn morgen			besuchen.
Ich	habe	ihn gestern	nicht		besuchen dürfen.

69 The English and the German Perfect

For any language-conscious American, the questions *Have you seen Mary?* and *Did you see Mary?* are not interchangeable. The sentence *Did you see Mary while you were in Berlin last month?* cannot possibly be changed to *Have you seen Mary while you were in Berlin last month?*. Nor can the sentence *I haven't seen Mary since her graduation* be changed into *I didn't see Mary since her graduation*. Why not?

If I want to refer to a period of time which began and ended in the past (*while you were in Berlin last month*), I can only say *Did you* . . . . If, on the other hand, I refer to a period which began in the past, but has not ended yet (*since her graduation*), I can only say *Have you* . . . . The following diagrams will make this situation clear:

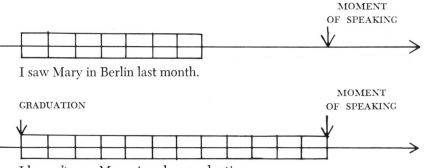

I saw Mary in Berlin last month.

I haven't seen Mary since her graduation.

If you look at this diagram, you will understand why only a fellow saint in heaven could make the statement *Washington has never told a lie* (implying willy-nilly that he might still do so), whereas *we*, knowing that he is dead, can only say *Washington never told a lie*.

The diagram also shows why the English perfect (*has done, has told*, etc.) is called a "present perfect"; it refers to a period which reaches right into the present.

The German perfect, on the other hand, is *not* a present perfect. It is the conversational tense used to talk about all past situations, regardless of when the time period involved came to an end. Thus,

Er hat drei Romane geschrieben

is ambiguous without context; it can mean either

He wrote three novels

or

He has written three novels.

To the English-speaking student, a German sentence like

Meyer ist vor einem Jahre gestorben
[Meyer has died a year ago]

will sound "unnatural" at first. And yet it is the normal way of saying what is meant by

Meyer died a year ago.

A German, on the other hand, has a hard time learning that he should not say in English

[I have seen her last year],

for he is constantly tempted to imitate the natural structure of the German sentence

Ich habe sie letztes Jahr gesehen.

Even a native German whose English is pretty good might surprise you by asking

[Is it true that Washington has never told a lie?]

Forgive him until you have mastered the next section.

70 Stretch-of-Time Phrases

While Germans use the perfect to express both *I did* and *I have,* they nevertheless have a way of expressing the difference; but they employ, as it were, a different code.

After all, each language is a coding system for saying "the same thing" in a different way. Both English and German have a system of indicating whether a certain stretch of time came to an end in the past, whether it reaches into the present, or whether it will end in the future. However, these two systems are not identical, and if you want to differentiate, in German, between

She has been in Berlin for three weeks
and
She was in Berlin for three weeks

you will have to *understand* the difference between the English system and the German system; mere memorization of pattern sentences will not be enough.

The English System
Taken by itself, an English stretch-of-time phrase like *for five years* contains no clue as to the location of these five years in relation to the moment

of speaking. The phrase *for five years* is correct in all three of the following situations.

ALL-PAST SITUATIONS

Both the beginning and the end of the five-year period are located in the past. We call this an "all-past" situation.

> Bill was hurt in an accident shortly after he left college, and *for five years* he *was* not able to drive.

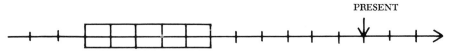

For five years he was not able to drive.

UP-TO-NOW SITUATIONS

The five-year period reaches right up to the moment of speaking (and the end of the predicament may not be in sight). We call this an "up-to-now" situation.

> Bill has some trouble with his eyes. He *has* not *been* able to drive *for five years.*

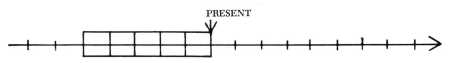

For five years he hasn't been able to drive.

INTO-THE-FUTURE SITUATIONS

The five-year period begins (practically) with the moment of speaking and will end five years later. We call this an "into-the-future" situation.

> Bill got his first license today. It *is* good *for five years.*

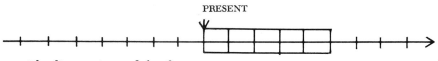

The license is good for five years.

Though he got his license in the past, the five-year period will end in the future. His license is still valid.

> Bill got his license two years ago. It *is* good *for five years.*

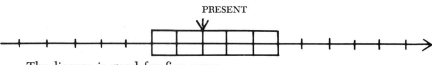

The license is good for five years.

The examples show that it is not the time phrase (*for five years*) itself, but the English verb tense which determines the location of a stretch of time in relation to a moment of speaking. The simple past (*was*) creates all-past situations; the present perfect (*has been*) creates up-to-now situations; and the present (*is*) creates into-the-future situations.

The German System

Since German

Washington hat . . . . gelogen

is ambiguous and can mean either Washington *told a lie* or *has told a lie*, German, in contrast to English, cannot use the difference between the simple past and the perfect to differentiate between an all-past and an up-to-now situation. The difference between the two is expressd by means of different time phrases:

ALL-PAST SITUATIONS

Onkel Fritz hat *nie* gelogen.
Uncle Fritz never *told a lie*. (He *was* that kind of man.)

Ich habe *drei Jahre* nicht geraucht.
I *didn't smoke* for three years.

Letzten Sommer hat es hier *wochenlang* nicht geregnet.
Last summer it *didn't rain* here for weeks.

UP-TO-NOW SITUATIONS

Onkel Fritz hat *noch nie* gelogen.
Uncle Fritz *has* never yet *told a lie*. (He *is* that kind of man.)

Ich habe *seit drei Jahren* nicht eine Zigarette geraucht.
I *haven't smoked* a cigarette for three years.

Hier hat es *schon wochenlang* nicht geregnet.
We *haven't had* any rain here for weeks.

INTO-THE-FUTURE SITUATIONS

Aber das weiß ich: Onkel Fritz lügt *nie*.
But this I know: Uncle Fritz *will* never *tell a lie*.

Ich darf *drei Jahre* nicht rauchen.
I *can't smoke* for three years.

Es soll *wochenlang* nicht regnen.
It *isn't supposed to rain* for weeks.

The following table shows the difference between the two sets of time phrases used to express the difference between all-past and into-the-future phrases on the one hand and up-to-now phrases on the other.

ALL-PAST AND INTO-THE-FUTURE TIME PHRASES	UP-TO-NOW TIME PHRASES	
lange	schon lange	for a long time
	seit langem	
	schon seit langem	
	seitdem	since
zwei Stunden (lang)	schon zwei Stunden (lang)	for two hours
	seit zwei Stunden	
	schon seit zwei Stunden	
drei Wochen (lang)	schon drei Wochen (lang)	for three weeks
	seit drei Wochen	
	schon seit drei Wochen	
fünf Jahre (lang)	schon fünf Jahre (lang)	for five years
	seit fünf Jahren	
	schon seit fünf Jahren	
stundenlang	schon stundenlang	for hours
wochenlang	schon wochenlang	for weeks
	seit Wochen	
	schon seit Wochen	
jahrelang	schon jahrelang	for years
	seit Jahren	
	schon seit Jahren	
nie	noch nie	never
		never yet
je, jemals, mal	schon (ein)mal	ever

NOTE: All time phrases starting with **seit, schon,** or **schon seit** are up-to-now phrases. English *since,* when used as a preposition, is always followed by a date or by a point in time. German **seit** is used the same way:

seit drei Uhr	since three o'clock
seit gestern	since yesterday
seit Anfang Mai	since the beginning of May

However, German **seit** can also be followed by a stretch-of-time, which is not possible with English *since.* **Seit zwei Jahren,** *for these last two years,* means "during all that stretch of time which started two years ago."

Darauf haben Sie schon lange gewartet:
Eine Suppe für den großen Hunger.

The Tense of the Verb in Up-to-Now Situations

The German examples for up-to-now situations given above all appear in the perfect. Actually, the tense used in up-to-now situations can be either the present or the perfect, depending on the type of situation involved.

UP-TO-NOW TIME PHRASES WITH THE PRESENT TENSE

The verb may express a regular habit or a continuous, uninterrupted act —that is, an action (or the absence of an action) which is regarded by the speaker not so much as an activity but as a state of affairs which has been in existence for some time and which can be expected to continue. In such situations, the present tense is used together with an up-to-now time phrase:

Ich rauche schon seit Jahren nur Zigarren.
For years, I've been been smoking only cigars.

   (I am by habit a cigars-only smoker and I don't intend to change.)

Ich rauche schon seit Jahren nicht mehr.
I haven't smoked for years.

   (I am no longer in the habit of smoking. I used to smoke, but I gave it up years ago and I don't intend to take up smoking again.)

Wir wohnen seit drei Jahren in München.
We've been living in Munich for three years.

> (Three years ago we moved to Munich; we've lived there ever since, and we don't intend to move in the near future.)

UP-TO-NOW TIME PHRASES WITH THE PERFECT TENSE

If the action expressed by the verb does not constitute an uninterrupted state of affairs which can be expected to continue, the perfect is used. This can happen

(a) if the up-to-now period ends with the moment of speaking:

Ich muß sagen, so gut habe ich schon lange nicht mehr gegessen.
I must confess, I haven't eaten this well for a long time.

> (The guest is folding his napkin. The period of "not eating this well" has come to an end.)

In contrast, the statement

So gut wie früher essen wir schon lange nicht mehr.
For a long time we haven't been able to eat as well as we used to.

would express a state of affairs which can be expected to continue.

So einen Pelzmantel habe ich mir schon lange gewünscht.
This is just the fur coat I've wanted for a long time.

> (The lady has just unwrapped a Christmas gift; the period of "wanting" has come to an end.)

In contrast, the statement

So einen Pelzmantel wünsche ich mir schon lange.
I've been wanting a fur coat like this for years.

could be made in front of a shop window with a most discouraging price tag on the fur coat.

(b) if the time span covered by the up-to-now phrase is not viewed as a continuum *and* if the action expressed by the verb occurs only intermittently or at no point at all.

Er hat mich schon oft besucht.
He has visited me often.

> (Frequent, intermittent action—not uninterrupted, continuous action.)

Seitdem habe ich nicht eine Zigarre mehr geraucht.
Since then, I haven't smoked a single cigar.

> (My doctor forbade me to smoke cigars, and I haven't had one at any time since.)

Er hat mich noch nie besucht.
He hasn't visited me yet.

  (The act of "visiting" has not taken place at any point at all.)

(c) in sentences with **schon immer.** In such sentences, the perfect is used
even if a continuous state is involved.

Du bist schon immer ein Pessimist gewesen.
You always have been (and still are) a pessimist.

Er hat schon immer Arzt werden wollen.
He's always wanted to become a doctor.

Note that in all the examples under (a), (b), and (c) English also uses
the perfect. But in contrast to English, the German examples contain
up-to-now time phrases that cannot be used in all-past situations. Note the
difference between **lange** and **schon lange** in the following situations.

Wir haben uns schon lange ein Mädchen gewünscht.
We've wanted a girl for a long time.

  (The smiling father has just been informed that the new baby is a girl. The act of
  "wishing" reaches into the moment of speaking and ends there.)

Wir haben uns lange ein Mädchen gewünscht.
For a long time we were hoping to get a girl.

  (But after seven boys in a row we gave up hope.)

71 Further Notes on Time Phrases

As in English, all time phrases are either adverbs, prepositional phrases,
or time nouns like **Sonntag** used without a preposition. Some of these are:

Adverbs **oft, gestern, heute, morgen, heute morgen, gestern abend, jetzt,**
     etc.

Prepositional Phrases **nach einem Jahr** (*after one year*); **um drei Uhr** (*at*
     three o'clock); **vor einem Jahr** (*a year ago*).

Time Nouns **Sonntag, jeden Sonntag, nächsten Sonntag, jede Woche,**
     dieses Jahr, letztes Jahr, nächstes Jahr, jedes Jahr, alle drei Jahre
     (*every three years*).

NOTE:
1. Time nouns used without a preposition show the accusative case of the
der-words belonging to them. Thus **jeden Sonntag** is the accusative of
jeder Sonntag. If a preposition is used, this preposition determines the
case: **nach einem Jahr** (**nach** always governs the dative); **für einen Monat**
(**für** always governs the accusative).

2. Phrases with **vor** may be misleading to the beginner. German **vor** is not equivalent to English *for;* **vor** means *in front of.* Therefore, **vor einem Jahr** means "at a point just in front of one year," or, simply, *a year ago.*

3. Time phrases with **für** and **auf** (used, interchangeably, with the accusative) are also apt to mislead the student.

Usually, English *for a week* does not correspond to German **für** (**auf**) **eine Woche.** In most cases, *for a week* is either **eine Woche** or **seit einer Woche** (see **70**).

> **Ich habe eine Woche in Berlin gearbeitet.**
> **Ich arbeite seit einer Woche in Berlin.**
> **Ich will eine Woche in Berlin arbeiten.**

However, the phrase **für eine Woche** does occur in the meaning of *for a week.*

> **Ich fahre für** (**auf**) **eine Woche nach Berlin.**

In this sentence (1) there is a directive, and (2) **für eine Woche** means "with the intention of staying for a week." It is not safe to use **für** (**auf**) **eine Woche** without a directive and without this meaning.

AMERICANISM	[**Wir haben für einen Monat in München gewohnt.**]
CORRECT	**Wir haben einen Monat in München gewohnt.**
	We lived in Munich for a month.
AMERICANISM	[**Wir wollen für einen Monat reisen.**]
CORRECT	**Wir wollen einen Monat** (**lang**) **reisen.**
	We want to travel for a month.

4. Germans love to use **schon.** It basically means *already*—that is, "earlier than expected," "further in the past than you think," or "as early as."

> **Er ist schon vor drei Jahren gestorben.**
> **Er ist schon gestern gekommen.**

72 Replacement of **er, sie, es** by **der, die, das**

In informal but perfectly acceptable German, nouns and names are frequently replaced by **der, die, das** instead of by **er, sie, es.** When used in this function, **der, die,** and **das** are not articles, but demonstrative pronouns, and the dative plural is **denen,** not **den.** These demonstrative pronouns may be stressed or unstressed.

Wem gehört denn der Wagen?	**Der Wagen gehört mir.**
	Er gehört mir.
	Der gehört mir.

Wo hast du denn den *Hut* gekauft?   Den habe ich in *Mün*chen gekauft.
Wo hast du denn *den* gekauft?   *Den* habe ich in *Mün*chen gekauft, aber *den*
                                                 hier habe ich in Ber*lin* gekauft.

Kennen Sie Frau Dr. Walter?   Ja, die habe ich in Ber*lin* kennengelernt.
                                                 Ja, mit *der* gehe ich heute abend ins The-
                                                 ater.

Note that if stressed, these demonstrative pronouns may mean *this one* and *that one*.

For the time being, do not use either the personal pronouns or the demonstrative pronouns after a preposition, unless they refer to persons.

73 es and das, Followed by Plural Verb Forms

A daughter recognizing that a certain lady on the TV screen is her mother, can say

> It's my mother!
> That's my mother!

This impersonal *it* or *that* is used in sentences identifying somebody or something for the first time. *She is my mother,* on the other hand, is used when *she* has already been talked about and a further statement is being made about her. German makes the same distinction:

> **Es ist meine Mutter!**
> **Das ist meine Mutter!**

But:

> **Kennen Sie Frau Bertram?**
> **Natürlich, sie ist meine Mutter!**

In contrast to English *it* and *that*, German **es** and **das** are followed by plural verb forms when the identifying nouns are in the plural:

> **Es sind die Kinder.**   It's the children.
> **Das sind die Kinder.**   That's the children.

EXERCISES

A. Give negative answers to the following questions.

SEE LAB
EXERCISES
4.1–4.2

(p. 625)

1. Bist du glücklich mit ihm?
2. Wohnt ihr noch in Berlin?
3. Mußt du denn morgen nach Paris fahren?

4. Trinkt Meyer Bier?
5. Trinkt er Kaffee?
6. Will Erika ihn heiraten?
7. Ist sie nicht noch ein Kind?
8. Ist Erika schon hier?
9. Wollt ihr morgen zu Hause bleiben?
10. Sind die Laternen schon an?
11. Machst du das Licht aus?
12. Hast du noch Geld?
13. Hat sie Geld?
14. Redet Frau Müller noch immer soviel?
15. Ist Erika intelligent?
16. Geht Fritz schon in die Schule?
17. Lebt Meyer noch?
18. Brauchst du *auch* einen Hut? (Use contrast intonation.)
19. Brauchst du auch einen *Hut*? (Use contrast intonation.)
20. Regnet es schon?

B. Replace the dative or accusative pronouns in italics by the proper form of the nouns in parentheses.

1. Ich will *es* nicht lesen. (Buch)
2. Kennst du *ihn*? (mein Vater)
3. Ich kann *ihn* schon sehen. (Zug)
4. Kennt er *sie*? (deine Frau)
5. Tante Amalie will mit *ihr* nach Italien fahren. (unsere Tochter)
6. Die Uhr gehört *ihr*. (meine Frau)
7. Liebt sie *ihn* denn nicht? (ihr Mann)
8. Liebt er *sie* denn nicht? (seine Frau)
9. Ich will nicht für *ihn* arbeiten. (Herr Meyer)
10. Bei *der* möchte ich nicht wohnen. (deine Tante)
11. *Dem* glaube ich nicht. (dein Vater)
12. Ich will *ihn* meiner Frau schenken. (Hut)
13. Mit *dem* kannst du nicht in die Kirche gehen. (dieser Hut)
14. Tante Amalie fährt mit *ihnen* nach Italien. (unsere Kinder)
15. Man kann *ihn* nicht trinken. (dieser Wein)

SEE LAB
EXERCISES
4.3–4.4

(p. 625)

C. Express the following sentences in German. This is not meant to be a translation exercise; the English sentences should "trigger" their German equivalents. Practice the sentences orally, until you can produce them without hesitation. Only then should you try to write them down.

1. That is my house.
2. It (the house) belongs to me.
3. It (the house) belongs to you?
4. Yes, to me.

SEE LAB
EXERCISES
4.5–4.6

(p. 625)

5. This house belongs to Hans.
6. It (the house) belongs to him.
7. It (the house) belongs to her.
8. The car belongs to her.
9. It (the car) belongs to her.
10. It is her car.
11. It is her hat.
12. It is their newspaper.
13. Is that your hat, Mr. Jones?
14. Yes, the hat belongs to me.
15. Yes, it (the hat) belongs to me.
16. Yes, that is my newspaper.
17. The book belongs to my aunt.
18. It (the book) belongs to my aunt.
19. It (the book) belongs to her.
20. It is her book.

D. Replace nouns and names by personal pronouns.

Ich fahre mit meinem Freund Fritz.
Ich fahre mit ihm.

1. Er wohnt bei seiner Tante.
2. Er will zu seinem Vater.
3. Er hilft seiner Mutter.
4. Er hilft seiner Freundin.
5. Er hilft seinem Freund.
6. Er kommt von seinem Freund Hans.
7. Er arbeitet für seinen Bruder.
8. Er arbeitet heute ohne seinen Freund.
9. Außer Erika sind wir alle hier.
10. Bei meiner Tante bin ich gern.
11. Ich komme mit meiner Freundin.
12. Ich komme ohne meine Freundin.
13. Er besucht seine Freundin.
14. Er antwortet seiner Freundin nicht.
15. Er dankt seinem Freund nicht.
16. Er geht zu seiner Tante.
17. Sie geht zu ihrer Tante.
18. Sie wohnt bei ihrer Tante.
19. Sie kommt ohne ihre Tante.
20. Er kommt ohne seine Tante.

E. Complete the following sentences by using either **nach, zu,** or **bei.** Use contractions with articles where necessary.

1. Ich gehe _____ Bahnhof.
2. Er wohnt _____ seiner Tante.
3. Wir gehen _____ Meyers.
4. Sie sind _____ Hans.
5. Wir fahren _____ Europa.
6. Wir fahren _____ Universität.
7. Wir fahren _____ Bahnhof.
8. Wir fahren _____ München.
9. Man spricht nicht _____ Essen.
10. Oskar wohnt _____ Schmidts.
11. Wir gehen heute abend _____ Schmidts.
12. Kommen Sie heute _____ Abendessen zu uns?

F. Complete the following sentences by using the correct *personal* pronouns.

1. Hier ist die Zeitung; sie ist für _Sie_, Herr Meyer.
2. Erika ist krank; ich muß ohne _sie_ ins Kino gehen.
3. „Fahren Sie ohne Ihren Mann nach Casablanca?" „Ohne _ihn_? Nie!"
4. Du Hans! Heute mußt du leider ohne _sie_ ins Theater gehen.
5. Fritz Müller möchte gern für _Sie_ arbeiten, Herr Doktor.
6. Inge ist doch sehr interessant. Was hast du denn gegen _sie_?
7. Du brauchst doch nicht in ein Hotel zu gehen. Du kannst bei uns wohnen. Etwas zu essen haben wir immer für _dich_.

G. In the following sentences, the inner field is left empty. Fill the inner field with each of the several series of words by rearranging them in the correct word order.

1. Ich habe _es ihm gestern_ geschenkt. _to give present_

    (a) es, gestern, ihm
    (b) das Buch, gestern, ihm _ihm das Buch gestern_
    (c) ein Buch, gestern, meinem Vater _meinem Vater ein Buch gestern_
    (d) es, gestern, meinem Vater _es meinem Vater gestern_

2. Wir haben _____ ins Haus geschickt. _to send_

    (a) ihr, gestern, Blumen _ihr Blumen gestern_
    (b) die Blumen, gestern, ihr _ihr die Blumen gestern_
    (c) sie (die Blumen), ihr, gestern _sie ihr gestern_
    (d) unserer Tante, gestern, Blumen _unserer Tante gestern Blumen_

3. Willst du _____ schenken? _give_

    (a) einen Hund, deiner Freundin _deiner Freundin einen Hund_
    (b) den Hund, deiner Freundin _deiner Freundin den Hund_
    (c) deiner Freundin, ihn _ihn deiner Freundin_
    (d) einen Hund, ihr _ihr einen Hund_
    (e) ihn, ihr _ihn ihr_

SEE LAB EXERCISE 4.7 (p. 625)

4. Wollen Sie _____ schicken?
    (a) Ihrem Vater, das Buch
    (b) ein Buch, ihm (Ihrem Vater)
    (c) es, ihm
    (d) Ihrem Vater, es
    (e) das Buch, ihm

5. Er hat _____ gekauft.
    (a) einen Hund, mir
    (b) den Hund, mir
    (c) mir, ihn
    (d) seiner Frau, ein Haus in Berlin
    (e) seiner Frau, einen Hut, in Berlin
    (f) ihr, den Hut, in Berlin
    (g) ihr, ihn, in Berlin

6. Ich habe _____ mitgebracht.
    (a) ein Buch, meiner Freundin, aus Berlin
    (b) aus Berlin, ein Buch, ihr
    (c) das Buch, ihr, aus Berlin
    (d) ihr, es, aus Berlin

7. Darf ich _____ ins Haus schicken, Herr Doktor?
    (a) morgen, Ihnen, den Wein
    (b) die Blumen, morgen, Ihrer Frau
    (c) sie (die Blumen), ihr (Ihrer Frau), morgen
    (d) sie (die Blumen), morgen, Ihrer Frau
    (e) Blumen, Ihrer Frau, morgen
    (f) Blumen, ihr, morgen
    (g) die Blumen, ihr, morgen

H. Restate the following sentences by using the perfect tense.

SEE LAB
EXERCISE
4.8

(p. 625)

1. Er arbeitet auch sonntags.
2. Sie bleibt Sonntag zu Hause.
3. Wieviel Geld brauchst du?
4. Inge fährt heute nach München.
5. Ich gehe mit Tante Amalie ins Museum.
6. Außer mir glaubt dir das kein Mensch.
7. Wir haben in München ein Haus.
8. Seine Kinder hassen ihn.
9. Ihr Mann kommt zurück.
10. Ich kenne ihn.
11. Das Wasser kocht schon.
12. Er kommt heute spät nach Hause.
13. Was sagt er denn?—Nichts! Er lacht!

14. Bei Meyer lerne ich nichts.
15. Liebt sie ihren Mann denn nicht?
16. Was machst du denn Sonntag?
17. Regnet es in Hamburg?
18. Er studiert Medizin.
19. Ich verstehe ihn nicht.
20. Er wird Arzt.
21. Das wissen wir nicht.
22. Wo wohnt ihr denn?
23. Zahlst du für den Wein?
24. Wann rufst du sie an?
25. Du antwortest ihm?
26. Wann machst du das Licht aus?
27. Ich bringe Erika nach Hause.
28. Natürlich danke ich ihm.
29. Dich frage ich nicht.
30. Warum gibst du mir kein Geld?
31. Dieses Haus gehört meinem Vater.
32. Warum helft ihr ihm denn nicht?
33. Ich kaufe mir eine Zeitung.
34. Er will nicht arbeiten.
35. Ich rauche nie.
36. Meine Frau redet wieder viel zuviel.
37. Was schenkst du ihr denn?
38. Wem schicken Sie denn das Buch?
39. Er schreibt mir nicht.
40. Wo sitzt sie denn?
41. Wir warten bis drei Uhr.
42. Nein, nein, ich sterbe noch nicht.
43. Er will nicht sterben.
44. Ich muß auch arbeiten.
45. Wann besuchst du ihn?
46. Wir essen heute im Hotel Berlin.
47. Das will ich nicht sagen.
48. Wann heiratest du denn?
49. Was hörst du von Erika?
50. Nicht einmal ihr Mann darf sie besuchen.
51. Ich lasse meinen Hut heute zu Hause.
52. Meyer lebt auch nur für sein Geld.
53. Er braucht nicht zu arbeiten.
54. Er schläft jeden Morgen bis zehn.
55. Wann siehst du sie denn wieder?
56. Wein trinkt er heute nicht.
57. Ich zwinge dich zu nichts.

58. Wann fährt der Zug denn ab?
59. Lernt diese Frau fahren?
60. Wie heißt sie denn?
61. Wann macht er denn das Licht aus?
62. Wann kommt sie denn wieder?
63. Wann fährt er denn zurück?
64. Wird Meyer wieder gesund?
65. Ist Meyer schon wieder krank?

I. Complete the following sentences:

1. Wir haben das Haus gesehen, aber gekauft (haben wir es nicht).
2. Seine Freundin ist intelligent, aber interessant _____.
3. Ich gehe oft ins Theater, aber ins Kino _____.
4. Er hat den Professor gehört, aber verstanden _____.
5. Ich fahre mit dir nach Hamburg, aber nach Casablanca _____.
6. _____ nicht glücklich, aber unglücklich ist sie auch nicht.
7. _____ keinen Wein, aber Bier möchte er auch nicht.
8. _____ nach Berlin, aber nach München will er nicht.
9. _____ gekauft, aber gelesen habe ich es nicht.
10. _____ etwas getrunken, aber gegessen habe ich nichts.

J. Read the following sentences aloud several times and supply, first, the correct personal pronoun and then the correct **der-die-das** substitute.

Das Haus gehört einem Herrn Schmidt. Kennen Sie ihn? Kennen Sie den?

1. Ich wohne bei Frau Hollmann.
   Kennst du _____? Kennst du _____?
2. Wir wohnen im Hotel Berlin.
   Kennen Sie _____? Kennen Sie _____?
3. Du, Hans! Hier kommt mein Bruder.
   Kennst du _____? Kennst du _____?
4. Peter, hier kommt Tante Amalie.
   Kennst du _____ noch? Kennst du _____ noch?
5. Heute kommt Frau Müller zu uns.
   Möchtest du _____ kennenlernen? Möchtest du _____ kennenlernen?
6. So! Das ist Dr. Fischer!
   Ihr fahrt mit _____ nach Paris, nicht wahr?
   Und mit _____ fahrt ihr nach Paris, nicht wahr?
7. So, das ist Herr Meyer?
   Und der VW gehört _____? Und _____ gehört der VW?

8. Erika ist seine Freundin.
   Er will _____ eine Uhr schenken. _____ will er die Uhr schenken.

9. Fritz ist Erikas Freund.
   Sie will _____ eine Uhr schenken. _____ will sie die Uhr schenken.

10. Meyer redet viel zuviel.
    Glaubst du _____? Glaubst du _____?

11. Meyer hat geschrieben.
    Ich muß _____ antworten. Aber _____ brauche ich nicht zu antworten.

SEE LAB
EXERCISES
4.9–4.12
(pp. 625-626)

12. Natürlich kenne ich Meyers gut.
    Aber ich kann doch nicht bei _____ wohnen!
    Aber bei _____ kann ich doch nicht wohnen!

13. Das ist Oskar Meyer.
    Dein Vater arbeitet für _____, nicht wahr?
    Für _____ möchte ich nicht arbeiten.

14. Das soll ein Hut sein?
    Und du willst _____ deiner Frau schenken?
    Mit _____ kann sie aber nicht in die Kirche gehen.

15. Fritz und Hans sind meine Freunde.
    Ich fahre mit _____ nach Italien.
    Mit _____ fahre ich morgen nach Italien.

K. Express in German:

1. The train to Cologne left at 4:07.
2. At 7:05 we'll be in Cologne.
3. I want to visit him tomorrow.
4. I wanted to visit him yesterday.
5. This house once belonged to my father.
6. Mr. Lenz, I can't believe you.
7. Why don't you want to believe me?
8. I don't have to help them.
9. I didn't have to help them.
10. He gave his girl friend a watch.
11. He gave the watch to his girl friend.
12. He gave it (the watch) to her.
13. He is coming from the movies.
14. Are you living with your aunt, Erika?
15. Were you living with your aunt at that time?
16. Why did you come home so late?
17. Meyer bought a car in Berlin.
18. Meyer bought a house (which stands) in Berlin.
19. (While) in Berlin, he bought a house.

20. He lived in Bonn, but he worked in Cologne.
21. They could see us, but they could not hear us.
22. Where have you been, Erika?
23. I went to the movies with my girl friend.
24. He worked yesterday, and we all helped him.
25. They went to Berlin today.
26. I bought myself the book yesterday. But I haven't read it yet.
27. Have you already read the paper?
28. No, I have not read it yet.
29. The train has not left yet.
30. I know she is no longer a child.
31. For a long time I did not know that.
32. I have known that for a long time.
33. Last year I didn't smoke one (single) cigarette. But now I smoke ten each (*accusative*) day.
34. Since the beginning of May I have not smoked one (single) cigarette.
35. I haven't been smoking any more for two years.
36. I did not smoke for two years.
37. Two years ago, I smoked too much.
38. You are still smoking too much.
39. Yes, I believe in God. But for a long time I did not believe in God.
40. Meyer died three years ago.
41. Meyer died a year ago.
42. Meyer has been sick for years.
43. Meyer has been sick for two years.
44. Two weeks ago, Meyer became sick.
45. When did you learn how to drive, Mrs. Meyer?
46. When did you meet (get acquainted with) your husband, Mrs. Meyer?
47. Haven't you turned off the light yet?
48. Did you turn off the light yesterday?
49. I, too, had to work.
50. He has never had to work yet.

VOCABULARY

das Abendessen supper
acht eight
Ägypten Egypt
anfangen (fängt an, hat angefangen) to begin, to start
  der Anfang, ⸚e beginning, start

anrufen (hat angerufen) to call up (on the telephone)
antworten (*plus dative of person*) to answer
der April′ April
die Arbeit, –en work
aus out of
außer besides, except for

außerdem moreover
der Bahnhof, ⸚e railway station
  zum Bahnhof to the station
  im Bahnhof within the station
  auf dem Bahnhof on the platform

befehlen (befiehlt, hat befohlen) (*plus dative of person*) to command, to order

bei at, with, near

bei Schmidts at the Schmidts

beim Essen while eating

besetzen to occupy

besetzt busy (telephone)

das Bild, –er picture

bis until, up until; up to, as far as

bis gestern until yesterday

bis Köln as far as Cologne

bis zum Winter (up) until winter

bis zum Bahnhof as far as the station

zwei bis drei two to three

die Blume, –n flower

böse mad, angry at; bad, evil

der Brief, –e letter

der Briefträger, – mailman

bringen (hat gebracht) to bring

ich bringe dich nach Hause I'll take you home

damals at that time

danken (*plus personal dative*) to thank

danke! thank you, thanks

vielen Dank! thank you very much

durch through

einmal (*colloquial* **mal**) once, at some time

zweimal twice

dreimal three times

viermal, etc.

(noch) *nicht* **einmal** not even

nicht *einmal* not once

fragen to ask

die Frage question

früh early

früher earlier; formerly

geben (gibt, hat gegeben) to give

gehören (*plus personal dative*) to belong to (property)

gehören zu to belong to (membership)

gern(e) gladly

ich esse gern(e) I like to eat

ich möchte gern(e) etwas essen I'd like to eat something

das Gesetz, –e law

gestern yesterday

glauben an (*with acc.*) to believe in

helfen (hilft, hat geholfen) (*plus personal dative*) to help

das Hotel, –s hotel

der Hut, –̈e hat

die Idee', die Ide'en idea

je, jemals ever

jung young

lang long

lange for a long time

jahrelang for years

fünf Jahre lang for five years

der Lärm (*no plural*) noise; din

letzt last

letzten Mai last May

letzte Woche last week

letztes Jahr last year

der Mai May

die Minu'te, –n minute

der Mo'nat, –e month

der Montag, –e Monday

die Nacht, –̈e night

heute nacht this coming night; last night

but: **gestern abend** last night (before going to bed), yesterday evening

neben next to, beside

neun nine

die Nummer, –n number

der Onkel uncle

die Physik' (*no pl.*) physics

recht right

rechts to the right

das ist mir recht that's all right with me

reden to talk, to speak

richtig correct, accurate

schenken to give (as a present)

schicken to send

schreiben (hat geschrieben) to write

die Schule, –n school

sehr very

seit since

seitdem since (*conj.*); since then, since that time (*adv.*)

seit langem for a long time

seit Anfang Mai since the beginning of May

sieben seven

sitzen (hat gesessen) to sit

der Sommer, – summer

die Stadt, –̈e town, city

sterben (stirbt, ist gestorben) to die

der Tag, –e day

das Telefon, –e telephone

am Telefon on the telephone

telefonieren (mit) to talk on the phone (with); to make a phone call

die Universität', –en university

vor before; in front of; ago

vor einem Jahr a year ago

wählen to choose; to dial

warten auf (*with acc.*) to wait for

die Woche, –n week

woher from where

zeigen to show

die Zigar're, –n cigar

die Zigaret'te, –n cigarette

zwanzig twenty

REVIEW

The following sections contain only structural patterns introduced in Units 1–4, but some new vocabulary is introduced. Read the sentences carefully; then do the exercises following each section.

Verbal Patterns with a Second Prong

Sie gehen *in die Kirche.*
Er geht mit Inge *ins Kino.*
Er fährt mit Gisela *nach Alexandria.*
Ich möchte das Buch *lesen.*
Sie darf ihren Mann heute *besuchen.*
Ich habe den Mann schon *kennengelernt.*
Erika möchte heute abend *zu Hause bleiben.*

Form the negative of the above sentences by starting with the italicized parts and using contrast intonation.

SEE
ANALYSIS
27–35
(pp. 45–55)

Modals

Herr Bauer muß heute in Köln arbeiten.
Morgen braucht er nicht zu arbeiten.
Wir können heute abend leider nicht kommen.
Es ist erst ein Uhr; er kann noch zu Hause sein.
Hans will schon wieder mit Inge ins Kino gehen.
Wir wollen erst essen und dann ins Theater gehen.
Aber, Willi, du *sollst* doch nicht so viel rauchen.
Tante Amalie kommt um drei, und wir sollen alle zum Bahnhof kommen.
Warum darf ich meinen Mann denn nicht besuchen, Herr Doktor?
Hoffentlich dürfen wir Sonntag zu Hause bleiben.
Danke, ich möchte heute keinen Wein.
Möchten Sie noch eine Tasse Kaffee, Frau Bertram?

SEE
ANALYSIS
48–54
(pp. 87–91)

Express in German:

He can't come yet.
Thank goodness we can go home now.
Meyer has to go to Berlin today.
I hope you don't have to go to Berlin.

You must learn to drive, Inge.
He wants to meet my husband.
He would like to meet my husband.
You mustn't come too late.
He is supposed to go to Berlin again.

Dative and Accusative

SEE
ANALYSIS
20–22:
58–64

(pp. 40–43;
120–128)

Kennen Sie *Meyers?*
Kennen Sie *Frau Meyer?*
Er hat *das Licht* schon ausgemacht.
Hast du *meinen Freund* gesehen?
Der Wagen gehört *meinem Vater.*
Hast du *Herrn und Frau Enders* schon geschrieben?
Hast du *deiner Mutter* schon geschrieben?
Durch *Herrn Enders* habe ich meine Frau kennengelernt.
Ich fahre mit *Frau Lenz* nach Köln.
Heute geht Hans ohne *Gisela* ins Kino.
Außer *Erika* sind alle hier.
Heute abend sind Schmidts bei *Meyers.*
Werner hat lange bei *Tante Amalie* gewohnt.
Er bringt *seiner Freundin* immer Blumen.
Sie geht nie ohne *ihren Freund* ins Theater.

In the above sentences, replace the italicized nouns and names by pronouns.

UNIT 5: Numbers—The Past—The Pluperfect—Verb-Last Position—Open Conditions—**um . . . zu**—**mit**—Word Formation

PATTERNS

[1] Cardinal Numbers

Learn the numbers; then go through the drills as indicated.

Null, eins, zwei, drei, vier, fünf, sechs, sieben, acht, neun, zehn, elf, zwölf, dreizehn, vierzehn, fünfzehn, sechzehn, siebzehn, achtzehn, neunzehn, zwanzig.

SEE ANALYSIS 74 (pp. 169-170)

eins und eins ist zwei	eins plus eins ist zwei
eins und zwei ist . . .	eins plus zwei ist . . .
eins . . .	eins . . . . .
zwanzig weniger eins ist neunzehn	zwanzig minus eins ist neunzehn
neunzehn weniger eins . . .	zwanzig minus zwei ist . . .
achtzehn . . .	zwanzig . . .
Wieviel Uhr ist es?	Es ist zehn Uhr dreizehn.
Wie spät ist es?	Es ist zehn Uhr dreizehn.
Wann kommt der Zug an?	Um sechs Uhr siebzehn.
Um wieviel Uhr kommt der Zug an?	Um sechs Uhr siebzehn.
Wann fährt der Zug ab?	Um sieben Uhr sechzehn.
Um wieviel Uhr fährt der Zug ab?	Um sieben Uhr sechzehn.
Wann fängt das Theater an?	Um acht Uhr funfzehn.

[2] Past Tense of Weak Verbs

In order to practice the forms of the past tense, vary these sentences by substituting the subjects in parentheses.

SEE ANALYSIS 75-76, 79 (pp. 170-172, 174-176)

Leider glaubte sie mir nicht.	Unfortunately, she did not believe me. (you)
Beim Frühstück sagte er nichts von einer Reise nach München.	At breakfast he said nothing about a trip to Munich. (they)

(*Facing*) **Schlafwagenschaffner**

Nach dem Krieg heiratete er ein Mädchen aus Berlin.	After the war he married a girl from Berlin. (I)
Vor dem Theater warteten Hans und Inge auf mich.	Outside the theater Hans and Inge were waiting for me. (Hans)
Damals brauchte ich nicht so oft nach Berlin zu fahren.	At that time I didn't have to go to Berlin so often. (we)
Die Tochter lachte gerade wie ihr Vater.	The daughter laughed just like her father. (the daughters)
Ingelheim liebte seine Kinder sehr.	Ingelheim loved his children very much. (Hans and Inge)
Wir machten damals oft Reisen.	At that time we often went on trips. (I)
Vor dem Krieg lebte Ingelheim in Berlin.	Before the war Ingelheim lived in Berlin. (we)
Rosemarie studierte damals in München.	At that time Rosemarie studied in Munich. (Rosemarie and I)
In München wohnten wir immer im Hotel Regina-Palast.	In Munich we always stayed at the Hotel Regina-Palast. (they)

[3] The Past Forms of the Modals

Vary these sentences by substituting the subjects in parentheses.

SEE
ANALYSIS
76

(p. 172)

Ich konnte gestern leider nicht kommen; ich mußte zu Hause bleiben.	Unfortunately, I couldn't come yesterday; I had to stay home. (we)
Er wollte nicht mit Tante Amalie ins Museum gehen.	He didn't want to go to the museum with Aunt Amalie. (I)
Warum wolltest du denn nicht ins Theater gehen?	Why didn't you want to go to the theater? (they)
Warum mußtet ihr denn nach Berlin fahren?	Why did you have to go to Berlin? (you, sing.)
Hans sollte mir helfen, aber er wollte nicht.	Hans was supposed to help me, but he didn't want to. (Hans and Inge)
Wir wollten mitgehen, aber wir durften nicht.	We wanted to go along, but we weren't allowed to. (they)
Sie sollten doch schon gestern hier sein, Herr Lorenz.	You were supposed to be here yesterday, Herr Lorenz. (Hans)

[4] Past Tense of **haben**

Form your own variations.

SEE
ANALYSIS
76

(p. 172)

| Ich fahre *heute* nach Bonn; *ges*tern hatte ich keine *Zeit*. | I am going to Bonn today; yesterday I didn't have time. |

Warum *hat*test du denn keine Zeit? | Why didn't you have any time?

Herr Lenz hatte *auch* keine Zeit. Wir hatten *al*le zu viel zu tun. | Herr Lenz had no time either. We all had too much to do.

Was, ihr hattet keine *Zeit?* | What, you had no time?

Sie hatten *al*le zu viel zu tun. | They all had too much to do.

Hatten Sie gestern *auch* so viel zu tun, Herr Lohmann? | Did you also have so much to do yesterday, Mr. Lohmann?

[5] Past Tense of **sein**

Form your own variations.

Herr Lenz ist heute in *Bonn.*—*G*estern war er in *Köln.* | Herr Lenz is in Bonn today.—Yesterday he was in Cologne.

Wo warst *Du* gestern, Inge?—*Ich* war in *Frank*furt. | Where were you yesterday, Inge?—I was in Frankfurt.

Ist Fritz heute *auch* hier?—Nein, er war *ges*tern hier; *heu*te ist er in *Frank*furt. | Is Fritz here too today?—No, he was here yesterday; today he is in Frankfurt.

Wir waren gestern *auch* in Frankfurt.—Wo wart *ihr* gestern? | We were in Frankfurt, too, yesterday.—Where were you yesterday?

Wo waren *Sie* denn, Herr Lenz? | Where were you, Herr Lenz?

SEE ANALYSIS 77 (p. 173)

[6] Past Tense of Strong Verbs

Vary these sentences by substituting the subjects in parentheses.

Er fuhr jeden Morgen um sieben Uhr ab. | He left every morning at seven o'clock. (we)

Ich rief sie damals jede Woche an. | I called her every week then. (she)

Ich bekam jede Woche drei Briefe von ihr. | I got three letters from her every week. (she)

Sonntags blieb er immer zu Hause. | On Sundays he always stayed home. (they)

Damals brachte ich sie jeden Abend nach Hause. | At that time, I took her home every night. (he)

Sie luden uns oft zum Essen ein. | They often invited us to dinner. (she)

Wir aßen damals oft im Regina. | We often ate at the Regina then. (I)

Er fuhr jeden Sommer nach Italien. | He went to Italy every summer. (we)

Wir fanden ihn in der Regina-Bar. | We found him in the Regina Bar. (they)

Ich gab ihm jede Woche zwanzig Mark. | I gave him twenty marks every week. (we)

Sonntags gingen wir nie ins Kino. | On Sundays we never went to the movies. (he)

Wir halfen ihm damals oft bei seiner Arbeit. | We often helped him with his work. (she)

Damals hieß sie noch Schmidt. | At that time, her name was still Schmidt. (my)

SEE ANALYSIS 77 (p. 173)

Ich kannte sie gut.	I knew her well. (we)
Er kam immer spät nach Hause.	He always came home late. (they)
Wir ließen unsere Kinder zu Hause.	We left our children at home. (they)
Er lief nach Hause.	He ran home. (she)
Ich dachte damals oft an sie.	I often thought of her then. (we)
Er schien mich nicht zu kennen.	He didn't seem to know me. (they)
Er schlief oft bis elf Uhr.	He often slept until eleven o'clock. (I)
Sie schrieb ihm jede Woche drei Briefe.	She wrote him three letters every week. (he)
Ich saß im Garten und las ein Buch.	I was sitting in the garden reading a book. (he)
Von Erika sprach er nie.	He never talked about Erika. (she)
Er stand vor dem Kino und wartete auf mich.	He was standing in front of the movie house waiting for me. (she)
Leider trank er.	Unfortunately he drank. (she)
Und dann tat er jahrelang nichts.	Then he didn't do a thing for years. (she)
Er starb drei Jahre später.	He died three years later. (she)
Jeden Sommer verschwand er auf eine Woche.	Every summer he disappeared for a week. (they)
Sie verstand ihn einfach nicht.	She simply didn't understand him. (they)
Sie wurde Ärztin.	She became a doctor. (he)
Sie wußte nichts von seiner Reise.	She didn't know anything about his trip. (we)

[7] Two Past Forms in One Sentence

Read these sentences carefully and note their narrative character.

SEE
ANALYSIS
75–79

(pp. 170-176)

Er kaufte ein Buch und schenkte es seiner Freundin.	He bought a book and gave it to his friend.
Hans kam um zehn Uhr aus dem Theater und fuhr nach Hause.	At ten o'clock, Hans got out of the theater and drove home.
Inge fuhr nach Berlin und besuchte dort ihren Vater.	Inge went to Berlin and there visited her father.
Hans ging mit Inge ins Kino; dann brachte er sie nach Hause.	Hans went to the movies with Inge; then he took her home.
Erika besuchte ihre Mutter in Stuttgart; dann fuhr sie nach Berlin.	Erika visited her mother in Stuttgart; then she went to Berlin.
Herr Kunz trank ein Glas Wein und las die Zeitung.	Herr Kunz drank a glass of wine and read the paper.
Ernst hörte seinen Freund, aber er sah ihn nicht.	Ernst heard his friend, but did not see him.

Er hörte, was ich sagte, aber er glaubte mir nicht.	He heard what I said, but he did not believe me.
Ferdinand Schulz studierte in Bonn und arbeitete in Köln.	Ferdinand Schulz studied in Bonn and worked in Cologne.
In Hamburg regnete es, aber in Casablanca schien die Sonne.	It was raining in Hamburg, but in Casablanca the sun was shining.

[8] Verb-Last Position in Dependent Clauses

By leaving out the main clauses, change the dependent clauses into assertions or questions.

Ich weiß, daß er Geld   hat.

Ich weiß, daß er Geld   hatte.

Ich weiß, daß er Geld   gehabt hat.

SEE
ANALYSIS
84-88

(pp. 178-185)

Ich weiß nicht, ob Fritz mit dem Auto zum Bahnhof   fährt.

Ich wußte, daß er immer mit dem Auto zur Arbeit   fuhr.

Ich glaube nicht, daß er mit dem Auto zum Bahnhof   gefahren ist.

Ich möchte, daß du morgen vernünftig   bist.

Ich hoffe, daß du gestern vernünftig   warst.

Ich weiß, daß du immer vernünftig   gewesen bist.

Ich möchte wissen, warum sie nie Tee   trinkt.

Alle wußten, warum sie nie Wein   trank.

Gut, daß ich heute abend keinen Kaffee   getrunken habe.

Wissen Sie, ob Meyers hier   wohnen?

Wir wußten, daß Meyers da   wohnten.

Wie soll ich wissen, wo Meyers   gewohnt haben?

Weiß er, daß er dir helfen   soll?

Er wußte, daß er mir helfen   sollte.

Weißt du, warum Frau Enders nicht kommen   will?

Ich wußte, warum Frau Enders nicht kommen   wollte.

[9] The Pluperfect

Form your own variations.

Als ich ihn kennenlernte, war er gerade aus Afrika zurückgekommen.	When I met him, he had just come back from Africa.
Er bekam die Gelbsucht, weil er zuviel gegessen hatte.	He got jaundice because he had eaten too much.

SEE
ANALYSIS
82-83

(pp. 177-178)

Ich schrieb ihr einen Brief, weil ich gelesen hatte, daß ihr Mann verschwunden war.	I wrote her a letter because I had read that her husband had disappeared.
Wir wußten nicht, daß er Soldat geworden war.	We didn't know that he had become a soldier.
Er war zwei Jahre lang in Norwegen gewesen, als man ihn an die Westfront schickte.	He had been in Norway for two years when he was sent to the Western Front.
Als ich Hans nach dem Krieg wiedersah, war er Schriftsteller geworden.	When I saw Hans again after the war, he had become a writer.
Bei Kriegsende hatten ihn die Amerikaner gefangengenommen, aber man schickte ihn bald nach Hause, weil er Hepatitis hatte.	At the end of the war, the Americans had taken him prisoner, but they sent him home soon because he had hepatitis.

[10] Open Conditions

Try to reverse the order of conditions and conclusions. You may have to make some logical changes.

SEE
ANALYSIS
89
(pp. 185-187)

Wenn es morgen nicht regnet, können wir arbeiten.
Wir können morgen nur arbeiten, wenn es nicht regnet.
Wenn ich kann, komme ich.
Wenn ich nach Köln muß, kann ich heute abend nicht kommen.
Wenn er dich liebt, Ingrid, dann heiratet er dich auch.
Wenn sie Ja sagt, heirate ich sie.
Ich fahre nur nach Casablanca, wenn du auch fährst.
Wenn du nach Casablanca fährst, fahre ich auch.
Wenn Herr Büttner hier ist, soll er zu mir kommen.
Wenn du kein Geld hast, helfe ich dir gerne.
Ich trinke nie Wein, wenn ich Auto fahren muß.

[11] um . . . zu

After studying 90, replace the um . . . zu clauses by either weil clauses or open conditions.

SEE
ANALYSIS
90
(p. 187)

Inge fuhr nach Frankfurt, um ins Theater zu gehen.
Er fuhr nach Kairo, um dort einen Roman zu schreiben.
Sie ging ins Theater, um *Hamlet* zu sehen.
Er studierte Englisch, um Shakespeare lesen zu können.

Herr Lenz ging in die Stadt, um seiner Frau ein Buch zu kaufen.

Ich bin nicht nach Köln gekommen, um mir hier ein Haus zu kaufen.

Aber Ingrid, ich kann doch nicht von Köln nach München fahren, nur um dich zu besuchen!

Um nach Casablanca fahren zu können, muß man viel Geld haben.

Um eine Frau verstehen zu können, muß man sie lieben.

[12] Rapid Reading Practice

Read these sentences aloud at normal speed.

Er ist intelligent.

Ich weiß, er ist intelligent.

Ich hoffe, er ist intelligent.

Ich glaube, er ist intelligent.

Ich hoffe, daß er intelligent ist.

Ich weiß nicht, ob er intelligent ist.

Ich glaube nicht, daß er intelligent ist.

Daß er intelligent ist, weiß ich.

Daß er intelligent ist, das weiß ich.

Ob er intelligent ist, weiß ich nicht.

Ich möchte wissen, ob er intelligent ist.

Daß er intelligent ist, glaube ich nicht.

Daß er intelligent ist, kann ich nicht glauben.

Morgen fährt er nach Berlin.

Ich weiß, er fährt morgen nach Berlin.

Ich glaube, er fährt morgen nach Berlin.

Ich hoffe, er fährt morgen nach Berlin.

Ich weiß, daß er morgen nach Berlin fährt.

Ich weiß, daß er morgen nicht nach Berlin fährt.

Ich glaube, daß er morgen nicht nach Berlin fährt.

Ich glaube, er fährt morgen nicht nach Berlin.

Ich hoffe, er fährt morgen nicht nach Berlin.

Ich hoffe, daß er morgen nicht nach Berlin fährt.

Ich weiß nicht, ob er morgen nach Berlin fährt.

Ob er morgen nach Berlin fährt, weiß ich nicht.

Daß er morgen nach Berlin fährt, weiß ich auch.

Wann er morgen nach Berlin fährt, weiß ich nicht.

Warum er morgen nach Berlin fahren will, weiß ich nicht.

Warum er morgen nach Berlin fahren will, brauche ich nicht zu wissen.

,,Er geht heute abend mit seiner Freundin ins Kino.''

Geht er heute abend nach Stuttgart ins Kino?

Geht er heute abend *nicht* nach Stuttgart ins Kino?

Er geht heute abend nach Stuttgart ins Kino.

Er geht heute abend *nicht* nach Stuttgart ins Kino.

Heute abend geht er nach Stuttgart ins Kino.

Heute abend geht er *nicht* nach Stuttgart ins Kino.

Nach Stuttgart ins *Ki*no geht er heute abend *nicht*.

Ich weiß, er geht heute abend nach Stuttgart ins Kino.

Ich weiß, er geht heute abend *nicht* nach Stuttgart ins Kino.

Ich weiß, heute abend geht er nach Stuttgart ins Kino.

Ich weiß, heute abend geht er *nicht* nach Stuttgart ins Kino.

Ich weiß, nach Stuttgart ins *Ki*no geht er heute abend *nicht*.

Ich weiß, daß er heute abend nach Stuttgart ins Kino geht.

Ich weiß, daß er heute abend *nicht* nach Stuttgart ins Kino geht.

Ich weiß nicht, ob er heute abend nach Stuttgart ins Kino geht.

Ob er heute abend nach Stuttgart ins Kino geht, weiß ich nicht.

Warum er heute abend *nicht* nach Stuttgart ins Kino geht, weiß ich nicht.

Geht er heute abend mit seiner Freundin ins Kino?

Geht er heute abend mit seiner Freundin *nicht* ins Kino?

Er geht heute abend mit seiner Freundin ins Kino.

Er geht heute abend mit seiner Freundin *nicht* ins Kino.

Heute abend geht er mit seiner Freundin ins Kino.

Heute abend geht er mit seiner Freundin *nicht* ins Kino.

Mit seiner *Freun*din geht er *heute* abend ins Kino.

Mit seiner *Freun*din geht er heute abend *nicht* ins Kino.

Ins *Ki*no geht er mit seiner Freundin heute abend *nicht*.

Ich weiß, er geht heute abend mit seiner Freundin ins Kino.

Ich weiß, er geht heute abend mit seiner Freundin nicht ins Kino.

Ich weiß, heute abend geht er mit seiner Freundin ins Kino.

Ich weiß, heute abend geht er mit seiner Freundin nicht ins Kino.

Ich weiß, mit seiner *Freun*din geht er *heute* abend ins Kino.

Ich weiß, ins *Ki*no geht er mit seiner Freundin heute abend *nicht*.

Ich weiß, daß er heute abend mit seiner Freundin ins Kino geht.

Ich weiß, daß er heute abend mit seiner Freundin *nicht* ins Kino geht.

Ich weiß nicht, ob er heute abend mit seiner Freundin ins Kino geht.

Ob er heute abend mit seiner Freundin ins Kino geht, weiß ich nicht.

Warum er heute abend mit seiner Freundin ins Kino geht, weiß ich nicht.

Warum er heute abend mit seiner Freundin *nicht* ins Kino geht, das weiß ich nicht.

Dr. Schmidt hat seinem Sohn ein Auto gekauft.

Dr. Schmidt hat seinem Sohn kein Auto gekauft.

Seinem Sohn hat Dr. Schmidt ein Auto gekauft.

Seiner Frau hat er nichts gekauft.

Ich glaube, Dr. Schmidt hat seinem Sohn ein Auto gekauft.

Ich hoffe, Dr. Schmidt hat seinem Sohn kein Auto gekauft.

Ich weiß, Dr. Schmidt hat seinem Sohn ein Auto gekauft.

Ich weiß nicht, ob Dr. Schmidt seinem Sohn ein Auto gekauft hat.

Ich möchte wissen, ob Dr. Schmidt seinem Sohn ein Auto gekauft hat.

Wie soll ich wissen, ob Dr. Schmidt seinem Sohn ein Auto gekauft hat?

Ich kann nicht glauben, daß Dr. Schmidt seinem Sohn ein Auto gekauft hat.

Ich weiß nicht, warum Dr. Schmidt seinem Sohn ein Auto gekauft hat.

Wann Dr. Schmidt seinem Sohn ein Auto gekauft hat, weiß ich nicht.

Daß Dr. Schmidt seinem Sohn ein Auto gekauft hat, habe ich nicht gewußt.

Ob Dr. Schmidt seinem Sohn ein Auto gekauft hat, kann ich Ihnen nicht sagen.

CONVERSATION

I

FRAU A: Weißt du, ob Hans und Maria das Haus hier in Bonn schon *gekauft* haben? Wenn sie es *nicht* gekauft haben, möchten *wir* es gerne kaufen.

FRAU B: Leider kann ich dir nicht *sagen*, ob sie es gekauft haben. Aber daß *ihr* es wollt, ist mir *neu*. Ich dachte, ihr wolltet euch ein Haus in *Köln* kaufen.

FRAU A: Das *wollten* wir auch. Aber *Fritz* und *ich* sind gestern nach *Köln* gefahren und haben das Haus noch einmal ge*sehen*. Wir wollen es *doch* nicht kaufen. Wir wollen *hier*bleiben. Übrigens habe ich mir in Köln einen *Hut* gekauft.

FRAU B: *So*, und das Haus in Köln habt ihr *nicht* gekauft! *Gut*, daß ihr *hier*bleibt. Und den *Hut* mußt du mir *zeigen*.

II

REPORTER: Wie lange sind Sie schon in Kairo, Herr Schmidt-Ingelheim?

SCHMIDT-INGELHEIM: Seit vierzehn Tagen*—seit Anfang April.

REPORTER: Und wie lange wollen Sie noch hierbleiben?

SCHMIDT-INGELHEIM: Das kann ich Ihnen noch nicht sagen; ich wollte noch zwei, drei Wochen hier arbeiten, aber gerade hat mich ein Freund angerufen und wollte wissen, ob ich mit nach Casablanca fahren will. Er hat eine Jacht, wissen Sie, und weil ich schon lange nicht mehr auf einem Schiff gewesen bin, dachte ich, ich fahre vielleicht mit.

REPORTER: Das kann nur Mr. Thistlethwaite gewesen sein, oder?

SCHMIDT-INGELHEIM: Sie haben recht—aber wie wußten Sie denn, . . . ?

REPORTER: Ich habe ihn vor drei oder vier Wochen zufällig kennengelernt und habe ihn seitdem zwei- oder dreimal besucht. Von ihm weiß ich auch, daß Sie hier sind. Er hat viel von Ihnen und von Ihrer Frau gesprochen—wie schön Ihre Frau ist, und wie intelligent—und er hat mir auch erzählt, daß Sie wieder an einem Roman arbeiten.

SCHMIDT-INGELHEIM: Ja, mein Roman! Um diesen Roman zu schreiben, bin ich nach Kairo gekommen, wissen Sie—ich mußte ein paar† Wochen allein sein, um arbeiten zu können. Und außerdem wollte ich Afrika wiedersehen, —der Roman hat viel mit Afrika zu tun.

REPORTER: Es ist also wieder ein Kriegsroman, Herr Schmidt-Ingelheim?

SCHMIDT-INGELHEIM: Ja, ja,—*Ende bei Karthago* heißt er. Ich arbeite jetzt schon seit zwei Jahren an diesem Roman, aber wissen Sie, wenn man immer so zu Hause sitzt, dann . . .

* **vierzehn Tage** in German, the usual way of expressing *two weeks*.
† **ein paar** a few

REPORTER:	Das kann ich gut verstehen, Herr Schmidt-Ingelheim.—Sie mußten eine Reise machen; Sie mußten nach Afrika kommen, um über ihren Roman nachdenken zu können; Sie mußten einmal verschwinden . . .
SCHMIDT-INGELHEIM:	Richtig! Kein Telephon, kein Briefträger, keine Reporter—verstehen Sie, ich möchte wirklich einmal verschwinden, spurlos verschwinden. Nur so für vierzehn Tage oder drei Wochen. Aber so ist das Leben leider nicht. Und der Briefträger kommt auch; heute morgen zum Beispiel habe ich einen Brief von meiner Tochter bekommen—sie schreibt, sie will nach Kairo kommen.
REPORTER:	Von Ihrer Tochter? Das habe ich nicht gewußt, daß Sie eine Tochter haben.
SCHMIDT-INGELHEIM:	Oh, doch,—von meiner ersten* Frau; sie wird Ende Mai zwanzig und studiert in Mainz Archäologie. Ich habe sie seit zehn Jahren nicht gesehen.
REPORTER:	Das ist ja interessant.—Aber ich möchte Sie noch etwas fragen, Herr Ingelheim. Ihr Roman—können Sie mir nicht noch etwas von ihrem Roman erzählen?
SCHMIDT-INGELHEIM:	Möchte ich ja gern, aber ich muß jetzt wirklich gehen; man erwartet mich zum Frühstück;—und wissen Sie, ohne meinen Frühstückskaffee ist das Leben nur halb so schön.

READING

Viel Lärm um nichts? (Schluß)

KAPITEL DREI: Ein Brief an Frau Schmidt–Ingelheim

Katharina Schmidt

65 Mainz/Rhein
Riedbachstraße 4
den 12. Mai

Sehr geehrte Frau Schmidt-Ingelheim!

Gerade habe ich in der† Zeitung gelesen, daß Ihr Mann seit drei Wochen in Afrika spurlos verschwunden ist.

Ich weiß, was Sie durchmachen. Mein Mann war auch einmal drei Wochen spurlos verschwunden. Aber wenn Sie diesen Brief bekommen, ist Hans vielleicht schon wieder zu Hause und sagt Ihnen 5 beim Frühstück: „Ohne deinen Kaffee, Ingrid, wäre das Leben nur halb so schön."

Sehr geehrte Standard form of address: literally "very honored Mrs. Schmidt-Ingelheim"

wäre would be

* **ersten** first
† The use of dative or accusative after prepositions like *an* and *in* will be discussed in Unit 7.

Woher ich weiß, daß er das sagt? Ich bin Frau Schmidt Nummer
eins, und ich glaube, Sie sind Frau Schmidt Nummer zwei oder
drei. Ich weiß nicht, wie oft Hans geheiratet hat, und ich möchte
es auch nicht wissen. Ich möchte aber, daß Sie warten, bis Hans
wiederkommt, und daß er nicht mehr in die Zeitung kommt. Sie ₅
brauchen nicht zu fürchten, daß ihm etwas passiert ist. Ihrem Hans
passiert nie etwas; ich kenne ihn. Ich habe ihn einmal geliebt,
wissen Sie; und oft, wenn ich sehe, wie seine Tochter mit einem
Lachen in den Augen zum Frühstück kommt, gerade wie früher
ihr Vater, dann frage ich mich, ob ich ihn nicht vielleicht doch noch ₁₀
liebe.

Nein, passiert ist ihm nichts. Wie habe ich Angst gehabt, als er
1939 Soldat wurde. Damals wußte ich noch nicht, daß ich keine
Angst zu haben brauchte. Man schickte ihn in ein Städtchen hinter
der Westfront, und da hat er ein Jahr lang Brieftauben gefüttert. ₁₅
Gerade als es 1940 im Westen gefährlich wurde, schickte man ihn
nach Hause, weil er Hepatitis bekam.

Wir heirateten.

Hans hatte aber keine Hepatitis. Er hatte nur Gelbsucht, weil er
zu gut gegessen und zu viel getrunken hatte; und so wurde er 1941 ₂₀
wieder Soldat. Man schickte ihn, wieder mit Brieftauben, nach
Norwegen. Seine Briefe sprachen im Sommer vom Fischen, und im
Winter vom Schilaufen. Bei Kriegsende war er zufällig in Ingelheim,
und die Amerikaner nahmen ihn gefangen. Jetzt bekam er wirklich
Hepatitis, und man schickte ihn nach Hause. Dreiundzwanzig ₂₅
Schüler haben 1931 mit ihm das Abitur gemacht. Von den dreiundzwanzig leben heute noch sechs, und ihm allein ist im Krieg
nichts passiert.

Hans wurde Schriftsteller. Seinen Kriegsroman *Wie das Gesetz es
befahl* habe ich auf der Maschine geschrieben. Er machte damals oft ₃₀
Reisen, ohne mich, und wohin, weiß ich nicht. Ich habe ihn auch
nie gefragt. Er mußte, so sagte er, zwei oder drei Wochen allein sein,
um seine Romane schreiben zu können. Aber er kam immer wieder,
mit seinem Lachen in den Augen, und trank seinen Kaffee, wie man
Rheinwein trinkt. Aber dann passierte ihm doch etwas. Als er von ₃₅
einer Reise zurückkam, sagte er beim Frühstück: „Ohne deinen
Kaffee, Gisela, wäre das Leben nur halb so schön." Ich weiß nicht,
wer Gisela war, aber ich fuhr mit meiner Tochter zu meiner Mutter.

Noch einmal, sehr geehrte Frau Schmidt, Ihrem Hans ist nichts
passiert. Ich weiß, er lebt und ist gesund. Seit Sie geheiratet haben, ₄₀
war er wohl noch nie so lange „spurlos verschwunden". Ich gratuliere Ihnen; Sie müssen interessant sein, interessanter als ich. Aber
wenn er wieder zu Hause ist, dann fragen Sie ihn doch beim

1939: neunzehnhun-
dertneununddreißig

1940: neunzehnhun-
dertvierzig

Gelbsucht jaundice
1941: neunzehnhun-
derteinundvierzig

1931: neunzehnhun-
derteinunddreißig
Abitur comprehensive
examination at the end
of German secondary
school

Frühstück: „Wie war Giselas Kaffee? Oder hieß sie diesmal nicht Gisela?" Vielleicht verschwindet er dann drei Wochen mit Ihnen. Auf keinen Fall aber dürfen Sie mit Ihren Kindern zu Ihrer Mutter fahren. Ich habe damals einen Fehler gemacht; ich hoffe, Sie machen diesen Fehler nicht. ₅

Auf . . . Fall under no circumstances.

Ihre
Katharina Schmidt

KAPITEL VIER: Frau Schmidt-Ingelheim wieder am Telefon

Ah, Herr Behrens; gut, daß Sie wieder anrufen. Wissen Sie was? Der Briefträger hatte wirklich zwei Briefe von meinem Mann. Und seine Tochter, die Jutta, war *doch* in Kairo. . . .

Nein, Johannes wußte es auch nicht. Sie studiert doch Archäologie ₁₀ und war gerade in Ägypten, und zufällig war sie in Kairo, als mein Mann in Kairo war. Die Welt ist doch wirklich klein, nicht? . . .

Und diese Männer! Er hatte mir geschrieben, daß er nicht mit der Lufthansa nach Casablanca wollte. Thistlethwaite hatte ihn eingeladen, mit ihm auf seiner Jacht nach Casablanca zu fahren. Und ₁₅ dann nimmt der Mann den Brief mit aufs Schiff, und gefunden hat er ihn erst in Casablanca im Hotel. . . .

Nein, nein, alles ist OK; ich fahre morgen nach Zürich und hole ihn ab. . . .

Ja, so sind die Männer, aber ich bin ja so glücklich, daß er gesund ₂₀ ist. . . .

Ja, mit dem Nekrolog müssen Sie jetzt natürlich noch warten. . . .

Natürlich, ich sage ihm morgen, daß Sie angerufen haben. Ich danke Ihnen, Herr Behrens. Auf Wiederhören!

ANALYSIS

74 Cardinal Numbers

The numbers from 0 to 20 are:

null	sieben	vierzehn
eins	acht	fünfzehn
zwei	neun	sechzehn
drei	zehn	siebzehn
vier	elf	achtzehn
fünf	zwölf	neunzehn
sechs	dreizehn	zwanzig

HOTEL VIER JAHRESZEITEN
RESTAURANT HAERLIN
HAMBURG

TELEFON HAMBURG (0411) 34 941
TELEX 021 1629

☎ — ☎ — ☎

HAUSANSCHLÜSSE

Zentrale	0	Tischbestellung	0
Auskunft	8	Gepäck	8
Portier	8	Autovermietung	8
Empfang	9	Zeitungen	699
Post	8	Bank	698
Reisedienst	684	Friseur	688
Theaterkarten	8	Wecken	8

Für Zimmerkellner und Mädchen
ab 7 Uhr
bitte die Klingel benutzen

HOTEL VIER JAHRESZEITEN
RESTAURANT HAERLIN
HAMBURG

TELEFON HAMBURG (0411) 34 941
TELEX 021 1629

☎ — ☎ — ☎

HOUSE EXTENSIONS

Operator	0	Table Order	0
Information	8	Luggage	8
Hall Porter	8	Car Hire	8
Reception	9	Newspapers	699
Mail Department	8	Money Exchange	698
Theater Tickets	8	Wake-Up-Calls	8
Travel Service	684	Barber Shop & Beauty Parlour	688

For room-service and chambermaid
as from 7:00 a.m.
please ring the bell

Note the difference in spelling:

sechs,   but   **sechzehn**
sieben,   but   **siebzehn**

One can say either

zwei und zwei ist vier   or   **zwei plus zwei ist vier,**

and

vier weniger zwei ist zwei   or   **vier minus zwei ist zwei.**

Plus and **minus** are mathematical terms; **und** and **weniger** are used in non-mathematical everyday language.

75 The Past Tense of Weak Verbs

Just as the present-tense form **ich gehe** may mean both *I go* and *I am going,* the past-tense form **ich ging** may mean both *I went* and *I was going;* in other words, German does not have progressive forms in any tense.

It was pointed out in Unit 4 that "weak" verbs form their participles by prefixing **ge-** and adding **-t** to the stem, whereas "strong" verbs form their participles by prefixing **ge-** and adding **-en** to the stem:

WEAK	STRONG
lieben, geliebt	bleiben, geblieben
lachen, gelacht	lesen, gelesen
kennen, gekannt	sein, gewesen

There is also a difference in the way "weak" and "strong" verbs form the past tense.

Weak verbs form the past tense by adding a personal ending starting with **-t-** to the unchanged (or only slightly changed) stem:

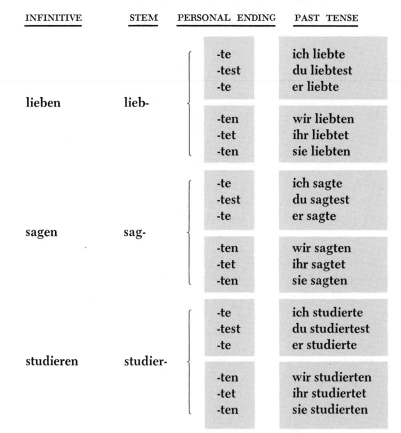

INFINITIVE	STEM	PERSONAL ENDING	PAST TENSE
lieben	lieb-	-te	ich liebte
		-test	du liebtest
		-te	er liebte
		-ten	wir liebten
		-tet	ihr liebtet
		-ten	sie liebten
sagen	sag-	-te	ich sagte
		-test	du sagtest
		-te	er sagte
		-ten	wir sagten
		-tet	ihr sagtet
		-ten	sie sagten
studieren	studier-	-te	ich studierte
		-test	du studiertest
		-te	er studierte
		-ten	wir studierten
		-tet	ihr studiertet
		-ten	sie studierten

Thousands of verbs follow the pattern of **lieben, sagen,** and **studieren** without any deviation. Some deviations are regular and will be discussed in the next paragraph. The few irregular deviations will be found in the tables of irregular verbs which, from now on, will follow the vocabulary of each unit.

76 Regular Deviations in the Past of Weak Verbs

Three slight deviations will not appear in the tables of irregular verbs:

Modals

The modals lose the umlaut found in the infinitive:

dürfen	ich durfte
können	ich konnte
müssen	ich mußte
sollen	ich sollte
wollen	ich wollte

We will not use, for a while, the past tense forms belonging to **ich möchte.** Note the difference between **ich konnte,** *I was able to,* and **ich kannte,** *I knew.*

Verbs with an **-e-** before the Ending **-te**

The endings **-te, -test, -te, -ten, -tet,** and **-ten** must be clearly audible. Therefore, verbs with a stem ending in **-d** or **-t,** like **arbeiten** and **reden,** insert an **-e-** between the stem and the ending.

ich arbeitete	ich redete
du arbeitetest	du redetest
er arbeitete	er redete
wir arbeiteten	wir redeten
ihr arbeitetet	ihr redetet
sie arbeiteten	sie redeten

For similar reasons, an **-e-** before the ending **-t** is also found in the past forms of verbs like **regnen, atmen** (*to breathe*), and **rechnen** (*to figure, to calculate*):

es regnete
er atmete
er rechnete

The Verb **haben**

ich hatte	wir hatten
du hattest	ihr hattet
er hatte	sie hatten

NOTE: In the past tense, the third person singular of a weak verb *never* ends in **-t.**

77 Past Tense of Strong Verbs

To form the past, strong verbs add the following endings to the changed stem:

ich:	—	wir:	-en
du:	-st	ihr:	-t
er:	—	sie:	-en

The change in the stem is unpredictable, and the best way to master these forms is to memorize them as they appear in the tables of irregular verbs.

INFINITIVE	CHANGED STEM	ENDING	PAST TENSE
		-	ich ging
		-st	du gingst
		-	er ging
gehen	ging-		
		-en	wir gingen
		-t	ihr gingt
		-en	sie gingen
		-	ich war
		-st	du warst
		-	er war
sein	war-		
		-en	wir waren
		-t	ihr wart
		-en	sie waren

Like the weak verbs whose stems end in -d or -t, strong verbs ending in -d or -t insert an -e- between the stem and the ending in the du-form and the ihr-form.

INFINITIVE	CHANGED STEM	ENDING	PAST TENSE
		-	ich fand
		-est	du fandest
		-	er fand
finden	fand		
		-en	wir fanden
		-et	ihr fandet
		-en	sie fanden

NOTE: In the past tense, the first and third persons singular of a strong verb *never* have an ending.

78 The Principal Parts of Strong and Irregular German Verbs

One can form all the tenses of an English verb like *to sing* if one knows the three forms

sing   sang   sung.

These three forms are called the "principal parts" of *to sing*.

The student learning German must learn two additional forms:

1. the **er**-form of verbs like **fahren**—that is, of strong verbs with a vowel change in the second and third persons singular. (Weak verbs never change their stem vowel in the present tense.)

2. the auxiliary (**haben** or **sein**) used to form the perfect.

Thus the principal parts of **kennen, schreiben,** and **fahren,** arranged in the traditional way, are:

kennen	kannte	hat gekannt	kennt
schreiben	schrieb	hat geschrieben	schreibt
fahren	fuhr	ist gefahren	fährt

The verb **kennen** is a weak verb. However, it changes the vowel in the past and in the perfect in an unpredictable way and therefore appears in the table of irregular verbs.

The verbs **schreiben** and **kennen** show no vowel change in the **du**-form or **er**-form. Therefore, one really does not have to memorize **er schreibt** or **er kennt**. But since one learns more easily if all irregular verbs appear in a certain rhythmical pattern, **er schreibt** and **er kennt** will be given as principal parts.

The verb **fahren** is a strong verb. The past tense **fuhr** (**ich fuhr, du fuhrst, er fuhr**) cannot be derived from the infinitive **fahren,** and neither can the participle **gefahren** or the third person singular present **er fährt**. In this case, therefore, all four principal parts have to be memorized.

79 The Difference in the Use of the Perfect and the Past

The verbs **schlafen** and **essen** have the principal parts

| schlafen | schlief | hat geschlafen | er schläft |
| essen | aß | hat gegessen | er ißt |

A native speaker of English is tempted to express the ideas

Did you eat at the Regina last night?
Did you sleep well last night?

by the Anglicisms

Beware!   [Aßt ihr gestern abend im Regina?]   DO NOT USE!
Americanism!   [Schliefst du heute nacht gut?]

The native speaker of English talks about "all-in-the-past" events (see **71**) by using the simple past tense, and he quite naturally transfers this habit to German. However, a German will ask only

Habt ihr gestern abend im Regina gegessen?
Hast du gut geschlafen?

The forms

    ich aß   and   **ich habe gegessen**
    ich schlief   and   **ich habe geschlafen**

are not interchangeable. As long as people are engaged in a conversation, (and telling a story is *not* conversation), they use the German perfect:

  A: **Wohnt Dr. Müller noch hier?**
  B: **Nein, Dr. Müller ist vor einem Jahr gestorben, und seine Frau ist nach München gezogen.** (ist gezogen—*has moved*)

     Not: [**Dr. Müller starb vor einem Jahr, und seine Frau zog nach München.**]

However, the sentence

Dr. Müller starb, und seine Frau zog nach München

is possible when the speaker turns into an author, when the conversational partner becomes a passive reader or listener, when two-way conversation changes to one-way storytelling. For then the storyteller uses the simple past tense to enumerate step by step those events, and only those events, which are part of the progressing story.

> **Hans wurde Schriftsteller. Seinen Kriegsroman *Wie das Gesetz es befahl* habe ich auf der Maschine geschrieben. Er machte damals oft Reisen, ohne mich, und wohin, weiß ich nicht. Ich habe ihn auch nie gefragt. Er mußte, so sagte er, zwei oder drei Wochen allein sein, um seine Romane schreiben zu können. Aber er kam immer wieder, mit seinem Lachen in den Augen, und trank seinen Kaffee, wie man Rheinwein trinkt. Aber dann passierte ihm doch etwas. Als er von einer Reise zurückkam, sagte er beim Frühstück: „Ohne deinen Kaffee, Gisela, wäre das Leben nur halb so schön." Ich weiß nicht, wer Gisela war, aber ich fuhr mit meiner Tochter zu meiner Mutter.**

Most of the verb forms in this passage are past-tense forms. These forms narrate, step by step, the events of the story. The perfect forms **habe ich auf der Maschine geschrieben** and **Ich habe ihn auch nie gefragt** are parenthetical remarks which interrupt the story. The two present forms **ich weiß nicht** refer to the time of writing the letter, not to what the author knew while the past was going on. Such shifts from the narrative past to a present or to a perfect are quite normal. The present or perfect forms in such cases interrupt the story and reestablish a connection with the present:

> **Auf dem Rückweg erzählte sie mir eine Geschichte, über die ich seitdem viel nachgedacht habe.**

> On the way back she told me a story about which I have thought a lot since then.

80 The Use of the Past Tense of **haben, sein,** and the Modals

What has been said about the difference between the past and the perfect is not applicable to **haben, sein,** and the modals. The perfect tense of these verbs is used primarily in up-to-now situations. In all-past situations, the simple past is preferred. This means that, as far as **haben, sein,** and the modals are concerned, the German use of tenses is parallel to English usage.

A: **Wo warst du denn gestern? Ich habe dich überall gesucht.**
Where were you yesterday? I looked for you everywhere.

B: **Ich hatte gestern Kopfschmerzen und bin zu Hause geblieben** (*or* **. . . und konnte nicht kommen** *or* **. . . und mußte zu Hause bleiben**).
I had a headache yesterday and stayed at home (*or* . . . and I couldn't come *or* . . . and I had to stay at home).

A: **Ich habe nie Kopfschmerzen.**
I never have headaches.

B: **Hast du wirklich noch nie Kopfschmerzen gehabt?**
You mean you've really never had a headache?

A: **Nein, aber ich habe schon zweimal die Mumps gehabt.**
No, but I've had the mumps twice.

81 The Use of the Past in Dependent Clauses

Frequently a perfect form in the main clause is accompanied by a past form in the dependent clause (see **84–87**). This is virtually obligatory in **als**-clauses and in other dependent clauses which fix the time of an event or describe the circumstances that brought the event about:

> **Ich habe bis elf gewartet. Aber als er dann immer noch nicht kam, bin ich ins Bett gegangen.**
> I waited until eleven. But when he still did not come, I went to bed.

Als wir in Köln wohnten, sind wir oft in den Dom gegangen.	When we lived in Cologne, we frequently went to the cathedral.
Warum hat sie ihn denn geheiratet, wenn sie ihn nicht liebte?—Weil sie wußte, daß er Geld hatte.	Why did she marry him if she didn't love him?—Because she knew he had money.

NOTE: If the action of the dependent clause occurs while the action of the main clause is in progress, the past tense may be used in both clauses.

Als ich meine Frau kennenlernte, wohnte sie in München.

82 The Formation of the Pluperfect

The German pluperfect is formed by combining the simple past of **haben** or **sein** with the participle of the main verb. Verbs which use **sein** for the perfect, like

bleiben   blieb   ist geblieben   bleibt,

also form their pluperfect with **sein: ich war geblieben** (*I had stayed*). Verbs which, like

schreiben   schrieb   hat geschrieben   schreibt,

use **haben** for the perfect, also use **haben** for the pluperfect: **ich hatte geschrieben** (*I had written*).

83 The Use of the Pluperfect

Like the English past perfect, the German pluperfect is the tense used to describe events or situations which precede events or situations that occurred in the past.

Hans hatte die Gelbsucht, weil er monatelang zu gut gegessen und zu viel getrunken hatte.	Hans had jaundice, because for months he had been eating and drinking too much.
Es war Abend geworden, und es regnete.	Night had come and it was raining.

When the sentence

Erich wohnt jetzt schon drei Jahre in München und geht jede Woche einmal ins Theater

becomes part of a narrative, it will appear as

Erich wohnte damals schon drei Jahre in München und ging jede Woche einmal ins Theater.

The "up-to-now" situation of the first sentence has become an "up-to-then" situation in the second sentence.

Similarly, an up-to-now perfect form changes to a pluperfect when it becomes part of a narrative.

Ich kannte sie schon lange, aber ich hatte noch nie mit ihr gesprochen.	I had known her a long time, but I had never talked with her.
Ich wußte damals nicht, daß sein Vater ein Jahr krank gewesen war.	I didn't know at the time that his father had been ill for a year (but was no longer ill).

But:

Ich wußte damals nicht, daß sein Vater seit einem Jahr krank war.	I didn't know at the time that his father had been ill for a year (and was still ill).

84 Dependent Clauses

Dependent clauses are syntactical units of main clauses. They can function as any part of the main clause: as subject, predicate noun, object, adverb, etc.

SUBJECT	*The winner* gets the prize.
	Whoever wins gets the prize.
PREDICATE NOUN	This is not *the expected result.*
	This is not *what I had expected.*
OBJECT	I'll never know *your thoughts.*
	I'll never know *what you think.*
ADVERB	He met John *during his stay in New York.*
	He met John *while he stayed in New York.*

Dependent clauses are usually introduced by a connecting word: a subordinating conjunction (*while, because, if,* etc.), a relative pronoun (*who, whom, what,* etc.), or an interrogative pronoun (*who, what, when, why,* etc.).

I have to go home, *because* I am tired.
This is the man *whom* we saw at the station.
I'd like to know *when* he will be there.

After certain introductory phrases containing a verb of thought, the connecting word can be left out:

I am sure (that) he'll come.
I thought (that) you'd be there.
I believe (that) he is sick.

In English, the word order in both introduced and unintroduced dependent clauses is usually the same as the word order of a main clause.

She took him to the airport.
I know she took him to the airport.
I know that she took him to the airport.

In German, *only unintroduced dependent clauses have the same structure as main clauses.* We have had many examples of this type.

> **Meyer arbeitet heute in Bonn.**
> **Ich glaube, Meyer arbeitet heute in Bonn.**

All unintroduced dependent clauses in German have verb-second position. They normally start with the subject, and the introductory main clause is never negated. If the main clause is negated, a major change takes place which has no parallel in English (see **85**).

85 Verb-Last Position

By now you are familiar with the most characteristic feature of German syntax—the tendency to separate a semantic unit into two parts and to use these parts as brackets to establish a larger unit. Thus the two prongs of the predicate enclose the inner field.

A similar bracket principle is used in all dependent clauses which are introduced by a subordinating conjunction, a relative pronoun, or an interrogative. The introductory word is used as the first bracket and, of all things, the first prong is moved out of its usual position and is used as the second bracket. The rest of the sentence, including the second prong, remains unchanged. This means that the first prong now follows the second prong and stands at the end of the clause if there is no end field. We therefore speak of "verb-last position."

	FRONT FIELD	1st Prong	INNER FIELD	2nd Prong	
MAIN CLAUSE	Er	ist	heute	hier	
UNINTRODUCED DEPENDENT CLAUSE	Ich glaube, er	ist	heute	hier	
INTRODUCED DEPENDENT CLAUSE	Ich glaube, daß er		heute	hier	ist

NOTE: Verbal complements like **an, aus, ab,** and any others that are written as one word with an infinitive, must also be connected in verb-last position.

> **Die Laternen gehen an.**—**Wenn die Laternen angehen,** . . .
> **Er macht das Licht aus.**—**Daß er das Licht ausmacht,** . . .
> **Er lernte sie in Bonn kennen.**—**Als er sie in Bonn kennenlernte,** . . .

All introduced dependent clauses follow this pattern of verb-last position.
In this unit, three groups of connecting words are used:

Subordinating Conjunctions

Ich weiß,	*daß*	er seit drei Wochen	verschwunden	*ist.*
Er will erst schreiben,	*wenn*	er wieder	zu Hause	*ist.*
Ich mußte warten,	*bis*	Herr Behrens mich	angerufen	*hatte.*
Er schrieb erst,	*als*	er von seiner Reise	zurückgekommen	*war.*
Er blieb zu Hause,	*weil*	er nicht	ins Kino gehen	*wollte.*
Er redet nicht viel,	*seit*	er aus Afrika	zurückgekommen	*ist.*

Interrogative Conjunctions

Sie wußte nicht mehr,	*wer*	ihr das Buch	gegeben	*hatte.*
Ich weiß nicht,	*was*	er in Norwegen	gemacht	*hat.*
Wissen Sie,	*wo*	er bei Kriegsende		*war?*
Ich weiß nicht,	*woher*	er	gekommen	*ist.*
Er sagte uns nicht,	*wohin*	er	gehen	*wollte.*
Er trank Kaffee,	*wie*	man Rheinwein		*trinkt.*

NOTE: Any German word question can be changed into a dependent clause by changing word order:

> Wann ist er nach Hause gekommen?
> Ich weiß nicht, wann er nach Hause gekommen ist.

> Wo wohnt er?
> Ich weiß nicht, wo er wohnt.

> Was will er?
> Ich weiß nicht, was er will.

The Conjunction ob

Any German yes-or-no question can be changed into a dependent **ob**-clause by changing word order:

> Hat Meyer Geld?
> Weißt du, ob Meyer Geld hat?

> Ist Meyer gestorben?
> Ich weiß nicht, ob Meyer gestorben ist.

> Hat sie geheiratet?
> Weißt du, ob sie geheiratet hat?

NOTE: In English, yes-or-no questions can be changed into dependent clauses by using either *whether* or *if:*

	Is he here?
Do you know whether	he is here?
Do you know if	he is here?

Every English *if* which can be replaced by *whether* must be expressed by **ob** in German. This **ob** cannot be replaced by **wenn.**

In all the above examples, the dependent clause follows the main clause. *If the dependent clause precedes the main clause, it is considered the first element of the main clause; that is, it occupies the front field of the main clause—and must therefore be followed by the first prong of the main clause* to conform to the principle of verb-second position. This means that, separated by a comma, the finite verb of the main clause immediately follows the finite verb of the dependent clause.

In Hamburg	**bin**	ich jeden Abend	ins Kino	gegangen.
Als ich in Hamburg war,	**bin**	ich jeden Abend	ins Kino	gegangen.
Seit Kriegsende	**hat**	er drei Romane	geschrieben.	
Seit er zurück ist,	**hat**	er drei Romane	geschrieben.	

Frequently, especially after **wenn**-clauses, the dependent clause—that is, the first element of the main clause—is repeated and summed up at the beginning of the main clause by either **dann** or **so**. This **dann** or **so** immediately precedes the first prong—that is, the second element of the main clause.

Wenn ich seine Tochter sehe,
        1

              dann | *weiß* ich, daß ich ihn immer noch liebe.
              1a   2

Wenn ich Ihnen sage, daß ich Frau Schmidt bin,
        1

                         so | *müssen* Sie mir das glauben.
                         1a   2

English uses a similar construction in such sentences as
    Well, if you won't sell, then there's nothing more to be said.

86 Position of the Subject in Dependent Clauses

In most dependent clauses, the subject follows the connecting word. (See all the above examples). However, a noun subject may be preceded by pronoun objects:

> Ich weiß, daß *Herr Meyer seiner Frau* einen Sportwagen geschenkt hat.
> Ich weiß, daß *Herr Meyer ihr* einen Sportwagen geschenkt hat.
> Ich weiß, daß *ihr Herr Meyer* einen Sportwagen geschenkt hat.

In order to increase the news value of a noun subject, it may be moved toward the end of the inner field. Thus, in the following sentences, the news value is shifted from the time element to the subject:

> Ich kann nicht glauben, daß *die Laternen* hier schon um vier Uhr angehen.
> Ich kann nicht glauben, daß hier schon um vier Uhr *die Laternen* angehen.

Read the following sentences, taken from the reading section of this unit, carefully and analyze their structure.

1. Gerade habe ich im *New York Star* gelesen, daß Ihr Mann seit drei Wochen spurlos verschwunden ist.
2. Ich weiß, was Sie durchmachen.
3. Wenn Sie diesen Brief bekommen, ist Hans vielleicht schon wieder zu Hause.
4. Woher ich weiß, daß er das sagt?
5. Ich glaube, Sie sind Frau Schmidt Nummer zwei.
6. Ich weiß nicht, wie oft Hans geheiratet hat.
7. Ich möchte aber, daß Sie warten, bis Hans wiederkommt, und daß er nicht mehr in die Zeitung kommt.
8. Sie brauchen keine Angst zu haben, daß ihm etwas passiert ist.
9. Als es im Westen gefährlich wurde, schickte man ihn nach Hause, weil er Hepatitis bekam.
10. Ich habe ihn einmal geliebt, wissen Sie; und oft, wenn ich sehe, wie seine Tochter mit einem Lachen in den Augen zum Frühstück kommt, gerade wie früher ihr Vater, dann frage ich mich, ob ich ihn nicht vielleicht doch noch liebe.

87 Intonation of Dependent Clauses

It was pointed out in Unit 1 that when a German assertion sinks down at the end to level 1 of the three intonation levels, as it does in

Wir blei-ben heu-te na-tür-lich zu Hau-se,

the fall to level 1 means "this is the end of the sentence."

Whenever an assertion is followed by a dependent clause, the speaker has several possibilities.

1. He may want to indicate that everything important has already been said in the main clause. In that case the entire dependent clause may have level 1 intonation, and the preceding main clause shows the usual 2–3–1 intonation pattern.

Ich war schon im Bett, als er nach Hau-se kam.

Du kannst kom-men, wenn du willst.

2. He may pack *all* the news value into the dependent clause and speak the preceding main clause entirely on level 2:

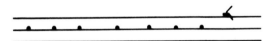

Ich war doch schon hier, als er kam.

Du kannst doch ge-hen, wann du willst.

3. He may want to distribute the news value over the main clause and the dependent clause by placing (at least) *one* stressed syllable in the main clausé and (at least) *one* stressed syllable in the dependent clause. He can use either the pattern

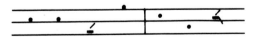

Du kannst kom-men , wann du willst.

or the equally idiomatic pattern

Du kannst kom-men , wann du willst.

The intonation patterns in (1) and (2) contain nothing new (they simply represent a "long-breath" variation of **Es regnet**), but the intonation patterns under (3) illustrate a new principle:

The main clause and the dependent clause are usually separated by a slight pause; and at the end of the main clause the pitch of the unstressed syllables does not sink to level 1 (which would signal the end of the sentence), but is spoken on level 3. This lack of a drop in pitch is a signal meaning: "This is not the end of the sentence; wait for the next clause." The last stressed syllable of the main clause can be either on level 3 or on level 1.

The high-pitch last-syllable intonation is also characteristic for dependent clauses which precede a main clause. Again, the last stressed syllable of the first clause can be either on level 1 or on level 3.

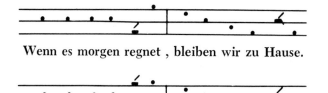

Wenn es morgen regnet , bleiben wir zu Hause.

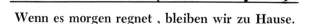

Wenn es morgen regnet , bleiben wir zu Hause.

88   Review: The Position of the German Finite Verb

We have now introduced three positions in which finite verbs can appear in German: verb-second position, verb-first position, and verb-last position.

Verb-Second Position

ASSERTIONS

Ich	bleibe	heute abend	zu Hause.
Heute abend	bleibe	ich	zu Hause.
Wenn es regnet,	bleibe	ich	zu Hause.

UNINTRODUCED DEPENDENT CLAUSES

| Ich weiß, er | bleibt | heute abend | zu Hause. |
| Glaubst du vielleicht, er | bleibt | heute abend | zu Hause? |

WORD QUESTIONS

| Wann | sind | Sie | zu Hause? |
| Wo | bist | du | gewesen? |

Verb-First Position

YES-OR-NO QUESTIONS

Bleibst	du heute	zu Hause?
Hast	du sie	gesehen?
Können	Sie mich	anrufen?

IMPERATIVES

| Rufen | Sie mich | an. |
| Kommen | Sie doch | morgen. |

Verb-Last Position, in Introduced Dependent Clauses

Ich weiß,	daß	er	nach Hause	kommt.	
Ich glaube nicht,	daß	sie	ins Kino gehen	will.	
	Als	er	nach Hause	kam,	war sie schon da.

89 Open Conditions

A condition is an event or a situation without which another event or situation cannot take place. Thus, in the statement *If the weather is good tomorrow, we can go to the beach,* good weather is the prerequisite for the trip to the beach. The *if*-clause (the grammatical "condition") does not indicate whether or not the weather will be good; it simply states that unless the weather is good, the second part of the statement (the grammatical "conclusion") will not become a reality.

Similarly, if someone says, *I haven't seen my old teacher for years. If he is still alive he was fifty years old last Monday,* this means that the speaker does not know whether the teacher is still alive, and that consequently he doesn't know whether the teacher was able to celebrate his fiftieth birthday. *The question as to the reality of the facts is left open.* However, this question *is not left open* if someone says, *If my teacher were still alive, he would have turned fifty last Monday.* The speaker now implies that the teacher is dead. In other words: The situation described in the condition is known to be unreal and to exist only in the speaker's thought and imagination.

The difference in meaning between "if he is alive" and "if he were alive" depends entirely on verb forms. The *is* leaves the question of the actual facts open; the *were* expresses the unreality of the situation imagined.

From now on, we shall use the terms "open conditions" and "irreal" or "contrary-to-fact conditions" to indicate whether the question of the facts is open or whether these facts are contrary to reality and merely assumed in imagination.

In Unit 5, only open conditions are introduced. Irreal conditions, which require the use of the subjunctive, will be discussed in Unit 6. German *if*-clauses are introduced by the subordinating conjunction **wenn.** As dependent clauses, they require verb-last position.

> **Wenn Inge kommen kann, gehe ich mit ihr ins Museum.**
> **Wenn ihm nichts passiert ist, muß er schon zu Hause sein.**
> **Ich schenke dir den Roman gern, wenn du ihn haben möchtest.**
> **Wenn Sie diesen Brief bekommen, müssen Sie mir sofort antworten.**
> **Ich habe keine Angst, wenn mein Mann nach Afrika fährt.**

NOTE: Without context, some of these sentences, especially the last two,

Wenn es in Europa regnet…

…scheint im Libanon die Sonne

are ambiguous, since **wenn** means both *when* and *if*. Thus the last sentence may mean

> I won't be afraid if my husband goes to Africa

or

> I am not afraid when my husband goes to Africa.

However, the **wenn** in the illustration on p. 186 can only mean *when*. Why would *if* be illogical in this case?

90 um . . . zu, in order to

We have introduced a number of situations in which an infinitive must be used with the preposition **zu**:

> **Er braucht heute nicht zu arbeiten.**
> **Er scheint zu glauben, daß Meyer intelligent ist.**

There is another type of infinitive construction, as, for example, in the English sentence

> We eat to stay alive,

which can be expanded into

> We eat in order to stay alive.

Whenever this English expansion is possible, German *must* introduce the infinitive phrase with the preposition **um**:

> **Wir essen, um zu leben.**

This construction with **um . . . zu** must be separated from the main clause by a comma. When it is expanded by other syntactical units, **um** stands at the beginning and the infinitive stands at the end of the phrase:

> **Er fuhr nach Kairo,** *um* **dort einen Roman** *zu schreiben.*
> **Sie ging nach Mainz,** *um* **dort Archäologie** *zu studieren.*
> *Um* **das Haus kaufen** *zu können,* **braucht er Geld.**

Usually, the **um . . . zu** phrase occupies either the end or the front field.

NOTE: If the **um . . . zu** clause follows the main clause, it can be replaced by a clause of the type **weil . . . er will** (**wollte**); if it precedes the main clause, it can be replaced by an open condition.

> **Er braucht Geld, um nach Berlin zu fahren.**
> **Er braucht Geld, weil er nach Berlin fahren will.**

> **Um nach Berlin fahren zu können, braucht man Geld.**
> **Wenn man nach Berlin fahren will, braucht man Geld.**

91   **mit** as a Verbal Complement

The preposition **mit** is frequently used as a verbal complement, meaning *along*. It forms the second prong of the predicate:

> **Rosemarie geht** *auch* **mit.**
> Rosemarie is coming along too.

If the sentence is negated, **mit** is preceded by **nicht**:

> **Rosemarie geht diesmal leider nicht mit.**

Mit is often used with, and always precedes, directives:

> **Sie geht wieder mit nach Deutschland.**

Mit alone can never occupy the front field:

> IMPOSSIBLE: [Mit geht sie diesmal nicht.]

If used with an infinitive, **mit** and the infinitive are written as one word.

> **Sie möchte wieder mitgehen.**

If the sentence contains a prepositional phrase with **mit**, the verbal complement **mit** is not used.

> **Ich gehe mit ihr nach Deutschland.**

92   Word Formation

The native speaker of any language not only has an active and a passive vocabulary at his disposal, but also knows how to construct new words from known stems. Thus, by adding the suffix *-ing* to the stem of "love," English derives the form "loving"; by adding the suffix *-er*, English forms the agent noun "lover," and by adding the prefix *be-* plus the suffix *-ed,* the adjective "beloved" is formed. The suffix *-er* can not only be added to the stem *lov-;* it also appears in "worker," "reader," "listener," "drinker," "driver," and many other agent nouns. The suffix *-er* is a very important part of our active vocabulary. We know how to use it, we know its semantic function, and anyone who doesn't know how to use the suffix *-er* cannot use English properly.

In German, even more frequently than in English, prefixes and suffixes are used to form derivatives. It is therefore important to learn when and how to apply the German prefixes and suffixes. From now on we shall present in most lessons a section on word formation.

93 The Suffixes -chen and -lein

These suffixes are added to nouns to form diminutive nouns, all of which are neuter. Thus the nouns **Vater, Mutter, Bruder, Haus, Stadt,** and **Mann** are the base for the diminutives

Väterchen	**Väterlein**
Mütterchen	**Mütterlein**
Brüderchen	**Brüderlein**
Häuschen	**Häuslein**
Städtchen	**Städtlein**
Männchen	**Männlein**

Diminutives umlaut the stem vowel and remain unchanged in the plural. The suffix **-chen** is standard, **-lein** is rather poetic.

If added to nouns referring to persons, diminutives express either smallness or affection; if added to nouns designating things they express either smallness or polite "belittling":

ein Täßchen Kaffee	**ein Städtchen**
ein Gläschen Wein	**ein Häuschen**

NOTE: The noun **Fräulein** now means *Miss;* the nouns **Männchen** and **Weibchen** are zoological terms meaning the male and the female (of the species).

94 The Suffix -er

The German suffix **-er** corresponds to the English suffixes *-er* and *-or*. It is added to verb stems to form agent nouns, which denote the person or instrument that performs the action implied.

denken	**der Denker**	the thinker
lesen	**der Leser**	the reader
zeigen	**der Zeiger**	the hand (of a clock)

In some cases, the agent noun shows a vowel change from **a** to **ä**.

schlafen	**der Schläfer**	the sleeper (sleeping person).

If agent nouns refer to human beings, the suffix **-in** is added to the suffix **-er** to form feminine agent nouns.

lesen	**der Leser, -**	**die Leserin, -nen**

NOTE: The suffix **-in** may also be added to other nouns:

der Student, -en	**die Studentin, -nen**
der Freund, -e	**die Freundin, -nen**

95 Infinitives as Neuter Nouns

German infinitives can be used as neuter nouns.

Das Leben ist schön.	Life is beautiful.
mit einem Lachen	with a smile

These neuter nouns denote the activity expressed by the verb. **Beim (bei dem)**, followed by such a verbal noun, always means "in the process (or act) of" or "while."

beim Fahren	in the act of driving
beim Essen	while eating
beim Trinken	while drinking

96 Compound Nouns

Both in English and in German two nouns can be combined to form a compound noun. For example, *house* and *dog* can form two combinations—*house dog* and *doghouse,* a house dog being a kind of dog and a doghouse being a kind of house. The second part of the compound is always the basic form, which is modified by the first part. For this reason, German compounds derive their gender from the second part. Thus:

das Haus	**der Hund**	**der Haushund**
der Hund	**das Haus**	**das Hundehaus.**

Other examples found in Unit 5 include:

der Krieg	**der Roman**	**der Kriegsroman**
der Brief	**die Taube**	**die Brieftaube**
der Brief	**der Träger**	**der Briefträger**
der Westen	**die Front**	**die Westfront**
das Militär	**der Arzt**	**der Militärarzt**
der Rhein	**der Wein**	**der Rheinwein**

Try to guess the meaning and determine the gender of the following compounds:

Kaffeetasse	**Stadttheater**
Damenhut	**Sonnenblume**
Morgenzeitung	**Monatsanfang**
Theaterschule	**Liebesbrief**

NOTE: In many such compounds, a letter is inserted between the two parts—for example, **Kriegsroman, Damenhut, Liebesbrief.** While there are some historical grammatical explanations for these formations, there are no general rules. It is best, therefore, to memorize these compounds as they occur.

EXERCISES

A. Read the following problems:

2 + 4 = 6	1 + 14 = 15	19 − 12 = 7
12 + 4 = 16	9 + 11 = 20	16 − 10 = 6
7 + 3 = 10	18 + 1 = 19	8 − 5 = 3
7 + 10 = 17	16 + 2 = 18	20 − 3 = 17
5 + 8 = 13	17 + 2 = 19	11 − 11 = 0

B. The following is an excerpt from a railroad timetable. Form questions and statements using the information given.

> **Wann fährt der Zug nach München in Köln ab?—Um 2 Uhr.**
> **Der Zug kommt um 8 Uhr 16 in Ulm an.**
> **Wie lange ist der Zug in Frankfurt?—12 Minuten.**

Köln	ab	2.00	München	ab	1.20
Bonn	an	2.18	Ulm	an	4.04
	ab	2.20		ab	4.05
Frankfurt	an	4.15	Stuttgart	an	5.08
	ab	4.20		ab	5.14
Heidelberg	an	5.12	Heidelberg	an	8.02
	ab	5.17		ab	8.06
Stuttgart	an	7.01	Frankfurt	an	9.08
	ab	7.06		ab	9.20
Ulm	an	8.16	Bonn	an	11.17
	ab	8.17		ab	11.20
München	an	10.03	Köln	an	12.00

SEE LAB
EXERCISE
5.1

(p. 626)

C. This exercise is meant as a quick drill of the present, past, and perfect forms of weak verbs. Transform according to the following pattern:

> **antworten — er antwortet, er antwortete, er hat geantwortet**

arbeiten	—	ich	heiraten	— wir
brauchen	—	wir	hoffen	— ich
danken	—	er	kochen	— sie
fragen	—	sie	lachen	— er
gehören	—	es	leben	— wir
glauben	—	du	lernen	— wir
hassen	—	er	lieben	— ich

SEE LAB
EXERCISE
5.2

(p. 626)

machen	—	wir	studieren	—	er
rauchen	—	er	tanzen	—	wir
reden	—	sie	wählen	—	ich
regnen	—	es	warten	—	du
sagen	—	ich	wohnen	—	wir
schenken	—	er	zahlen	—	er
schicken	—	wir	zeigen	—	sie

D. Restate the following sentences in the past tense. In each sentence, add **damals,** as in the following example:

> **Erika studiert in München.—Erika studierte damals in München.**

SEE LAB
EXERCISES
5.3–5.5

(pp. 626-627)

1. Hans hat nie Hunger.
2. Er besucht seinen Vater in Berlin.
3. Wir kaufen ein Haus in München.
4. Dieses Haus gehört meinem Vater.
5. Er antwortet mir nicht.
6. Ist deine Mutter nicht in Berlin?
7. Wir können leider nicht kommen.
8. Ich will ihm die Stadt zeigen.
9. Er soll zu Hause bleiben.
10. Ich darf es ihm nicht sagen.
11. Wir müssen leider nach Hause fahren.
12. Er braucht nicht zu arbeiten.

E. Form the present, past, and perfect. All verbs in this exercise are irregular.

> **bleiben   —   wir bleiben, wir blieben, wir sind geblieben**

anfangen	—	ich	scheinen	—	es
anrufen	—	er	schlafen	—	er
bringen	—	er	schreiben	—	ich
essen	—	er	sehen	—	er
fahren	—	du	sein	—	ihr
geben	—	er	sitzen	—	wir
gehen	—	wir	sprechen	—	ich
helfen	—	er	sterben	—	er
heißen	—	sie	trinken	—	wir
kennen	—	ich	tun	—	ich
kommen	—	wir	verstehen	—	er
lassen	—	er	werden	—	er
lesen	—	er	wissen	—	du

F. Restate the following sentences in the past tense:

SEE LAB
EXERCISES
5.6–5.9

(p. 627)

1. Inge geht zum Bahnhof.
2. Er versteht Professor Hansen sehr gut.
3. Hans hört mich nicht.
4. Erika hilft mir bei der Arbeit.
5. Ingelheim antwortet nicht.
6. Herr Bergmann kommt um 9 Uhr aus dem Kino.
7. Herr Lenz fährt mit seinem Freund durch die Stadt.
8. Ich sehe meine Mutter in Berlin.
9. Er trinkt keinen Wein.
10. Ich hole ihn in Köln ab.
11. Er bekommt jeden Tag einen Brief von seiner Freundin.
12. Hans lädt mich oft zum Essen ein.
13. Er denkt lange nach.
14. So etwas passiert nicht oft.
15. Hans und Inge stehen vor dem Theater.

G. Transform the twenty sentences of this exercise according to the following pattern:

Er wohnt in Berlin.
a. Ich glaube, er wohnt in Berlin.
b. Ich glaube nicht, daß er in Berlin wohnt.
c. Ich möchte wissen, ob er in Berlin wohnt.

1. Hans studiert Mathematik.
2. Der Wagen gehört Frau Lenz.
3. Sie kann sie sehen.
4. Er will mir die Stadt zeigen.
5. Frau Lenz geht mit Frau Hoffmann ins Kino.
6. Er muß heute nach Hamburg.
7. Hans will ohne Inge ins Theater gehen.
8. Herr Meyer hat zu viel Wein getrunken.
9. Sie sind gestern in Berlin gewesen.
10. Er hat in Berlin einen Freund besucht.
11. Er mußte gestern zu Hause bleiben.
12. Schmidt hat seiner Frau ein Auto geschenkt.
13. Ingelheim ist wirklich spurlos verschwunden.
14. Es regnet schon wieder.
15. Er hat viel Geld.
16. Sie wollten in Köln ein Haus kaufen.
17. Er hat heute abend nur Tee getrunken.
18. Herr Müller hat ihn verstanden.
19. Morgen müssen wir viel arbeiten.
20. Er hat viel Deutsch gelernt.

H. Ask correct questions for the following answers. Your questions should ask for the italicized parts of the answers.

> **Er geht *heute abend* ins Kino.**
> **Wann geht er ins Kino?**

Then restate the question, starting with **Ich möchte wissen:**

> **Ich möchte wissen, wann er ins Kino geht.**

1. Ihr Mann ist *gestern* nach Köln gefahren.
2. Erika war gestern *in Berlin.*
3. Es (das Buch) gehört *meinem Vater.*
4. Er will dir die Stadt *morgen* zeigen.
5. Er will es *seiner Freundin* schicken.
6. Er hat ihr *ein Buch* geschenkt.
7. Ihr Mann arbeitet in *Bonn.*
8. Er heißt *Fritz.*
9. *Mein Vater* hat das gesagt.
10. Er geht *mit Inge* ins Kino.

I. Join the following pairs of sentences to form open conditions. The first sentence should always become the **wenn**-clause.

> **Es regnet morgen. Wir gehen ins Kino.**
> **Wenn es morgen regnet, gehen wir ins Kino.**

SEE LAB
EXERCISES
5.10–5.12

(p. 627)

1. Du hast Geld. Du kannst ein Haus kaufen.
2. Du hast kein Geld. Du kannst das Haus nicht kaufen.
3. Er studiert Mathematik. Er muß intelligent sein.
4. Nancy ist intelligent. Sie lernt Deutsch.
5. Morgen regnet es nicht. Wir besuchen euch.
6. Ihr wollt ins Kino gehen. Wir gehen mit.
7. Herr Meyer wohnt in Berlin. Ich kann ihn besuchen.
8. Er ist dein Freund. Er hilft dir bestimmt.
9. Du liebst mich. Du fährst nicht nach Casablanca.
10. Man hat kein Geld. Man kann nicht an die Riviera fahren.

J. Of the following pairs of sentences, change the second to an infinitive with **um . . . zu.**

> **Inge fuhr nach Frankfurt. Sie wollte ins Theater gehen.**
> **Inge fuhr nach Frankfurt, um ins Theater zu gehen.**

SEE LAB
EXERCISES
5.13–5.14

(p. 627)

1. Ingelheim fuhr nach Afrika. Er wollte einen Roman schreiben.
2. Er kam nach Frankfurt. Er wollte seinen Vater besuchen.
3. Seine Tochter ging nach Mainz. Sie wollte Archäologie studieren.
4. John fuhr nach Deutschland. Er wollte Deutsch lernen.
5. Hans ging zum Telephon. Er wollte Inge anrufen.
6. Werner hat mich gestern angerufen. Er wollte mich ins Kino einladen.
7. Der Reporter folgte ihm ins Hotel. Er wollte mit ihm sprechen.
8. Ich besuchte Ingelheim. Ich wollte seine Frau kennenlernen.
9. Ich fuhr nach Hause. Ich wollte mit Tante Amalie ins Museum gehen.
10. Ingelheim hat geheiratet. Er wollte nicht mehr allein frühstücken müssen.

K. Express in German. Where appropriate, defend your choice of the German past or perfect.

1. Are you taking her along?
2. Hans went along to Cologne.
3. Does he want to go along to Berlin, too?
4. At that time the house belonged to my father.
5. I simply couldn't believe it.
6. I'd like to know why you couldn't believe it.
7. If you want to, you may go.
8. I don't know where he was.
9. I don't know whether he was in Berlin.
10. At that time I didn't know he was in Berlin, too.
11. It is ten after eleven, and I must go home.
12. At that time, he was visiting his friend in Berlin.
13. Today he visited his friend.
14. They went to Berlin today.
15. I bought the book yesterday, but I haven't read it yet.
16. Unfortunately, I didn't understand him.
17. He never needed much money.
18. Why didn't you stay home yesterday, Karl?
19. The train left at 8:11.
20. I didn't understand why she didn't want to come.
21. How am I supposed to know whether he went to Casablanca?
22. We would like to know why she does not drink wine.
23. I hope I'll never see him again.
24. Do you believe that Karl is very intelligent?
25. *That* he is intelligent I know.
26. But that he is *very* intelligent, I cannot believe.
27. Whether Meyer really went to Casablanca (that) I cannot tell you.
28. Why he wanted to go to the movies with Inge, I don't know.
29. I cannot believe that you only do what you want to do.
30. If you are home tomorrow I would like to visit you.
31. I'd like to visit Ingrid, but I don't know whether she is at home.
32. If you want (me to), I'll come along to the movies.

33. Before the war he was a writer.
34. Then he became a soldier.
35. I married him because I loved him.
36. I didn't meet him at that time, for he was in Norway.
37. I know he is here, but I haven't seen him yet.
38. She has never been afraid yet.
39. Not until three weeks later did he tell us his story.
40. He had not visited us for years when I accidentally saw him in Berlin.
41. I have known her for a long time, but I don't know who she is.
42. When he met her in Berlin she was still a child.
43. He only wants to go if I go too.
44. He didn't want to tell us where he wanted to go.
45. I'd like to know when he'll come home.
46. I've just read in the paper that her friend has been in Africa for three months.
47. You don't need to tell me how often he goes to the theater.
48. If I see him, I'll tell him that you were here and that you wanted to speak with him.
49. I wanted to visit him (in order) to thank him, but unfortunately he wasn't home.
50. I can't visit you tomorrow, because tomorrow I have to be in Munich.

VOCABULARY

abholen to pick up, to call for
das Abitur final comprehensive examination in the secondary school
achtzehn eighteen
als when; than; as
  als er kam when he came (single event in the past)
  mehr als more than
  ich als dein Vater I as your father
der Amerikaner, – American
die Angst, ¨e fear, anxiety
  Angst haben vor to be afraid of
ankommen to arrive
das Auge, –n eye
bekommen to get, to receive
das Bett, –en bed
die Brieftaube, –n carrier pigeon
diesmal this time
der Dom, –e cathedral
dort there

dreizehn thirteen
durchmachen to go through, to suffer
einfach easy, simple
einladen to invite
elf eleven
das Ende, –n end
erwarten to expect
erzählen to tell, to relate
der Fehler, – mistake
finden to find
der Fisch, –e fish
fischen to fish
das Fräulein, – Miss, young lady
das Frühstück, –e breakfast
  frühstücken to eat breakfast
fünfzehn fifteen
fürchten to fear
füttern to feed
der Garten, ¨ garden
gefährlich dangerous
gerade just; straight

gratulieren to congratulate
halb half
hinter behind
das Kapi'tel, – chapter
klein little
der Kopf, ¨e head
  die Kopfschmerzen (*pl.*) headache
das Lachen laughter
laufen to run
das Leben, – life
das Mädchen, – girl
die Maschi'ne, –n machine, typewriter
die Mathematik' mathematics
nachdenken to reflect, to meditate
nehmen to take; to seize
  gefangennehmen to capture, to take prisoner
neu new
  das ist mir neu that's news to me

neunzehn nineteen
Norwegen Norway
null zero
ob whether
passieren to happen
plus plus
recht haben to be right
die Reise, –n trip
    eine Reise machen to take
    a trip
der Roman, –e novel
das Schiff, –e ship, boat
schilaufen to ski
schön beautiful, pretty; good,
    OK
der Schriftsteller, – writer
der Schüler, – pupil, student
    (in a secondary school)

sechzehn sixteen
siebzehn seventeen
der Soldat, –en soldier (de-
    clined like der Mensch)
die Sonne, –n sun
die Spur, –en trace
    spurlos without a trace
stehen to stand
die Straße, –n street
suchen to look for, to seek, to
    search
der Tee tea
tragen to carry
über over
überall everywhere
um . . . zu in order to
vernünftig reasonable

verschwinden to disappear
    verschwunden (adj.) lost
vielleicht perhaps
vierzehn fourteen
weil (conj.) because
die Welt, –en world
weniger minus, less
der Westen the West
    die Westfront the Western
    Front
Auf Wiederhören! Good-by!
    (telephone)
Auf Wiedersehen! Good-by!
    (in person)
wohl well; probably
zufällig by coincidence, by
    chance, accidentally
zwölf twelve

LIST OF STRONG AND IRREGULAR VERBS

abfahren to depart, to leave
    fuhr ab, ist abgefahren, er
    fährt ab
anfangen to begin, to start
    fing an, hat angefangen, er
    fängt an
angehen to go on
    ging an, ist angegangen, er
    geht an
ankommen to arrive
    kam an, ist angekommen,
    er kommt an
anrufen to call up (on the
    telephone)
    rief an, hat angerufen, er
    ruft an
ausgehen to go out
    ging aus, ist ausgegangen,
    er geht aus
befehlen to order, to com-
    mand
    befahl, hat befohlen, er be-
    fiehlt
beginnen to begin, to start
    begann, hat begonnen, er
    beginnt
bekommen to get, to receive

bekam, hat bekommen, er
    bekommt
bleiben to stay, to remain
    blieb, ist geblieben, er
    bleibt
bringen to bring
    brachte, hat gebracht, er
    bringt
denken to think
    dachte, hat gedacht, er
    denkt
einladen to invite
    lud ein, hat eingeladen, er
    lädt ein
essen to eat
    aß, hat gegessen, er ißt
fahren to drive, to go (by
    train, boat, plane, car)
    fuhr, ist gefahren, er fährt
finden to find
    fand, hat gefunden, er
    findet
geben to give
    gab, hat gegeben, er gibt
gefangennehmen to capture,
    to take prisoner
    nahm gefangen, hat ge-

fangengenommen, er
    nimmt gefangen
gehen to go, to walk
    ging, ist gegangen, er geht
haben to have
    hatte, hat gehabt, er hat
heißen to be called; to mean
    hieß, hat geheißen, er heißt
helfen to help
    half, hat geholfen, er hilft
kennen to know, to be ac-
    quainted with
    kannte, hat gekannt, er
    kennt
kommen to come
    kam, ist gekommen, er
    kommt
lassen to let, to leave
    ließ, hat gelassen, er läßt
laufen to run
    lief, ist gelaufen, er läuft
lesen to read
    las, hat gelesen, er liest
lügen to tell a lie
    log, hat gelogen, er lügt
nachdenken to reflect, to me-
    ditate

dachte nach, hat nachge-
dacht, er denkt nach
nehmen to take, to seize
nahm, hat genommen, er
nimmt
scheinen to seem; to shine
schien, hat geschienen, er
scheint
schilaufen to ski
lief Schi, ist schigelaufen,
er läuft Schi
schlafen to sleep
schlief, hat geschlafen, er
schläft
schreiben to write
schrieb, hat geschrieben, er
schreibt
sehen to see
sah, hat gesehen, er sieht

sein to be
war, ist gewesen, er ist
sitzen to sit
saß, hat gesessen, er sitzt
sprechen to speak, to talk
sprach, hat gesprochen, er
spricht
stehen to stand
stand, hat gestanden, er
steht
sterben to die
starb, ist gestorben, er
stirbt
tragen to carry
trug, hat getragen, er trägt
trinken to drink
trank, hat getrunken, er
trinkt

tun to do
tat, hat getan, er tut
verschwinden to disappear
verschwand, ist verschwunden, er verschwindet
verstehen to understand
verstand, hat verstanden,
er versteht
werden to become
wurde, ist geworden, er
wird
wiedersehen to see again
sah wieder, hat wiederge-
sehen, er sieht wieder
wissen to know
wußte, hat gewußt, er weiß
zwingen to force
zwang, hat gewungen, er
zwingt

REVIEW

The following sentences review the use of **schon, kein . . . mehr, nicht mehr, noch, immer noch.** Analyze them carefully and form your own variations.

Erika ist noch nicht hier.
Erika ist schon hier.
Erika ist noch hier.
Nein, Erika ist nicht mehr hier.
Sie ist gestern schon (schon gestern) wieder nach Hause gefahren.

Ist Fritz schon Arzt?
Fritz ist doch erst zwanzig.
Er kann doch noch kein Arzt sein!

Fritz ist erst vor zwei Stunden abgefahren.
Fritz kann noch nicht in Paris sein.
Fritz muß jetzt schon in Paris sein.
Fritz ist noch in Paris.
Fritz ist noch immer (immer noch) in Paris.
Nein, Fritz ist jetzt nicht mehr in Paris.
Fritz ist noch nie in Paris gewesen.

Ich habe die Zeitung schon gelesen.
Ich habe die Zeitung noch nicht gelesen.
Ich habe noch keine Zeit gehabt.

Meyer ist schon letztes Jahr gestorben.
Meyer ist schon vor zwei Jahren gestorben.

Weißt du noch, wo sie wohnen?
Weißt du nicht mehr, wo sie wohnen?
Wir wohnen schon seit zwei Jahren in Köln.
Wir wohnen schon zwei Jahre hier.

Er ist schon immer ein Idealist gewesen.
Intelligent ist sie schon immer gewesen.

Aber Mutter, ich bin doch kein *Kind* mehr.
Doch, du bist *doch* noch ein Kind.

SEE
ANALYSIS
45
(pp. 85–86)

VOCABULARY CHECK LIST, UNITS 1-5

This is a complete list of the vocabulary used in Units 1–5.

ab
der Abend, –e
abends
aber
abfahren
abholen
das Abitur
ach so
acht
achtzehn
alle
allein
alles
als
also
der Amerikaner, –
an
der Anfang, ⸚e
anfangen
angehen
die Angst, ⸚e
Angst haben
ankommen
anmachen
anrufen
antworten
der April'
arbeiten
    die Arbeit, –en
der Arzt, ⸚e
auch
das Auge, –n
aus
ausgehen
ausmachen
außer
außerdem'
das Auto, –s

der Bahnhof, ⸚e
    zum Bahnhof
    im Bahnhof
    auf dem Bahnhof
bald
befehlen
beginnen
bei

das Beispiel, –e
    zum Beispiel
    (z. B.)
bekommen
besetzen
besetzt
besuchen
das Bett, –en
das Bier, –e
das Bild, –er
bis
bitte
bleiben
die Blume, –n
böse
brauchen
der Brief, –e
die Brieftaube, –n
der Briefträger, –
bringen
der Bruder, ⸚
das Buch, ⸚er
das Büro, –s
die Butter

da
damals
die Dame, –n
danken
    danke!
    vielen Dank!
dann
darum
daß
denken
denn
Deutsch
    Deutschland
dieser, diese, dieses
diesmal
doch
der Dok'tor, –en
der Dom, –e
dort
drei
dreizehn
der Dummkopf, ⸚e
durch

durchmachen
dürfen

egoistisch
einfach
einladen
einmal
eins
elf
das Ende, –n
erst
    erst dann
erwarten
erzählen
essen
das Essen
etwas

fahren
    fahren lernen
der Fehler, –
der Film, –e
finden
der Fisch, –e
    fischen
fragen
    die Frage, –n
die Frau, –en
das Fräulein, –
frei
der Freund, –e
    die Freundin, –nen
früh
früher
das Frühstück, –e
    frühstücken
fünf
für
fünfzehn
fürchten
füttern

der Garten, ⸚
geben
gefährlich
gefangennehmen
gegen
gehen

gehören
    gehören zu
das Geld
gerade
gern(e)
das Gesetz, –e
gestern
gesund
das Glas, ⸚er
glauben
das Glück
glücklich
gottseidank
der Gott, ⸚er
gratulieren
gut

haben
halb
hassen
das Haus, ⸚er
    ich gehe nach Hause
    ich bin zu Hause
heiraten
heißen
helfen
der Herr, –en
heute
    heute abend
    heute morgen
hier
hinter
hoffen
hoffentlich
hören
das Hotel, –s
der Hund, –e
der Hunger
    ich habe Hunger
    hungrig
der Hut, ⸚e

die Idee', die Ide'en
immer
    immer noch
    noch immer
in

intelligent'
die Intelligenz'
interessant'
Ita'lien
Italie'nisch

ja
die Jacht, –en
das Jahr, –e
je, jemals
jeder, jede, jedes
jetzt
jung

der Kaffee
kalt
das Kapi'tel, –
kaufen
kein
kennen
  kennenlernen
das Kind, –er
das Kino, –s
  ich gehe ins Kino
die Kirche, –n
  ich gehe in die
    Kirche
klein
kochen
kommen
können
der Kopf, ⸚e
  die Kopfschmerzen
kosten
krank
der Krieg, –e

das Lachen
lachen
lang
  lange
  jahrelang
der Lärm
lassen
die Later'ne, –n
laufen
leben
das Leben, –
leider
lernen
lesen
letzt–
  letztes Jahr

die Leute
das Licht, –er
die Liebe
lieben
lieber
lügen

das Mädchen, –
machen
der Mai
man
der Mann, ⸚er
die Mark
die Maschine, –n
die Mathematik'
die Medizin'
  Medizin'
mehr
  mehr als
der Mensch, –en
die Minute, –n
mit
mögen
der Monat, –e
der Morgen, –
  morgen
  morgen abend
  guten Morgen!
das Muse'um, die
  Muse'en
müssen
die Mutter, ⸚

na und?
nach
nachdenken
nächst–
  nächstes Jahr
die Nacht, ⸚e
  heute Nacht
die Natur, –en
natür'lich
neben
nehmen
nein
neu
  das ist mir neu
neun
neunzehn
nicht
  noch nicht
  nicht mehr

nichts
nie
noch
Norwegen
null
die Nummer, –n
nur

ob
oder
oft
ohne
der Onkel, –

passieren
die Physik'
plus
prima
der Profes'sor, die
  Professo'ren
die Psychologie'

rauchen
recht
  das ist mir recht
  recht haben
rechts
reden
regnen
  der Regen
die Reise, –n
  eine Reise machen
richtig
der Roman, –e

sagen
scheinen
schenken
schicken
das Schiff, –e
schilaufen
schlafen
schon
schön
schreiben
der Schriftsteller, –
die Schule, –n
der Schüler, –
  die Schülerin, –nen
sechs
sechzehn
sehen

sehr
sein
seit
  seit langem
der September
sieben
siebzehn
sitzen
so
sofort
der Sohn, ⸚e
der Soldat, –en
sollen
der Sommer, –
die Sonne, –n
der Sonntag, –e
  Sonntag abend
  Sonntag morgen
  jeden Sonntag
  sonntags
spät
  später
sprechen
die Spur, –en
  spurlos
die Stadt, ⸚e
stehen
sterben
die Straße, –n
der Student, –en
  die Studentin, –nen
studier'en
die Stunde, –n
suchen

der Tag, –e
die Tante, –n
tanzen
die Tasse, –n
das Taxi, –s, die
  Taxe, –n
der Tee
telefonieren
  das Telefon, –e
das Theater, –
das Tier, –e
die Tochter, ⸚
tragen
trinken
tun

über

überall
übrigens
die Uhr, –en
   um sechs Uhr
   wieviel Uhr
um
um . . . zu
und
die Universität', –en

der Vater, ¨
die Vernunft
vernünftig
verschwinden
verschwunden
verstehen
viel
   soviel
   zuviel
vielleicht

vier
vierzehn
von
vor
   vor einem Jahr

der Wagen, –
wählen
wahr
wann
warten auf
warum
was
das Wasser, –
weil
der Wein, –e
die Welt, –en
weniger
wenn
wer

werden
das Wetter
der Westen
   die Westfront
wie
wieder
wiedersehen
   Auf Wiedersehen!
   Auf Wiederhören!
wieviel
   wieviel Uhr
der Winter, –
   im Winter
wirklich
wissen
wo
die Woche, –n
woher
wohin
wohl

wohnen
wollen

zahlen
zehn
zeigen
die Zeit, –en
die Zeitung, –en
die Zigar're, –n
die Zigaret'te, –n
zu
zufällig
der Zug, ¨e
zurück
   wieder zurück
zwanzig
zwei
zwingen
zwischen
zwölf

frische
Junghennen
Eier
10 Stück
7.98

NEW LAID DUTCH EGGS

UNIT 6: The Future Tense—The Subjunctive

[1] The Future Tense

Ich glaube, ich werde sie nie wiedersehen.	I believe I will never see them (her) again.	SEE ANALYSIS 97
Diesen Sonntag werde ich nie vergessen.	I shall never forget this Sunday.	
Diesen Sonntag werde ich leider nie vergessen können.	Unfortunately, I shall never be able to forget this Sunday.	(pp. 220-221)

Ich weiß nicht, was Sie tun werden, Frau Ingelheim. Aber ich hoffe, Sie werden nicht zu Ihrer Mutter fahren.

I don't know what you will do, Mrs. Ingelheim. But I hope you will not return to your mother.

Nein, Herr Behrens, ich werde es nicht vergessen. Ich werde Sie morgen um 9 Uhr 10 anrufen.

No, Mr. Behrens, I shall not forget it. I'll give you a ring at 9:10 tomorrow.

Nächste Woche, meine Damen und Herren, werde ich über das Problem sprechen, ob Tiere nur Intelligenz oder auch Vernunft haben.

Next week, ladies and gentlemen, I shall talk about the problem of whether animals possess only intelligence, or whether they have reason, too.

Meyer war schon vor zwanzig Jahren ein Realist, und er wird heute auch noch ein Realist sein.

Meyer was already a realist twenty years ago, and he probably still is a realist.

Inge ist schon vor einer Stunde abgefahren, also wird sie jetzt schon lange zu Hause sein.

Inge left an hour ago, so she has probably been home for a long time now.

So, Ingelheim schreibt schon wieder einen Roman? Ich möchte wissen, was er dieses Mal schreibt. Von seinen Brieftauben wird er bestimmt nicht schreiben.

So Ingelheim is writing another novel? I should like to know what he is writing this time. I'm sure he won't write about his carrier pigeons.

Ich möchte wissen, warum Hans mich immer noch nicht angerufen hat; ob er mir böse ist?—Warum soll er dir böse sein? Er wird (wohl) noch schlafen.

I'd like to know why Hans hasn't called me up yet. I wonder whether he's mad at me.—Why should he be mad at you? He's probably still asleep.

(Facing) **Kleiner Mann bei großem Einkauf**

Den Emil habe ich schon wochenlang nicht gesehen. Wo kann der denn nur sein?— Er wird wieder in Bonn arbeiten müssen.

I haven't seen Emil in weeks. Where could he be?—He probably has to work in Bonn again.

[2] The Subjunctive—Wishes with **Ich wollte** or **Ich wünschte** (Present Time)

Be prepared to produce orally the subjunctive statement when you hear the indicative statement, and vice versa.

SEE ANALYSIS 98–102

(pp. 221-232)

Ich wollte, wir wären in Italien, aber wir sind nicht in Italien.

I wish we were in Italy, but we are not in Italy.

Ich wünschte, sie hätte Geld, aber sie hat kein Geld.

I wish she had money, but she doesn't have any money.

Ich wollte, mein Vater kaufte mir ein Auto (würde mir ein Auto kaufen), aber er kauft mir kein Auto (wird mir kein Auto kaufen).

I wish my father would buy me a car, but he won't buy me a car.

Ich wünschte, wir machten diesen Sommer wieder eine Reise, aber wir machen keine Reise (werden keine Reise machen).

I wish we were going to take another trip this summer, but we aren't going on a trip.

Ich wollte, Monika studierte Physik oder Psychologie, aber sie studiert Medizin.

I wish Monika were studying physics or psychology, but she is studying medicine.

Ich wünschte, wir brauchten nicht nach Köln zu fahren, aber wir müssen.

I wish we didn't have to go to Cologne, but we have to.

Ich wollte, er bliebe noch eine Woche hier (würde noch eine Woche hierbleiben), aber er bleibt nicht hier.

I wish he'd stay here for another week, but he isn't going to.

Ich wünschte, er brächte Monika mit (würde Monika mitbringen), aber er bringt sie nicht mit.

I wish he'd bring Monika along, but he won't.

Ich wünschte, mein Mann äße auch einmal mit *mir* im Regina (würde auch einmal mit *mir* im Regina essen), aber im Regina ißt er nur mit seinen Freunden.

I wish my husband would take *me* to dinner at the Regina, for a change, but at the Regina he only eats with his friends.

Ich wünschte, du tränkst nicht soviel Kaffee (würdest nicht soviel Kaffee trinken). Du trinkst zu viel Kaffee.

I wish you didn't (wouldn't) drink so much coffee. You drink too much coffee.

Ich wünschte, wir könnten jedes Jahr nach Italien fahren; Meyers können jedes Jahr fahren.

I wish we could go to Italy every year; the Meyers can go every year.

Ich wollte, du müßtest auch jeden Tag um sechs aufstehen, aber du brauchst erst um acht aufzustehen.

I wish you had to get up at six o'clock every day, too, but you don't have to get up until eight.

[3] Wishes with **Ich wollte** or **Ich wünschte** (Past Time)

Be prepared to produce orally the subjunctive statement when you hear the indicative statement, and vice versa.

Ich wünschte, ich hätte nicht soviel gegessen; aber ich habe leider zuviel gegessen.

I wish I hadn't eaten so much. However, I have eaten too much.

SEE ANALYSIS 102

(pp. 231-232)

Ich wollte, er wäre noch eine Woche hiergeblieben, aber er ist nicht hiergeblieben.

I wish he had stayed for another week, but he didn't.

Ich wünschte, er wäre nicht so jung gestorben, aber er ist jung gestorben.

I wish he hadn't died so young, but he did.

Ich wollte, mein Mann wäre auch einmal mit *mir* nach Kairo gefahren, aber mit *mir* ist er *nie* nach Kairo gefahren.

I wish my husband had taken me to Cairo, too, for a change, but he never did.

Ich wollte, du hättest mir mehr Geld geschickt, aber du hast mir nur zehn Mark geschickt.

I wish you had sent me more money, but you sent me only ten marks.

Ich wünschte, ich hätte sie nie kennengelernt, aber leider habe ich sie kennengelernt.

I wish I had never met her, but unfortunately I did.

Ich wollte, er wäre zu Hause geblieben, aber leider ist er nicht zu Hause geblieben.

I wish he'd stayed home, but unfortunately he didn't.

Ich wünschte, ich hätte *auch* einen Monat in Casablanca bleiben können, aber ich konnte nicht.

I wish I, too, had been able to stay in Casablanca for a month, but I couldn't.

Ich wollte, ich hätte letzten Sommer nicht nach Casablanca zu fahren brauchen, aber ich mußte.

I wish I hadn't had to go to Casablanca last summer, but I had to.

Ich wollte, deine Tochter hätte uns einmal besuchen dürfen, aber sie durfte nicht.

I wish your daughter had been permitted to visit us, but she wasn't.

Ich wünschte, sie hätte nicht jeden Abend tanzen wollen, aber sie wollte immer tanzen.

I wish she hadn't wanted to go dancing every night, but she always wanted to dance.

[4] Wishes Introduced by **Es wäre nett, wenn . . .**

After studying these sentences, complete the variations at the end of the section.

SEE
ANALYSIS
102

(pp. 231-232)

Ich hoffe, wir finden sofort eine Wohnung. Es wäre nett, wenn wir sofort eine Wohnung fänden (finden würden).	I hope we'll find an apartment right away. It would be nice if we found a place to live immediately.
Ich hoffe, du fliegst. Dann bist du in zwei Stunden in Hamburg, nicht wahr? Es wäre nett, wenn du fliegen würdest (flögst). Dann wärst du in zwei Stunden in Hamburg, nicht?	I hope you'll take a plane. Then you'll be in Hamburg in two hours, won't you? It would be nice if you went by plane. Then you would be in Hamburg in two hours, wouldn't you?
Ich hoffe, wir frühstücken morgen nicht wieder um sechs. Es wäre nett, wenn wir morgen erst um acht frühstückten (frühstücken würden).	I hope we are not going to have breakfast at six again tomorrow. It would be nice if we didn't have breakfast until eight tomorrow.
Ich hoffe, sie lädt uns ein. Es wäre nett, wenn sie uns einlüde (einladen würde).	I hope she invites us. It would be nice if she invited us (if she'd invite us).
Ich stehe von Montag bis Freitag jeden Tag um sechs Uhr auf und mache dir das Frühstück. Es wäre nett, wenn du samstags und sonntags *vor* mir aufständest und *mir* das Frühstück machtest.	I get up at six every day, Monday through Friday, and fix breakfast for you. It would be nice if on Saturdays and Sundays you would get up before me and fix breakfast for me.
Letztes Jahr hast du meinen Geburtstag vergessen. Es wäre nett, wenn du ihn dieses Jahr einmal nicht vergäßest (vergessen würdest).	Last year you forgot my birthday. It would be nice if this year you would not forget it for a change.

VARIATIONS

Ich hoffe, du kommst morgen. Es wäre nett, wenn _____.

Ich hoffe, du kannst morgen kommen. _____.

Ich hoffe, du besuchst uns bald. _____.

Ich hoffe, er braucht morgen nicht zu arbeiten. _____.

Ich hoffe, du bringst mir etwas mit. _____.

Invent further variations of your own.

[5] Irreal Conditions

SEE
ANALYSIS
98, 103

(pp. 221-222,
232-234)

Sie schreibt mir nicht. Ich schreibe ihr auch nicht.

    Wenn sie mir schriebe, schriebe ich ihr auch.

    Wenn sie mir schriebe, würde ich ihr auch schreiben.

    If she wrote to me, I'd write to her, too.

Sie hat mir nicht geschrieben. Ich habe ihr auch nicht geschrieben.

    Wenn sie mir geschrieben hätte, hätte ich ihr auch geschrieben.

    If she had written to me, I would have written to her, too.

Das Essen ist schlecht. Ich bleibe nicht hier.

    Wenn das Essen nicht so schlecht wäre, bliebe ich hier.

    Wenn das Essen nicht so schlecht wäre, würde ich hierbleiben.

    If the food weren't so bad, I would stay here.

Das Essen war schlecht. Ich bin nicht dageblieben.

    Wenn das Essen nicht so schlecht gewesen wäre, wäre ich dageblieben.

    If the food hadn't been so bad, I would have stayed.

Es regnet. Wir können nicht arbeiten.

    Wenn es nicht regnete, könnten wir arbeiten.

    If it weren't raining, we could work.

Gestern hat es geregnet, und wir konnten nicht arbeiten.

    Wenn es gestern nicht geregnet hätte, hätten wir arbeiten können.

    If it hadn't rained yesterday, we could have worked.

[6] Irreal Conditions in Context

Inges Vater hat Geld. Sie kann jede Woche ins Theater gehen, und ich muß zu Hause bleiben. Wenn mein Vater mehr Geld hätte, könnte ich auch jede Woche ins Theater gehen und brauchte nicht zu Hause zu bleiben.—Inges Vater hatte Geld. Inge konnte jede Woche ins Theater gehen, und ich mußte zu Hause bleiben. Wenn mein Vater mehr Geld gehabt hätte, hätte ich auch jede Woche ins Theater gehen können und hätte nicht zu Hause zu bleiben brauchen.

Inge's father has money. She can go to the theater every week, and I have to stay at home. If my father had more money, I, too, could go to the theater every week and would not have to stay at home.— Inge's father had a lot of money. Inge could go to the theater every week, and I had to stay at home. If my father had had more money, I, too, could have gone to the theater every week and would not have had to stay at home.

SEE ANALYSIS 103
(pp. 232-234)

Ich weiß nicht, warum mein Mann nach Kairo gefahren ist. Und wenn ich es wüßte, Herr Behrens, würde ich es Ihnen doch nicht sagen.—Ich wußte ja nicht, warum mein Mann nach Kairo gefahren war. Und wenn ich es gewußt hätte, Herr Behrens, hätte ich es Ihnen doch nicht gesagt.

I don't know why my husband went to Cairo. If I knew, Mr. Behrens, I wouldn't tell you anyway.—I really didn't know why my husband had gone to Cairo. If I had known, Mr. Behrens, I wouldn't have told you anyway.

Nein, heute werde ich dich nicht nach
Hause bringen. Ich habe keine Zeit.
Wenn ich Zeit hätte, brächte ich dich
natürlich nach Hause (würde ich dich
natürlich nach Hause bringen).—Nein,
gestern habe ich Inge nicht nach Hause
gebracht. Ich hatte keine Zeit. Wenn ich
Zeit gehabt hätte, hätte ich sie natürlich
nach Hause gebracht.

No, I am not going to take you home today.
I have no time. If I had the time, I would
take you home, of course.—No, yesterday
I did not take Inge home. I had no time.
If I had had the time, I would have taken
her home, of course.

[7] hätte in Dependent Clauses with Double Infinitive

SEE
ANALYSIS
103, 108

(pp. 232-234,
239-240)

Wenn Inge nicht hätte nach München
fahren müssen, hätte Meyer sie nie kennengelernt.*

If Inge hadn't had to go to Munich, Meyer
would never have met her.

Wenn du nicht hättest kommen können,
wäre ich sehr unglücklich gewesen.

If you had not been able to come, I would
have been very unhappy.

Wenn er gestern abend nicht hätte zu
Hause bleiben müssen, hätte er mit uns
ins Kino gehen können.

If he had not had to stay home last night,
he could have gone to a show with us.

VARIATIONS

Hans konnte nicht kommen. Es wäre nett gewesen, wenn _____.

Erika durfte nicht mitgehen. Es wäre nett gewesen, wenn _____.

Fritz mußte zu Hause bleiben. Es wäre nett gewesen, wenn _____.

Sie hat nie zu kochen brauchen. Es wäre nett gewesen, wenn sie auch einmal _____

_____.

[8] Irreal If-Clauses to Express Desires

Be prepared to formulate subjunctive statements when you hear indicative
statements, and vice versa.

> Ich kann nicht gut schlafen.
> Wenn ich nur gut schlafen könnte!

SEE
ANALYSIS
104

(pp. 234-235)

Wenn ich doch nur einmal gut schlafen
könnte! Aber ich kann einfach nicht mehr
so schlafen wie früher.

If only I could sleep well for once! But I
simply can't sleep the way I used to.

Wenn Meyers doch nur endlich nach Hause
gehen wollten! Aber sie gehen nicht nach
Hause. Sie bleiben hier.

If the Meyers would only go home! But
they won't. They are staying here.

* In irreal **wenn**-clauses, **nicht müssen** is used rather than **nicht brauchen zu**.

Wenn doch nur endlich wieder einmal die Sonne schiene! Aber es regnet, und die Sonne scheint nicht.	If only the sun would shine again! But it is raining, and the sun isn't shining.
Wenn er doch nur diese Frau nicht geheiratet hätte! Aber er hat sie geheiratet.	If only he hadn't married that woman! But he did.
Wenn der Zug doch nur endlich abführe (abfahren würde, abfahren wollte)! Aber er fährt erst um sechs.	If only the train would leave! But it won't leave until six.

[9] Irreal Conclusions without *If*-Clauses (Wishes)

After studying these sentences, express the variations at the end of this section in German.

Meyers fahren jedes Jahr nach Italien. Ich führe *auch* gerne einmal mit dir nach Italien (würde *auch* gerne einmal mit dir nach Italien fahren).	The Meyers go to Italy every year. Some day I'd like to go to Italy with you, *too*.	SEE ANALYSIS **105** (pp. 235-236)
Meine Freunde haben alle einen Wagen. Ich hätte *auch* gerne einen Wagen.	My friends all have a car. I'd like to have a car, *too*.	

,,Ich weiß, Meyers wohnen jetzt in München. Wir wohnten natürlich auch lieber in München.''

Ich weiß, Meyers wohnen jetzt in München. Natürlich wohnten wir *auch* lieber in München (würden wir *auch* lieber in München wohnen).

I know Meyers live in Munich now. Of course, we, too, would rather live in Munich.

Was willst *du* denn werden, Fritz?—Am liebsten würde ich Arzt (werden). Mein Bruder wird *auch* Arzt.

What are you going to be, Fritz?—I'd like very much to become a doctor. My brother is also going to be (become) a doctor.

Was sollen wir denn heute *a*bend machen, Fritz? *Ich* ginge am liebsten ins Kino (würde am liebsten ins Kino gehen).— *Ich* bliebe am liebsten zu Hause und arbeitete (würde am liebsten zu Hause bleiben und arbeiten).

What do you think we should do tonight, Fritz? I'd very much like to go to the movies.—I would really like to stay at home and work.

Meyers sind heute morgen nach Italien gefahren. Ich wäre auch gerne mit dir nach Italien gefahren.

The Meyers went to Italy this morning. I would have liked to go to Italy with you, too.

Wir wohnten damals in Augsburg. Natürlich hätten wir lieber in München gewohnt.

At that time we lived in Augsburg. Of course, we would have preferred to live in Munich.

Müssen wir wirklich noch hierbleiben, Fritz? Ich ginge am liebsten nach Hause (würde am liebsten nach Hause gehen). —Ich wäre gerne schon vor einer Stunde nach Hause gegangen; und am liebsten wäre ich gar nicht gekommen.

Do we really have to stay here any longer, Fritz? I would much rather go home.—I wanted to go home an hour ago, and I really didn't want to come at all.

VARIATIONS

I'd like to go to Italy next summer.

I'd like to have a car.

I'd like to live in Munich.

I'd rather live in Berlin.

I'd like best of all to live in Cologne.

I would have liked to go to the theater.

I would rather have read the newspaper.

[10] Irreal Conclusions without *If*-Clauses (Polite Requests)

Invent variations of your own.

SEE
ANALYSIS
105
(pp. 235-236)

Könnte (Kann) ich noch eine Tasse Kaffee haben?

Could I have another cup of coffee?

Warum jeder, der im Wirtschaftsleben steht, eine American Express Karte haben sollte

Guten Abend! Hätten (Haben) Sie vielleicht noch ein Zimmer frei?	Good evening! Do you by any chance still have a room available?
Dürfte (Darf) ich Sie zu einem Gläschen Wein einladen?—Vielen Dank, aber ich möchte jetzt nichts trinken.	May I invite you to (have) a glass of wine (with me)?—Thanks very much, but I don't want to drink anything now.
Könnten (können) Sie mir vielleicht sagen, ob die Maschine aus Hamburg schon angekommen ist?	Could you perhaps tell me whether the flight from Hamburg has arrived yet?
Dürfte ich Sie bitten, mir den Wein ins Haus zu schicken?	Could I ask you to deliver the wine to my house?
Guten Morgen! Könnten Sie mir bitte Zimmer 6 geben? Danke schön!	Good morning! Would you connect me with Room 6, please? Thank you.
Könnten (Würden) Sie mich morgen um zehn anrufen?	Could you call me up at ten tomorrow?
Ich hätte gerne einen Kriminalroman.	I would like to have a detective story.
Ich hätte gerne ein Glas Wasser.	I'd like to have a glass of water.
Haben Sie noch ein Zimmer frei? Ich hätte gern ein Zimmer mit Bad.	Do you still have a room available? I would like to have a room with bath.

[11] Indirect Discourse: Present and Future Time

Be prepared to change orally all statements in direct discourse to indirect discourse, and vice versa.

Hans sagte: „Mein Vater bleibt noch in Berlin."
    Hans sagte, sein Vater bliebe noch in Berlin.
    Hans sagte, sein Vater würde noch in Berlin bleiben.

Frau Lenz sagte: „Erika wohnt nicht mehr in Köln."
    Frau Lenz sagte, du wohntest nicht mehr in Köln.
    Frau Lenz glaubte, du würdest wohl nicht mehr in Köln wohnen.

SEE ANALYSIS 106 (pp. 236-238)

Er sagte: „Mein Freund will morgen abend doch nicht mitgehen."
    Er sagte, sein Freund wollte morgen abend doch nicht mitgehen.
    Er meinte, sein Freund würde morgen abend doch nicht mitgehen wollen.

Inge sagte: „Erika fährt morgen nach Frankfurt."
    Inge sagte, Erika führe morgen nach Frankfurt.
    Inge sagte, Erika würde morgen nach Frankfurt fahren.
    Inge sagte, daß Erika morgen nach Frankfurt führe.
    Inge sagte, daß Erika morgen nach Frankfurt fahren würde.

Er sagte, seine Frau lernte jetzt fahren.
Er sagte, er studierte Medizin.
Er sagte, das Buch gehörte ihm nicht.
Er sagte, er wohnte zwischen Köln und Bonn.

Er sagte, er wollte seinen Vater besuchen.
Er sagte, er könnte leider nicht mitgehen.
Er sagte, er dürfte keinen Wein trinken.
Er sagte, er müßte morgen arbeiten.
Er sagte, er brauchte nicht nach Köln zu fahren.

Er sagte, der Film wäre sehr gut.
Er sagte, der Wein wäre alle.
Er sagte, das wäre ihm recht.

Er sagte, ich hätte sein Buch.
Er sagte, Erika hätte heute keine Zeit.

Er sagte, er ginge mit Inge ins Kino.
Er sagte, sie kämen heute sehr spät nach Hause.
Er sagte, seine Frau tränke nie Wein.
Er sagte, Sie führen mit, Herr Müller.
Er sagte, er würde mich nie wieder küssen.

[12] Indirect Questions: Present and Future Time

Be prepared to transform orally all direct questions into indirect questions, and vice versa.

SEE
ANALYSIS
106

(pp. 236-238)

Er fragte: „Ist dein Vater heute abend zu Hause?"
Er fragte, ob mein Vater heute abend zu Hause wäre.

Er fragte: „Wohin geht ihr heute abend zum Essen?"
Er fragte, wohin wir heute abend zum Essen gingen.

Er fragte: „Wo studiert Fritz denn jetzt?"
Er wollte wissen, wo Fritz denn jetzt studierte.

Er fragte, ob ich krank wäre.
Er fragte, ob ich kein Geld hätte.
Er fragte, ob das Buch mir oder meinem Vater gehörte.
Er fragte, ob Karl mitgehen könnte.

Er fragte, ob wir das Haus in Köln kaufen wollten.
Er fragte, ob er mich zum Bahnhof bringen dürfte.

Er fragte mich, warum ich denn nicht mit nach Köln führe.
Er fragte Fritz, wann sein Vater nach Hause käme.
Er fragte sie, wie sie hieße.

Er wollte wissen, ob Maria zu Hause wäre.
Er wollte wissen, warum Hans nicht mitgehen könnte.
Er wollte wissen, ob ich Angst hätte.

[13] Indirect Discourse: Past Time

Be prepared to transform direct statements into indirect statements, and vice versa.

SEE
ANALYSIS
106

(pp. 236-238)

Er sagte: „Ich war in Köln."
Er sagte, er wäre in Köln gewesen.

Er sagte: „Ich bin in Köln gewesen."
Er sagte, er wäre in Köln gewesen.

Er sagte: „Ich war gerade in Köln gewesen."
Er sagte, er wäre gerade in Köln gewesen.

Er sagte: „Ich arbeitete damals in Hamburg."
Er sagte, daß er damals in Hamburg gearbeitet hätte.

Er sagte: „Ich habe damals in Hamburg gearbeitet."
Er sagte, daß er damals in Hamburg gearbeitet hätte.

Er sagte: „Ich hatte gerade eine Woche in Hamburg gearbeitet."
Er sagte, daß er gerade eine Woche in Hamburg gearbeitet hätte.

Er sagte, außer Ernst und seiner Frau wäre niemand da gewesen.
Er sagte, kein Mensch hätte ihm geglaubt.
Er sagte, er hätte ihm sein Büro gezeigt.

Er sagte, sie hätte das Buch meiner Mutter geschickt.
Er sagte, seine Frau hätte ihm das Buch geschenkt.

Er sagte, daß er seitdem nichts mehr von ihr gehört hätte.

Er sagte, daß er mich leider nicht verstanden hätte.

Er schrieb, daß er Inge gestern abend nach Hause gebracht hätte.

Frau Schmidt sagte, ihr Mann hätte nach Afrika fahren wollen.

Frau Schmidt sagte, sie hätten erst nach dem Kriege heiraten können.

Frau Schmidt sagte, Johannes hätte nach Kairo fahren müssen.

[14] Indirect Questions: Past Time

Be prepared to transform direct questions into indirect questions, and vice versa.

SEE
ANALYSIS
106

(pp. 236-238)

Er fragte: „Warum sind Sie denn gestern nicht nach Köln gefahren?"

Er fragte, warum ich denn gestern nicht nach Köln gefahren wäre.

Er fragte: „Sind Sie gestern in Köln gewesen?"

Er fragte, ob ich gestern in Köln gewesen wäre.

Er fragte: „Hatten Sie damals oft Hunger?"

Er wollte wissen, ob ich damals oft Hunger gehabt hätte.

Er fragte: „Mit wem warst du denn gestern abend im Theater?"

Er wollte wissen, mit wem ich gestern abend im Theater gewesen wäre.

Er wollte wissen, wieviel die Zigarren gekostet hätten.

Er wollte wissen, wie lange ich für die Lufthansa gearbeitet hätte.

[15] Position of **hätte** with Double Infinitive in Indirect Discourse

Be prepared to produce orally the other two sentences of each group when you hear one.

SEE
ANALYSIS
108

(pp. 239-240)

Er sagte: „Ich wollte gestern eigentlich hierbleiben."

Er sagte, er hätte gestern eigentlich hierbleiben wollen.

Er sagte, daß er gestern eigentlich hätte hierbleiben wollen.

Er sagte: „Ich habe Inge nie verstehen können."

Er sagte, er hätte Inge nie verstehen können.

Er sagte, daß er Inge nie hätte verstehen können.

Er sagte: „Leider mußte ich gestern abend zu Hause bleiben."

Er sagte, er hätte leider gestern abend zu Hause bleiben müssen.

Er sagte, daß er leider gestern abend hätte zu Hause bleiben müssen.

Er sagte: „Kurz vor dem Kriege mußte ich Soldat werden."

Er sagte, kurz vor dem Krieg hätte er Soldat werden müssen.

Er sagte, daß er kurz vor dem Krieg hätte Soldat werden müssen.

CONVERSATION

Frau Ingelheim has just met her husband at the airport upon his return from Africa.

FRAU SCHMIDT-INGELHEIM:	Und dann hat der Herr Behrens angerufen und wollte wissen, ob du wirklich spurlos verschwunden wärst.
SCHMIDT-INGELHEIM:	Behrens? Den kenne ich nicht.
FRAU SCHMIDT-INGELHEIM:	Doch, du kennst ihn. Er hat mir gesagt, er hätte dich in Afrika kennengelernt.
SCHMIDT-INGELHEIM:	Ach, der Reporter. Du hast ihm doch hoffentlich gesagt, daß du von mir gehört hättest,—daß ich dir geschrieben hätte, ich käme heute.
FRAU SCHMIDT-INGELHEIM:	Ja, aber erst, als er mich wieder anrief. Denn als er das erste Mal* anrief, wußte ich noch nicht, daß du in Casablanca warst; der Briefträger kam gerade, als ich mit ihm sprach. Und ich hatte doch Angst, verstehst du; vierzehn Tage hatte ich nichts von dir gehört.
SCHMIDT-INGELHEIM:	Du hast ihm also nicht gesagt, ich wäre *nicht* verschwunden. Das war unvernünftig. Das hättest du nicht tun sollen.
FRAU SCHMIDT-INGELHEIM:	Aber Hans, ich dachte doch nur . . .
SCHMIDT-INGELHEIM:	Du solltest nicht immer denken. Es wäre mir viel lieber, wenn du nicht immer so viel reden würdest. Du kanntest doch diesen Behrens gar nicht.
FRAU SCHMIDT-INGELHEIM:	Er war aber sehr nett zu mir. Hätte ich ihm vielleicht sagen sollen, ich wüßte, wo du bist? Ich wußte es doch nicht.
SCHMIDT-INGELHEIM:	Du hättest ihm aber *sagen* sollen, daß du es wüßtest.
FRAU SCHMIDT-INGELHEIM:	Und dann hätte er mich gefragt, *wo* du wärst. Ich war ja so glücklich, als er mir sagte, er hätte dich gesehen. Ich dachte, er wäre vielleicht ein Freund von dir. Er sagte, er wollte auch Käthe anrufen . . .
SCHMIDT-INGELHEIM:	Käthe! Woher wußte denn dieser Mensch, daß ich schon einmal verheiratet war? Hast *du* ihm das gesagt?
FRAU SCHMIDT-INGELHEIM:	Nein, ich habe es ihm *nicht* gesagt, aber er sagte, die Zeitung wüßte alles.
SCHMIDT-INGELHEIM:	„Alles?" Was heißt „alles"! Wenn du nur nicht immer so viel erzählen würdest, Inge.

* the first time

FRAU SCHMIDT-INGELHEIM: Nun, alles hat er doch nicht gewußt. Zum Beispiel, daß du eine Tochter hast und daß diese Tochter in Mainz Archäologie studiert. Ich habe ihm gesagt, daß deine Tochter zufällig auch in Kairo gewesen wäre und zufällig auch in deinem Hotel gewohnt hätte.

SCHMIDT-INGELHEIM: Das hättest du ihm nicht sagen sollen! Das kommt morgen bestimmt in die Zeitung, und es wäre viel besser, wenn es *nicht* in die Zeitung käme.

FRAU SCHMIDT-INGELHEIM: Ja, Hans.

SCHMIDT-INGELHEIM: Und du hättest ihm sagen können, du wüßtest gar nichts, und er sollte warten, bis ich zurückkäme. Du weißt doch, daß ich nicht einfach spurlos verschwinde. Ich muß nur allein sein, wenn ich arbeite. Aber das braucht die Zeitung doch nicht zu wissen. Ich bin doch schon so oft allein zum Arbeiten weggefahren, daß du eigentlich wissen müßtest, was du tun sollst.

FRAU SCHMIDT-INGELHEIM: Ja, Hans.
(Pause)
Du, Hans!

SCHMIDT-INGELHEIM: Ja?

FRAU SCHMIDT-INGELHEIM: Hans,—wie war denn Giselas Kaffee?

READING

Zwei und zwei ist fünf

EINE UNMÖGLICHE GESCHICHTE

von Johannes Schmidt-Ingelheim

eine unmögliche Geschichte an impossible story

Hinter unserem Haus haben wir eine Terrasse. Sie ist fünf Meter breit und zehn Meter lang. Ich habe die Platten für diese Terrasse letzten Winter in Italien gekauft; sie sind alle ein Meter breit und ein Meter lang.

Ich bin nie auf den Gedanken gekommen, diese Platten zu zählen. 5 Ich weiß, es müssen fünfzig sein. Und als meine Frau vor einem Monat doch auf den Gedanken kam, die Platten zu zählen, und mir dann sagte, es wären einundfünfzig (51), da wußte ich, daß sie beim Zählen einen Fehler gemacht hatte. Denn wenn es wirklich

einundfünfzig wären, dann—nun, man kann den Gedanken einfach
nicht zu Ende denken; man würde den Verstand verlieren, wenn
man es versuchte.

Aber nach diesem Wochenende weiß ich nicht mehr, ob fünf mal
zehn wirklich immer fünfzig ist. Natürlich wird mir kein Mensch 5
glauben, was ich dieses Wochenende erlebt habe. Aber wahr ist es
doch.

Die Geschichte fing Freitag morgen in Tripolis an, das heißt,
eigentlich hat sie schon angefangen, als wir noch mit Rommel in
Afrika gegen die Amerikaner kämpften.   10

Mein Schulfreund Hermann Schneider, Erich Karsten und ich wohnten damals in Tripolis bei dem Ägypter Ali und seiner Frau Busuq.
Ali war ungefähr sechzig; Busuq war mindestens achtzig. Vor Busuq
hatten wir alle Angst. Wenn wir mit ihr sprachen, hatten wir das
Gefühl: sie sieht dich nicht nur an, sie sieht durch dich durch. Nur 15
Erich hatte keine Angst vor ihr. Für ihn war diese Frau eine
Königin. Er brachte ihr immer etwas mit, wenn er ins Haus kam,
und man sah, es machte ihn glücklich, wenn sie seine Geschenke
annahm.

Einmal, als wir nicht weit von der Stadt an unserem Wagen ar- 20
beiteten, erschienen plötzlich ein paar englische Tiefflieger. Wir
warfen uns zu Boden, aber nicht schnell genug. Als wir wieder auf-
standen, blieb Erich mit einer Kopfwunde wie tot liegen.

Wir warfen uns zu Boden we threw ourselves on the ground

Wir fuhren mit ihm nach Tripolis zurück. Als Busuq Erichs Wunde
sah, befahl sie uns, ihn ins Haus zu bringen. Wir hatten, wie immer, 25
Angst vor ihr. Darum gehorchten wir und brachten ihn ins Haus.
Wir konnten aber nicht bei ihm bleiben und kamen erst nach
vierzehn Tagen wieder zurück. Erich war noch schwach, aber die
Wunde war gottseidank geheilt.

Doch Erich war nicht mehr unser Erich. Er redete nicht mehr so viel 30
wie früher, und seine Augen schienen sagen zu wollen: Ich weiß
etwas, was ihr nicht wißt. Außerdem sah er oft stundenlang irgendwohin in die Ferne und war sozusagen einfach nicht da.

Nun, Hermann und ich hatten keine Zeit, Erich zu analysieren. Die
Situation in Afrika war damals schon gefährlich, und wir fragten uns 35
oft: Wie kommt ihr nur zurück nach Deutschland?

Zwei oder drei Wochen später saßen Hermann und ich in Alis Haus
und schrieben Briefe. Erich saß bei uns und war wieder einmal
sozusagen nicht da. Aber plötzlich sah er mich mit seinem Ich-weiß-
etwas-was-du-nicht-weißt Blick an und sagte: „Weißt du, daß deine 40

Frau dir gerade einen Brief schreibt, um dir zu erzählen, daß deine
Tochter schon bis fünf zählen kann?" Niemand lachte. Ich wußte
nicht, was ich denken sollte.

Ungefähr zehn Tage später flog man Hermann und mich nach
Deutschland. Erich blieb in Afrika zurück. Wie lange er noch bei   5
der Ägypterin gewesen ist, weiß ich nicht. Ich habe ihn erst dieses
Wochenende wiedergesehen.

Kurz vor dem Abflug nach Deutschland aber bekam ich damals noch
einen Brief von meiner Frau. Was sie schrieb, machte mich unruhig.
„Es wäre wirklich nett," schrieb sie, „wenn Du* hier wärst. Du   10
hättest sehen sollen, wie Dein Töchterchen heute morgen an den
Fingern bis fünf gezählt . . . Du, Hans, was ich gerade erlebt habe,
ist wirklich unglaublich, und ich muß mich zwingen, ruhig zu
bleiben. Ich hatte beim Schreiben plötzlich das Gefühl, daß jemand
hinter mir stand. Ich fühlte es. Ich wußte einfach, daß jemand   15
hinter mir stand. Ich saß eine Zeitlang still, dann sprang ich auf.
Niemand war im Zimmer. Aber Hans, auf dem Boden waren Fußabdrücke, wie Du sie machst, wenn Du mit Deinen Militärschuhen
nach Hause kommst. Du darfst nicht lachen. Ich weiß, was ich Dir
schreibe, kann einfach nicht passieren. Aber es *ist* passiert!—Oder   20
ist es doch nicht passiert? Hans, ich bin einfach zu viel allein."

(Fortsetzung folgt)

* In letters, all pronouns of direct address must be capitalized (**Du**, **Dich**, **Dein**,
Ihr, etc.).

ANALYSIS

97 The Future

Formation

The German future is formed by using **werden** as an auxiliary in the
first prong and any infinitive in the second prong.

Ich werde	. . . sein	ich werde	. . . haben	ich werde	. . . fahren
du wirst	. . . sein	du wirst	. . . haben	du wirst	. . . fahren
er wird	. . . sein	er wird	. . . haben	er wird	. . . fahren
wir werden	. . . sein	wir werden	. . . haben	wir werden	. . . fahren
ihr werdet	. . . sein	ihr werdet	. . . haben	ihr werdet	. . . fahren
sie werden	. . . sein	sie werden	. . . haben	sie werden	. . . fahren

Use

Since the present tense can refer to future time, the future tense is comparatively rare. One usually hears

Ich fahre morgen nach Berlin,

not

Ich werde morgen nach Berlin fahren.

However, if a sentence contains no time phrase, the future is used more frequently:

Ihr werdet ja sehen, wie es ist.   You'll see how it is.

Very frequently, future forms express not futurity but present probability. Such a probability statement often contains adverbs such as **wohl** (probably), **sicher** (certainly), **vielleicht** (perhaps), and **wahrscheinlich** (probably).

Es ist jetzt sieben. Inge wird wohl   It's seven o'clock now. Inge is probably at
(sicher, wahrscheinlich) schon zu   home by now.
Hause sein.

98 Irreal (Contrary-to-Fact) Conditions in English

It was pointed out in Unit 5 that the open condition

If his parents *are* still alive, they *are* now fifty

leaves the question of whether or not the parents are alive entirely unanswered. *If they are still alive* means "they may or may not be alive." By substituting *were* for *are* in the *if*-clause, and *would be* for *are* in the conclusion, the open condition changes into the irreal or contrary-to-fact condition

If his parents *were* still alive, they *would* be fifty now.

Now the question as to whether or not the parents are alive is no longer left undecided. *If his parents were alive* contains the unmistakable implication "they are dead," and *they would be fifty now* implies that they did not live to be fifty.

A similar change from an open condition to an irreal condition can occur when reference is made not to present time, but to past or future time:

PAST TIME, OPEN CONDITION:

John always did things in a big way. I therefore suspect that *if he stole, he stole* at least a million.

PAST TIME, IRREAL CONDITION:

John always did things in a big way. *If he had stolen, he would have stolen* at least a million.

FUTURE TIME, OPEN CONDITION:

I will not forget this, even *if I live* to be a hundred.

FUTURE TIME, IRREAL CONDITION:

I would not forget this, even *if I lived* to be a thousand years old.

As can be seen from the sentences quoted, the change from an open condition to an irreal condition is accomplished in English by changing the verb forms

(a) in the *if-clause* from the indicative to the subjunctive, and

(b) in the *conclusion* from the indicative to the conditional.

IF-CLAUSE

	OPEN POSSIBILITY (Indicative)	IMPLIED IRREALITY (Subjunctive)
PAST TIME	if he stole	if he had stolen
PRESENT TIME	if they are alive	if they were alive
FUTURE TIME	if I go	if I ever went

CONCLUSION

	OPEN POSSIBILITY (Indicative)	IMPLIED IRREALITY (Conditional)
PAST TIME	he stole	he would have stolen
PRESENT TIME	they are now fifty	they would be fifty now
FUTURE TIME	I will go	I would go

The question now is: Does German also shift from the indicative to the subjunctive in the *if*-clause and from the indicative to the conditional in the conclusion? Before we can answer this question, we have to analyze the English subjunctive in greater detail.

99 The English Subjunctive

The subjunctive found in English irreal *if*-clauses (and in wishes of the type "I wish they were here") consists of a very interesting set of forms. If the speaker refers to *past time,* he always uses a form which looks as if it were the past perfect.

REALITY	IRREALITY
(Past Perfect Indicative)	(Past Subjunctive)
I suddenly realized that *I had lost* my wallet.	If *I had lost* my wallet I'd really be upset now.

If the speaker refers to *present* or *future time,* he uses forms like *had, lost,* or *loved,* that is, forms which look as if they were past indicatives:

REALITY	IRREALITY
(Past Indicative)	(Present Subjunctive)
When I was a child, *we had* a mountain cabin.	If *we had* a mountain cabin, we could spend our vacations there.
I know *he loved* me as long as he lived.	If *he loved* me he would marry me.
We lost the last game.	It would be too bad if *we lost* this game.

It is perhaps surprising, but nevertheless a fact, that forms like *had, lost,* and *loved,* if taken out of context, have no time reference built into them at all. The time reference depends entirely on context.

If these forms are used in a context of reality to express real events or open possibilities, they refer to past time:

We *lost* the last game.

They are then used in the indicative (reality) mood, and they are in the past tense.

However, if these forms are used in a context of irreality to describe something which exists only in thought, imagination, or desire, they refer to present or future time:

It would be too bad if we *lost* this game.

Although *had, lost,* and *loved* still remind us by their "looks" of the past indicative, they are now used in the subjunctive (irreality) mood, and we shall call them the present tense of the subjunctive. Like all present tenses, the present tense of the subjunctive may, as it does in the case of *lost,* take on a future meaning.

Schematically, one might represent this situation as follows:

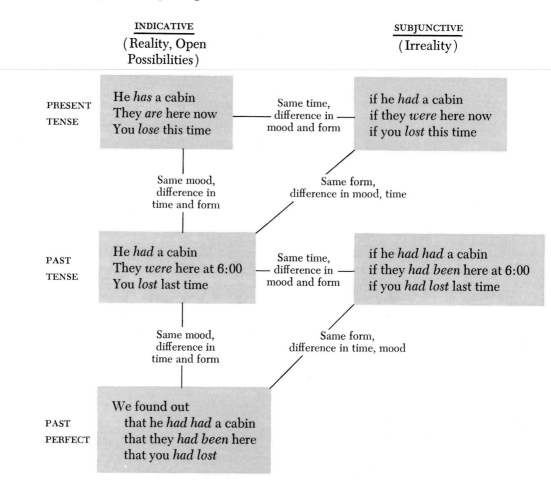

For the sake of convenience, let us call this distribution of forms the *had : had* pattern, the first *had* referring to the indicative and the second to the subjunctive. The past indicative *had* of *I know he had a cabin* is identical with the present subjunctive *had* of *I wish he had a cabin*, and it is the same with other verbs.

There is only one verb which does not follow the *had : had* pattern; this is the verb *to be*.

Although one hears people say (systematically following the *had : had* pattern)

If she was only a little older, I'd like her better

this is generally considered substandard English; the accepted form is

If she were only a little older, . . .

Because the past indicative *was* is, in this case, not identical with the present subjunctive *were*, we shall call this arrangement the *was : were* pattern. It is an exception in English and occurs only in the singular of one verb: *if I were* and *if he were.* In German, however, the *was : were* pattern is very common.

An interesting fact about the *had : had* pattern form is that it makes *if*-clauses ambiguous. The sentence

If he had money, he must have squandered it

is an open condition. But the sentence

If he had money, he would surely squander it

is an irreal condition.

This means that the irreal *if*-clause *if he had money* has its subjunctive (irreality) flavor not by virtue of its own linguistic character, but through the character of the following conclusion *he would surely squander it.*

Similarly, in English *if*-clauses referring to past time, phrases like *if he had done it* are also "neutral," that is, by themselves they are neither indicatives nor subjunctives. They acquire subjunctive character if they are followed (or preceded) by a conditional:

I was curious to find out *if he had done it.* (Indicative)
If he had done it, he would have told me about it. (Subjunctive)

On the other hand, the *if*-clause *If she were only a little older* is never ambiguous; for *if she were,* which follows the *was : were* model, can only be a present subjunctive; and therefore it can only be followed by a conditional.

Summary of the English Subjunctive in Irreal *If*-Clauses

1. Without context, all *had : had* pattern forms are ambiguous and have no time reference built into them.

2. The *was : were* pattern forms are never ambiguous.

3. The ambiguous *had : had* pattern forms in *if*-clauses acquire an unmistakable irreality (subjunctive) character

    (a) when they are followed by a conditional verb form in the conclusion: *If he had money, he would surely squander it.*

    (b) when they appear in a fixed "if-only" frame, as in *If I only had some money.*

This summary is valid not only for English but also for German. Let us see now how German derives its conditional, its *had : had* pattern, and its *was : were* pattern forms.

100 The Forms of the Conditional and of the Present Subjunctive

The Conditional

The German conditional is derived from the future indicative.

FUTURE INDICATIVE	CONDITIONAL
ich werde gehen	ich würde gehen
du wirst gehen	du würdest gehen
er wird gehen	er würde gehen
wir werden gehen	wir würden gehen
ihr werdet gehen	ihr würdet gehen
sie werden gehen	sie würden gehen

There are—gottseidank—no deviations from this pattern. These *würde*-forms are definitely subjunctives; they cannot be anything else.

The use of **würde**-forms in **wenn**-clauses is still rare; however, they are frequently found in the conclusion. They can refer either to present or to future time.

PRESENT TIME

Wenn ich Geld hätte, würde ich jetzt auch an der Riviera wohnen.
    If I had money, I'd live on the Riviera, too, now.

Wenn es nicht so neblig wäre, würden wir jetzt die Berge sehen können.
    If it weren't so foggy, we'd be able to see the mountains now.

FUTURE TIME

Wenn wir Geld hätten, würden wir diesen Sommer heiraten.
    If we had money, we'd get married this summer.

The Present Subjunctive of Weak Verbs

Weak verbs use the same forms for the past indicative and the present subjunctive; in other words, they are parallel to the English *had : had* pattern.

PAST INDICATIVE	PRESENT SUBJUNCTIVE
ich lebte	ich lebte
du lebtest	du lebtest
er lebte	er lebte
wir lebten	wir lebten
ihr lebtet	ihr lebtet
sie lebten	sie lebten

This means that **wenn**-clauses like

Wenn es regnete, . . .
Wenn wir lachten, . . .

are intolerably ambiguous. One doesn't know whether the forms **regnete** and **lachten** are past indicatives meaning

Whenever it rained, . . .
Whenever we laughed, . . .

or whether they are present subjunctives meaning

If it were raining . . .
If we were to laugh . . .

These forms can therefore be used only in contexts which resolve this ambiguity (see **102, 103**).

The Present Subjunctive of the Modals

The present subjunctive of the modals is formed by adding the endings of the past tense to the *unchanged* stem.

PAST INDICATIVE	PRESENT SUBJUNCTIVE
ich wollte	ich wollte
ich sollte	ich sollte
ich mußte	ich müßte
ich konnte	ich könnte
ich durfte	ich dürfte

This table shows that **wollen** and **sollen** have ambiguous *had : had* pattern forms, whereas **müssen, können,** and **dürfen** have unambiguous *was : were* pattern forms. The form **ich möchte,** which we have been using since Unit 3, is a polite subjunctive which is now used as if it were an indicative. The indicative form **ich mag** is discussed in Unit 9.

Sentences with **wollte** and **sollte** are therefore ambiguous unless they are clarified by context (see **102** and **107.**)

The Present Subjunctive of Strong Verbs

Strong verbs form the present subjunctive by adding **-e, -est, -e, -en, -et, -en** (that is, the endings of **leb-te** minus **-t-**) to the stem of the past, which is umlauted whenever possible—that is, whenever the stem vowel is *a, o, u,* or *au*. The endings **-est** and **-et** are often shortened to **-st** and **-t**.

PAST INDICATIVE	PRESENT SUBJUNCTIVE
ich war	ich wär-e
du war-st	du wär-est, wär-st
er war	er wär-e
wir war-en	wir wär-en
ihr war-t	ihr wär-et, wär-t
sie war-en	sie wär-en
ich ging	ich ging-e
du ging-st	du ging-est, ging-st
er ging	er ging-e
wir ging-en	wir ging-en
ihr ging-t	ihr ging-et, ging-t
sie ging-en	sie ging-en

This system leads to both *had : had* and *was : were* pattern forms.

    1. *had : had* pattern forms

2. *was : were* pattern forms

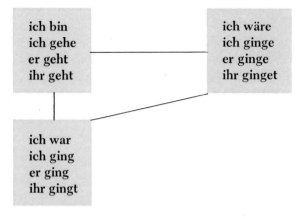

This means again that a **wenn**-clause like

Wenn wir nach Hause gingen, ...

is ambiguous. It may mean

Whenever we went home, ...

or:

If we were to go home (should go home).

Context will resolve this ambiguity (see **102, 103**).

Irregular Forms

A few weak verbs umlaut their subjunctive forms, and occasionally a strong verb changes the stem vowel in an irregular way. The following forms must therefore be memorized.

PAST INDICATIVE	PRESENT SUBJUNCTIVE
ich hatt-e	ich hätt-e
du hatt-est	du hätt-est
er hatt-e	er hätt-e
wir hatt-en	wir hätt-en
ihr hatt-et	ihr hätt-et
sie hatt-en	sie hätt-en
ich wußt-e	ich wüßt-e
du wußt-est	du wüßt-est
er wußt-e	er wüßt-e
wir wußt-en	wir wüßt-en
ihr wußt-et	ihr wüßt-et
sie wußt-en	sie wüßt-en

PAST INDICATIVE	PRESENT SUBJUNCTIVE
ich bracht-e	ich brächt-e
du bracht-est	du brächt-est
er bracht-e	er brächt-e
wir bracht-en	wir brächt-en
ihr bracht-et	ihr brächt-et
sie bracht-en	sie brächt-en
ich kannt-e	ich kennt-e
du kannt-est	du kennt-est
er kannt-e	er kennt-e
wir kannt-en	wir kennt-en
ihr kannt-et	ihr kennt-et
sie kannt-en	sie kennt-en
ich half	ich hülfe
du halfst	du hülfest
er half	er hülfe
wir halfen	wir hülfen
ihr halft	ihr hülfet
sie halfen	sie hülfen
ich wurde	ich würde
du wurdest	du würdest
er wurde	er würde
wir wurden	wir würden
ihr wurdet	ihr würdet
sie wurden	sie würden

All these irregular forms are *was : were* forms; they can clearly be recognized as subjunctives.

NOTE:

1. Distinguish between the following forms:

ich konnte	I was able to
wenn ich könnte	If I were able to
ich kannte	I knew
wenn ich kennte	If I knew

2. The present subjunctive of **sein** (**wäre**) and **haben** (**hätte**) occurs more frequently than the corresponding conditional forms **würde sein** and **würde haben**. The conditional of the modals (**würde müssen, würde können**) is hardly ever used.

101 The Past Subjunctive

The German past subjunctive is formed from the pluperfect indicative as illustrated by the following table.

PLUPERFECT INDICATIVE	PAST SUBJUNCTIVE
ich war gegangen	ich wäre gegangen
du warst gegangen	du wär(e)st gegangen
er war gegangen	er wäre gegangen
wir waren gegangen	wir wären gegangen
ihr wart gegangen	ihr wär(e)t gegangen
sie waren gegangen	sie wären gegangen
ich war gewesen	ich wäre gewesen
du warst gewesen	du wär(e)st gewesen
er war gewesen	er wäre gewesen
wir waren gewesen	wir wären gewesen
ihr wart gewesen	ihr wär(e)t gewesen
sie waren gewesen	sie wären gewesen
ich hatte gehabt	ich hätte gehabt
du hattest gehabt	du hättest gehabt
er hatte gehabt	er hätte gehabt
wir hatten gehabt	wir hätten gehabt
ihr hattet gehabt	ihr hättet gehabt
sie hatten gehabt	sie hätten gehabt.

As this table shows, all German past subjunctive forms follow the *was : were* pattern and can be clearly recognized as subjunctives. Modals follow the same pattern:

ich hatte gekonnt	ich hätte gekonnt
ich hatte gehen können	ich hätte gehen können

NOTE: The past subjunctives of modals usually correspond to English statements starting with *could have, should have,* and *would have.*

Ich hätte gehen können.	I could have gone.
Ich hätte gehen sollen.	I should have gone.
Ich hätte gehen müssen.	I would have had to go.

102 Wishes Starting with **Ich wollte** or **Ich wünschte**

The easiest way to start practicing German subjunctives is by means of the patterns

Ich wollte, es regnete morgen.
Ich wollte, es würde morgen regnen.

The short introductory clauses **ich wollte** or **ich wünschte**, which are interchangeable, are present subjunctives and follow the obsolescent English pattern

Oh, would I were a boy again,

where *would* is also a subjunctive referring to present time.

Ich wollte, wir wohnten in München.	I wish we were living in Munich.
Ich wollte, es wäre schon Frühling.	I wish it were already spring.
Ich wollte, es regnete morgen (würde morgen regnen).	I wish it would rain tomorrow.
Ich wollte, es hätte gestern geregnet.	I wish it had rained yesterday.

Note that the structure of these sentences is fixed: they always start with **ich wollte** or **ich wünschte**, which are then followed by an unintroduced dependent clause. The subjunctive flavor (and thereby reference to present or future time) depends on this fixed structure. That is why **Ich wollte, es regnete** (*I wish it were raining*) is always unambiguous, although **regnete** by itself is a *had : had* pattern form which could also be indicative. The subjunctive flavor disappears if **ich wollte** or **ich wünschte** is followed by a **daß**-clause:

Ich wollte, er heiratete.	I wish he would get married.
Ich wollte, daß er heiratete.	I wanted him to get married.

Wishes are also expressed by using the introductory phrase **Es wäre nett, wenn . . .** followed by a subjunctive.

Es wäre nett, wenn du morgen kommen könntest.	It would be nice if you could come tomorrow.
Es wäre nett, wenn wir nächstes Jahr nach Deutschland führen (fahren würden).	It would be nice if we went to Germany next year.
Es wäre nett gewesen, wenn du meinen Geburtstag nicht wieder vergessen hättest.	It would have been nice if you had not forgotten my birthday again.

103 Irreal (Contrary-to-Fact) Conditions

Irreal conditions refer either to present and future time or to past time.

Present and Future Time

We have seen (**99**) that, with the exception of some forms of the verb *to be* (the *was : were* pattern), all the verb forms which appear in irreal *if*-clauses in present-day English speech are ambiguous *had : had* pattern forms which, in a different context, could just as well be indicatives. For this reason, any *if*-clause like *if they lost this game* hangs in the air until it is rescued by a preceding or following conclusion.

If this conclusion is *it was their own fault,* then the *lost* of the *if*-clause is a past indicative; but in *It would be too bad if they lost this game,* the *lost* of the *if*-clause is a subjunctive.

The necessity to rescue the otherwise ambiguous *if*-clauses of contrary-to-fact conditions has forced English to use only conditional forms with *would* or *should* in the conclusion. For when used with *if*-clauses, these conditional forms are unambiguous subjunctives which guarantee that the ambiguous *had : had* forms in the *if*-clauses will also be interpreted as subjunctives.

German, too, prefers to use only unambiguous subjunctive forms in the conclusions belonging to contrary-to-fact **wenn**-clauses. But the conditional **würde**-forms, which English-speaking students are tempted to prefer, are not the only unambiguous subjunctives:

ich könnte		ich würde können
ich müßte		ich würde müssen
ich dürfte		ich würde dürfen
ich hätte	are just as unambiguous as	ich würde haben
ich wäre		ich würde sein
ich ginge		ich würde gehen
ich führe		ich würde fahren

On the whole, the shorter forms, especially the shorter forms of **haben, sein,** and the modals, are preferred. Thus, one will usually hear

Wenn ich Geld hätte, könnte ich heiraten.
, wäre ich schon lange nicht mehr hier.
, führe ich auch nach Deutschland.

However, it is permissible to say

Wenn ich Geld hätte, würde ich auch nach Deutschland fahren.

Even such ambiguous forms as **brauchte** and **wohnte,** which can be either past indicatives or present subjunctives, can appear in contrary-to-fact conclusions as long as the **wenn**-clause contains an unambiguous subjunctive:

Wenn ich Geld hätte, brauchte ich nicht zu arbeiten.
, wohnte ich auch an der Riviera.

The **würde**-forms are mandatory only

1. if a weak verb refers to the future:

    Wenn ich Geld hätte, würde ich heiraten.
    (not: **heiratete ich.**)

2. if two ambiguous weak verbs would otherwise follow each other:

    Wenn es regnete, würden wir nicht arbeiten.
    (Not: **arbeiteten wir nicht.**)

As a matter of fact, the sentence

   Wenn es regnete, arbeiteten wir nicht

would be interpreted to mean

   Whenever it rained, we didn't work.

Past Time

To express past time, use only the past subjunctive (**hätte** or **wäre** plus participle) for both the *if*-clause and the conclusion. Do not try to imitate English conditionals like *would have died*, which refer to past time. If you want to express English *would have* plus a participle, you must use **hätte** or **wäre** plus a participle in German. Since all these forms are un-ambiguous *was : were* forms, no complications will arise.

Wenn es gestern geregnet hätte, wären wir zu Hause geblieben.	If it had rained yesterday, we would have stayed at home.
Wenn du hier gewesen wärst, wäre mein Bruder nicht gestorben.	If you had been here, my brother would not have died (John 11:21). (King James Version: If thou hadst been here, my brother had not died.)

104   *If*-Clauses to Express Desires

If a speaker is dissatisfied with the situation as it actually exists, he may express what he would like the facts to be or to have been. Such wishes-contrary-to-fact may assume the form of an irreal *if-clause* used by itself without a conclusion, as in English *If he would only come!*

If German *if*-clauses of this type refer to present or future time, either the present subjunctive or the conditional may be used, but remember that the conditional of **sein, haben,** and the modals is rare. If they refer to past time, only the past subjunctive (**hätte** or **wäre** plus participle) should be used. *If*-clauses that express wishes must contain at least a **nur** or **doch nur;** if the speaker is anxiously looking forward to something, he uses **nur endlich, doch endlich,** or **doch nur endlich.** (This **endlich** does not mean *finally;* it merely expresses impatience.) As sentence adverbs, these little inserts stand between elements without news value and elements with news value.

Wenn es doch nur endlich regnen würde!	If it would only rain!
Wenn ich doch nur mehr Geld hätte!	If only I had more money!
Wenn ich nur nicht soviel Kaffee getrunken hätte!	If only I had not had so much coffee!

105 Irreal Conclusions without *If*-Clause

The English sentence

> I would like to have a cup of coffee

is an irreal conclusion. The irreal *if*-clause is not expressed, but the use of the subjunctive implies "if this should be possible."

Such irreal conclusions express a wish or a polite request. In German, they frequently contain the adverbs **gerne** (*with pleasure*), **lieber** (*rather, preferably*), or **am liebsten** (*what I would like most of all . . .*). If these irreal conclusions express something the speaker would look forward to, they frequently contain **einmal,** which, literally, means *at some time* or *once,* but which usually adds the flavor of "if this were possible" and replaces the suppressed *if*-clause. Polite requests, in the form of a question, frequently contain **vielleicht.** Examples:

Wishes

Ich führe auch gerne einmal nach Italien (würde auch gerne einmal nach Italien fahren).	I would like to go to Italy too, sometime.
Wir wohnten auch lieber in München (würden auch lieber in München wohnen).	We too would rather live in Munich.
Am liebsten wäre ich nach Köln gefahren.	Most of all, I would have liked to go to Cologne.
Wir hätten auch lieber in München gewohnt.	We, too, would rather have lived in Munich.

Polite Requests

Ich hätte gerne ein Zimmer mit Bad.	I should like to have a room with bath.
Ich hätte gerne noch eine Tasse Kaffee.	I should like to have another cup of coffee.
Könnte ich noch eine Tasse Kaffee haben?	Could I have another cup of coffee?
Hätten Sie vielleicht noch ein Zimmer frei?	Would you perhaps still have a room?
Würdest du mich bitte morgen zum Flughafen bringen?	Would you please drive me to the airport tomorrow?

106 The Subjunctive in Indirect Discourse

The English System

When I, the speaker, want to report to one person, my wife for instance, what another person, for instance my father, has just told me over the phone, I can freely choose between two syntactical patterns:

I can use quotation marks and repeat verbatim what my father said. If he said, "Fred, I am sick," I can report, *Father just called and said, "Fred, I am sick."* Such "direct discourse" presents no problems. One simply quotes verbatim what one hears.

I may also use the "indirect discourse" pattern—that is, I may change the original statement into a dependent clause: *Father just called and said he was sick.* In this case the original words *I am sick* change into *he was sick.* If the original is "I was sick last week," I may report: *Father just called and said he had been sick last week.*

The rule governing English indirect discourse is usually formulated as follows: If the opening verb (*said, told, reported, maintained, read*) is in the past tense, then any *present tense* in the words to be reported is normally changed to *past tense* and any *past tense* (simple past, present perfect, past perfect) is normally changed to *past perfect.*

Schematically, this English system can be represented as follows:

	DIRECT DISCOURSE	INDIRECT DISCOURSE
PRESENT TENSE	I am sick	He said he was sick
	I have money	He said he had money
ANY PAST TENSE	I was sick	He said he had been sick
	I have broken my arm	He said he had broken his arm
	I had not thought of it	He said he had not thought of it.

In learning German, you will find it helpful to regard this shift in verb forms not as a shift in tense but as a shift from the indicative to the subjunctive, a shift which in English follows the *had : had* pattern all the way through. You will then automatically do what you ought to do: shift from the German indicative to the German subjunctive.

The German System

AFTER AN OPENING VERB IN ONE OF THE PAST TENSES

If the original statement (that is, the statement in quotation marks) referred to the present time, the present subjunctive is used, and such *had : had* forms as **wohnte** and **liebte** do not have to be replaced by **würde**-forms.

If the original statement referred to the future, one can use either the present subjunctive or the future subjunctive; *had : had* pattern forms like **heiratete**—that is, weak verbs with a future meaning—are usually replaced by a **würde** form.

„Ich bin krank."	Er sagte, er wäre krank.
„Ich wohne in München."	Er sagte, er wohnte in München.
„Ich kann kommen."	Er sagte, er könnte kommen.
„Ich werde zu Hause bleiben."	Er sagte, er würde zu Hause bleiben (bliebe zu Hause).
„Ich komme morgen."	Er sagte, er käme morgen (würde morgen kommen).
„Ich heirate sie bestimmt."	Er sagte, er würde sie bestimmt heiraten.
„Fährst du morgen nach Köln?"	Er wollte wissen, ob ich morgen nach Köln führe.

If the original statement was made in any past tense, one shifts to the past subjunctive (**wäre** or **hätte** plus participle).

„Ich war krank."	Er sagte, er wäre krank gewesen.
„Ich bin krank gewesen."	Er sagte, er wäre krank gewesen.
„Bei uns schien die Sonne."	Er sagte, bei ihnen hätte die Sonne geschienen.
„Eva ist schon nach Hause gegangen."	Er sagte, Eva wäre schon nach Hause gegangen.

If the original statement contained a subjunctive, no change is possible:

„Wenn wir Geld hätten, würden wir sofort heiraten."	Er sagte, wenn sie Geld hätten, würden sie sofort heiraten.
„Wenn ich das gewußt hätte, wäre ich nicht gekommen."	Er sagte, wenn er das gewußt hätte, wäre er nicht gekommen.

AFTER AN OPENING VERB IN THE PRESENT TENSE

If the opening verb is in the present tense, a change from indicative to subjunctive is possible though not as frequent in spoken German as in literary German. However, after an **ich**-form in the present tense, the subjunctive is apt to indicate deceit.

„Meyer ist intelligent."	Fritz meint, Meyer ist intelligent.
	Fritz meint, Meyer wäre intelligent.
	Ich sage, Meyer ist intelligent.
	Ich sage ihm einfach, Meyer wäre intelligent.
„Meyer ist nicht gekommen."	Fritz sagt, Meyer ist nicht gekommen.
	Fritz sagt, Meyer wäre nicht gekommen.
	Ich sage, Meyer ist nicht gekommen.

NOTE:

1. If the speaker wants to emphasize that the words reported refer to a fact, he uses the indicative:

Er wollte wissen, warum Erika so oft nach Berlin fährt.

But:

Er wollte wissen, ob Erika immer noch so oft nach Berlin führe.

Wer hat Ihnen denn gesagt, daß mein Mann in Afrika ist?

But:

Wer hat Ihnen denn gesagt, mein Mann wäre in Afrika?

2. In most of the examples above, indirect discourse appears in the form of unintroduced clauses with verb-second position. These clauses can, however, be introduced by **daß** and then show verb-last position:

Er sagte, daß in Hamburg die Sonne schiene.

107 sollte

German **sollte** is one of the ambiguous *had : had* pattern forms which can be used either as a past indicative or as a present subjunctive.

Past Indicative

Jedes Mal, wenn du mit mir ins The-ater gehen solltest, hattest du Kopf-schmerzen.	Every time you were supposed (Every time I wanted you) to go to the theater with me, you had a headache.
Wir sollten schon um acht in Köln sein. Jetzt ist es neun, und wir sind immer noch in Bonn.	We were supposed to be in Cologne at eight. Now it is nine, and we are still in Bonn.

Present Subjunctive

In the *if*-clause, the present subjunctive denotes a future possibility which the speaker does not expect to materialize. The conclusion shows the indicative.

Wenn es morgen regnen sollte, bleiben wir zu Hause.	If it should rain tomorrow, we'll stay at home.

In the conclusion, the present subjunctive denotes an as yet unfulfilled obligation. The *if*-clause shows the indicative.

Wenn du kannst, solltest du ihm helfen.	If you can, you should (ought to) help him.
Du solltest nicht soviel rauchen.	You should not (ought not to) smoke so much.

Sentences with the modal subjunctives **sollte, müßte, könnte** frequently contain the word **eigentlich;** such sentences express the notion *I ought to* (*should, could*), *but I guess I won't.*

Morgen sollte ich eigentlich nach Köln fahren.	I really ought to go to Cologne tomorrow. (But I probably won't.)
Ich hätte gestern eigentlich nach Köln fahren sollen.	I really ought to have gone to Cologne yesterday. (But I didn't.)

108 Position of **hätte** in Connection with "Double Infinitives"

It was pointed out before that when the modals and **brauchen** are used with a dependent infinitive, the participles look like infinitives: **Ich habe sie noch nicht besuchen können.** As a result, **besuchen können** looks like a double infinitive. If subjunctive sentences like

Er hätte zu Hause bleiben können,   or
Er hätte nicht zu Hause bleiben sollen,

are changed into dependent clauses which should show verb-last position, the **hätte** does not go to the end, but follows **nicht** and precedes the second prong.

Wenn ich doch nur hätte zu Hause bleiben können.

Es wäre nett gewesen, wenn ich gestern nicht hätte zurückzufahren brauchen.

NOTE: This exception to the principle of verb-last position occurs also in those rare cases when the indicative is used:

Sie war mir böse, weil ich sie noch nie hatte besuchen können.

109   The Prefix **un-**

The prefix **un-** is added to many adjectives and a few nouns to form antonyms.

glücklich	unglücklich
interessant	uninteressant
vernünftig	unvernünftig
das Wissen (knowledge)	das Unwissen (ignorance)
das Glück (happiness, good luck)	das Unglück (misfortune, accident)

110   The Suffix **-lich** Added to Nouns

Like the English suffix -*ly*, the German suffix **-lich** is added to nouns. It forms adjectives with the meaning of "having the qualities one associates with things or people of such a nature." The stem vowel of the noun is usually umlauted.

der Freund	friend	freundlich	friendly
die Mutter	mother	mütterlich	motherly
das Kind	child	kindlich	childlike
die Welt	world	weltlich	worldly, secular
die Natur	nature	natürlich	naturally

111   The Suffixes **-lich** and **-bar** Added to Verb Stems

Added to verb stems, **-bar** and **-lich** form passive adjectives corresponding to English adjectives in -*able* and -*ible*.

glauben	to believe	unglaublich	unbelievable
brauchen	to use	brauchbar	usable
vergessen	to forget	unvergeßlich	unforgettable

Some of the adjectives formed by **-lich** have an active meaning. (Compare English *durable*.)

sterben	to die	sterblich	mortal, apt to die
vergessen	to forget	vergeßlich	forgetful

EXERCISES

A. Change the following sentences from affirmative to negative and vice versa:

1. Sie ist schon in der Schule.
2. Wir wohnen nicht mehr in Köln.
3. Er ist noch nicht aufgestanden.
4. Wir haben keine Zeit mehr.
5. Ich habe sie noch nicht angerufen.
6. Bist du schon einmal in Paris gewesen?
7. Sie hat noch nie gelogen.
8. Wir haben noch kein Haus gefunden.
9. Rauchst du immer noch Zigaretten?
10. Brauchst du nicht mehr jeden Freitag nach Berlin zu fahren?

SEE LAB
EXERCISES
6.1–6.4

(p. 627)

B. Change the following sentences to wishes starting with **Ich wollte.** Change from affirmative to negative, and from negative to affirmative.

> **Wir haben noch kein Haus an der Riviera.**
> **Ich wollte, wir hätten schon ein Haus an der Riviera.**

1. Seine Nummer ist immer besetzt.
2. Er fährt morgen leider nach Kairo.
3. Ich habe mein Buch zu Hause gelassen.
4. Ich bin zu meiner Mutter gefahren.
5. Wir haben das Haus gekauft.
6. Wir haben uns noch kein Haus gekauft.
7. Ich kann ihn nicht verstehen.
8. Ich habe ihn nicht besuchen können.
9. Wir sind ins Theater gegangen.
10. Sie ist noch nicht zu Hause.
11. Er ist nicht mehr so glücklich wie letztes Jahr.
12. Wir haben keine Butter mehr.
13. Der Winter hat schon begonnen.
14. Bei euch ist es so kalt.
15. Fritz hat das Licht schon ausgemacht.
16. Du hast gestern abend zuviel geredet.
17. Ich habe sie kennengelernt.
18. Sie hat mich nicht angerufen.
19. Ich kann mir kein Buch kaufen.
20. Die Menschen sind leider so egoistisch.
21. Er hat Kriegsromane geschrieben.
22. Ich weiß nicht, was er von mir denkt. (Change only *weiß*.)

SEE LAB
EXERCISES
6.5–6.7

(p. 628)

23. Ich durfte sie nicht nach Hause bringen.
24. Wir konnten letztes Jahr keine Reise machen.
25. Wir mußten gestern abend zu Hause bleiben. (Use either *müssen* or *brauchen*.)

C. Change the following short statements into irreal *if*-clauses. Change negative statements to affirmative *if*-clauses, and affirmative statements to negative *if*-clauses. Add **nur.** Use the **würde**-form only if you want to stress future meaning.

> **Ich habe kein Geld.—Wenn ich nur Geld hätte.**
> **Ich hatte kein Geld.—Wenn ich nur Geld gehabt hätte.**

SEE LAB
EXERCISE
6.8

(p. 628)

1. Er kommt nicht.
2. Sie ist nicht intelligent.
3. Sie haben keine Kinder.
4. Wir haben ihn gestern besucht.
5. Wir müssen zu Hause bleiben.
6. Er bringt mich nicht nach Hause.
7. Ich darf nicht ins Kino.
8. Ihr wart nicht zu Hause.
9. Er geht nicht nach Hause.
10. Sie ist nicht gesund.
11. Er hat nichts gegen mich.
12. Ich habe sie nicht kennengelernt.
13. Er kann nicht mehr lachen.
14. Sie hat fahren gelernt.
15. Sie liebt ihn nicht.
16. Ich darf keinen Kaffee trinken.
17. Ich kann dich nicht besuchen.
18. Du rauchst zuviel.
19. Du hast ihr keine Blumen geschickt.
20. Ihr habt uns nicht geschrieben.

D. Change the following statements to wishes or requests in the subjunctive. Add **gerne, auch gerne einmal, am liebsten, bitte,** or **vielleicht,** as indicated. Whenever the wishes demand the present subjunctive, use the **würde**-form as well.

> **Ich fahre nach Italien.—Ich führe auch gerne einmal nach Italien.**
> **Ich würde gerne nach Italien fahren.**
> **Kann ich morgen nach Bonn fahren?—Könnte ich vielleicht morgen nach Bonn fahren?**
> **Ich habe eine Tasse Kaffee.—Ich hätte gerne eine Tasse Kaffee.**

1. Darf ich ein Glas Wein haben?   (bitte)
2. Ich bin nach Bonn gefahren.   (auch gerne)
3. Hans blieb zu Hause.   (gerne)
4. Ich habe meine Mutter besucht.   (am liebsten)
5. Haben Sie ein Zimmer für mich?   (vielleicht)
6. Ich esse im Hotel Regina.   (auch gerne einmal)
7. Darf ich auf meinem Zimmer frühstücken?   (vielleicht)
8. Können Sie mir jetzt das Frühstück bringen?   (bitte)
9. Ich rauche nach dem Essen eine Zigarette.   (auch gerne)
10. Ich rauchte nach dem Essen eine Zigarette.   (auch gerne)
11. Ich gehe mit einer Freundin ins Kino.   (am liebsten)
12. Darf ich Sie nach Hause bringen, Ingrid?   (vielleicht)
13. Ich habe Ingrid nach Hause gebracht.   (am liebsten)
14. Haben Sie ein Buch für mich?   (vielleicht)
15. Ich habe ein Buch für meine Tochter.   (gerne)

E. Change the following pairs of sentences to irreal conditions. Affirmative statements must then appear in negative form and negative statements in affirmative form. Use the first statements for the **wenn**-clause. In the conclusion, use either the subjunctive or, if possible, the **würde**-form.

> **Ich habe kein Geld. Ich kann nicht nach Paris fahren.**
> **Wenn ich Geld hätte, könnte ich nach Paris fahren.**

1. Es regnet. Wir können jetzt nicht arbeiten.
2. Es regnet nicht. Wir können jetzt arbeiten.
3. Wir haben keine Zeit. Wir fahren morgen nicht an den Rhein.
4. Ich kann nicht arbeiten. Ich bin unglücklich.
5. Ich wohne nicht in München. Ich gehe nicht jeden Tag ins Theater.
6. Wir haben viel zu tun. Wir können nicht in die Stadt fahren.
7. Ingelheim ist nicht glücklich verheiratet. Er fährt allein nach Kairo.
8. Ich liebe dich. Ich habe dich geheiratet.
9. Ich liebe ihn nicht. Ich heirate ihn nicht.
10. Ich habe keinen Wagen. Ich kann dich nicht nach Köln bringen.
11. Tante Amalie kommt nicht. Ich brauche ihr die Stadt nicht zu zeigen.
12. Ingelheim war Soldat. Er konnte einen Kriegsroman schreiben.
13. Der Krieg ist gekommen. Ich habe nicht Medizin studiert.
14. Vater hat uns geholfen. Wir konnten heiraten.
15. Er war krank. Er brauchte nicht Soldat zu werden.

F. The following sentences contain a dependent clause introduced by **weil**. Changing the **weil**-clause into a **wenn**-clause, transform the sentences into irreal conditions.

> **Ich kann nicht arbeiten, weil ich krank bin.**
> **Ich könnte arbeiten, wenn ich nicht krank wäre.**

SEE LAB
EXERCISES
6.9–6.11

(p. 628)

1. Weil ich nicht soviel Geld habe wie Meyer, kann ich nicht an der Riviera wohnen.
2. Weil in Hamburg die Sonne nicht schien, bin ich nach Afrika gefahren.
3. Er kam so spät nach Hause, weil er im Kino war.
4. Weil er Geld hatte, hat sie ihn geheiratet.
5. Weil Frau Meyer Frau Meyer ist, kann man nicht mit ihr sprechen.
6. Weil das Essen nicht gut war, fuhren wir nach Hause.
7. Weil er Hepatitis bekam, schickte man ihn nach Hause.
8. Wir wohnen in der Stadt, weil wir keine Kinder haben.
9. Er wurde Soldat, weil er mußte.
10. Weil ich dich geheiratet habe, konnte ich Anton nicht heiraten.

G. Restate the following sentences in the past subjunctive, starting with **Es wäre nett gewesen, wenn . . .**

SEE LAB
EXERCISES
6.12–6.13

(p. 628)

1. Ich kann ihn besuchen.
2. Ich darf nach Köln fahren.
3. Ich kann arbeiten.
4. Ich kann meinem Vater einen Brief schreiben.
5. Ich kann mit ihr ins Museum gehen.
6. Ich brauche das Buch nicht zu lesen.
7. Ich kann dich von Berlin aus anrufen.
8. Ich darf mit nach Casablanca fahren.
9. Wir können mit der Lufthansa fliegen.
10. Er braucht heute nicht zu arbeiten.
11. Er kann es tun.
12. Ich kann das Haus kaufen.
13. Er darf seinen Freund mitbringen.
14. Ich kann nach Hause fahren.
15. Ich brauche heute nicht ins Museum zu gehen.

H. Change the following sentences to indirect discourse, starting with **Er sagte, daß . . .** Change pronouns as appropriate.

1. Meyer wohnt in Köln.
2. Ich brauche kein Geld.
3. Wir arbeiten heute nicht.
4. Ich brauche nicht nach Bonn zu fahren.
5. Ich bleibe heute abend zu Hause.

6. Ich gehe heute abend mit meiner Freundin ins Kino.
7. Ich bin heute abend nicht zu Hause.
8. Wir haben schon ein Haus.
9. Ingelheim fährt nach Afrika, um einen Roman zu schreiben.
10. Ich heiße Behrens.
11. Ich verstehe Sie nicht.
12. Ich komme zu Ihnen.
13. Das weiß ich auch.
14. Das kann ich Ihnen nicht glauben.
15. Ich will ihn in Berlin besuchen.
16. Ich möchte mit dir ins Kino gehen.
17. Ich muß Ingelheims Roman lesen.
18. Ich darf mit meinem Vater nach Afrika fahren.
19. Karl soll dir helfen.
20. Ich kann Sie nicht verstehen.

I. Change the following sentences to indirect discourse, starting with **Er sagte, . . .** Change pronouns as appropriate.

1. Man hat ihn nach Norwegen geschickt.
2. Leider war sie viel zu intelligent.
3. Leider hatte sie zuviel Geld.
4. Er ist nicht mit uns nach Berlin gefahren.
5. Ich mußte nach Casablanca fliegen.
6. Wir konnten das Haus in Köln nicht kaufen.
7. Ich habe zuviel Kaffee getrunken.
8. Er konnte uns gestern nicht besuchen.
9. Leider mußte ich damals Brieftauben füttern.
10. Den Roman von Ingelheim habe ich noch nicht gelesen.
11. Leider bin ich zu meiner Mutter gefahren.
12. Leider habe ich den Brief mit nach Casablanca genommen.
13. Er hat uns nie eingeladen.
14. Natürlich mußte ich mit ihr ins Museum gehen.
15. Leider konnte ich ihn nicht verstehen.
16. Leider habe ich vergessen, meine Frau anzurufen.
17. Ich habe sie noch nicht angerufen.
18. Meine Freundin wohnt jetzt in Berlin.
19. Erika durfte nicht mitgehen.
20. Das hast du mir nie gesagt.

SEE LAB
EXERCISES
6.14–6.16

(pp. 628-629)

J. Change the following questions to indirect yes-or-no questions. First start with **Ich wüßte gerne, ob . . .** (indicative), and then with **Er fragte mich, ob . . .** (subjunctive).

1. Fährt Erika morgen bestimmt nach Berlin?
2. Sind Sie verheiratet?

3. Wohnen Sie in München?
4. Haben Sie noch ein Zimmer frei?
5. Kennst du meine Freundin?
6. Kannst du mich morgen anrufen?
7. Darf ich Sie einladen?
8. Gehen Sie gerne fischen?
9. Ist sein Vater auch Arzt?
10. Sind Sie in Deutschland geboren?

K. Change to direct questions. Change pronouns as appropriate.

1. Er wollte wissen, ob ich nach Berlin kommen könnte.
2. Er wollte wissen, ob mein Vater Schriftsteller wäre.
3. Er wollte wissen, was er mir schenken sollte.
4. Er wollte wissen, ob mein Vater bald nach Hause käme.
5. Er wollte wissen, ob ich ihm vielleicht zwanzig Mark geben könnte.
6. Er wollte wissen, warum ich Angst vor ihm hätte.
7. Er wollte wissen, wann ich ihn einmal besuchen könnte.
8. Er wollte wissen, ob ich ihn nicht anrufen könnte.
9. Er wollte wissen, wem der Wagen gehörte.
10. Er wollte wissen, warum alle Professoren so vergeßlich wären.

L. Change to indirect questions (past time). Start with **Er fragte mich, . . .** Change pronouns as appropriate.

1. Waren Sie damals auch Student?
2. Warst du gestern abend in der Universität?
3. Hattest du kein Geld bei dir?
4. Stand da drüben nicht früher ein Hotel?
5. W*arum* hattest du eigentlich nie Geld?
6. Wie lange war Hans denn in Afrika?
7. Warum konntest du nicht nach Hause kommen?
8. Warum ist Inge nicht mitgegangen?
9. Wen wolltest du denn in Berlin besuchen?
10. Mußtest du gestern abend schon wieder arbeiten?
11. Warum hattest du ihm nie geantwortet?
12. Hast du gestern arbeiten müssen?
13. Hast du ihm schon für die Bücher gedankt?
14. Hast du deine Mutter mitgenommen?
15. Haben Sie ein Taxi genommen?
16. Was hast du ihm denn erzählt?
17. Wann habt ihr geheiratet?
18. Hat Fritz dir nicht helfen können?
19. Wem hat denn das Haus gehört?
20. Mit wem bist du gestern abend im Kino gewesen?

M. Change to direct questions:

1. Er fragte, ob viele Leute dagewesen wären.
2. Er fragte, ob ich gestern krank gewesen wäre.
3. Er fragte, ob es wahr wäre, daß es im Winter hier immer so kalt ist.
4. Er fragte, ob ich auch Hepatitis gehabt hätte.
5. Er fragte, wie lange ich in Afrika gewesen wäre.
6. Er fragte, warum ich um neun Uhr noch im Bett gelegen hätte.
7. Er fragte, warum Inge nicht hätte mit nach Italien fahren dürfen.
8. Er fragte, warum Erika gestern abend hätte zu Hause bleiben müssen.
9. Er fragte, warum ich ihr nicht hätte schreiben können.
10. Er fragte, ob sein Sohn nicht hätte zu Hause bleiben können.

N. Express in German:

1. When it began to rain, we couldn't work any more.
2. If it begins to rain now, we can't work any more.
3. If it began to rain now, we wouldn't be able to work any more.
4. I was often unhappy; but when I saw her, I was always happy.
5. I'd like to know whether he is really a writer.
6. I wish he weren't a writer.
7. I don't understand why you always want to eat here.
8. I wish we could always eat here.
9. I wish we'd eat at home tonight.
10. It would have been nice if you had stayed at home.
11. Why did Ingelheim go to Africa alone?
12. It was not against the law.
13. I really should (ought to) invite him, but I have no time.
14. I really should have invited him, but I had no time.
15. Not until yesterday did I hear from him.
16. Not until yesterday did he ask me whether I could go to Bonn with him.
17. She told me she would go to Bonn with me.
18. If only we could go to Bonn again!
19. Thank goodness I've always been healthy.
20. He said he had never been in Berlin.
21. I'd like to have a cup of coffee.
22. When Ingelheim became twenty, he got hepatitis.
23. You should have seen him three years ago.
24. If only she had learned to drive.
25. Has he found the mistake yet?—No, not yet.
26. He told us that Ingelheim had disappeared in Africa without a trace.
27. I shall never be able to forget you.
28. I wish he didn't always forget my birthday.
29. I wish you hadn't forgotten my birthday again.
30. Whenever I needed her, she came immediately.

31. I know that he went to Cairo alone.
32. But I also know that he wasn't alone in Cairo.
33. I mustn't forget to send my wife flowers.
34. When he met her, she was only twenty.
35. He met her in Berlin before the war.
36. She lived in Cologne at that time, but she studied in Bonn.
37. I know Aunt Amalie is unreasonable.
38. In three weeks they saw sixteen cities; now they believe they know Europe.
39. He knows he should have stayed at home.
40. If he hadn't lived in Munich at that time, he would never have met her.

VOCABULARY

achtzig eighty
anfangen to begin
  es fängt an zu regnen it is beginning to rain
annehmen to accept; to assume, to take on
ansehen to look at
baden to bathe
das Bad, ⁻er bath
begleiten to accompany
besser better
bestimmt definitely
bitten um to request, to ask for
blicken to look, to glance
der Blick, –e look, glance; view
der Boden, ⁻ ground; floor
breit broad, wide
danke schön thank you very much
drüben over there
eigentlich actually, really
das Ende, –n end
  zu Ende to an end, to a conclusion
endlich at last, finally
erleben to experience
erscheinen to appear
fern far away, distant
  die Ferne distance
der Finger, – finger
fliegen to fly

der Flieger, – flyer
der Tiefflieger, – strafing plane
der Flug, ⁻e flight
der Abflug, ⁻e departure
der Flughafen, ⁻ airport
frei unoccupied, free
der Freitag, –e Friday
fühlen to feel
  das Gefühl, –e feeling
fünfzig fifty
der Fußabdruck, ⁻e footprint
gar nicht not at all
geboren born
  ich bin geboren I was born
die Geburt, –en birth
  der Geburtstag, –e the birthday
der Gedanke, –n thought, idea
  auf den Gedanken kommen to hit upon the idea
gehorchen to obey
genug enough
die Geschichte, –n story, history
heilen to heal
  geheilt healed, well
heiraten to marry
  verheiratet married
  ich bin verheiratet I am married

hinter behind, beyond, on the other side of
irgendwohin somewhere
jemand somebody, someone (*dat.:* jemand, jemandem; *acc.:* jemand, jemanden)
kämpfen to fight
der König, –e king
kurz short
küssen to kiss
lieber (*adverb*) rather
  am liebsten (to like) most of all
liegen to lie (flat); to be situated
dieses Mal this time
  noch einmal once more
  manchmal sometimes
  jedesmal every time
  diesmal this time
  zwei mal zwei two times two
das Meter, – meter (measure of length)
mindestens at least
möglich possible
der Montag, –e Monday
nett nice
niemand nobody, no one (*dat.:* niemand, niemandem; *acc.:* niemand, niemandem)
nun now

das Paar, –e pair, couple
  ein paar a few
die Platte, –n (phonograph)
  record; flagstone
plötzlich suddenly
das Problem', –e problem
der Rhein the Rhine
ruhig quiet, restful
  unruhig restless
der Samstag, –e Saturday
  samstags on Saturdays
schenken to present, to give
  das Geschenk, –e present,
  gift
schlecht bad
schnell fast, rapid
der Schuh, –e shoe

schwach weak
sechzig sixty
sicher certain, sure; probably
die Situation, –en* situation
springen to jump
  aufspringen to jump up
stehen to stand
  aufstehen to arise, to get
  up, to rise
still quiet, still
die Terras'se, –n terrace
tot dead
ungefähr approximate(ly),
  about
vergessen to forget
verlieren to lose

der Verstand (no pl.) mind,
  reason
versuchen to try, to attempt
wahrscheinlich probably
weg away
  wegfahren to drive away,
  to leave
weit far
werfen to throw
das Wissen knowledge
die Wohnung, –en apartment
die Wunde, –n wound
wünschen to wish
zählen to count
eine Zeitlang for a while
  (not: for a long time)
das Zimmer, – room

* All foreign nouns in -tion are feminine and are declined like **Situation**.

STRONG VERBS

anfangen to begin
  fing an, hat angefangen, er
  fängt an
annehmen to accept; to assume, to take on
  nahm an, hat angenommen,
  er nimmt an
ansehen to look at
  sah an, hat angesehen, er
  sieht an
bitten to ask for, to request
  bat, hat gebeten, er bittet
erscheinen to appear
  erschien, ist erschienen, er
  erscheint
fliegen to fly

  flog, ist geflogen, er fliegt
liegen to lie (flat); to be
  situated
  lag, hat gelegen, er liegt
springen to jump
  sprang, ist gesprungen, er
  springt
  aufspringen to jump up
  sprang auf, ist aufge-
  sprungen, er springt
  auf
stehen to stand
  stand, hat gestanden, er
  steht
  aufstehen to get up, to
  rise, to arise

  stand auf, ist aufge-
  standen, er steht auf
vergessen to forget
  vergaß, hat vergessen, er
  vergißt
verlieren to lose
  verlor, hat verloren,
  er verliert
wegfahren to drive away, to
  leave
  fuhr weg, ist weggefahren,
  er fährt weg
werfen to throw
  warf, hat geworfen, er
  wirft

REVIEW

Negation: Use of Front Field

Restate the following sentences in negative form, starting with the parts in parentheses; use contrast intonation if you want to.

> **Es hat (gestern) geregnet.**
> **Gestern hat es nicht geregnet.**

1. Ich will (heute abend) ausgehen.
2. Mein Mann fährt (nächstes Jahr) nach Amerika.
3. Herr Schmidt ist (gestern) zu Hause geblieben.
4. Ich möchte (dieses Buch) lesen.
5. Ich habe (seinen Vater) gekannt.
6. Ich kann (um eins) am Bahnhof sein.
7. Wir gehen (heute) in den Dom.
8. Meyer ist (leider) in Berlin.
9. Ich habe (gestern) Wein getrunken.
10. Wir sind (gestern) nach dem Kino ins Café Kranzler gegangen.

SEE ANALYSIS 43 (pp. 83–85)

Negation: Use of Contrast Intonation

Negate the following sentences and start with the underlined parts. Use contrast accent and write down a statement implied by contrast accent.

> **Sie ist intelligent.**
> **Intelligent ist sie nicht. Sie ist dumm.**

1. Wir gehen heute abend ins Kino.
2. Ich habe deinen Freund angerufen.
3. Ihr Mann arbeitet in Köln.
4. Herr Bertram muß heute in Köln arbeiten.
5. Er will in Frankfurt Medizin studieren.
6. Ich kann dir das Buch schon heute abend geben.
7. Erika möchte heute abend Tee trinken.

SEE ANALYSIS 55–56 (pp. 91- 93)

8. Herr Müller will <u>morgen</u> kommen.
9. Meine Tochter will <u>Ärztin</u> werden.
10. Hildegard ist <u>glücklich</u>.

Word Order in Dependent Clauses

Introduce the following statements by **Ich weiß, daß.** . . . Remember that in dependent clauses the subject usually follows the conjunction.

SEE
ANALYSIS
84–86
(pp. 178–182)

1. Nach Hause begleiten will er mich nicht.
2. Ein Bild von mir hat sie nicht.
3. Einen Hut hat er seiner Frau nicht gekauft.
4. In der Regina-Bar kann man gut tanzen.
5. Er hat das Licht noch nicht angemacht.
6. Das hat er in der Zeitung gelesen.
7. Erika sollten wir Blumen ins Haus schicken.
8. Überall sprach man von seinem Roman.
9. Frühstücken kannst du auch auf deinem Zimmer.
10. Meinen Vater hätte ich nicht anzurufen brauchen.
11. So interessant ist die Regina-Bar nicht.
12. Hier gehen schon um sechs die Laternen an.
13. An der Westfront nahmen ihn die Amerikaner gefangen.
14. Damals mußte er Soldat werden.
15. Im Mai hat er geschrieben, er wollte nach Casablanca.

Prepositions with the Dative—Prepositions with the Accusative

Vary the first sentence of each group by using the words in parentheses.

SEE
ANALYSIS
62–64
(pp. 124–125)

Er wohnt bei seiner Tante.

bei _____ (sein Vater)
bei _____ (seine Tochter)
bei _____ (Frau Schmidt)
bei _____ (Schmidts)
bei _____ (sie)
bei _____ (wir)
bei _____ (ich)

Ich bin mit Inge ins Kino gegangen.

mit _____ (mein Vater)
mit _____ (meine Freundin)
mit _____ (Fräulein Lenz)
mit _____ (unsere Kinder)
mit _____ (sie)
mit _____ (er)

Außer ihr ist kein Mensch gekommen.
Außer _____ (wir)
Außer _____ (unser Onkel)
Außer _____ (meine Freundin)
Außer _____ (Schmidt)
Außer _____ (die zwei Mädchen)
Außer _____ (seine Studenten)

Hans ist zum Bahnhof gegangen.
     zu _____ (sein Freund)
     zu _____ (seine Freundin)
     zu _____ (Erika)
     zu _____ (Meyers)
     zu _____ (ihr)
     zu _____ (sie)
     zu _____ (er)
     zu _____ (du)

Ich habe das Buch für dich gekauft.
     für _____ (er)
     für _____ (sie)
     für _____ (wir)
     für _____ (ich)
     für _____ (meine Frau)
     für _____ (meine Kinder)
     für _____ (mein Mann)
     für _____ (meine Studenten)
     für _____ (eine Dame)

Er ist ohne mich nach Casablanca gefahren.
     ohne _____ (er)
     ohne _____ (seine Frau)
     ohne _____ (sein Sohn)
     ohne _____ (Geld)

UNIT 7: Prepositions with Dative or Accusative—The Genitive Case—**Ein**–Words without Nouns—The Indirect–Discourse Subjunctive

PATTERNS

[1] Prepositions with either Dative or Accusative

Analyze the use of case after the prepositions. Be prepared to produce the answers orally in class when you hear the questions.

Wo fahrt *ihr* denn hin?—*Wir* fahren an den *Rhein*.
  Where are *you* going?—*We* are going to the *Rhine*.

SEE
ANALYSIS
112–114
(pp. 272-276)

Wo *wart* ihr denn gestern?—Wir waren gestern am *Rhein*.
  Where *were* you yesterday?—We were at the *Rhine* yesterday.

Wohin fuhr er denn mit seiner Frau?—Er fuhr mit ihr an die Riviera.
  Where did he go with his wife?—He went to the Riviera with her.

Wo wohnt er denn?—Er wohnt an der Riviera.
  Where does he live?—He lives on the Riviera.

Wo hat er sie denn hingefahren?—Er hat sie ans Theater gebracht.
  Where did he take her?—He took her to the theater.

Wo wartete ihr Freund?—Er wartete am Theater.
  Where was her friend waiting?—He was waiting at the theater.

Wo hat er denn seinen Hut hingelegt?—Er hat ihn aufs Bett gelegt.
  Where did he put his hat?—He put it on the bed.

Wo lag denn sein Hut?—Er lag auf dem Bett.
  Where was his hat?—It was lying on the bed.

Wohin hat er seine Frau denn gebracht?—Er hat sie aufs Schiff gebracht.
  Where did he take his wife?—He took her to the ship.

Wo hast du ihn denn gesehen?—Ich habe ihn auf dem Schiff gesehen.
  Where did you see him?—I saw him on the ship.

(Facing) **Universität München**

Was hat er denn mit seinem Geld gemacht?—Er hat es auf die Bank gebracht.
 What did he do with his money?—He took it to the bank.

Wo hast *du* dein Geld?—*Ich* habe mein Geld *auch* auf der Bank.
 Where do *you* have your money?—I have my money in the bank, *too*.

Wo hast du den Wagen denn hingestellt?—Hinter das Haus.
 Where did you put the car?—Behind the house.

Wo steht denn dein Wagen?—Hinter dem Haus.
 Where is your car?—Behind the house.

Was habt *ihr* denn gestern gemacht?—*Wir* sind gestern ins Theater gegangen.
 What did *you* do yesterday?—*We* went to the *theater*.

Wo wart ihr denn gestern abend?—Im Theater.
 Where were you last night?—At the theater.

Wo wohnst du denn, wenn du in München bist?—In München gehe ich immer
 ins Hotel Regina.
 Where do you stay in Munich?—In Munich I always go to the Hotel Regina.

Wo wohnst du denn, wenn du in München bist?—Ich wohne in München
 immer im Hotel Regina.
 Where do you stay in Munich?—In Munich I always live at the Hotel Regina.

Was hast du denn mit meiner Zeitung gemacht?—Ich habe sie neben deinen
 Hut gelegt.
 What did you do with my paper?—I put it by your hat.

Neben meinem Hut liegt sie aber nicht.—Wo kann sie denn sein?
 But it isn't by my hat.—Where can it be?

Wie seid ihr nach Deutschland geflogen?—Wir sind nonstop über den Atlantik
 geflogen.
 How did you fly to Germany?—We flew nonstop across the Atlantic.

Und wo habt ihr gefrühstückt?—Über dem Atlantik.
 And where did you have breakfast?—Over the Atlantic.

Wie seid ihr denn nach Wiesbaden gefahren?—Wir sind von Mainz über den
 Rhein gefahren.
 How did you drive to Wiesbaden?—We drove from Mainz across the Rhine.

Wo fährt die Untergrundbahn in Chicago?—Über der Straße.
 Where does the subway run in Chicago?—Above the street.

Wo sind denn meine *Schu*he?—Unter dem *Bett*.—*Wo* sind sie?
　Where are my *shoes?*—Under the *bed.*—*Where* are they?

Sie sieht immer unter das Bett, wenn sie ins Bett geht.
　She always looks under the bed when she goes to bed.

Es regnete, und wir hielten unter der Brücke.
　It was raining, and we stopped under the bridge.

Es regnete, und wir liefen unter die Brücke.
　It was raining, and we ran under the bridge.

Wo hast du Rosemarie denn gesehen?—Vor dem Hotel.
　Where did you see Rosemarie?—In front of the hotel.

Bringst du mir bitte den Wagen?—Ja, ich bringe ihn dir vor das Hotel.
　Would you please bring me the car?—Yes, I'll bring it to the hotel for you.

Ich war schon vor dem Krieg in Afrika.
　I was in Africa even before the war.

Vor zehn Jahren stand hier ein Haus.
　Ten years ago there was a house here.

Sollen wir vor oder nach dem Theater essen?
　Shall we eat before or after the theater?

Vor einem Jahr kam Ingelheim nach Hause.
　A year ago Ingelheim came home.

Ich möchte vor dem Essen noch einen Brief schreiben.
　I'd like to write a letter before dinner.

Wo lag denn der Brief?—Er lag zwischen den Zeitungen, und ich konnte ihn
　nicht finden.
　Where was the letter?—It was lying among the newspapers, and I couldn't
　find it.

Er konnte den Brief lange nicht finden; seine Frau hatte ihn zwischen die
　Zeitungen gelegt.
　He couldn't find the letter for a long time; his wife had put it among the
　newspapers.

[2] Prepositions with the Genitive

Während des Krieges war Schmidt in Frankreich.
　During the war Schmidt was in France.

SEE
ANALYSIS
115, 116
(pp. 276-281)

Während dieser Zeit hat er viel durchgemacht.
  During that time he went through a lot.

Während der Woche kannst du mich nicht besuchen.
  During the week you can't visit me.

Ihr könnt doch wegen des Regens nicht zu Hause bleiben.
  You can't stay at home because of the rain.

Ich fürchte, er will sie nur wegen ihres Geldes heiraten.
  I am afraid he only wants to marry her because of her money.

Wir haben trotz des Regens gestern gearbeitet.
  We worked yesterday in spite of the rain.

Wir haben trotz dem Regen gestern gearbeitet.
  We worked yesterday in spite of the rain.

Try to form sentences of your own using **während, wegen,** and **trotz.**

[3] The Attributive Genitive

Rephrase the German sentences by using the elements indicated in parentheses.

SEE
ANALYSIS
116
(pp. 279-281)

Am Abend ihres Geburtstages ging er mit ihr ins Theater.
  On the evening of her birthday he went to the theater with her.
  (on the evening of his birthday)

Gegen Ende des Jahres kam er aus Afrika zurück.
  Toward the end of the year he came back from Africa.
  (toward the end of the week)

Gegen Gottes Gesetz ist der Film des Jahres.
  Against God's Law is the movie of the year.
  (the book of the month)

Die Integrität des Menschen ist das Thema dieses Buches.
  The theme of this book is the integrity of man.
  (the intelligence of our children)

Herr Behrens ist ein Freund meines Mannes.
  Herr Behrens is a friend of my husband.
  (the son of my friend)

Ingrid Overhoff ist die Tochter eines Architekten.
  Ingrid Overhoff is the daughter of an architect.
  (the wife of a writer)

Das war am Anfang des Krieges.
> That was at the beginning of the war.
> (at the beginning of the month)

Werners Freundin kenne ich nicht.
> I don't know Werner's girl friend.
> (Ingrid's aunt)

Schmidt-Ingelheims Roman habe ich nicht gelesen.
> I haven't read Schmidt-Ingelheim's novel.
> (father's books)

Hast du Mutters Hut gesehen?
> Have you seen mother's hat?
> (Karl's car)

Wo ist denn Antons Frau?
> Where is Anton's wife?
> (Maria's husband)

Das ist Doktor Müllers Haus.
> That's Doctor Müller's house.
> (Professor Meyer's daughter)

Den Vater dieses Mädchens kenne ich sehr gut.
> I know this girl's father very well.
> (his friend's mother)

Die Tochter deines Bruders habe ich nie kennengelernt.
> I've never met your brother's daughter.
> (your sister's son)

Dr. Schmidt ist ein Schüler meines Mannes.
> Dr. Schmidt is a student of my husband's.
> (a friend of my father's)

Die Sekretärin meines Mannes hat mir Blumen geschenkt.
> My husband's secretary has given me flowers.
> (my daughter's friend)

Von dem Geld meines Vaters habe ich nie etwas gesehen.
> I've never seen anything of my father's money.
> (my wife's money)

Der Arzt meines Mannes hat mir befohlen, nicht mehr zu rauchen.
> My husband's doctor has ordered me to stop smoking.
> (my wife's doctor)

Hannelore? Das ist doch die Freundin von Werner Schlosser!

    Hannelore? She's Werner Schlosser's friend, isn't she?
    (Hans Wagner's wife)

Sie müssen das Buch von Schmidt-Ingelheim lesen.

    You must read Schmidt-Ingelheim's book.
    (see Bergman's film)

Herr Behrens ist ein Freund von meinem Mann.

    Herr Behrens is a friend of my husband's.
    (Frau Behrens; of my wife's)

Herr Behrens ist ein Freund von Johannes.

    Herr Behrens is a friend of Johannes'.
    (Frau Behrens; a friend of Inge's)

Nein, das ist doch der Wagen von seinem Vater; *ihm* gehört der nicht.

    No, that's his father's car; it doesn't belong to him.
    (my aunt's hat; to me)

Wo sind denn die Schuhe von den Kindern?

    Where are the children's shoes?
    (your father's letter)

Und die Tochter von *diese*n Leuten willst du heiraten?—Na und?

    And you want to marry the daughter of *those* people?—Well, so what?
    (the son of *that* man?)

Maria ist eine von Dieters Freundinnen.

    Maria is one of Dieter's girl friends.
    (Fritz; Karl's friends)

[4] von plus Dative as a Genitive Substitute

Note the difference in the use of the genitive and of **von** plus dative in the
following sentences. When is the **von**-phrase obligatory?

SEE
ANALYSIS
116

(pp. 279-281)

Ingelheims Kinder sind noch klein.

    Ingelheim's children are still little.

Die Kinder von Ingelheim sind noch klein.

    Ingelheim's children are still little.

Die Kinder von Hans und Ingrid Ingelheim sind noch klein.

    Hans and Ingrid Ingelheim's children are still little.

Die Kinder von Ingelheims sind noch sehr klein.
  The Ingelheims' children are still very little.

Ingrids Kinder sind noch sehr klein.
  Ingrid's children are still very little.

Die Kinder von Ingrid sind noch sehr klein.
  Ingrid's children are still very little.

Sie war eine Freundin von Overhoffs Frau.
  She was a friend of Overhoff's wife.

Er war der Vater von dreizehn Kindern.
  He was the father of thirteen children.

Ich bin kein Freund von Rheinwein.
  I don't like Rhine wine.

Jeder Leser von Kriegsromanen weiß, wer Schmidt-Ingelheim ist.
  Every reader of war novels knows who Schmidt-Ingelheim is.

Ist das nicht die Freundin von Karls Frau?
  Isn't that the friend of Karl's wife?

[5] Special Constructions

Er ist ein Freund von mir.

SEE
ANALYSIS
116

(pp. 279-281)

  von _____ (du)
  von _____ (er)
  von _____ (sie)
  von _____ (wir)
  von _____ (ihr)
  von _____ (Sie)
  von _____ (meine Mutter)
  von _____ (mein Vater)

Möchten Sie noch eine Tasse Tee?
  Would you like another cup of tea?

Haben Sie schon gewählt?—Ja, ich hätte gerne ein Glas Mosel.
  Have you decided yet?—Yes, I'd like a glass of Moselle.

Meine Frau würde gerne ein Glas Wasser trinken.
  My wife would like to drink a glass of water.

[6] Ein-Words without Nouns

Form variations of your own.

SEE
ANALYSIS
117

(p. 281)

Ich habe leider kein Buch mitgebracht. Hast du eins bei dir?
  Unfortunately, I didn't bring a book along. Do you have one with you?

Keiner von seinen Freunden hat ihn besucht.
  None of his friends visited him.

Haben Sie noch zwei Zimmer frei?—Nein, leider nur noch eins.
  Do you still have a couple of rooms?—No, unfortunately only one.

Ingrid ist auch eine von den Frauen, die glauben, daß eine Frau nicht intelligent zu sein braucht.
  Ingrid, too, is one of those women who believe that a woman doesn't have to be intelligent.

Obermann ist leider auch einer von den Männern, die nie sagen, was sie denken.
  Obermann, unfortunately, is also one of those men who never say what they think.

Hier ist das Buch von Fritz.—Nein, das ist meins.
  Here is Fritz's book.—No, that's mine.

Mir gehört das Buch nicht; es muß deins sein.
  That book doesn't belong to me. It must be yours.

Wem gehört denn der Mercedes? Ist das Ihrer, Frau Ingelheim?
  Who owns that Mercedes? Is it yours, Frau Ingelheim?

Einen Ihrer Romane habe ich gelesen.
  I have read one of your novels.

Einen von Ihren Romanen habe ich gelesen.
  I have read one of your novels.

Eine seiner Töchter studiert jetzt Medizin.
  One of his daughters is studying medicine now.

Eine von seinen Töchtern studiert jetzt Medizin.
  One of his daughters is studying medicine now.

Keiner seiner Söhne ist Schriftsteller geworden.
  Not one of his sons has become a writer.

Keiner von seinen Söhnen ist Schriftsteller geworden.
  Not one of his sons has become a writer.

[7] The Indirect-Discourse Subjunctive

After studying these sentences, form statements in indirect discourse using the assertions printed below the pattern sentences. If possible, use both forms of the subjunctive.

„Ich bin nur zwei Tage in München.“
Sie sagte, sie wäre nur zwei Tage in München.
Sie sagte, sie sei nur zwei Tage in München.

SEE
ANALYSIS
118, 119
(pp. 281-283)

„Ich habe ein Zimmer im Regina.“
Sie sagte, sie hätte ein Zimmer im Regina.
Sie sagte, sie habe ein Zimmer im Regina.

„Sind Sie schon zwanzig?“
Er fragte mich, ob ich schon zwanzig wäre.
Er fragte mich, ob ich schon zwanzig sei.

„Wann bist du denn gestern abend nach Hause gekommen?“
Er fragte mich, wann ich gestern abend nach Hause gekommen wäre.
Er fragte mich, wann ich gestern abend nach Hause gekommen sei.

München. Ludwigstraße von der Feldherrnhalle

„Wenn du willst, komme ich um elf ins Hotel."
Er sagte, wenn ich wollte, käme er um elf ins Hotel.
Er sagte, wenn ich wolle, komme er um elf ins Hotel.

„Dann können wir zusammen frühstücken."
Er sagte, wir könnten dann zusammen frühstücken.

„Kannst du mit mir frühstücken?"
Er fragte, ob ich mit ihm frühstücken könnte.
Er fragte, ob ich mit ihm frühstücken könne.

„Ich muß morgen abend um sieben bei Schmidts sein."
Er sagte, er müßte morgen abend um sieben bei Schmidts sein.
Er sagte, er müsse morgen abend um sieben bei Schmidts sein.

„Ich mußte gestern nach Berlin fahren."
Er sagte, er hätte gestern nach Berlin fahren müssen.
Er sagte, er habe gestern nach Berlin fahren müssen.

„Ich brauche gottseidank nicht nach Berlin zu fahren."
Er sagte, er brauchte gottseidank nicht nach Berlin zu fahren.
Er sagte, er brauche gottseidank nicht nach Berlin zu fahren.

„Ihr braucht nicht auf mich zu warten; ich komme erst morgen."
Er sagte, wir brauchten nicht auf ihn zu warten; er käme erst morgen.
Er sagte, wir brauchten nicht auf ihn zu warten; er komme erst morgen.

„Der Wolf ist gekommen und hat sie alle gefressen."
Er sagte, der Wolf wäre gekommen und hätte sie alle gefressen.
Er sagte, der Wolf sei gekommen und habe sie alle gefressen.

Transform the following statements into indirect discourse in accordance with the examples above:

„Er ist seit langem wieder zu Hause."
„Morgen habe ich keine Zeit."
„Ich kann dich morgen leider nicht besuchen."
„Leider muß ich morgen nach Berlin fahren."
„Fahren *Sie* doch morgen nach Köln, Herr Müller."
„Ich darf meinen Mann noch nicht besuchen."
„Ich will nicht studieren."
„Liebst du mich, und findest du mich schön?"
„Wann fährst du nach Berlin?"
„Du rauchst zuviel."
„Der Mantel ist ganz neu."
„Ich muß mal telefonieren."

CONVERSATION

TELEFONISTIN:	Hotel Regina, guten Morgen.
KLAUS:	Guten Morgen. Ich hätte gerne Zimmer 641 (sechseinundvierzig).
TELEFONISTIN:	Einen Augenblick, bitte.
ROSEMARIE:	Ja, bitte?
KLAUS:	Rosemarie? Guten Morgen.
ROSEMARIE:	Klaus? Guten Morgen. Du hättest aber wirklich nicht so früh anzurufen brauchen. Ich schlafe ja noch.
KLAUS:	Das höre ich.
ROSEMARIE:	Wieviel Uhr ist es denn? Sieben? Oder ist es schon acht?
KLAUS:	Acht? Es ist zwanzig nach zehn.
ROSEMARIE:	Nein, das ist nicht möglich—zwanzig nach zehn?
KLAUS:	Doch, das *ist* möglich. Wenn es *nicht* schon so spät wäre, hätte ich dich nicht angerufen.
ROSEMARIE:	Ja, und wenn wir gestern abend nicht so lange getanzt hätten, wäre ich auch schon lange auf.
KLAUS:	Aber wer wollte denn gestern so lange tanzen, du oder ich?
ROSEMARIE:	Ich, natürlich. Wenn ich nur zwei Tage in München bin, will ich doch auch etwas sehen.
KLAUS:	Na, *so* interessant ist die Regina-Bar ja *auch* nicht!
ROSEMARIE:	Du, Klaus, wo bist du denn eigentlich? Hier im Hotel?
KLAUS:	Nein, ich bin noch zu Hause. Aber wenn du willst, komme ich um elf ins Hotel. Dann können wir zusammen frühstücken. Du könntest natürlich auch auf deinem Zimmer frühstücken, und ich komme erst um zwölf,—wie du willst.
ROSEMARIE:	Nein, das möchte ich nicht. Wenn ich nur drei Nächte in München bin, will ich mit *dir* frühstücken.
KLAUS:	Gut, Rosemarie,—ich bin um elf in der Hotelhalle,—und es wäre schön, wenn du nicht erst um zwölf kämst: ich habe Hunger, ich bin schon seit acht Uhr auf.
ROSEMARIE:	Aber Klaus, du weißt doch, daß du nie auf mich zu warten brauchst. Gestern hast du auch gesagt, daß ich um acht Uhr da sein müßte oder wir kämen nicht mehr in das Restaurant—wie hieß es doch?

KLAUS: Feldherrnkeller.

ROSEMARIE: Ja richtig,—wir kämen nicht mehr in den Feldherrnkeller, weil dort
                immer so viele Leute seien. Na, und wann war ich da? Um zehn vor acht.
                —Übrigens, Klaus, wie ist denn das Wetter? Ich habe noch nicht aus dem
                Fenster gesehen, aber es wäre schön, wenn heute die Sonne schiene.

KLAUS: Das Wetter könnte nicht besser sein. Heute morgen sah es ja aus, als
                ob es wieder regnen würde,—und wenn du nicht hier wärst, hätte es
                heute bestimmt geregnet.

ROSEMARIE: Vielen Dank für das Kompliment, Klaus. Aber wenn es geregnet hätte,
                das hätte auch nichts gemacht. Wir hätten ja in ein Museum gehen
                können. Aber weißt du was? Ich ginge nach dem Frühstück gerne durch
                die Stadt; ich möchte mir doch einen Mantel kaufen, und es wäre nett,
                wenn wir das zusammen machen könnten.

KLAUS: Gut;—und was machen wir, wenn wir den Mantel gekauft haben?

ROSEMARIE: Dann können wir eine Stunde auf einer Bank in der Sonne sitzen.

KLAUS: Im Hofgarten:* Das wäre prima. Wir gehen eine Stunde in den Hof-
                garten, und dann gehen wir essen.

* The Royal Gardens, a public park in the center of Munich.

ROSEMARIE: Du, aber bitte in ein Restaurant, wo keine Touristen sind, ja, Klaus? Ich wollte, in München wären nicht immer so viele Touristen.

KLAUS: Ja, was wäre München ohne die Touristen! Aber ich kenne ein Restaurant bei der Universität; da ist noch nie ein Tourist gewesen, nur Studenten. Wie wäre das, Rosemarie?

ROSEMARIE: Du, das wäre nett; da möchte ich essen. Übrigens, hast du gestern nicht gesagt, daß es heute abend die *Fledermaus** gibt?

KLAUS: Ja, im Theater am Gärtnerplatz. Das ist eine Idee. Wie wäre es, wenn wir heute abend ins Theater gingen?

ROSEMARIE: Gerne, ich habe die *Fledermaus* noch nie gesehen. Und dann könnten wir nach Schwabing† gehen und tanzen, ja?

KLAUS: Und ein Glas Wein trinken,—und jetzt ist es halb elf‡, und wenn ich jetzt nicht gehe, bist du um elf Uhr *doch* nicht in der Halle. Oder soll ich doch lieber erst um zwölf kommen?

ROSEMARIE: Nein, nein—ich bin bestimmt da.

* Operetta by Strauss—literally, *The Bat; es gibt* they are playing.
† Artists' and students' quarter near the University of Munich.
‡ halb elf = zehn Uhr dreißig.

NATIONALTHEATER

Tageskasse Nationaltheater, Maximilianstraße
Telefon 29 72 04

1. 1.   Die Meistersinger von Nürnberg

2. 1.   Die Zaubergeige
3. 1.   Fidelio
4. 1.   Rigoletto – 3. Mi.-Platzm. – blau
5. 1.   Der Freischütz
6. 1.   Der fliegende Holländer
7. 1.   Don Carlos
8. 1.   Der Rosenkavalier

9. 1.   Lucia di Lammermoor / (Geschl. Vorstell.)
10. 1. Lohengrin – (Geschl. Vorstellung)
11. 1. Nabucco
12. 1. Karl V. – (Geschl. Vorstellung)
13. 1. Ein Maskenball – 2. Fr.-Platzm. – blau
14. 1. Othello / Gastspiel Kammersänger
        Wolfgang Windgassen
15. 1. Ballett: Dornröschen – 3. So.-Platzm., rot

16. 1. Fidelio – 4. Mo.-Platzm. – weiß
17. 1. Lucia di Lammermoor
        4. Di.-Platzm. – weiß
18. 1. Hänsel und Gretel – 4. Mi.-Platzm., weiß
19. 1. Ballett: Serenade – Der grüne Tisch –
        Medea – 4. Do.-Platzm. – weiß
20. 1. PREMIERE: Anna Boleyn
21. 1. Madame Butterfly
22. 1. Anna Boleyn – 4. So.-Platzm. – weiß

23. 1. Rigoletto (Geschl. Vorstellung)
24. 1. Rigoletto – 3. Di.-Platzm. – rot
25. 1. Tristan und Isolde – Gastspiel:
        Kammersänger Wolfgang Windgassen
        3. Mi.-Platzm. – rot
26. 1. Don Pasquale – 3. Do.-Platzm. – rot
27. 1. Ballett: Dornröschen – 3. Fr.-Platzm., rot
28. 1. Die Walküre
29. 1. Tosca (ital.)

30. 1. Lucia di Lammermoor
31. 1. Der Freischütz – 3. Di.-Platzm. – blau

THEATER AM GÄRTNERPLATZ

BAYERISCHES STAATSTHEATER
Gärtnerplatz 3, Telefon 26 12 32

1. 1.   19.30   Die Fledermaus

2. 1.   19.30   Das Land des Lächelns
3. 1.   19.30   Zar und Zimmermann
                3. Platzm. – Vorst. weiß
4. 1.   19.30   Hoffmanns Erzählungen
5. 1.   19.30   Der Arzt wider Willen
6. 1.   19.30   Zar und Zimmermann
                3. Platzm. – Vorst. grün
7. 1.   19.30   Die Fledermaus
8. 1.   14.30   Die Fledermaus
        19.30   Die Fledermaus

9. 1.   19.30   Die Feenkönigin
10. 1. 19.30   Manon Lescaut
11. 1. 19.30   Zar und Zimmermann
                3. Platzm. – Vorst. rosa
12. 1. 19.30   Die Feenkönigin
13. 1. 19.30   Gräfin Mariza
14. 1. 19.30   Hoffmanns Erzählungen
15. 1. 14.30   Die Fledermaus
        19.30   Die Fledermaus

16. 1. 19.30   Zar und Zimmermann
                3. Platzm. – Vorst. gelb
17. 1. 19.30   Eine Nacht in Venedig
18. 1. 19.30   Die verkaufte Braut
19. 1. 19.30   Der Walzerkrieg
20. 1. 19.30   Zar und Zimmermann
                3. Platzm. – Vorst. orange
21. 1. 19.30   Martha
22. 1. 19.30   Hoffmanns Erzählungen

23. 1. 19.30   Gräfin Mariza
24. 1. 19.30   Die Feenkönigin
25. 1. 19.30   Boccaccio
26. 1. 19.30   Zar und Zimmermann
27. 1. 19.30   Geschlossene Vorstellung
                Eine Nacht in Venedig
28. 1. 19.30   Gräfin Mariza
29. 1. 14.30   Das Land des Lächelns
        19.30   Das Land des Lächelns

30. 1. 19.30   Banditenstreiche
31. 1. 19.30   Die lustigen Weiber von Windsor

READING

Zwei und zwei ist fünf (Fortsetzung)

Ich wußte sofort, daß meine Frau diesen Brief an dem Tag geschrieben hatte, als ich mit Erich und Hermann bei Ali gesessen
hatte und Erich plötzlich sagte: „Du Hans, deine Frau schreibt
dir bestimmt gerade einen Brief." Aber wie gesagt, ich wußte damals
nicht, wo Erich war, und habe ihn erst letzten Freitag in Tripolis 5
wiedergesehen.

Ich arbeitete gerade an meinem Roman *Das Ende bei Karthago* und
war nach Afrika geflogen, um noch einmal die Gegend zu besuchen,
wo wir damals gegen die Amerikaner gekämpft haben. Es war darum

ganz natürlich, daß ich, sofort nachdem ich in Tripolis angekommen
war, zu Busuqs Haus gehen wollte. Es steht tatsächlich noch. Ich
wollte gerade mit meiner Leica eine Aufnahme machen (hätte ich
diese Aufnahme doch nur gemacht!), als jemand aus dem Haus
kam. Es war Erich.   5

Erich, der mich jahrelang immer nur in Uniform gesehen hatte,
erkannte mich nicht. Er sah nur einen Mann mit einer Kamera—
und war auf einmal verschwunden. Verschwunden, sage ich: er ging
nicht um die Ecke, er ging nicht ins Haus zurück, er war plötzlich
einfach nicht mehr da. „Diese Sonne", dachte ich, „die macht einen 10
noch ganz verrückt." Dann ging ich ins Haus. Ali saß im Garten. Er
war jetzt über achtzig. Er erzählte mir, daß seine Frau kurz nach dem
Ende des Krieges gestorben sei und daß mein Freund Erich ihn jedes
Jahr einmal besucht habe. Ja, Erich wäre gerade vor ein paar
Minuten im Haus gewesen und habe ihm, wie jedes Jahr um diese 15
Zeit, fünf Goldstücke dagelassen. Tatsächlich stand Ali auf, nahm
einen Stein aus der Wand des Hauses, griff in ein Loch hinter dem
Stein und zeigte mir fünf Goldstücke, fünf Zwanzigmarkstücke.
„Also war es wirklich Erich, den du gesehen hast und der dann
einfach nicht mehr da war", sagte ich mir; und plötzlich wußte ich: 20
hier ist etwas nicht in Ordnung.

Ich ging ins Hotel zurück, um nachzudenken. Im Hotel wartete ein
Brief von Hermann Schneider aus Hamburg auf mich. „Lieber
Hans," schrieb Hermann, „ich habe Dich zwar seit Ende des Krieges
nicht mehr gesehen, aber ich habe alle Deine Bücher gelesen. Ich 25
gratuliere Dir zu Deinen Detektivromanen, die ich viel besser finde
als Deine Kriegsromane. Dein Verleger ist ein Freund von mir und
hat mir versprochen, Dir diesen Brief nachzuschicken. Aber da er
mir nicht sagen wollte, wo Du bist, weiß ich nicht, wo und wann
Dich mein Brief erreichen wird. Ich habe eine Bitte an den Detektiv 30
in Dir.

Wie Du vielleicht weißt, bin ich in Hamburg Direktor der Hansa-
Bank. In unserer Bank verschwinden seit zehn Jahren jedes Jahr um
diese Zeit fünf Zwanzigmarkstücke. Natürlich sind hundert Mark
in Gold nicht viel Geld. Aber es ist doch seltsam, daß jemand in 35
unserer Bank jedes Jahr fünf Goldstücke stiehlt. Ich will noch nicht
die Polizei anrufen, denn ich habe das Gefühl, ich stehe hier vor
irgendeinem Geheimnis. Ich bitte Dich daher, die Sache zu untersuchen. Du könntest ein paar Wochen lang in der Bank ‚arbeiten'
und versuchen, den Dieb zu finden. Mein Privatsekretär ist übrigens 40
unser Freund Erich Karsten."

Erich Karsten!

---

der (*relative pronoun*) who. (Relative pronouns will be discussed in Unit 8.)

achtzig eighty

den whom

Lieber Hans Dear Hans

die which
Verleger publisher

irgendein some kind of

Erich Karsten! Gerade vor einer Stunde war er bei Ali gewesen und
hatte ihm, „wie jedes Jahr um diese Zeit", fünf Goldstücke gegeben.
Und damals hatte er mit seinen Militärschuhen hinter meiner Frau
gestanden und den Brief gelesen.

Es wäre nicht gerade intelligent gewesen, Hermann Schneider von ₅ **nicht gerade** not
Tripolis aus anzurufen. Wenn Erich der Dieb war—und er mußte   exactly
es sein—durfte er auf keinen Fall wissen, daß ich gerade heute in
Tripolis war, als er Ali fünf Goldstücke ins Haus getragen hatte.

Ich nahm daher ein Taxi zum Flughafen, bekam auf der Maschine
nach Paris noch einen Platz und rief Hermann Schneider von Paris ₁₀
aus an. Da ich nicht wußte, ob Erich bei Hermann war oder nicht,
erzählte ich Hermann, ich sei ein paar Tage in der Normandie
gewesen, hätte gerade seinen Brief bekommen und werde gegen
sechs in Hamburg ankommen. Ich gab meinem Freund die Flug-
nummer und bat ihn, mich abzuholen. „Natürlich hole ich dich ab", ₁₅ **Hamburger** When
sagte Hermann. „Ich wohne nicht weit vom Hamburger Flughafen.   city names are used
Es ist zwar sehr heiß hier in Hamburg, aber gottseidank habe ich   attributively, they
hinter dem Haus ein Schwimmbecken."   have the ending **-er**.

Es war ungefähr sieben Uhr, als wir vor Hermanns Haus hielten.
Vor dem Haus stand ein Volkswagen. „Das ist Gerdas Wagen", sagte ₂₀
Hermann. „Sie hat deine Romane gelesen und wollte dich gerne
kennenlernen; übrigens werden wir nächste Woche heiraten. Ich—"

Hinter dem Haus schrie eine Frau. Sie schrie, daß mir fast das Herz
stillstand. Bevor ich wußte, was geschah, hatte Hermann einen
Revolver aus dem Wagen geholt und lief hinter das Haus. Ich folgte ₂₅
ihm. Am Schwimmbecken stand ein Mädchen, blond, schön, und
mit einer Figur, wie man sie sonst nur im Film sieht. Auf dem
Wasser schwamm ein Hut. Sie zitterte, zeigte auf den Hut und
sagte: „Er ist weg,—oh, ich hasse diesen Menschen."

(Fortsetzung folgt)

*Der Wolf und die sieben Geißlein**

Es war einmal eine alte Geiß, die hatte sieben junge Geißlein, und ₃₀ **eine alte Geiß** an old
hatte sie lieb, wie eine Mutter ihre Kinder lieb hat. Eines Tages   goat. (For the time be-
wollte sie in den Wald gehen und etwas zu essen holen. Da rief   ing, pay no attention
sie alle sieben ins Haus und sprach: „Liebe Kinder, ich will in den to the adjective end-
Wald. Wenn der Wolf kommt, dürft ihr ihn nicht ins Haus lassen.   ings.)

* This story is taken, with very few changes, from the famous collection of
fairy tales by the brothers Grimm. The German of these fairy tales is highly
sophisticated and yet of classic simplicity. Every German child grows up with
Grimm. The syntactical range of these stories just about coincides with the
level the student is reaching with Unit 7.

Wenn er hereinkommt, so frißt er euch alle. Der Bösewicht verstellt
sich oft, aber an seiner Stimme und an seinen schwarzen Füßen
werdet ihr ihn gleich erkennen." Die Geißlein sagten: „Liebe
Mutter, du brauchst keine Angst zu haben." Da meckerte die Alte
und ging in den Wald.   5

Es dauerte nicht lange, so klopfte jemand an die Haustür und rief:
„Macht auf, ihr lieben Kinder, eure Mutter ist da und hat jedem
von euch etwas mitgebracht." Aber die Geißlein hörten an der
Stimme, daß es der Wolf war. „Wir machen nicht auf," riefen sie,
„du bist nicht unsere Mutter, die hat eine feine und liebliche   10
Stimme, aber deine Stimme ist rauh; du bist der Wolf." Da ging der
Wolf fort und kaufte ein Stück Kreide; die aß er und machte damit
seine Stimme fein. Dann kam er zurück, klopfte an die Haustür und
rief: „Macht auf, ihr lieben Kinder, eure Mutter ist da und hat
jedem von euch etwas mitgebracht." Aber der Wolf hatte seinen   15
schwarzen Fuß in das Fenster gelegt; das sahen die Kinder und
riefen: „Wir machen nicht auf, unsere Mutter hat keinen schwarzen
Fuß, wie du; du bist der Wolf." Da lief der Wolf zu einem Bäcker
und sprach: „Ich habe etwas an meinem Fuß, kannst du etwas Teig
auf meinen Fuß streichen?" Und als der Bäcker den Teig auf seinen 20
Fuß gestrichen hatte, so lief er zum Müller und sprach: „Kannst du
etwas Mehl auf meinen Fuß streuen?" Der Müller dachte: „Der
Wolf will einen betrügen", und wollte es nicht tun; aber der Wolf
sprach: „Wenn du es nicht tust, so fresse ich dich." Da bekam der
Müller Angst und machte ihm den Fuß weiß. Ja, so sind die   25
Menschen.

Nun ging der Bösewicht wieder zu der Haustür, klopfte an und
sprach: „Macht auf, Kinder, euer liebes Mütterchen ist zurück und
hat jedem von euch etwas aus dem Wald mitgebracht." Die Geißlein
riefen: „Du mußt uns erst deinen Fuß zeigen, sonst wissen wir   30
nicht, ob du unser liebes Mütterchen bist." Da legte er den Fuß
ins Fenster, und als sie sahen, daß er weiß war, so glaubten sie,
es wäre alles wahr, was er sagte, und machten die Tür auf. Wer
aber hereinkam, das war der Wolf.

Da bekamen sie alle Angst. Das eine sprang unter den Tisch, das   35
zweite ins Bett, das dritte in den Ofen, das vierte in die Küche, das
fünfte in den Schrank, das sechste unter die Waschschüssel, das
siebte in den Kasten der Wanduhr. Aber der Wolf fand sie alle und
fraß sie eins nach dem andern; nur das jüngste in dem Uhrkasten
fand er nicht. Als der Wolf die Sechs gefressen hatte, ging er fort, 40
legte sich draußen vor dem Haus unter einen Baum und fing an
zu schlafen.

Der Bösewicht . . . oft the rascal often disguises himself

meckern to bleat

rauh rough
damit with it

Teig dough

streuen sprinkle
betrügen deceive

Waschschüssel washbowl

Es dauerte nicht lange, da kam die alte Geiß aus dem Wald wieder
nach Hause. Ach, was mußte sie da sehen! Die Haustür stand auf,
Tisch, Stühle und Bänke waren umgeworfen. Sie suchte ihre Kinder,
aber sie konnte sie nicht finden. Sie rief sie alle bei Namen, aber
niemand antwortete. Endlich, als sie an das jüngste kam, da rief 5
eine feine Stimme: „Liebe Mutter, ich bin im Uhrkasten." Sie holte
es heraus, und es erzählte ihr, daß der Wolf gekommen wäre und
die anderen alle gefressen hätte. Da könnt ihr denken, wie sie über
ihre armen Kinder geweint hat.*

Endlich ging sie hinaus, und das jüngste Geißlein lief mit. Als sie 10
vor das Haus kam, so lag da der Wolf unter dem Baum und
schnarchte, daß die Äste zitterten. „Ach Gott," dachte sie, „vielleicht
leben meine Kinder doch noch." Da mußte das Geißlein ins Haus
laufen und Schere, Nadel und Zwirn holen. Dann schnitt sie dem   **Schere, . . . Zwirn**
Bösewicht den Bauch auf, und kaum hatte sie einen Schnitt getan, 15 scissors, needle, and
so steckte schon ein Geißlein den Kopf heraus, und als sie weiter   thread
schnitt, so sprangen sie alle sechs heraus, und waren noch alle am
Leben. Das war eine Freude! Die Alte aber sagte: „Jetzt wollen
wir Steine suchen, mit denen füllen wir dem Bösewicht den Bauch,
solange er noch schläft." Da brachten die sieben Geißlein Steine 20
herbei und steckten sie ihm in den Bauch. Dann nähte ihn die Alte
wieder zu.

Als der Wolf endlich ausgeschlafen hatte, stand er auf, und weil
ihn die Steine in seinem Bauch durstig machten, so wollte er zu
einem Brunnen gehen und trinken. Als er aber an den Brunnen kam 25
und trinken wollte, da zogen ihn die Steine in den Brunnen hinein,
und er mußte ertrinken. Als die sieben Geißlein das sahen, da kamen   **da . . . herbeigelaufen**
sie herbeigelaufen, riefen laut: „Der Wolf ist tot! der Wolf ist tot!" they came running
und lachten und tanzten mit ihrer Mutter um den Brunnen.

* Observe the change of tense: this sentence is not part of the story.

ANALYSIS

112   Prepositions with either Dative or Accusative

Nouns or pronouns following the prepositions **aus, außer, bei, mit, nach,
seit, von, zu** must always be in the dative case:

Ich komme von meiner Tante.
Ich komme von ihr.

Nouns or pronouns following **durch, für, gegen, ohne** must always be in the accusative:

Ich gehe ohne meinen Freund.
Ich gehe ohne ihn.

In both groups, it is the preposition alone that determines the case of the following noun or pronoun.

There is, however, a group of prepositions which can be used with either dative or accusative, and the case of the noun or pronoun following these prepositions depends on the particular situation.

These prepositions are:

an, auf, hinter, in, neben, über, unter, vor, zwischen.

These nine prepositions are used to describe local areas in relation to some fixed point of reference. Thus, the English phrases *under the sofa* and *behind the sofa* describe different areas in relation to a stationary object.

To a native speaker of English, the phrase *under the sofa* is not ambiguous; it can be used without danger of confusion in such sentences as

The dog slept under the sofa.

and

The dog crawled under the sofa.

However, the same speaker of English will usually distinguish between *in* and *into* in such sentences as

The dog slept in the house.—The dog ran into the house.
He moved in high circles.—He moved into high circles.
He slipped in his slippers.—He slipped into his slippers.

The areas designated by *into* are the goals toward which the actions of running, moving, and slipping are directed; and in each case, the action stops when that goal has been reached. On the other hand, the area *in the house* is not reached by sleeping there. The dog was in the house when he started to sleep; and the poor fellow who slipped in his slippers had already slipped into his slippers and was in his slippers when he started to slip in his slippers.

A German will argue that the difference between

sleeping in the house

and

running into the house

is exactly parallel to the difference between

    sleeping under the sofa

and

    crawling under the sofa.

Germans are very conscious of this difference because their language forces them to distinguish not only between *in*-situations and *into*-situations, but also between the two kinds of *under*-situations. The distinction is made in German not by the use of different prepositions like *in* and *into* but by the use of different cases following one and the same preposition.

If the area described by one of the nine prepositions above functions as the end-point or goal reached by the action (of crawling under the sofa), the noun following this preposition shows the accusative case.

If the area is the place where the entire action (of sleeping under the sofa) goes on from beginning to end, the noun following the preposition shows the dative.

This means that a German will always distinguish between **unter das Sofa** and **unter dem Sofa:**

Der Hund schläft unter dem Sofa.	**Der Hund springt unter das Sofa.**
Der Hund schläft hinter dem Sofa.	**Der Hund springt hinter das Sofa.**
Der Hund schläft auf dem Sofa.	**Der Hund springt auf das Sofa.**

It is important to realize that the distinction between dative and accusative after these nine prepositions is not one of rest versus motion. In both situations there may be motion (*He walked in the garden* and *He walked into the garden*). The determining factor is whether or not, in the course of the verbal action, a borderline is crossed by either the subject or the object. If such a borderline is crossed, the accusative must be used; if not, the dative must be used. This "borderline" may be real or imagined. Thus, the area **vor dem Haus** does not have a clearly defined border, but there is nevertheless common consent as to the meaning of **vor dem Haus.** If this area **vor dem Haus** is entered in the course of the verbal action, the accusative must be used: **Er fuhr vor das Haus** (*He drove up to the house*). If the entire verbal action takes place within the area **vor dem Haus,** the dative must be used: **Er hielt vor dem Haus** (*He stopped in front of the house*).

On the other hand, after verbs which cannot imply motion, such as **sein** and **bleiben,** the dative is always required with these nine prepositions.

    Er ist schon im Bett.
    Er muß im Haus sein.

NOTE:

1. The preposition corresponding to English *on* is **auf,** not **an.** German **an** describes an area "leaning against and touching" the point of reference. Thus it is **Frankfurt am Main** and **Köln am Rhein** (cf. *Stratford-on-Avon*). One speaks of a bed which stands **an der Wand** (**an** plus dative) after it has been pushed **an die Wand** (**an** plus accusative).

2. Unless the article is stressed, the following contractions are customary: **an dem = am; an das = ans; in dem = im; in das = ins.** The contractions **aufs, hinterm, übers, unterm** also occur in colloquial German.

3. If used with the accusative, **über** means either *over* with the implication "into the territory across," or it means *via* or *by way of.*

> **Er sprang über *den* Zaun.**   He jumped over the fence (into the neighbor's garden).
>
> **Er ist über *die* Schweiz nach Italien gefahren.**   He went to Italy via Switzerland.

When **über** means *via*, the corresponding interrogative is **wie?**, not **wohin?**

> **Wie seid ihr nach Italien gefahren, über Österreich oder über die Schweiz?**   How did you go to Italy, via Austria or via Switzerland?

but

> **Wohin seid ihr gefahren?**   Where did you go?
> **Nach Italien! Und zwar über die Schweiz!**   To Italy—and by way of Switzerland.

(Note that the article *must* be used with **Schweiz,** but is not used with the names of most other countries.)

4. As you already know, the preposition **vor** frequently means *ago*. If so used, it must be followed by the dative: **vor drei Jahren** (*three years ago*).

113 Wo and Wohin

The difference between **unter dem Sofa** and **unter das Sofa** reappears in the difference between **wo** and **wohin.** If you ask a **wo**-question, chances are that the answer will contain one of the nine "local area" prepositions with the dative; if you ask a **wohin**-question, chances are that the answer will contain one of those prepositions with the accusative:

> **Wo warst du denn?—In der Stadt.**
> **Wohin willst du denn?—In die Stadt.**

114 The Splitting of **wohin, woher, dahin,** and **daher**

In spoken German, the interrogatives **wohin** (*to which place*) and **woher** (*from which place*) and the demonstratives **dahin** (*to that place*) and **daher** (*from that place*) are usually split in such a way that **hin** and **her** become part of the second prong. They are then treated as if they were complements like **ab** or **an** and thus join a following verb form.

UNSPLIT POSITION	SPLIT POSITION
Wohin *gehst* du?	Wo gehst du *hin?*
Wohin willst du *gehen?*	Wo willst du denn *hingehen?*
Woher *kommst* du?	Wo kommst du *her?*
Woher ist der Brief ge*kommen?*	Wo ist denn der Brief *her*gekommen?
Dahin *will* ich nicht.	Da will ich gar nicht *hin.*
Daher komme ich *auch.*	Da komme ich *auch* her.

This splitting is colloquial, but not substandard. In the Lutheran translation of the Bible, Ruth 1:16 still reads:

> Wo du hingehst, da will ich auch hin; wo du bleibst, da bleibe ich auch. Dein Volk ist mein Volk, und dein Gott ist mein Gott.

These "split" forms are very commonly used. When a German unexpectedly meets a friend, he asks,

> Wo kommst *du* denn her?

not:

> Woher kommst du?

and if the answer is „**Aus dem Kino**", your rejoinder might be

> Da komme ich *auch* gerade her.

not:

> Daher komme ich auch.

115 The Genitive Case

The English phrases *John Miller's house* and *the house of John Miller* are interchangeable. Both forms are "possessives" and answer the question *whose?* But *John Miller's* is called a genitive form, and *of John Miller* is a prepositional phrase used as a substitute for that genitive form. Forms like *John's* are normally used when referring to persons or to personifications; phrases with *of* are used in English when referring to things or ideas. It is normal to say *the purpose of the experiment,* not *the experiment's purpose.* Phrases with *of* are much more prevalent than forms with *'s.*

In this unit the German genitive case is introduced. It is important to recognize from the very beginning two areas where German differs from English:

1. Phrases like *John's father* as well as phrases like *the purpose of the experiment* can be expressed in German by genuine genitive forms—that is, without the use of a preposition. German, in other words, does not make any distinction between persons and things. For example, **das Haus meines Vaters** and **der Titel meines Romans** correspond structurally to *my father's house* and *my novel's title*.

2. There is a growing tendency in German, especially in the spoken language, to avoid the genitive and to replace it with a prepositional phrase with **von,** again without any distinction between persons and things. It is very important, therefore, that you memorize thoroughly the patterns demonstrating these constructions, and that you keep in mind the fact that quite often the same English phrase can be expressed in two different ways in German.

ein Freund meines Mannes	or	**ein Freund von meinem Mann**
das Ende dieses Romans	or	**das Ende von diesem Roman**

Forms of the Genitive Case

INTERROGATIVE PRONOUNS

NOM.	**wer**	was
GEN.	*wessen*	
DAT.	**wem**	was
ACC.	**wen**	was

NOTE: **Was** has no genitive of its own. The dative **was** is used only after prepositions governing the dative, for example, **Von *was* habt ihr geredet?**

DEFINITE AND INDEFINITE ARTICLES

	MASC.	FEM.	NEUT.	PLUR.
NOM.	der	die	das	die
	ein	eine	ein	(keine)
GEN.	*des*	*der*	*des*	*der*
	eines	*einer*	*eines*	(*keiner*)
DAT.	dem	der	dem	den
	einem	einer	einem	(keinen)
ACC.	den	die	das	die
	einen	eine	ein	(keine)

GENITIVE OF NOUNS

Feminine nouns have the same form throughout the singular; there is no special ending for the genitive.

NOM.	die Frau	die Zeitung
GEN.	der Frau	der Zeitung
DAT.	der Frau	der Zeitung
ACC.	die Frau	die Zeitung

The majority of masculine and neuter nouns add the ending **-es**, if their stem consists of one syllable, and **-s**, if their stem consists of two or more syllables.

NOM.	der Mann	der Bahnhof	das Buch
GEN.	des Mannes	des Bahnhofs	des Buches
DAT.	dem Mann	dem Bahnhof	dem Buch
ACC.	den Mann	den Bahnhof	das Buch

Some masculine nouns, for example, **der Student, der Mensch, der Polizist′** (the policeman) have the ending **-en** in the genitive; this ending **-en** in such nouns occurs in all forms but the nominative singular.

	SINGULAR	PLURAL
NOM.	der Student	die Studenten
GEN.	des Studenten	der Studenten
DAT.	dem Studenten	den Studenten
ACC.	den Studenten	die Studenten

There are a few nouns that are irregular in the singular, for example, **das Herz** (the heart).

	SINGULAR	PLURAL
NOM.	das Herz	die Herzen
GEN.	des Herzens	der Herzen
DAT.	dem Herz(en)	den Herzen
ACC.	das Herz	die Herzen

The genitive plural of nouns has the same form as the nominative plural and the accusative plural. Remember that the dative plural of most German nouns ends in **-n** (see **58**).

NOM.	die Männer	die Frauen	die Bücher
GEN.	der Männer	der Frauen	der Bücher
DAT.	den Männern	den Frauen	den Büchern
ACC.	die Männer	die Frauen	die Bücher

116 Use of the Genitive

Prepositions Governing the Genitive

There are a number of prepositions which must be used with the genitive, but only three of these are of importance to the beginner: **während** (during); **wegen** (because of); and **trotz** (in spite of).

> **Während des Krieges war Schmidt in Norwegen.**
> **Wegen des Regens bleiben wir zu Hause.**
> **Trotz des Regens fahren wir nach Köln.**

With **trotz** and **wegen**, there is a tendency to replace the genitive with the dative, but this is still considered colloquial (**trotz dem Regen**). The compound **trotzdem** (in spite of that, nevertheless) has become standard.

We have now introduced all the major German prepositions. Remember that they *must* be used with specific cases. There are four different groups:

WITH THE GENITIVE:	**während, wegen, trotz**
WITH THE DATIVE:	**aus, außer, bei, mit, nach, seit, von, zu**
WITH THE ACCUSATIVE:	**durch, für, gegen, ohne**
WITH EITHER DATIVE OR ACCUSATIVE:	**an, auf, hinter, in, neben, über, unter, vor, zwischen**

The Genitive of Time

Occasionally, the genitive is used to express indefinite time. In contrast to English *one day* (past) and *some day* (future), **eines Tages** can be used for both past and future. Similarly: **eines Morgens, eines Abends**, and, by analogy, **eines Nachts** (and not **einer Nacht**).

The Attributive Genitive

By far the most common occurrence of the genitive is its use as an attribute. It then modifies a noun in the same way that an adjective does. When so used, the genitive is always part of another sentence element. Compare these English sentences:

> *The government's decision* did not come unexpectedly.
> (*government's* is an attribute of the subject *the decision*)
> The Thurbers expected Joan's cousin to arrive momentarily.
> (*Joan's:* attribute of the direct object *cousin*)

In these sentences, the "possessive" attributes can be eliminated without impairing the basic structure of the sentence; in other words, even without the attributes, the sentences are complete units of thought.

> The decision did not come unexpectedly.
> The Thurbers expected (the) cousin momentarily.

In German, the use of the attributive genitive is considered standard in the written language. It is used in two positions:

1. If the genitive form is a proper name, it *precedes* the noun it modifies:
   Schmidt-Ingelheims Roman war eine Sensation.
   Werners Freundin kannte er nicht.

Note that German does not use an apostrophe with this personal genitive.

2. If the genitive form is a common noun, it *follows* the noun it modifies.
   Am Abend ihres Geburtstages ging er mit ihr ins Theater.
   Die Integrität des Menschen ist das Thema seines Romans.

This means that *the woman's husband* must be rendered by **der Mann der Frau** and *the girl's father* by **der Vater des Mädchens.**

In the spoken language, the situation is far more complicated. While the attributive genitive is still considered standard German by most educated speakers, there is a steady erosion of these forms. The genitive most frequently replaced is the real possessive genitive in such forms as *my father's house* (expressing ownership: *My father owns the house.*) The German equivalent is **das Haus meines Vaters,** but the variant **das Haus von meinem Vater** also occurs and is used even by many well-educated Germans.

Von plus dative is always used when the genitive would not be recognizable—that is, primarily in the absence of an article or of a **der-** or **ein-** word.

die Bücher von Studenten	students' books
der Vater von zehn Kindern	the father of ten children
eine Freundin von Müllers Frau	a friend of Müller's wife

With **Freund** and other nouns expressing similar relationships, **von** plus dative is used as the equivalent of the English phrases

He is a friend of mine.
Er ist ein Freund von mir.
He is a friend of Karl's.
Er ist ein Freund von Karl.
Meyer is a colleague of mine.
Meyer ist ein Kollege von mir.

The idea *one of* in such sentences as *He is one of my friends* is expressed by **einer (eine, eins) von** (see **117**).

Er ist einer von meinen Freunden.
Sie ist eine von Karls Freundinnen.

In such phrases as *a cup of coffee, a glass of wine, a pound of butter,* where the first noun denotes a measure and the second something measured, the second German noun shows no case.

eine Tasse Kaffee
ein Glas Wein
ein Pfund Butter

If more than one measured unit is involved, only feminine nouns are used in the plural; masculines and neuters retain the singular form.

zwei Tassen Kaffee
zwei Glas Wein
zwei Pfund Butter

Compounding of nouns is another means by which German very frequently expresses the equivalent of English phrases with *of,* for example, *the production of leather goods:* **die Produktion von Lederwaren** or **die Lederwarenproduktion.** English, of course, uses the same device, but usually without spelling the compound as one word: *wheat production, book publishing,* etc.

117 Ein-Words without Nouns

When **ein**-words are not followed by nouns, their declension is exactly the same as that of the **der**-words. The neuter ending is usually -s instead of -es.

Inges Freund heißt Hans, und *meiner* heißt Werner.
Ich habe leider kein Buch. Hast du *eins?*

118 The Indirect-Discourse Subjunctive

In addition to the subjunctive forms introduced in Unit 6, German has a second set of subjunctive forms which we shall call the indirect-discourse subjunctive. This set is not complete. It is sufficient to know the following forms:

PRESENT INDIRECT-DISCOURSE SUBJUNCTIVE

	sein	All other verbs						
		haben	werden	können	wollen	lieben	nehmen	fahren
ich	sei	habe	werde	könne	wolle	liebe	nehme	fahre
du	—	—	—	—	—	—	—	—
er	sei	habe	werde	könne	wolle	liebe	nehme	fahre
wir	seien	—	—	—	—	—	—	—
ihr	—	—	—	—	—	—	—	—
sie	seien	—	—	—	—	—	—	—

PAST INDIRECT-DISCOURSE SUBJUNCTIVE

ich sei gekommen	ich habe gegessen
er sei gekommen	er habe gegessen
wir seien gekommen	_____
sie seien gekommen	_____

NOTE:

1. The **ich**-form is always identical with the **er**-form.

2. The past indirect-discourse subjunctive replaces the past and the perfect of the indicative.

119   The Use of the Indirect-Discourse Subjunctive

As stated in Unit 6, the forms of the regular subjunctive can *always* be used in indirect discourse. It is not possible to formulate any definite rule stating when the indirect-discourse subjunctive should be used. It simply exists as an alternative preferred by some and almost completely avoided by others. In spoken German, the regular subjunctive is constantly gaining ground. Of the **ich**-forms listed above, the forms of **sein** and the modals are clearly recognizable as subjunctive forms; all other **ich**-forms are indistinguishable from the present-tense indicative (**ich liebe** can be either subjunctive or indicative).

Those who do use the indirect-discourse subjunctive usually follow this rule: the forms not recognizable as subjunctive occur only in indirect questions.

    Sie fragte mich, ob ich sie liebe.

In an indirect assertion, the unrecognizable **ich liebe** is replaced by the regular subjunctive **ich liebte:**

    Ich sagte ihr, daß ich sie liebte.

To illustrate the range of choice, let us assume that somebody asks the following question:

    Liebst du mich denn, und findest du mich schön?

By using the regular subjunctive only, this question could be reported in the form:

    Sie fragte mich, ob ich sie denn liebte und schön fände.

By using the new set only, one could write:

    Sie fragte mich, ob ich sie denn liebe und schön finde.

Most probably, one will find a mixture: thus (in Heinrich Böll, *Ansichten eines Clowns*):

> **Sie fragte mich, ob ich sie denn liebe und schön fände,**

is followed, at the end of the same paragraph, by:

> **Ich murmelte** [mumbled], **ja, ja, ich fände sie schön und liebte sie,**

and preceded, a few pages earlier, by:

> **Sie fragte mich, ob ich sie denn schön fände und sie liebte.**

DIRECT DISCOURSE	REGULAR SUBJUNCTIVE	INDIRECT DISCOURSE SUBJUNCTIVE
PRESENT		
Vater wohnt in Berlin	Vater wohnte in Berlin	Vater wohne in Berlin
Vater ist in Berlin	Vater wäre in Berlin	Vater sei in Berlin
Vater hat Geld	Vater hätte Geld	Vater habe Geld
PAST		
Vater wohnte in Berlin	Vater hätte in Berlin gewohnt	Vater habe in Berlin gewohnt
Vater war in Berlin	Vater wäre in Berlin gewesen	Vater sei in Berlin gewesen
Vater hatte Geld	Vater hätte Geld gehabt	Vater habe Geld gehabt

NOTE:

1. If the original statement was made in the regular subjunctive, it cannot be changed.

> „Es wäre schön, wenn heute die Sonne schiene.“
> Er sagte, es wäre schön, wenn heute die Sonne schiene.

2. To put an imperative into indirect discourse, **sollen** is used.

> „Seien Sie mir nicht böse.“
> Er sagte, ich sollte ihm nicht böse sein.
> Er sagte, ich solle ihm nicht böse sein.

120 The Suffix **-ung**

The suffix **-ung** is added to many verb stems. It forms feminine nouns, the plural form being **-ungen**. Comparable to English derivatives in *-tion*, these nouns designate the verbal act as such (cf. English *the foundation* *of Rome*) or the result of a verbal act (*the foundations of the cathedral*) or something which causes the verbal act (*his letter was a real consolation*).

die Einladung	invitation
die Erwartung	expectation
die Erzählung	story, narration
die Hoffnung	hope
die Untersuchung	investigation
die Versuchung	temptation

A special case is

die Wohnung	living quarters, apartment.

EXERCISES

A. Read aloud, then write out the numbers.

SEE LAB EXERCISES 7.1–7.3 (p. 629)

$1 + 10 = 11$	$4 + 9 = 13$
$6 + 10 = 16$	$2 + 3 = 5$
$12 + 5 = 17$	$7 + 8 = 15$
$14 + 6 = 20$	$18 + 1 = 19$

$20 - 19 = 1$	$13 - 7 = 6$
$18 - 16 = 2$	$11 - 4 = 7$
$17 - 14 = 3$	$10 - 2 = 8$
$16 - 12 = 4$	$9 - 0 = 9$
$15 - 10 = 5$	$16 - 6 = 10$

Es ist jetzt 7 Uhr 20. (7^{20} Uhr)
Es ist jetzt 8 Uhr 19.
Es ist jetzt 9 Uhr 18.
Es ist jetzt 10 Uhr 17.
Es ist jetzt 11 Uhr 16.
Es ist jetzt 12 Uhr 15.
Es ist jetzt 1 Uhr 07.
Es ist jetzt 6 Uhr 14.
Es ist jetzt 5 Uhr 13.
Es ist jetzt 4 Uhr 12.
Es ist jetzt 3 Uhr 16.
Es ist jetzt 2 Uhr 17.

B. Form questions for the following statements, using either **wo** or **wohin.**

1. Ich habe den Tisch an die Wand gestellt.
2. Gestern habe ich im Theater Frau Lenz gesehen.
3. Ich wollte mir auf dem Bahnhof eine Zeitung kaufen.
4. Im Sommer war er mit Rosemarie an der Mosel.
5. Morgen fährt er mit Rosemarie nach Bonn.
6. Seine Tochter ist in Mainz in die Schule gegangen.
7. Seine Tochter war in Mainz.
8. Meine Frau liest die Zeitung immer im Bett.
9. Zu Hause trinkt Anton immer Tee.
10. Meyer hat uns zum Bahnhof gefahren.
11. Das Städtchen lag fünf Kilometer hinter der Front.
12. Unser Hund schläft immer unter dem Tisch.
13. Unter dieser Brücke dürfen Sie nicht schlafen.
14. Ich werde Rosemarie im Hotel Regina abholen.
15. Vor Meyers Haus steht nie ein Wagen.

C. Answer the following questions, using in your answers one of the prepositions that can take either the dative or the accusative.

1. Wohin hat er seinen Hut gelegt?
2. Wo hast du sie gesehen?
3. Wo waren Sie während des Krieges, Herr Schmidt?
4. Wo steht denn euer Wagen?
5. Wo geht ihr heute abend hin?
6. Wo wohnen Sie in München, Herr Schneider?
7. Was tut Anton Meyer denn mit seinem Geld?
8. Wie seid ihr nach Italien gefahren?
9. Was hast du denn mit meinem Hut getan?
10. Wo hast du heute gefrühstückt?
11. Wo hast du denn das Geld gefunden, Hans?
12. Wo warst du denn gestern?
13. Wo ist sie denn gestern hingefahren?
14. Wo las Frau Ingelheim, daß ihr Mann verschwunden war?
15. Wo ist Vater?

D. Express in German:

1. He is my friend.
2. He is Karl's friend.
3. He is my sister's friend.
4. He is a friend of my sister's.
5. He is one of my sister's friends.

SEE LAB
EXERCISES
7.4–7.8

(p. 629)

6. He is my father.
7. He is Mary's father.
8. He is my wife's father.
9. He is her son.
10. He is Inge's son.
11. He is my brother's son.
12. Karl is one of my brother's sons.
13. Ernst is one of the sons of Mr. Bertram.
14. Fritz is her friend.
15. Fritz is a friend of hers.
16. Fritz is one of her friends.
17. Her daughters are very intelligent.
18. Ingrid's daughter is also very intelligent.
19. Ingelheim's daughters are intelligent.
20. The Ingelheims' daughters are intelligent.

E. Give appropriate answers to the following questions, using either the genitive or **von** plus dative:

1. Wessen Buch ist das?
2. Mit wessen Wagen bist du denn nach Köln gefahren?
3. Mit *wes*sen Freundin warst du im Theater?
4. Von wessen Roman sprecht ihr denn?
5. Wessen Haus habt ihr gekauft?
6. Wessen Tochter hat er geheiratet?
7. Wessen Freundin ist das?
8. Wessen Vater hast du besucht?
9. Für wessen Haus willst du so viel Geld bezahlen?
10. Durch wessen Freundin hast du ihn kennengelernt?

F. Fill the blanks with appropriate **ein**-words.

SEE LAB
EXERCISES
7.9–7.10

(pp. 629-630)

1. Ich habe leider kein Buch. Hast du _____?
2. Ich habe meinen Wagen nicht hier, Hans. Wo ist denn _____?
3. Habt ihr schon ein Haus? Nein, wir haben noch _____.
4. Hast du Zeit? Ich habe _____.
5. Das ist _____ von den Büchern, die mein Vater mir geschickt hat.
6. Er ist auch _____ von den Soldaten, die nicht über den Krieg sprechen wollen.
7. Ich habe nicht _____ von seinen Büchern gelesen.
8. _____ seiner Romane habe ich mir gekauft.
9. Mein Hut ist das nicht; es muß _____ sein, Frau Bertram.

G. Supply the missing words:

SEE LAB
EXERCISES
7.11

(p. 630)

1. Ich habe heute morgen meine Frau _____ Bahnhof gebracht.
2. Woher wissen Sie denn, daß Johannes schon _____ verheiratet war?
3. Mein Mann spricht oft _____ seiner Tochter.
4. In Frankreich war Ingelheim nur während _____ Krieges.
5. Ich habe gerade gelesen, daß Sie _____ drei Wochen in München wohnen.
6. Liegt er immer noch _____ Bett?
7. Von Ingelheims Kriegsroman spricht heute _____ Mensch mehr.
8. Ich bin nicht Soldat geworden, um Brieftauben _____ füttern.
9. Der Arzt glaubte, Ingelheim _____ Hepatitis, aber er _____ nur zu viel getrunken.
10. Ich weiß, daß Anton nach Berlin gefahren _____.
11. Kannst du mir sagen, _____ Ingelheims Kinder haben?
12. Er ist einer _____ Ingelheims Söhnen.
13. Ich möchte wissen, _____ du mich eigentlich geheiratet hast.
14. Können Sie mir sagen, _____ der Zug nach Köln fährt?
15. _____ der Krieg anfing, studierte Schmidt in Frankfurt Medizin.
16. Man kann doch nicht im Garten arbeiten, _____ es regnet.
17. Er fragte mich, ob ich heute abend auch ins Kino _____.
18. Ich wollte, ich _____ dich nie gesehen.
19. Wenn er nicht nach Deutschland gefahren _____, hätte ich ihn nie kennengelernt.
20. Ich habe das Haus nicht kaufen _____.

H. Rewrite Hermann Schneider's letter to Ingelheim (page 269) in indirect discourse, using either the normal subjunctive or, when possible, the indirect-discourse subjunctive.

SEE LAB
EXERCISES
7.12, 7.13

(p. 630)

I. Express in German:

1. We really ought to put (stellen) that little table (-chen) between our beds.
2. The people who sit on these benches here have no money in the bank.
3. I don't believe that they sit here because they have no money in the bank.
4. Do you always have to put your books on the breakfast table?
5. Why can't they lie on the breakfast table?
6. During the war Ingelheim was on the Western Front.
7. At that time he was happy that he did not have to go to Africa.
8. It is cold tonight; I wish you hadn't forgotten your overcoat.
9. One of them asked Ingelheim if he had been in Cairo during the war.
10. If only that woman hadn't been so unfriendly!
11. If only I hadn't accepted the money!
12. You should have given him more money.
13. I wish I weren't so far away from you.

J. Write a brief paragraph in German containing the following ideas; use the past tense. Do *not* translate the passage; just use it as an outline. Use your own words, but do not attempt to use any construction or any vocabulary that you haven't had yet.

Hermann Schneider drove to the Hansa-Bank at 7 A.M. It was hot, and he would much rather have stayed at home by his swimming pool. But he had to go to the bank, because Karsten had just called to tell him that five gold pieces had disappeared again. Schneider didn't understand why this could happen every year. The thief had to be somebody who worked in the bank, but Schneider did not want to call the police yet. He would rather discuss the matter with Karsten first, he thought.

K. Now write a brief dialogue between Schneider and his fiancée Gerda, taking place in the evening of the same day.

Hermann tells Gerda about the theft of the gold pieces. She wants to know whether he has told Karsten about it, and whether Karsten had any ideas. Yes, he has, and Karsten thought it was somebody who works in the bank, but he was very much against calling the police. Gerda has an idea: What about Hermann's friend Ingelheim? He has written detective stories, and perhaps he can help Hermann. But Hermann hasn't seen Ingelheim since the war and doesn't know where he is. Gerda suggests that he call Ingelheim's publisher, which Hermann promises to do the next morning. Gerda is pleased, because she has wanted to meet Ingelheim for a long time.

VOCABULARY

ach oh
ander– other
  eins nach dem anderen one after the other
arm poor
der Ast, ⁀e branch
auf on, on top of; up; open
  auf sein to be up (out of bed)
  aufmachen to open
die Aufnahme, –n picture, photo
der Augenblick, –e moment
ausschlafen to get enough sleep
aussehen to look, give the appearance
backen to bake
  der Bäcker, – baker

die Bank, ⁀e bench
die Bank, –en bank
der Bauch, ⁀e stomach, belly
der Baum, ⁀e tree
bevor (*conj.*) before
die Bitte, –n request
die Brücke, –n bridge
der Brunnen, – well, fountain
da (*conj.*) since
daher therefore; from there, from that place
dahin there, toward that place
dauern to last, to take (time)
der Dieb, –e thief
draußen (*adverb*) outside
durstig thirsty
die Ecke, –n corner

erkennen (an) to recognize (by)
erreichen to reach, attain
ertrinken to drown
der Fall, ⁀e case; fall
  auf jeden Fall in any case, at any rate
  auf keinen Fall in no case, under no circumstances
fast almost
fein fine
das Fenster, – window
folgen (*with dative*) to follow
fort away
Frankreich France
fressen to eat (said of animals)
die Freude, –n joy
füllen to fill

der Fuß, ⸚e foot
ganz whole, entire
gegen sechs Uhr around six
  o'clock
die Gegend, –en area
geheim secret
  das Geheimnis, –se secret
die Geiß, –en goat
geschehen to happen, occur
gleich equal; (time adverb)
  immediately, presently
greifen to grasp, reach out
  (for something)
die Halle, –n hall, lobby
halten to hold; stop
heiß hot
her toward the speaker (in
  the sense of "hither")
  herauskommen to come out
  hereinkommen to come in
  herkommen to come here
das Herz, –en heart
  (gen.: des Herzens; dat.:
  dem Herzen)
hin away from the speaker
  hineingehen to go in
  hinfahren to go there
der Hof, ⸚e (royal) court;
  yard
  der Hofgarten the Royal
  Gardens
  der Bahnhof, ⸚e station
holen to get, fetch
hundert hundred, a hundred
der Kasten, ⸚ chest, box
kaum (adverb) hardly
klopfen to knock
  anklopfen to knock (at the
  door)
die Kreide chalk
die Küche, –n kitchen
laut loud
legen to lay, place

lieb dear
  liebhaben to love
  lieblich lovely
das Loch, ⸚er hole
es macht nichts it doesn't
  matter
der Mantel, ⸚ coat, overcoat
das Mehl flour
möglich possible
  unmöglich impossible;
  (sentence adverb) not
  possibly
der Müller, – miller
na! well! (interj.)
nachdem (conj.) after
nachschicken to forward
  (mail)
nähen to sew
der Name, –n name
  (gen.: des Namens; dat.:
  dem Namen; acc.: den
  Namen)
die Ordnung, –en order
  in Ordnung in order, all
  right, O.K.
das Pfund, –e pound
der Platz, ⸚e place, seat
die Polizei police
  der Polizist, –en policeman
rufen to call
die Sache, –n thing, matter
schnarchen to snore
schneiden to cut
  der Schnitt, –e the cut
der Schrank, ⸚e cupboard,
  wardrobe
schreien to scream, cry out
schwarz black
die Schweiz Switzerland
schwimmen to swim
  das Schwimmbecken, –
  swimming pool
der Sekretär', –e secretary

selten rare, seldom
seltsam strange, peculiar
solange (conj.) as long as
sonst otherwise
stecken to stick, put
stehlen to steal
der Stein, –e stone
stellen to place, put (upright)
die Stimme, –n voice
streichen to spread (as
  paint), stroke
das Stück, –e piece
  das Goldstück, –e gold coin
der Stuhl, ⸚e chair
tatsächlich actual(ly)
der Tisch, –e table
trotz in spite of
die Tür, –en door
unter under
  die Untergrundbahn, –en
  subway
untersu'chen to investigate
der Verleger, – publisher
verrückt crazy
versprechen to promise
das Volk, ⸚er people
von (Paris) aus from (Paris)
während during
der Wald, ⸚er woods, forest
die Wand, ⸚e wall
wegen because of
weinen to cry
weiß white
werfen to throw
  umwerfen to knock over
wie gesagt as I said
der Wolf, ⸚e wolf
ziehen to pull; to move
zittern to tremble, shake
zusammen together
zwar to be sure

IRREGULAR VERBS

ausschlafen to get enough
  sleep
  schlief aus, hat ausge-
  schlafen, er schläft aus
backen to bake
  backte, hat gebacken, er
  backt
erkennen to recognize
  erkannte, hat erkannt, er
  erkennt
ertrinken to drown
  ertrank, ist ertrunken, er
  ertrinkt
fressen to eat (said of animals)
  fraß, hat gefressen, er
  frißt

geschehen to happen, occur
  geschah, ist geschehen, es
  geschieht
greifen to grasp
  griff, hat gegriffen, er
  greift
halten to hold, stop
  hielt, hat gehalten, er hält
rufen to call
  rief, hat gerufen, er ruft
schneiden to cut
  schnitt, hat geschnitten, er
  schneidet
schreien to scream, cry out
  schrie, hat geschrie(e)n, er
  schreit
schwimmen to swim

schwamm, ist geschwom-
  men, er schwimmt
stehlen to steal
  stahl, hat gestohlen, er
  stiehlt
streichen to spread (as
  paint), stroke
  strich, hat gestrichen, er
  streicht
versprechen to promise
  versprach, hat ver-
  sprochen, er verspricht
werfen to throw
  warf, hat geworfen, er
  wirft
ziehen to pull, move
  zog, hat gezogen, er zieht

REVIEW

Demonstrative Pronouns

Read these sentences carefully and observe that in spoken German **der, die, das** are preferred to **er, sie, es** to pick up an item from the immediately preceding sentence. This demonstrative **der, die, das** may be stressed or unstressed.

Nein, mit *dem* Hut kannst du nicht nach Berlin fahren; *der* bleibt hier.

Ich soll mit *Hans* ins Theater? Nein, mit *dem* gehe ich nicht, der *re*det mir zu viel.

Soll Frau *Schmidt auch* kommen?—Nein, *die* brauchst du nicht einzuladen; mit *der* will ich nichts zu tun haben.

Hast du in Frankfurt auch deinen Freund *Hans* besucht?—Nein, den habe ich *nicht* besucht; der wohnt doch jetzt in *Mün*chen.

Mit *dem* Kugelschreiber (*ball-point pen*) hier kann ich nicht schreiben. Wo hast du *den* denn gekauft?—Den *ha*be ich gar nicht gekauft; den hat mir Tante Amalie ge*schenkt*.

Der Wein ist nicht schlecht. Hat dein *Mann* den gekauft?—Mein *Mann*? *Der* versteht doch nichts von Wein.

Wo ist denn *Franz* heute abend?—Der wollte heute abend zu *Hau*se bleiben. Wa*rum*, hat er mir nicht ge*sagt*.

Ist das nicht Frau *Ra*demacher da in dem Mercedes?—Das kann doch nicht Frau *Ra*demacher sein; die ist doch gestern nach I*ta*lien gefahren; außerdem fährt sie nur einen *Volks*wagen.

Ich höre, der Edgar will die Barbara *doch* nicht heiraten.—Hm, aber die Barbara will *ihn* heiraten, und wenn *die* etwas will, dann be*kommt* sie es auch.

Kennen Sie Herrn und Frau *West*berg?—Natürlich! Durch die habe ich doch meine *Frau* kennengelernt.

Present, Past, and Perfect

Restate these sentences (a) in the present, (b) in the perfect.

1. Hans fuhr um sechs Uhr ab.
2. Er studierte auch in Heidelberg.
3. Wann fing denn das Theater an?
4. In Berlin kaufte er seiner Frau einen Hut.
5. Die Amerikaner nahmen ihn gefangen.

6. Ich kannte sie nicht.
7. Ernst kam um sechs Uhr nach Hause.
8. Der Wagen hielt vor dem Hotel.
9. Ingelheim verschwand spurlos.
10. Sein Sohn wurde auch Arzt.
11. Das wußte ich leider nicht.
12. Er sprach oft mit meinem Vater.
13. Er stellte seinen Wagen immer vor das Haus.
14. Ich stand lange vor dem Haus und wartete auf Inge.
15. Im Theater saß er oft neben mir.
16. Sie schrieb ihm fast jeden Tag einen Brief.
17. Wir brauchten oft tagelang nicht zu arbeiten.
18. Er mußte oft allein nach Afrika fahren.
19. Sie konnte leider nicht kommen.
20. Wollte er wirklich heute abend kommen?

Irreal Conditions

State the facts implied by the following irreal conditions; use **daher** or **weil** to connect your sentences.

> **Wenn er hier wäre, wäre ich nicht unglücklich.**
> **Er ist nicht hier; daher bin ich unglücklich.**

or:

> **Weil er nicht hier ist, bin ich unglücklich.**

1. Wenn das Essen nicht so schlecht wäre, blieben wir noch hier.
2. Wenn ich Zeit hätte, würde ich dich gerne besuchen.
3. Hans würde gerne mitfahren, wenn er nicht krank wäre.
4. Wenn es nicht schon wieder regnete, könnten wir heute im Garten arbeiten.
5. Erich wäre gestorben, wenn Busuq ihm nicht geholfen hätte.
6. Ingelheim wäre nicht so reich geworden, wenn er keine Kriegsromane geschrieben hätte.
7. Ich hätte ihn nicht am Flughafen abholen können, wenn er nicht von Frankfurt aus angerufen hätte.
8. Wenn er mir nicht geschrieben hätte, wüßte ich nicht, daß er jetzt in Hamburg wohnt.

Time Phrases

Express in German; use the perfect whenever possible.

1. A year ago he lived in Munich.
2. He lived in Munich for two years.

3. We've been living in Munich for two years.
4. Now he wants to live in Munich for two years.
5. We've been living in Munich only since the beginning of May.
6. He has gone to Munich for a week.
7. He has been in Munich for a week.
8. He was in Munich for a week.
9. He was in Munich a week ago.
10. He hasn't been in Munich for years.

UNIT 8: Relative Pronouns—wann, ob, als, wenn—gar—da–Compounds—wo–Compounds—Prepositional Objects

PATTERNS

[1] Definite Relative Pronouns

Analyze carefully the relative clauses contained in these sentences.

Mein Vater, der nicht studiert hatte, konnte nicht verstehen, warum ich Schriftsteller werden wollte.

SEE ANALYSIS 121 (pp. 316-318)

> My father, who had not gone to the university, could not understand why I wanted to become a writer.

Maria ist auch eine von den Frauen, die ihren Mann nicht verstehen.

> Maria is also one of those women who don't understand their husbands.

Sein Vater, dessen Frau aus Leningrad kam, sprach gut Russisch.

> His father, whose wife came from Leningrad, spoke Russian well.

Seine Frau, deren Vater aus Leningrad kam, sprach gut Russisch.

> His wife, whose father came from Leningrad, spoke Russian well.

In Mainz besuchte Ingelheim das Goethe-Gymnasium, dessen Direktor damals Schiller hieß.

> In Mainz Ingelheim went to the Goethe Gymnasium, the director of which at the time was a man named Schiller.

Kennen Sie meinen Freund Müller?—Meinen Sie den Müller, dem das Corona-Hotel gehört?

> Do you know my friend Müller?—Do you mean the Müller who owns the Corona Hotel?

Ist das der Hut, den dir dein Mann aus Paris mitgebracht hat?

> Is that the hat your husband brought you from Paris?

Habe ich dir schon die Omega gezeigt, die ich in Zürich gekauft habe?

> Have I shown you the Omega (that) I bought in Zurich?

(Facing) **In einem schwäbischen Gasthof**

295

Das Essen, das wir hier bekommen, ist so gut, daß wir noch eine Woche bleiben wollen.

The food we get here is so good that we want to stay another week.

Ich wußte natürlich, woher die Goldstücke kamen, die bei Ali in einem Loch in der Wand lagen.

I knew, of course, where the gold pieces came from that were lying in a hole in the wall at Ali's.

Ich wollte Ali und Busuq wiedersehen, deren Gast ich während des Krieges gewesen war.

I wanted to see Ali and Busuq again, whose guest I had been during the war.

Ist das der Wagen, mit dem du nach Italien gefahren bist?

Is that the car you went to Italy in?

Hermann, durch den ich meine Frau kennengelernt habe, ist jetzt Bankdirektor in Hamburg.

Hermann, through whom I met my wife, is now director of a bank in Hamburg.

Wer waren denn die drei Herren, Ingrid, mit denen ich Sie gestern abend gesehen habe?

Who were the three gentlemen with whom I saw you last night, Ingrid?

Wer sind eigentlich diese Schmidts, von denen du immer redest?

Who are those Schmidts, anyway, that you always talk about?

Wer sind eigentlich diese Schmidts, ohne die du nicht mehr nach Italien fahren willst?

Who are those Schmidts, anyway, without whom you don't want to go to Italy any more?

Ihre Töchter, für die sie so schwer gearbeitet hat, wollen heute nichts mehr von ihr wissen.

Today her daughters, for whom she worked so hard, don't want to have anything to do with her any more.

Während der Kämpfe in der Normandie, über die Ingelheim so realistisch schrieb, war er in Norwegen und fütterte Brieftauben.

During the battles in Normandy, about which he wrote so realistically, Ingelheim was in Norway, feeding carrier pigeons.

Der Mann, ohne dessen Hilfe ich heute nicht Arzt wäre, ist Professor Schmidt.

The man without whose help I wouldn't be a doctor today is Professor Schmidt.

[2] Indefinite Relative Pronouns

Wer Geld hat, hat auch Freunde.
Wer Geld hat, der hat auch Freunde.

> (He) who has money has friends, too.

SEE
ANALYSIS
121
(pp. 316-318)

Was Ingelheim gestern abend zu erzählen hatte, war wirklich nicht viel.
Was Ingelheim gestern abend zu erzählen hatte, das war wirklich nicht viel.

> What Ingelheim had to say last night really wasn't very much.

Hans hat mich zum Essen eingeladen, was ich sehr nett finde.

> Hans has invited me to dinner, which I think is very nice.

Ich habe leider nicht alles verstanden, was sie gesagt hat.

> Unfortunately, I did not understand everything she said.

Professor Schmidt hat wirklich nichts gesagt, was ich nicht schon wußte.

> Professor Schmidt really didn't say anything that I didn't already know.

Ich habe dieses Wochenende in Afrika etwas erlebt, was man eigentlich nicht erleben kann.

> This weekend I experienced something in Africa that one really cannot experience.

[3] wann

Form other questions with **wann** and transform them into dependent clauses.

„Wann ist Fritz denn gestern abend nach Hause gekommen?"
Fritz, Vater möchte wissen, wann du gestern abend nach Hause gekommen bist.

SEE
ANALYSIS
122
(pp. 318-320)

„Wann fahrt ihr denn nach Berlin?"
Ich kann dir noch nicht sagen, wann wir nach Berlin fahren.

„Wann waren Sie an der Westfront, Herr Ingelheim?"
Er hat mich gefragt, wann ich an der Westfront gewesen wäre.

„Wann will Heidi denn heiraten?"
Ich weiß nicht, wann sie heiraten will.

[4] ob

Form other yes-or-no questions and transform them into dependent clauses.

„Fährst du nach Berlin?"
Mutter will wissen, ob du nach Berlin fährst.

SEE
ANALYSIS
122
(pp. 318-320)

„Haben Sie die Platten schon einmal gezählt?"
Ich möchte wissen, ob er die Platten schon einmal gezählt hat.

„War Erich wirklich in Tripolis?"
Ich habe nie erfahren können, ob Erich wirklich in Tripolis war.

„Kann deine Tochter schon bis fünf zählen?"
Er fragte mich, ob meine Tochter schon bis fünf zählen könne.

„Liegt Hermanns Haus direkt am Atlantik?"
Weißt du, ob Hermanns Haus direkt am Atlantik liegt?

[5] als ob, als wenn, als

Form parallel examples. Be prepared to produce orally **Er tut, als ob er schliefe,** when you hear **Er schläft.**

SEE
ANALYSIS
122

(pp. 318-320)

Er tut, als ob er schliefe. Er tut, als schliefe er.	He acts as if he were asleep.
Er tat, als ob er schliefe. Er tat, als schliefe er.	He acted as if he were asleep.
Er tut, als ob er geschlafen hätte. Er tut, als hätte er geschlafen.	He acts as if he had been alseep.
Er tat, als ob er geschlafen hätte. Er tat, als hätte er geschlafen.	He acted as if he had been asleep.
Er tat, als wenn er schliefe.	He acted as if he were asleep.
Er tat, als wenn er geschlafen hätte.	He acted as if he had been asleep.
Gerda sah aus, als wäre sie krank.	Gerda looked as if she were sick.
Die Frau sieht aus, als ob sie viel Geld hätte.	That woman looks as if she had a lot of money.
Er redet immer, als wüßte er alles.	He always talks as if he knew everything.
Er tat, als ob er mich nie gesehen hätte.	He acted as if he had never seen me.
Er aß, als hätte er eine Woche lang nichts gegessen.	He ate as if he hadn't eaten for a week.
Es sah aus, als wenn es regnen wollte.	It looked as if it were going to rain.
Tat ich das? Ich konnte so tun, als täte ich es.	Did I do that? I could act as if I were doing it.

[6] als with the Comparative

Form parallel sentences with **besser als** and **mehr als.**

Du bist auch nicht besser als er.	You are no better than he is.	SEE ANALYSIS 122 (pp. 318-320)
Das ist besser als nichts.	That is better than nothing.	
Geben ist besser als Nehmen.	Giving is better than taking.	
In New York wohnen mehr Menschen als in Berlin.	More people live in New York than in Berlin.	
Frau Behrens hat in Casablanca mehr Geld verloren, als sie wollte.	Frau Behrens lost more money in Casablanca than she intended to.	
Er wußte bestimmt mehr, als er uns gesagt hat.	I'm sure he knew more than he told us.	

[7] The Conjunction als

Als Ingelheim ins Hotel kam, wartete ein Brief auf ihn.

Als wir in Tripolis waren, wohnten wir bei Ali und Busuq.

Hermann und ich saßen bei Ali, als Erich von meiner Frau sprach.

Wir wollten gerade ins Haus gehen, als eine Frau laut schrie.

SEE ANALYSIS 122 (pp. 318-320)

[8] wenn

Form parallel sentences with **wenn,** in the meaning of both *if* and *whenever.*

Wenn es morgen regnet, bleiben wir zu Hause.

Wenn er schon hier ist, können wir ihn besuchen.

Wenn er wirklich in Köln war, muß er den Dom gesehen haben.

Wenn er wirklich in Köln gewesen wäre, hätte er auch den Dom sehen müssen.

Wenn er schon hier wäre, könnten wir ihn besuchen.

Wenn der Sommer kam, fuhren unsere Eltern immer mit uns an den Rhein.

Jedesmal, wenn Tante Amalie uns besuchte, mußte ich mit ihr ins Museum gehen.

Wenn ich in München bin, gehe ich abends immer ins Theater.

Von jetzt an nehme ich dich immer mit, wenn ich wieder nach Kairo fahren muß.

SEE ANALYSIS 122 (pp. 318-320)

[9] gar nicht, gar kein, gar nichts

Study these sentences carefully. Note that whenever **gar** is stressed, it denies an immediately preceding idea. Be prepared to form your own examples.

Meyer ist gar nicht *dumm;* er weiß immer, was er will.

    Meyer isn't at all stupid; he always knows what he wants.

SEE ANALYSIS 123 (pp. 320-321)

Was, Heidi will heiraten? Das habe ich gar nicht ge*wuß*t.

    What? Heidi wants to get married? I didn't have any idea of that.

Was hast du mir denn mitgebracht?—*Gar* nichts; ich hatte keine Zeit, dir etwas zu kaufen.

    What did you bring me?—Nothing at all; I didn't have time to buy you anything.

Er spricht so leise, daß man ihn gar nicht ver*ste*hen kann.

    He speaks so softly that you can't understand him at all.

Wie hast du denn geschlafen?—Ich habe *gar* nicht geschlafen.

    How did you sleep?—I didn't sleep at all.

Was habt ihr denn heute gelernt?—*Gar* nichts, wir haben nur gespielt.

    What did you learn today?—Nothing at all, we only played.

Ingelheim *war* gar kein General; er war nur Leutnant.

    Ingelheim wasn't a general at all; he was only a lieutenant.

Ich weiß gar nicht, warum ich schon *wie*der nicht *schla*fen konnte. Ich habe gestern abend doch gar keinen *Kaf*fee getrunken.

    I just don't know why I couldn't sleep again. I didn't drink any coffee at all last night.

[10] da-Compounds with unstressed da-

SEE ANALYSIS 124 (pp. 321-322)

Wo ist denn mein Kugelschreiber?—Ich schreibe gerade damit.

    Where is my ballpoint pen?—I'm writing with it.

Wir haben *auch* ein Haus mit einer Garage dahinter.

    We, too, have a house with a garage behind it.

Das ist die Marienkirche, und in dem Haus da*ne*ben hat früher mein Bruder gewohnt.

    That's St. Mary's, and my brother used to live in the house next to it.

Das Häuschen stand am Ende der Straße, und in dem Garten davor saßen wir oft auf einer Bank.

    The little house was at the end of the street, and in the garden in front of it we often sat on a bench.

Das Haus steht noch immer. Aber die Menschen, die darin einmal glücklich waren, sind fast alle gestorben.

    The house still stands. But almost all the people who once were happy in it have died.

Haben Sie Ingelheims Roman gelesen?—Nur den Anfang davon.

    Have you read Ingelheim's novel?—Only the beginning of it.

Ich höre, Müller will euer Haus kaufen. Was will er euch denn dafür geben?
I understand Müller wants to buy your house. What has he offered you for it?

Natürlich möchte ich morgen nicht arbeiten, aber was kann ich dagegen tun?
Of course I don't want to work tomorrow, but what can I do about it?

Er ist nie *für* eine Sache; er ist immer nur da*gegen*.
He is never *for* something; he is always *against* it.

Form sentences with the following prepositional phrases; then substitute **da**-compounds:

mit dem Geld   (machen)
in dem Haus   (wohnen)
für zwei Mark   (kaufen)
gegen Kopfschmerzen   (tun)
mit diesem Wagen   (fahren)
beim Arbeiten   (singen)
sofort nach dem Essen   (ins Bett gehen)
von Biologie   (etwas verstehen)

[11] Stressed and unstressed **da**-Compounds—Split **da**-Compounds —**der hier, der da**

Be prepared to produce orally the statements containing **da**-compounds when you hear the initial statements or questions of each group.

(a) *Den* Kugelschreiber kannst du zurückbringen.
     *Da*mit (mit *dem*) kann ich nicht schreiben.
     Da kann ich nicht mit schreiben.

(b) Was soll ich denn mit einem *Ku*gelschreiber?
     *Da*mit kann man doch nicht *schrei*ben!
     Da kann man doch nicht mit *schrei*ben!

(c) Dieser Kugelschreiber hier ist mir zu schwer. Darf ich mal *den* da versuchen?

(a) Was? Einen Mer*ce*des soll ich dir kaufen? Nein!
     *Da*für habe ich kein Geld.
     Da habe ich kein Geld für.

(b) Wir können doch nicht schon *wie*der nach Italien fahren.
     *Da*für haben wir doch gar kein *Geld*.
     Da haben wir doch gar kein *Geld* für.

(c) Ich glaube, ich nehme *doch die*sen Wagen. Er ist zwar etwas alt, aber *der* da ist mir zu teuer, für *den* habe ich nicht genug Geld.

SEE ANALYSIS 124–128 (pp. 321-324)

(a) *Das* Bett hier ist zu *kurz* für mich.
     *Da*rin kann ich nicht schlafen.
     Da kann ich nicht drin schlafen.

(b) Sie sehen doch, daß das Bett zu *kurz* für mich ist.
     Darin kann ich doch nicht *schla*fen.
     Da kann ich doch nicht drin *schla*fen.

(c) Das Bett da vor dem Fenster ist zu kurz für mich. Aber das Rokokoding
     [rococo thing] da bei der *Tür* ist in Ordnung. In *dem* kann ich be*stimmt*
     schlafen.

(a) In die *O*per brauchst du mit Tante Amalie *nicht* zu gehen.
     *Da*bei schläft sie immer ein.
     Da schläft sie immer bei *ein*.

(b) Für eine *Wag*ner-Oper ist Tante Amalie doch zu alt.
     Das dauert doch sechs Stunden; dabei muß sie ja *ein*schlafen.
     Da muß sie ja bei *ein*schlafen.

(c) Sonntag im Kino ist sie *auch* eingeschlafen.—Aber im Gloria-Palast läuft
     heute abend ein Hitchcock-Film. Bei *dem* schläft sie be*stimmt* nicht ein.

(a) So, der Frankenwein* war Ihrem Mann *doch* zu sauer? Dann nehmen Sie
     doch mal einen *Mo*sel.
     *Da*mit ist er bestimmt zufrieden.
     Da ist er bestimmt mit zufrieden.

(b) Den *Fran*kenwein hätte ich nicht kaufen sollen.
     Damit war mein Mann *gar* nicht zufrieden.
     Da war mein Mann *gar* nicht mit zufrieden.

(c) Wenn Ihnen der Mosel zu *teu*er ist, dann nehmen Sie doch einen
     Remstaler.† Mit *dem* ist Ihr Mann be*stimmt* zufrieden.

[12] wo-Compounds

SEE
ANALYSIS
129

(pp. 324-325)

Wofür brauchst du denn so viel Geld? Was willst du denn kaufen?
     What do you need so much money for? What do you want to buy?

Für was brauchst du denn das Geld?
     What do you need the money for?

Ich weiß nicht, wofür er das Geld ausgegeben hat.
     I don't know what he spent the money for.

Der Karl hat mich gerade angerufen. Ich soll ihm wieder einmal helfen.—
     Wobei denn?—Beim Transponieren.—Bei *was?*—*Wo*bei?
     Karl just called me. I am supposed to help him again.—With what?—
     Transposing.—With what?

---

* wine from Franken (Franconia)
† wine from the Rems valley in Württemberg

Ich verstehe das alles nicht. Wovon sprecht ihr denn eigentlich?
> I don't understand all that. What are you talking about anyway?

Worüber habt ihr denn den ganzen Abend geredet?
> What did you talk about all evening?

Wozu willst du denn nach Italien fahren?
> What do you want to go to Italy for?

War der Briefträger immer noch nicht da?—Warum fragst du denn schon wieder? Auf was (worauf) wartest du denn eigentlich, auf einen Brief von deiner Freundin?
> Hasn't the mailman been here yet?—Why are you asking again? What are you waiting for anyway, a letter from your girl friend?

[13] Prepositional Objects

After memorizing these verbs with their prepositions, form variations of your own.

SEE
ANALYSIS
130–132
(pp. 325-329)

Angst haben vor

Hast du Angst vor ihm?—Nein, nicht vor ihm, aber vor seiner Intelligenz.
> Are you afraid of him?—No, not of him, but of his intelligence.

antworten auf

Sie hat immer noch nicht auf meinen Brief geantwortet.
> She still hasn't answered my letter.

bitten um

Dürfte ich Sie um eine Tasse Kaffee bitten?
> Could I ask you for a cup of coffee?

danken für

Ich hätte ihm natürlich schon längst für die Blumen danken sollen.
> Of course I should have thanked him for the flowers long ago.

denken an   and   **nachdenken über**

Weißt du, daß ich noch oft an unsre Reise denke?
> Do you know that I still think about our trip very often?

Über *dieses* Problem habe ich *auch* schon nachgedacht.
> I've thought about this problem, too.

einladen zu

Darf ich Sie zu einem Glas Wein einladen?
> May I invite you to (have) a glass of wine (with me)?

fragen nach

Hat jemand nach mir gefragt?—Du kannst dir doch denken, daß sie alle nach dir gefragt haben.

> Did anybody ask about me?—Don't you know that they all asked about you?

gehören zu

Diese Schlüssel gehören zu unserem VW.

> These keys belong to our VW.

Weißt du, daß Meyer jetzt zur Antivivisektionsliga gehört?

> Do you know that Meyer belongs to the Anti-Vivisection League now?

glauben an

Ein Athe*ist* glaubt nicht an Gott.

> An atheist doesn't believe in God.

halten von, halten für

Was halten Sie von Meyer? Ich halte ihn für sehr intelligent.—Ich nicht, ich halte ihn gar nicht für intelligent.

> What do you think of Meyer? I think he is very intelligent.—I don't; I don't think he's intelligent at all.

Und was halten Sie von Ingelheims Kriegsromanen?—Die halte ich für ganz gut. Sie sind gar nicht schlecht.

> And what do you think of Ingelheim's war novels?—I think they're pretty good. They're not bad at all.

hoffen auf

Ich weiß, ihr Touristen hofft, daß morgen wieder die Sonne scheint. Aber die Leute hier hoffen auf Regen.

> I know you tourists hope that the sun is going to shine again tomorrow. But the people here are hoping for rain.

hören von

Seit dem Kriege habe ich nichts mehr von Meyer gehört.

> Since the war, I haven't heard anything from Meyer (of Meyer, about Meyer).

Ich habe erst gestern von der Sache gehört.

> I didn't hear about it until yesterday.

lachen über   (to laugh at, about)

Ich lache gar nicht über dich; ich lache nur über deinen Akzent.

> But I'm not laughing at you; I'm only laughing at your accent.

auslachen   (to laugh at, jeer at, make fun of)

Sie haben ihn einfach ausgelacht.
> They simply laughed at him.

Wenn ein Humorist gut ist, lacht man über ihn; wenn er schlecht ist, lacht man ihn aus.
> If a humorist is good, you laugh at him; if he is bad, you jeer at him.

reagieren auf

Wie reagieren denn Ihre Leser auf diesen Kriegsroman?
> How do your readers react to this war novel?

Wie hat er denn auf dich reagiert?
> How did he react to you?

sein für, sein gegen

Sind Sie etwa für die Vivisektion?—Nein, ich bin dagegen.
> Are you by any chance for vivisection?—No, I'm against it.

Wer nicht für mich ist, ist gegen mich.
> Whoever is not for me, is against me.

sprechen von

Von seiner Frau hat er nicht gesprochen.
> He didn't talk about his wife.

Ich weiß nicht, warum er nie von seinen Romanen spricht.
> I don't know why he never talks about his novels.

sprechen über

Heute abend spricht Professor Leid über Psychoanalyse.
> Tonight Professor Leid will speak about psychoanalysis.

verstehen von

Du weißt doch, daß ich nichts von Archäologie verstehe.
> You know, don't you, that I know nothing about archeology.

warten auf

Wie lange wartest du denn schon auf Fritz?
> How long have you been waiting for Fritz?

wetten (um)

Wir haben (um) eine Flasche Wein gewettet, daß Ingelheim *doch* wieder allein nach Kairo fährt.
> We've bet a bottle of wine that Ingelheim will go to Cairo all by himself again after all.

wissen von

Leider weiß ich gar nichts von Ingelheim.
  Unfortunately I know nothing about Ingelheim.
Was weißt *du* denn von den Kämpfen in der Normandie?
  What do *you* know about the fighting in Normandy?

[14] Syntactical Variations with **warten**

SEE
ANALYSIS
130–132
(pp. 325-329)

Worauf wartest du denn?—Auf Geld.—Wartest du schon lange darauf?

Einen Liebesbrief habe ich von dir ja leider nie bekommen; aber gewartet habe ich lange darauf.

Das glaube ich nicht, daß du darauf gewartet hast.

Liebesbriefe soll ich dir schreiben? Nein, *da*rauf kannst du *lang*e warten.

Warum hast du dir denn das Buch ge*kauft?* Du wußtest doch, ich wollte es dir zum Geburtstag schenken.—Ich weiß, aber *da*rauf habe ich leider nicht *war*ten können.

Ich warte auf meine Frau.

Ich warte hier, bis meine Frau kommt.

Ich warte auf einen Brief von ihr.

Ich warte immer noch darauf, daß sie mir einen Brief schreibt.

Worauf wartest du denn eigentlich?

Heute ist mein Mann endlich gekommen; ich habe wochenlang auf ihn gewartet.

Heute ist mein Mantel endlich gekommen; ich hatte wochenlang darauf gewartet.

Leider können wir Ihnen den Mantel erst in einer Woche schicken.—*Da*rauf kann ich aber nicht warten.

Ich habe wochenlang darauf gewartet, endlich wieder einmal etwas von ihr zu hören.

Wenn ich gewußt hätte, daß Erika immer zu spät kommt,* hätte ich nicht auf sie gewartet.

Du weißt, ich kann nicht lange auf dich warten.

Ich habe leider nicht auf dich warten können.

Ich wollte, ich hätte nicht auf dich zu warten brauchen.

Er sagte, er könnte nicht auf mich warten.

Er sagte, er hätte gestern leider nicht auf mich warten können.

Er sagte, daß er gestern leider nicht hätte auf mich warten können.

---

* **zu spät kommen**   to arrive too late; to be late (for a date, for an appointment, for school, etc.)

Weil er auf Erika zu warten schien, habe ich nicht mit ihm gesprochen.

Er hat mir versprochen, auf Erika zu warten.

Ich warte nicht auf einen Liebesbrief; ich warte auf Geld.

Ich wartete damals nicht auf Liebesbriefe; ich wartete immer nur auf Geld.

Ich habe noch nie auf Liebesbriefe gewartet.

Ich weiß nicht, ob er auf einen Liebesbrief wartet oder auf Geld.

Ich wußte nicht, ob er auf Liebesbriefe wartete oder auf Geld.

Mir hat damals kein Mensch geschrieben. Wenn ich dich damals gekannt hätte, Heidemarie, dann hätte ich jeden Tag auf einen Brief von dir gewartet.

Herr Meyer, so lange kann ich auf das Geld leider nicht warten.

Weil ich gestern schon in Berlin sein mußte, habe ich auf Ihren Brief leider nicht warten können. Ich hoffe, meine Frau schickt ihn mir nach.

[15] Rapid Reading Practice: Syntactical Variations with Prepositional Objects

SEE ANALYSIS 130–132 (pp. 325-329)

Wir haben gerade von Meyer gesprochen.

Wir haben gerade davon gesprochen, daß du den Meyer heiraten willst.

Er spricht nie von seinen Kriegserlebnissen.

Du willst wissen, was ich im Kriege erlebt habe? Davon spreche ich nicht.

Wir haben gestern davon gesprochen, diesen Sommer nach Italien zu fahren.

Morgen abend spricht Professor Erdmann.—Worüber spricht er denn?—Er spricht über den Materialismus im Deutschland der Nachkriegszeit.—Da bleibe ich zu Hause; *dar*über habe ich ihn schon *drei*mal sprechen hören.

Meine Damen und Herren, wir sprachen gestern darüber, daß der Glaube an den Fortschritt heute nicht mehr so stark ist wie früher. Wir sprachen auch darüber, ob es nicht besser wäre, diesen Glauben ganz aufzugeben.

Herr Doktor, glauben Sie, daß ich Hepatitis habe?—Nein, Hepatitis haben Sie nicht, aber Sie haben zu viel gegessen und zu viel getrunken.

Ingelheims Frau meint, er hätte Hepatitis.—Ich glaube nicht daran, daß er Hepatitis hat.

Ich hoffe sehr auf Ihre Hilfe, Herr Engels.

Ich hoffe sehr, daß Sie uns helfen werden, Herr Engels.

Ich hoffe immer noch darauf, daß Herr Engels uns hilft.

Ich habe in der Zeitung gelesen, daß es bald regnen soll und daß die Leute hier darauf hoffen, daß es regnet. Hoffen *Sie* darauf, daß es bald regnet?— Nein, ich hoffe, es regnet nicht.

Ich habe Rosemarie lange nicht gesehen, aber ich hoffe, sie in München wiederzusehen.—Ich verstehe wirklich nicht, warum du darauf hoffst, sie wiederzusehen. Du weißt doch, sie lacht nur über dich.—Aber sie lacht doch gar
nicht über mich; sie lacht nur darüber, daß ich immer noch einen Akzent
habe, wenn ich Deutsch spreche.

Darf ich Sie um Ingelheims Romane bitten?

Dürfte ich Sie darum bitten, mir Ingelheims Romane ins Hotel zu schicken?

Ich habe Sie schon einmal darum gebeten, mir alle Romane von Ingelheim zu
schicken.

Darf ich Sie bitten, Montag abend mein Gast zu sein?

Wo ist denn der Brief an die Hansa-Bank? Der Herr Direktor hat schon danach
gefragt.—Hat er auch nach den Briefen nach München gefragt?—Nein,
*da*nach hat er *nicht* gefragt; nur nach dem Brief an die *Ha*nsa-Bank.—
Fräulein Schmitz, der Herr Direktor hat schon wieder danach gefragt, ob Sie
den Brief an die Hansa-Bank schon geschrieben haben.

Ich habe meinem Vater gestern abend gesagt, daß wir im Juni heiraten wollen.
—Und was hat er darauf geantwortet?

Ich habe ihm immer noch nicht auf seinen Brief geantwortet.

Er hat mir einen Brief geschrieben, und ich habe ihm auch schon darauf geantwortet.—Was hast du ihm denn geantwortet?—Ich habe ihm geantwortet,
daß ich nicht daran denke, ihn zu heiraten.

Lieber Hans, ich danke Dir sehr für deine Hilfe.

Liebe Emma, ich danke Ihnen sehr, daß Sie meiner Frau geholfen haben.
Und nun möchte ich Ihnen noch einmal dafür danken, daß Sie meiner Frau
geholfen haben.

Denkst du auch daran, daß Rosemarie morgen Geburtstag hat?—Morgen? Ich
dachte, sie hätte erst im September Geburtstag.

Erika hat mir erzählt, du führst mit ihr nach Italien.—Ich? Mit Erika? Ich denke
ja nicht daran. Ich war vor einem Jahr mit ihr in Italien,—und ich kann nur
sagen: Einmal und nie wieder.

Wir wohnen zu weit weg von Köln. Ich möchte nicht mehr jeden Tag in die
Stadt fahren müssen. Wir denken daran, uns in der Stadt ein Haus zu kaufen.

Wie wäre es, wenn wir im Regina-Palast zu Mittag essen würden?—Das wäre
sehr schön, aber ich habe leider kein Geld bei mir.—Das macht nichts, ich
lade Sie ein.

Ich wollte dir nur sagen, daß ich heute nicht zum Essen nach Hause komme.
Müller hat mich eingeladen, mit ihm im Regina-Palast zu essen.

So, *dein* Mann kommt heute *auch* nicht nach Hause? Hat Müller ihn etwa *auch* dazu eingeladen, im Regina-Palast zu Mittag zu essen?

Was halten Sie davon, daß mein Sohn Arzt werden will?—Davon halte ich *gar* nichts.

Er hat mir gar nicht ge*sagt*, daß er nach Italien fahren will.
Er hat mir gar nichts davon ge*sagt*, daß er nach Italien fahren will.
Davon, daß er nach I*ta*lien fahren will, hat er mir nichts ge*sagt*.
Daß er nach I*ta*lien fahren will, davon hat er mir nichts ge*sagt*.
Daß der Schmidt, wie er uns immer erzählt, in der Normandie gekämpft hat, daran glaube ich nicht.

Davon, daß er sich in Köln ein Haus bauen will, hat er nicht gesprochen.
Daran, daß sie schon fünfzig ist, habe ich gar nicht gedacht.

Ich bin seit zwanzig Jahren mit ihm verheiratet; und daß er mir einmal das Frühstück ans Bett bringt, darauf hoffe ich schon lange nicht mehr.

Vor dreißig Jahren, als ich ihn gerne geheiratet hätte, meinte er, er wäre zu jung zum Heiraten. Aber daß er heute immer noch daran denkt, mich heiraten zu wollen, darüber kann ich nur lachen.

CONVERSATION

Snatches of Conversation Overheard by the Hat-Check Girl at the Regina Bar

FRAUENSTIMME 1: Und als er dann endlich erschienen ist, habe ich gesagt: „Jetzt hättest du aber wirklich nicht mehr zu kommen brauchen." Und weißt du, was er mir darauf geantwortet hat? Ich hätte ja nicht auf ihn zu warten brauchen!

FRAUENSTIMME 2: Na so was! Wenn er *mir* das gesagt hätte, dann hätte ich ihm aber ...

MANN 1: Nein, wirklich? Auf *den* Gedanken wäre ich nie gekommen. Im Schlafzimmer, sagen Sie?

MANN 2: Ja, wissen Sie, eine Zeitlang dachte ich ja, so ein Ding könnte man nur ins Wohnzimmer stellen. Außerdem hatte ich es ihr zum Geburtstag geschenkt, und da wollte sie natürlich, daß alle unsere Freunde es sehen sollten.

MANN 1: Ja, ja, ich kenne das, meine Frau ist auch so. Aber ich verstehe immer noch nicht, warum Sie es jetzt ins Schlafzimmer ...

REGINA-PALAST-HOTEL MÜNCHEN

5-Uhr-Tanz-Tee mit namhaften Kapellen

Cocktail-Stunde in der kleinen Bar mit Jonny van Dyck an der Hammondorgel

Täglich ab 21 Uhr in der ›Großen Regina-Bar‹ *Tanz*

MANN 2: Weil es zu groß ist! Über zwei Meter lang, und in *der* Wohnung, . . . na, ich sage Ihnen, diese Wohnungen heute! Vor ein paar Tagen hat meine Frau zehn Leute zum Abendessen eingeladen, und da war einfach kein Platz mehr, und seitdem spielen wir im Schlafzimmer Klavier. Es ging gerade zwischen die Betten und die Wand . . .

FRAU A: Wer? Der mit dem Hut? Das soll Schmidt-Ingelheim sein?

FRAU B: Nein, nicht *der. Der* da, mit dem Mantel über dem Arm.

FRAU A: Glaubst du wirklich, daß er das ist?

FRAU B: Ganz bestimmt. Gestern war doch sein Bild in der Zeitung. Er ist gerade aus Afrika zurückgekommen.

FRAU A: *Der* sieht aber gut aus, den möchte ich kennenlernen.

FRAU B: Du, ob das wohl seine Frau ist, die da neben ihm steht?

FRAU A: Nein, bestimmt nicht, die ist doch viel zu jung für ihn;—vielleicht seine Tochter.

MANN: . . . mir viel zu heiß war! Im Theater ist es mir immer zu heiß, und dann auch noch Wagner. Da schläft man ja bei ein. Fünf Stunden hab' ich da gesessen, und am liebsten wär' ich schon nach zehn Minuten aufgestanden und nach Hause gegangen. Acht Stunden im Büro sitzen und dann noch Wagner! Nee, da mach' ich nicht mehr mit. Das nächste Mal bleibe ich zu Hause und lese meine Zeitung.

FRAU: Von mir aus kannst du ruhig zu Hause bleiben. Dann gehe ich eben allein. Ach, ich liebe doch Wagner so sehr . . .

MÄNNERSTIMME: Der sollte sein Geld lieber auf die Bank bringen, statt seiner Frau schon wieder einen Mercedes zu kaufen.

HERR 1: Das war aber wirklich nett von Ihnen, daß Sie mich noch so spät am Abend am Flugplatz abgeholt haben.

HERR 2: Ja, wenn Sie mich von Frankfurt aus nicht angerufen hätten, hätten Sie mit dem Bus in die Stadt fahren müssen. Ich wollte nämlich heute abend eigentlich ins Theater gehen.

HERR 1: Sie haben hoffentlich nicht sehr lange warten müssen.

MÄDCHEN A: Niemand weiß etwas davon—kein Mensch. Außer dir habe ich das noch niemandem erzählt, und du mußt mir versprechen, daß du mit keinem darüber redest, auch mit Fritz nicht.

MÄDCHEN B: Natürlich nicht! Mit wem könnte ich über so etwas reden? Du kennst mich doch. Übrigens, weißt du, daß die Erika den Hans jetzt *doch* heiraten will?

MÄDCHEN A: Ach was! Wirklich? Das hätte ich nicht gedacht.

MÄDCHEN B: Ja, doch! Sie hat mir's gestern erzählt, es soll aber noch niemand etwas davon wissen.

MANN A: Ach was! Ein Glas Wein können Sie doch mit uns trinken, es ist doch erst halb zwölf.

MANN B: Danke, sehr nett von Ihnen, aber ich möchte wirklich lieber auf mein Zimmer gehen; ich will noch ein Bad nehmen, und ich muß auch noch meine Frau anrufen, um ihr zu sagen, daß ich . . . .

MÄNNERSTIMME I: Plötzlich waren schon wieder ein paar Tiefflieger da. Ich denke, ich werde verrückt. Ich drücke mich auf den Boden, einer von den

Tieffliegern sieht mich und kommt herunter. . . . Hier ist mein Hut, Fräulein. Was bekommen Sie dafür? Ach so, erst wenn wir weggehen. . . . Ja, wo war ich, also der kommt herunter, und ich denke, jetzt ist alles zu Ende, aber da fliegt er plötzlich nach rechts weg und. . . .

MÄNNERSTIMME II: Müssen Sie hier stehenbleiben und mit den Händen reden? Fräulein, meinen Mantel, bitte. . . .

MÄNNERSTIMME I: Ja, also, das hätten Sie erleben sollen, damals in Afrika. Dagegen war die Westfront gar nichts. Und dann war da noch dieser Erich Karsten, das müßte ich Ihnen wirklich noch erzählen. Also, wir haben nämlich damals bei einem Ägypter gewohnt, wissen Sie, Ali hieß. . . .

EIN MANN: Ingelheim, Ingelheim, Ingelheim, müßt ihr denn den ganzen Abend von Ingelheim reden? Als ob es sonst keine Schriftsteller mehr in Deutschland gäbe! Also, wenn ich den Namen Ingelheim noch einmal höre, könnt ihr allein Wein trinken gehen, ohne mich, ich kann den Namen nicht mehr hören. Ingelheim, Ingelheim, Ingelheim. . . .

READING

Zwei und zwei ist fünf (Schluß)

„Wer ist weg?" fragte Hermann. „Herr Karsten", antwortete das Mädchen. Hermann führte sie zu einem der Gartenstühle, versuchte, ganz ruhig zu sein, und sagte: „Gerda, dies ist mein Freund Schmidt-Ingelheim. Ich habe ihn gerade am Flugplatz abgeholt", und als sie nicht auf seine Worte reagierte, sagte er: „Gerda, könntest du dich 5 zwingen, mir und Hans jetzt zu erzählen, was hier geschehen ist?"

Es dauerte doch noch ein paar Minuten, bis Gerda ruhig sprechen konnte. Dann erzählte sie: „Ich bin kurz nach fünf mit meiner Mutter hier angekommen. Wir sahen, daß du noch nicht zurück warst. Mutter ist spazierengegangen, und ich wollte schwimmen, 10 bis du kamst. Als ich ins Wasser sprang, war niemand hier, das weiß ich bestimmt. Aber als ich aus dem Wasser wollte, stand Herr Karsten oben und hielt mir die Hand hin, um mir zu helfen. Ich erschrak, schrie laut und sprang zurück. Herr Karsten fiel ins Wasser. Als ich auf dieser Seite aus dem Wasser kam, war Herr 15 Karsten weg. Aber da schwimmt sein Hut."

hielt . . . hin held out his hand

Hermann, dem ich auf dem Weg vom Flughafen erzählt hatte, was in Tripolis geschehen war, sah mich an, dann ging er ins Wohnzimmer, holte ein Telefon, stellte es auf den Gartentisch beim Schwimmbecken, wählte eine Nummer und wartete. Gerda und ich hörten, wie es am anderen Ende klingelte. Dann gab mir Hermann 5 den Hörer. „Hier Karsten", sagte eine Männerstimme. Und obwohl ich seit dem Kriege nicht mit Erich gesprochen hatte, erkannte ich seine Stimme sofort. Ich log und sagte ihm, ich riefe vom Flughafen aus an.

Ich hätte gehofft, Hermann könnte mich abholen, er sei aber nir-10 gends zu sehen, und zu Hause sei er auch nicht. „Er wollte dich auch abholen", sagte Erich, „aber vielleicht ist er nicht so schnell durch die Stadt gekommen, wie er wollte. Ich rufe ihn trotzdem sofort noch einmal an und sage ihm, daß du da bist. Aber er ist bestimmt nicht mehr zu Hause." 15

Einen Augenblick später klingelte das Telefon. Wir antworteten nicht. „Wie weit ist es von hier bis zu Erichs Wohnung?" fragte ich Hermann. „Mit dem Wagen mindestens eine Stunde", war die

Antwort. Ich sagte nichts, auch Gerda schwieg; aber ich glaube,
sie fühlte, daß Hermann und ich mehr wußten, als wir sagten.

Endlich meinte Hermann: „Gerda, die Geschichte, die du uns da
erzählt hast, ist einfach unmöglich. Wem der Hut auf dem Wasser
gehört, weiß ich nicht. Aber Erich kann er nicht gehören, Erich kann 5
nicht hier gewesen sein. Wenn er hier gewesen wäre, könnte er
jetzt nicht zu Hause sein. Weißt du was, wir warten, bis deine
Mutter zurückkommt, und dann fahre ich euch beide in meinem
Wagen nach Hamburg zurück. Hans kann mit deinem VW hinter   **hinter uns herfahren**
uns herfahren.“   10 follow us

Es war schon ungefähr neun, als wir Gerda und ihrer Mutter gute
Nacht sagten. Gerda hatte versprochen, ein Bad zu nehmen, eine
Tasse Tee mit Kognak zu trinken und dann ins Bett zu gehen. Um   **um halb zehn**   at half-
halb zehn saßen wir bei Hermann, tranken einen Whisky und re-   past nine
deten von den Fußabdrücken hinter dem Stuhl meiner Frau, von 15
den fünf Goldstücken hinter dem Stein in Alis Haus und von Erichs
Hut in Hermanns Schwimmbecken. Wir versuchten, etwas zu erklären, was man einfach nicht erklären kann.

Da klingelte das Telefon; Hermann nahm den Hörer ab. Lange
sagte er nichts, und ich wußte nicht, mit wem er sprach. „Wir 20
kommen sofort, Gerda“, sagte er dann, legte den Hörer auf und
sprang auf. „Aber so etwas ist doch einfach unmöglich!“ rief er.
„Was ist unmöglich?“ fragte ich und versuchte, ruhig zu bleiben.
Das Telefon klingelte wieder. Diesmal ging ich in Hermanns Ar-
beitszimmer, wo noch ein Telefon stand, und hörte mit.   25

„Hier ist Elisabeth Meyer“, hörte ich eine Frauenstimme sagen. „Bei
mir in der Wohnung wohnt ein Herr Karsten. Soviel ich weiß, ist
er Ihr Privatsekretär. Herr Direktor, Ihrem Sekretär muß irgendetwas passiert sein. Er ist heute noch gar nicht weggewesen. Seit
dem Frühstück sitzt er auf seinem Zimmer. Vor ein paar Minuten 30
habe ich an seine Tür geklopft, um ihn zu fragen, ob er nicht etwas
essen wollte. Während ich klopfte, hörte ich einen lauten Schrei,
und dann war es still im Zimmer. Ich habe die Polizei schon angerufen, aber es wäre vielleicht gut, wenn Sie auch kämen. Er ist
doch ein Freund von Ihnen.“ „Ich komme sofort, Frau Meyer“, sagte 35
Hermann und legte auf. Dann sagte er zu mir: „Hans, das ist zum
Verrücktwerden. Du mußt sofort zu Gerda fahren. Die zwei Frauen
dürfen heute abend nicht allein in ihrer Wohnung sein. Du kannst
meinen Wagen nehmen, und ich fahre mit einer Taxe zu Erichs
Wohnung. Ich sehe dich dann später bei Gerda. Sie soll dir erzählen, 40
was dort passiert ist.“ „OK“, sagte ich. Dann liefen wir aus dem
Haus.

Gerda und ihre Mutter waren erstaunt, mich allein zu sehen.
„Hermann ist zu Erich gefahren", sagte ich. „Erichs Wirtin hat ihn
vor einer halben Stunde laut schreien hören, und sie meint, ihm sei
etwas passiert."

vor einer halben Stunde half an hour ago

„Aber Erich war doch vor einer halben Stunde hier", sagte Gerda. 5
„Hat Ihnen Hermann denn nichts davon erzählt?"—„Unmöglich!
Wie kann er vor einer halben Stunde hier gewesen sein, wenn er
vor einer halben Stunde in seinem Zimmer laut geschrien hat?
Gerda, ich glaube, Sie hätten keinen Kognak trinken sollen."

Aber Gerda lachte nicht. „Hans, Sie wissen mehr als Sie sagen", 10
meinte sie, und dann erzählte sie mir, was passiert war. „Nachdem
Sie beide heute abend weggegangen waren, nahm ich, wie ich versprochen hatte, ein Bad. Als ich nach zehn Minuten aus der Badewanne stieg, stand plötzlich der Karsten wieder vor mir. Wie er ins
Badezimmer gekommen ist, weiß ich nicht. Niemand hat geklingelt, 15
und meine Mutter hat niemand hereingelassen. Auch durch den
Garten kann er nicht gekommen sein, sonst hätte bestimmt der Hund
gebellt. Fitzi schläft nämlich auf der Terrasse, wissen Sie. Aber
trotzdem stand Karsten in der Badezimmertür und fragte: ‚Wo
haben Sie meinen Hut?' Ich wurde wütend, nahm meinen Schuh 20
und schlug ihm damit auf den Kopf. Und dann war er plötzlich weg,
gerade wie heute nachmittag im Schwimmbecken. Und mein Schuh
ist auch weg."—„Ich glaube, wir sollten jetzt wirklich eine Tasse
Tee mit Kognak trinken", sagte ich zu den Frauen, „oder noch
besser einen Kognak ohne Tee." Dann warteten wir auf Hermann. 25

Es war schon eins, als er kam. „Eine unglaubliche Geschichte", fing
er an, „einfach unmöglich. Als ich vor Erichs Wohnung hielt, war
die Polizei gerade angekommen. ‚Aber ich sage Ihnen doch, er hat
laut geschrien', hörte ich die Wirtin sagen, ‚gerade als ich an die
Tür klopfte, um ihn zu fragen, ob ich ihm etwas zu essen bringen 30
könnte. Als er mir dann nicht antwortete, habe ich Sie sofort angerufen, und ich habe hier vor der Tür gestanden, bis Sie kamen.'—
Es dauerte fast zehn Minuten, bis die Polizisten endlich die Tür
aufmachen konnten. Dann gingen wir alle ins Zimmer. Erich war
weg; kein Mensch war im Zimmer, aber auf dem Tisch stand eine 35
Tasse Kaffee, der noch warm war. Die Polizisten wußten nicht, was
sie von der Sache halten sollten. Ich konnte ihnen nicht helfen, denn
wenn ich ihnen erzählt hätte, was seit gestern geschehen ist, hätten
sie bestimmt gedacht, ich wäre verrückt."

Ich wäre nicht erstaunt gewesen, wenn Gerda jetzt hysterisch ge- 40
worden wäre, aber sie blieb ruhig, erzählte noch einmal, daß Erich
in der Tür zum Badezimmer gestanden und sie nach seinem Hut

gefragt habe, daß sie ihm mit einem Schuh auf den Kopf geschlagen
hätte, und daß Erich plötzlich einfach nicht mehr dagewesen sei.

Hermann, die zwei Frauen und ich redeten, bis es Tag wurde.

Dann frühstückten wir zusammen—Gerdas Kaffee war übrigens unglaublich gut—und fuhren nach Hause.   5

Gestern abend waren Gerda und ihre Mutter wieder bei uns. Wir
saßen gerade beim Abendessen, als das Telefon klingelte. Ich hörte
wieder mit. Es war die Polizei, aber nicht die Hamburger Polizei.
Es war Interpol in Tripolis. Vor dem Haus eines Ägypters habe*
man am Morgen einen Mann gefunden, tot und mit einer Wunde 10
im Kopf. Die Untersuchung durch die Polizei hätte bis jetzt zu
nichts geführt. Einen Paß habe der Mann nicht gehabt; in seiner
Tasche wäre ein Brief gewesen, adressiert an Hermann, aber
außer hundert Mark wäre in dem Brief nichts gewesen. Niemand
wisse, wer der Mann sei; in keinem der Hotels in Tripolis kenne 15
man ihn, und so sei nur die eine Spur da, die zu Hermann führe,
und ob er wüßte, wer der Mann sein könnte. Übrigens habe man
neben ihm—wie seltsam—einen Damenschuh gefunden, und sonst
gar nichts.

Hermann zitterte. „Das könnte mein Privatsekretär Erich Karsten 20
sein", sagte er, „er ist seit gestern abend spurlos verschwunden. Ich
werde sofort die Polizei hier in Hamburg anrufen." Dann legte er
auf. Er zitterte noch immer.

Heute nachmittag fliege ich nach Hause. Meine Frau holt mich, wie
immer, am Flughafen ab. Und morgen, noch vor dem Frühstück, 25
werde ich etwas tun, was ich vor einem Monat nicht tun wollte:
Ich werde die Steinplatten auf unserer Terrasse zählen.

Und was tue ich, wenn es wirklich einundfünfzig sind?

* Note that the use of the subjunctive is sufficient to indicate indirect discourse;
no introductory statement such as **Man sagte uns,** . . . is necessary.

ANALYSIS

121 Relative Pronouns

The Definite Relative Pronoun

The German relative pronouns are **der, die, das.** Their forms are the same
as those of the definite article, except that the singular genitive and the
plural genitive and dative add the ending **-en.** This **-en** necessitates

doubling the -s- in the masculine and neuter forms in order to keep the preceding -e- short.

	MASC.	FEM.	NEUT.	PLURAL
NOM.	der	die	das	die
GEN.	dessen	deren	dessen	deren
DAT.	dem	der	dem	denen
ACC.	den	die	das	die

Relative pronouns must agree in gender and number with their antecedent; but their case depends on their function within the relative clause. The German relative pronouns are never omitted. All relative clauses are thus introduced dependent clauses and therefore have verb-last position.

Kennst du den Mann, *der* **gestern hier war?**
Do you know the man who was here yesterday?

Kennst du die Frau, *die* **gestern hier war?**
Do you know the woman who was here yesterday?

Kennst du das Mädchen, *das* **gestern hier war?**
Do you know the girl who was here yesterday?

Sein Vater, *dessen* **Frau aus Leningrad kam, sprach gut Russisch.**
His father, whose wife came from Leningrad, spoke Russian well.

Seine Frau, *deren* **Vater aus Leningrad kam, sprach gut Russisch.**
His wife, whose father came from Leningrad, spoke Russian well.

Wer war denn der Junge, mit *dem* **ich dich gestern gesehen habe?**
Who was the boy I saw you with (with whom I saw you) yesterday?

Wer war denn die Dame, mit *der* **ich dich gestern gesehen habe?**
Who was the lady I saw you with (with whom I saw you) yesterday?

Wer war denn das Mädchen, mit *dem* **ich dich gestern gesehen habe?**
Who was the girl I saw you with (with whom I saw you) yesterday?

Der Junge, *den* **du gestern gesehen hast, ist mein Sohn.**
The boy (whom) you saw yesterday is my son.

Die Dame, *die* **du gestern gesehen hast, ist meine Tante.**
The lady (whom) you saw yesterday is my aunt.

Das Mädchen, *das* **du gestern gesehen hast, ist meine Schwester.**
The girl (whom) you saw yesterday is my sister.

Kennst du die Leute, *die* **gestern hier waren?**
Do you know the people who were here yesterday?

Wer waren denn die Mädchen, mit *denen* **ich dich gestern gesehen habe?**
Who were the girls I saw you with (with whom I saw you) yesterday?

Die Mädchen, *die* **du gesehen hast, waren meine Schwestern.**
The girls (whom) you saw were my sisters.

Relative clauses do not always follow their antecedents immediately. If only a few words are needed to complete the governing clause, this clause is not interrupted by a relative clause.

> **Ich wollte Hermann Schneider besuchen, mit dem ich während des Krieges in Afrika gewesen war.**
> I wanted to visit Hermann Schneider, with whom I had been in Africa during the war.
>
> (*Not:* **Ich wollte Hermann Schneider, mit dem ich während des Krieges in Afrika gewesen war, besuchen.**)

The Indefinite Relative Pronoun

The German indefinite relative pronouns are **wer** and **was.** They are always used if there is no antecedent:

> *Wer* **Geld hat, hat auch Freunde.**
> Whoever (He who) has money has friends too.
> *Wer* **nicht für mich ist, ist gegen mich.**
> Whoever is not for me is against me.
> *Was* **er zu erzählen hatte, war nicht viel.**
> What he had to tell was not much.
>
> **Was er zu erzählen hatte, das war nicht viel.**
> **Wer Geld hat, der hat auch Freunde.**
> **Wer mich liebt, den liebe ich auch.**

In the last three examples, **das, der,** and **den** repeat the relative clause.

Was is also used to refer to an entire clause or to **alles, nichts,** or **etwas.**

> **Hans hat mich zum Essen eingeladen, was ich sehr nett finde.**
> **Ich habe nicht alles verstanden, was er gesagt hat.**
> **Er hat nichts gesagt, was ich nicht schon wußte.**
> **Ich habe etwas erlebt, was man eigentlich nicht erleben kann.**

122   wann, ob, als, wenn

Wann is an interrogative, meaning *when.* It is used

1. to introduce a question:

> **Wann fährst du nach Köln?**
> When are you going to Cologne?

2. as an interrogative conjunction when a **wann**-question is changed into a dependent clause:

Mutter will wissen, wann du nach Köln fährst.
Mother wants to know (the answer to the question) when you are going
  to Cologne.

Ob is a conjunction used to change a yes-or-no question into a dependent
clause:

Fährst du nach Berlin?
Mutter will wissen, ob du nach Berlin fährst.

Als is used in the following ways:

1. As a particle in comparisons, it means *than* and is used only to compare what is *not* equal:

Er trinkt mehr als du.
He drinks more than you (drink).
Ich habe nicht mehr als hundert Mark.
I don't have more than a hundred marks.

2. As a conjunction, **als** means *when* and introduces dependent clauses
referring to *one single event or situation in the past* (English *when* has
a much wider usage):

Als mein Mann noch lebte, gingen wir oft ins Theater.
When my husband was still alive, we often went to the theater.

3. **Als** may be the short version of **als ob** or **als wenn,** both meaning
as if. When so used, **als** or **als ob** is followed either by the normal subjunctive or, less frequently, by the indirect-discourse subjunctive.

If **als** is equivalent to **als ob,** the verb of the dependent clause follows
immediately after **als.**

Er tat, als ob er schliefe.   He acted as if he were asleep.
Er tat, als schliefe er.
Er tat, als schlafe er.

Er tat, als wenn er alles wüßte.   He acted as if he knew everything.
Er tat, als wüßte er alles.

Wenn is troublesome to the beginner, because it introduces both conditional and time clauses.

1. In conditional clauses, **wenn** always corresponds to English *if;* and any
if which cannot be replaced by *whether* must be rendered by **wenn.**

2. In time clauses, **wenn** basically means *whenever* and presents no difficulties as long as it is used with this meaning.

3. Trouble arises because English *when* is apt to be a source of interference. English *when* is used as an interrogative and then corresponds
to German **wann**. English *when* can also be a time conjunction meaning
"at the time when." In this latter function, *when* corresponds to ***als*** if the
clause refers to one single event in the past, and it corresponds to **wenn**
if the clause refers to present or future time. The following table summarizes the situation:

	IF (condition)	IF (whether)	WHENEVER	WHEN (interrogative)	WHEN (conjunction)
PAST	wenn	ob	wenn	wann	als
PRESENT	wenn	ob	wenn	wann	wenn
FUTURE	wenn	ob	wenn	wann	wenn

NOTE. The student can eliminate all interference caused by his own
speech habits if he realizes that

(a) in the sentence *I'd like to know when he came home,* the *when* is an
interrogative replaceable by "the answer to the question when"; *when*
therefore corresponds to German **wann:**

   Ich möchte wissen, wann er nach Hause gekommen ist.

(b) in *When my husband was still alive, we often went to the theater,*
when is a conjunction replaceable by "at the time when"; *when* therefore
corresponds to German **als,** because it refers to a single event or situation
in the past:

   Als mein Mann noch lebte, sind wir oft ins Theater gegangen.

(c) in *When he comes home from the war, we will get married, when* is
also a conjunction replaceable by "at the time when." But this time it
refers to the future and corresponds to German **wenn.**

   Wenn er aus dem Krieg nach Hause kommt, heiraten wir.
   When he comes home from the war, we will get married.

Since **wenn** also corresponds to English *if,* this last sentence is ambiguous
from an English point of view; only the context makes the meaning clear.
There are no linguistic means in German of distinguishing between *when*
and *if* as long as *when* refers to the future.

123 gar nicht, gar kein, gar nichts

The particle **gar** is used in connection with a following **nicht, kein,** or
nichts either to add the idea "contrary to expectation" or to strengthen
the negative particle in the same way in which *at all* strengthens the
not in *not at all.* This is shown on the next page.

Meyer ist gar nicht so dumm, wie du denkst.
Meyer isn't as stupid as you think.

Ich habe heute nacht gar nicht geschlafen.
I didn't sleep at all last night.

124 da-Compounds

You should by now be thoroughly familiar with the forms of the personal
pronouns and of the demonstrative pronouns.

	SINGULAR			PLURAL
NOM.	er	sie	es	sie
DAT.	ihm	ihr	ihm	ihnen
ACC.	ihn	sie	es	sie

	SINGULAR			PLURAL
NOM.	der	die	das	die
DAT.	dem	der	dem	denen
ACC.	den	die	das	die

We have used both personal and demonstrative pronouns as substitutes
for names and nouns. When these pronouns referred to persons, we have
used them freely, even if they were preceded by prepositions:

Du gehst mit Meyers ins *Kino*?
Du gehst mit ihnen ins *Kino*?
Mit *de*nen gehst du ins *Kino*?

However, when these pronouns referred to things or ideas, we have tried
to avoid using them after prepositions.

The reason is this: While it is quite possible to use *demonstrative* pronouns after prepositions, even if they refer to things, the *personal* pronouns, if referring to things, cannot follow a preposition.

This means that, in talking about a hat or a car, it is possible to say

Mit dem fahre ich nicht nach Paris.

However, the **ihm** in

Ich fahre nicht mit ihm nach Paris

can only refer to a person, and not to a hat or a car.

If you do want to refer to a hat or a car, you must use a "**da**-compound";
that is, you must replace the noun by **da-** followed by the preposition.
Thus the **damit** in

Damit kannst du doch nicht nach Paris fahren

is a substitute for **mit dem Hut** or **mit dem Wagen**; and this **damit** cannot
possibly refer to a person.

This **da-** can be a substitute for any noun in the dative or accusative case. Therefore, the questions

Was soll *ich* denn	mit diesem Schlüssel?
	mit dieser Uhr?
	mit diesem Buch?
	mit diesen Büchern?

all become

Was soll *ich* denn   damit?

Similarly, the questions

Was hast du denn	für diesen Wein	
	für diese Uhr	be*zahlt?*
	für dieses Haus	
	für diese Blumen	

all become

Was hast du denn   dafür   be*zahlt?*

The **da-** of the above examples is unstressed, just as the nouns replaced by **da-** are unstressed. The preposition is usually unstressed, too, but occasionally it may become the stress point of the sentence:

Ich habe nichts da*gegen*, aber ich bin auch nicht da*für*.

125 **da**-Compounds with Stressed **da-**

The preceding section dealt with the replacement by **da-** of unstressed nouns denoting things. If stressed nouns denoting things and preceded by a preposition are to be replaced, one has a choice. One can use either the stressed demonstrative pronoun *after* a preposition or a stressed **da-** *preceding* the preposition.

Thus

Was soll ich denn	mit *dem* Schlüssel?
	mit *der* Uhr?
	mit *dem* Buch?
	mit *den* Büchern?

may become either

Was soll ich denn	mit *dem?*
	mit *der?*
	mit *dem?*
	mit *denen?*

or

Was soll ich denn	*da*mit?

In assertions, **da**-compounds with a stressed **da-** usually occupy the front field and carry contrast intonation:

> Was soll ich denn mit *dem* Hut? *Da*mit gehe ich *nicht* in die Kirche.
> So, Jutta hat ge*hei*ratet? *Da*von habe ich nichts ge*wußt*.

NOTE:

1. The second example above shows that **da**-compounds are used not only to refer to things, but also to refer to entire sentences.

2. Do not replace directives like **ins Haus, zum Bahnhof, nach Berlin** with **da**-compounds. Such directives are sometimes replaced by **hin** or **dahin.**

> Mußt du zum Bahnhof? Ich bringe dich gerne *hin.*
> Ich soll nach Kairo fahren? Nein, *da*hin fahre ich nicht.
> Sie fahren nach Berlin? Da möchte ich *auch* gerne mal hinfahren.

126 Table of **da**-Compounds

If the preposition starts with a vowel, **dar-** is used instead of **da-**.

dadurch	dabei	dahinter
dafür	damit	daneben
dagegen	danach	daran
	daraus	darauf
	davon	darin
	dazu	darüber
		darunter
		davor
		dazwischen

Note that **ohne, außer, seit** and the prepositions governing the genitive (**während, wegen, trotz**) do not form **da**-compounds. **Außer** forms **außerdem** (*besides*), **seit** forms **seitdem** (*since then*, conj. *since*), and **trotz** forms **trotzdem** (*in spite of that, nevertheless*).

127 Split **da**-Compounds

In the spoken language, **da**-compounds may be split. The **da**- (stressed or unstressed) then stands in the front field, and the preposition becomes the first part of the second prong.

*D*amit	war	mein Mann *gar* nicht		zufrieden
Da	war	mein Mann *gar* nicht	mit	zufrieden

If the preposition begins with a vowel, **daraus** does not become **da . . . aus**, but **da . . . draus**; **daran**: **da . . . dran**; **darauf**: **da . . . drauf**; etc.

128 **der hier** and **der da**

In spoken German, the contrast *this one: that one* is expressed by **der hier** (or **dieser hier**): **der da** (or **dieser da**). Formerly, **dieser** and **jener** were used to express this contrast.

> **Dieses Haus hier möchte ich nicht, aber das da hätte ich gerne.**
> **Dieser Kugelschreiber hier ist mir zu schwer. Mit dem kann ich nicht schreiben. Kann ich den da mal versuchen?**
> **Die hier (diese Uhr hier) ist mir zu teuer. Darf ich die da mal sehen?**

German **jener** is a **der**-word; it is now a literary word used only with the meaning of *that* or *those* in such sentences as

> **Sie trug eines von jenen Sportkleidern, die zwar einfach geschnitten sind, aber doch viel kosten.**
> She was wearing one of those casual dresses that are cut very simply but cost a lot of money.

129 **wo**-Compounds

If the question word **was** is preceded by a preposition, it may be replaced by **wo** (**wor-** in front of vowels) compounded with and followed by the preposition in question. One may ask

EITHER	OR
An was glaubst du?	Woran glaubst du?
An was denkst du?	Woran denkst du?
Auf was wartest du?	Worauf wartest du?

Also the indefinite relative pronoun **was** may be replaced by **wo-:**

Ich möchte wissen, auf was du noch wartest.
Ich möchte wissen, worauf du noch wartest.

130 Prepositional Objects

It was pointed out in Unit 2 that prepositions can be used to form compound verbs—that is, irreducible verbal patterns which constitute separate dictionary entries.

You have to turn off the light.
Du mußt das Licht ausmachen.

We now have to introduce a number of semantic units which consist of a verb plus a whole prepositional phrase rather than of a verb and just a preposition.

We are not thinking of time phrases like **vor einem Jahr,** of directives like **ins Kino,** or of place phrases like **zu Hause.** To be sure, directives and phrases like **zu Hause** are second-prong complements; however, **zu Hause bleiben, im Bett bleiben,** and **bei Schmidts bleiben** are not separate dictionary entries; they are examples of the use of **bleiben,** which, when used without such complements, is almost as devoid of independent meaning as **sein.**

What we are thinking of is the type of prepositional phrase occurring in such sentences as

She waited for him.
She waited on him.

where *to wait for somebody* and *to wait on somebody* are clearly separate dictionary entries: A woman may be willing to wait *for* a man, but that does not necessarily mean that she is also willing to wait *on* him. The phrase *on him* forces a meaning on the verb *to wait* which is clearly different from the meaning of the same verb in *to wait for somebody:*

| *She waited on him* | means | *She served him;* |
| *She waited for him* | means | *She expected him.* |

Clearly, the relationship between *served* and *him* and between *expected* and *him* is similar to that between *waited* and *on him* and between *waited* and *for him.*

$$\frac{\text{served}}{\text{him}} = \frac{\text{waited}}{\text{on him}}$$

$$\frac{\text{expected}}{\text{him}} = \frac{\text{waited}}{\text{for him}}$$

Therefore, if we call *him* the object of *expected*, we call *on him* or *for him* the object of *waited*. We shall call phrases like *on him* and *for him*, when they occur in such semantic units as *to wait on somebody* and *to wait for somebody*, "prepositional objects."

Both English and German have literally hundreds of such fixed combinations of verbs plus prepositional objects. Unfortunately, however, the prepositions used with the German verbs hardly ever correspond to the prepositions used with the English verbs. Compare the following sentences:

Ich bin *in* sie verliebt.	I'm in love *with* her.
Ich bin *mit* ihr verlobt.	I'm engaged *to* her.
Ich warte *auf* sie.	I'm waiting *for* her.
Ich lache *über* sie.	I'm laughing *at* her.
Ich glaube *an* sie.	I believe *in* her.
Ich habe Angst *vor* ihr.	I'm afraid *of* her.
Ich bin stolz *auf* sie.	I'm proud *of* her.

Note that the prepositional objects sometimes belong to such compound verbs as **Angst haben** or **stolz sein**.

131 Frequent Prepositional Objects

Memorize the following verbs with their prepositions:

Angst haben vor (*dat.*)	to be afraid of
antworten auf (*acc.*)	to reply to (something)
bitten um (*acc.*)	to ask for (something)
danken für	to thank (someone) for
denken an (*acc.*)	to think of, to remember
nachdenken über (*acc.*)	to think, meditate about
einladen zu	to invite to
fragen nach	to ask about, inquire about
gehören zu	to be part or a member of, to belong to
glauben an (*acc.*)	to believe in
halten von	to have an opinion about; to think (highly, a great deal, not much, etc.) of (somebody or something)
halten für	to think that something (or somebody) is (something)
hoffen auf (*acc.*)	to hope for, to trust in, to look forward to
hören von	to hear from somebody or about something
lachen über (*acc.*)	to laugh about
jemanden auslachen	to laugh at (make fun of) somebody
reagieren auf (*acc.*)	to react to (something or somebody)

sein für or **sein gegen**	to be for or against
sprechen von	to talk of, to mention
sprechen über (*acc.*)	to talk in detail about a topic
verstehen von	to understand about
warten auf (*acc.*)	to wait for
wetten (**um**)	to bet (something)
wissen von	to know about

NOTE: A number of these prepositional objects use the prepositions **an, auf, über**. In all cases listed, **an, auf,** and **über** are used with the accusative, even though these phrases are not directives answering the question **wohin**. There are other cases where the dative *must* be used—for example, with **Angst haben vor**. From now on, the correct case will be indicated in the vocabulary. How important it is to use the correct case can be seen from the following example:

> **Ich warte auf** *die* **Straßenbahn**

means

> I am waiting for the streetcar,

whereas

> **Ich warte auf** *der* **Straßenbahn**

could only mean

> I am waiting on top of the streetcar.

132 The Syntax of Prepositional Objects

Preposition plus Noun or Personal Pronoun

The prepositional object constitutes the second prong. Under contrast intonation, it can be placed in the front field.

> **Ich glaube nicht an Gott.**
> **Ich glaube nicht an den Fortschritt.**
> **Ich warte auf sie.**
> **Auf Fritz brauchst du heute abend nicht zu warten.**
> **Auf mich brauchst du nach dem Theater nicht zu warten.**
> **An meinen Geburtstag hast du natürlich nicht gedacht.**

Replacement of Nouns and Pronouns by Demonstratives

The stressed demonstratives used to replace nouns or names are usually placed in the front field.

> **Erika? Von der hat kein Mensch gesprochen.**
> **Erika? Auf die brauchst du nicht zu warten.**

Meyers? Von denen haben wir lange nichts gehört.

Meyers? Auf die brauchst du nicht zu warten.

Das ist ein *Wein!* Mit *dem* werden Sie be*stimmt* zufrieden sein! Gegen *den* kann auch ein *Kenner* nichts sagen.

Prepositional **da**-Compounds

The **da**-compounds with an unstressed **da**- appear in the first box of the second prong. The compounds with a stressed **da**- appear in the front field, with contrast intonation.

*Da*ran *glau*be ich nicht.

Ich *glau*be noch nicht daran.

*Da*rauf kann ich nicht *war*ten.

Ich hoffe, ich brauche nicht darauf zu *war*ten.

Prepositional **wo**-Compounds

Like all questions, questions introduced by a **wo**-compound can be changed into dependent clauses.

Auf was wartet er denn?

Worauf wartet er denn?

Ich weiß nicht, auf was er wartet.

Ich weiß nicht, worauf er wartet.

da-Compounds with an Anticipatory Function

The prepositional object may be replaced by a dependent clause or an infinitive phrase. If this is the case, a **da**-compound anticipating or repeating this dependent clause frequently appears in the main clause:

Ich habe gar nicht daran gedacht, daß   It had slipped my mind that you too live in
   du ja auch in Köln wohnst.   Cologne.

or

Daran, daß du ja auch in Köln wohnst,
   habe ich gar nicht gedacht.

or

Daran habe ich gar nicht gedacht, daß
   du ja auch in Köln wohnst.

Ich möchte Ihnen noch einmal dafür   I would like to thank you once more (for
   danken, daß Sie gekommen sind.   the fact that you came) for your coming.

Ich hoffe immer noch darauf, sie wie-   I still hope to see her again.
   derzusehen.

These anticipatory **da**-compounds are especially frequent if the ideas contained in the dependent clause or in the infinitive phrase have, in some form, existed before and are not news either for the speaker or for the listener.

133 Feminine Nouns Ending in **-in**

Masculine nouns denoting persons (and a few animals), especially agent nouns in **-er**, form corresponding feminines ending in **-in** (plural **-innen**).

der Freund	die Freundin
der Lehrer	die Lehrerin
der Student	die Studentin
der Tänzer	die Tänzerin
der Koch	die Köchin
der Arbeiter	die Arbeiterin
der Sänger	die Sängerin

NOTE: These **-in** derivatives are apt to denote professional status. If my wife is not a professional singer, I'll say **Meine Frau singt gut** rather than **Meine Frau ist eine gute Sängerin**.

EXERCISES

A. Each of the following incomplete sentences contains a blank for a relative pronoun. Fill in the correct forms.

1. das Haus, aus _____ er kam
2. die Betten, zwischen _____ der Tisch stand
3. der Blick, mit _____ er mich ansah
4. die vielen Aufnahmen, _____ ich von ihm gemacht habe
5. die Leute, _____ zu uns kamen
6. der Herr, nach _____ Sie fragen
7. der Materialismus, gegen _____ wir kämpfen
8. das Haus, in _____ wir wohnen
9. das Theater, vor _____ ich sie treffen wollte
10. die Familie, bei _____ du wohnst
11. das Haus, vor _____ wir unseren Wagen stellten
12. seine Frau, _____ Vater in Berlin Architekt war
13. meine Bücher, ohne _____ ich nicht leben kann
14. der Zug, mit _____ du fahren willst
15. die Blicke, _____ sie mir zuwarf
16. die Ecke, an _____ er stand

SEE LAB
EXERCISE
8.1

(p. 630)

17. die Stadt, von ＿＿＿＿＿＿ wir sprachen
18. das Fenster, aus ＿＿＿＿＿＿ sie heraussah
19. ihr Mann, ＿＿＿＿＿＿ Vater in Berlin Architekt war
20. die zwei Fußabdrücke, ＿＿＿＿＿＿ wir neben dem Haus fanden
21. die Gefühle, mit ＿＿＿＿＿＿ ich vor ihr stand
22. die Menschen, von ＿＿＿＿＿＿ wir sprachen
23. viele Gedanken, ＿＿＿＿＿＿ man schon bei Platon findet
24. die Geschichte, ＿＿＿＿＿＿ er nun erzählte
25. die Eltern, ＿＿＿＿＿＿ Kinder aufs Gymnasium gehen
26. mein Freund, durch ＿＿＿＿＿＿ ich sie kennengelernt habe
27. seine Frau, für ＿＿＿＿＿＿ er den Mercedes gekauft hat
28. der Garten, in ＿＿＿＿＿＿ wir saßen
29. Menschen, ＿＿＿＿＿＿ man gerne hilft
30. ein Mädchen, ＿＿＿＿＿＿ Vater sie nicht versteht
31. ein Mädchen, ＿＿＿＿＿＿ Mutter sie nicht versteht
32. eine Frau, ＿＿＿＿＿＿ jeder gerne hilft
33. Gott, ohne ＿＿＿＿＿＿ Wissen nichts geschieht
34. ein Buch, mit ＿＿＿＿＿＿ Sie zufrieden sein werden
35. der Tisch, ＿＿＿＿＿＿ neben der Tür stand
36. das Haus, von ＿＿＿＿＿＿ ich gerade sprach
37. Inge, ＿＿＿＿＿＿ damals erst achtzehn war
38. das Land, durch ＿＿＿＿＿＿ wir fuhren
39. die Mädchen, ＿＿＿＿＿＿ ich kenne
40. das Kind, ＿＿＿＿＿＿ Vater bei meinem Mann im Büro arbeitete
41. Werner, ＿＿＿＿＿＿ damals schon dreißig war
42. der Roman, von ＿＿＿＿＿＿ du mir erzählt hast
43. die Stadt, in ＿＿＿＿＿＿ wir wohnen
44. die Sachen, ＿＿＿＿＿＿ mir gehören
45. Schmidts, ohne ＿＿＿＿＿＿ Hilfe ich nie gesund geworden wäre
46. ein Tag, ＿＿＿＿＿＿ ich nie vergessen kann
47. Kinder, ＿＿＿＿＿＿ Väter sie nicht verstehen
48. die Stadt, in ＿＿＿＿＿＿ wir fuhren
49. die Stadt, durch ＿＿＿＿＿＿ wir gingen
50. ein Mensch, ＿＿＿＿＿＿ jeder gerne hilft

B. Join the following pairs of sentences by changing one of them into a relative clause.

SEE LAB
EXERCISES
8.2–8.12

(p. 630)

1. Werners Vater sprach gut Englisch. Er hatte lange in Amerika gelebt.
2. Werners Vater sprach gut Englisch. Seine Frau kam aus London.
3. Ich habe dich gestern abend im Theater mit einem jungen Mann gesehen. Wer war denn der junge Mann?
4. In Mainz besuchte ich meinen Freund Emil. Ich bin mit ihm aufs Gymnasium gegangen.
5. Ich fuhr nach Hamburg, um Hermann wiederzusehen. Während des Krieges war ich mit Hermann in Afrika.

6. Wer ist denn eigentlich dieser Schmidt? Du redest schon seit Tagen von ihm.
7. Der Brief lag vor ihr auf dem Tisch. Ihr Mann hatte ihn aus Kairo geschickt.
8. Ich kann diese Vase doch nicht wegwerfen. Tante Amalie hat sie mir geschickt.

C. By starting with **Er fragte, . . .** , change the following questions to dependent clauses. Change pronouns as appropriate.

1. Hat Else schon geheiratet?
2. Wann soll ich ihn abholen?
3. Nimmt er wirklich an, daß Erich das Geld gestohlen hat?
4. Wann kann ich mir die neuen Wintermäntel ansehen?
5. Wann ist er denn zum Flughafen gefahren?

D. Restate the following sentences by starting with **Er sah aus, als ob . . .** and **Er sah aus, als. . . .**

1. Er hat die Gelbsucht.
2. Er hat nicht gut geschlafen.
3. Er hat viel erlebt.
4. Er ist unglücklich.
5. Er war krank.
6. Er kann nicht bis fünf zählen.
7. Er hat seit Tagen nichts gegessen.
8. Er war ungefähr fünfzig.
9. Er hat den Verstand verloren.
10. Er ist seit Tagen nicht ins Bett gekommen.

E. Using the comparative, complete the following sentences.

> **Meyer ist sehr intelligent, aber seine Frau ist noch intelligenter als er.**

1. Ich habe im Kasino viel Geld verloren, aber meine Frau hat noch _____.
2. Ich weiß, du stehst früh auf, aber ich muß noch viel _____.
3. Natürlich ist Inge schön, aber meine Freundin ist doch noch _____.
4. In Rom ist es im Sommer sehr heiß, aber in Casablanca ist es noch _____.
5. Hier ist es dir zu laut? Im Regina-Palast war es doch noch viel _____.
6. Ich weiß, von hier nach Hamburg ist es weit, über 220 km,* aber ich glaube, von hier nach München ist es noch viel _____.

---

* **Kilometer,** abbreviated **km,** not capitalized and without a period.

F. Restate the following sentences in the past tense. Note that with the change from present tense to past tense, **wenn** must be in some cases changed to **als**.

1. Wir können erst ins Theater gehen, wenn Else kommt.
2. Jedesmal, wenn Tante Amalie hier ist, muß ich mich zwingen, nett zu ihr zu sein.
3. Wenn mein Zug in München ankommt, bist du schon in Chicago.
4. Wenn meine Wohnung groß genug wäre, könnte ich auch fünfundzwanzig Leute einladen.
5. Wenn Hans geht, gehe ich auch.
6. Wenn ich daran denke,—und ich denke oft daran—, daß unser Hans diese Magda heiraten will, werde ich ganz unruhig.
7. Wenn es nicht so spät wäre, bliebe ich gerne noch eine Stunde hier.
8. Jedesmal, wenn ich ihn sehe, hat er eine neue Freundin.
9. Wenn Franz versuchen würde, mit *dem* Wagen nach Italien zu fahren, käme er sicher nicht weit.

G. In the following sentences, supply **als, als ob, ob, wann,** or **wenn.**

1. Hermann schrieb, es sähe so aus, _____ hätte Erich das Geld gestohlen.
2. Ich weiß, jemand hat hinter mir gestanden, _____ ich den Brief schrieb.
3. Warum hast du denn nichts gesagt, _____ du wußtest, daß Anton hier in Berlin war?
4. _____ ich gewußt hätte, daß sie nicht schwimmen konnte, wäre ich natürlich nicht mit ihr fischen gegangen.
5. Können Sie mir sagen, _____ der Zug aus Köln ankommt?
6. Können Sie mir sagen, _____ der Zug aus Köln schon angekommen ist?
7. Ich stand gerade vor Erichs Zimmer, _____ er mit Hermann telefonierte.
8. Ich wußte nicht, _____ Erich mich erkannt hatte; jedenfalls tat er, _____ hätte er mich nicht gesehen.
9. Ich kann Ihnen leider nicht sagen, _____ Ingelheims Romane auch in England erschienen sind.
10. Ich bin so müde. _____ ich nur endlich einmal lange schlafen könnte!
11. Ich bin nicht sicher, _____ ich das Geschenk annehmen soll oder nicht.
12. Was? Tante Amalie will uns schon wieder besuchen? _____ kommt sie denn?
13. Aber Liebling, du tust ja, _____ *du* immer mit ihr ins Museum gehen müßtest.
14. Wir waren gerade nach Hause gekommen, _____ Gerda anrief.
15. Du weißt doch, ich komme erst um 7 Uhr nach Hause. _____ soll ich denn essen, _____ das Theater schon um 7 Uhr 30 anfängt?

H. Read the following sentences and supply either **nicht** or **nichts,** or the correct form of **kein.**

SEE LAB
EXERCISES
8.13–8.15

(p. 631)

1. Nein, danke, ich möchte heute gar _____ Kaffee.
2. Ich habe seit gestern morgen gar _____ gegessen.
3. Ich bin schon seit vier Wochen in München und habe von der Stadt gar _____ gesehen.

4. Daß du in Italien warst, habe ich gar _____ gewußt.
5. Hast du denn mit deiner neuen Kamera noch gar _____ Aufnahmen gemacht?
6. Leider haben wir gar _____ Moselwein im Haus.
7. So viele Autostunden sind es doch gar _____ von Köln bis München.
8. Es ist doch dumm, daß er uns gar _____ geschrieben hat, wann er ankommt.
9. Aber der Hund hat doch gar _____ gebellt.
10. Jetzt habe ich dir so viel von Erika erzählt. Dumm, daß ich gar _____ Bild von ihr habe.

I. Fill in each blank by using a form of the demonstrative **der, die, das.**

1. Sollen Inge und Gerda auch kommen?—Nein, _____ brauchst du nicht einzuladen; _____ können zu Hause bleiben; mit _____ will ich nichts mehr zu tun haben.
2. Kennen Sie _____ Friedrich Bertram?—Aber natürlich; mit _____ war ich doch in Mainz auf der Schule.
3. Diese Schuhe hier möchten Sie also doch nicht, gnädige Frau?—Nein, ich nehme lieber _____ da.
4. Nein, Maria; mit _____ Hut kannst du dich in Paris nicht sehen lassen. _____ läßt du beser zu Hause.—Aber Paul, _____ kommt doch aus Paris. _____ hast du mir doch letztes Jahr aus Paris mitgebracht.
5. Dieser Kaffee ist aber gut. Wo hast du _____ denn gekauft?—_____ hat mein Mann gekauft.—Dein Mann? Versteht _____ was von Kaffee?
6. Wie geht's denn deiner Freundin Gertrud?— _____ geht's gut. _____ hat einen Architekten geheiratet.
7. Kennen Sie Hermann Schneider und seine Frau?—Natürlich kenne ich _____; mit _____ waren wir doch letztes Jahr in Sizilien.
8. Ich höre, _____ Barbara hat geheiratet.—Ja, und weißt du, wen sie geheiratet hat? _____ Enders.—Meinst du _____, dem das Hotel Krone gehört? Ich dachte, _____ wäre schon verheiratet.

J. In the following sentences, substitute a **da-**compound for the italicized prepositional phrases.

1. Der Garten *hinter dem Haus* braucht viel Wasser.
2. *Mit dem Hut* kannst du dich nicht sehen lassen.
3. Und *vor dem Wohnzimmer* ist eine grosse Terrasse.
4. Er hat viel Geld *für das Haus* bezahlt.
5. Aber den Namen *unter dem Bild* kann ich nicht lesen.
6. Was hast du denn *gegen meine Reise nach Italien?*
7. Kurz *vor dem Abflug nach Deutschland* bekam ich einen Brief von meiner Frau.
8. Und ich hatte *beim Schreiben* das Gefühl, daß jemand hinter mir stand.
9. Ich habe nichts *von seiner Reise* gewußt.

SEE LAB
EXERCISES
8.16–8.17

(p. 631)

K. In the following sentences, substitute for the prepositional phrase in the front field (a) a stressed **da**-compound, and (b) the preposition plus demonstrative article.

> **Für *den* Wein hast du zuviel bezahlt.**
> (a) ***Dafür* hast du zuviel bezahlt.**
> (b) **Für *den* hast du zuviel bezahlt.**

1. Mit *dem* Wagen fahre ich nicht.
2. Mit *die*sem Hut kann ich nichts anfangen.
3. In *die*sem Bett kann ich nicht schlafen.
4. Für *den* Wagen bezahle ich keine zweitausend Mark.
5. Mit *mei*ner Leica kann ich auch bei Nacht Aufnahmen machen.
6. Bei *sei*nen Romanen kann ich immer gut einschlafen.
7. Mit *die*sem Wein hier ist Ihr Mann bestimmt zufrieden.
8. Auf *die*sen Film habe ich schon lange gewartet.
9. Auf *den* Brief hat er noch nicht geantwortet.
10. Und für *die*se Blumen hast du acht Mark ausgegeben?

L. Write down the questions to which the following sentences would be the answers. Start each question with (a) a **wo**-compound and (b) the preposition plus demonstrative article.

> **Meine Tochter hat Angst vor der Schule.**
> (a) **Wovor hat sie denn Angst?**
> (b) **Vor was hat sie denn Angst?**

SEE LAB
EXERCISES
8.18

(p. 631)

1. Wir warten auf schönes Wetter.
2. Ich brauche das Geld für einen neuen Wagen.
3. Wir haben um eine Flasche Wein gewettet.
4. Meyer glaubt an den Fortschritt.
5. Wir haben gerade von dem neuen Hitchcock-Film gesprochen.
6. Ich denke gerade daran, daß Vater morgen Geburtstag hat.
7. Sie hofft immer noch darauf, daß Gustav eines Tages wiederkommt.
8. Professor Meyer hat schon wieder über Kafka gesprochen.
9. Ich habe ihn an seiner Stimme erkannt.
10. Sie lacht über nichts.

M. Read the following sentences aloud and supply the missing prepositions.

SEE LAB
EXERCISE
8.19

(p. 631)

1. Ich glaube _____ Gott.
2. Wir haben _____ unserer Reise gesprochen.
3. Denkst du auch noch _____ mich?
4. Hast du schon _____ den Brief geantwortet?

5. Hast du auch nicht vergessen, ihn _____ seiner Frau zu fragen?
6. Ich danke Ihnen _____ Ihre Hilfe.
7. Meyer hat mich _____ einem Glas Wein eingeladen.
8. Dürfte ich Sie _____ eine Zigarette bitten?
9. Ich wette nie _____ Geld.
10. _____ wen warten Sie denn?
11. Was, Professor Meyer will schon wieder _____ Kafka sprechen?
12. Ich habe lange _____ deinen Brief nachgedacht.
13. Warum lacht ihr denn immer _____ mich?
14. _____ ein Wiedersehen hoffe ich schon lange nicht mehr.
15. Ich halte ihn nicht _____ sehr intelligent.
16. Ich halte nicht viel _____ ihr.
17. Ich denke noch oft _____ meinen Vater.
18. Ich habe gestern auf dem Bahnhof lange _____ dich gewartet.
19. Kannst du nicht deine Freundin Emma _____ Hilfe bitten?
20. Was halten Sie _____ Picasso?

N. Read the following sentences aloud and supply the missing articles or possessives.

1. Wir warten auf _____ Zug aus Köln.
2. Wir warten auf _____ Bahnhof.
3. Meyer glaubt nicht an _____ Fortschritt.
4. Ingelheim hat viel über _____ Krieg geschrieben.
5. Erich stand an _____ Ecke und wartete auf _____ Freundin.
6. Ich muß in _____ Universität über _____ Krieg zwischen Rom und Karthago sprechen.
7. Ich halte nicht viel von _____ Film.
8. Wir hoffen sehr auf _____ Mitarbeit Ihres Mannes, Frau Becker.
9. Frau Direktor, als Sie an die Tür kamen, habe ich Sie für _____ Tochter gehalten.
10. Sie hat den ganzen Abend nicht von _____ Mann gesprochen.

O. Using the verbs in parentheses, form main clauses containing a **da**-compound anticipating the dependent clause.

(schon lange nachdenken), wo ich dieses Jahr hinfahren soll.
Ich denke schon lange darüber nach, wo ich dieses Jahr hinfahren soll.

1. (sehr hoffen), daß er morgen kommen kann.
2. (gerade sprechen), daß er im Sommer nach Italien fahren will.
3. (warten), daß mein Mann endlich nach Hause kommt.
4. (nicht viel halten), daß meine Tochter Psychologie studieren will.
5. (wohl bitten dürfen), daß Sie um acht Uhr im Büro sind.
6. (oft denken), wie wir als Kinder zusammen gespielt haben.

SEE LAB
EXERCISES
8.20–8.22

(p. 631)

7. (noch nie fragen), ob ich schon einmal verheiratet war.
8. (immer noch nicht glauben können), daß er jetzt verheiratet ist.
9. (noch einmal danken), daß er meinem Sohn geholfen hat.
10. (sehr glücklich sein), daß Professor Erdmann mein Lehrer ist.

P. Expand the prepositional objects in the following sentences into dependent clauses.

> **Ich warte auf einen Brief von ihr.**
> **Ich warte darauf, daß sie mir schreibt.**

1. Ich möchte Ihnen noch einmal für Ihre Hilfe danken.
2. An seinen Geburtstag gestern habe ich gar nicht gedacht.
3. Ich glaube an Gottes Liebe zu den Menschen.
4. Wir sind sehr unglücklich über die Heirat unserer Tochter.
5. Lacht sie immer noch über seinen Akzent?
6. Die Leute hier warten alle auf Regen.
7. Meine Frau spricht immer von einer Italienreise im nächsten Sommer.
8. Ich halte nichts von deinem Plan, eine Doktorarbeit über deutsche Syntax schreiben zu wollen.

Q. Expand the prepositional objects in the following sentences into infinitive phrases.

> **Erika denkt gar nicht an eine Italienreise.**
> **Erika denkt gar nicht daran, nach Italien zu fahren.**

1. Darf ich Sie zu einem Glas Wein einladen, Herr Müller?
2. Ich habe meinen Freund um Ingelheims Romane gebeten.
3. Hoffst du immer noch auf ein Wiedersehen mit ihr?
4. Ich hoffe auf ein Wiedersehen mit Ihnen.
5. Ich habe wochenlang auf einen Brief von ihr gewartet.

R. Read the following sentences starting with each of the italicized words and rearrange the syntax accordingly.

1. Ich möchte Ihnen noch einmal *dafür* danken, daß Sie meiner Frau so schön geholfen haben.
2. Ich glaube nicht *daran, daß* er während des Krieges Brieftauben gefüttert hat.
3. Daran, *daß* wir heute vor zehn Jahren geheiratet haben, hast *du natürlich* nicht gedacht.
4. Natürlich bin *ich* nicht *glücklich darüber, daß* Heidi so jung heiraten will.
5. Mir hat *er gestern* nichts *davon* gesagt, daß er bald heiraten will.

S. Express in German:

(a) 1. I am waiting for my son.
    2. I am waiting for him.
    3. I am not waiting for her, I am waiting for her mother.
    4. I am not waiting for you.
    5. I am waiting for her to come.
    6. I am waiting for her father to come home.

(b) 1. Why don't you invite him?
    2. Why haven't you invited him?
    3. I'd like to invite him.
    4. May I invite you to dinner?
    5. May I invite you to go to the movies with us?
    6. I have invited him to go to the movies with us.
    7. It would be nice if we invited him to go to the movies with us.

(c) 1. Thank you, Mr. Meyer.
    2. Did you thank Mr. Meyer?
    3. Did you thank him for the book?
    4. I should like to thank you, Mr. Meyer.
    5. I should like to thank you again for having done so much for us.

T. Express in German:

1. Until yesterday I had heard nothing from him.
2. Not until yesterday did he ask me whether I wanted to marry him.
3. The man with whom Mrs. Ingelheim is talking is called Behrens.
4. Ingelheim's daughter sat at the breakfast table and drank her coffee as if it were Rhine wine.
5. Not every human being can say at the end of his life: I have never done anything which I should not have done.
6. When they had eaten, they were already over the Atlantic.
7. If the walls in this room could talk, we would never have to read a novel again.
8. Hans wanted to know whether I could pick him up at the station.
9. When did you pick him up?
10. Can you tell me when you picked him up? (indicative)
11. Every time she picked me up at the airport she had to wait for a long time.
12. When I arrived, she was not there yet.
13. He acted as if I were his secretary and not his wife.
14. He acted as if the house belonged to him.
15. He looked as if he hadn't slept well.
16. I can't give you more than I have given him.
17. You know him better than her, don't you?

SEE LAB EXERCISE 8.23

(p. 631)

18. That was more than I had expected.
19. When I wrote you, I suddenly felt that somebody was standing behind me.
20. If it hadn't been so hot in Cairo, we would not have flown back to Germany.
21. If we had not stopped in front of Ali's house, Erich would have died.
22. If I hadn't seen the footprints, I wouldn't have been afraid.
23. That was a moment I shall not forget.
24. The man I saw in front of the house was Erich.
25. Behind the stone was a hole in which Ali had five goldpieces.
26. Not one of my friends with whom I was in Africa has come back.
27. Is he also one of those men who from time to time disappear without a trace?
28. Writers who haven't been in the war shouldn't write about the war.
29. Hermann, in whose house I was supposed to live, was the director of a bank in Hamburg.
30. But I don't need to count the tiles at all; I know there are fifty.
31. He said that he had seen nothing at all.
32. If I'm not there at three o'clock, you'll simply have to wait for me.
33. She looked as if she hadn't slept well.
34. When I knocked at the door, Erich didn't answer.
35. He showed us the picture of a girl who was at least eighteen.
36. And this is a picture of our house.—And where is your swimming pool?— That's behind it.
37. Every time I think of it I am afraid again.
38. In front of the garage stood a Mercedes; next to it stood a Volkswagen.
39. Of that I would never have thought.
40. We were standing in front of the door, and we knew that somebody stood behind it.
41. May I invite you to a cup of tea?
42. Then we were all silent and hoped that the phone would ring.
43. Can you think of something with which I could make her happy?
44. Where would you like to go tonight, darling?—I'd like to go somewhere where nobody knows us.
45. I'm so tired tonight; I don't want to read.
46. Although I had never met him, I knew who he was.
47. Was it really a woman who screamed?
48. My wife became very restless, because she thought she had forgotten the keys.
49. That's correct. At approximately two o'clock he left (went away). He said he wanted to go to the city in order to buy something for his wife.
50. When I went to bed, he wasn't home yet; he didn't come home until four o'clock.
51. This time we flew to New York via London.
52. He had not slept well and wanted to go to bed early.

die **Adresse, –n** address
   adressieren to address
alt old
die **Antwort, –en** answer,
   reply
der **Arm, –e** arm
aufgeben to give up; mail (a
   letter)
auslachen to laugh at, make
   fun of
die **Badewanne, –n** bathtub
bauen to build
beide both
bellen to bark
bezahlen to pay
das **Ding, –e** thing
dreißig thirty
drücken to push, press
dumm stupid, dumb
eben just
einschlafen to fall asleep
die **Eltern** parents
erfahren to find out, learn
erklären to explain
das **Erlebnis, –se** experience,
   adventure
erschrecken to be frightened
erstaunt astonished
etwa about; by any chance
fallen to fall, drop
die **Familie, –n** family
die **Flasche, –n** bottle
der **Fortschritt, –e** progress,
   advance, improvement
führen to lead, guide
ganz gut pretty good, not bad
der **Gast, ─e** guest
der **General', ─e** general
der **Glaube** (*no pl.*) belief,
   faith
   (*gen.:* **des Glaubens;** *dat.:*
   dem Glauben; *acc.:* **den
   Glauben**)
groß big, great, tall
das **Gymnasium, die Gymna-
   sien** (German secondary
   school, grades 5–13)
halten für to consider

halten von to have an opinion
   about; to think (highly,
   a great deal, not much,
   etc.) of
die **Hand, ─e** hand
die **Hilfe** help
der **Hörer, –** (telephone receiver; listener
irgendetwas something, anything
der **Junge, –n** boy
der **Juni** June
kämpfen to fight
   der **Kampf, ─e** fight, battle
das **Klavier, –e** piano
klingeln to ring (said of a
   bell)
die **Kugel, –n** ball, globe;
   bullet
   der **Kugelschreiber, –**
   ball-point pen
längst, schon längst for a long
   time, a long time ago
leise soft, without noise
der **Leutnant, –e** lieutenant
der **Liebling, –e** darling, favorite
meinen to mean, to have an
   opinion; to say
mitmachen to go along, to
   cooperate
der **Mittag, –e** noon
   der **Nachmittag, –e** afternoon
müde tired
na so was! (expression of
   astonishment) You don't
   mean it! What do you
   think of that!
nämlich namely; that is to
   say; you know
nee (*colloquial*) = **nein** no
nirgends nowhere
oben up (above); upstairs;
   on top
obwohl although
die **O'per, –n** opera; opera
   house

der **Paß, die Pässe** passport;
   pass
der **Plan, ─e** plan
reagieren auf to react to
reich rich
ruhig quiet, calm; (*sentence
   adverb*) it won't bother
   me, I'll stay calm about it
russisch Russian
sauer sour
schlagen to beat, hit
der **Schluß** end; conclusion
der **Schlüssel, –** key
der **Schrei, –e** scream
schweigen to be silent, say
   nothing
schwer heavy; hard (difficult)
die **Schwester, –n** sister
die **Seite, –n** page; side
singen to sing
   der **Sänger** singer
so etwas something like this
soviel (*conjunction*) as far as
spazierengehen to go for a
   walk
spielen to play
stark strong
statt (*with genitive*) instead
   of
   statt zu (kaufen) instead
   of (buying)
stehenbleiben to stop (walking or moving)
steigen to climb
der **Stolz** (*no pl.*) pride
   stolz proud
die **Straßenbahn, –en** streetcar
die **Tasche, –n** pocket; handbag; briefcase
tausend thousand, a thousand
teuer expensive
trotzdem in spite of that;
   nevertheless
die **Vase, –n** vase (*v* pronounced similar to
   English *v*)
verliebt in love

verlobt engaged
von (jetzt) an from (now) on
von (mir) aus as far as I am
    concerned
während (*conjunction*) while

warm warm
der Weg, –e way; path
wetten (um) to bet
der Wirt, –e innkeeper, land-
    lord

das Wort, ⸚er (or –e) word
wütend mad, angry
zufrieden satisfied, content
zu'hören (*with dative*) to
    listen to

IRREGULAR VERBS

aufgeben to give up; mail
    gab auf, hat aufgegeben,
    er gibt auf
einschlafen to fall asleep
    schlief ein, ist einge-
    schlafen, er schläft ein
erfahren to find out, learn
    erfuhr, hat erfahren, er
    erfährt
erschrecken to be frightened
    erschrak, ist erschrocken, er
    erschrickt

fallen to fall
    fiel, ist gefallen, er fällt
schlagen to beat, hit
    schlug, hat geschlagen, er
    schlägt
schweigen to be silent, say
    nothing
    schwieg, hat geschwiegen,
    er schweigt
singen to sing
    sang, hat gesungen, er singt

spazierengehen to go for a
    walk
    ging spazieren, ist spazie-
    rengegangen, er geht
    spazieren
stehenbleiben to stop (walk-
    ing or moving)
    blieb stehen, ist stehenge-
    blieben, er bleibt stehen
steigen to climb
    stieg, ist gestiegen, er steigt

REVIEW

The verbs in the following examples all have short, one-word complements which are prefixed to the verb if verb and complement stand next
to one another. Review these patterns thoroughly; then use the list at the
end of this section to form sentences of your own, alternating between
the various positions.

Present and Past

Wann fängt das Theater an?
Den Schmidt lade ich nicht ein.
Ich schickte dir den Brief nach.
Ich nehme an, daß er Englisch spricht.
Plötzlich sprang Hermann auf und lief zum Telephon.
Die Zeit steht nie still.
Heidemarie fuhr sofort zurück.
Ihre Mutter holte sie am Bahnhof ab.

Perfect

Wann ist Tante Amalie denn angekommen?
Warum hast du ihn denn nicht eingeladen?
Ich habe sie noch nicht kennengelernt.
Zu spät! Er ist schon weggegangen.
Sie ist leider schon zurückgefahren.
Karl ist schon gestern abend weggefahren.
Hat es schon angefangen zu regnen?

Verb-Last Position

Weißt du, wann das Theater anfängt?
Ich möchte nicht, daß du den Meyer einlädst.
Ich kann Ihnen leider nicht sagen, wann der Zug nach Köln abfährt.
Was hat denn deine Mutter gesagt, als du sie von München aus anriefst?
Das war aber nett von dir, daß du mich abgeholt hast.
Schön, daß Erika auch mitgekommen ist.
Ich danke Ihnen, daß Sie mir so lange zugehört haben.

Ich möchte wissen, warum meine Uhr schon wieder stehengeblieben ist.
Gut, daß man mir den Brief aus Berlin nachgeschickt hat.

Infinitives without **zu**

Weißt du, ob Fritz mitgehen will?
Wann soll denn das Theater anfangen?
Ich weiß auch nicht, warum ich gestern abend nicht einschlafen konnte.
Heute abend kann ich dich leider nicht abholen.
Darf ich deine Freundin einmal kennenlernen?

Infinitives with **zu**

Sie saß vor ihm und schien ihm zuzuhören.
Heute brauche ich gottseidank nicht mitzugehen.
Else ist zum Bahnhof gegangen, um ihren Vater abzuholen.
Es ist schwer, ihm jeden Tag zwei Stunden zuzuhören.
Es ist schwer, ihm jeden Tag zwei Stunden zuhören zu müssen.
Ich habe Erika gebeten, morgen mitzugehen.
Ich habe Erika gebeten, morgen mit ins Theater zu gehen.

Now form sentences of your own with the following verbs:

abfahren	aufmachen	kennenlernen
abholen	aufspringen	nachdenken (über)
anfangen	aufstehen	nachschicken
angehen	ausgehen	spazierengehen
anklopfen	ausmachen	stehenbleiben
ankommen	aussehen	stillstehen
anmachen	durchmachen	wegfahren
annehmen	einladen	zuhören
anrufen	einschlafen	zurückfahren
ansehen	gefangennehmen	zurückkommen

UNIT 9: Nicht in the Inner Field—nicht A, sondern B—
Present and Past Infinitives—Subjective and Objective
Use of Modals—The Reflexive Pronoun sich—
Contrary-to-Fact Conditions without wenn

PATTERNS

[1] nicht in the Inner Field

Study these sentences carefully; then follow the instructions at the end of this
section.

SEE
ANALYSIS
134

(pp. 370-372)

Aber du kannst doch nicht den ganzen Tag schlafen!
But you can't sleep all day!

Warum denn nicht? Ich habe die ganze Nacht nicht geschlafen.
Why not? I didn't sleep all night.

Ich möchte nicht mit Rosemarie ins Theater gehen.
I don't want to go to the theater *with Rosemarie*.

Ich möchte mit Rosemarie nicht ins Theater gehen.
I don't want to go *to the theater* with Rosemarie.

Meyer war krank und hat lange nicht arbeiten können.
Meyer was sick, and for a long time he couldn't work.

Heute haben wir nicht lange arbeiten können.
Today we couldn't work very long.

Du brauchst nicht auf dem Sofa zu schlafen. Wir haben ein Bett für dich.
You don't have to sleep on the sofa. We have a bed for you.

Ich kann in diesem Bett einfach nicht schlafen. Es ist zu kurz.
I simply can't sleep in this bed. It is too short.

(Facing) **München. Leopoldstraße**

345

Geschlafen habe ich. Aber ich habe nicht gut geschlafen.
>   I slept. But I didn't sleep well.

Ich fahre oft nach Hamburg. Aber ich fahre nicht gerne nach Hamburg.
>   I often go to Hamburg. But I don't like to go to Hamburg.

Man konnte ihn verstehen. Aber man konnte ihn nicht gut verstehen.
>   One could understand him. But one couldn't understand him well.

Ingelheim war in Kairo. Aber! War er allein in Kairo, oder war er nicht allein in Kairo?
>   Ingelheim was in Cairo. But—was he alone in Cairo, or was he not alone in Cairo?

Ja, wir sind geflogen. Aber wir sind nicht mit der Lufthansa geflogen.
>   Yes, we flew. But we didn't fly Lufthansa.

Gut, daß du hier bist. Wir haben dich so lange nicht gesehen.—Ich bin auch froh, daß ich hier bin. Aber leider kann ich nicht lange bleiben.
>   Good that you are here. We haven't seen you for so long.—I am glad, too, to be here. But, unfortunately, I can't stay long.

Ich höre, ihr seid erst um halb zwei nach Hause gekommen.—Nein, wir sind nicht erst um halb zwei nach Hause gekommen. Um halb zwei lagen wir schon im Bett.
>   I hear you didn't get home until half-past one.—No, we didn't come home at (as late as) half-past one. At half-past one we were already in bed.

Form sentences parallel to the model

> **Man konnte ihn verstehen, aber man konnte ihn nicht gut verstehen.**

Note that the second clause contains a **nicht** which does not negate the verb.

[2] nicht A, sondern B

Study these sentences; then follow the instructions below.

SEE
ANALYSIS
134
(pp. 370-372)

Ich wartete nicht auf Inge. Ich wartete auf Erika.
Ich wartete damals nicht auf Inge, sondern auf Erika.
Ich habe nicht auf Inge, sondern auf Erika gewartet.
Ich habe nicht auf Inge gewartet, sondern auf Erika.
Nicht auf Inge, sondern auf Erika habe ich gewartet.
Du weißt doch, daß ich nicht auf Inge, sondern auf Erika gewartet habe.
Du weißt doch, daß ich nicht auf Inge gewartet habe, sondern auf Erika.

Nicht *er,* sondern sein *Bru*der ist gestern nach Berlin gefahren.
Nicht *er* ist gestern nach Berlin gefahren, sondern sein *Bru*der.

Er ist nicht *ges*tern, sondern erst *heu*te nach Berlin gefahren.
Er ist nicht *ges*tern nach Berlin gefahren, sondern erst *heu*te.

Wir haben uns keinen Volkswagen, sondern einen Mercedes gekauft.
Wir haben uns kein *Haus* gekauft, sondern ein *Häus*chen.

Er ist gestern nicht nach Ber*lin,* sondern nach *Ham*burg gefahren.
Er ist gestern nicht nach Ber*lin* gefahren, sondern nach *Ham*burg.

Wir sind gestern nicht nach Hamburg ge*flo*gen, sondern ge*fah*ren.

Ich habe nicht *sie,* sondern sie hat *mich* geheiratet.
Ich habe nicht *sie* geheiratet, sondern sie hat *mich* geheiratet.

Ich liebe Erika nicht.
Ich liebe nicht Erika, sondern ihre Freundin.

Inge ist nicht nur schön, sondern auch intelligent.
Weißt du, daß Inge nicht nur schön, sondern auch intelligent ist?
Weißt du, daß Inge nicht nur schön ist, sondern auch intelligent?

Be prepared to produce orally sentences of your own. They should contain the **nicht A** part in the front field, in the inner field, or in the second prong. In each case, the **sondern B** part can either follow the **nicht A** part immediately or be placed in the end field.

[3] Numbers from 1 to 100

zwanzig, einundzwanzig, zweiundzwanzig, dreiundzwanzig, vierundzwanzig, fünfundzwanzig, sechsundzwanzig, siebenundzwanzig, achtundzwanzig, neunundzwanzig, dreißig, einunddreißig, zweiunddreißig, vierzig, dreiundvierzig, vierundvierzig, fünfundvierzig, fünfzig, fünfundfünfzig, sechsundfünfzig, sechzig, sechsundsechzig, siebenundsechzig, siebzig, siebenundsiebzig, achtundsiebzig, achtzig, achtundachtzig, neunundachtzig, neunzig, hundert (einhundert)

ein mal zwei ist zwei
zwei mal zwei ist vier
drei mal zwei ist sechs
vier mal zwei ist acht
fünf mal zwei ist zehn
sechs mal zwei ist zwölf

SEE ANALYSIS 135 (p. 372)

sieben mal zwei ist vierzehn
acht mal zwei ist sechzehn
neun mal zwei ist achtzehn
zehn mal zwei ist zwanzig

hundert (geteilt) durch zehn ist zehn
neunzig (geteilt) durch zehn ist neun
achtzig (geteilt) durch zehn ist acht
siebzig (geteilt) durch zehn ist sieben
sechzig (geteilt) durch zehn ist sechs
fünfzig (geteilt) durch zehn ist fünf
vierzig (geteilt) durch zehn ist vier
dreißig (geteilt) durch zehn ist drei
zwanzig (geteilt) durch zehn ist zwei
zehn   (geteilt) durch zehn ist eins

To practice these numbers, recite the multiplication tables from 2 to 10. It is a well-known fact that counting easily and naturally in a foreign language is the last thing you will learn to do. When you reach that point you have become bilingual.

[4] Past Infinitives

SEE
ANALYSIS
136

(pp. 373-374)

Er scheint zu schlafen.
Er scheint gut geschlafen zu haben.

Er schien in Paris zu sein.
Er schien in Paris gewesen zu sein.

Sie scheint Geld zu haben.
Sie scheint Geld gehabt zu haben.

Sie scheint gerade fahren zu lernen.
Sie scheint schon fahren gelernt zu haben.

Meyer schien sehr glücklich zu sein.
Meyer scheint sehr glücklich gewesen zu sein.

Sie scheint ihn jeden Tag anzurufen.
Sie scheint ihn heute noch nicht angerufen zu haben.

Wer Arzt werden will, muß sechs Jahre studieren.
Wer Arzt ist, muß sechs Jahre studiert haben.

Ich muß um sechs Uhr meine Brieftauben füttern.
Ich muß um sechs Uhr meine Brieftauben gefüttert haben.

[5] The Objective Use of **müssen** (Review)

Read these sentences carefully and review the forms of **müssen**. Then go through the variations below. You should be able to do these and similar variations without hesitation.

SEE
ANALYSIS
137

(pp. 374-380)

Jetzt habe ich keine Zeit. Ich muß erst die Kinder in die Schule schicken und dann noch die Betten machen.

> I have no time now. First I have to send the children off to school, and then I still have to make the beds.

Sie sagte, sie hätte keine Zeit. Sie müßte erst die Kinder in die Schule schicken und dann noch die Betten machen.

> She said she had had to send the children off to school first.
> and then she still had to make the beds.

Sie sagte, sie hätte erst die Kinder in die Schule schicken müssen.

> She said she had had to send the children off to school first.

Die Erika hat's gut. Sie hat eine Hilfe und hat noch nie ein Bett zu machen brauchen.

> Erika is well off. She has a maid and hasn't ever had to make a bed.

Um eins kommt mein Mann nach Hause. Bis dahin muß ich in der Stadt gewesen sein und das Mittagessen gekocht haben.

> My husband is coming home at one. By then I must be back from downtown and have dinner ready.

Wenn Meyer morgens um neun ins Büro kam, mußte seine Sekretärin schon die Post gelesen haben.

> When Meyer got to the office at nine in the morning his secretary had to have read the mail already. (= he expected his secretary to have read the mail already.)

VARIATIONS

> I have to be downtown at one o'clock.
> Um ein Uhr muß ich in der Stadt sein.

> She said she had to be downtown at one o'clock.
> Sie sagte, um ein Uhr _____.

> At one o'clock I had to be downtown.
> Um ein Uhr _____.

> She said she had had to be downtown at one o'clock.
> Sie sagte, um ein Uhr hätte _____.

> I must be back from (have been) downtown at one o'clock.
> Um ein Uhr _____.

Form similar variations with:

>   Morgen—das Buch lesen
>   Um drei Uhr—mit Meyer sprechen
>   Jeden Morgen um neun—die Betten machen

[6] The Subjective Use of müssen

Study the subjective use in these sentences; then follow the instructions below.

SEE
ANALYSIS
137

(pp. 374-380)

Diesen Brief habe ich heute von einem Herrn Brandt bekommen. Er muß Amerikaner sein. Er schreibt: „Gestern ich war in Berlin und habe gekauft Ihren Roman."

>   I got this letter from a Mr. Brandt today. He must be an American. He writes, "Yesterday I was in Berlin and bought your novel."

Ich hörte sofort, daß Herr Brandt trotz seines Namens Amerikaner sein mußte, denn er sagte: „Morgen ich kann nicht kommen, weil ich muß fahren nach Berlin."

>   I heard immediately that Mr. Brandt had to be an American in spite of his name, for he said, "Tomorrow I can't come because I have to go to Berlin."

Ich verstehe nicht, warum er noch nicht hier ist. Sein Zug müßte schon vor einer Stunde angekommen sein.

>   I don't understand why he isn't here yet. His train should have arrived an hour ago.

Sie ist doch in Stuttgart aufs Gymnasium gegangen. Sie muß also Englisch können und Faulkner gelesen haben.

>   But she went to the Gymnasium in Stuttgart. So she must know English and must have read Faulkner.

Sie ist doch in Stuttgart aufs Gymnasium gegangen. Sie müßte eigentlich Englisch können und Faulkner gelesen haben.

>   But she went to the Gymnasium in Stuttgart. So she ought to know English and ought to have read Faulkner.

Ich wußte, sie war in Stuttgart aufs Gymnasium gegangen. Sie mußte also Englisch können und Faulkner gelesen haben.

>   I knew she had gone to the Gymnasium in Stuttgart. So she had to know English and had to have read Faulkner.

Ich wußte, sie war in Stuttgart aufs Gymnasium gegangen, und sie hätte eigentlich Englisch können müssen.

>   I knew she had gone to the Gymnasium in Stuttgart and should have known English.

VARIATIONS

Following the pattern of the examples below, answer the questions by using a subjective form of **müssen**; try to support your conclusion with a sentence starting with **denn**.

> (a) **Ist sie wirklich schon achtzehn?—**
> **Sie muß achtzehn sein, denn sie will nächste Woche heiraten.**
>
> (b) **Waren Meyers wirklich an der Riviera?—**
> **Sie müssen an der Riviera gewesen sein, denn sie sind so braun wie Kaffee.**

1. Hat Meyer wirklich so viel Geld?
2. Ist Inge wirklich intelligent?
3. War Ingelheim wirklich Soldat?
4. War Ingelheim schon einmal verheiratet?
5. Woher wußtest du, daß er Amerikaner war?
6. Glaubst du, er liebt sie wirklich?

[7] wollen

Study these sentences carefully and determine whether **wollen** is used subjectively or objectively; then follow the instructions below.

Tante Amalie will uns nächste Woche besuchen.

 Tante Amalie wants to visit us next week.

SEE
ANALYSIS
137
(pp. 374-380)

Geht Tante Amalie wirklich allein ins Museum?

Früher habt ihr alle über Ingelheim geredet. Jetzt, wo er den Literaturpreis bekommen hat, will niemand etwas gesagt haben.

> You all used to talk about Ingelheim. Now that he has gotten the literature prize, everybody pretends to have said nothing.

Ich habe dich noch nie gebeten, mir zu helfen. Und jetzt, wo ich dich brauche, sagst du nein. Und du willst mein Freund sein!

> I have never asked you to help me, and now that I need you, you say no. And you claim to be my friend!

Er will in der Normandie gekämpft haben? Das glaube ich nicht.

> He says he has fought in Normandy? I don't believe that.

Hans hat mich gerade angerufen. Er will Erich vor einer Stunde in Tripolis gesehen haben.—Aber das ist doch unmöglich. Erich war heute morgen bei mir im Büro.

> Hans just called me. He says that he saw Erich in Tripoli an hour ago.— But that's impossible. Erich was in my office this morning.

Hast du nicht gesagt, du wolltest morgen nach Hamburg fahren?

> Didn't you say you wanted to go to Hamburg tomorrow?

Um acht wollte ich schon gefrühstückt haben. Und jetzt ist es zehn, und ich liege immer noch im Bett.

> I wanted to have finished my breakfast by eight. Now it's ten, and I'm still in bed.

Als Ingelheim den Preis bekam, wollte natürlich jeder seinen Roman schon gelesen haben. *Ich* hatte ihn *wirk*lich gelesen.—So?—Und ich wollte, ich hätte ihn *nicht* gelesen.

> When Ingelheim got the prize, everybody pretended to have read his novel already, of course. *I* really *had* read it.—Really?—And I wish I *hadn't* read it.

VARIATIONS

Change the following sentences according to the pattern of the example.

> **Er behauptet, ein Freund des Direktors zu sein.**
> **Er will ein Freund des Direktors sein.**

1. Er behauptet, ein Freund des Direktors gewesen zu sein.
2. Er behauptete, ein Freund des Direktors zu sein.
3. Er behauptete, ein Freund des Direktors gewesen zu sein.
4. Er behauptet, ein Haus an der Riviera zu haben.

5. Er behauptet, ein Haus an der Riviera gehabt zu haben.
6. Er behauptete, ein Haus an der Riviera zu haben.
7. Er behauptete, ein Haus an der Riviera gehabt zu haben.
8. Herr Direktor, dieser Mann behauptet, ihren Sekretär zu kennen.
9. Herr Direktor, dieser Mann behauptet, ihren Sekretär gekannt zu haben.
10. Der Mann behauptete, meinen Sekretär zu kennen.
11. Der Mann behauptete, meinen Sekretär gekannt zu haben.
12. Er behauptet, noch nie ein Mädchen geküßt zu haben.

[8] sollen

Read the following sentences carefully and decide which express obligation or "a plan of operation made for the grammatical subject," and which express "hearsay about the grammatical subject." Then follow the instructions below.

SEE
ANALYSIS
137
(pp. 374-380)

Du sollst nicht stehlen.
    Thou shalt not steal.

Wir sollen morgen um acht auf dem Bahnhof sein.
    We are supposed to be at the station at eight tomorrow.

Er sagte, wir sollten morgen um acht Uhr auf dem Bahnhof sein.
    He said we were to be at the station at eight tomorrow.

Ich weiß, ich sollte nicht soviel rauchen.
    I know I shouldn't smoke so much.

Das werde ich nie vergessen! Und wenn ich hundert Jahre alt werden sollte!
    I'll never forget that, even if I should live to be a hundred.

Die Brücke sollte schon letztes Jahr fertig sein, aber sie ist immer noch nicht fertig.
    The bridge was supposed to be finished last year, but it still isn't finished.

Ich verstehe nicht, Herr Schmidt, warum Sie immer noch nicht wissen, wo das "nicht" stehen muß. Nach zwei Semestern Deutsch sollten Sie das wirklich gelernt haben.
    I don't understand, Mr. Schmidt, why you still don't know what the position of "nicht" is. After two semesters you really ought to have learned that.

Wenn du Erich sehen solltest, dann darfst du nicht vergessen, ihm zu sagen, daß er mich besuchen soll.
    If you should see Erich, you mustn't forget to tell him that he should (is to) visit me.

Damals suchte IBM zwanzig Ingenieure. Alle sollten Deutsch können und mindestens vier Semester Elektronik studiert haben.

At that time, IBM was looking for twenty engineers. They all were supposed to know German and to have had four semesters of electronics.

Wo ist denn der Erich?—Der soll schon wieder an der Riviera sein.

Where is Erich?—Supposedly he is on the Riviera again.

Hast du etwas von Inge gehört?—Die soll im Juni geheiratet haben. Ihr Mann soll Ingenieur sein.

Have you heard anything about Inge?—I've heard that she got married last June. I understand her husband is an engineer.

Hast du gehört? Der Ingelheim soll schon wieder einen Roman geschrieben haben.

Have you heard that Ingelheim is supposed to have written another novel?

So, Meyer hat geheiratet?—Ja, aber er soll gar nicht glücklich sein, und trinken soll er auch.

So, Meyer has got married?—Yes, but I've heard that he isn't happy at all, and supposedly he is drinking, too.

VARIATIONS

Change the following sentences according to the pattern of the example.

> **Ich höre, Meyer wohnt in Berlin.—Meyer soll in Berlin wohnen.**

Ich höre, er ist schon wieder in Afrika.
Ich höre, er ist noch nie in Afrika gewesen.
Ich höre, seine Frau war krank.
Ich höre, Erika hat geheiratet.
Ich höre, er muß schon wieder nach Amerika fahren.
Ich höre, er hat viel Geld verdient und braucht nicht mehr zu arbeiten.

[9] können

Read the following sentences and determine whether **können** is used objectively or subjectively; then follow the instructions below.

SEE
ANALYSIS
137

(pp. 374-380)

Meyer ist krank und kann leider nicht kommen.

Meyer is sick and unfortunately can't come.

Heute ist ja schon Donnerstag. Bis Samstag kann ich den Roman nicht gelesen haben.

But today is Thursday already. I can't possibly have read the novel by Saturday.

Intelligent kann sie nicht sein. Wenn sie intelligent wäre, würde sie nicht für Meyer arbeiten.

She can't be intelligent. If she were intelligent, she wouldn't work for Meyer.

Mit Erich hatte ich gerade vor fünf Minuten telefoniert. Erich konnte es also nicht gewesen sein.

I had talked to Erich on the phone just five minutes earlier. Therefore it couldn't possibly have been Erich.

Sie war fast noch ein Kind und konnte nicht älter sein als siebzehn.

She was still almost a child and couldn't have been any older than seventeen.

Wenn Meyer kein Geld hätte, könnte er keinen Mercedes 300 fahren.

If Meyer didn't have any money, he couldn't drive a Mercedes 300.

Seine Frau sagte, er sei krank und könne leider nicht kommen.

His wife said he was sick and unfortunately wouldn't be able to come.

Könnte ich vielleicht ein Zimmer mit Bad haben?

Could I have a room with bath?

Ich glaube, wir sollten heute im Garten arbeiten. Morgen könnte es regnen.

I think we should work in the garden today. It could (might) rain tomorrow.

Und der Herr, der mich sprechen wollte, hat nicht gesagt, wie er heißt? Wer kann das nur gewesen sein? Er sprach mit einem Akzent, sagen Sie? Hm, das könnte Mr. Taylor gewesen sein.

And the gentleman who wanted to talk to me didn't tell you his name? Who could that have been? You say he had an accent? Hm, that could have been Mr. Taylor.

Die Zimmer sind *gut*. Aber das *Essen* könnte *bes*ser sein.

The rooms are OK. But the food could be better.

Die Zimmer waren *gut*. Aber das *Essen* hätte *bes*ser sein können.

The rooms were OK. But the food could have been better.

Ich hätte auch Medizin studieren können. Aber ich wollte nicht.

I could have studied medicine too. But I didn't want to.

Ich habe noch nie nach Italien fahren können. Ich habe einfach nicht die Zeit dazu.

    I have never been able to go to Italy. I simply don't have the time.

VARIATIONS

Change the following sentences according to the pattern of the example.

> **Ist er schon hier?**
> **Nein, er kann noch nicht hier sein. Es ist doch erst acht.**

Ist sie schon verheiratet?
Nein, _____ Sie ist doch erst sechzehn.

War er gestern abend im Kino?
Nein, _____ Er war gestern abend bei Meyers.

Woher wußtest du denn, daß es nicht Erich war?
Erich _____ Der war doch damals in Hamburg.

Bist du sicher, daß es Erich war?
Nein, sicher bin ich nicht, aber _____

[10] dürfen

Study the use of **dürfen** in these sentences and determine whether it is used objectively or subjectively.

SEE
ANALYSIS
137

(pp. 374-380)

Darf ich Sie nach dem Theater nach Hause bringen, Fräulein Schumacher?
    May I take you home after the theater, Fräulein Schumacher?

Darf ich heute abend ins Kino gehen, Mutti?
Kann ich heute abend ins Kino gehen, Mutti?
    May I go to the movies tonight, Mom?

Ich fragte sie, ob ich sie nach Hause bringen dürfte.
    I asked her whether I could (might) take her home.

Rauchen darf man hier leider nicht.
    Unfortunately smoking is not permitted here.

Sie dürfen nicht mehr so viel Kaffee trinken, Frau Emmerich.
    You mustn't (shouldn't) drink so much coffee any more, Frau Emmerich.

Wann ist er denn weggefahren?—Vor zwei· Stunden.—Dann dürfte er jetzt
schon in Frankfurt sein.

When did he leave?—Over two hours ago.—Then we can assume that he
is in Frankfurt by now.

Ich möchte wissen, wer mich gestern abend um elf noch angerufen hat.—Das
dürfte Erich gewesen sein; der ruft doch immer so spät an.

I wonder who called me last night at eleven.—I suppose that was Erich;
he always calls that late, doesn't he?

[11] mögen

Acquaint yourself with the indicative use of **mögen,** both as a non-modal and as
a subjective modal. Then follow the instructions below.

SEE
ANALYSIS
137
(pp. 374-380)

Ingelheims Romane sind ja ganz gut, aber als Mensch mag ich ihn gar nicht.

Ingelheim's novels aren't bad, but as a person I don't care for him at all.

Ich mochte ihn schon nicht, als wir während des Krieges in Afrika waren.

I disliked him already when we were in Africa during the war.

Meine Frau hat ihn auch nie gemocht.

My wife never liked him either.

Danke, Schweinefleisch mag ich nicht; ich esse lieber ein Steak.

Thanks, I don't care for pork; I'd rather have a steak.

Glaubst du, daß Erich wirklich der Dieb war?—Das mag schon sein.

Do you think that Erich really was the thief?—That's quite possible.

Mag sein, daß er nur seinem Freund Ali helfen wollte.

Maybe (It may be that) he only wanted to help his friend Ali.

Wie alt ist seine Tochter eigentlich?—Oh, ich weiß nicht. Sie mag achtzehn
oder neunzehn sein.

How old is his daughter?—Oh, I don't know, maybe eighteen or nineteen.

Er mochte damals etwa dreißig sein.

At that time, he was probably about thirty.

Was mag ihm nur passiert sein?

I wonder what has happened to him?

Er mag gedacht haben, ich hätte ihn nicht gesehen.

He may have thought that I hadn't seen him.

Er mochte gedacht haben, ich hätte ihn nicht gesehen.

He had probably thought that I hadn't seen him.

VARIATIONS

Change the following sentences according to the pattern of the example.

> **Ich glaube, sie ist etwa zwanzig.—Sie mag etwa zwanzig sein.**

Ich glaubte, sie war zwanzig.—Sie _____.

Ich glaube, sie war damals etwa zwanzig.—Sie _____.

Ich glaube, er hat mich nicht gesehen.—Er _____.

Ich glaube, das ist Zufall.—Das _____.

Ich glaube, das war Zufall.—Das _____.

Das kostet vielleicht dreißig Mark.—Das _____.

Es hat vielleicht dreißig Mark gekostet.—Es _____.

Er gab mir ein Buch, das vielleicht dreißig Mark gekostet hatte. Das Buch, das er mir gab, _____.

[12] hätte fliehen können vs. könnte geflohen sein

After studying **138** carefully, try to find the various ways in which these sentences can be expressed in English.

SEE ANALYSIS 138

(pp. 380-384)

Meyer hätte fliehen können, aber er wollte nicht.

Wahrscheinlich ist er noch im Lande, aber er könnte natürlich auch geflohen sein.

Natürlich hätte ich das Geld stehlen können, aber ich bin doch kein Dieb.

Sie können doch gar nicht wissen, ob mir das Geld wirklich gehört; ich könnte es ja auch gestohlen haben.

Ich habe dich leider nicht anrufen können; ich hatte einfach keine Zeit.

Nein, Herr Behrens, um sieben Uhr kann mein Mann Sie noch nicht angerufen haben; da hat er noch geschlafen.

Du willst Anglist sein und hast nie Chaucer gelesen? Als Anglist müßtest du doch Chaucer gelesen haben.

Da hast du ganz recht; wir hätten ihn schon auf dem Gymnasium lesen müssen.

Du wolltest das Feuerwerk sehen? Da hättest du schon um acht Uhr hier sein müssen.

Er hat das Feuerwerk gesehen? Dann muß er schon um acht Uhr hier gewesen sein.

Wir waren dumm; wir hätten uns einen Volkswagen kaufen sollen.
Meyers sollen schon wieder einen Mercedes gekauft haben.

Und hier hat es den ganzen Sommer geregnet? Ihr hättet mit uns nach Rom
   fahren sollen.
Was, ihr wart noch nie in Rom? Ihr solltet schon lange einmal dort gewesen
   sein.

Ich habe schon immer Deutsch lernen wollen, aber ich habe nie genug Zeit
   dazu gehabt.
Er will in drei Wochen Deutsch gelernt haben. Glaubst du das?

[13] The Reflexive Pronoun sich

Er hat mir ein Auto gekauft.
Er hat sich ein Auto gekauft. (He bought himself a car.)

SEE
ANALYSIS
139
(p. 384)

Ich wasche mir die Hände.
Er wäscht sich die Hände.

Ich will mir einen Mantel kaufen.
Sie will sich einen Mantel kaufen.

Wir haben uns ein Haus gebaut.
Sie haben sich ein Haus gebaut.

Das kann ich mir denken.
Das hätte er sich doch denken können.

Ich konnte es mir einfach nicht erklären.
Er konnte es sich einfach nicht erklären.

Ich wollte mir in Köln eine Wohnung suchen.
Er hat sich in Köln eine Wohnung gesucht.

Ich will mich noch baden.
Hat sie sich schon gebadet?

Ich lege mich bald ins Bett.
Er hat sich schon ins Bett gelegt.

Ich halte ihn für dumm,
aber er hält sich für sehr intelligent.

Ich habe mich neben sie gestellt.
Er hat sich neben mich gestellt.

VARIATIONS

> **Er hat sich ein Auto gekauft.—Ich habe mir ein Auto gekauft.**

Er hat sich schon gebadet?—Du _____?
Er hat sich schon gebadet?—Ihr _____?
Das konnte er sich doch denken.—Das konntest du _____.
Das konnte er sich doch denken.—Das konntet ihr _____.
Er hat sich ins Bett gelegt.—Ich _____.
Er hat sich ins Bett gelegt.—Wir _____.
Sie haben sich ein Haus gebaut.—Ich _____.
Sie haben sich ein Haus gebaut.—Wir _____.
Sie haben sich ein Haus gebaut.—Er _____.

Using the phrase **ein Haus bauen,** form sentences, with and without modals, negative and affirmative, using the reflexive **sich.**

[14] Contrary-to-Fact Conditions without **wenn**

SEE
ANALYSIS
140
(p. 385)

Wäre Ingelheim nicht Soldat gewesen, so hätte er keine Kriegsromane schreiben können.

> If Ingelheim hadn't been a soldier, he couldn't have written war novels.

Hätte Erich seinen Hut nicht verloren, so hätte niemand geglaubt, was Gerda erzählte.

> If Erich hadn't lost his hat, nobody would have believed what Gerda was saying.

Hätte Hans mich an meinem Geburtstag angerufen, dann hätte ich gewußt, wo er war.

> If Hans had called me on my birthday, I would have known where he was.

Wäre Ingrid nicht gerade mit ihrer Mutter in München gewesen, hätte sie ihren Mann nie kennengelernt.

> If Ingrid hadn't happened to be in Munich with her mother, she would never have met her husband.

Hätten wir uns dieses Wochenendhaus nicht gekauft, dann könnten wir jetzt jeden Sommer nach Italien fahren.

> If only we hadn't bought this weekend house, we could go to Italy every summer now.

Wenn Otto nur nicht so *dumm* wäre!
> If only Otto weren't so *stupid!*

Wenn nur *Ot*to nicht so dumm wäre!
> If only *Otto* weren't so stupid!

Wenn meine Frau nur nicht so viel Geld brauchte!
> If only my wife didn't need so much money!

Wenn du wenigstens Kaffee kochen könntest!
> If only you could at least make coffee!

Wenn sie nur nicht so oft ins Kino gehen wollte!
> If only she didn't want to go to the movies so often!

Wenn ich damals nur *Geld* gehabt hätte!
> If only I had had *money* then!

Wenn ich das Geld nur *damals* gehabt hätte!
> If only I had had the money *then!*

Ja, wenn nur damals der Krieg nicht gekommen wäre!
> If only the war hadn't come then!

Wenn du mir wenigstens geschrieben hättest!
> If at least you had written to me!

Wenn ich das nur gewußt hätte!
> If I'd only known that!

Hättest du mir doch nur geschrieben, daß du Geld brauchtest! Du weißt doch, daß ich dir gerne geholfen hätte.
> If only you had written that you needed money! You know that I would have been glad to help you.

Hätte ich doch nur gewußt, daß Meyer krank war! Ich hätte ihn gerne besucht.
> Had I only known that Meyer was sick! I would have been glad to visit him.

Wäre er doch nur zu Hause geblieben! In einer Nacht wie dieser schickt man doch keinen Hund auf die Straße.
> If only he had stayed home! You wouldn't put a dog out on a night like this.

Wäre ich nur heute abend nicht ins Theater gegangen! Ich wußte doch, daß Ilse Bruckner heute die Desdemona spielt.
> If only I hadn't gone to the theater tonight! I knew that Ilse Bruckner was playing Desdemona tonight.

VARIATIONS

Transform the following sentences into wishes. Shift the position of **nur** or
wenigstens.

> Er hat meine Freundin nicht eingeladen.
> Wenn er nur meine *Freun*din eingeladen hätte!
> Wenn er meine Freundin nur *ein*geladen hätte!
> Hätte er doch nur meine *Freun*din eingeladen!
> Hätte er meine Freundin doch nur *ein*geladen!

1. Er war gestern nicht hier.
2. Er ist mit seiner Frau nach München gefahren.
3. Er hat meiner Frau Blumen geschickt.
4. Hans hatte zu viel getrunken.

CONVERSATION

We took a tape recorder to a German university and listened to students talking
between lectures and in the university cafeteria. Here are some of the results,
slightly edited.

I

STUDENT: Wie geht's?

STUDENTIN: Ach, ganz gut. Das war vielleicht eine Arbeit mit dem Referat![1] Ich hab'
vier Nächte dran gearbeitet. Das hat was gekostet, diese ganze Literatur
durchzuarbeiten. Aber ich hab' doch viel dabei gelernt.

STUDENT: Ja, aber man kann nur eins: entweder Referat schreiben oder Vorlesungen[2]
besuchen. Und wenn man am Proseminar teilnimmt,[3] *muß* man ein Referat
schreiben, oder man bekommt keinen Seminarschein.[4] Ich werd' mir wohl
noch einen holen, wenn ich auch nicht weiß, wie ich das machen soll.—
Übrigens, was hat denn der Burkhardt zu deinem Referat gesagt?

STUDENTIN: Zum Referat? Also, er hat gesagt, ich brauchte keine Angst zu haben; die
Arbeit sei gut, und ich könne ruhig an mein Referat für das Romantik-
Seminar gehen. Er sagte, das und das sei ganz richtig gesehen, aber—na
ja, dann kamen die „Aber".

[1] **Referat**   term paper
[2] **Vorlesung**   university lecture
[3] **teil'nehmen**   to take part
[4] **Seminarschein**   certificate of participation in a seminar

STUDENT: Ist ja eigentlich alles Unsinn,—so zu arbeiten. Die Hannelore Schneider, die hat doch jetzt ein Semester lang Latein gepaukt,[5] und dann hat sie am Tag der Prüfung[6] so gezittert, daß sie nicht hingehen konnte. „Jetzt werd' ich nicht Studienrätin,[7] jetzt werd' ich Mittelschullehrerin", hat sie gesagt.

II

STUDENT A: Kennst du die Gisela Wiesner? Das ist so 'ne Blonde; die macht jetzt Examen.[8]

STUDENT B: Ja, die kenne ich; die hab' ich auf einer Party kennengelernt; die muß doch mindestens zwölftes Semester sein.

STUDENT A: Ist sie auch; es ist Zeit, daß die endlich mal Examen macht.—Und Peter Lemmert, kennst du den? Aus München.

STUDENT B: Ach der—ich dachte früher immer, das wär' ein Engländer.

STUDENT A: Ja, ich dachte auch, das wäre ein Engländer—der rollte das „r" am Ende so—ich hör' manchmal englische Sender—daher weiß ich das. Aber dann war ich mit ihm zusammen bei Hornemann im Seminar, und als er das erste Mal den Mund aufgemacht hat, wußte ich, der kommt aus München.

[5] **pauken**   to cram
[6] **prüfen**   to test, to examine
[7] **der Studienrat**   teacher at a Gymnasium
[8] **Examen machen**   to take a (final) examination

Universität Frankfurt

III

A: Wie spät ist es eigentlich?

B: Also die Uni-Uhren gehen alle nach dem Mond.[9] Die im Audi-Max[10] geht anders als die hier im Seminar, und die im Hauptgebäude geht noch anders.

A: Ach so—na ja; es muß so gegen zehn vor elf sein.—Sag mal,[11] was hältst du eigentlich von Parties?

B: Nicht viel.

A: Wir wollen nämlich eine machen—es braucht ja nicht gerade eine Cocktail-Party zu sein—mit Tanz und so . . .

B: Ich weiß (a) nicht, wer „wir" sind—und (b) glaube ich, ich muß endlich mal was für die Uni tun.

IV

STUDENT 1:   Ich soll morgen zu Dr. Schober in die Sprechstunde[12] kommen. Er hat mir für meine Arbeit eine 2[13] gegeben. Die beste Arbeit, hat er gesagt.

STUDENT 2:   Herzlichen Glückwunsch![14] Das war aber auch ein Thema![15]

STUDENT 1:   Das kann man schon sagen. Aber hören Sie mal, haben Sie schon mit der Übersetzung angefangen? Das sind acht Zeilen. Erst dachte ich, das ginge ganz leicht—zwei Zeilen hab ich rausbekommen,[16] dann hab' ich das Ding in die Ecke geworfen. Man kann auch nirgends nachsehen.[17] Ich weiß nicht, was Verb ist und was Substantiv.

STUDENT 2:   Hoffentlich läßt er keine Klausur[18] schreiben,—mündlich ist besser.

V

STUDENT: Kommen Sie, wir wollen uns weiter vorne hinsetzen—dann schlaf' ich wenigstens nicht ein. An der Vorlesung hab' ich wirklich keine Freude.

STUDENTIN: Ich kriege gottseidank immer die Notizen[19] für alle Vorlesungen von Kurt Müller—das ist schick,[20] da brauche ich nie mitzuschreiben. Übrigens, wo ist denn Ihre Freundin heute?

[9] **die . . . Mond**   the university clocks are all off
[10] **Audi-Max**   Auditorium Maximum
[11] **Sag mal**   tell me
[12] **die Sprechstunde**   office hours
[13] **2**   corresponds to a B on the American grading scale (1 = A)
[14] **Herzlichen Glückwunsch**   congratulations
[15] **das Thema**   topic
[16] **herausbekommen**   to figure out
[17] **nachsehen**   to look up
[18] **Klausur**   written test
[19] **Notizen**   (lecture) notes
[20] **schick** (*colloq.*)   great, fine, sharp

STUDENT: Ach, das ist eigentlich gar nicht meine Freundin, das ist eine Bekannte.[21]— Ich muß mir doch mal Ihren Namen aufschreiben; fünf Buchstaben, genau wie meiner. Und wie war noch Ihr Vorname? Ich vergesse das immer.

STUDENTIN: Helga.

STUDENT: Wollen Sie jetzt hier wirklich zuhören? Wollen wir nicht lieber Kaffee trinken gehen?

STUDENTIN: Warum eigentlich nicht? So interessant ist der Paulsen ja nun auch nicht.

VI

STUDENT: Ich muß abends um halb elf zu Hause sein, sonst meckert[22] meine Wirtin. Aber gestern habe ich gekündigt.[23] Ich habe gesagt, das wäre besser für sie und für mich,—dann brauchte sie keine Anfälle[24] mehr zu haben über mich. Es war ihr ja nicht ganz recht, daß ich kündigte,—weil sie dann vielleicht keine Miete[25] kriegt für einen Monat—und die hundert Mark will sie natürlich haben.

STUDENTIN: Warum mußt du denn so früh zu Hause sein?

STUDENT: Wegen ihrer Tochter, die bekommt sonst nicht genug Schlaf. Und die wacht schon auf, wenn ich den Schlüssel ins Schlüsselloch stecke.

STUDENTIN: Wie alt ist die denn?

STUDENT: Och, die ist wohl so fünfunddreißig oder achtunddreißig—schon uralt.[26] Aber lieber schlaf' ich irgendwo auf dem Fußboden[27] als *da* bleiben.

STUDENTIN: Ich hab' jetzt Forsythien in der Vase. Du mußt mich mal besuchen. Aber bei mir ist das so kalt!

STUDENT: Dann mußt du heizen.

STUDENTIN: Das kann ich nicht—und zwar, weil ich Zentralheizung habe.

STUDENT: Dann ist die Heizung kaputt.

STUDENTIN: Nein, das ist es nicht, aber mein Zimmer ist sechs Meter lang und zwei Meter breit. An der einen zwei-Meter-Seite ist das Fenster, an der anderen— also sechs Meter weit weg—ist die Heizung. Und davor steht noch 'ne Kommode.

STUDENT: Was ist denn das für'n Zimmer?[28]

STUDENTIN: Das ist kein Zimmer—das ist ein Schlauch.[29]

[21] **Bekannte**   acquaintance
[22] **meckern**   here: to complain
[23] **kündigen**   to give notice
[24] **der Anfall**   seizure, attack; fit
[25] **die Miete**   rent
[26] **uralt**   ancient
[27] **der Fußboden**   floor
[28] **Was . . . Zimmer?**   What kind of a room is that?
[29] **der Schlauch**   tube, hose

"Dear Abby" auf Deutsch

The following exchange of letters was taken, with only minor changes, from the "Dear Abby" column of a German newspaper.

Liebe Frau Erika,

als Max (mein Mann) und ich uns vor drei Jahren verlobten, kauften wir uns zwei Goldringe. Ich war stolz auf meinen, und er war stolz auf seinen Ring.

wir verlobten uns we got engaged

Nun sind wir seit zwei Jahren verheiratet. Als wir in die Kirche gingen, trugen wir die Ringe an der linken Hand. Und als wir dann 5 freudestrahlend aus der Kirche kamen, trug jeder seinen Ring an der rechten Hand.

an der linken Hand on the left hand
strahlen to beam

Wir waren glücklich und sind auch heute noch glücklich. Aber, mein Mann legte seinen Ring kurz nach der Hochzeit in seine Schublade, in dieselbe Schublade, in der auch sein Rasierapparat 10 liegt. „Der Ring", meinte er, „hindert mich beim Arbeiten." Er ist nämlich Automechaniker, wissen Sie, und ich kann es verstehen, daß er den Ring nicht gerne bei der Arbeit trägt. Aber auch samstags und sonntags, wenn er nicht arbeitet, will er ihn nicht mehr tragen. Ich habe ihm den Ring auf den Frühstückstisch gelegt, aber 15 er schiebt ihn einfach auf die Seite und liest die Zeitung.

die Hochzeit wedding
die Schublade drawer
dieselbe the same
der Rasierapparat razor
hindern to hinder, be in the way

Vor einem Monat habe ich meinen Ring auch in die Schublade gelegt. Wenn er seinen Ring nicht tragen will, brauche ich auch keinen Ring zu tragen, habe ich mir gesagt. Und wissen Sie was, liebe Frau Erika? Max hat es gar nicht gemerkt, daß ich seit einem 20 Monat keinen Ring mehr trage. Meine Freundinnen haben es natürlich sofort gemerkt und fragen immer, was denn mit uns los wäre.

Was ist los? What's the matter?

Was soll ich tun? Es wäre doch *so* nett, wenn Max und ich beide unsere Ringe trügen! Bitte geben Sie mir Ihren Rat.

raten to advise; **der Rat** advice

Annemarie S., Dortmund

Liebe Frau Annemarie,

Ich bin auch seit Jahren glücklich verheiratet, und mein Mann 25 trägt auch keinen Ring. Nicht weil der Ring ihn beim Arbeiten hindert, sondern weil seine Finger nicht mehr so schlank sind wie früher. Aber das macht mir gar nichts aus. Legen Sie Ihrem Mann den Ring sonntags nicht wieder auf den Frühstückstisch. Aber

schlank slender
macht...aus doesn't bother me at all

Soll die Ehe glücklich sein, kauf bei KURTZ die Ringe ein!

machen Sie den Kaffee besonders gut und fahren Sie mit ihm übers
Wochenende in die Berge. Und wenn Sie mit Ihrem Max in ein
Restaurant gehen, dann stecken Sie Ihren Ring vorher an den Finger.
Oder sind Ihre Finger nicht mehr schlank genug für Ihren Ring?
Das wäre schade.   5

Soll man allein auf Parties gehen?

In the same newspaper, a mother had written to the editor, complaining that
her daughter, in order to be invited to parties, had to have a boy friend. The
paper received a large number of replies, both agreeing and disagreeing with
the mother. A few of these letters follow.

Es ist doch ganz natürlich, daß man nur zu zweit auf eine Party **zu zweit** two to-
geht. Ich habe schon bei Parties erlebt, daß Mädchen, die keine gether
Partner hatten, durch ihre Melancholie die Partystimmung ver- **die Stimmung** mood,
darben. Man muß doch erwarten, daß ein Junge, der ein Mädchen fun
eingeladen hat, nur mit diesem Mädchen tanzt. Ich selbst, sechzehn 10 **verderben, verdarb,
Jahre (Gymnasiastin), gehe oft zu Parties und gebe auch oft eine verdorben** to spoil
Party. **Gymnasiast** student
in a Gymnasium

Hella S., Kassel

Auch ich gehe oft zu Parties. Niemals ist es passiert, daß ein Junge **niemals** = nie
oder ein Mädchen zuviel oder zuwenig war. Es wäre auch dumm,
wenn man die Gäste nicht paarweise einlüde, denn oft ist es ja so, 15 **paarweise** by couples
daß ein Junge sich nur für ein Mädchen interessiert. Für ein Mäd-
chen, das keinen Jungen hat, wird der Abend ganz uninteressant.
Frau X fragte, ob die Pärchen immer so zusammensitzen müßten.
Das ist doch vom Gastgeber und seinen Freunden schon geplant. **der Gastgeber** host

Die laden nur die Mädchen ein, die den Gastgeber und seine
Freunde interessieren. Oft gehen diese Parties allerdings zu weit.
Darüber will ich jedoch diesmal nicht schreiben. Ich bin siebzehn
Jahre alt und gehe noch zur Schule.

Rita L., Mannheim

Es ist heute fast überall so: Man lädt zu einer Party fast nur Pärchen 5
ein. Hat ein Mädchen keinen Freund, so bekommt sie einfach keine
Einladung. Lädt man sie doch ein, so sagt man ihr, daß sie einen
Jungen mitbringen soll. Ich finde so etwas unglaublich. Man kann
doch von einem Mädchen nicht erwarten, nur wegen einer Party
einen Freund zu haben. Ich bin der Meinung, daß man sich nicht 10
zu früh fest binden sollte.

Heidemarie M., Duisburg (sechzehn Jahre)

Ich finde es sehr dumm, wenn auf Parties nur Paare zusammen
tanzen. In unserem Kreis (Gymnasiasten, achtzehn bis zwanzig
Jahre) laden wir nicht nur Paare ein, sondern auch Jungen und
Mädchen, die keinen Partner haben. Da tanzt eben jeder mit jedem. 15
Bleiben die Paare einmal doch zu sehr zusammen, so machen wir
einfach Abklatschen oder ein Tanzspiel. Bei uns ist der ameri-   **Abklatschen machen**
kanische Einfluß des "going steady" noch nicht so stark.   to cut in

Doris D., Bremen

Guten Morgen! Was möchten Sie gern
zum Frühstück, bitte?

Portion Kaffee — Nescafé — Tee — Schokolade
mit Butter, Konfitüre, Marmelade, Honig, Brot,
Brötchen, Hörnchen, Zwieback   3,50

Eierspeisen

1 weichgekochtes Ei   —,60
2 Eier im Glas   1,20
2 Stück Rühreier oder Spiegeleier   1,50
2 Spiegeleier mit Schinken oder Speck   2,50

Diverses

Käse nach Wahl   1,30
Porridge mit Sahne und Zucker   1,50
Cornflakes mit Sahne oder Milch   1,50
Joghurt mit Zucker   1,—

Kleine Fleischbeilage

Wurstaufschnitt   1,30
Spezial-Frühstücksteller (unser Titelfoto)   1,50
Gekochter Schinken   1,80
Roher Räucherschinken   2,—
Roastbeef   2,—

Fruchtsäfte und Früchte

Orangensaft, frisch gepreßt   1,50
Grapefruitsaft   1,25
Tomatensaft   1,25
Karottensaft, frisch   1,50
Frische halbe Pampelmuse   1,—
Geeiste Melone   nach Jahreszeit
Gemischtes Kompott oder Backpflaumen mit Sahne   2,—
Frisches Obst   zum Tagespreis

15 % Etage · Etagenaufschlag pro Person DM 0,50 · 10 % Service

Ich war letztes Jahr zu einer Neujahrsparty eingeladen. Als ich
ankam, sagte man mir, daß der Partner, den man mir zugedacht
hatte, wegen einer Autopanne von einer Reise nicht rechtzeitig
zurückgekommen sei. Von den vier Pärchen, die da waren, hat
keiner versucht, mir zu zeigen, daß ich nicht überflüssig sei: nicht 5
einer hat mit mir getanzt. Als ich um dreiundzwanzig Uhr heimlich
verschwand, haben die andern wohl gedacht, das wäre selbstverständlich, denn bis heute hat mich noch niemand nach dem Grund
meines Verschwindens gefragt.

Steffi B., Lübeck

die Panne (mechan-
ical) breakdown

überflüssig superflu-
ous
heimlich secretly
selbstverständlich
self-understood, as it
ought to be
Grund reason

Woher wußten Sie denn, daß ich Amerikanerin bin?

Ich weiß, mein Deutsch ist gut und fast akzentfrei; und wenn ich 10
nach Deutschland fahre, glaubt man oft, daß ich in Deutschland
geboren bin. Aber letztes Jahr habe ich gelernt, daß man mehr als
die Sprache können muß, wenn man nicht will, daß jeder sofort
weiß, daß man Amerikaner ist.

Ich war mit meinem Mann in Hamburg, und wir wohnten in den 15
„Vier Jahreszeiten". Morgens im Frühstückszimmer saßen wir kaum
an unserem Tisch, als der Kellner kam und uns fragte: „And what
would you like for breakfast?" Woher wußte er, daß wir Amerikaner
waren?

Vier Jahreszeiten
Four Seasons

Good morning!
What would you like for breakfast, please?

Coffee — Nescafé — tea — chocolate
compl. with butter, jam, marmelade, honey,
rolls, recent-rolls, bread, biscuits   3,50

Egg - dishes

1 soft boiled egg   —,60
2 boiled eggs in a glass   1,20
Scrambled eggs or fried eggs   1,50
2 fried eggs with ham or bacon   2,50

Sundries

Assorted cheese   1,30
Porridge with cream and sugar   1,50
Cornflakes with cream or milk   1,50
Yoghurt with sugar   1,—

Small meat supplements

Sausages cold meat   1,30
Assorted cold meat   1,50
Boiled ham   1,80
Smoked ham   2,—
Roastbeef   2,—

Fruit and fruit-juices

Orange juice, fresh   1,50
Grapefruit juice   1,25
Tomato juice   1,25
Carrots juice, fresh   1,50
Fresh half grapefruit   1,—
Mixed fruits or stewed prunes with cream   2,—
Fresh fruit   price of day

15 % room-service · room-tax per person DM 0,50 · 10 % service

Mein Kleid hatte ich am Tage vorher in Hamburg gekauft; ich hatte
keinen Lippenstift an, und meine Dauerwelle hatte ich mir in Köln
machen lassen. Außerdem las mein Mann eine Hamburger Zeitung.
Und trotzdem sagte der Kellner: „What would you like for breakfast?" Ich war neugierig und fragte: „Herr Ober, woher wissen ₅
Sie, daß wir Amerikaner sind?"

der Lippenstift lip-
stick
die Dauerwelle per-
manent
neugierig curious

„Wenn man seit dreißig Jahren Kellner ist, dann sieht man das
sofort, gnädige Frau", sagte er auf Deutsch. „Als Sie Platz nahmen,
hat Ihnen Ihr Mann den Stuhl gehalten,—und das tut man in
Deutschland nicht. Und als ich an Ihren Tisch kam, habe ich sofort ₁₀
gesehen, daß Sie Ihren Ring an der linken Hand tragen,—und das
tut man in Deutschland nur, solange man verlobt ist."

„Und woher wußten Sie, daß wir verheiratet sind?"

„Gnädige Frau, das darf ich Ihnen wirklich nicht sagen."

„Das brauchen Sie auch nicht", sagte mein Mann, der bis jetzt ₁₅
hinter seiner Zeitung gesessen und nichts gesagt hatte. Er grinste,
faltete die Zeitung zusammen, gab sie dem Kellner und sagte:
„Herr Ober, Sie sind ein Menschenkenner.—Also: zwei Orangensaft, Spiegeleier mit Schinken, Toast und Kaffee."

grinsen to grin
zusammenfalten to
fold
der Saft juice
das Ei, -er egg; **das
Spiegelei** fried egg,
sunny side up
der Schinken ham

„In other words, an American breakfast", sagte der Ober und ver-₂₀
schwand.

ANALYSIS

134 The Use of **nicht**

nicht in the Inner Field

As was pointed out in **43, nicht,** if placed at the end of the inner field
in front of the second prong, negates the predicate.

Ich	bin	sehr oft	nicht	zu Hause

I am very often not at home

means basically *I am not at home,* and this *not being at home* happens
very often.

It was also pointed out that if **nicht** is placed within the inner field, the validity of the predicate is untouched. The sentence

Ich	bin	nicht	sehr oft	zu Hause

I am not very often at home

means basically *I am at home,* but this *being at home* happens *not very often.*

Up to this unit, we have not used many sentences of the second type because we wanted to establish firmly the habit of putting **nicht** in front of the second prong. From now on we shall feel free to use **nicht** within the inner field—that is, in sentences in which the predicate is not negated.

The difference in meaning between the two positions of **nicht** is sometimes rather startling. Compare

Er wollte Priester werden. Und darum hat er freiwillig nicht geheiratet.	He wanted to become a priest. For this reason he voluntarily did not marry.
Ihre Eltern haben sie gezwungen, einen Mann zu heiraten, den sie nicht liebte. Sie hat nicht freiwillig geheiratet.	Her parents forced her to marry a man she did not love. She did not marry voluntarily.

nicht Followed by sondern

The English pattern "not A, but B," which occurs in such sentences as

You are not my friend, but my enemy

is expressed in German by **nicht A, sondern B.**

Das war nicht gestern, sondern vorgestern.
That was not yesterday, but the day before yesterday.

Such sentences use contrast intonation. The element introduced by **nicht** (or **kein**) has a rising stress (_⌐/), and the element introduced by **sondern** has a falling stress (⌐\ ). The **nicht** (or **kein**) and the **sondern** are normally unstressed.

The element introduced by **nicht** can stand

(a) in the front field
(b) in the inner field
(c) in front of the second prong, negating that part of the second prong which has the _⌐/ -type stress.

The element introduced by **kein** should not be placed in the front field.

The element introduced by **sondern** can either stand behind the second prong in the end field, or it can follow immediately upon the **nicht A** element:

> **Ich war nicht gestern in Berlin, sondern vorgestern.**
> **Ich war nicht gestern, sondern vorgestern in Berlin.**

The **nicht A, sondern B** pattern can even be distributed over two clauses; in this case, the **nicht A** part stands in the first clause and **sondern,** as a coordinating conjunction, introduces the second clause, which, as a unit, forms element B.

> **Ich habe nicht sie geheiratet, sondern sie hat mich geheiratet.**

As the example shows, this use of **nicht** and **sondern** is possible only if the second clause reverses the subject-object relation of the first.

135 Numbers from 1 to 100

The German system is quite similar to English. From 0 to 12, each number has its own name; from 13 on, and with the exception of 100, the numbers are either compounded or are derived from the basic set 1–9. Note that from 21 to 29, 31 to 39, etc. German reverses the English pattern: *twenty-one* becomes **einundzwanzig.**

null		zwanzig	
eins		einundzwanzig	
zwei		zweiundzwanzig	*zwanzig*
drei	dreizehn	dreiundzwanzig	*dreißig*
vier	vierzehn	vierundzwanzig	vierzig
fünf	fünfzehn	fünfundzwanzig	fünfzig
sechs	*sechzehn*	sechsundzwanzig	*sechzig*
sieben	*siebzehn*	siebenundzwanzig	*siebzig*
acht	achtzehn	achtundzwanzig	achtzig
neun	neunzehn	neunundzwanzig	neunzig
zehn			(ein)hundert
elf			
zwölf			

Particular attention must be paid to the spelling and pronunciation of the italicized numbers in the table.

136 Present and Past Infinitives

In any sentence containing an infinitive, there is always a time relation between this infinitive and the inflected verb. Consider the sentences

| Er scheint zu schlafen. | He seems to be asleep. |
| Er schien zu schlafen. | He seemed to be asleep. |

Clearly the inflected verbs (**scheint** and **schien**) and the infinitive (**schlafen**) refer to the same time.

If the infinitives, compared to the time of the inflected verb, refer to the same time, they are called present infinitives, *even if* (as in **er schien zu schlafen**) both the inflected verb and the infinitive refer to past time compared to the moment of speaking. Up to now, only such present infinitives have been used in this book.

The situation is quite different in sentences such as

Er scheint gut geschlafen zu haben.
He seems to have slept well.

Er behauptet, General gewesen zu sein.
He claims to have been a general.

Here the infinitives **geschlafen zu haben** (to have slept) and **gewesen zu sein** (to have been) refer to a point in time which precedes the time of the inflected verb. The compound infinitives used in such cases are called past infinitives.

In German past infinitives, the participle (**geschlafen; gewesen**) precedes the infinitive of the auxiliary, which is always either **haben** or **sein**. The **zu** stands between the participle and **sein** or **haben. Zu** is, of course, not used after modals.

PRESENT INFINITIVE	PAST INFINITIVE
haben	gehabt (zu) haben
sein	gewesen (zu) sein
essen	gegessen (zu) haben
schlafen	geschlafen (zu) haben
lieben	geliebt (zu) haben
ausgehen	ausgegangen (zu) sein
abfahren	abgefahren (zu) sein
kennenlernen	kennengelernt (zu) haben
glücklich sein	glücklich gewesen (zu) sein.

To some extent, the use of present and past infinitives in German is parallel to their use in English:

Wer ist denn dagegen?	Who is against it?
Meyer scheint dagegen zu sein.	Meyer seems to be against it.
Wer war denn dagegen?	Who was against it?
Myer scheint dagegen gewesen zu sein.	Meyer seems to have been against it.

However, this parallelism almost evaporates when it comes to German modals (see **138**).

137 The Subjective Use of Modals

In such sentences as

Alle Menschen müssen sterben.	All humans must die.
Ich muß morgen arbeiten.	I must (have to) work tomorrow.

both English *must* and German **müssen** express an unavoidable necessity. It is important to point out that this necessity exists for the grammatical subject (which is sometimes the speaker himself). The speaker, in such cases, reports in an objective way what exists in the world of facts and objects. He is using the modals *must* and **müssen** "objectively."

The situation is quite different in sentences like

See the smoke coming out of the Meyers' chimney?
They must be home!

Meyer fährt jetzt einen Mercedes 300.
Er muß Geld haben.

The *must* and the **muß** in these sentences do not mean that the Meyers are compelled to be at home or that Herr Meyer is compelled to have money. Rather, the modal expresses inferences: the speaker has analyzed the visible facts and arrived at an unavoidable conclusion. The *must* and the **muß** express the speaker's subjective judgment. He is now using the modal "subjectively."

In spite of the fact that the subjective use of **müssen** is usually parallel to the use of English *must*, we have until now carefully avoided the subjective use of the German modals. For very good reasons. First of all, German modals, when used subjectively, are frequently followed by a past infinitive, and past infinitives are used for the first time in this unit. Second, some of the German modals have subjective meanings which do not occur in English. We shall therefore have to look systematically into the subjective use of all the German modals.

müssen

When used subjectively, **müssen** occurs only in the present and past tenses. This subjective use, as stated above, is almost completely parallel to the use of English *must*. Almost, not quite.

1. **Müssen** has a subjective past indicative **er mußte** which corresponds to *he had to.*

> **Ich hörte sofort, daß Herr Brandt Amerikaner sein mußte, denn er sagte: „Morgen ich kann nicht kommen, weil ich muß fahren nach Berlin."**
> I heard immediately that Mr. Brandt had to be an American, for he said, "I can't come tomorrow, because I have to go to Berlin."

2. The present indicative

> **Er muß schon angekommen sein.**
> He must have arrived by now.

can be changed to the subjunctive to express the notion that, though the inference *He must have arrived* is logical, it is nevertheless uncertain. The use of **eigentlich** underscores the uncertainty of the inference:

> **Er müßte eigentlich schon angekommen sein.**
> He really ought to have arrived by now.

This subjunctive **müßte** is very frequent in German and has no structural parallel in English.

3. The past infinitive occurs with both the objective and the subjective use of **müssen.**

OBJECTIVE

> **Wer Medizin studieren will, muß Latein gelernt haben.**
> Whoever wants to enter medical school, must have learned Latin.

This sentence expresses an objective *present* necessity which compels the grammatical subject, not to take Latin, but to have taken Latin by the time he wants to enter a medical school.

SUBJECTIVE

The Meyers don't answer the doorbell; I notice that there is no longer any furniture in the living room and that the house is for sale. I say:

> **Sie müssen umgezogen sein.**
> They must have moved.

Nobody compelled the Meyers to move, but the observable physical facts compel the speaker to assume *now* (present tense) that they have moved.

**Eine Reise um die Welt
muß nicht ein Vermögen kosten PAN AM
und nicht ewig dauern.**

wollen

When used subjectively, **wollen** assumes the meaning *to claim:*

> **Er will Arzt sein und in Wien studiert haben.**
> He claims to be a doctor and to have studied in Vienna.

It is only context, not structure, that will show whether **wollen** is used subjectively or objectively. Thus

> **Sie wollen alle dabei gewesen sein**

may mean, subjectively,

> They all claim to have been there.

It may also mean, objectively,

> They all want to be able to say, "I was there."

sollen

The basic meaning of **sollen** can be defined as "a plan of operation not made by the grammatical subject."

> **Er soll morgen nach Berlin fahren.**
> He is supposed to go to Berlin tomorrow.
> **Die Brücke soll nächstes Jahr fertig sein.**
> The bridge is supposed to be finished by next year.

The sentences quoted denote a plan of operation and therefore may contain a connotation of hearsay:

> I understand that he is going to Berlin tomorrow.
> I have heard that the bridge is to be finished by next year.

This suggestion of hearsay—both for German **sollen** and for English *to be supposed to*—may become the predominant meaning:

> **Meyer soll viel Geld haben.**
> Meyer is supposed to have a lot of money.
> (It is common gossip that he has a lot of money.)
> **Meyer soll früher viel Geld gehabt haben.**
> Meyer is said to have had a lot of money.

On the other hand, since plans of operation are often made by authorities, **sollen** frequently expresses obligation.

> **Wir sollen um elf zu Hause sein.**
> We are to be home at eleven.

NOTE: The present subjunctive **sollte** is frequently found with the same meaning of *ought to* as the present subjunctive **müßte**, especially when accompanied by **eigentlich.**

> **Er sollte eigentlich schon angekommen sein.**
> He really ought to have arrived by now.

können

When used objectively, **können** expresses the ability of the grammatical subject to do something.

> **Können Sie schwimmen?**
> Can you swim?
> (Are you able to swim?)
> **Leider konnte sie nicht schwimmen.**
> Unfortunately she couldn't (wasn't able to) swim.

When used subjectively, **können** expresses a possibility inferred by the speaker on the basis of observable facts. English expresses such inferred possibility by using *can* or *may* in the present and by using *could* or *might* in the past or in the subjunctive.

> **Das kann nicht Frau Müller sein; die ist doch in München.**
> That can't be Mrs. Müller; she's in Munich, you know.
> **Vielleicht ist er in München; er kann aber auch in Berlin sein.**
> Perhaps he is in Munich; but, of course, he may also be in Berlin.
> **Sie war noch so jung; sie konnte höchstens siebzehn sein.**
> She was so young; she could have been seventeen at the most.

The subjunctive is used to express an inference which is not so certain.

> **Es könnte Erich gewesen sein.**
> It might have been Erich.

dürfen

Of the six modals, **dürfen** has the lowest frequency. When used objectively, it expresses the idea that the grammatical subject has been given permission. Since nobody wants to be bossy or be bossed around, **dürfen**, like **erlauben,** is not used very often. Even a child prefers

> **Kann ich heute abend ins Kino gehen?**

to the obedient

> **Darf ich heute abend ins Kino gehen?**

The real "live" use of **dürfen** therefore tends to be restricted to situations where no person giving permission is involved:

Darf man hier rauchen?	Is smoking permitted here?
Meine Damen und Herren, ich darf wohl annehmen, daß Sie alle wissen, wer Ingelheim ist.	Ladies and gentlemen, I suppose I may assume that you all know who Ingelheim is.

or where **dürfen** really means "it would be wise":

Sie dürfen abends keinen Kaffee mehr trinken.	You mustn't drink coffee at night any more.
Man darf nicht vergessen, daß Ingelheim jahrelang in Norwegen gewesen ist.	One mustn't forget that Ingelheim was in Norway for years.

The only subjective meaning of **dürfen** is the use of the subjunctive **dürfte** to express probability:

Erika dürfte jetzt schon in Frankfurt sein.	Erika is probably already in Frankfurt by now.

mögen

Up to this point, we have used only the forms **ich möchte, du möchtest,** etc. But although these **möchte**-forms are the ones used most frequently, **mögen,** like the other modals, has a complete set of forms:

PRESENT INDICATIVE	PRESENT SUBJUNCTIVE
ich mag	ich möchte
du magst	du möchtest
er mag	er möchte
wir mögen	wir möchten
ihr mögt	ihr möchtet
sie mögen	sie möchten

PAST INDICATIVE	PAST SUBJUNCTIVE
ich mochte	Ich hätte ... (infinitive) mögen
du mochtest	du hättest ” ”
er mochte	er hätte ” ”
wir mochten	wir hätten ” ”
ihr mochtet	ihr hättet ” ”
sie mochten	sie hätten ” ”

PERFECT WITH DEPENDENT INFINITIVE	PERFECT WITHOUT INFINITIVE
ich habe ... mögen	ich habe gemocht
du hast ... mögen	du hast gemocht
etc.	etc.

The verb **mögen** can be used without a following infinitive. If so used, it means *to like* and takes an accusative object:

Sie mag ihn nicht.	She doesn't like him.
Wir mögen kein Schweinefleisch.	We don't like pork.
Wir mochten ihn nicht.	We did not like him.
Ich habe sie nie gemocht.	I never liked her.

When used as a modal—that is, with a dependent infinitive, **mögen** has an objective and a subjective meaning.

Used objectively, **mögen** plus infinitive expresses the fact that the grammatical subject has a desire. This use, for all practical purposes, is restricted to the **möchte**-forms—that is, to the present subjunctive (*would like*). Occasionally you will find the past subjunctive **hätte** ... (infinitive) **mögen** (*would have liked*) in your reading. In colloquial German, **hätte mögen** is replaced by **hätte gerne (am liebsten) getan**.

„Oskar hätte ihn anschreien mögen." (Grass)	Oscar would have liked to shout at him.
Oskar hätte ihn am liebsten angeschrien.	
„Ich bin ein alter Arzt und möchte niemandem Böses getan haben." (Dürrenmatt)	I am an old doctor and I would like to be sure that I have not done any harm to anybody.

When used subjectively, as in **Das mag sein** (*That may be*), **mögen** means *may* and denotes that the speaker presents his statement with the reservation that what he reports "may be" the case. As a matter of fact, **Mag sein!**, used as a sentence by itself, does mean *Maybe!*

This subjective use of **mögen** occurs quite frequently in modern literature. The present indicative **mag** denotes a present possibility, and **mochte**, the past indicative, a past possibility. The use of the past infinitive is frequent. The following examples are taken from modern literature:

Man mag es nicht glauben wollen.	You may not want to believe it.
Er sang den Text, wie er es auf dem Priesterseminar gelernt haben mochte.	He sang the text as he had probably learned it (might have learned it) in the seminary.
Was mochte passiert sein?	What could possibly have happened?
Das mag einer der Punkte gewesen sein.	That may have been one of the points.
Eineinhalb Jahre alt mag ich gewesen sein.	I was probably (possibly) a year and a half old.
Dann begann ich zu verstehen, wo ich war, und zu überlegen, was mit mir geschehen sein mochte.	Then I began to understand where I was and to think about what might have happened to me.
Sie mögen gedacht haben, ich bin ein Staatssekretär.	Maybe they thought that I was a secretary of state.
Das mochte wirklich Zufall gewesen sein.	Perhaps that was really a coincidence.
Und die Gäste des Cafés mögen bemerkt haben, wer da saß.	And the guests of the café probably noticed who was sitting there.
Er mag geglaubt haben, ich verstände ihn.	He may have thought that I understood him.

138 The Use of Past Infinitives after Modals

You are by now familiar with such sentences as

Meyer konnte fliehen, aber er wollte nicht.
Meyer could (was able to) escape, but he didn't want to (wouldn't).

By using the past-tense forms **konnte** and *could* and the present infinitives **fliehen** and *escape*—infinitives that express simultaneity, just as in **Er schien zu schlafen**—both English and German refer to a chance in the past to do something (to escape) while this chance was good. The chance involved can be defined as "a past chance for somebody to do something."

The parallelism between

Er konnte fliehen

and

He could escape

disappears if the sentence above is expressed as a contrary-to-fact condition:

Er hätte fliehen können, wenn er gewollt hätte.
He could have escaped if he had wanted to.

Note that

Er konnte	fliehen		Er hätte	fliehen	können

becomes

He could	escape		He could	have escaped

In German, the past indicative **konnte** is replaced by the past subjunctive **hätte können** while the present infinitive **fliehen** is retained; English, on the other hand, changes from the present infinitive *escape* to the past infinitive *have escaped* (and, to be technical about it, the *could* in the first sentence, which is a past indicative, is changed to a *had : had* modal present subjunctive *could* in the second sentence.)

Since the chance involved in the sentence

Er hätte fliehen können, wenn er gewollt hätte

must still be defined as "a past chance for somebody to do something," the use of the past infinitive *have escaped* in English seems utterly illogical to a German; and your German teacher might point out with glee that

He could	have escaped

can be replaced by the "more logical"

He would have been able to	escape

which actually shows a present infinitive.

For the English-speaking student, the pattern *could have escaped* constitutes a serious source of interference. He is always tempted to say

Er könnte	**geflohen sein.**

This is a perfectly good German sentence without a single grammatical mistake, but, unfortunately, it doesn't mean *He would have been able to flee*, although it may mean—and we are not being facetious—*He could have fled*. The fact is that *could have fled* is an ambiguous phrase and can refer to two entirely different situations.

Situation A. Imagine the following news item: "The police are still looking for the elegantly dressed young woman who shot the Prime Minister last night. Of course, she *could* conceivably *have fled* the country, but since all airports were alerted immediately, it is assumed that she is still in the country." German, in this situation, would use a structural pattern parallel to English:

> **Sie könnte   geflohen sein**

> She could (might)   have fled

The subjunctives **könnte,** *could* (*might*)—all used subjectively—suggest that the possibility (a *present* possibility) is slim and almost imaginary. The past infinitives are used, because the chance involved must here be defined as "a chance that somebody has already done something." The sentences mean "It is at present considered unlikely that the assassin has fled."

The subjunctive sentences
> **Sie könnte geflohen sein**
> She might have fled

belong to the present indicative sentences
> **Sie kann geflohen sein**
> She may have fled.

In all four of these sentences, the modals are used subjectively; that is, they express an inference.

The difference between the subjunctive and the indicative is mainly a difference in degree, not in meaning. **Kann** and *may* are more positive than **könnte** and *might*.

Situation B. The news item above could have read: "The young lady who shot the Prime Minister was arrested as she tried to board a small private plane. If the police had not been tipped off, she could have fled the country."

Here we are back to the past chance to do something, to the objective use of **können,** and to the difference between the past indicative

Sie konnte   fliehen

She could (was able to)   escape

and the past subjunctive

Sie hätte   fliehen   können

She could   have escaped

which was discussed above.

You will now realize, we hope, that you must learn to distinguish between a chance to do something and a chance that somebody has done something. Subjunctive sentences involving modals are apt to confuse you unless you clearly understand the following table:

CHANCE TO DO SOMETHING

INDICATIVE   SUBJUNCTIVE (irreality)

Sie konnte   fliehen   **Sie hätte   fliehen   können**

CHANCE THAT SOMEBODY HAS DONE SOMETHING

INDICATIVE   SUBJUNCTIVE (uncertainty)

Sie kann   geflohen sein   **Sie könnte   geflohen sein**

NOTE: The same difference between English and German can also be observed in sentences with **sollen** and **müssen.**

Ich hätte nicht so viel Kaffee   trinken   sollen.

I should not   have drunk   so much coffee.

Ich hätte eigentlich schon gestern in Berlin sein **müssen.**

I actually should have been in Berlin yesterday.

139 The Reflexive Pronoun **sich**

Very often the subject and the object of a verb are one and the same
person or thing:

> He hated himself.
> History never repeats itself.
> I bought myself a car.

In all these cases, English uses reflexive pronouns for the object. In a
way, this is linguistic luxury. "I bought me a car," though considered substandard, is just as clear as "I bought myself a car." German gets along
without reflexive pronouns for all first and second persons:

Ich habe mich gebadet.	**Ich kaufe mir ein Auto.**
Du hast dich gebadet.	**Du kaufst dir ein Auto.**
Wir haben uns gebadet.	**Wir kaufen uns ein Auto.**
Ihr habt euch gebadet.	**Ihr kauft euch ein Auto.**

The situation is different in all third persons. Whereas the difference
between *me* and *myself* is luxury, the difference between *him* and *himself*
may be the difference between murder and suicide: *he killed him; he
killed himself.*

German has only the one reflexive pronoun **sich** for all third-person cases.
This **sich** serves both as a dative and as an accusative, both as a singular
and as a plural.

Er hat sie vergiftet.	He poisoned her.
Sie hat ihn vergiftet.	She poisoned him.
Er hat sich vergiftet.	He poisoned himself.
Sie hat sich vergiftet.	She poisoned herself.
Sie haben sich vergiftet.	They poisoned themselves.
Er hat ihr ein Auto gekauft.	He bought her a car.
Sie hat ihm ein Auto gekauft.	She bought him a car.
Er hat sich ein Auto gekauft.	He bought himself a car.
Sie hat sich ein Auto gekauft.	She bought herself a car.
Sie haben sich ein Auto gekauft.	They bought themselves a car.

140 Contrary-to-Fact Conditions without **wenn**

In contrary-to-fact conditions, the conjunction **wenn** may be omitted. In contemporary German, and particularly in the spoken language, this pattern occurs almost exclusively in past time.

> **Wenn Ingelheim nicht Soldat gewesen wäre, hätte er keine Kriegs-romane schreiben können.**

> **Wäre Ingelheim nicht Soldat gewesen, dann hätte er keine Kriegs-romane schreiben können.**

The clause with the omitted **wenn** always shows verb-first position and usually precedes the conclusion. The conclusion is usually introduced by **dann** or **so**.

If the condition stands alone to express a wish or desire, the **wenn** can also be omitted, but again primarily in past time.

> **Wenn er mir nur geschrieben hätte!**
> **Hätte er mir doch nur geschrieben!**

NOTE: These wishful **wenn**-clauses are independent syntactical units and almost always contain a **nur** or **doch nur** or a **wenigstens**. Like all sentence adverbs, this **nur** or **wenigstens** shifts position as follows: The elements preceding *nur, doch nur,* or *wenigstens* are unstressed and include all those things which have already been talked about; the elements following *nur, doch nur,* or *wenigstens* are all news items.

> **Ich wollte ja studieren. Wenn ich nur das Geld dazu gehabt hätte!**
> **Jetzt habe ich das Geld. Wenn ich das Geld nur früher gehabt hätte!**

141 ja

The most obvious use of **ja**, of course, is to answer a question. Frequently, however, it is used in the same position and with the same affirmative function, even if there is no question or previous conversation. Similar to English *well*, this **ja** can precede any reaction.

> **Ja, das ist aber schön, daß ihr doch noch gekommen seid.**
> Well, how nice that you came after all.

> **Ja, das habe ich nicht erwartet.**
> Well, I didn't expect *that*.

> **Ja, was machen wir denn jetzt?**
> Well, what are we going to do now?

As an unstressed sentence adverb, **ja** occurs very frequently. It has two functions:

1. The speaker wants to express the idea that the facts asserted are well known and accepted by both speaker and listener.

> **Bei uns regnet es im Sommer ja sehr oft.**
> As you know, we have lots of rain during the summer.

> **Wir müssen ja alle einmal sterben.**
> We've all got to die, you know.

2. In sentences spoken with emphatic stress, **ja** heightens the emotional flavor.

> **Das ist ja wunderbar.**
> **Das ist ja himmlisch.**
> **Ich komme ja schon.**
> **Du rauchst ja schon wieder zu viel.**
> **Ich bin ja so glücklich.**
> **Das ist ja nicht möglich.**
> **Das ist ja nicht zu glauben.**

When used as a sentence adverb, **ja** follows items of no news value and precedes items with news value, unless the verb itself is stressed.

142 Adverbs in **-erweise**

These sentence adverbs are formed from adjectives and express a judgment.

glücklicherweise	fortunately, it is fortunate that
möglicherweise	possibly, it is possible that
normalerweise	normally, as a rule, it is normal that

143 Adverbs in **-ens**

The following derivatives are frequently used:

frühstens	at the earliest
spätestens	at the latest
höchstens	at most
meistens	in most cases, mostly
nächstens	in the near future

EXERCISES

A. Without changing word order, negate the following sentences by using **nicht** in at least two different positions.

1. Ich möchte mit Rosemarie ins Theater gehen.
2. Meyer hat lange arbeiten können.
3. Hans ist lange in Berlin gewesen.
4. Ich bin oft ins Kino gegangen.
5. Du kannst doch mit diesem Wagen nach Italien fahren.
6. Ich kann aber auf dem Sofa schlafen.
7. Sie wollte aber den Meyer heiraten.
8. Ich habe lange mit dem Direktor sprechen können.

SEE LAB
EXERCISES
9.1, 9.2

(p. 631)

B. Using the **nicht A, sondern B** pattern, combine the following pairs of sentences.

> Wir fahren nicht im Juli nach Berlin. Wir fahren im August.
> (a) Wir fahren nicht im Juli, sondern im August nach Berlin.
> (b) Wir fahren nicht im Juli nach Berlin, sondern im August.

1. Ich habe nicht meine Mutter besucht. Ich habe meinen Vater besucht.
2. Er hat nicht acht Stunden gearbeitet. Er hat nur zwei Stunden gearbeitet.
3. Gestern abend hat Erich keinen Wein getrunken. Er hat nur Bier getrunken.
4. Er hat mir kein Buch geschenkt. Er hat mir einen Hut geschenkt.

SEE LAB
EXERCISES
9.3

(p. 632)

C. (a) Using the pattern

> ein mal zwei ist zwei
> zwei mal zwei ist vier, etc.

SEE LAB
EXERCISES
9.4, 9.5

(p. 632)

go through the multiplication table up to 10.

(b) Using the pattern

> hundert durch zehn ist zehn
> neunzig durch zehn ist neun, etc.

go through the table from 10 to 2.

(c) Read and write down the following:

1, 2, 3, 7, 11, 13, 17, 19, 23, 31, 37, 41, 43, 47, 53, 59, 61, 67, 71, 73, 79, 83, 87, 89, 93, 97.

D. In the following ten sentences, change the present infinitives to past infinitives.

> **Maria muß schon aufstehen.**
> **Maria muß schon aufgestanden sein.**

1. Meyer muß nach Berlin fahren.
2. Er scheint sehr freundlich zu sein.
3. Mein Vater scheint sehr viel von ihm zu halten.
4. Sie kann doch nicht schon wieder spazierengehen.
5. Ihr Mann muß sehr viel Geld verdienen.
6. Er muß schon um sechs Uhr hier sein.
7. Inge scheint Englisch zu lernen.
8. Das kann er ihr doch nicht sagen.
9. Er muß den Brief heute bekommen.
10. Man braucht nicht zu studieren, um hier arbeiten zu können.

E. Change the following ten sentences, all containing objective modals, from present indicative to present subjunctive and add **eigentlich** in the place indicated by /. (**Eigentlich** follows the pronouns and elements of no news value.) Then translate these sentences into English.

1. Ich soll / um sechs Uhr zu Hause sein.
2. Hans muß / hierbleiben.
3. Wir müssen heute abend / schon wieder ausgehen.
4. Wir können / auch einmal ins Theater gehen.
5. Ich kann ja / auch mit *Inge* spazierengehen.
6. Ich muß / einmal mit ihm reden.
7. Ihr sollt / Russisch lernen.
8. Du kannst mir / eine Tasse Kaffee machen.
9. Ich soll / morgen in Berlin sein.
10. Ich darf / keinen Wein trinken.

F. Change the following ten sentences to the past.

SEE LAB EXERCISE 9.6 (p. 632)

1. Ich kann es ihm noch nicht sagen.
2. Wir müssen auch schwer arbeiten.
3. Ich darf ihn nie wieder besuchen.
4. Ich will nie wieder nach Berlin fahren.
5. Und trotzdem muß ich immer wieder freundlich zu ihr sein.
6. Ich kann dich heute leider nicht anrufen.
7. Meine Frau darf nie an die Nordsee fahren.
8. Wir wollen euch ja schon lange einmal besuchen.
9. Wir können den Redner einfach nicht verstehen.
10. Ich brauche ihn nie um etwas zu bitten.

G. The following sentences represent frequently used modal patterns. Study them carefully. Then put the two sentences below through the same six modal patterns (see **137**).

(a) Er ist Arzt, muß also sehen, daß Ingelheim keine Hepatitis hat.
       He is a doctor; he must see that Ingelheim doesn't have hepatitis.

(b) Er ist Arzt, müßte also eigentlich sehen, daß Ingelheim keine Hepatitis hat.
       He is a doctor; he ought to see that Ingelheim doesn't have Hepatitis.

(c) Er ist Arzt, muß also gesehen haben, daß Ingelheim keine Hepatitis hatte.
       He is a doctor; he must have seen that Ingelheim didn't have hepatitis.

(d) Er ist Arzt, müßte also eigentlich gesehen haben, daß Ingelheim keine Hepatitis hatte.
       He is a doctor; he ought to have seen that Ingelheim didn't have hepatitis.

(e) Er war Arzt, mußte also sehen, daß Ingelheim keine Hepatitis hatte.
       He was a doctor; he had to see that Ingelheim didn't have hepatitis.

(f) Er war Arzt, hätte also eigentlich sehen müssen, daß Ingelheim keine Hepatitis hatte.
       He was a doctor; he ought to have seen that Ingelheim didn't have hepatitis.

1. Sein Vater ist Psychologe; er muß also wisssen, daß sein Sohn nicht intelligent ist.
2. Es ist elf Uhr; er kann schon im Büro sein.

H. Change the following sentences in two ways: (a) Change the modal to the perfect; (b) keep the modal in the present and change the infinitive to a past infinitive. Then translate the two resulting sentences so as to show the difference in meaning.

> **Er soll um acht Uhr zu Hause sein.**
>
> (a) **Er hat um acht Uhr zu Hause sein sollen.**
>   He had to be at home at eight.
>
> (b) **Er soll um acht Uhr zu Hause gewesen sein.**
>   He is said to have been at home at eight.

1. Er kann nicht in Berlin arbeiten.
2. Ingelheim muß Soldat werden.
3. Ingeborg muß heiraten.
4. Meyer will ein Haus an der Riviera kaufen.
5. Ingelheim soll Arabisch lernen.

SEE LAB
EXERCISE
9.7

(p. 632)

I. By using the proper forms of modals, express in one sentence each of the following ideas:

1. There is a rumor that five gold pieces have disappeared.
2. Ingelheim claims that he fought in Africa.
3. I came to the conclusion that he was living in Berlin.
4. I have arrived at the conclusion that he has been in America.
5. You should have gone to Berlin two years ago.
6. There was a rumor that she had gone to Berlin.

7. It is possible that he is still here.
8. It is not possible that he was in Berlin.
9. It has never been possible for him to go to Berlin.
10. He tries to give the impression that he was a friend of my father.

J. Change the following ten sentences from the past indicative to the past subjunctive. Add **eigentlich** in the place indicated by /.

> **Ich mußte gestern nach Berlin fahren.**
> **Ich hätte gestern eigentlich nach Berlin fahren müssen.**

1. Ich sollte gestern / meine Mutter besuchen.
2. Ich durfte es Ihnen / nicht sagen.
3. Ich brauchte / gar nichts zu sagen.
4. Ich konnte damals / auch nach Casablanca fliegen.
5. Mir konntest du das ja / erzählen.
6. Damals sollte ich / den Meyer heiraten.
7. Er mußte / schon lange zu Hause sein.
8. Sie durfte / nicht an die Nordsee fahren.
9. Er mußte / ins Krankenhaus.
10. Du brauchtest / nicht bei Nacht nach München zu fahren.

K. In the following sentences, change the modals from indicative to subjunctive. Add **eigentlich** when appropriate.

SEE LAB EXERCISES 9.8–9.14 (p. 632)

1. Er kann, wenn er will.
2. Ich kann auch mitgehen.
3. Ich muß auch einmal nach Italien fahren.
4. Sie sollen nicht so viel rauchen.
5. Sein Sohn sollte in Heidelberg studieren.
6. Sie war krank und mußte im Bett bleiben.
7. Ich darf keinen Kaffee trinken.
8. Damals hatte ich viel Geld; wenn ich wollte, konnte ich jedes Jahr an die Riviera fahren.
9. Wenn Tante Amalie ins Museum gehen wollte, mußte ich natürlich mitgehen.

L. The following sentences contain a dependent clause introduced by **weil.** By changing the **weil**-clause, first into a conditional clause with **wenn** and then without **wenn,** transform the sentences into contrary-to-fact conditions. Start all sentences with the conditional clause.

> **Weil er krank war, konnte er nicht arbeiten.**
> (a) **Wenn er nicht krank gewesen wäre, hätte er arbeiten können.**
> (b) **Wäre er nicht krank gewesen, dann hätte er arbeiten können.**

1. Weil ich nicht so viel Geld hatte wie Meyer, konnte ich nicht an der Riviera wohnen.
2. Weil es mir in Hamburg zu kalt war, bin ich nach Afrika gefahren.
3. Er kam spät nach Hause, weil er ins Kino gegangen war.
4. Er hat sie geheiratet, weil sie Geld hatte.
5. Weil das Essen so schlecht war, fuhren wir nach Hause.
6. Weil ich nie Soldat gewesen bin, kann ich natürlich keine Kriegsromane schreiben.
7. Weil er mich nicht richtig verstanden hat, hat er wahrscheinlich einen Fehler gemacht.
8. Weil Ingelheim keine Hepatitis hatte, mußte er wieder Soldat werden.

M. Change the following statements to wishes contrary to fact, using either **doch nur** or **doch nur nicht** and starting with **wenn** and then without **wenn**. (Like **eigentlich, doch nur** follows the pronouns and elements of no news value.)

> **Er ist nach Italien gefahren.**
> (a) **Wenn er doch nur nicht nach Italien gefahren wäre.**
> (b) **Wäre er doch nur nicht nach Italien gefahren.**

1. Er kam so oft.
2. Er hat mir nicht geschrieben, daß er Geld braucht.
3. Sie hat mir gesagt, daß sie Thusnelda heißt.
4. Die Desdemona konnte ich leider nicht spielen.
5. Ich habe nicht gewußt, daß du auch in Berlin warst.
6. Wir sind *gestern* abend ins Theater gegangen.
7. Ich habe zu viel Kaffee getrunken.
8. Schwimmen hatte sie leider nie gelernt.

SEE LAB
EXERCISE
9.15

(p. 632)

N. Express in German:

1. Yes, I know them. I got to know them in Mainz before the war.
2. He must have waited for me for three hours.
3. He had to wait for me for three hours.
4. He can't have slept long. I called him up at seven o'clock, but I couldn't reach him any more.
5. I won't drive back until tomorrow; I wanted to drive home this morning already, but then Tante Amalie invited me to supper (*Abendessen*).
6. He doesn't seem to be at home. Where can he be? He can't have gone to the movies yet.
7. You should have sent the letter to me immediately.
8. Had he sent the letter to me, I could have answered him immediately.
9. His letter must have arrived when I had already gone to Munich.
10. What you claim to have experienced cannot have happened.
11. He has always wanted to go to Africa.
12. He cannot have been in Africa.
13. Erich must have recognized me.

14. Erika seems to have arrived already.
15. I must have slept a few hours when the phone rang.
16. If I didn't *have* to go out tonight, I would rather stay home in this rain.
17. I don't think much of him.
18. I often think of you.
19. You really ought not to act as if you knew everything. (Use **so** in front of **tun**)
20. He ought to have arrived an hour ago.
21. Dr. Schmidt was at the Meyers' too; you must have met him there.
22. It could not have been Erich, for I knew that Erich had gone to the airport to pick up Ingelheim.
23. Could I have another cup of coffee, please?
24. Could you work in the garden yesterday?
25. Of course we could have gone to the movies, but we didn't want to.
26. She claims to be thirty; she looks as if she were thirty-five; but she is said to be forty.
27. If you should see Hans tomorrow, would you please tell him that I don't want to work this weekend.
28. She may have thought that Erich wanted to help her.

O. Write a conversation between two students, Doris Weise and Günter Hartmann, using the following outline:

Doris has just seen Professor Niemann to talk to him about a term paper she has just written for his seminar. Günter wants to know what Professor Niemann told her; he has heard that Niemann is very nice and likes to talk to students. But Doris doesn't agree with him; she was so nervous that she trembled when she talked to Niemann. It turns out, however, that her paper was really very good, and she didn't need to be afraid at all. Günter congratulates her and suggests that they go and have a cup of coffee. Doris thinks that she ought to go to Professor Neuhof's lecture, but Günter thinks that she can easily get somebody else's lecture notes; after all, that lecture isn't all that interesting. Doris agrees, and Günter uses the occasion to invite her to a party that he and some friends are giving the following week.

VOCABULARY

allerdings however
der Anglist', –en anglicist
die Ankunft arrival
aufschreiben to write down, note
der August' August
behaupten to maintain, claim
bemerken to notice, mention, note, say

der Berg, –e mountain
besonders especially
binden to bind, tie
braun brown
der Buchstabe, –n letter (of the alphabet)
der Donnerstag, –e Thursday
der Einfluß, die Einflüsse influence

entweder ... oder either ... or
weder ... noch neither ... nor
fertig ready, complete
fest firm(ly)
das Feuer, – fire
das Feuerwerk, –e fireworks
fliehen to escape, flee
freiwillig voluntary

froh glad, gay
frühstens at the earliest
genau exact(ly)
das Gebäude, – building
  das Hauptgebäude, – main building
glücklicherweise fortunately, happily
heizen to heat
  die Heizung heating system, radiator
  die Zentralheizung central heating
der Himmel heaven, sky
  himmlisch heavenly
höchstens at the most
der Ingenieur', –e engineer
irgendwo somewhere
jedoch however
der Juli July
der Kellner, – waiter
  der Oberkellner, – head-waiter
  Herr Ober (usual way of addressing a waiter)
das Kleid, –er dress
der Kreis, –e circle
kriegen (*colloquial*) = **bekommen** to get
das Land, ̈er the land, country
lehren to teach
  der Lehrer, – teacher

leicht easy, light (in weight)
die Meinung, –en opinion
meistens usually, mostly
merken to notice
das Mittagessen, – dinner (noon meal, the main meal in Germany)
möglicherweise possibly
der Mond, –e moon
der Mund mouth
  mündlich oral
Mutti Mom, Mommy
nächstens in the near future
der Name, –n name
  der Vorname, –n first name
  der Nachname, –n last name
normalerweise normally
Platz nehmen to sit down, have a seat
die Post mail; post office
der Preis, –e price; prize
der Punkt, –e point; period (in punctuation)
der Ring, –e ring
rollen to roll
schade too bad
schieben to push, shove
das Schwein, –e pig
  das Schweinefleisch (*no pl.*) pork
  das Fleisch (*no pl.*) meat

senden to send; broadcast
  der Sender, – sender; broadcasting station
sondern (**nicht A, sondern B**) but (not A but B)
spätestens at the latest
teilen to divide
  geteilt durch divided by
überlegen (**sich**) to think about, meditate
überset'zen to translate
  die Überset'zung, –en translation
umziehen to move (change residence)
der Unsinn nonsense
verdienen to earn, deserve
vergiften to poison
verkaufen to sell
vorgestern day before yesterday
vorher (*adv.*) before, earlier
vorne (*adv.*) in front
waschen to wash
wenigstens at least
Wien Vienna
wunderbar wonderful, marvelous
die Zeile, –n line (of print, poetry, verse)
der Zufall, ̈e accident, coincidence
  durch Zufall by accident

IRREGULAR VERBS

binden to bind, tie
  band, hat gebunden, er bindet
fliehen to flee, escape
  floh, ist geflohen, er flieht
schieben to push, shove

  schob, hat geschoben, er schiebt
senden to send; broadcast
  sandte, hat gesandt, er sendet
umziehen to move (change

residence)
  zog um, ist umgezogen, er zieht um
waschen to wash
  wusch, hat gewaschen, er wäscht

REVIEW

The sentences in this section represent a systematic review of all possible positions of the German verb.

Verb-First Position

YES-OR-NO QUESTIONS

Bleibst du noch eine Stunde hier?
Holen Sie Ihren Mann am Flughafen ab?
Ist Erich schon abgefahren?
Möchtest du noch eine Tasse Kaffee?

wenn-CLAUSES WITHOUT *wenn*

Hätte ich doch nur ihren Geburtstag nicht vergessen!
Hättest du mich damals doch nur angerufen!
Hätte ich nur mein Geld nicht verloren!
Wäre ich damals nur nicht an der Westfront gewesen!
Wären wir doch nur nach Köln gezogen, dann brauchtest du nicht jeden Tag
    zwei Stunden auf dem Zug zu sitzen.

Verb-Second Position

QUESTIONS

Wie bist du denn auf *den* Gedanken gekommen?
Mit wem warst *du* denn gestern abend im Theater?
Mit wessen Wagen seid ihr denn gefahren?
*Wor*über spricht Prof. Schmidt heute abend?
Mit wem bist du denn *ges*tern abend ausgegangen?

ASSERTIONS

Ingelheim fuhr nach seiner Ankunft in Hamburg nicht sofort ins Hotel.
Ingelheim ist nach seiner Ankunft in Hamburg sofort ins Hotel gefahren.

Sofort nach seiner Ankunft in Hamburg fuhr Ingelheim ins Hotel.
Nach seiner Ankunft in Hamburg wollte Ingelheim sofort ins Hotel fahren.
Ingelheim hätte nach seiner Ankunft sofort ins Hotel fahren sollen.
Ingelheim, der mit der Sechs-Uhr Maschine aus Frankfurt angekommen war,
    fuhr vom Flughafen aus sofort ins Hotel.
Nachdem Ingelheim in Hamburg angekommen war, fuhr er sofort ins Hotel.

VARIANT: SUMMING-UP OF DEPENDENT CLAUSE (THE 1–1A–2 PATTERN)

Daß Erich uns wieder einmal besuchen will, daran glaube ich schon lange nicht
    mehr.
Warum er nicht sofort ins Hotel gefahren ist, das kann ich dir nicht sagen.
Daß die Erika den Meyer geheiratet haben soll, das kann ich nicht glauben.
Wäre er sofort ins Hotel gefahren, dann hätte er mich noch erreicht.
Wenn du nicht gekommen wärst, dann hätte ich heute abend bestimmt ange-
    rufen.
Hätte er mich vom Flugplatz aus angerufen, so hätte ich ihn natürlich abge-
    holt.
Wer glaubt, was der Meyer behauptet, der muß verrückt sein.
Was nicht ist, das kann noch werden.

Verb-Last Position

IN NORMAL DEPENDENT CLAUSES

Obwohl es gestern den ganzen Tag regnete, haben wir gearbeitet.
Er erzählte mir, daß seine Eltern sehr erstaunt gewesen wären.
Ich weiß, daß Ingrid gut kochen kann.
Er ging nicht mit, weil er sich endlich einmal ausschlafen wollte.
Hans war noch nicht da, als Erich in Berlin ankam.

VARIANT: *als ob—als*

Er sah aus, als ob er schliefe.
Er sah aus, als schliefe er.
Er tat, als ob er auf mich gewartet hätte.
Er tat, als hätte er auf mich gewartet.

VARIANT: DEPENDENT CLAUSE WITH DOUBLE INFINITIVE

Hans sagte, daß er den ganzen Tag hätte arbeiten müssen.
Erika wäre sicher sehr unglücklich gewesen, wenn sie nicht hätte mit nach
    Deutschland fahren können.
Er sagte, daß er eigentlich schon am Freitag hätte nach Hause fahren wollen.

The End Field

Er kann doch nicht in die Stadt gefahren sein bei diesem Regen.
Das Bier ist wirklich gut hier in München.
Ich habe ihn leider nicht länger sehen können als eine Stunde.
Mein Vater hat Deutschland viel besser gekannt als ich.
Meyers sind *doch* nicht nach Italien gefahren, sondern in die Schweiz.
Das weiß doch jeder, daß das Bier gut ist hier in München.
Du weißt doch, daß sie viel intelligenter ist als er.

REVIEW EXERCISE

Connect the following pairs of sentences by means of the words in parentheses. Which of the connecting words are adverbs, which are coordinating conjunctions, and which are subordinating conjunctions?

1. Ich habe nichts davon gewußt. Er hat mir nicht geschrieben. (weil)
2. Er stand lange vor der Tür. Er klopfte endlich an. (dann)
3. Er wollte nicht mit Prof. Müller sprechen. Er hatte Angst vor ihm. (denn)
4. Er war krank. Ich konnte ihn nicht besuchen. (daher)
5. Ich konnte ihn nicht besuchen. Er war krank. (da)
6. Ich rief von Paris aus an. Erich sollte nicht wissen, daß ich in Afrika gewesen war. (weil)
7. Er fuhr sofort nach Hamburg. Er hatte meinen Brief bekommen. (nachdem)
8. Sollen wir ins Kino gehen? Sollen wir zu Hause bleiben? (oder)
9. Tante Amalie kommt morgen. Wir gehen bestimmt wieder ins Museum. (Wenn . . . , dann)
10. Erich hat die Goldstücke gestohlen. Ich kann es nicht glauben. (Daß . . . , das)
11. Ich habe Erich nicht mehr gesehen. Wir waren zusammen in Afrika. (seit)
12. Ich war mit Erich zusammen in Afrika. Ich habe ihn nicht mehr gesehen. (seitdem)
13. Er ist nicht mit ins Kino gegangen. Er hat seiner Frau einen Brief geschrieben. (sondern)
14. Der Meyer will mich heiraten. Ich kann nur lachen. (Daß . . . , darüber)
15. Er hätte eigentlich um zehn nach Hause gehen sollen. Er blieb bis elf. (trotzdem)
16. Er blieb bis elf. Er sollte um zehn zu Hause sein. (obwohl)
17. Ich habe ihn lange gesucht. Ich habe ihn nicht finden können. (aber)
18. Er hat mir nicht geschrieben. Ich habe ihm auch nicht mehr geschrieben. (darum)
19. Gestern bei Meyers habe ich eine Frau kennengelernt. Ihr Mann soll Arabisch sprechen. (deren)

UNIT 10: Adjectives

[1] Attributive Adjectives, Nominative Singular

Read the analysis first; then try to visualize the slots while you read these examples:

Der alte Mann kam aus der Tür.	The old man came out of the door.
Ein junger Mann wartete auf ihn.	A young man was waiting for him.
Die junge Frau hieß Barbara.	The young woman's name was Barbara.
Eine junge Frau stand neben ihm.	A young woman was standing next to him.
Das kleine Mädchen hieß auch Barbara.	The little girl's name was also Barbara.
Barbara war noch ein kleines Mädchen, als Paul sie kennenlernte.	Barbara was still a little girl when Paul met her.
Mein lieber Vater!	My dear Father: (Salutation)
Meine liebe Mutter!	My dear Mother:
Mein liebes Kind!	My dear Child:
Lieber Vater!	Dear Father:
Liebe Mutter!	Dear Mother:
Liebes Kind!	Dear Child:
Das ist wirklich ein guter Wein!	That is really a good wine!
Guter Wein ist teuer.	Good wine is expensive.
Klare Fleischsuppe ist eine Spezialität unseres Hauses.	Clear broth is a specialty of the house.
Eine gute Suppe gehört zu jeder Mahlzeit.	A good soup belongs with every meal.
Unsere italienische Gemüsesuppe ist auch nicht schlecht.	Our Italian vegetable soup isn't bad either.
Frisches Obst ist immer gut.	Fresh fruit is always good.
Das italienische Obst ist nicht mehr so teuer wie früher.	Italian fruit is no longer as expensive as it used to be.
Ich empfehle Ihnen Dortmunder Union; das ist ein gutes Bier.	I recommend Dortmunder Union; that's a good beer.

SEE
ANALYSIS
144–149

(pp. 422-426)

(Facing) **Bischofsheim in der Rhön**

VARIATIONS

Der Mann war sehr alt. Es war ein sehr _____.

Sie ist intelligent. Sie ist _____ Mädchen.

Der Wein ist wirklich gut. Das ist wirklich ein _____.

Sie ist immer noch schön. Sie ist immer noch _____ Frau.

Das Wasser ist aber kalt. Das ist aber _____.

Ist das Obst auch frisch? Ist das auch wirklich _____?

Das Bier hier ist gut. Das ist wirklich ein _____.

Diese Suppe kommt aus Italien. Es ist _____.

So klein ist eure Barbara nicht mehr. Sie ist kein _____ Kind mehr.

Gestern war es kalt. Gestern war _____ Tag.

[2] Attributive Adjectives, Accusative Singular

SEE
ANALYSIS
144–149
(pp. 422-426)

Hast du den alten Mann gesehen?	Did you see the old man?
Nein, einen alten Mann habe ich nicht gesehen.	No, I haven't seen an old man.
Ich kenne die junge Dame leider nicht.	I don't know the young lady, unfortunately.
Paul hatte das junge Mädchen lange nicht gesehen.	Paul hadn't seen the young girl for a long time.
Schmidts haben gestern ein kleines Mädchen bekommen.	The Schmidts had a little girl yesterday.
Für wirklich guten Wein muß man in diesem Restaurant mindestens zwanzig Mark bezahlen.	For really good wine you have to pay at least twenty marks in this restaurant.
Nehmen Sie ein heißes Bad und gehen Sie früh ins Bett.	Take a hot bath and go to bed early.

VARIATIONS

Gestern war das Wetter schlecht. Gestern hatten wir _____.

Gestern war es kalt. Gestern hatten wir einen _____ Tag.

Der Wein war gut. Wir haben einen _____ getrunken.

Das Bier ist wirklich gut. Wo habt ihr denn dieses _____ Bier gekauft?

Meyers Frau ist jung. Meyer hat _____.

Das ist aber ein hübsches Mädchen. Kennst du das _____?

Das ist meine neue Freundin.—Was, du hast schon wieder _____?

Mein neuer Freund heißt Hans.—Was, du hast schon wieder _____?

Ist der Mantel neu?—Ja, ich habe mir endlich _____ gekauft.

Ist das Wasser auch warm? Ich möchte kein Zimmer ohne _____.

Ihre Stimme ist zu schwach für diese Rolle, Fräulein Karsten. Sie haben eine zu

_____.

[3] Attributive Adjectives, Dative Singular

Mit *dem* alten Wagen fahre ich aber nicht in die Schweiz.	I won't drive to Switzerland with *that* old car.	SEE ANALYSIS 144–149 (pp. 422-426)
Was soll ich denn mit einem alten Wagen?	What am I supposed to do with an old car?	
Am nächsten Abend kam er in San Franzisko an.	He arrived in San Francisco the next evening.	
Wir wohnten damals in einer kleinen Stadt.	At that time we lived in a small town.	
Meyers Vater ist gestern nach langer Krankheit gestorben.	Meyer's father died yesterday after a long illness.	
Ingrid ist aus guter Familie.	Ingrid comes from a good family.	
Wir wohnten damals in einem kleinen Städtchen am Rhein.	We then lived in a small town on the Rhine.	
Ich hätte gern ein Zimmer mit fließendem Wasser.	I'd like to have a room with running water.	

VARIATIONS

Gibt es hier warmes Wasser?—Ja, wir haben nur Zimmer mit _____.

Ihr Wagen ist neu? Wohin wollen Sie denn mit _____ fahren?

Das Haus ist alt. Wir wohnen in einem _____ Haus.

Die Stadt ist klein. Wir wohnen in _____.

Sie war lange krank. Sie ist nach _____ Krankheit gestorben.

Das Wetter ist schlecht. Bei dem _____ Wetter bleibe ich zu Hause.

Wenn das Wetter gut ist, arbeiten wir im Garten. Bei _____ Wetter arbeiten wir im Garten.

Seit wann ist Inge denn blond?—Sie meint, mit _____ Haar sieht sie besser aus.

Das Theater ist dort rechts. Es ist auf der _____ Seite der Straße.

[4] Attributive Adjectives, Genitive Singular

Während des letzten Krieges mußte Ingelheim Brieftauben füttern.	During the last war, Ingelheim had to feed carrier pigeons.	SEE ANALYSIS 144–149 (pp. 422-426)
Ingrid war die Tochter eines bekannten Architekten in Berlin.	Ingrid was the daughter of a well-known architect in Berlin.	
Der Besuch der alten Dame ist ein Stück von Dürrenmatt.	*The Visit of the Old Lady* is a play by Dürrenmatt.	
Wegen des schlechten Wetters konnten wir in Frankfurt nicht landen.	Because of the bad weather we couldn't land in Frankfurt.	

VARIATIONS

Sein neuer Roman heißt *Eva*. Der Titel _____ ist *Eva*.

Die Reise war lang, aber trotz _____ war ich gar nicht müde.

Ein intelligenter Mann raucht PRIVAT. PRIVAT, die Zigarette des _____ Mannes.

Jede moderne Frau wünscht sich eine elektrische Küche. Eine Elektroküche von Bosch ist der Wunsch jeder _____ Frau.

Denken Sie modern? Der Preis eines _____ Hauses ist nicht so hoch, wie Sie denken.

[5] Attributive Adjectives, Plural

SEE ANALYSIS 144–149 (pp. 422-426)

Die ersten Fluggäste kamen aus dem Zoll.	The first passengers were coming out of customs.
Meine amerikanischen Freunde wohnen in Chicago.	My American friends live in Chicago.
Liebe Eltern!	Dear Parents:
Barbara war die Mutter der beiden Kinder.	Barbara was the mother of the two children.
Eines der kleinen Mädchen hieß Barbara.	One of the little girls was called Barbara.
In dieser Schule sind fast nur Kinder reicher Leute.	In this school you find practically only children of rich people.
In dieser Schule sind fast nur Kinder von reichen Leuten.	In this school you find practically only children of rich people.
Sie wußten nicht, was sie von den amerikanischen Soldaten zu erwarten hatten.	They didn't know what to expect of the American soldiers.
In seinen müden Augen war Angst.	In his tired eyes there was fear.
Für die deutschen Soldaten war der Krieg im Mai zu Ende.	For the German soldiers the war was over in May.
Niemand liest seine letzten Romane.	Nobody reads his last novels.
Er brachte ihr rote Rosen.	He brought her red roses.
Sie hat zwei intelligente Kinder.	She has two intelligent children.
Nach dem Krieg konnte man für amerikanische Zigaretten alles kaufen.	After the war, one could buy everything for American cigarettes.

VARIATIONS

Meyers Kinder sind intelligent. Meyer hat _____.

Rot ist meine Lieblingsfarbe; daher bringt er mir immer _____ Rosen.

Ich habe Freunde in Amerika. Ich fliege morgen zu meinen _____ Freunden.

So, Sie haben Freunde in Amerika? Was denken denn Ihre _____ Freunde darüber?

Unsere Kinder sind noch klein; und _____ trinken viel Milch.

Sie geht auf eine deutsche Schule. Sind die _____ Schulen so gut wie die amerikanischen?

Sie kennen doch Amerika, nicht wahr? Was halten Sie denn von den _____ Schulen?

Meyers? Die sind doch reich. Für diese _____ Leute ist nichts zu teuer.

Gottseidank sind meine Mitarbeiter alle sehr intelligent; mit _____ Menschen kann man gut arbeiten.

Bei uns wohnten damals Amerikaner. Einer _____ Soldaten hieß Paul Suhl.

[6] Series of Attributive Adjectives

SEE ANALYSIS 150–151 (pp. 427-428)

Der blonde junge Mann da drüben heißt Suhl.	The name of the blond young man over there is Suhl.
Zuerst kam ein blonder junger Mann aus dem Zoll.	First a blond young man came out of customs.
Die blonde junge Dame ist seine Frau.	The blond young lady is his wife.
Zuerst kam eine blonde junge Dame aus dem Zoll.	First a blond young lady came out of customs.
Das kleine blonde Mädchen hieß Barbara.	The name of the blond little girl was Barbara.
Vor dem Hause saß ein blondes kleines Mädchen.	A blond little girl was sitting in front of the house.
Die Eltern der blonden jungen Dame kamen aus Leningrad.	The parents of the blond young lady came from Leningrad.
Die Eltern des netten jungen Mannes kamen aus Leningrad.	The parents of the nice young man came from Leningrad.
Die Eltern des hübschen kleinen Mädchens kamen aus Leningrad.	The parents of the pretty young girl came from Leningrad.
In unserem kleinen alten Städtchen gibt es kein modernes Hotel.	In our little old town there is no modern hotel.
Mit deinem alten grauen Mantel kannst du dich in Berlin nicht sehen lassen.	With your old gray coat you can't let yourself be seen in Berlin.
Ich nehme an, Sie kennen den netten jungen Mann da drüben.	I assume you know the nice young man over there.
Ich habe keinen blonden jungen Mann gesehen.	I haven't seen any blond young man.
Ich habe keine blonde junge Dame gesehen.	I haven't seen any blond young lady.
Ich habe kein blondes kleines Mädchen gesehen.	I haven't seen any blond little girl.
Bei klarem schönem Wetter fuhren wir ab.	We left in clear, beautiful weather.

Die hellen, kurzen Sommernächte Nor-
wegens hat er nie vergessen können.

He has never been able to forget the bright,
short summer nights of Norway.

Helle kurze Sommernächte wie in Norwegen gibt es in Afrika nicht.

In Africa, there are no bright, short summer
nights as in Norway.

Wir fuhren über eine breite neue Brücke in
die Stadt.

We drove into the city across a wide new
bridge.

Mit seinen langen, sentimentalen Romanen
hat er viel Geld verdient.

He has made a lot of money with his long,
sentimental novels.

Mit langen, sentimentalen Romanen kann
man heute kein Geld mehr verdienen.

Today you can't make money any more with
long, sentimental novels.

Zimmer mit fließendem warmen und kalten
Wasser.

Rooms with running hot and cold water.

VARIATIONS

Insert the adjectives **neu** and **automatisch** in the following sentences:

Ich wollte, ich hätte eine Waschmaschine.

Der Preis einer Waschmaschine ist gar nicht so hoch.

Die Preise unserer Waschmaschinen sind gar nicht so hoch.

Mit dieser Waschmaschine ist Ihre Frau bestimmt zufrieden.

Ist das eure Waschmaschine?

Diese Waschmaschinen sind gar nicht teuer.

Waschmaschinen sind gar nicht teuer.

Wir können nur noch Waschmaschinen verkaufen.

Meyer hat mit Waschmaschinen viel Geld verdient.

Ohne diese Waschmaschinen hätte Meyer nicht so viel Geld verdient.

[7] der-Words

SEE
ANALYSIS
152
(pp. 428-429)

Bei diesem schlechten Wetter bleibe ich zu
Hause.

In this bad weather I'll stay home.

Ohne dieses kleine Stückchen Papier hätte
ich euch nie gefunden.

Without this little piece of paper I would
never have found you.

Bei welcher amerikanischen Division waren
Sie denn?

With which American division were you?

Welche deutschen Städte haben Sie denn
gesehen?

Which German cities did you see?

In welcher deutschen Stadt habt ihr denn
damals gewohnt?

In which German town did you live then?

Jeder junge Mensch sollte einmal ein Jahr
lang im Ausland leben.

Every young person ought to live abroad for
a year.

In Deutschland gibt es in jeder großen Stadt ein Stadttheater.	In Germany, there is a municipal theater in every big city.
Von hier aus fährt jede halbe Stunde ein Zug nach Stuttgart.	From here, a train goes to Stuttgart every half-hour.
Dort haben wir schon manchen schönen Tag verbracht.	We've spent many a beautiful day there.
Manche von den jungen Soldaten waren erst siebzehn Jahre alt.	Some of the young soldiers were only seventeen years old.
Mancher von den jungen Soldaten wußte gar nicht, wofür er kämpfte.	Many a young soldier didn't know at all what he was fighting for.

Wenn mancher Mann wüßte,
wer mancher Mann wär',
gäb 'mancher Mann manchem Mann
manchmal mehr Ehr'!
(German proverb)

VARIATIONS

Express in German:

Who is this young man?
Which young man? (*nom.*)
Which young man do you mean?
This young man! (*acc.*)

Who are these young men?
Which young men?
Which young men do you mean?
These young men!

In which hotel does he live?
He always lives in this old hotel.
These old hotels are not expensive.
Every good hotel should have rooms with running water.

[8] solcher, solch, so

So einen guten Freund finde ich so bald nicht wieder.	Such a good friend I will not find again soon.	**SEE ANALYSIS 153**
Wie kann ein so intelligenter Mensch nur so dumm sein!	How can a man who is that intelligent be so stupid!	(pp. 429-430)
Und für so einen alten Wagen will der tausend Mark haben?	And for such an old car he wants to have a thousand marks?	

Für einen so alten Wagen bekommst du bestimmt keine tausend Mark.	I'm sure you won't get a thousand marks for a car as old as that.
Für solch einen Wagen bezahlen Sie mindestens zwanzigtausend Mark.	For such a (fancy) car you'll have to pay at least twenty thousand marks.
Ich wußte gar nicht, daß er noch so kleine Kinder hat.	I didn't know that his children are still that little.
Solche Kinder wie die möchte ich auch haben.	I'd like to have children like that too.
Mit so kleinen Kindern geht man doch nicht ins Theater.	You don't take children that little to the theater.

Using such combinations as **gute Freundin, schönes Haus, hübsche Kinder,** form your own variations.

[9] all, ganz

SEE ANALYSIS 154 (pp. 430-431)

Aller Anfang ist schwer.	All beginning is difficult.
Alles Gute zum neuen Jahr wünscht Dir Deine Luise.	All good wishes for the New Year. Yours, Louise.
Was hilft ihm jetzt all sein schönes Geld? Er muß doch sterben.	What good does all his lovely money do him now? He's got to die anyway.
Was hilft ihm denn jetzt das ganze Geld?	What good does all that money do him now?
Was sollen wir denn mit all dem Brot?	What are we going to do with all that bread?
Ich habe alle meine alten Freunde besucht.	I visited all my old friends.
All meine Freunde sind im Krieg gefallen.	All my friends were killed in the war.
Warum liest du eigentlich all diese dummen Romane?	Why do you read all these stupid novels anyway?
Ich habe alle seine Romane gelesen.	I have read all his novels.
Ich habe seine Romane alle gelesen.	I have read all his novels.
Warum liest du eigentlich seine ganzen Romane?	Why do you read all his novels?
Kannst du für uns alle *Kar*ten kaufen?	Can you buy tickets for all of us?
Kannst du Karten für uns *al*le kaufen?	Can you buy tickets for all of us?
Ich habe alle Karten gekauft, die noch zu haben waren.	I've bought all the tickets that were still to be had.
Alle guten Karten waren schon ausverkauft.	All the good tickets were sold out already.
Was sollen wir denn mit all den Karten?	What are we supposed to do with all those tickets?
Was sollen wir denn mit den ganzen Karten?	What are we supposed to do with all those tickets?

Das Geld ist alle.	The money is all gone.
Der Wein ist alle.	The wine is all gone.
Die Dummen werden nicht alle.	There'll always be some stupid people.
Wir alle sind dir dankbar.	We are all grateful to you.
Wir sind dir alle dankbar.	We are all grateful to you.
Er hat den ganzen Tag auf mich gewartet.	He waited for me all day.
In zwei Stunden kann ich doch nicht das ganze Buch lesen.	I can't read that whole book in two hours.
Fritzchen hat einen ganzen Apfel gegessen.	Fritzchen has eaten a whole apple.
Sie war ganz allein.	She was all alone.
Das Wetter war heute ganz gut.	The weather wasn't bad today.
Wie geht's dir denn?—Danke, ganz gut.	How are you?—Thanks, pretty well.
Wir sind durch ganz Deutschland gefahren.	We drove through all of Germany.

Form variations of your own on all but the first two examples above.

[10] Adjectives Used as Nouns

Wo ist denn der Alte?	Where is the Old Man (the Boss)?	SEE ANALYSIS 155 (pp. 431-432)
Hast du den Alten schon gesehen?	Have you seen the Old Man yet?	
In dem Zimmer lag ein Toter.	A dead man was lying in the room.	
Die Polizei fand einen Toten im Zimmer.	The police found a dead man in the room.	
Kein Mensch wußte, wer der Tote war.	Nobody knew who the dead man was.	
Von Toten soll man nur Gutes reden.	One should say only good things about the dead.	
Wer ist denn die Blonde da drüben?	Who is the blonde over there?	
Der junge Deutsche auf Zimmer Eins ist erst gestern angekommen.	The young German in Room 1 arrived only yesterday.	
Auf Zimmer Eins wohnt ein junger Deutscher.	A young German lives in Room 1.	
John wohnt mit einem jungen Deutschen auf Zimmer Eins.	John lives in Room 1 with a young German.	
Den jungen Deutschen habe ich noch nicht kennengelernt.	I haven't met the young German yet.	
Auf Zimmer Eins wohnen zwei junge Deutsche.	Two young Germans are living in Room 1.	
Die beiden jungen Deutschen habe ich noch nicht kennengelernt.	I haven't met the two young Germans yet.	
Er spricht ein gutes Deutsch.	He speaks good German.	
Sie haben recht, er spricht wirklich gut Deutsch.	You are right, he really does speak German well.	

Auf Wiedersehen, und alles Gute.	Good-bye and good luck.
Er hat viel Gutes getan.	He has done much good.
Könnte ich noch etwas Warmes zu essen bekommen?	Could I still get something warm to eat?
Ich habe gestern etwas sehr Schönes erlebt.	Yesterday I experienced something very beautiful.
Ich hoffe, ich habe nichts Wichtiges vergessen.	I hope I haven't forgotten anything important.

By changing gender, number, or case, form variations on all those examples above that refer to persons.

[11] Participles Used as Adjectives and Nouns

SEE
ANALYSIS
156
(p. 433)

Es war nicht leicht, in einer zerstörten Stadt zu leben.	It was not easy to live in a destroyed city.
Erich brachte die gestohlenen Goldstücke seinem ägyptischen Freund.	Erich took the stolen gold coins to his Egyptian friend.
Er kam mit einem gebrochenen Bein vom Schilaufen zurück.	He returned from skiing with a broken leg.
Sein gebrochenes Bein ist immer noch nicht geheilt.	His broken leg is still not healed.
Sie kam mit gebrochenem Herzen vom Schilaufen zurück.	She returned from skiing with a broken heart.
Er war bei uns immer ein gern gesehener Gast.	He was always a welcome guest at our house. (Literally: he was a gladly seen guest.)
Meyer ist ein guter Bekannter von uns.	Meyer is a close acquaintance of ours.
Frau Meyer ist eine gute Bekannte von meiner Frau.	Mrs. Meyer is a close acquaintance of my wife's.
Haben Sie Bekannte hier in der Stadt?	Do you have acquaintances here in town?
Gestern abend war ich mit meinen alten Bekannten im Löwen.	Last night I was at the Lion Inn with my old friends.
Gestern abend war ich mit alten Bekannten im Löwen.	Last night I was at the Lion Inn with old friends.
Haben Sie Verwandte in Deutschland?	Do you have relatives in Germany?
Nein, ich habe keine Verwandten in Deutschland.	No, I have no relatives in Germany.
Otto Müller ist ein Verwandter von mir.	Otto Müller is a relative of mine.
Heidi ist eine entfernte Verwandte von mir.	Heidi is a distant relative of mine.
Das ist der amerikanische Gesandte.	That is the American ambassador.

Sein Vater war ein hoher Beamter bei der Bundesregierung.

His father was a high official in the Federal Government.

In Deutschland bekommt jeder Beamte, wenn er fünfundsechzig wird, eine Pension vom Staat.

In Germany, every official (civil servant) gets a pension from the state when he turns sixty-five.

Alle deutschen Lehrer sind Beamte.

All German teachers are civil servants.

Hier auf der Post arbeiten über hundert Beamtinnen.

More than a hundred women civil servants work here at the post office.

Auch Frau Meyer ist eine Beamtin.

Mrs. Meyer is a civil servant too.

Form variations of your own.

[12] -d Adjectives

Wer war denn der gut aussehende junge Mann gestern abend?

Who was the good-looking young man last night?

Er hatte so ein gewinnendes Lächeln.

He had such a winning smile.

Alles um sich her vergessend, saßen sie mit klopfendem Herzen unter der blühenden Linde; und ihre vielsagenden Blicke aus leuchtenden Augen sagten mehr als ihre zurückhaltenden Worte.
(from: Schmidt-Ingelheim, *Die Frau mit dem Flamingo*, p. 97)

Forgetting everything around them, they sat under the blooming linden tree, with their hearts pounding, and the meaningful glances of their shining eyes said more than their reserved words.

SEE ANALYSIS 157 (p. 434)

[13] derselbe

Ist das derselbe Wein, den wir gestern abend getrunken haben?

Is that the same wine that we drank last night?

Wir wohnen in demselben Hotel, in dem Schmidts gewohnt haben.

We are staying in the same hotel in which the Schmidts stayed.

Hans und Katharine waren auf derselben Schule.

Hans and Katharine were in the same school.

Seit Jahren trägt sie jeden Sonntag dasselbe Kleid.

For years she's been wearing the same dress every Sunday.

Hans und ich wohnen schon lange in derselben Stadt.

Hans and I have lived in the same town for a long time.

Er hat lange im selben Haus gewohnt wie ich.

He and I lived in the same house for a long time.

Wir saßen gestern mit Meyers am selben Tisch.

Yesterday we sat at the same table with the Meyers.

Form variations of your own.

SEE ANALYSIS 158 (p. 434)

[14] was für

SEE
ANALYSIS
159

(pp. 434-435)

Was ist denn das für ein Wagen?
Was für ein Wagen ist das?
} What kind of car is that?

Was hast du dir denn für einen Wagen
  gekauft?
Was für einen Wagen hast du dir denn
  gekauft?
} What kind of car did you buy?

Mit was für einem Wagen bist du denn
  gefahren?
What kind of car did you go in?

Was lesen Sie denn da für eine Zeitung?
Was für eine Zeitung lesen Sie denn da?
} What (kind of) newspaper are you read-
  ing?

In was für einer Zeitung haben Sie das denn
  gelesen?
In what (kind of) paper did you read that?

Was hast du dir denn für ein Buch gekauft?
Was für ein Buch hast du dir denn gekauft?
} What kind of book did you buy?

Was hast du denn für Bücher mitgebracht?
Was für Bücher hast du denn mitgebracht?
} What kind of books did you bring along?

Das sind aber alles teure Häuser; was für
  Leute wohnen hier?
Those are all expensive houses; what kind
  of people live here?

Was wohnen denn hier für Leute?
What kind of people live here?

Ich muß noch immer daran denken, was
  für wunderbare Tage wir an der See
  verbracht haben.
I still remember what wonderful days we
  spent at the seashore.

Ich muß noch immer daran denken, was
  für einen unvergeßlichen Tag wir an der
  Mosel verbracht haben.
I still remember what an unforgettable day
  we spent by the Mosel.

,,Mit was für einem Wagen
bist du denn gefahren?''

,,. . . was für einen unvergeßlichen Tag wir an der Mosel verbracht haben!''

Was für ein herrlicher Tag das war! Was das für ein herrlicher Tag war!	What a marvelous day that was!

Hast du gesehen, was für einen unmöglichen Hut die Anita schon wieder aufhat?

Did you see what an impossible hat Anita has on again?

Weißt du noch, mit was für einem unmöglichen Hut sie damals im Theater war?

Do you remember with what an impossible hat she came to the theater?

By changing nouns, form variations on each of the examples above.

[15] viel, wenig

Meyer hat viel Geld.

Meyer has a lot of money.

Ja, aber das viele Geld macht ihn auch nicht glücklich.

Yes, but all that money doesn't make him happy either.

Sein vieles Geld macht ihn nicht glücklich.

All his money doesn't make him happy.

Emma ging mit viel Geld ins Kasino und kam mit wenig Geld nach Hause.

Emma went to the Casino with a lot of money and came home with little money.

Was machen sie nur mit dem vielen Geld?

What are they doing with all that money?

Wo hat denn der Edgar die vielen Bücher her?—Die hat ihm jemand geschenkt.

Where did Edgar get all these books?— Somebody gave them to him.

Heute ist Sonntag, und viele Leute fahren heute spazieren.

Today is Sunday, and many people go for a ride today.

Was haben Sie denn während der vielen langen Winternächte in Norwegen gemacht?

What did you do during the many long winter nights in Norway?

SEE ANALYSIS 160

(pp. 435-436)

Ich habe viel zu wenig Geld, um jedes Jahr in die Schweiz fahren zu können.

I have far too little money to be able to go to Switzerland every year.

Mit dem wenigen Geld, das du mir schickst, kann ich nicht viel kaufen.

With the little money you send me I can't buy much.

Wir haben dieses Wochenende nur wenige Gäste im Hause. Bei dem Wetter bleiben die Leute zu Hause.

We have only a few guests here this weekend. In this weather, people stay at home.

VARIATIONS

Insert the correct form of **viel**.

Ich habe nicht _____ Geld.

Was tut sie denn mit ihrem _____ Geld?

Sein _____ Geld hat er nicht mitnehmen können.

Wie _____ Kinder habt ihr denn?

Wie _____ Reisen haben Sie dieses Jahr denn schon gemacht?

Wie _____ Bier habt ihr denn getrunken?

Was machst du denn jetzt mit deinen _____ Büchern?

Er hat schon immer _____ gelesen.

[16] ander-

SEE
ANALYSIS
161
(pp. 436-437)

Wir hatten gedacht, es würde ein so schöner Sommer werden, und nun ist alles ganz anders gekommen.

We had thought it would be such a beautiful summer, and now everything has turned out quite differently.

So geht das nicht; das mußt du anders machen.

It won't work that way; you'll have to do it differently.

Aber Erich, du bist ja ganz anders als früher.

But Erich, you are so different from the way you used to be.

Erich soll ein ganz anderer Mensch geworden sein.

Erich supposedly has become a completely different person.

Er spricht von nichts anderem als von seiner Amerikareise.

He talks about nothing (else) but his trip to America.

Den einen Herrn kannte ich, aber wer war denn der andere?

One of the gentlemen I knew, but who was the other one?

Den anderen Herrn kenne ich auch nicht.

I don't know the other gentleman either.

Das muß jemand anders gewesen sein.

That must have been somebody else.

Das kann niemand anders gewesen sein als Meyer.	That can have been nobody (else) but Meyer.
Das kann kein anderer gewesen sein als Meyer.	That can't have been anybody but Meyer.
Anderen hat er geholfen; sich selbst kann er nicht helfen.	Others he has helped; himself he cannot help.
Keiner will es getan haben; es sind immer die anderen gewesen.	Nobody will admit having done it; it was always "the others."

VARIATIONS

Insert the correct form of **ander-.**

Es war ganz _____ als ich gedacht hatte.

Wer waren denn die _____ Herren?

Wir wollen gar keine _____ Waschmaschine haben.

Sie wohnen in einem _____ Hotel.

Ich war es nicht; es war jemand _____.

Dieses Buch war es nicht; es war ein _____.

Ich habe leider keinen _____ Mantel.

Alle _____ gingen nach Hause.

Wir blieben noch da, aber viele _____ gingen nach Hause.

Ich hätte lieber etwas _____.

[17] ein paar, einige, mehrere

„In ein paar Tagen bin ich wieder hier", hatte er gesagt. Aber dann wurden aus den paar Tagen ein paar Jahre.	"I'll be back in a few days," he had said. But then the few days turned into a few years.	SEE ANALYSIS 162 (pp. 437-438)
Es waren nur ein paar Leute da.	Only a few people were there.	
Mit den paar Mark kannst du doch nicht nach Italien fahren.	You can't go to Italy with those few marks.	
Ein paar schöne Tage haben wir ja gehabt, aber die meiste Zeit hat es geregnet.	We did have a few nice days, but most of the time it rained.	
Ich hätte gerne ein paar kleine Würstchen zum Frühstück.	I'd like to have a few sausages for breakfast.	
Bringen Sie mir doch bitte ein Paar Würstchen.	Could I have a couple of sausages (frankfurters), please?	

Ich habe nur zwei Paar gute Schuhe mitgebracht.	I've only brought two pairs of good shoes.
Anton und Emma waren ein schönes Paar.	Anton and Emma were a lovely couple.
Einige von unseren Lesern möchten wissen, ob Ingelheim noch in Konstanz wohnt.	Some of our readers would like to know whether Ingelheim still lives in Constance.
Wir kamen durch mehrere zerstörte Dörfer.	We came through several destroyed villages.
Einige der Soldaten wohnten im Hause des Pfarrers.	Some of the soldiers lived in the pastor's house.
Im Löwen kann man für ein paar Mark gut essen.	At the Lion Inn one can eat well for a few marks.
Ich habe auch schon einige Male da gegessen.	I've eaten there several times, too.
Letzte Woche habe ich mehrere Male im Löwen gegessen.	Last week I ate at the Lion several times.

Form variations of your own.

READING

Ankunft in Deutschland

Wir wollen annehmen, daß Sie während der Nacht über den Atlantik geflogen sind und morgens auf dem Rhein-Main Flughafen bei Frankfurt ankommen, vielleicht nach einer Zwischenlandung in Paris oder London.

Wenn Sie non-stop fliegen, ist die Flugzeit von New York etwa 5 sieben Stunden, von Chicago neun Stunden und von San Franzisko etwa dreizehn Stunden. Dazu kommt aber der Zeitunterschied zwischen Amerika und Europa. Wenn Sie in New York abfliegen, ist es vielleicht 7 P.M. EST oder EDST, und wenn Sie in Frankfurt ankommen, ist es 8 oder 7 Uhr MEZ. MEZ heißt Mitteleuropäische 10 Zeit. Wenn es in Frankfurt Mitternacht ist, ist es im Sommer in New York erst 7 Uhr abends, und um 7 Uhr abends sind Sie ja abgeflogen. Das heißt, Sie kommen in Frankfurt um 2 Uhr nachts an, aber nach New Yorker Zeit EST, und in Frankfurt ist es dann schon 8 Uhr morgens, oder, im Sommer, 7 Uhr morgens, weil es in Deutschland 15 keine Sommerzeit (Daylight Saving Time) mehr gibt.

Vielleicht bleiben Sie oft bis zwei Uhr morgens auf, aber es ist doch spät und eigentlich Zeit, schlafen zu gehen. Aber die Nacht ist vorbei, für immer verloren. Sie haben im Flugzeug ein amerikanisches

Dinner gegessen, von acht bis zehn Uhr abends, und dann tat man,
als käme jetzt eine lange Nacht. Alle Lichter gingen aus, und weil
es dunkel war, haben Sie versucht zu schlafen. Vielleicht haben Sie
auch eine Stunde geschlafen, aber dann hielt Ihnen die Stewardess
plötzlich ein Glas Orangensaft unter die Nase und tat, als ob es 5
sechs Uhr morgens wäre. Frühstück um Mitternacht ist eigentlich
verrückt, aber es war ja in Wirklichkeit sechs Uhr morgens, nur
war es nicht 6 A.M. EDST, sondern 6 Uhr MEZ.

der Saft, ⁼e juice

Und jetzt landen Sie also in Frankfurt. „Bitte anschnallen", lesen
Sie über Ihrem Sitz und „Nicht rauchen", und über den Laut- 10
sprecher hören Sie: „Wir möchten Sie bitten sitzenzubleiben, bis
die Maschine völlig zum Stillstand gekommen ist." Gottseidank wie-
derholt die Stewardess das auf Englisch: „Please remain seated
until the plane has come to a complete stop."

anschnallen to fasten
the seat belt

völlig completely

Dann hält die Maschine, aber vom Flugzeug zum Empfangsgebäude 15
ist es mindestens eine halbe Meile,—nein, Sie denken jetzt schon
ganz europäisch und sagen zu Ihrer netten Nachbarin: „Das ist ja

der Empfang, ⁼e re-
ception; **das Gebäude**
building

fast ein Kilometer! Müssen wir denn jetzt dahin laufen?" „Nein, nein", lacht die Nachbarin, die gerade ein Jahr als Austauschstudentin in Amerika studiert hat, „da kommen schon die Busse."

der Austausch exchange

Auf vielen europäischen Flughäfen holen Busse die Fluggäste direkt am Flugzeug ab und bringen sie zum Empfangsgebäude. Man hat 5 dann nur noch ein paar Meter zu gehen und ist schon an der Paßkontrolle. Die Formalitäten sind schnell erledigt; der Beamte sieht Ihren Paß kaum an. Dann kommt der Zoll. Die deutsche Studentin ist vor Ihnen an der Reihe. „Haben Sie etwas zu verzollen?" „Nein, gar nichts." „Dann machen Sie doch bitte einmal Ihren 10 Koffer auf." Eine halbe Minute, und die Studentin ist fertig; sie hatte wirklich nichts zu verzollen. Jetzt kommen Sie an die Reihe. Der Zollbeamte sieht schon, daß Sie Amerikaner sind. (Die meisten Amerikaner in Europa sehen aus, als ob sie Amerikaner wären.) "Anything to declare?" fragt er. "Coffee, tea, cigarettes?" Aber 15 weil Sie nicht rauchen und auch keinen Kaffee trinken, können Sie ruhig sagen: „Nein, gar nichts". "OK", sagt der Beamte, „danke schön", und dann sagt er noch: „Viel Spaß", was so viel heißt wie "Have fun."

erledigen to take care of, to settle

verzollen to pay duty on

Spaß fun, pleasure

Dann gehen Sie durch eine große Glastür, und da steht Ihre Kusine 20 Emma und sagt: „Da bist du ja endlich." Und Sie sind froh, daß Sie eine Kusine Emma haben, die jetzt alles für Sie tun wird, weil sie ein praktisches Mädchen ist und weiß, daß man um drei Uhr morgens sehr müde ist.

Aber nicht alle haben eine Emma.   25

Wenn Sie nun keine Kusine in Frankfurt haben, dann haben Sie noch viel zu tun, bevor Sie sich schlafen legen können. Zunächst brauchen Sie deutsches Geld. Sie gehen also zu einer Wechselstube. Solche Wechselstuben gibt es auf allen deutschen Flughäfen und in den großen Bahnhöfen. Der Dollarkurs ist nicht ganz 1:4 (eins 30 zu vier); für einen Reisescheck über $20 bekommen Sie DM 78,80. (DM heißt „ Deutsche Mark".) Der Bankbeamte sagt „Achtundsiebzig Mark achtzig" und gibt Ihnen einen Fünfzigmarkschein, einen Zwanzigmarkschein, ein Fünfmarkstück, ein Zweimarkstück, ein Markstück, ein Fünfzigpfennigstück und drei Zehnpfennigstücke. 35 Sie haben also jetzt statt Ihres amerikanischen Reiseschecks deutsches Bargeld in der Hand.

die Stube, –n room; **wechseln** to change, exchange
der Kurs, –e rate of exchange
der Scheck, –s check

der Schein, –e bill

das Bargeld cash

Es gibt nun drei Möglichkeiten: Erstens—und das ist die vernünftigste Möglichkeit—Sie haben schon von Amerika aus in Frankfurt ein Zimmer bestellt und schlafen sich zunächst aus. Zweitens: Sie 40 wollen vielleicht mit der Bahn weiterfahren, sagen wir nach Koblenz,

die Bahn = Eisenbahn

weil Sie am nächsten Tag mit dem Schiff den Rhein hinunter fahren
wollen. Drittens, wenn *Ihre* Kusine Emma in München wohnt, dann
müssen Sie natürlich noch am gleichen Tag nach München weiterfliegen.

Sie gehen also zum Lufthansaschalter und geben einer der jungen   5   **der Schalter, –**   ticket
Damen Ihren Flugschein.   window, counter
                                                         der Schein, –e   ticket

„Ich komme gerade aus New York und möchte nach München
weiterfliegen."

„Haben Sie schon einen Platz gebucht?"

„Ja, für heute nachmittag."   10

„Das ist Flug Nummer 604, Abflug 13.45 Uhr (dreizehn Uhr fünfundvierzig), Ankunft in München um 14.30 Uhr. Warteraum B   **der Raum, ⸚e**   room
bitte,—der Flug wird um 13.15 Uhr aufgerufen."

Die junge Dame wiegt Ihren Koffer, dann gibt sie Ihnen Ihr Ticket
zurück, und Sie können nun in aller Ruhe etwas essen, eine Zeitung 15
lesen (vielleicht die *Frankfurter Rundschau*, die *Frankfurter Allgemeine* oder einen Artikel im *Spiegel*) und die Leute beobachten.
Um halb zwei gehen Sie zum Ausgang B 6, dann fahren Sie wieder   **pünktlich**   prompt(ly),
mit dem Bus zum Flugzeug, und pünktlich um dreiviertel zwei   punctual(ly)
startet Ihre Maschine zum Flug nach München.   **dreiviertel zwei**   a
                                                        20 quarter of two

Ein Mann kommt nach San Franzisko*
von Mathias Koch

I Epilog als Vorspiel

das Vorspiel prologue

Flughafen San Franzisko, November 1962

Die Lufthansa-Maschine aus Frankfurt ist gerade angekommen:
Abflug in Frankfurt um zwei Uhr, kurze Zwischenlandung in Mont-
real, am gleichen Abend in Kalifornien,—was sind schon† zwölf-
tausend Kilometer. Man kauft sich eine Flugkarte, steigt ein, ißt
zwei Mahlzeiten, schläft ein bißchen, und dann ist plötzlich nur 5
noch der Zoll da, der einen von der neuen Welt trennt.

einen accusative of **man**

Vor dem Zollausgang stehen zehn, zwölf Leute und warten: eine
Frau wartet auf ihren Mann, Eltern auf ihre Kinder; ein Mädchen
wartet auf ihren Vater, eine Braut auf ihren Bräutigam. Endlich
kommen die ersten Fluggäste aus dem Zoll; zuerst eine große blonde 10

* In this text, we have purposely retained certain grammatical constructions,
such as reflexives and passives, that will be introduced systematically in Units
11–13. These constructions, as well as some other grammatical points and some
vocabulary, appear in the margins.
† **schon** here: *a mere* (used as a sentence adverb expressing a shoulder-shrugging
so-what attitude of the speaker).

Frau, dann ein junger Mann, dann wieder eine Frau, eine Familie
mit vier Kindern, dann zwei junge Leute, Touristen, wie es scheint,
man sieht es an ihren Koffern. Alle reden und lachen, man hört
Englisch und Deutsch, und langsam verlieren sich alle den langen,
hellen Korridor hinunter.   5

Minutenlang bleibt die Tür zum Zoll geschlossen. Dann öffnet sie   **sich öffnen** to open
sich noch einmal, langsam diesmal, so langsam, als hätte der, der sie
öffnet, Angst davor, das Flugzeug zu verlassen und in eine Welt
zu treten, die er nicht kennt. Für ihn war der Flug sicher keine
Reise, wie man sie so macht, wenn man Geld und Zeit dazu hat. 10
Grau ist er, der Mann, der jetzt in der Tür steht, und er sieht aus,
als fröre er. Seine Augen sind müde; Angst ist darin, als er jetzt
nach links sieht und dann nach rechts. Seine Hände zittern, als ob
ihm Koffer und Tasche zu schwer wären. Oder zittert er, weil er
Angst hat? Lange steht er so. Dann sieht er noch einmal nach links 15
und nach rechts und geht langsam weiter.

Da kommt plötzlich ein junger Mann den Korridor herunter, und
hinter ihm eine junge Frau. Der junge Mann mag fünfunddreißig
Jahre alt sein, höchstens vierzig, und sie muß ungefähr fünfund-
zwanzig sein. Sie laufen auf den alten Mann zu. Der sieht sie nicht 20   **auf . . . zu** toward
kommen. Sie bleiben vor ihm stehen; sie sprechen mit ihm, aber er
scheint sie nicht zu hören. Die Angst ist immer noch in seinem
Gesicht, in seinen Augen und in seinen zitternden Händen. Der
junge Mann nimmt ihm den Koffer aus der Hand. Der alte Mann
will es nicht, aber als das Mädchen (oder ist es die Frau des 25
jungen Mannes?) auch noch seine Tasche nimmt, läßt er es geschehen. Wie ein Kind führen ihn die beiden den Korridor hinunter.
Dort, wo der Korridor in das Empfangsgebäude hineinführt, stehen
zwei Kinder, ein Junge und ein Mädchen, vielleicht drei Jahre alt,
und bei ihnen steht ein älteres Ehepaar.   30   **das Ehepaar, –e**
                                                                         married couple

Als die letzten Fluggäste den Korridor herunterkommen, sehen sie
den Mann auf dem Boden knien, in jedem Arm eines der beiden   **knien** to kneel
Kinder. Von dem kleinen Mädchen sieht er hinauf zur Mutter (es
muß die Mutter sein), und von der Mutter wieder zur Tochter, und
zu beiden sagt er immer wieder: „Barbara!", so, als hätte er den 35
Namen noch nie gehört. Der junge Mann und das ältere Ehepaar
stehen dabei und lächeln, und der Mann sieht gar nicht mehr so
grau und müde aus, und auch nicht mehr so alt wie vor ein paar
Minuten, als er dort unten durch die Tür kam. Er steht plötzlich
auf, zieht ein Stück Papier aus der Tasche und gibt es dem jungen 40
Mann. „Hier", sagt er, „hier, das ist es. Wenn ich das nicht gehabt
hätte, hätte ich euch nie gefunden". Er zittert wieder, aber die
Angst ist aus seinen Augen verschwunden.

II

Mai 1945

Angefangen hatte es damit, daß Paul Suhl aus St. Louis, nachdem
er ein Jahr lang Japanisch gelernt hatte, nach Deutschland geschickt
wurde. Zur Landung in der Normandie war er zu spät gekommen;
im November 1944 kam er zu einer Infanterie-Kompanie in der
Nähe von Aachen. Danach verpaßte er nichts mehr; die Ardennen- 5
schlacht, den Rheinübergang bei Remagen, und dann die Kapitu-
lation. Überall zerstörte Brücken und Dörfer, zerbombte Städte.
Quer durch Deutschland fuhr er seinen Jeep, vom Rhein nach
Kassel, von Kassel nach Leipzig. Es wurde Frühling, während er
mit dem Krieg nach Osten fuhr. Die braune Erde wurde grün; 10
manchmal sah man Frauen auf den Feldern arbeiten, oder alte
Männer oder Kinder; auf den Straßen zogen deutsche Soldaten nach
Westen in die Kriegsgefangenenlager.

Am 20. April, an Hitlers letztem Geburtstag, besetzten die Amerikaner Leipzig. Am 21. April, seinem eigenen Geburtstag—einund- 15
zwanzig Jahre wurde er alt—, fuhr Paul Suhl mit seiner Kompanie
wieder nach Südwesten, in den Thüringer Wald. Manchmal, wenn
er die Straßenschilder las, dachte er an seinen Großvater, der aus
dieser Gegend gekommen war (er war in Saalfeld an der Saale
geboren und in den neunziger Jahren nach Amerika ausgewandert): 20
„Naumburg 12 km, Jena 23 km, Weimar 39 km", las er auf einem
Schild; und später: „Gotha 45 km, Eisenach 61 km."

Das Dorf lag im Thüringer Wald, nicht weit von Ilmenau, an der
Eisenbahn von Erfurt nach Meiningen. In einem langen Tal, Wald
auf beiden Seiten, zog es sich an der Straße hin, alt und grau; im 25
Zentrum das Rathaus, die Schule, eine einfache Kirche; daneben
das Pfarrhaus, vor dem selbst in diesem Frühling ein paar Blumen
blühten. Von den Bewohnern sah man nicht viel, als Paul das erste
Mal mit seinem Jeep durch das Dorf fuhr; sie hielten sich zurück,
wußten nicht, was sie von den fremden Soldaten denken sollten. 30

Die Soldaten wurden in der Schule untergebracht, aber die Schule
war nicht groß genug für die ganze Kompanie. Paul und zwei andere
wohnten in einem Haus nicht weit vom Pfarrhaus. Der Bauer, ein
alter Mann, sagte etwas von einem gefallenen Sohn und von Stalingrad; dann machte er den Mund nicht mehr auf; auch seine Frau 35
sagte kein Wort. Paul, Bill und Joe bewohnten das Wohnzimmer und
das Schlafzimmer. Wo der Bauer und seine Frau schliefen, wußten
sie nicht; irgendwo mußte wohl noch ein Zimmer sein, vielleicht das
Zimmer des gefallenen Sohnes. Am nächsten Morgen merkten sie,
daß noch andere Menschen bei dem Bauern wohnten; in der 40

---

geschickt wurde was
sent

verpassen to miss
die Ardennen Forest
of Ardennes; **die
Ardennenschlacht**
Battle of the Bulge
der Übergang, ⁼e
crossing
quer durch straight
across
nach Osten eastward
das Feld, –er field
**das Kriegsgefangenen-
lager** P.O.W. camp
20. = zwanzigsten

nach Südwesten
southwestward
Straßenschild road
sign
**in den neunziger
Jahren** in the (18)90's
auswandern to emi-
grate

das Tal, ⁼er valley

zog . . . hin it stretched
along the road

das Pfarrhaus, ⁼er
parsonage
selbst even
der Bewohner, – in-
habitant; **bewohnen**
to inhabit

**wurden . . . unter-
bracht** were billeted

Scheune lebten zwei oder drei Flüchtlingsfamilien, aus dem Osten wahrscheinlich, vielleicht auch aus Berlin oder Leipzig. Paul sah die Frauen manchmal über den Hof gehen, sie kamen ihm vor wie dürres Laub, das der Wind über die Straße fegt. Auf einer Bank vor der Scheune saß ein alter Mann und blickte ins Leere. Er bemerkte nicht einmal die Kinder, die auf dem Hof und auf der Straße spielten.

die Scheune, –n the barn
die Flüchtlingsfamilie, –n refugee family
sie kamen ihm vor they looked to him
dürres Laub dry leaves
fegen to sweep
leer empty; ins Leere into space

III

Für die Amerikaner: No fraternizing; Fraternisieren verboten. Für die Deutschen: No loitering; Herumstehen verboten.—Wer die Bestimmungen der Militärregierung übertritt, wird bestraft.—Den Anordnungen des amerikanischen Ortskommandanten ist unbedingt Folge zu leisten, Zuwiderhandelnde werden bestraft.

Nur die Kinder waren von Anfang an ausgenommen.

Wer ... bestraft Whoever transgresses the orders of the military government will be punished.
Den Anordnungen ... bestraft Orders issued by the American local commander are to be obeyed under all circumstances; offenders will be punished.
ausgenommen exempted
zögern to hesitate

Das Mädchen mochte neun Jahre alt sein. Sie blieb immer im Hintergrund, wenn die anderen zu den Soldaten kamen. Paul hatte sie zum ersten Mal gesehen, als er mit Joe und Bill abends auf der Bank vor dem Haus saß. Die Flüchtlingskinder aus der Scheune, die auf dem Hof gespielt hatten, zögerten zuerst, als Joe mit ihnen sprach; aber als er ihnen Schokolade hinhielt, kamen sie doch. Die Soldaten lachten, und Bill meinte, man hätte den ganzen Krieg mit Schokolade führen sollen, alle Deutschen wären mit Schokolade zu kaufen. Nur das schlanke dunkelblonde Mädchen wollte nicht näherkommen. „Was ist denn mit Eurer Freundin los?" fragte Paul. „Will die denn keine Schokolade?" „Ach die", sagte eines der Mädchen, „die weint immer nur, weil ihre Mutti tot ist.—Mein Vater ist auch tot, aber ich kriege bald einen neuen." „Mein Pappi ist auch in Rußland gefallen", rief ein sechs- oder siebenjähriger Junge dazwischen, „und mit der Barbara spielen wir gar nicht mehr." Joe und Bill wollten wissen, wovon die Kinder sprachen, aber Paul konnte sich nicht dazu bringen zu übersetzen. Aber von da an beobachtete er die kleine Barbara. Sie war fast immer allein; und auch, als die Soldaten anfingen, jeden Morgen zwei oder drei der Kinder im Jeep mitzunehmen, wenn sie zur Schule fuhren, wollte sie nie mitfahren.

Was ist los? What's the matter?

Bis Paul und Bill sie eines Nachmittags allein vor dem Haus fanden. „Na, Barbara, möchtest du nicht auch mal ein Stück mitfahren? Du brauchst doch keine Angst vor uns zu haben", sagte Paul und hielt ihr ein Stück Schokolade hin. „Hör auf, Mensch", meinte Bill, „die kannst du auch mit Schokolade nicht kaufen; das ist so'n richtiger kalter Fisch." Das Kind mußte gefühlt haben, daß Bill ihm da kein Kompliment machte. Sie drehte sich um und rannte die Straße hinunter. Man konnte sehen, daß sie weinte. Bill lachte und ging ins

hör auf stop (leave her alone)
das ist ... Fisch she's a real cold fish
sich umdrehen to turn around

Haus. Paul stieg in den Jeep und fuhr hinter ihr her. Sie mußte ihn
kommen hören, aber sie drehte sich nicht um. Er hielt neben ihr, sie
sah zu ihm herüber, ohne etwas zu sagen; dann mußte sie lächeln.
Langsam kam sie zu ihm und setzte sich wortlos neben ihn in den
Wagen. Paul fuhr aus dem Dorf hinaus; die Straße führte neben der ₅   **nicht recht** not quite
Eisenbahn ins Tal. Er wußte nicht recht, was er sagen sollte. Er
konnte ihr ja nicht erklären, daß sie ihm leid tat, weil ihre Mutter
tot war, und daß sie ihn an seine kleine Schwester erinnerte. Dieser   **erinnern an** to remind
verdammte Krieg—aber sie war ja nur ein Kind und hatte mit all   of
dem nichts zu tun. Und irgend jemand mußte sich doch um sie küm- ₁₀   **verdammt** damn
mern. Man sollte einen Brief nach Hause schreiben: Liebe Eltern,   **sich kümmern um** to
ich habe ein Kind gefunden, erinnert mich an Kathy, Mutter tot, wo   take care of
der Vater ist, weiß ich nicht. Man kann das Kind doch nicht einfach
allein lassen. Aber mitnehmen kann ich sie auch nicht, sie ist doch
eine Deutsche. „Du, ich weiß, wo es hier Walderdbeeren gibt", sagte ₁₅   **die Erdbeere, –n**
Barbara plötzlich, dann fuhren sie eine Seitenstraße hinauf in den   strawberry
Wald. Eine halbe Stunde suchten sie unter den Bäumen herum,   **es gibt** there are
Erdbeeren fanden sie nicht, aber er war froh, daß sie „du" zu ihm
sagte. Er hatte ihr eigentlich die Schokolade wieder anbieten wollen,   **anbieten** to offer
aber dann dachte er daran, wie Bill gesagt hatte, man könne alle ₂₀
Deutschen mit Schokolade kaufen; und er ließ die Schokolade in
der Tasche.

(Fortsetzung folgt)

ANALYSIS

144 Predicate Adjectives and Adverbs

Most English adjectives can be transformed into adverbs by adding the
suffix *-ly*, for example, *high—highly, beautiful—beautifully;* for some
others, there is a separate adverbial form, for example, *good—well;* and
only a few have the same form both as adjectives and as adverbs, for
example, *fast.*

In German, there is no distinction between the predicate adjective and
the adverb.

> **Seine Frau soll *schön* sein.**
> His wife is supposed to be very *beautiful.*
> **Sie soll auch sehr *schön* singen können.**
> Supposedly she can also sing very *beautifully.*

145 Predicate Adjectives and Attributive Adjectives

The predicate adjective, as the name implies, is part of the predicate; it constitutes a verbal complement and thus forms the second prong of the predicate.

Das Wetter war wochenlang schlecht.

The attributive adjective is an attribute of a following noun.

Im Januar war wochenlang *schlechtes Wetter.*
Bei diesem *schlechten Wetter* bleibe ich zu Hause.
Der *junge Mann* hieß Suhl.

The German predicate adjective never has an ending; the German attributive adjective *must* take an ending. These endings are determined by a variety of factors: gender, number, case, and the presence or absence of a **der**-word or **ein**-word.

146 Strong Endings

The endings of the definite article, **der, die, das,** are most important. This set of endings is generally referred to as "strong" adjective endings.

	Singular			Plural
	MASCULINE	FEMININE	NEUTER	ALL GENDERS
NOM.	der	die	das	die
GEN.	des	der	des	der
DAT.	dem	der	dem	den
ACC.	den	die	das	die

You are already used to the fact that when these endings are unstressed, as in the forms of **dieser,** the long **-ie** of **die** becomes **-e** and the **-as** of **das** becomes **-es.**

	Singular			Plural
	MASCULINE	FEMININE	NEUTER	ALL GENDERS
	-er	-e	-es	-e
	-es	-er	-es	-er
	-em	-er	-em	-en
	-en	-e	-es	-e

147 Weak Endings

Attributive adjectives following a definite article must take what are generally referred to as "weak" endings. There are only two weak endings,
-e and **-en.** The ending is **-en** in all cases except five: the three nominative
singular forms, and the accusative feminine and neuter.

	Singular			Plural
	MASCULINE	FEMININE	NEUTER	ALL GENDERS
NOM.	-e	-e	-e	-en
GEN.	-en	-en	-en	-en
DAT.	-en	-en	-en	-en
ACC.	-en	-e	-e	-en

Note that there is a similarity between these weak endings and the strong
endings: Only the masculine singular distinguishes between nominative
and accusative.

If we assign definite positions (or slots) for each of the three words in
the phrase **der alte Herr,** then slot 1 contains the **der**-word—that is, the
strong ending—slot 2 contains the attributive adjective with the weak
ending, and slot 3 contains the noun. Note again that only the masculine
singular distinguishes between nominative and accusative.

	SLOT 1	SLOT 2	SLOT 3
MASC.			
NOM.	*der*	*alte*	Herr
GEN.	des	alten	Herrn
DAT.	dem	alten	Herrn
ACC.	*den*	*alten*	Herrn
FEM.			
NOM.	*die*	*alte*	Dame
GEN.	der	alten	Dame
DAT.	der	alten	Dame
ACC.	*die*	*alte*	Dame
NEUTER			
NOM.	*das*	*junge*	Mädchen
GEN.	des	jungen	Mädchens
DAT.	dem	jungen	Mädchen
ACC.	*das*	*junge*	Mädchen

	SLOT 1	SLOT 2	SLOT 3
PLURAL, ALL GENDERS			
NOM.	*die*	*alten*	Herren
GEN.	der	alten	Herren
DAT.	den	alten	Herren
ACC.	*die*	*alten*	Herren

148 Attributive Adjectives after **ein**-Words

The **ein**-words (**ein, kein, mein, dein, sein, ihr, unser, euer, ihr**) are declined like the definite article, that is, they have strong endings. However, in three forms they have no ending at all: nominative masculine and nominative and accusative neuter.

	Singular		Plural
MASCULINE	**FEMININE**	**NEUTER**	**ALL GENDERS**
ein	eine	ein	keine
eines	einer	eines	keiner
einem	einer	einen	keinen
einen	eine	ein	keine

The basic rule governing phrases containing **der-** or **ein-** words followed by attributive adjectives is that *there must be a strong ending* in slot 1. With **der**-words, this is simple: since **der**-words have strong endings in all forms, they always occupy slot 1.

SLOT 1	SLOT 2	SLOT 3
der	alte	Mann

All **ein**-words *with* an ending follow the same pattern: they occupy slot 1.

SLOT 1	SLOT 2	SLOT 3
einem	alten	Mann

In the three forms, however, in which the **ein**-word does not have an ending, the following shift takes place:

The **ein**-word is moved forward, as it were, into slot 0 (reserved for introductory words without endings); thus, slot 1 is vacated, and the adjective moves into it and takes a strong ending. Slot 2 then remains empty:

SLOT 0	SLOT 1	SLOT 2	SLOT 3
ein	der alter	alte	Mann Mann

If we compare the singular forms of phrases starting with **der**-words and of phrases starting with **ein**-words, this shift becomes quite clear:

	der-words				ein-words			
	SLOT 0	SLOT 1	SLOT 2	SLOT 3	SLOT 0	SLOT 1	SLOT 2	SLOT 3
MASC.								
NOM.		der	alte	Herr	ein	alter		Herr
GEN.		des	alten	Herrn		eines	alten	Herrn
DAT.		dem	alten	Herrn		einem	alten	Herrn
ACC.		den	alten	Herrn		einen	alten	Herrn
FEM.								
NOM.		die	alte	Dame		eine	alte	Dame
GEN.		der	alten	Dame		einer	alten	Dame
DAT.		der	alten	Dame		einer	alten	Dame
ACC.		die	alte	Dame		eine	alte	Dame
NEUTER								
NOM.		das	junge	Mädchen	ein	junges		Mädchen
GEN.		des	jungen	Mädchens		eines	jungen	Mädchens
DAT.		dem	jungen	Mädchen		einem	jungen	Mädchen
ACC.		das	junge	Mädchen	ein	junges		Mädchen

149 Attributive Adjectives without **der-** or **ein-**Words

If there is neither a **der**-word nor an **ein-** word to fill slot 1, the adjective must always occupy slot 1. Both slot 0 and slot 2 are then empty.

SLOT 0	SLOT 1	SLOT 2	SLOT 3
	Lieber Liebe Liebes		Vater! Mutter! Kind!

150 Series of Attributive Adjectives

If two or more attributive adjectives stand together, they all occupy the same slot and show the same endings.

SLOT 0	SLOT 1	SLOT 2	SLOT 3
ein	der blonder junger eine das gutes deutsches	blonde junge kleine alte beste deutsche	Mann Mann Stadt Bier Bier

NOTE: Adjectives in a series may be separated by a comma; such commas have the same function as **und** would have. Thus **ein blonder junger Mann** is a young man who happens to be blond, whereas **ein langer, sentimentaler Roman** is a novel which is both long and sentimental.

151 Variations

1. In the dative masculine and neuter, the sequence **-em -en** is so ingrained that of two or more adjectives not preceded by a strong ending only the first tends to take on the strong ending:

	SLOT 0	SLOT 1	SLOT 2	SLOT 3
Bei **Bei**		diesem nebligem	nebligen kalten kalten	Wetter Wetter

2. In the genitive masculine and neuter, with adjectives not preceded by a **der**-word or an **ein**-word, the strong endings have been replaced by weak endings. These forms, however, do not, as a rule, occur in the spoken language.

	SLOT 0	SLOT 1	SLOT 2	SLOT 3
Trotz **Trotz**			starken schlechten	Nebels Wetters

The spoken language prefers the regular pattern with the dative:

	SLOT 0	SLOT 1	SLOT 2	SLOT 3
Trotz		starkem		Nebel
Trotz		schlechtem		Wetter

3. Adjectives ending in **-el** and **-er** drop the **-e-** if an attributive ending is added.

Das Zimmer war dunkel.

Sie saßen in einem dunklen Zimmer.

Die Zimmer hier sind aber sehr teuer.

Wir wohnten in einem teuren Zimmer.

4. The adjective **hoch** drops the **-c-** if an ending is added, and the **h** becomes silent.

Der Baum war sehr hoch.

The tree was very tall.

Vor dem Haus stand ein hoher Baum.

A tall tree stood in front of the house.

152 der-Words

The following are declined like the definite article; that is, they take strong endings:

dieser, this

jeder, each, every

welcher, which, what

mancher, many a; plural: some

(a) The neuter singular **dieses** may be used without an ending (**dies**) in the nominative and accusative.

Dies Buch hier ist wirklich gut.

In identifying or in introducing phrases, **dies** must be used:

Gerda, dies ist mein Freund Hans.

Und dies, meine Damen und Herren, war das Schlafzimmer des Königs.

(b) **Jeder** has no plural forms. The plural of **jeder Mensch** is **alle Menschen.**

(c) **Welcher** is normally used as an interrogative: **in welcher Stadt?** *in which (what) city?* In poetic German, **welcher** may be used without an ending, if it corresponds to English *what* in such exclamations as *What luck!*

SLOT 0	SLOT 1	SLOT 2	SLOT 3
	Welches		Glück!
Welch			Glück!
Welch ein			Glück!

Note the use of **welch** in the last stanza of Goethe's "Willkommen und Abschied":

Doch ach, schon mit der Morgensonne	But alas, with the morning sun
Verengt der Abschied mir das Herz:	parting already constricted my heart.
In deinen Küssen welche Wonne!	What delight was in your kisses,
In deinem Auge welcher Schmerz!	what pain in your eyes!
Ich ging, du standst und sahst zur Erden,	I went, you stood looking at the ground,
Und sahst mir nach mit nassem Blick:	and looked after me with wet eyes.
Und doch, welch Glück, geliebt zu werden!	And yet, what bliss to be loved,
Und lieben, Götter, welch ein Glück!	and to love, gods, what bliss!

(d) **Mancher** is also occasionally used without an ending, and must be so used if followed by **ein**.

SLOT 0	SLOT 1	SLOT 2	SLOT 3
	mancher	junge	Mensch
manch	junger		Mensch
manch ein	junger		Mensch

153 so, solch

In the singular, both **so ein** and **ein so** are usually followed by adjectives.

so ein intelligentes Mädchen	such an intelligent girl
ein so intelligentes Mädchen	a girl who is so intelligent
Sie ist doch so ein intelligentes Mädchen.	She is such an intelligent girl.
Ein so hübsches Mädchen müßte doch einen Mann finden.	A girl who is that pretty ought to be able to find a husband.

In the plural, **so** is immediately followed by an adjective.

so kleine Kinder	children who are that little
Ich wußte gar nicht, daß er noch so kleine Kinder hat.	I didn't know that his children are still so little.

It is advisable to use **solch** only with a strong ending and without a following adjective; it then means "such a degree of" (cf. English *with such force*) or "that kind of."

| Warum hast du denn immer solche Angst? (so große Angst?) | Why are you always so afraid? |
| Mit solchen Menschen will ich nichts zu tun haben. | I don't want to have anything to do with that kind of people. |

154 all, ganz

All is used with or without endings. When there is an ending, it is always strong.

SINGULAR

(a) Forms with an ending are not used very frequently. They occur, immediately followed by a noun, in stereotyped phrases:

   Ich wünsche dir alles Gute

and in proverbial expressions:

   Aller Anfang ist schwer.

(b) If used without an ending, **all** must be followed by a **der**-word or a possessive adjective:

   all das schöne Geld
   all mein Geld

Such phrases express bulk quantity, and **all** can be replaced by the attributive adjective **ganz**:

   das ganze schöne Geld
   mein ganzes Geld.

PLURAL

(a) **All** with an ending is the plural of **jeder** and means *every single one of them;* it precedes nouns and follows pronouns.

   Alle meine Brüder sind im Krieg gefallen.
   Wir alle haben ihn gestern besucht.

In the spoken language, it is usually separated from its noun or pronoun and placed in the inner field preceding the first item of news value:

   Meine Brüder sind im Krieg alle gefallen.
   Wir haben ihn gestern alle besucht.
   Gestern haben wir ihn alle besucht.

(b) **All** without an ending refers again to bulk quantity and means *the whole bunch of them*. Again, it must be followed by a **der-** or an **ein-**word.

> Ich habe all meine Bücher verloren.

Again, this "bulk" meaning of **all** can be replaced by the attributive adjective **ganz**.

> Ich habe meine ganzen Bücher verloren.

NOTE: **Alle** may be used predicatively to mean *all gone*.

> Das Geld ist alle.
> Der Wein ist alle.
> Die Dummen werden nicht alle.
> There will always be stupid people.

Ganz, if not used as a replacement for **all**, is used in the following ways:

(a) as an attributive adjective meaning *whole* or *entire*.

> Er hat den ganzen Tag auf mich ge-   He waited for me all day.
> wartet.

(b) as an adverb, meaning *completely*, modifying an adjective.

> Sie war ganz allein.   She was all alone.

(c) as an *unstressed* adverb, meaning *quite* or *rather*, modifying such "praising" adjectives as **gut, glücklich, intelligent**.

> Das Wetter war ja ganz gut, aber es   The weather wasn't bad, but it could have
> hätte besser sein können.   been better.

Do not thank your hostess by saying **Das Essen war ganz gut.** This would mean that the food wasn't bad, but certainly nothing to rave about.

(d) without an ending and preceding geographical names. It then means *all of*.

> Wir sind durch ganz Deutschland gefahren.

155 Adjectives Used as Nouns

In such English phrases as

> the idle rich   *Gentlemen Prefer Blondes*
> he helped the poor   *The Naked and the Dead*,

the adjectives *rich, poor, blonde, naked,* and *dead* are used as plural nouns. In German, many more adjectives can be used as nouns than in English, and, unlike English, they very often occur in the singular. If so used, they are capitalized, but are otherwise treated like attributive adjectives.

SLOT 0	SLOT 1	SLOT 2	SLOT 3	
	der	Reiche		the rich man
	die	Alte		the old woman
	das	Gute		the good
mein	Alter			my old man
	die	Armen		the poor
	der	Tote		the dead man
	die	Tote		the dead woman
	die	Toten		the dead
ein	Toter			a dead man

Note the use of adjectives as nouns in the last eight lines of Goethe's *Faust:*

Alles Vergängliche	Everything transitory
ist nur ein Gleichnis;	is but a simile;
Das Unzulängliche,	Here, the unattainable
hier wird's Ereignis;	becomes event;
Das Unbeschreibliche,	Here, the indescribable
hier ist es getan;	is fully achieved;
Das Ewig-Weibliche	The eternally feminine
zieht uns hinan.	draws us upward.
	(Transl. by B. Q. Morgan)

When an adjective follows **nichts, etwas,** or **wenig,** as in the English *nothing new* or *something important,* the German adjective is capitalized and has a strong neuter singular ending.

Es gibt leider nichts Neues.
Ich habe etwas Wichtiges vergessen.
Das führt zu nichts Gutem.

NOTE: Of all nouns indicating nationality, **Deutsch** is the only one declined like an adjective.

der Deutsche, the German (man)
die Deutsche, the German (woman)

156   Participles Used as Adjectives

In German, as in English, participles can be used as attributive adjectives.

SLOT 0	SLOT 1	SLOT 2	SLOT 3	
	die	**zerstörte**	**Stadt**	the destroyed city
	eine	**zerstörte**	**Stadt**	a destroyed city
	zerstörte		**Städte**	destroyed cities
ein	**gestohlenes**		**Goldstück**	a stolen gold coin
	das	**gestohlene**	**Goldstück**	the stolen gold coin
mein	**geliebter**		**Sohn**	my beloved son

Both German and English can use participles as plural nouns:

die Verwundeten   the wounded
die Besiegten   the conquered

Unlike English, however, German can also use participles as singular nouns:

SLOT 0	SLOT 1	SLOT 2	SLOT 3
ein	**der Verwundeter**	**Verwundete**	
	die der	**Verwundeten amerikanische Gesandte**	
	der	**Gekreuzigte***	
	der	**Erwählte**†	
	die	**Betrogene**‡	

Similarly:

der Bekannte, acquaintance—from: **bekannt sein,** to be (well) known
die Bekannte
der Verwandte, relative—from: **verwandt sein,** to be related
die Verwandte
der Beamte, official, civil servant—from: **das Amt,** office
    (originally: **der Beamtete,** one who is given an office)
but:
die Beamtin

* The crucified one (Christ)
† The chosen one (title of Thomas Mann's novel *The Holy Sinner*)
‡ The deceived one (title of Thomas Mann's novel *The Black Swan*)

157 -d Adjectives

In principle, any German verb can form an adjective corresponding to English adjectives in *-ing* simply by adding the suffix **-d** to the infinitive. These **-d** derivatives can be used safely only as attributive adjectives.

	SLOT 0	SLOT 1	SLOT 2	SLOT 3
		das	lachende	Kind
	ein	lachendes		Kind
	ein	gewinnendes		Lächeln
mit		klopfendem		Herzen
		ihre	leuchtenden	Augen
	ein	hungerndes		Kind

158 derselbe

There are two German adjectives to express English *the same:* **der gleiche** and **derselbe.** The forms of **derselbe** are written as one word unless the article is contracted with a preposition. Both **der** and **selb-** must be declined.

> Ist das derselbe Wein wie gestern?
> Ist das der gleiche Wein wie gestern?
> Wir trinken heute wieder denselben Wein wie gestern.
> Wir wohnen in derselben Stadt.
> Wir wohnen im selben Hotel.
> Wir wohnen im gleichen Hotel.
> Wir wohnen in demselben Hotel.

Strictly speaking, **der gleiche** expresses similarity (the same kind), and **derselbe** expresses identity (the very same). However, this distinction is rapidly disappearing.

159 was für

There is no English structural equivalent for the very frequently used construction with **was für.** It is not declined, nor does **für** have any influence on the case of the following adjective or noun. **Was für** means *what kind of* or *what.*

In the nominative and accusative, **was** occupies the front field; **für** plus the noun or pronoun may either follow the **was** immediately or stand in the inner field, usually right before the second prong.

Was für ein Wagen ist denn das da drüben?
Was ist denn das für ein Wagen da drüben?*
Was ist denn das da drüben für ein Wagen?

Was für einen Wagen hast du dir denn gekauft?
Was hast du dir denn für einen Wagen gekauft?

Ich weiß nicht, *was für einen Wagen* er sich gekauft hat.
Ich weiß nicht, *was* er sich *für einen Wagen* gekauft hat.

Was für Bücher hast du mir denn mitgebracht?
Was hast du mir denn für Bücher mitgebracht?

Was für ein Wetter das heute wieder ist!
Was das heute wieder für ein Wetter ist!
Was für ein Wetter ist das heute wieder!
Was ist das heute wieder für ein Wetter!

In the dative, the **was für** construction cannot be split. Nor can it be split
if it is preceded by a preposition.

Was für einem Mann gehört denn der Wagen?
Mit was für einem Wagen bist du denn gefahren?
Durch was für Dörfer seid ihr denn gefahren?
Auf was für einen Mann wartest du denn?

160 viel, wenig

Viel (*much;* plural: *many*) and **wenig** (*little;* plural: *few*) have the same
characteristics. Their use is in a state of flux, but it is safe to use them in
the following ways.

(a) In the singular, **viel** and **wenig** express bulk and are usually used
without endings.

Wieviel Fisch habt ihr gegessen? (wieviel—one word)
Wir haben damals viel Fisch und wenig Fleisch gegessen.

Adjectives used after these endingless forms have strong endings:

Ich habe noch viel deutsches Geld.
Ich habe nur noch wenig deutsches Geld.

After possessive adjectives and definite articles, **viel** and **wenig**, still indicating bulk, take attributive adjective endings: **sein vieles Geld, das
viele Geld.**

NOTE: **Vielen Dank,** *thank you very much,* is an exception.

(b) In the plural, **viele** means *many* and **wenige** *few*. They are then treated
as attributive adjectives.

* da drüben is end field; remember the sentence **Das Bier ist gut hier in München.**

SLOT 1	SLOT 2	SLOT 3
viele junge die wenigen	vielen jungen	Leute Leute Worten

mit

(c) **Viel** and **wenig** may be used as adverbs preceding comparatives:

> Er war viel älter als sie.
> Er war nur wenig älter als sie.
> Er hatte viel mehr Geld als ich.

Viel must not be confused with the adverb **sehr** (*very*) which sometimes corresponds to an English *very much*.

Ich habe sie sehr geliebt.	I loved her very much.
Ich ginge sehr gerne mit nach Köln.	I'd like very much to go along to Cologne.
Er war sehr krank.	He was very sick.
Die Amerikaner essen sehr viel Fleisch.	Americans eat very much meat.
Ich war sehr dagegen.	I was very much against it.
Es waren sehr viele Leute dort.	There were very many people there.

Note that German and English are not always parallel:

geliebt	sehr geliebt	loved very much
gerne	sehr gerne	very gladly
krank	sehr krank	very sick
viel Fleisch	sehr viel Fleisch	very much (a lot of) meat
dagegen	sehr dagegen	very much against it
viele Leute	sehr viele Leute	very many people

English *very* always precedes *much, many,* or some other adjective or adverb. German **sehr**, on the other hand, is an independent adverb and does not have to be followed by anything: **Sie liebte ihn sehr.**

161 ander-

Ander- means *other, different,* or *else*. If used attributively or after **etwas** or **nichts**, it takes the same endings as any other attributive adjective and is often preceded by **ganz**.

> Das eine Buch kenne ich, aber das andere habe ich noch nicht gelesen.
> Erika kenne ich ja, aber wer war denn die andere Dame?
> Dieser Herr war es nicht, es muß ein anderer gewesen sein.
> Das ist natürlich etwas anderes. (something else)
> Das ist etwas ganz anderes. (something quite different)

NOTE: For some unfathomable reason, no form of **ander-** is ever capitalized.

If **ander-** is used as an adverb or a predicate adjective, it always has the form **anders.**

> **Ich hätte das ganz anders gemacht.** I would have done that quite differently.
> **Es ist alles ganz anders gekommen, als wir dachten.**
> **Er ist anders, als er früher war.**

Note also the following frequently used phrases:

> **Das kann nicht mein Bruder gewesen sein, das muß _jemand anders_ [somebody else]
> gewesen sein.**
> **Das kann _niemand anders_ [nobody else] gewesen sein als Anton Meyer.**

162 mehrere, einige, ein paar

All three of these terms mean _more than two, but not many._

Mehrere and **einige** are never used with an article, as is possible with English _the several states._ They therefore take strong endings.

Mehrere means _several,_ **einige** (literary) and **ein paar** mean _a few_ (_some, a bunch_).

SLOT 0	SLOT 1	SLOT 2	SLOT 3
	mehrere junge		Leute
	einige deutsche		Bücher
ein paar	junge		Leute
ein paar	deutsche		Bücher

Do not confuse _few_ (_not many_), **wenige,** with _a few_ (_some_), **ein paar.**

> **Wenige Menschen wußten, wer er wirklich war.**
> **Ein paar Menschen wußten, wer er wirklich war.**

After the article or a possessive adjective, **ein paar** becomes **paar.**

Neither **paar** (_few_) nor **ein paar** (_a few_) is ever declined, nor does either of them have any influence on the ending of a following adjective.

	SLOT 0	SLOT 1	SLOT 2	SLOT 3
	(ein paar)	alte		Hemden
		die (paar)	alten	Hemden
mit	(ein paar)	alten		Hemden
mit		den (paar)	alten	Hemden
		meine (paar)	alten	Hemden
mit		meinen (paar)	alten	Hemden
mit	(ein paar)	alten		Hemden

Bring mir doch bitte ein paar Zigaretten mit.
Ich komme in ein paar Minuten.
Er wollte in Berlin ein paar Freunde besuchen.
Er ist ein paar Tage in Berlin gewesen.
Wir haben ein paar schöne Tage an der Riviera verbracht.
Die paar schönen Tage an der Riviera waren viel zu kurz.
In den paar kurzen Tagen konnte ich nicht viel arbeiten.

Note the difference between **ein paar** (*a few*) and **ein Paar** (*a pair, a couple*):

Wir aßen Suppe mit ein paar Würstchen.
Wir aßen Suppe mit einem Paar Würstchen.
Anton und Emma waren ein schönes Paar.

163   Word Formation: Nouns of Action Derived from Weak Verbs

The stem of some weak verbs appears as a masculine noun of action—
that is, a noun denoting the activity expressed by the verb. Feel free to
use the nouns listed, but do not try to invent your own—they may not
exist. Most of these nouns are masculine, but there are also a few feminines and neuters.

antworten	die Antwort, –en	das war eine gute Antwort
baden	das Bad, ─er	ein heißes Bad
besuchen	der Besuch, –e	Der Besuch der alten Dame (Dürrenmatt)
blicken	der Blick, –e	ein vielsagender Blick
danken	der Dank (*no pl.*)	vielen Dank
fragen	die Frage, –n	das kommt nicht in Frage (that's out of the question)
glauben	der Glaube (*no pl.*)	Glaube, Liebe, Hoffnung
grüßen	der Gruß, ─e	viele Grüße aus den Bergen
hassen	der Haß (*no pl.*)	Ohne Liebe kein Haß (Ingelheim)
heiraten	die Heirat	ich bin gegen diese Heirat
kaufen	der Kauf, ─e	ein guter Kauf
küssen	der Kuß, die Küsse	mit Gruß und Kuß, Dein Julius
lieben	die Liebe (*no pl.*)	Liebe macht blind
reden	die Rede, –n	er hielt eine lange Rede
suchen	die Suche (*no pl.*)	die Suche nach dem Dieb
tanzen	der Tanz, ─e	der Tanz um das goldene Kalb
versuchen	der Versuch, –e	ein chemischer Versuch
wünschen	der Wunsch, ─e	alle guten Wünsche zum Neuen Jahr

The most common nouns of action are the feminine nouns in **-ung** (see **120**).

164 Nouns of Action Derived from Strong Verbs

Theoretically, any one of the various forms of the stem of a strong verb can occur as a noun denoting the action of the verb, or the result of such action, or the thing used for such action.

> Action: **der Schlaf** sleep
> Result of action: **der Fund** the find
> Thing used for action: **der Sitz** the seat

Again, it is safe to use the nouns listed, but do not invent your own. Note that of the nouns ending in **-t** and **-e**, most are feminine.

abfahren	die Abfahrt, –en	departure
anfangen	der Anfang, ̈e	beginning
ankommen	die Ankunft, ̈e	arrival
annehmen	die Annahme, –n	reception; assumption
anrufen	der Anruf, –e	phone call
ansehen	die Ansicht, –en	view, sight
aufgeben	die Aufgabe, –n	task, homework
ausgeben	die Ausgabe, –n	expense, delivery
aufnehmen	die Aufnahme, –n	reception; photograph
ausgehen	der Ausgang, ̈e	exit
aussehen	die Aussicht, –en	expectation, view
befehlen	der Befehl, –e	order, command
beginnen	der Beginn (*no pl.*)	beginning
bitten	die Bitte, –n	request
brechen	der Bruch, ̈e	break, fracture, fraction
fahren	die Fahrt, –en	drive, trip
fallen	der Fall, ̈e	fall, case
geben	die Gabe, –n	gift
	das Gift, –e	poison
	die Mitgift (*no pl.*)	dowry
gehen	der Gang, ̈e	gait, corridor, gear (in a motor)
gewinnen	der Gewinn, –e	profit, gain
greifen	der Griff, –e	handle; grasp
helfen	die Hilfe	help
lesen (to read, to gather)	die Weinlese, –n	grape harvest
	„Spätlese"	a wine made from overripe grapes
liegen	die Lage, –n	situation

raten	der Rat	advice
scheinen	der Schein (*no pl.*)	appearance, light
	der (Geld)schein, –e	banknote
schlafen	der Schlaf (*no pl.*)	sleep
schlagen	der Schlag, –̈e	strike, stroke, hit
schneiden	der Schnitt, –e	cut
schreiben	die Schrift, –en	(hand)writing
	die Heilige Schrift	Bible, Holy Writ
sehen	das Gesicht, –er	face
sitzen	der Sitz, –e	seat
sprechen	die Sprache, –n	language, speech
springen	der Sprung, –̈e	jump
stehen	der Stand, –̈e	stand
trinken	das Getränk, –e	beverage
tun	die Tat, –en	deed
	die Tatsache, –n	(actual) fact
verbieten	das Verbot, –e	prohibition
verlieren	der Verlust, –e	loss
verstehen	der Verstand (*no pl.*)	reason, intelligence
ziehen	der Zug, –̈e	train

165   The Suffix -ig

This suffix may be added to nouns to form adjectives corresponding to English derivatives of the type *stone: stony, meat: meaty.*

der Stein	steinig	stony
die Güte	gütig	good, kind
die Ecke	eckig	angular
das Dreieck (triangle)	dreieckig	three-cornered, triangular
das Viereck (rectangle)	viereckig	four-cornered, rectangular
die Seite	-seitig	-sided
	einseitig	onesided
	ein gleichseitiges Dreieck	an equilateral triangle

Frequently, the suffix **-ig** is added to time expressions to form adjectives. Most of these adjectives cannot be imitated in English.

die Zeit	zeitig	in (good) time
	rechtzeitig	on time, at the right time
das Jahr	-jährig	
	dreijährig	three years old, lasting for three years

	ein dreijähriges Kind	a three-year-old child
	eine dreitägige Wanderung	a three-day hike
heute	heutig	of today
	die heutige Zeitung	today's paper
jetzt	jetzig	of today, present, contemporary
	der jetzige Bürgermeister heißt Böttle	the name of the present mayor is Böttle
damals	damalig	then
	der damalige Bürgermeister hieß Meyer	the then mayor's name was Meyer

Note also:

hier	hiesig	
	die hiesige Bevölkerung	the local population

EXERCISES

A. Insert the adjectives given in parentheses into the following sentences:

1. Meyer ist mit einer Frau verheiratet. (sehr intelligent)
2. Eine Frau ist sie *nicht*. (intelligent)
3. Er ist dumm, aber er hat eine Frau geheiratet. (intelligent)
4. Sie ist dumm, aber sie hat einen Mann geheiratet. (intelligent)
5. Er ist ein Mensch. (intelligent)
6. Wer *ist* denn der Mann, von dem ihr da sprecht? (intelligent)
7. Sie ist ein Kind. (intelligent)
8. Wer *ist* denn das Mädchen, von dem ihr da sprecht? (intelligent)
9. Von einem Mädchen hätte ich das nicht erwartet. (so intelligent)
10. Mein Sohn hat ein Mädchen geheiratet. (intelligent)
11. Meyers haben drei Kinder. (intelligent)
12. Frauen wissen immer, was sie wollen. (intelligent)
13. Mit Studenten kann man gut arbeiten. (intelligent)
14. Was machen Sie denn mit den Kindern in Ihrer Schule? (intelligent)
15. Sie ist mit einem Mann verheiratet. (intelligent)

SEE LAB EXERCISE 10.1 (p. 633)

B. Restate the following sentences, leaving out the italicized **der-** or **ein-**words.

1. *Jeder* gute Wein ist teuer.
2. *Alle* intelligenten Frauen wissen, was sie wollen.
3. Das ist wirklich *ein* guter Wein.
4. *Diese* italienische Gemüsesuppe ist eine Delikatesse.

5. *Dieses* deutsche Bier ist sehr gut.
6. *Mein* lieber Vater!
7. *Das* frische Obst ist jetzt zu teuer.
8. Bei *dem* starken Regen fahre ich nicht in die Stadt.
9. Er ist nach *einer* langen Krankheit gestorben.

C. Place the word in parentheses in front of the adjective.

SEE LAB
EXERCISES
10.2, 10.3

(p. 633)

1. Das Zimmer mit fließendem Wasser bekomme *ich*. (dem)
2. Für intelligente Kinder tun wir viel zu wenig. (unsere)
3. Automatische Uhren sind teuer. (diese)
4. Ingrid ist aus guter Familie. (einer)
5. Nach kurzer Pause fuhren wir weiter. (einer)
6. Für amerikanische Zigaretten konnten wir damals alles kaufen. (unsere)
7. Beide Kinder gingen damals schon in die Schule. (seine)
8. Westfälischer Schinken ist eine Spezialität unseres Hauses. (dieser)

D. Restate the following sentences by changing the italicized nouns to the singular and by making the corresponding changes in the **der**-words and adjectives.

SEE LAB
EXERCISE
10.4

(p. 633)

1. Siehst du *die jungen Mädchen* da drüben?
2. Woher hast du denn *die schönen Bücher?*
3. *Diese neuen Maschinen* fliegen tausend Kilometer in der Stunde.
4. *Die ersten Fluggäste* kamen aus dem Zoll.
5. Wir fragten *die jungen Männer,* wo sie herkämen.
6. *In den zerstörten Städten* gab es kein Wasser.
7. *Die kleinen Dörfer* lagen im Schwarzwald.
8. *Die amerikanischen Soldaten* kamen in ein Dorf im Schwarzwald.
9. Er sprach nicht einmal *mit den kleinen Kindern.*
10. Ich werde *mit meinen deutschen Verwandten* sprechen. (feminine)
11. Niemand gab *den Kleinen* etwas zu essen. (masculine)
12. Niemand gab *den Kleinen* etwas zu essen. (feminine)
13. Sie wollte nicht *mit den amerikanischen Soldaten* fahren.

E. Restate the following sentences by changing the nouns to the singular. Change the adjective ending as required and place an **ein**-word before the adjective.

SEE LAB
EXERCISES
10.5–10.7

(p. 633)

1. Ich habe Verwandte in Frankfurt.
2. Bei uns wohnen jetzt amerikanische Soldaten.
3. Vor ihm saßen zwei blonde Mädchen.
4. Er rauchte amerikanische Zigaretten.
5. Meyers sind gute Freunde von mir.
6. Das waren schöne Sommermonate an der See.
7. Wer nach dem Krieg gute Freunde in Amerika hatte, brauchte nicht zu hungern.
8. *Gute* Romane hat er noch *nie* geschrieben.

F. In the following sentences, insert an appropriate **der-** or **ein-**word (if necessary) and the correct form of the adjective in parentheses.

1. Mit _____ _____ Roman hat er viel Geld verdient. (letzt)
2. Wir wohnen in _____ _____ Haus. (neu)
3. Er brachte mir ein Glas _____ Wasser. (kalt) [see **116**]
4. Er hält sich für _____ _____ Mann. (groß)
5. Ich hätte gern etwas _____ Obst. (frisch)
6. Gestern abend habe ich _____ _____ Professor kennengelernt. (deutsch)
7. Du hast in _____ _____ Zeit zu viel gearbeitet. (letzt)
8. Ich freue mich auf _____ Sonntag. (nächst)
9. Mein Mann ist gerade von _____ _____ Reise zurückgekommen. (lang)
10. Bei _____ Wetter bleiben wir zu Hause. (schlecht)
11. Mit _____ _____ Schreibmaschine kann ich nicht schreiben. (alt)
12. Wann soll _____ _____ Brücke denn fertig sein? (neu)
13. Wegen _____ _____ Nebels konnten wir in Chicago nicht landen. (stark)
14. Mit _____ _____ Mantel kannst du nicht nach Paris fahren. (alt)
15. Bist du mit _____ _____ Sekretärin zufrieden? (neu)
16. Barbara war die Mutter _____ _____ Kinder. (beid)
17. Für _____ _____ Soldaten war der Krieg zu Ende. (deutsch)
18. In _____ _____ _____ Städtchen gibt es keine Hotels. (klein, alt)
19. Ich möchte ein Zimmer mit _____ Wasser. (fließend)
20. Haben Sie etwas _____ gehört? (neu)
21. Er hat viel _____ getan. (gut)
22. Er hat zwei _____ Romane geschrieben. (gut)

G. Express in German:

1. We have two small children.
2. He lived with his old mother.
3. I hope you'll marry an intelligent woman.
4. We paid good money for that.
5. How expensive is your new car?
6. She wrote him a long letter.
7. Her long letter arrived only yesterday.
8. She never read his long letters.
9. I don't like to write long letters. (Don't use *mögen.*)
10. She wrote him many long letters.
11. Good coffee is very expensive.
12. I can't go to Europe without a new coat.
13. He is an old friend of mine.
14. She is a good friend of mine.
15. Is that the new hotel?
16. Last week I was in Berlin.
17. Last Monday I was in Berlin.

SEE LAB
EXERCISES
10.8, 10.9

(p. 633)

18. During the last war he was in Norway.
19. I am living with my German relatives.
20. I have a German aunt.
21. Did you drive to Italy with that old car?
22. For this old car he wants three thousand marks.
23. Do you know that we have a new director?
24. Dear Hans!
25. Dear Elisabeth!
26. Dear Children!
27. Our dear old Aunt Amalie died last week.
28. In which hotel did you live?
29. She really is a very interesting woman.
30. In this city we don't have one single good hotel.
31. Every large German city has at least one theater.
32. We all went to the movies last night.
33. I have read all his novels.
34. All really good wines are expensive.
35. This is really a good wine.
36. My old friends are all dead.
37. All my old friends are dead.
38. She has married a young German.
39. He married a young German.
40. In the room above me lives a young German (man).
41. In the room above me lives a young German (woman).
42. I have forgotten something very important.
43. Today I experienced something very beautiful.
44. When a man is thirty-nine, he is no longer a young man in the eyes of a young girl.

H. Change singular nouns in the following sentences to plurals.

1. Was für einen herrlichen Tag wir gehabt haben!
2. Was für ein Buch möchtest du denn gerne haben?
3. Was für eine schöne Tochter Sie haben!
4. Was für ein Haus ist denn das?
5. Was für ein interessantes Kleid hat sie sich denn diesmal gekauft?
6. In was für einem Hotel wollen Sie denn wohnen?
7. Sie glauben gar nicht, was ich für einen netten Menschen in Berlin kennengelernt habe.

I. Change the plural nouns in the following sentences to singulars.

1. Was für schöne Kinder das sind!
2. Was müssen das für Menschen sein!
3. Was für herrliche Tage das waren!
4. Was für Bücher liest du denn in der Schule?
5. Was für interessante Kleider die Anita anhat!

J. Express in German:

1. What kind of man did she marry?
2. To what kind of man is she married?
3. I don't know what kind of cars those (das) are.
4. To (auf) what kind of school did you go?
5. You don't know what a beautiful girl Rosemary is.
6. I didn't know what a dumbbell he is.
7. Why didn't you tell me what an interesting husband she has?
8. What interesting people one can meet in Casablanca!
9. What kind of shoes are you taking along?

K. Insert the words italicized in the first sentence as adjectives into the second sentence.

1. Die Deutschen hatten die Brücke *zerstört*. Wir konnten nicht über die _____ Brücke fahren.
2. Dieses Wasser ist *kalt*. Trinken Sie gerne _____ Wasser?
3. Erich hatte fünf Goldstücke *gestohlen*. Mit den _____ Goldstücken fuhr er nach Afrika.
4. Die Maschine aus London ist gerade *gelandet*. Die gerade _____ Maschine hat 35 Minuten Verspätung.
5. Die Goldstücke waren *verschwunden*. Niemand wußte, wo die _____ Goldstücke waren.
6. Er hatte einen langen Brief an sie *angefangen,* aber weil er nichts mehr von ihr hörte, ließ er den _____ Brief einfach liegen.
7. Ingelheim war in Afrika *verschwunden,* aber nach vierzehn Tagen kam der in Afrika _____ Ingelheim plötzlich zurück.
8. Meine Tante ist nach Amerika *ausgewandert.* Von meiner nach Amerika _____ Tante haben wir nie wieder etwas gehört.

L. Change the italicized inflected form of the verb into a **-d** adjective and insert it into the second sentence.

1. Der *sieht* aber gut *aus*. Er ist ein gut _____ junger Mann.
2. Die Linden *blühten* noch; sie saßen unter einer _____ Linde.
3. Das Kind *schlief,* als er abfuhr. Er sah noch einmal auf das _____ Kind und fuhr dann ab.
4. Die Kinder *spielten* auf der Straße, aber der alte Mann sah die _____ Kinder nicht.
5. Die Menschen *hungerten*. Man sah viele _____ Menschen.
6. Jedesmal, wenn sie ihn sah, *klopfte* ihr das Herz. Mit _____ Herzen sah sie ihn kommen.
7. Wir *sprechen* hier alle Deutsch. Es ist gut, wieder einmal unter Deutsch _____ Menschen zu sein.
8. Ihre Augen *leuchteten*. In ihren _____ Augen las er die Antwort auf seine Frage.

M. Express in German:

SEE LAB
EXERCISES
10.10–10.12
(p. 633)

1. Many young men went to war (ziehen in), but only few came back healthy.
2. Some have everything, and many have nothing.
3. A few went home, others stayed.
4. Yesterday was such a beautiful day.
5. On such a beautiful day one shouldn't work.
6. I think quite differently about that.
7. He has become quite a different person (Mensch).
8. Other people (Mensch) think differently.
9. She has done much good.
10. At that time we had little to eat.
11. Now we can eat as much as we want.
12. Could you give me some cigarettes? I've left mine at home.
13. We had to wait for several hours.
14. I don't want to have anything to do with such people.
15. Where do all these people come from?
16. They didn't all come.
17. Not all Germans speak (a) good German.
18. Only few Americans speak German well.
19. He was such a good husband.

N. Construct a conversation between yourself and your cousin Emma who has come to pick you up at the Frankfurt Airport. This is not an exercise in translation, but you should nevertheless follow the English outline. Use your imagination, but avoid using patterns that you are not thoroughly familiar with. Be prepared to produce a similar conversation orally in class.

Emma, of course, wants to know how you are, how the flight was, whether you are tired, and whether you would like to have breakfast before driving into town. You try to figure out what time it is in New York and you talk a bit about time differences. When Emma mentions MEZ, you are puzzled because you've never heard the term. Emma explains. Then you decide that you are really tired and ought to get to your hotel. She wants to know whether you have ordered a room, which, of course, you have done. Emma thinks it might be a good idea to call the hotel to be sure that you have the room. Since you have never made a phone call in Germany, you ask her whether she would please do that for you. While she telephones, you want to get some German money. She asks you to come to the exit in ten minutes, and she will get her car in the meantime.

Now, here is your first sentence: Emma: „Da bist du ja endlich."

anders different (See **161**)

der Apfel, ⸚ apple

ausgeben to spend

das Ausland foreign countries

  er lebt im Ausland he lives
  abroad

ausverkauft sold out

der Bauer, –n peasant, farmer

der Beamte, –n civil servant,
  (government) official
  (*gen.:* **des Beamten,** *dat.:*
  dem Beamten)

  die Beamtin, –nen
  official (female)

das Bein, –e leg

bekannt well known

  der Bekannte, –n
  acquaintance (see **156**)

beobachten to observe, watch

bestellen to order

der Besuch, –e visit

ein bißchen a bit, a little

blühen to bloom, blossom,
  flower

die Braut, ⸚e bride

  der Bräutigam, –e bridegroom

brechen to break

das Brot, –e bread

der Bus, –se bus

da drüben over there

dankbar grateful, thankful

derselbe the same (see **158**)

das Dorf, ⸚er village

dunkel dark

die Ehre, –n honor

eigen (*adjective*) own

einige some, several, a few

einsteigen to enter, board
  (a train or plane)

die Eisenbahn, –en railroad

empfehlen to recommend

entfernt distant

die Erde, –n earth

erstens first(ly)
  zweitens second(ly)
  drittens third(ly)
  etc.

Euro'pa Europe

europä'isch European

die Farbe, –n color

  die Lieblingsfarbe, –n
  favorite color

das Fleisch (*no pl.*) meat

fließen to flow

der Fluggast, ⸚e airplane
  passenger

das Flugzeug, –e airplane

fremd strange, alien

frieren to freeze

frisch fresh

der Frühling, –e spring

das Gemüse, – vegetable

der Gesandte, –n ambassador,
  envoy

das Gesicht, –er face

gewinnen to win

gleich (*adjective*) same,
  like

grau gray

der Großvater, ⸚er grandfather

grün green

grüßen to greet

  der Gruß, ⸚e greeting

das Haar, –e hair

hell light, bright

das Hemd, –en shirt

herrlich magnificent, splendid, marvelous

herum around

der Hintergrund, ⸚e background

hinunter down

  den (Rhein) hinunter
  down the Rhine

hoch high

hübsch pretty

immer wieder again and
  again

  immer größer bigger and
  bigger

  immer schöner more and
  more beautiful

der Januar January

die Karte, –n map, ticket

klar clear

der Koffer, – suitcase

die Krankheit, –en illness,
  disease

die Kusi'ne, –n (female)
  cousin

lächeln to smile

  das Lächeln smile

landen to land

langsam slow

leid tun to feel sorry

  sie tat ihm leid he felt
  sorry for her

  es tut mir leid I am sorry

leuchten to shine

link- left

  links left, on the left side

die Mahlzeit, –en meal

mancher many a (see **152**)

  manchmal sometimes

mehrere several

die Meile, –n mile

meist- most

die Milch (*no pl.*) milk

Mitternacht midnight

modern' modern

die Möglichkeit, –en possibility

der Nachbar, –n neighbor

nah near, close

  die Nähe proximity, closeness, nearness

die Nase, –n nose

der Nebel, – fog

  neblig foggy

der November November

das Obst (*no pl.*) fruit

öffnen to open

  offen (*adjective*) open

das Papier, –e paper

die Pause, –n pause, intermission

der Pfarrer, – pastor

der Pfennig pfennig, penny
  (100 to a Mark)

raten to advise; give counsel;
  guess

  der Rat advice, counsel;
  council; councilor

  das Rathaus, ⸚er town
  hall, city hall

rechtzeitig on time
die Regie'rung, –en govern-
    ment
    die Bundesregierung the
        Federal Government (of
        Germany)
die Reihe, –n row; series
    ich bin an der Reihe it's
        my turn
    ich komme an die Reihe
        I'm next
rennen to run
die Rose, –n rose
rot red
die Ruhe (*no pl.*) rest;
        quietness
    in aller Ruhe at leisure
Rußland Russia
der Schinken, – ham
schlank slender, slim
die Schokola'de, –n
        chocolate

der See, –n lake
die See (*no pl.*) sea, ocean
sentimental' sentimental
solcher such (see **153**)
der Staat, –en state
stark strong, heavy (as rain,
        wind, etc.)
die Suppe, –n soup
trennen to separate
treten to step
unten down, down below,
        downstairs
der Unterschied, –e differ-
        ence
verbieten to forbid, prohibit
verlassen to leave (some-
        body or something)
verbringen to spend (time)
die Verspätung, –en delay
    Verspätung haben to be
        late, not on schedule

verwandt related
    der Verwandte, –n relative
        (see **156**)
vorbei (*adverb*) gone, past
was für what kind of (see
        159)
welcher which
wenig little (See **162**)
wichtig important
wiederho'len to repeat
wiegen to weigh
die Wirklichkeit, –en
    reality
der Wunsch, ̈e wish
die Wurst, ̈e sausage
    Wurst cold cuts
    das Würstchen, – sausage
zerstören to destroy
der Zoll, ̈e customs; duty
zuerst first, at first
zunächst first, first of all

IRREGULAR VERBS

brechen to break
    **brach, hat gebrochen, er
        bricht**
empfehlen to recommend
    **empfahl, hat empfohlen, er
        empfiehlt**
fließen to flow
    floß, ist geflossen, er fließt
frieren to freeze
    fror, hat gefroren, er friert
gewinnen to win

    **gewann, hat gewonnen, er
        gewinnt**
leid tun to be sorry
    **tat . . . leid, hat . . . leid
        getan, es tut . . . leid**
raten to advise; to guess
    riet, hat geraten, er rät
rennen to run
    rannte, ist gerannt, er rennt
treten to step
    trat, ist getreten, er tritt

verbieten to forbid
    **verbot, hat verboten, er
        verbietet**
verbringen to spend (time)
    **verbrachte, hat verbracht,
        er verbringt**
verlassen to leave
    **verließ, hat verlassen, er
        verläßt**
wiegen to weigh
    **wog, hat gewogen, er
        wiegt**

VOCABULARY CHECK LIST, UNITS 1–10

This is a complete list of the vocabulary used in Units 1–10.

ab
der Abend, –e
abends
aber
abfahren
abholen
das Abitur'
ach
ach so
acht
achtzehn
achtzig
die Adresse, –n
adressieren
Ägyp'ten
alle
allein
allerdings
alles
als
also
alt
der Amerikaner, –
an
ander-
anders
der Anfang, ⏜e
anfangen
angehen
die Angst, ⏜e
Angst haben vor
ankommen
die Ankunft
anmachen
annehmen
anrufen
ansehen
die Antwort, –en
  antworten
der Apfel, ⏜
der April
arbeiten
die Arbeit, –en
der Arbeiter, –
arm
der Arm, –e
der Arzt, ⏜e
der Ast, ⏜e
auch

auf
auf sein
aufgeben
aufmachen
die Aufnahme, –n
aufschreiben
aufspringen
aufstehen
das Auge, –n
der Augenblick, –e
der August'
aus
ausgeben
ausgehen
auslachen
das Ausland
ausmachen
(sich) ausschlafen
aussehen
außer
außerdem
ausverkauft
das Auto, –s

backen
  der Bäcker, –
baden
das Bad, ⏜er
  die Badewanne, –n
der Bahnhof, ⏜e
  zum Bahnhof
  im Bahnhof
  auf dem Bahnhof
bald
die Bank, ⏜e
die Bank, –en
der Bauch, ⏜e
bauen
der Bauer, –n
der Baum, ⏜e
der Beamte, –n
  die Beamtin
befehlen
beginnen
begleiten
behaupten
bei
  beim Essen
beide

das Bein, –e
das Beispiel, –e
  zum Beispiel
bekannt
  der Bekannte
bekommen
bellen
bemerken
beobachten
der Berg, –e
besetzen
  besetzt
besonders
besser
bestellen
bestimmt
besuchen
  der Besuch, –e
das Bett, –en
bevor (*conjunction*)
bezahlen
das Bier, –e
das Bild, –er
binden
bis
ein bißchen
bitte
bitten um
die Bitte, –n
bleiben
blicken
  der Blick, –e
blühen
die Blume, –n
der Boden, ⏜
böse
brauchen
braun
die Braut, ⏜e
  der Bräutigam, –e
brechen
breit
der Brief, –e
  der Briefträger, –
die Brieftaube, –n
bringen
das Brot, –e
die Brücke, –n
der Bruder, ⏜

der Brunnen, –
das Buch, ⏜er
der Buchstabe, –n
das Büro, –s
der Bus, –se
die Butter

da (*adverb*)
da (*conjunction*)
da drüben
daher
dahin
damals
die Dame, –n
danken
  danke
  danke schön
  vielen Dank!
  dankbar
dann
darum
daß
dauern
denken
denn
derselbe
Deutsch
Deutschland
der Dieb, –e
dieser, diese, dieses
diesmal
das Ding, –e
doch
der Dok'tor, die
  Dokto'ren
der Dom, –e
der Donnerstag, –e
das Dorf, ⏜er
dort
draußen
drei
dreißig
dreizehn
drüben
drücken
dumm
der Dummkopf, ⏜e
dunkel
durch

durchmachen
dürfen
durstig

eben
die Ecke, –n
egoistisch
die Ehre, –n
eigen
eigentlich
einfach
der Einfluß, die
    Einflüsse
einige
einladen
einmal
eins
einschlafen
die Eisenbahn, –en
elf
die Eltern
empfehlen
das Ende, –n
endlich
entfernt
entweder . . . oder
    weder . . . noch
die Erde, –n
erfahren
erkennen (an)
erklären
erleben
das Erlebnis, –se
erreichen
erscheinen
erschrecken
erst
    erst dann
    zuerst
    erst gestern
erstaunt
erstens
    zweitens
    drittens
ertrinken
erwarten
erzählen
essen
das Essen, –
etwa
etwas
Euro'pa
    europä'isch

fahren
fahren lernen
der Fall, ¨-e
    auf jeden Fall
    auf keinen Fall
fallen
die Familie, –n
die Farbe, –n
    die Lieblingsfarbe
fast
der Fehler, –
fein
das Fenster, –
fern
die Ferne
fertig
fest
das Feuer, –
    das Feuerwerk, –e
der Film, –e
finden
der Finger, –
fischen
der Fisch, –e
die Flasche, –n
das Fleisch
fliegen
    der Flieger, –
    der Tiefflieger, –
    der Flug, ¨-e
    der Fluggast, ¨-e
    das Flugzeug, –e
    der Flughafen, ¨-
    der Abflug, ¨-e
fliehen
fließen
folgen
fort
der Fortschritt, –e
fragen
    die Frage, –n
Frankreich
die Frau, –en
das Fräulein, –
frei
der Freitag, –e
freiwillig
fremd
fressen
die Freude
der Freund, –e
frieren
frisch
froh (über)

früh
früher
frühestens
der Frühling, –e
das Frühstück, –e
    frühstücken
fühlen
    das Gefühl, –e
führen
füllen
fünf
fünfzehn
fünfzig
für
fürchten
der Fuß, ¨-e
der Fußabdruck, ¨-e
füttern

ganz
    ganz gut
gar (nichts)
der Garten, ¨-
der Gast, ¨-e
das Gebäude, –
    das Hauptgebäude
geben
geboren
    ich bin geboren
die Geburt, –en
    der Geburtstag, –e
der Gedanke, –n
die Gefahr, –en
gefährlich
gefangennehmen
gegen
die Gegend, –en
gehen
geheim
    das Geheimnis, –se
gehorchen
gehören
gehören zu
die Geiß, –en
das Geld
das Gemüse, –
genau
der General', ¨-e
genug
gerade
gern(e)
der Gesandte, –n
geschehen
die Geschichte, –n

das Gesetz, –e
das Gesicht, –er
gestern
gesund
geteilt durch
gewinnen
das Glas, ¨-er
glauben
der Glaube (no pl.)
gleich
das Glück
glücklich
    glücklicherweise
der Gott, ¨-er
gottseidank
gratulieren
grau
greifen
groß
der Großvater, ¨-
grün
grüßen
    der Gruß, ¨-e
gut
Guten Abend!
das Gymnasium,
        die Gymnasien

das Haar, –e
haben
halb
die Halle, –n
halten
    halten für
    halten von
die Hand, ¨-e
hassen
das Haus, ¨-er
    ich gehe nach Hause
    ich bin zu Hause
heilen
heiraten
heiß
heißen
heizen
die Heizung
    die Zenthralheizung
helfen
hell
das Hemd, –en
her
herauskommen
hereinkommen
herkommen

der Herr, –en
herrlich
herum
das Herz, –en
   (*gen.* des Herzens,
     dat. dem Herzen)
heute
   heute abend
   heute morgen
hier
die Hilfe
der Himmel
himmlisch
hin
hineingehen
hinfahren
hinter
der Hintergrund, ̈e
hinunter
   den (Rhein)
     hinunter
hoch
höchstens
der Hof, ̈e
   der Hofgarten
hoffen
hoffentlich
holen
hören
der Hörer, –
das Hotel, –s
hübsch
der Hund, –e
hundert
der Hunger
   ich habe Hunger
   hungrig
der Hut, ̈e

die Idee, die Ide'en
immer
   immer größer
   immer noch
   noch immer
in
der Ingenieur, –e
intelligent
die Intelligenz
interessant
irgend etwas
irgendwo
irgendwohin
Italien
   italienisch

ja
die Jacht, –en
das Jahr, –e
der Januar
je, jemals
jeder, jede, jedes
jedoch
jemand
jetzt
der Juli
jung
der Junge, –n
der Juni

der Kaffee
kalt
der Kampf, ̈e
kämpfen
das Kapitel, –
die Karte, –n
der Kasten, ̈
kaufen
kaum
kein
der Kellner, –
   der Oberkellner,
     „Herr Ober"
kennen
   kennenlernen
das Kind, –er
das Kino, –s
   ich gehe ins Kino
die Kirche, –n
   ich gehe in die
     Kirche
klar
das Klavier, –e
das Kleid, –er
klein
klingeln
klopfen
   anklopfen
kochen
der Koffer, –
kommen
der König, –e
können
der Kopf, ̈e
   die Kopfschmerzen
kosten
krank
die Krankheit, –en
die Kreide
der Kreis, –e

der Krieg, –e
kriegen
die Küche, –n
die Kugel, –n
   der Kugel-
     schreiber, –
kurz
Kusine, –n
küssen

lächeln
das Lächeln
lachen
   das Lachen
das Land, ̈er
landen
lang
lange
   jahrelang
langsam
längst
der Lärm
lassen
die Later'ne, –n
laufen
laut
leben
   das Leben, –
legen
lehren
der Lehrer, –
leicht
leider
leid tun
   es tut mir leid
   er tut mir leid
leise
lernen
lesen
letzt-
   letztes Jahr
leuchten
die Leute
der Leutnant, –e
das Licht, –er
lieb
   liebhaben
die Liebe
lieben
lieber
   am liebsten
der Liebling, –e
liegen

link-
   links
das Loch, ̈er
lügen

machen
   das macht nichts
das Mädchen, –
die Mahlzeit, –en
der Mai
mal
   dieses Mal
   einmal
   zweimal
   noch einmal
   manchmal
   jedesmal
   diesmal
   zwei mal zwei
man (*dat.* einem,
    accus. einen)
mancher
manchmal
der Mann, ̈er
der Mantel, ̈
die Mark
   zwei Mark
die Maschine, –n
die Mathematik'
die Medizin
   Medizin
das Mehl
mehr
   mehr als
mehrere
die Meile, –n
meinen
die Meinung, –en
meist
meistens
der Mensch, –en
merken
das Meter, –
die Milch
mindestens
die Minute, –n
mit
   mitmachen
der Mittag, –e
   der Nachmittag
   das Mittagessen
die Mitternacht
modern
mögen

möglich
   unmöglich
   möglicherweise
   die Möglichkeit,
      –en
der Monat, –e
der Mond, –e
der Montag, –e
der Morgen, –
   morgen
   morgen abend
   guten Morgen!
müde
der Müller, –
der Mund, –̈er
mündlich
das Muse'um,
   die Muse'en
müssen
die Mutter, –̈
   Mutti

na
na sowas!
na und?
nach
der Nachbar, –n
nachdem (conjunc-
   tion)
nachdenken
nachschicken
nächst-
   nächstens
die Nacht, –̈e
   gute Nacht
   heute nacht
die Nadel, –n
nah
   die Nähe
nähen
der Name, –n
   der Vorname, –n
   der Nachname, –n
nämlich
die Nase, –n
die Natur, –en
   natürlich
der Nebel, –
   neblig
neben
nee (colloquial)
nehmen
nein
nett

neu
   das ist mir neu
neun
neunzehn
neunzig
nicht
   nicht mehr
   noch nicht
nichts
nie
niemand
nirgends
noch
   noch einmal
normalerweise
Norwegen
der November
null
die Nummer, –n
nun
nur

ob
oben
das Obst (no pl.)
obwohl
oder
öffnen
   offen
oft
ohne
der Onkel, –
die Oper, –n
die Ordnung, –en
   in Ordnung

das Paar
   ein paar
das Papier, –e
der Paß, –̈e
passieren
die Pause, –n
der Pfarrer, –
der Pfennig, –e
das Pfund, –e
die Physik
der Plan, –̈e
die Platte, –n
der Platz, –̈e
   Platz nehmen
plötzlich
plus
die Polizei (no pl.)

der Polizist, –en
die Post
der Preis, –e
prima
das Problem', –e
der Profes'sor, die
   Professo'ren
die Psychologie
der Punkt, –e

raten
der Rat
   das Rathaus
rauchen
reagieren auf
recht
   das ist mir recht
   recht haben
   recht (sein)
   rechts
   rechtzeitig
reden
der Regen
   regnen
die Regie'rung, –en
   die Bundes-
      regierung, –en
reich
die Reihe, –n
   ich bin an der
      Reihe
   ich komme an die
      Reihe
die Reise, –n
   eine Reise machen
rennen
der Rhein
richtig
der Ring, –e
rollen
der Roman, –e
die Rose, –n
rot
rufen
die Ruhe (no pl.)
   ruhig
   unruhig
russisch
   Rußland

die Sache, –n
sagen
der Samstag, –e
   samstags

der Sänger, –
sauer
schade
scheinen
schenken
   das Geschenk, –e
schicken
schieben
das Schiff, –e
schilaufen
der Schinken, –
schlafen
schlagen
schlank
schlecht
der Schluß
der Schlüssel, –
schnarchen
schneiden
   der Schnitt, –e
schnell
die Schokola'de
schon
schön
der Schrank, –̈e
schreiben
schreien
   der Schrei, –e
der Schriftsteller, –
der Schuh, –e
die Schule, –n
der Schüler, –
schwach
schwarz
schweigen
das Schwein, –e
die Schweiz
schwer
die Schwester, –n
schwimmen
   das Schwimm-
      becken, –
sechs
sechzehn
sechzig
der See, –n
die See (no pl.)
sehen
sehr
sein
seit
   seit langem
   seitdem
die Seite, –n

der Sekretär, –e
selten
seltsam
senden
   der Sender, –
der September
sicher
sieben
siebzehn
singen
die Situation, –en
sitzen
so
   so etwas
   soviel (*conjunction*) soviel ich weiß
sofort
der Sohn, –̈e
solange (*conjunction*)
   solange du lebst
solcher
der Soldat, –en
sollen
der Sommer, –
sondern
die Sonne, –n
der Sonntag, –e
   Sonntag abend
   Sonntag morgen
   jeden Sonntag
   sonntags
sonst
spät
später
spätestens
spazierenfahren
spazierengehen
spielen
sprechen
springen
die Spur, –en
spurlos
der Staat, –en
die Stadt, –̈e
stark
statt
stecken
stehen
   stehenbleiben
stehlen
steigen
   einsteigen

der Stein, –e
stellen
sterben
still
die Stimme, –n
stolz
der Stolz (*no pl.*)
die Straße, –n
   die Straßenbahn, –en
streichen
das Stück, –e
   das Goldstück, –e
der Student, –en
studieren
der Stuhl, –̈e
die Stunde, –n
suchen
die Suppe, –n

der Tag, –e
die Tante, –n
tanzen
die Tasche, –n
die Tasse, –n
tatsächlich
tausend
das Taxi, –s, die Taxe, –n
der Tee
teilen
das Telefon, –e
   telefonieren
die Terrasse, –n
teuer
das Theater, –
das Tier, –e
der Tisch, –e
die Tochter, –̈
tot
tragen
trennen
treten
trinken
trotz
   trotzdem
tun
die Tür, –en

über
überall
(sich) überlegen
überset′zen

die Überset′zung, –en
übrigens
die Uhr
   um ein Uhr
   sechs Uhr
   wieviel Uhr
um
umziehen
um . . . zu
und
ungefähr
die Universität′, –en
der Unsinn
unten
unter
   die Untergrundbahn
der Unterschied, –e
untersuchen

die Vase, –n
der Vater, –̈
verbieten
verbringen
verdienen
vergessen
vergiften
verheiratet sein
verkaufen
verlassen
der Verleger, –
verliebt
verlieren
verlobt
die Vernunft
   vernünftig
verrückt
verschwinden
verschwunden
die Verspätung
   Verspätung haben
versprechen
der Verstand (*no pl.*)
verstehen
versuchen
verwandt
   der Verwandte
viel
   soviel
   zuviel
vielleicht
vier
vierzehn

vierzig
das Volk, –̈er
von
   von (Paris) aus
   von (mir) aus
   von (jetzt) an
vor
   vor einem Jahr
vorbei
vorgestern
vorher
vorne

der Wagen, –
wählen
wahr
während
wahrscheinlich
der Wald, –̈er
die Wand, –̈e
wann
warm
warten auf
warum
was
   was für
waschen
das Wasser, –
weg
   wegfahren
der Weg, –e
wegen
weil
der Wein, –e
weinen
weiß
weit
welcher
die Welt, –en
wenig
   weniger
   wenigstens
wenn
wer
werden
werfen
   umwerfen
der Westen
   die Westfront
wetten um
das Wetter
wichtig
wie
   wie gesagt

wieder
wiederho'len
wie'dersehen
   Auf Wiedersehen!
   Auf Wiederhören!
wiegen
Wien
wieviel
   wieviel Uhr
der Winter
wirklich
   die Wirklichkeit
der Wirt, –e
wissen
   das Wissen
wo

die Woche, –n
woher
wohin
wohl
wohnen
   die Wohnung, –en
der Wolf, ̈e
wollen
das Wort, ̈er and –e
die Wunde, –n
wunderbar
der Wunsch, ̈e
wünschen
die Wurst, ̈e
das Würstchen, –
wütend

zahlen
zählen
zehn
zeigen
die Zeile, –n
die Zeit, –en
   eine Zeitlang
die Zeitung, –en
zerstören
ziehen
die Zigar're, –n
die Zigaret'te, –n
das Zimmer, –
zittern
der Zoll, ̈e
zu

der Zufall, ̈e
   durch Zufall
zufällig
zufrieden
der Zug, ̈e
zuhören
zunächst
zurück
   wieder zurück
zusammen
zwanzig
zwar
zwei
zwingen
zwischen
zwölf

UNIT 11: Infinitive Constructions—**hin** and **her**—
Comparison of Adjectives—The Rhetorical **nicht**—Numbers

[1] **lernen** plus Infinitive

Observe the position of the dependent infinitives; then complete the variations
below.

Ingelheim kannte ich schon vor dem Kriege, aber seine Frau lernte ich erst kennen, als er
mit ihr nach München zog.

> I had known Ingelheim since before the war, but I met his wife only when he moved
> to Munich with her.

SEE
ANALYSIS
166, 167
(pp. 490-495)

Ingelheim kenne ich schon lange, aber seine Frau habe ich leider noch nicht kennengelernt. Ich möchte sie gerne kennenlernen.

> I've known Ingelheim for a long time, but his wife I haven't met yet. I'd like to meet
> her.

Ali war sehr intelligent, aber er hatte nie lesen gelernt.

> Ali was very intelligent, but he had never learned to read.

Viele Kinder lernen schon mit fünf Jahren lesen.

> Many children learn to read at the age of five.

Bevor Sie nach Kalifornien gehen, müssen Sie unbedingt Auto fahren lernen.

> Before you go to California, you absolutely must learn to drive.

Es wäre besser, wenn Sie Auto fahren gelernt hätten.

> It would be better if you had learned to drive.

VARIATIONS

Complete the following sentences by using the infinitives in parentheses. Use
more than one tense if possible.

> Es wäre besser, wenn sie _____ (kochen lernen).
> Ich möchte wissen, ob sie _____ (kochen lernen).

(Facing) **Der ,,Römer''—das Rathaus in Frankfurt**

Ich dachte, du _____ (schwimmen lernen).

Sie soll tatsächlich _____ (Auto fahren lernen).

Ich hoffe, daß er hier jemanden _____ (kennenlernen).

[2] **bleiben** plus Infinitive

Observe again the position of the dependent infinitives; then complete the variations below.

SEE
ANALYSIS
167
(pp. 491-495)

Bitte bleiben Sie doch sitzen, Herr Schmidt.

>   Please stay seated (don't get up).

Warum hat sie denn den Meyer geheiratet? Um nicht sitzenzubleiben?—Ja, weil sie nicht sitzenbleiben wollte.

>   Why did she marry Meyer? In order not to become an old maid?—Yes, because she didn't want to become an old maid.

Sie hat nicht sitzenbleiben wollen.

>   She did not want to become an old maid.

Du brauchst noch nicht aufzustehen; du kannst noch liegen bleiben.

>   You don't have to get up yet; you can still stay in bed.

Wem gehört denn das Buch da?—Das weiß ich nicht; es ist gestern abend hier liegengeblieben.

>   To whom does that book belong?—I don't know; it was left here last night.

Meine Uhr ist gestern abend plötzlich stehengeblieben.

>   My watch suddenly stopped last night.

Bitte gehen Sie weiter; Sie dürfen hier nicht stehenbleiben.

>   Please go on, you mustn't stop here.

VARIATIONS

Complete the following sentences, using the infinitives in parentheses. Use more than one tense, if possible.

>   Bitte _____, Herr Meyer! (sitzen bleiben).
>
>   Ich hoffe, meine Uhr _____ (stehenbleiben).
>
>   Ich glaube, meine Uhr _____ (stehenbleiben).
>
>   Ich dachte, meine Uhr _____ (stehenbleiben).
>
>   Er kommt heute nicht zum Frühstück. Er _____ (liegen bleiben).

[3] **gehen** and **fahren** plus Infinitive

Observe again the position of the dependent infinitives; then complete the variations that follow.

Wie wäre es, wenn wir jetzt essen gingen?

    How about going to eat now?

SEE
ANALYSIS
167
(pp. 491-495)

Fritz ist auch schon essen gegangen.

    Fritz has gone to eat too.

Können wir bald essen gehen?

    Can we go eat soon?

Du brauchst doch nicht schon wieder essen zu gehen; du hast doch gerade erst gefrühstückt.

    You don't need to go eat again; you just had breakfast, didn't you?

Wie wär's denn, wenn wir Sonntag baden gingen?

    Would you like to go swimming on Sunday?

Was habt ihr denn heute gemacht?—Erst sind wir schwimmen gegangen, und dann sind wir spazierengefahren.

    What did you do today?—First, we went swimming, and then we went for a ride.

VARIATIONS

Complete the following sentences by using the infinitives in parentheses. Use more than one tense, if possible.

    Es wäre nett, wenn wir morgen ——————— (schwimmen gehen).

    Ich dachte, ihr beide ——————— (schwimmen gehen).

    Er soll jeden Tag mit Erika ——————— (schwimmen gehen).

    Ist Hans schon im Bett?—Ja, er ——————— (schlafen gehen).

    Ich wollte, wir ——————— (schlafen gehen).

[4] hören and sehen plus Infinitive

Observe how **hören** and **sehen** behave like modals in these sentences. Then follow the instructions below.

Ich hörte ihn kommen.

    I heard him come.

SEE
ANALYSIS
167
(pp. 491-495)

Ich hörte ihn nach Hause kommen.

    I heard him come home.

Ich hörte ihn gestern abend nach Hause kommen.
Ich habe ihn gestern abend nach Hause kommen hören.
Ich habe gehört, wie er gestern abend nach Hause kam.

    I heard him come home last night.

Hinter dem Hause hörten wir eine Frau schreien.

    Behind the house we heard a woman scream.

Wir sahen sie in Berlin die Desdemona spielen.
> We saw her play Desdemona in Berlin.

Wir haben sie die Desdemona spielen sehen.
> We've seen her play Desdemona.

Wir sind nach Berlin gefahren, um sie die Desdemona spielen zu sehen.
> We went to Berlin to see her play Desdemona.

VARIATIONS

Form sentences with the following phrases, using modals, subjunctives, and various tenses:

> Emma einmal (noch nie) lachen sehen
> den Kleinen schreien hören
> die Maria nach Hause kommen hören

[5] lassen

The various uses of **lassen** are shown below, each followed by a short exercise.

SEE
ANALYSIS
167
(pp. 491-495)

Heute regnet es bestimmt nicht. Deinen Regenmantel kannst du zu Hause lassen.
> I'm sure it won't rain today. You can leave your raincoat at home.

Heute regnet es bestimmt nicht. Du hättest deinen Mantel zu Hause lassen können.
> I'm sure it won't rain today. You could have left your raincoat at home.

Ingelheims Romane lassen mich kalt.
> Ingelheim's novels leave me cold.

Bitte lassen Sie mich jetzt allein.
> Please leave me alone now.

Ich wollte, er ließe mich in Ruhe.
> I wish he'd leave me alone (in peace).

Express in German:
> I've left my coat at home.
> I wish I hadn't left it at home.
> Why do you always leave your coat at home?
> He has always left me cold (and still does).
> He left everything as it was.

Jetzt habe ich schon wieder meinen Mantel im Hotel hängenlassen.
> Now I've left my coat at the hotel again.

Und wo ist deine Handtasche?—Die habe ich bei Tante Amalie auf dem Tisch stehen-
lassen.

> Where is your bag? — I left it on the table at Aunt Amalie's.

Und deine Handschuhe hast du wohl auch irgendwo liegenlassen?

> And I suppose you left your gloves somewhere too?

Express in German (note that the infinitives **hängen, stehen, liegen** behave like
prefixes and do not change):

> I hope you won't leave your coat in the hotel again.
> I have left my gloves at Aunt Amalie's.
> You can't leave your car in front of the hotel.

Ich lasse dich nicht nach Berlin fahren.

> I won't let you go to Berlin.

Ich habe ihn doch nach Berlin fahren lassen.

> I have let him go to Berlin after all.

Ich wollte, ich hätte ihn nicht nach Berlin fahren lassen.

> I wish I hadn't let him go to Berlin.

Du kannst mich doch nicht ohne Geld nach Berlin fahren lassen.

> You can't let me go to Berlin without money.

Ich hätte ihn nicht allein nach Berlin fahren lassen sollen.

> I shouldn't have let him go to Berlin alone.

Warum darf *ich* nicht allein ins Kino gehen? *Müllers* lassen ihre Tochter allein ins Kino
gehen.

> Why can't I go to the movies alone? The Müllers let their daughter go to the movies
> alone.

Express in German:

> Why don't you let me study medicine?
> I wish you'd let me study medicine.
> I wish we had let him study medicine.
> We can't let him study medicine.
> We shouldn't have let him study medicine.
> We shall let him study medicine.

Müllers Frau ging es gestern abend so schlecht, daß er den Arzt kommen lassen mußte.

> Müller's wife was so unwell last night that he had to call the doctor (had to let the
> doctor come).

Meyer mußte gestern abend den Arzt kommen lassen.
>   Meyer had to have the doctor come last night.

Ich habe ihm sagen lassen, daß er mich morgen anrufen soll.
>   I left word for him to call me tomorrow.

Ich wollte ihn nicht anrufen; ich habe ihm ein Telegramm schicken lassen.
>   I didn't want to call him; I've had a telegram sent to him.

Ingelheim läßt seine Romane in München drucken.
>   Ingelheim has his novels printed in Munich.

Wo hast du dir die Haare schneiden lassen?
>   Where did you have your hair cut?

Frau Lenz hat sich schon wieder einen Mantel machen lassen.
>   Frau Lenz has had another coat made.

Du, *der* Mantel ist aber todschick; in *dem* kannst du dich sehen lassen.
>   Say, that coat is really something (great, fine); it really does something for you.

Der Wein ist gut; der läßt sich trinken.
>   This wine is good; it's quite drinkable. (Understatement)

Meyer tut, was er will. Der läßt sich nie etwas sagen.
>   Meyer does what he wants. You can't tell him a thing.

Ich lasse mir eine Tasse Kaffee aufs Zimmer bringen.
>   I'm having a cup of coffee brought to my room.

Ich habe mir eine Tasse Kaffee aufs Zimmer bringen lassen.
>   I've had a cup of coffee brought to my room.

Warum hast du dir denn nicht eine Tasse Kaffee aufs Zimmer bringen lassen?
>   Why didn't you have a cup of coffee brought to your room?

Warum hat sie sich denn den Kaffee nicht aufs Zimmer bringen lassen?
>   Why didn't she have the coffee brought to her room?

Nein, von Meyer lasse ich mich nicht nach München fahren; man sollte ihn überhaupt nicht Autofahren lassen.
>   No, I won't let Meyer take me to Munich; they shouldn't let him drive a car at all.

Hans ist doch Student; du kannst dir doch von ihm nicht immer das Essen bezahlen lassen.
>   But Hans is a student; you can't always let him pay for your meals.

Using the phrase **die Haare schneiden,** express in German:

>   I must get a haircut today.
>   I got a haircut yesterday.

I always have him cut my hair.

Why didn't you get a haircut today?

Yes, I'll get a haircut tomorrow.

François? I'll never have *him* cut my hair again.
    (Start with *Von dem* . . .)

[6] brauchen, scheinen, haben, sein

Observe the use of infinitives with **zu** depending on these verbs.

Du brauchst nicht auf mich zu warten; ich komme heute spät nach Hause.
    You don't need to wait for me; I'll come home late today.

Du hättest nicht auf mich zu warten brauchen.
    You needn't have waited for me.

Es scheint zu regnen.

Er scheint zu schlafen.

Er scheint nicht zu Hause zu sein.

Er scheint schon abgefahren zu sein.

Gut ge*schla*fen zu haben scheinst du *nicht.*

Er scheint heute nicht zu arbeiten zu brauchen.

Er scheint nichts zu sagen zu haben.

Ich kann leider nicht mitgehen; ich habe noch etwas zu tun.
    I'm sorry, but I can't come along; I still have something to do.

Ich hatte den ganzen Tag nichts zu tun.
    I didn't have anything to do all day.

SEE ANALYSIS 167

(pp. 491-495)

Wenn ich nicht so viel zu tun gehabt hätte, hätte ich dir gerne geholfen.

> If I hadn't had so much to do, I would gladly have helped you.

Nur um etwas zu tun zu haben, ging er jeden Abend ins Kino.

> Just to have something to do, he went to the movies every night.

Meyer ist nicht mein Chef, und er hat mir nichts zu sagen.

> Meyer is not my boss, and I don't have to take any orders from him.

Da ist nichts zu machen.

> There's nothing to be done (about it).

Hans war einfach nicht zu finden.

> Hans was simply not to be found.

Professor Mertens ist immer gut zu verstehen.

> Professor Mertens is always easy to understand.

Er soll gut zu verstehen gewesen sein.

> He is supposed to have been easy to understand. (I hear he was easy to understand.)

Es ist nicht zu erwarten, daß die Preise bald fallen.

> It is not to be expected that prices will come down soon.

VARIATIONS

Express in German:

> Don't you have anything to do?
> Don't you have anything to say?
> Why does he never have anything to say?
> It would be nice if I had nothing to do today.
> I wish I had something to do today.
> He seems to have nothing to do today.
> He seems to have married again.

[7] End-Field Infinitives (the Group **anfangen**)

In the following sentences, note that the clause to which the infinitive belongs has to be completed before the infinitive phrase can be started. Then complete the variations below.

SEE
ANALYSIS
168

(pp. 495-498)

Es fing an zu regnen.

> It began to rain.

Als es anfing zu regnen, gingen wir nach Hause.

> When it began to rain, we went home.

Es hat angefangen zu regnen.
    It has started to rain.

Es fing an, sehr stark zu regnen.
    It started to rain hard.

Als es anfing, sehr stark zu regnen, gingen wir nach Hause.
    When it started to rain very hard, we went home.

Kannst du nicht endlich aufhören zu arbeiten?
    Can't you finally stop working?

Ich finde es langweilig, jeden Abend stundenlang fernzusehen.
    I find it boring to watch TV for hours every night.

Weil ich vergessen hatte, ihm zu schreiben, kam er nicht zum Bahnhof.
    Because I had forgotten to write to him, he didn't come to the station.

Meyer soll seinem Sohn versprochen haben, ihm zum Geburtstag ein Auto zu schenken.
    Meyer supposedly promised his son to give him a car for his birthday.

Hast du denn nicht versucht, sie anzurufen?
    Didn't you try to call her?

Ingelheim behauptet, in der Normandie gekämpft zu haben.
    Ingelheim claims to have fought in Normandy.

Vor einer Stunde hat ein Herr Melzer angerufen. Er behauptete, ein Freund von Ihnen zu sein.
    A Mr. Melzer called an hour ago. He claimed to be a friend of yours.

VARIATIONS

Change the following sentences to infinitive clauses and use the verbs in parentheses to form introductory clauses.

Es regnet nicht mehr. (aufhören)
Es hat aufgehört zu regnen.

Er will in Paris gewesen sein. (behaupten)
Ich habe ihr nicht geschrieben. (vergessen)
Meyer will seiner Frau ein Auto schenken. (versprechen)
Ich möchte sie bald wiedersehen. (hoffen)
Ich wollte dich gestern abend anrufen (versuchen)
Ich muß jeden Tag zwei Stunden im Auto sitzen. (es dumm finden)
Ich kann meinen Vater nicht um Geld bitten. (es nicht wagen)

[8] End-Field Infinitives (the Group **befehlen**)

Observe the identity of the personal dative and the unmentioned subject of the end-field infinitive. Then complete the variations.

SEE
ANALYSIS
168

(pp. 495-498)

Er schlug mir vor, an die Nordsee zu fahren.
> He suggested that I go to the North Sea.

Wenn Sie mir nicht vorgeschlagen hätten, an die Nordsee zu fahren, hätte ich meinen Mann nie kennengelernt.
> If you hadn't suggested that I go to the North Sea, I would never have met my husband.

Ich rate dir, nicht mehr so viel zu rauchen.
> I advise you not to smoke so much any more.

Wir erlauben unseren Kindern nicht, jede Woche zweimal ins Kino zu gehen.
> We don't allow our children to go to the movies twice a week.

In Deutschland ist es verboten, im Kino zu rauchen.
> In Germany it is forbidden to smoke in the movie theater.

Niemand kann mir befehlen, einen Mann zu heiraten, den ich nicht liebe.
> Nobody can order me to marry a man I don't love.

Wir können Ihnen leider nicht gestatten, dieses Buch mit nach Hause zu nehmen.
> I'm sorry, but we can't permit you to take this book home.

Darf ich Ihnen empfehlen, gnädige Frau, einmal einen Mosel zu versuchen?
> May I recommend that you try a Moselle, Madam?

Vielen Dank, daß Sie mir geholfen haben, die Sachen ins Haus zu bringen.
> Thank you for helping me to bring the things into the house.

VARIATIONS

Change the following sentences to infinitive clauses and use the verbs in parentheses to form introductory clauses. Use **Er** and the perfect tense throughout.

> **Fahren Sie doch mal an die See. (raten)**
> **Er hat mir geraten, einmal an die See zu fahren.**

Trinken Sie jeden Abend vor dem Schlafengehen ein Glas Wein. (empfehlen)
Bleiben Sie morgen zu Hause. (erlauben)
Ich wünsche nicht, daß Sie mit meiner Tochter ins Theater gehen. (verbieten)
Fahren Sie doch mit mir nach München. (vorschlagen)

[9] End-Field Infinitives after Adjectives

After studying these sentences, complete the variations.

Inge war froh, ihren Mann wiederzusehen.
   Inge was glad to see her husband again.

SEE
ANALYSIS
168
(pp. 495-498)

Ich wußte, Inge wäre froh gewesen, ihren Mann wiederzusehen.
   I knew Inge would have been glad to see her husband again.

Ich bin immer bereit gewesen, ihm zu helfen.
   I have always been ready to help him.

Ich war sehr erstaunt, Erich aus dem Haus des Ägypters kommen zu sehen.
   I was very astonished to see Erich come out of the Egyptian's house.

Ich möchte wissen, ob er fähig ist, eine Frau wirklich zu lieben.
   I'd like to know whether he is capable of really loving a woman.

Es macht mich glücklich, Sie endlich kennenzulernen.
   It makes me happy to meet you at last.

Ich bin froh, Sie endlich kennengelernt zu haben.
   I am glad to have met you at last.

VARIATIONS

Change the following sentences to infinitive clauses. Use the subjects of these sentences and the adjectives in parentheses to form introductory clauses.

Inge sah ihren Mann wieder. (froh)
Inge war froh, ihren Mann wiederzusehen.

Gottseidank sind wir wieder zu Hause. (glücklich)
Erich half uns immer. (bereit)
Das Kind kann schon bis zehn zählen. (fähig)
Ich sah ihn letztes Wochenende in Hamburg wieder. (erstaunt)

[10] End-Field Infinitives after **da**-Compounds

Note that the subject of the inflected verb is also the unmentioned subject of the infinitive.

Ich denke nicht daran, mit Inge schwimmen zu gehen.
   I wouldn't think of going swimming with Inge.

SEE
ANALYSIS
168
(pp. 495-498)

Du weißt doch, daß ich gar nicht daran denke, mit Inge schwimmen zu gehen.
> Don't you know that I wouldn't think of going swimming with Inge?

Ich habe ja gar nicht daran gedacht, mit Inge schwimmen zu gehen.
> I hadn't any intention of going swimming with Inge.

Ich hätte nie daran gedacht, mit Inge schwimmen zu gehen.
> I would never have thought of going swimming with Inge.

Form similar sentences with **Angst haben vor, jemanden bitten um, hoffen auf.**

[11] End-Field Infinitives with **um . . . zu, ohne . . . zu, statt . . . zu**

Note how the German construction changes if the subject of the infinitive is not also the subject of the inflected verb.

SEE
ANALYSIS
168
(pp. 495-498)

Wir bleiben heute zu Hause, um endlich einmal arbeiten zu können.
> We're going to stay at home today in order to get some work done finally.

Wir bleiben heute zu Hause, damit mein Mann endlich einmal arbeiten kann.
> We're going to stay at home today in order that my husband can finally get some work done (so that my husband can finally get some work done).

Wir sind in die Stadt gezogen, um öfter ins Theater gehen zu können.
> We've moved to the city (in order) to be able to go to the theater more often.

Wir sind in die Stadt gezogen, damit mein Mann nicht mehr so weit ins Büro fahren muß.
> We've moved to the city so that my husband won't have to drive so far to the office.

Ohne auch nur einen Augenblick nachzudenken, lief Hermann hinter das Haus.
> Without a moment's thought, Hermann ran behind the house.

Ingelheim war nach Casablanca gefahren, ohne daß seine Frau etwas davon wußte.
> Ingelheim had gone to Casablanca without his wife knowing anything about it.

Ich hatte ihn oft gesehen, ohne zu wissen, wer er war.
> I had often seen him without knowing who he was.

Mit Meyer kann man nie sprechen, ohne daß seine Frau dabei ist.
> You can never talk to Meyer without his wife being there too.

Hast du schon wieder die ganze Nacht gelesen, statt zu schlafen?
> Have you read all night again instead of going to sleep?

Statt daß man *Meyer* nach Berlin geschickt hätte, muß *ich* schon wieder fahren.
> Instead of their having sent Meyer to Berlin (which they should have done and didn't), I have to go again.

[12] hin and her

Be prepared to produce orally the sentences on the left when you hear the
sentences on the right, and vice versa.

Ich fahre sofort hin.	Er kommt sofort her.	SEE ANALYSIS 169 (pp. 498-501)
Kannst du hinfahren?	Kannst du herkommen?	
Ich bin sofort hingefahren.	Er ist sofort hergekommen.	
Ich brauche nicht hinzufahren.	Er braucht nicht herzukommen.	
Wer hat dich denn dahingebracht?	Wer hat dich denn hierhergebracht?	
Wie bist du denn dahingekommen?	Wie bist du denn hierhergekommen?	
Sie fahren nach Köln? Dahin fahre ich auch.	Sie kommen von Köln? Daher komme ich auch.	

VARIATIONS

Form variations with the following pattern:

Den kenne ich noch von früher her.
(Literally: I've known him from an earlier time on.)

von der Schule
vom Kriege
von der Tanzstunde
von München

Form variations on the following situation with **vorher** and **nachher**:

**Gestern abend waren wir im Theater. Vorher haben wir im Regina ge-
gessen, und nachher waren wir bei Schmidts.**

Letzten Mittwoch war ich in Köln.
Um sieben haben wir zu Abend gegessen.
Morgen mittag besuche ich Tante Amalie.

Memorize the following sentences:

Weißt du was? Rosemarie hat vorhin angerufen.
Ich war vorhin bei Schmidts.

Diese Uhr hier ist hin,—die ist kaputt.
Meine Ruh' ist hin, mein Herz ist schwer. (Goethe)

Be prepared to produce the sentences on the left when you hear the sentences on the right, and vice versa:

Wohin gehst du denn?	Wo gehst du denn hin?
Woher kommst du denn?	Wo kommst du denn her?
Wohin ist er denn gegangen?	Wo ist er denn hingegangen?
Woher ist er denn gekommen?	Wo ist er denn hergekommen?
Wohin wollt ihr denn fahren?	Wo wollt ihr denn hinfahren?
Wohin kann sie denn gegangen sein?	Wo kann sie denn hingegangen sein?
Dahin gehe ich auch.	Da gehe ich auch hin.
Daher komme ich auch.	Da komme ich auch her.

In the following examples, note the difference in meaning between the forms with **hin-** and **her-** and the forms without **hin-** and **her-**.

Die Titanic ist untergegangen.
> The Titanic sank.

Die Sonne geht unter.
> The sun sets.

Wo seid ihr denn untergekommen?
> Where did you find a place to stay?

Das Licht ist ausgegangen.
> The light went out.

Die Sonne geht auf.
> The sun rises.

Zwanzig Gäste können wir hier nicht unterbringen.
> We can't put up twenty guests here.

Ich konnte ihn nicht mehr einholen.
> I couldn't catch up with him any more.

Mit zweihundert Mark im Monat kann ich nicht auskommen.
> I can't get along on two hundred marks a month.

Ich gehe ins Eßzimmer hinunter.
> I'm going down to the dining room.

Er kommt sofort herunter.
> He'll be down in a minute.

Ist er schon heruntergekommen?
> Has he come down yet?

Er ist gerade hinausgegangen.
> He just went out.

Herr Doktor Schmidt ist schon hinaufgegangen.
> Dr. Schmidt has already gone up.

Ich bringe Ihnen den Koffer hinunter.
> I'll take your suitcase down.

Hast du die Zeitung schon hereingeholt?
> Have you brought the paper in yet?

Ich habe ihn noch nicht herauskommen sehen.
> I haven't seen him come out yet.

Note the "prepositional brackets" in the following sentences:

Er kam aus dem Haus heraus.
Er ging ins Haus hinein.

Wir fahren durch den Panamakanal hindurch.
Wir stiegen auf den Berg hinauf.
Er sprang über den Zaun hinüber.

[13] Comparative Forms of Adjectives

Be prepared to produce orally the sentences on the right when you hear the sentences on the left.

Sie ist so alt wie ich.	Sie ist älter als ich.	SEE ANALYSIS 170 (pp. 501-504)
Hier ist es so kalt wie in Hamburg.	Hier ist es kälter als in Hamburg.	
Leider ist sie nicht so jung wie er.	Leider ist er jünger als sie.	
Hier ist es nicht so warm wie bei euch.	Bei euch ist es viel wärmer als bei uns.	
Die Alpen sind nicht so hoch wie die Sierras.	Die Sierras sind höher als die Alpen.	
Ingelheim ist nicht ganz so interessant wie Thomas Mann.	Thomas Mann ist etwas interessanter als Ingelheim.	
Du bist doch nicht so groß wie ich.	Doch, ich bin größer als du.	
Das Bier hier ist wirklich gut.	Ja, aber das Bier in München ist noch besser.	
Tante Dorothea redet genau so viel wie Tante Amalie.	Nee, nee, die redet noch mehr als Tante Amalie, noch viel mehr.	
Hier ist das frische Obst nicht so teuer wie bei uns.	Bei uns ist das Obst viel teurer als bei euch.	
Inges Haar war schon immer so dunkel wie meins.	Aber seit sie vierzig ist, wird es immer dunkler.	
Möchtest du dir gern den Faustfilm ansehen?	Nein, ich ginge viel lieber in einen Wildwestfilm.	

Form similar pairs with the following adjectives:

schnell, schneller	lang, länger
freundlich, freundlicher	oft, öfter
arm, ärmer	schwarz, schwärzer
hart, härter	stark, stärker
kurz, kürzer	nah, näher

[14] Superlative Forms of Adjectives

Read the following sentences and complete the variations:

Die Frau mit dem Flamingo ist sein bester Roman.
Ich halte *Die Frau mit dem Flamingo* für _____.

SEE ANALYSIS 170 (pp. 501-504)

Monika ist die interessanteste Frau, die ich kenne.
Von allen Frauen, die ich kenne, ist sie die _____.

San Franzisko soll die schönste Stadt der Welt sein.
Möchtest du nicht auch ein Haus in der _____ der Welt haben?

Im Februar ist es hier am kältesten.
Der Februar ist der _____ Monat des Jahres.

Im Dezember sind die Tage am kürzesten.
Der 21. Dezember ist der _____ Tag des Jahres.

In dieser Show sehen Sie Giganto, den stärksten Mann der Welt.
Giganto ist von allen Männern der _____.

Was ist Ingelheims bester Roman?
Mir gefällt *Die Frau mit dem Flamingo* am _____.

Hier ist es ja das ganze Jahr sehr schön, aber im Mai ist es hier doch am _____.

Spieglein, Spieglein an der Wand,
Wer ist die Schönste im ganzen Land?
    Frau Königin, Ihr° seid die Schönste hier,
    aber Schneewittchen hinter den Bergen,
    bei den sieben Zwergen,
    ist noch tausendmal schöner als Ihr.

[15] Comparatives and Superlatives: Advertising Slogans

You can find advertisements like these in German magazines.

Sie können natürlich mehr Geld ausgeben, aber es ist nicht sicher, ob Sie einen besseren
    Waschautomaten bekommen.

Gesünder und darum besser ist ein Cottona-Hemd.

Sie sollten nicht weniger für ihr Geld verlangen.
Sie sollten mehr verlangen: Ein VW ist der beste Kauf.

Cinzano on the rocks: der beste Anfang einer guten Sache.

In der ganzen Welt kennt man den Namen Pall Mall als Garantie für teuerste Tabake.
    Die Pall Mall Filter ist eine mild-aromatische Blendcigarette im King-Size-Format.
    20 Pall Mall Filter kosten DM 1,75.

Was trinken Sie am liebsten, wenn Sie mit Ihrer Frau abends fernsehen? Natürlich Löwen-
    bräu.

° **Ihr** is an obsolete polite form now replaced by **Sie**.

Wie gern essen wir ein Steak. Noch lieber ist es uns mit einem Schuß Ketchup. Am liebsten essen wir es aber mit Thomy's Tomaten-Ketchup. Es gehört zu den neun Thomy's
Delikatessen.

Statt für jeden etwas, etwas Besonderes für alle: Triumpf, die beste Schreibmaschine.

Jede moderne Frau weiß, wie man sich interessanter macht. Die interessantesten Frauen
tragen Elastiform.

[16] The Rhetorical **nicht**

Haben Sie einen *Bru*der?	Do you have a brother?	**SEE ANALYSIS 172**
Haben Sie keinen *Bru*der?	Don't you have a brother?	
Haben Sie nicht *einen Bru*der?	Don't you have a single brother?	(pp. 507-508)
Haben Sie nicht einen *Bru*der?	You have a brother, haven't you?	

Habe ich nicht einen intelligenten Sohn?

Ist sie nicht ein hübsches Mädchen?

Warst du nicht gestern abend mit Inge im Kino?

Habe ich dich nicht gestern im Theater gesehen?

Haben Sie nicht damals in Berlin die Desdemona gespielt?

Haben Sie nicht früher bei der Hansa-Bank gearbeitet?

Bin ich nicht schon immer dagegen gewesen?

Hat nicht unsere Partei seit Jahren immer wieder bewiesen, daß sie allein den Weg weiß
in eine bessere Zukunft?

Change the following statements into rhetorical questions:

Sie haben ihn schon vor dem Krieg kennengelernt, nicht wahr?

Seine Tochter hat den Fritz Müller geheiratet, nicht wahr?

Sie haben schon immer einmal nach Amerika fahren wollen, nicht wahr?

[17] Numbers

Read aloud and observe stress:

100 *hun*dert

101 hundert*eins*

102 hundert*zwei*

110 hundert*zehn*

120 hundert*zwan*zig

121 hundert*ein*und*zwan*zig

122 hundert*zwei*und*zwan*zig

SEE ANALYSIS 173 (pp. 508-510)

198 hundert*acht*und*neun*zig
199 hundert*neun*und*neun*zig
200 *zweihun*dert

100 *ein*hundert
200 *zwei*hundert
300 *drei*hundert
900 *neun*hundert
1.000 *taus*end

7.839 *sieb*entausend*acht*hundert*neun*und*dreiß*ig
1.000.000 eine Milli*on*
2.000.000 zwei Millionen
1.000.000.000 eine Milli*arde* (one billion)

Ich brauche zweihundert*ein*undvierzig *Mark.*
In unserer Stadt wohnen jetzt über *drei*hunderttausend *Men*schen.
Unsere Bibliothek hat mehrere Millionen *Mark* gekostet.
„Und Noah lebte nach der Flut *drei*hundertund*fünf*zig Jahre; alle Tage Noahs waren *neun*hundertund*fünf*zig Jahre, und er *starb*.“

0,7 *null* komma *sie*ben
0,17 *null* komma *sieb*zehn (*null* komma *eins sie*ben)
3,14159 *drei* komma *eins vier eins fünf neun*

Read the following numbers:

758
75,8
7,58
2,718282
232.493,00
232,493

DM   4,20 vier Mark zwanzig
DM 121,00 hunderteinundzwanzig Mark
DM 100,21 hundert Mark einundzwanzig
DM   0,75 fünfundsiebzig Pfennig
  $1.477,00 vierzehnhundertsiebenundsiebzig Dollar
             eintausendvierhundertsiebenundsiebzig Dollar
  $ 18,37 achtzehn Dollar siebenunddreißig

Und was kosten drei Dosen Orangensaft?

Am ersten und zweiten Februar waren wir in Berlin, am dritten und vierten in Hamburg und vom fünften bis zum zehnten in Bonn.

Berlin, den 1.2.1970 (den ersten Februar 1970)
Hamburg, 8.9.71 (den achten September 1971)

August Meyer
17. Aug. 1889—21. Sept. 1954.
R.I.P.
(geboren am siebzehnten August 1889,
gestorben am einundzwanzigsten September 1954.
Requiescat in Pace)

Read the following dates:

13.1.27	7.7.29	18.6.1962
8.2.25	20.8.54	22.2.1732
25.10.04	1.9.38	7.12.1941

Heinrich I. (Heinrich der Erste)
Friedrich Wilhelm IV. (Friedrich Wilhelm der Vierte)
Er war ein Sohn Friedrichs II. (Er war ein Sohn Friedrichs des Zweiten.)

Read the following:

Leo XIII. (1887–1903) (1887 bis 1903)
Pius X. (1903–1914)
Benedict XV. (1914–1922)
Pius XI. (1922–1939)
Pius XII. (1939–1958)
Johannes XXIII. (1958–1963) (der Dreiundzwanzigste)

Und hier, meine Damen und Herren, sehen Sie ein Bild von Herzog August III., der, wie Sie wissen, der Vater Sigismunds II. war. Seine Frau Mechthild, eine Tochter Augusts V. von Niederlohe-Schroffenstein, soll die schönste Frau ihrer Zeit gewesen sein.

Nein, nach Italien fahren will ich nicht. Erstens habe ich kein Geld, zweitens habe ich keine Lust, drittens mag ich Meyers nicht und viertens: meine Frau ist dagegen.

Nein, soviel kann ich nicht essen. Die Hälfte davon ist mehr als genug.

Hat Tante Amalie schon ihr Testament gemacht?—Ja, und ein Drittel von ihrem Geld bekommt das Museum.

Seine Frau erhielt zwei Drittel seines Vermögens, und das dritte Drittel ging an seine beiden Söhne.

GEÖFFNET:
MONTAG-FREITAG
                    8 30 - 18 30
SAMSTAG   8 30 - 14 00
jeden 1. Samstag des Monats
                    8 30   -   18 00

Ich hätte gerne ein halbes Pfund Butter.
Geben Sie mir bitte ein viertel Pfund Schinken.

Read aloud:

½   ⅓   ²/₇   ⁶/₈   ⁵/₁₂

[18] Time

SEE
ANALYSIS
174
(pp. 510-511)

11.00 Uhr	elf Uhr
11.05 Uhr	fünf nach elf
11.10 Uhr	zehn nach elf
11.15 Uhr	viertel nach elf; viertel zwölf
11.20 Uhr	zwanzig nach elf
11.25 Uhr	fünf vor halb zwölf
11.30 Uhr	halb zwölf
11.35 Uhr	fünf nach halb zwölf
11.40 Uhr	zehn nach halb zwölf
11.45 Uhr	dreiviertel zwölf; viertel vor zwölf
11.50 Uhr	zehn vor zwölf
11.55 Uhr	fünf vor zwölf
12.00 Uhr	zwölf Uhr

Read aloud and, where possible, in several ways:

9.05 (Uhr)	4.25 (Uhr)	12.45 (Uhr)
9.15	7.45	1.30
10.30	7.57	21.45

Eisenbahnterminologie

Es ist nicht leicht, einen deutschen Fahrplan zu lesen. Die folgende Tabelle (siehe Seite 480) ist eine Seite aus einem deutschen Kursbuch, und wir wollen versuchen, einen Zug von Frankfurt nach Koblenz zu finden.

Zunächst suchen wir Frankfurt (Zeile 11) und Koblenz (Zeile 23). 5 *Hbf.* steht für Hauptbahnhof. Der erste Zug hat die Nummer D 1269, d.h. es ist ein D-Zug oder Schnellzug, der nur auf größeren Bahnhöfen hält. Dieser Zug kommt um 13.57 Uhr in Koblenz an, aber er fährt nicht über Frankfurt, sondern direkt von Mannheim nach Mainz. Auch der nächste Zug, D 463, aus Basel in der Schweiz, 10 fährt nicht über Frankfurt. Jetzt kommt ein Eilzug (E 721), ab Frankfurt Hbf. um 12.32 Uhr und an Koblenz um 14.27 Uhr.

der Fahrplan, ¨e timetable
die Tabelle, –n table
das Kursbuch, ¨er complete book of timetables

die Zeile, –n line
das Haupt, ¨er head; **Haupt–** (in compounds) main
d.h. = das heißt that is (i.e.)

eilen to hurry

Bahnhof in Hamburg-Altona

Eilzüge halten öfter als Schnellzüge, aber nur Personenzüge halten auf allen Bahnhöfen. Außerdem gibt es noch F-Züge, d.h. Fernschnellzüge und TEE– (Trans-Europ-Express) Züge. TEE- und F-Züge haben nur 1. Klasse, alle anderen Züge haben 1. und 2. Klasse. Fahrkarten für die 1. Klasse kosten 12 Pf. pro km, für die 2. 5 Klasse 8 Pf./km. Außerdem gibt es Rückfahrkarten mit 10 bis 40% (Prozent) Ermäßigung. In F-Zügen und D-Zügen bezahlt man zum Fahrpreis noch einen besonderen Zuschlag von 2 bis 4 Mark.

Zurück zum Fahrplan: Die nächsten beiden Züge sind wieder Eilzüge (E 590 und E 297), aber der erste fährt von Bingerbrück aus 10 nach Saarbrücken, der zweite fährt rechtsrheinisch, d.h. auf der

Europ shortened form of **Europa**

die Ermäßigung, –en reduction, reduced price
der Zuschlag, –̈e surcharge

10 KARLSRUHE und FRANKFURT (Main)—KÖLN—DORTMUND*

No.	Station									
1	München Hbf.	ab	....	....	....	....	....	9.00	....	8.42
2	Stuttgart Hbf.	ab	....	....	....	....	....	11.55	....	
3	Basel Bad. Bf.	ab		9.18	....	....	....			....
	ZUG NR.		**D1269**	**D463**	**E721**	**E590**	**E297**	**D203**	**D1114**	**D455**
4	Karlsruhe Hbf.	ab	11.30	11.36	....	....	....	|		
5	Heidelberg Hbf.		|	|	....	....	....	13.15		
6	Mannheim Hbf.		12.06	12.13	....	....	....	13.34		
7	Ludwigshafen (Rh.)				....	....	....	13.50		
8	Worms Hbf.	ab			....	....	....			
9	Nürnberg Hbf.	ab			....	....	....		....	10.59
10	Würzburg Hbf.	ab			10.09	....	....		....	12.10
11	Frankfurt Hbf.	ab			12.32	12.42	13.14		14.00	14.04
12	Rüsselsheim		↓	↓	12.51	13.01			|	
13	Mainz Hbf.	ab	12.53	13.03	13.07	13.17	↓	14.37	14.29	
14	Mainz-Kastel	ab					13.40		an	|
15	Wiesbaden Hbf.						13.55		....	14.42
16	Eltville		von Freiburg			von Hof	14.07		....	|
17	Rüdesheim (Rh.)						14.20		....	15.06
18	Niederlahnstein	ab		↓	↓		15.10		....	
19	Bingen (Rhein)	ab	13.12		13.30	13.41		↓	....	
20	Bingerbrück		|		13.33	13.43		14.58	....	
21	St. Goar		|		13.57	an		|	....	Hellas-Express
22	Boppard		13.40		14.10		nach Saarbrücken	|	....	
23	Koblenz Hbf.		13.57	14.03	14.27			15.40	....	15.57
24	Andernach		|	|	14.40			|	....	
25	Remagen		|	|	14.58			|	....	
26	Bad Godesberg		|	|	15.08			|	....	
27	Bonn	an	14.35	14.40	15.14	↓		16.17	....	16.34
28	Neuwied	ab					15.29		....	
29	Linz (Rhein)						15.48		....	
30	Königswinter				....		16.01		....	
31	Beuel		↓	↓	....		16.09		....	
32	Troisdorf		↓	↓	....		16.16	↓	....	↓
33	KÖLN Hbf.	an	15.00	15.05	15.41	....	16.35	16.40	....	17.00
34	Aachen Hbf.	an	....	....	....		....	....	....	....
35	Mönchengladb. Hbf.	an	....	....	....		17.38	....	....	....
36	Krefeld Hbf.	an	....	....	....			....	....	....
	ZUG NR.					**E441**			**E315**	
37	Köln Hbf.	ab	15.05	15.10	15.47	16.13	....	16.45	16.48	17.10
38	Solingen-Ohligs	an	15.23			16.38			17.15	
39	Wuppertal-Elberf.	an	15.38			16.55			17.32	
40	Hagen	an	16.03			17.20			18.03	
41	Münster (Westf.)	ab	....	↓	↓	....	....	↓	....	↓

* Abbreviations

Hbf.—Hauptbahnhof
Bf.—Bahnhof
Bad. Bf.—Badischer Bahnhof
Nr.—Nummer
Rh.—am Rhein

St. Goar—Sankt Goar
Mönchengladb.—Mönchengladbach
Elberf.—Elberfeld
Westf.—Westfalen

östlichen Seite des Rheins, und Koblenz liegt auf der westlichen
Rheinseite, wo die Mosel in den Rhein mündet. Der D 203 (von | **münden** to flow into
München nach Dortmund) fährt nicht über Frankfurt, aber der
D 1114, ab Frankfurt um 14 Uhr, hat in Mainz Anschluß an diesen | **der Anschluß, ̈e**
Zug. Allerdings muß man dabei umsteigen und hat zwischen den ₅ | connection
beiden Zügen nur acht Minuten Zeit. | **umsteigen** to change (trains)

Der letzte Zug auf unserem Fahrplan ist die beste Verbindung von | **die Verbindung, –en**
Frankfurt nach Koblenz und auch der interessanteste Zug. Es ist der | connection
Hellas-Expreß, und er kommt aus Athen. | **Hellas** Greece

Fahrkarten bekommt man am Fahrkartenschalter. Man sagt: „Eine ₁₀
Fahrkarte erster Klasse nach Koblenz", oder als alter Eisenbahn-
fahrer: „Einmal erster Koblenz."

„Einfach oder hin und zurück?" | **einfach** (here) one way

„Einfach, bitte. Und einen D-Zug-Zuschlag." | **hin und zurück** round trip

„So, mein Herr, das macht 17,88 und 2 Mark für den Zuschlag: 19 ₁₅
Mark 88, bitte."

In Deutschland kann man nicht ohne Fahrkarte auf den Bahnsteig, | **der Bahnsteig, –** platform
sondern man muß zuerst durch die Sperre, wo ein Eisenbahnbeamter | **die Sperre, –n** gate
die Fahrkarte locht. Der Zug soll um 13.47 auf Gleis 12 ankommen, | **das Gleis, –e** track
aber kurz vorher hört man über den Lautsprecher: „Der Schnellzug ₂₀ | **planmäßig** scheduled, according to plan
aus München, planmäßige Ankunft 13.47 Uhr, hat voraussichtlich | **voraussichtlich** probably
30 Minuten Verspätung." Aber es dauert etwas länger als eine halbe | **Verspätung haben** to be late (not on schedule)
Stunde, und um halb drei heißt es endlich: „Der verspätete Schnell-
zug aus München läuft soeben auf Gleis 12 ein. Bitte von der Bahn- | **heißt es** it is announced
steigkante zurücktreten." Der Zug ist nicht stark besetzt, und es ist ₂₅ | **die Kante, –n** the edge
leicht, in einem Nichtraucherabteil erster Klasse einen Fensterplatz | **das Abteil, –e** compartment
zu bekommen. Der Zug hat eine elektrische Lokomotive; in großen | **der Dampf** steam
Teilen Deutschlands ist die Eisenbahn elektrifiziert, aber man sieht
auch Diesellokomotiven und noch Dampflokomotiven. Der Zug hat

Wagen erster und zweiter Klasse; in jedem Wagen gibt es zwölf
Abteile mit je sechs Sitzplätzen. In den meisten D-Zügen kann man   **je** (here) each, apiece
sich einen Platz reservieren lassen. Außerdem hat der Zug einen
Postwagen, einen Gepäckwagen und einen Speisewagen, aber keinen   **das Gepäck** baggage
Schlafwagen, denn er kommt schon um 19.06 in Dortmund an, fährt 5   **speisen** to dine
also nicht mehr über Nacht.

Ein Mann kommt nach San Franzisko (Fortsetzung)

IV

Juli 1945

„Woher können Sie eigentlich so gut Deutsch? Das haben Sie doch
nicht während der paar Wochen hier im Dorf gelernt."

„Ja, wissen Sie, Herr Pfarrer, meine Großeltern kommen aus
Deutschland, hier aus dieser Gegend. Mein Großvater ist nach 10
Missouri ausgewandert, und mein Vater ist lutherischer Pfarrer in
St. Louis. Bei uns zu Hause haben wir immer viel Deutsch ge-
sprochen; bis zum Krieg hat mein Vater sogar noch Deutsch ge-   **predigen** to preach
predigt. In den letzten zwei Jahren habe ich allerdings Japanisch
lernen müssen."   15

„Und deshalb hat man Sie wohl nach Deutschland geschickt. Aber
Spaß beiseite. Sie haben da einen Vorschlag gemacht, und Sie wollen   **Spaß** fun, kidding
meinen Rat wissen. Glauben Sie denn, daß Sie das überhaupt machen   **beiseite** aside
können?"

„Doch, bestimmt. Ich habe Ihnen ja gesagt, wir haben Verwandte 20
in Frankfurt,—einen Vetter mit seiner Frau,—denen habe ich geschrieben, und sie haben zurückgeschrieben und haben ja gesagt.
Meine Kompanie fährt in ein paar Tagen nach Frankfurt; Sie wissen
ja, die Amerikaner ziehen sich ganz aus Thüringen zurück, Thü-   **sich zurückziehen** to
ringen gehört ja zur russischen Zone."°   25 withdraw

„Ja, leider! Thüringen gehört zur russischen Zone. Dann ist es wohl
auf jeden Fall besser, wenn Sie Barbara mitnehmen. Und dem Kind
wird es in Frankfurt besser gehen als hier, wo die Kleine ganz allein
ist. Wenn nur die Mutter nicht gestorben wäre! Ich kannte sie ja   **der Flüchtling, –e**
kaum, die beiden waren erst ein paar Wochen hier, aus Breslau 30   refugee
kamen sie. Dieses Flüchtlingselend ist furchtbar; wir haben zweimal   **das Elend** (*no pl.*)
soviel Flüchtlinge im Dorf wie Einwohner. Wohin das noch führen   misery
soll!"

° At the end of the war, British and American troops had occupied large parts
of what later became East Germany. In August 1945, these troops were with-
drawn to a demarcation line which had been agreed upon at Yalta. This line
became the "Iron Curtain."

„Ich habe lange darüber nachgedacht, Herr Pfarrer. Ich habe meinem Vater davon geschrieben, und er meinte, ich solle tun, was ich für richtig halte; wir hätten ja jetzt lange genug gehaßt. Und wenn ich sehe, wieviel Haß es hier noch gibt; die Bauern hassen die Flüchtlinge, weil die ihnen das Brot wegessen; die Flüchtlinge 5 hassen die Bauern, weil es denen besser geht als ihnen, und sie alle hassen die Amerikaner, weil die ihnen das Land zerstört haben. Die Barbara hat mir neulich davon erzählt. ‚Ich soll dich auch hassen‘, hat sie gesagt, ‚aber das will ich nicht!‘ "

„Sie dürfen nicht vergessen, daß der Krieg erst seit acht Wochen zu 10 Ende ist. Geben Sie uns Zeit, Herr Suhl. Sie sind ja noch sehr jung; aber ich bin ein alter Mann, ich weiß, daß es kein Gefühl gibt, das die Zeit nicht ändern kann. Nehmen Sie die Kleine mit nach Frankfurt,—und wir wollen hoffen, daß sie noch jung genug ist, um zu vergessen, was hinter ihr liegt." 15

Am 15. Juli zog Barbara in ein Haus in der Bettinastraße in Frankfurt, von dem nur noch das Erdgeschoß und der erste Stock standen. Wenn es regnete, lief an allen Wänden das Wasser herunter. Aber Ernst und Irene Suhl, Pauls Verwandte, waren froh, überhaupt ein Dach über dem Kopf zu haben, auch wenn es nur die Decke ihrer 20 Wohnung war. „Das wird sich schon finden", meinte Ernst, als Paul ihn fragte, wie er sich denn eigentlich den nächsten Winter vorstelle; und als sie über die Zukunft der kleinen Barbara sprachen, hatte Ernst die gleiche optimistische Antwort.

das Erdgeschoß, –e ground floor

die Decke, –n ceiling
das wird sich schon finden it'll work out all right
sich vorstellen to imagine, picture

Bei seinem letzten Gespräch mit dem alten Pfarrer in Thüringen 25 hatte Paul Namen und Adresse seiner Verwandten auf ein Stück Papier geschrieben, und darunter seine eigene I.D.-Nummer. „Die Armee weiß immer, wo ich bin", hatte er gesagt, „und auf jeden Fall können Sie mich über meine Frankfurter Verwandten erreichen."

V

Frankfurt, September 1948

In der Bettinastraße läuft zwar das Wasser nicht mehr an den 30 Wänden herunter, aber das Haus besteht noch immer nur aus Erdgeschoß und erstem Stock. Ernst und Irene Suhl sind ganz gut durch die wilden Jahre nach dem Krieg durchgekommen; Paul hat nach seiner Entlassung aus der Armee von Amerika aus geholfen.

die Entlassung discharge
die Lebensmittelkarte, –n ration card

Die Zeit der Care-Pakete und der Lebensmittelkarten: Wer Freunde 35 in Amerika hatte, brauchte nicht zu hungern; die anderen bekamen, wenn sie Glück hatten, alle vier Wochen ein Ei; und die Milch war so blau wie der Himmel im November,—was wurde eigentlich aus der Butter? Die öffentlichen Bibliotheken waren überfüllt, weil es da warm war. Auf der Universität saßen die Studenten in alten Solda- 40

Frankfurt/Main, An der Hauptwache

tenmänteln und froren. Aber es ist nie so viel gearbeitet worden wie
in den ersten Semestern nach dem Kriege. Die Studenten froren,
und die Professoren froren mit ihnen. Im Theater fror das Publikum,
und die Schauspieler froren auf der Bühne. Und wenn† dann endlich
der Sommer kam, fror man zwar nicht mehr, aber man hungerte 5
immer weiter.

Care-Pakete, Lebensmittelkarten, Schwarzer Markt. Frankfurt war
eine Zentrale des Schwarzen Marktes in Deutschland, und der
Schwarze Markt war das Fieberthermometer von Westdeutschland.
Am Anfang kostete eine Zigarette fünfzig Pfennig,—dann stiegen 10
die Preise, aber die Währung war nicht etwa die Mark, sondern die
amerikanische Zigarette. Ein Pfund Butter für 200 Zigaretten, ein
Paar Nylonstrümpfe für 300 Zigaretten. Als Paul Suhl im März 1948
nach Deutschland zurückkam, stand die Zigarette bei etwa 4 bis 5
Mark, im Juni war sie auf 10 Mark gestiegen. Und bewacht wurde 15
das alles von der Militärregierung,—HICOG, was die Deutschen

es ist . . . worden
never has so much
work been done
das Publikum audi-
ence, public

die Zentra′le, –n
center
das Fieber fever
die Währung, –en
medium of exchange,
currency
der Strumpf, ∸e stock-
ing
bewacht wurde was
watched over
HICOG High Com-
missioner of Germany

† **wenn** rather than **als** is used here, because more than one summer is involved.

wie „Hickock" aussprachen. HICOG war eine Maschine mit vielen
Rädchen, und eines dieser Rädchen hieß seit März 1948 Paul Suhl.
Nachdem er sein Studium beendet und sein Japanisch völlig ver-
gessen hatte, bekam er eine Stellung bei der Militärregierung in
Deutschland und hatte nun ein Büro im I. G. Hochhaus‡ in Frank- 5
furt.

Auf der Kaiserstraße und im Hauptbahnhof beobachtete er oft die
Schwarzmarkthändler; er wanderte zu Fuß durch die zerstörte Stadt
und kletterte auf den Ruinenbergen zwischen dem Römer und dem
Dom herum, in dem viele deutsche Kaiser gekrönt worden waren. 10
Während der Hauptverkehrszeit stand er oft an der Hauptwache,
gegen fünf Uhr nachmittags, wenn die Straßenbahnen überfüllt
waren, um zu hören, worüber die Menschen sprachen. Und abends
besuchte er seinen Vetter Ernst, um mit ihm endlos zu diskutieren.

der Römer (name of
the Frankfurt city hall)
gekrönt worden waren
had been crowned
die Hauptwache
(square in the center
of Frankfurt)
diskutieren (here) to
have a bull session

‡ **I. G. Hochhaus**   Administration Building of I. G. Farben, the largest German
chemical trust until 1945. After the war, the building was used as headquarters
by the Americans.

**„und hatte nun ein Büro im I. G. Hochhaus
in Frankfurt."**

So wurde es April, und Mai, und Juni.—Das Fieberthermometer
kletterte immer mehr in die Höhe, und der Patient wäre gestorben,
wenn die Militärregierung nicht die Währungsreform§ befohlen
hätte. Am Montag, dem 20. Juni, gab es statt der alten „Reichsmark"
die neue „Deutsche Mark", und wer an dem Tage auf zehntausend 5
Reichsmark saß statt auf tausend Zigaretten, der hatte nur einen
Haufen nutzloses Papier, mit dem man noch nicht einmal gut Feuer
anmachen konnte.

der Haufen, – heap,
pile
Feuer anmachen to
light a fire

Und so wurde es Juli, und August, und September, und an diesen
Sommernachmittagen geschah es oft, daß, wenn Paul in die Bettina- 10
straße fuhr, Barbara vor dem Haus auf ihn wartete. Sie kam dann
zu seinem Wagen gerannt, steckte den Kopf durch das offene
Fenster und sagte: „Fahren wir heute ein bißchen?" Und dann
fuhr er mit ihr vor die Stadt, irgendwohin, wo es Felder gab und
Wiesen und Blumen und Bänke, auf denen man sitzen konnte und 15
wo Barbara lachen mußte, wenn Paul manchmal einschlief. „Erdbeeren essen gehen" nannten sie diese Expeditionen, und Barbara
fand das viel schöner als die „olle Schule", womit sie die Bettina-
Schule meinte, ein Gymnasium für Mädchen. Sie war in der Quarta
und erzählte Paul immer wieder, wie ihr Englischlehrer den ameri- 20
kanischen Akzent nachahmte. (Er hatte in Oxford studiert.) Aber
auch Paul erzählte in diesem Sommer viel, von Schiffen auf dem
Atlantik, von New York, von tagelangen Fahrten mit der Eisenbahn,
von St. Louis und von seinen Eltern, von seiner Schwester Kathy,
die auch zwölf Jahre alt war und auch immer Geschichten über ihre 25
Lehrer erzählte. An einem Freitagnachmittag, als er gerade versucht hatte, ihr zu erklären, wie breit der Mississippi ist, sagte sie
auf einmal: „Du, weißt du, da möchte ich auch mal hin." „Ja, dann
müssen wir ja wohl mal darüber reden", meinte er.

olle = alte
die Quarta third year
of the Gymnasium
(seventh grade)
nachahmen to imitate

VI

Ernst Suhl war fünfzehn Jahre älter als sein Vetter Paul. Er 30
war Diplomingenieur und hatte während des Krieges bei einer
Frankfurter Firma gearbeitet, die irgendwelche kriegswichtigen
Maschinen herstellte. Ernst hatte daher nie Soldat zu werden
brauchen. Neunzehnhundertdreiundvierzig war er Chefingenieur geworden und hatte einige Erfindungen gemacht, die seine Firma noch 35
kriegswichtiger machten als vorher. Aber nach dem 8. Mai 1945
brauchte in Deutschland kein Mensch mehr einen Chefingenieur,
und ganz bestimmt keinen, der kriegswichtige Erfindungen gemacht
hatte. Eine Zeitlang tat Ernst gar nichts; dann, kurz nachdem Bar-

der Diplomingenieur
engineer with a grad-
uate degree from a
technical university
die Firma, die Firmen
firm
herstellen to produce

§ The currency reform was a drastic devaluation of the currency. Each German,
on that day, could receive no more than 40 new "Deutsche Mark."

bara nach Frankfurt gekommen war, arbeitete er ein paar Monate
lang bei den Amerikanern in einer Soldatenküche, wo er Englisch
lernte. Später bekam er eine Stellung als technischer Zeichner bei
der Eisenbahn; eine Möglichkeit, in seinen alten Beruf zurück-
zukommen, gab es nicht. Schon lange bevor Paul wieder nach 5
Deutschland gekommen war, hatten Ernst und Irene daran gedacht
auszuwandern, sobald das wieder möglich sein würde. Und während der Sommermonate 1948 hatte Paul sie davon überzeugt, daß
Ernst in Amerika eine neue Zukunft finden könnte. Hatte man nicht
schon gleich nach dem Krieg viele deutsche Wissenschaftler in die 10
Staaten gebracht, die da weiterarbeiten durften, wo sie am Ende
des Krieges aufgehört hatten? Warum sollte Ernst das nicht können?

der Zeichner, – draftsman

der Wissenschaftler, – scientist

Die Frage war nur, was aus Barbara werden sollte. Das Leben in
Frankfurt war in der ersten Zeit nach dem Kriege nicht leicht gewesen für Barbara. Es hatte lange gedauert, bis sie sich in der 15
Bettinastraße zu Hause fühlte. Zuerst hatte sie kaum gesprochen,
wenn sie mit Irene allein war, gelacht hatte sie nur manchmal, wenn
Ernst da war. Aber dann hatte sie sich doch an die beiden gewöhnt,
und nach ein paar Monaten war sie ein völlig normales Kind geworden. Ihr Vater blieb verschwunden; alle Versuche, ihn zu finden, 20
waren erfolglos. Ernst hatte drei- oder viermal an den Pfarrer in
Thüringen geschrieben, aber der wußte nichts von Barbaras Vater.
Nach Breslau, an die alte Adresse, konnte man ja nicht schreiben:
Breslau hieß jetzt Wroclaw und war polnisch. Auch beim Roten
Kreuz konnten sie nichts erfahren, und so mußte man annehmen, 25
daß er, wie tausend andere, irgendwo in Osteuropa umgekommen
war. Im Juni, ein paar Tage vor der Währungsreform, machte Paul
einen letzten Versuch und schrieb noch einmal nach Thüringen.
Aber der Brief kam zurück: „Adressat verstorben." Der alte
Pfarrer, der einzige, der von der Sache wußte, war tot, und als die 30
Blockade Berlins begann, gab es überhaupt keine Verbindung mehr
nach drüben, zum Osten Deutschlands, zur russischen Zone.

sich gewöhnen an to get used to

das Rote Kreuz the Red Cross

umkommen to perish

Adressat verstorben addressee deceased

die Verbindung, –en connection, link

Wenn Irene und Ernst nach Amerika auswanderten, dann wollten
sie Barbara mitnehmen, und das ging nur, wenn sie sie adoptierten.
Es war ein schwerer Entschluß, denn sie wußten ja nicht bestimmt, 35
ob Barbaras Vater nicht doch noch lebte. Aber sie konnten sich ihr
Leben ohne Barbara nicht mehr vorstellen, und an dem Tage, an
dem Barbara auf dem Rückweg in die Stadt zu Paul gesagt hatte:
„Du, weißt du, da möchte ich auch mal hin", beschlossen sie, mit
ihr darüber zu sprechen. Nach dem Abendessen fing Paul ganz harm- 40
los an: „Sag mal, Barbara, wie wäre es, wenn wir nächstes Jahr mal
in St. Louis Erdbeeren essen gingen?"

der Entschluß, ⁔e decision

VII

Januar 1952

Viele von den deutschen Soldaten, die mit Oswald Kerner aus
Rußland zurückgekommen waren, waren so schnell wie möglich
nach Westdeutschland weitergefahren. Andere fuhren zu ihren
Familien in der Sowjetzone. Die meisten hatten seit Monaten oder
Jahren nichts von zu Hause gehört und hatten keine Ahnung, wo 5
sie ihre Eltern, ihre Frauen, ihre Kinder finden würden.

Kerner war im Februar 1945 in Pommern gefangengenommen
worden. Ein paar Tage vorher hatte er den letzten Brief von seiner
Frau bekommen. Sie war mit ihrer kleinen Tochter aus Breslau
geflüchtet und wohnte in einem Dorf im Thüringer Wald. Seitdem 10
hatte er nichts mehr gehört, aber er war trotzdem nach Thüringen
gefahren. Zwei Tage lang war er von einem Haus zum anderen
gegangen, aber niemand wußte etwas von seiner Frau und seinem
Kind. Schließlich hatte er den Bauern gefunden, in dessen Haus
Paul Suhl gewohnt hatte, und der konnte sich an die junge Frau aus 15
Breslau erinnern, die damals mit den anderen Flüchtlingen in seiner
Scheune gewohnt hatte. Schon bei ihrer Ankunft sei die Frau krank
gewesen und dann wäre sie auch bald gestorben; dann seien die
Amerikaner gekommen, und die hätten die Tochter mitgenommen.
Der Bauer wußte auch noch, daß einer der amerikanischen Soldaten 20
oft im Pfarrhaus gewesen war. Und so saß Oswald Kerner dann dem
Pfarrer gegenüber, im gleichen Stuhl, auf dem Paul gesessen hatte.
Nur war es nicht mehr derselbe Pfarrer.

„Ich kann Ihnen nur sagen, Herr Kerner, daß Ihre Frau am
28. März 1945 gestorben ist. Von Ihrer Tochter steht in unseren 25
Büchern nichts. Möglich, daß mein Vorgänger wußte, was aus ihr
geworden ist, aber der alte Herr ist vor vier Jahren gestorben und
hat keine Papiere hinterlassen. Ich bin erst nach seinem Tod hier
ins Dorf gekommen. Es tut mir leid, Herr Kerner. So gerne ich es
möchte, ich kann Ihnen leider nicht helfen."   30

Kerner sagte kein Wort. Er saß und starrte ins Leere. Der Krieg
war seit sieben Jahren vorbei, aber für ihn kam das Ende erst
jetzt. Als er ins Dorf gekommen war, war er schwach und hungrig
gewesen, aber was ihn sieben Jahre lang am Leben gehalten hatte,
hatte ihn immer noch getrieben: die Hoffnung auf ein Ende und auf 35
einen neuen Anfang. Das Ende war jetzt gekommen, aber statt eines
neuen Anfangs—nichts. Sieben Jahre Leben hatte er verloren, und
er hatte fast vergessen, was es heißt, sein eigenes Leben zu leben.
Aber das wäre alles nicht so schlimm gewesen, er hätte es vergessen
können. Aber jetzt?   40

Pommern Pomerania,
a province of Eastern
Germany
**war . . . gefangenge-
nommen worden** had
been taken prisoner

sich erinnern an to
remember

**dem Pfarrer gegen-
über** opposite the
pastor. (The noun
governed by **gegen-
über** usually precedes
the preposition.)
der Vorgänger, –
predecessor

ins Leere starren to
stare into space

treiben to drive

„Verstehen Sie, was das bedeutet, Herr Pfarrer? Sieben Jahre warten; sieben Jahre lang jeden Tag daran denken, wie es sein wird, wenn— Und dann gibt es auf einmal kein ‚wenn‘ mehr. Wissen Sie, Herr Pfarrer, daß ich eine fünfzehnjährige Tochter habe, und ich kenne sie gar nicht, und wenn ich zu ihr sage: Bar- 5 bara, ich bin dein Vater, dann denkt sie, wer ist der Mensch und was will er von mir? Aber ich habe ja gar keine Tochter mehr; die ist bei den Amerikanern, wenn sie überhaupt noch lebt. Nach Hause kommen, wieder zu Hause sein, das alles war nur ein Traum, Herr Pfarrer, wissen Sie: Lagerpsychose, Fata Morgana. Was ist richtig, 10 ‚Das Leben ein Traum‘ oder ‚Der Traum ein Leben‘?“

die Lagerpsychose prison psychosis
die Fata Morgana mirage
„Das Leben ein Traum" title of a play by Calderón
„Der Traum ein Leben" title of a play by Grillparzer
der Studienrat, ⸚e fully certified Gymnasium teacher
von vorne from the beginning

„Was sind Sie eigentlich von Beruf, Herr Kerner?“

„Sie meinen, was *war* ich von Beruf? Ich war Lehrer, Studienrat in Breslau, Deutsch und Geschichte. Neunzehnhundertvierzig bin ich Soldat geworden, und meine Schüler schrieben im Abitur über das 15 Thema: „Der ideale Mensch im idealen Staat.“

„Sie sollten das alles vergessen, Herr Kerner, und von vorne anfangen. Gehen Sie wieder in Ihren Beruf, man braucht doch überall Lehrer. Sie können noch so viel Gutes tun in ihrem Leben, Herr Kerner, unsere Jugend braucht Männer wie Sie, Männer, die nicht 20 nur das Leben kennen, sondern auch den Tod.“

„Danke, nein, Herr Pfarrer, das mache ich nicht mehr mit. Soll ich etwa meine Schüler wieder über den idealen Menschen und den idealen Staat schreiben lassen? Ich könnte doch nur sagen, Kinder, glaubt den Unsinn nicht; am Ende kommt nie eine bessere Welt, 25 sondern einfach nichts.—Nein, nein,—ich bleibe hier im Dorf, irgendeine Arbeit werde ich schon finden.“

etwas mitmachen to take part in something

Im Dorf fand er zwar keine Arbeit, aber vierzehn Tage später holte ihn Fritz Müller, Schreinerei, Möbel- und Sarglager VEB in die kleine Nachbarstadt. Als junger Mann hatte Oswald Kerner in seiner 30 Freizeit für Barbara Kindermöbel gemacht. Jetzt machte er vierzehn Monate lang Särge. „Sechs Bretter und zwei Brettchen“, das war schließlich auch klassische deutsche Literatur.

Schreinerei, Möbel- und Sarglager carpenter's shop, furniture and coffin depot
VEB = Volkseigener Betrieb business owned by the people. (Many firms in East Germany had been nationalized by that time.)
das Brett, ─er board; this is a line from Bürger's ballad *Lenore*. (Six boards and two little boards are needed to make a coffin.)

(Fortsetzung folgt)

166 The Position of Dependent Infinitives

The two German sentences

> **Er brauchte sie heute nicht anzurufen.**
> (He did not have to call her up today.)
>
> **Er versprach, sie heute nicht anzurufen.**
> (He promised not to call her up today.)

seem to have the same structure. But they don't. After **brauchte,** there is
no pause. But after **versprach,** the speaker stops for a split second before
he goes on to **sie heute nicht anzurufen.** The pause creates the impression
that the infinitive phrase which follows is something like a dependent
clause—an "infinitive clause." If the two sentences above are changed
from the past tense to the perfect, the second one shows a syntactical pattern which we have tried to avoid until now.

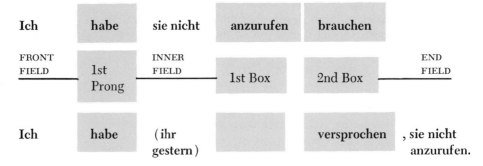

This diagram shows: The infinitive depending on **brauchen** stands in the
first box of the second prong, but if this same infinitive depends on **versprechen** it stands in the end field, together with the syntactical units that
belong to it.

The difference between the old pattern and the new one is just as striking
if we change from verb-second to verb-last position:

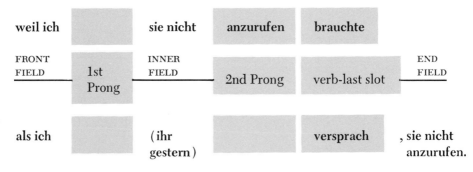

The diagram shows again: The infinitive depending on **versprechen** stands in the end field. *This end field cannot be started until the preceding clause has been completed.*

In the following paragraphs we shall discuss which infinitives belong in the second prong and which belong in the end field.

167   Second-Prong Infinitives

The most important group of verbs which are used together with an infinitive in the second prong are the modals and **brauchen**. Though **brauchen** has a dependent infinitive with **zu**, it behaves like the modals: the participle following the infinitive is **brauchen**, not **gebraucht**:

Ich habe sie heute noch nicht anrufen können.
Ich habe sie heute nicht anzurufen brauchen.

However, the modals and **brauchen** are not the only verbs which are used with a second-prong infinitive. There are others of which some govern an infinitive with **zu**, and some an infinitive without **zu.**

Second-Prong Infinitives without **zu**

LERNEN

The infinitives depending on **lernen** all take the second-prong position of **kennen** in **kennenlernen**, but only **kennenlernen** is spelled as one word:

lesen lernen	gehen lernen
schreiben lernen	fahren lernen
kochen lernen	Auto fahren lernen

Sie lernt jetzt fahren.	, weil sie jetzt fahren lernt.
Sie hat schon kochen gelernt.	, weil sie schon kochen gelernt hat.
Ich habe sie schon kennengelernt.	, weil ich sie schon kennengelernt habe.

NOTE: Though **lernen** is used with an infinitive without **zu**, it does not behave like a modal. If it did, **kochen gelernt hat** in the example above would have to be replaced by [**hat kochen lernen**].

BLEIBEN

The infinitives used most frequently with **bleiben** are **liegen, stehen,** and **sitzen.** As long as **liegen** means literally *lying,* **sitzen** *sitting,* and **stehen** *standing,* they are written separately.

Dieser Baum hier kann stehen bleiben.	This tree can stay here.
Du brauchst noch nicht aufzustehen, du kannst noch etwas liegen bleiben.	You don't have to get up yet; you can stay in bed for a while.

> In Deutschland dürfen die Herren sitzen bleiben, wenn die Hausfrau aus dem Wohnzimmer in die Küche geht.
>
> In Germany, the gentlemen may stay seated if the lady of the house goes from the living room to the kitchen.

Usually, however, these combinations are used with non-literal meanings and are spelled as one word. **Stehenbleiben** then means *to stop,* **liegenbleiben** means *to be left behind (forgotten),* and **sitzenbleiben** means *not to find a husband* or *not to be promoted into the next higher class in school.*

> **Der Hut ist gestern abend hier liegengeblieben.**
> **Meine Uhr ist gestern abend stehengeblieben.**
> **Kein Mädchen möchte gerne sitzenbleiben.**
> **Fritz ist schon wieder sitzengeblieben.**

GEHEN AND FAHREN

German **gehen** is frequently used with an infinitive which denotes some routine activity like **essen, schlafen, baden, schilaufen,** and others.

> **Wir gehen jetzt essen.**
> **Wir wollen morgen schwimmen gehen.**
> **Wir gehen jetzt schlafen.**
> **Er ist schon schlafen gegangen.**
> **Wir wollen morgen schilaufen gehen.**

The verb **spazieren** can mean *to promenade.* Today it is mostly used in **spazierenfahren** (*to go for a ride*) and in **spazierengehen** (*to go for a walk*):

> **Wir sind gestern spazierengefahren.**
> **Wir sind gestern spazierengegangen.**
> **Warum gehen wir nicht etwas spazieren?**

Observe again that **gehen** and **fahren** do not behave like modals. If they did, **gegangen** and **gefahren** in the above examples would have to be replaced by **gehen** and **fahren.**

HÖREN AND SEHEN

In the English sentence *I heard him come, him* is the object of the governing verb *heard* and at the same time the subject of the infinitive *come.* The corresponding German sentence **Ich hörte ihn kommen** shows the same relation: the **ihn** is at the same time the object of **hörte** and the subject of **kommen.** In both languages, the dependent infinitive is used without *to* or **zu.**

When used in this pattern, **hören** and **sehen** do behave like modals: their past participles are **sehen** and **hören**, not **gesehen** and **gehört**.

>**Ich habe ihn nie nach Hause kommen hören.**
>**Ich habe ihn kommen sehen.**
>**Das habe ich kommen sehen.**

LASSEN

The verb **lassen** is one of the most frequently used German verbs. It occurs with two different basic meanings: (1) *to leave* and (2) *to cause* or *to permit*.

1. **lassen** *to leave* (*behind*)

>**Ich habe meinen Mantel zu Hause gelassen.**
>**Ich hätte meinen Mantel nicht zu Hause lassen sollen.**

In combination with **hängen, liegen, stehen** (used like **kennen** in **kennenlernen**), **lassen** also means *to leave*. In this case the participle is either **lassen** or **gelassen**, but we advise you to use only **lassen**.

>**Ich habe meinen Mantel zu Hause hängenlassen.**
>**Ich habe mein Buch zu Hause liegenlassen.**
>**Ich habe meinen Schirm** (umbrella) **zu Hause stehenlassen.**

2. **lassen** *to cause* or *to permit*

When used (like **hören** and **sehen**) with a subject-infinitive construction, **lassen** means "to cause—*either* by permission *or* by request—somebody to do something."

>**Wir ließen ihn kommen.**
>We let (or had) him come.

When it means *to cause* or *to permit,* **lassen** behaves like a modal, that is, the participle is **lassen**, not **gelassen**.

>**Wir haben ihn kommen lassen.**
>We permitted (asked) him to come.

Compare also:

>**Ich lasse meinen Mann nicht allein nach Kairo fahren.**
>**Vater hat mich gestern abend nicht ins Kino gehen lassen.**
>**Meyers haben gestern den Arzt kommen lassen müssen.**

By *suppressing the subject* of the subject-infinitive construction, German arrives at a pattern which cannot be imitated in English:

>**Ich ließ mir eine Tasse Kaffee aufs Zimmer bringen.**
>I asked (somebody) to bring me a cup of coffee to my room.
>I had a cup of coffee brought to my room.

Ich ließ mir die Haare schneiden.
I asked (somebody) to give me a haircut.
I had my hair cut.

Wir haben uns ein Haus bauen lassen.
We asked (somebody) to build a house for us.
We had a house built.

The subject of the infinitive can also be expressed by **von** plus noun or pronoun. Again the result is a construction not possible in English:

Wir lassen uns von Meyer ein Haus bauen.
We're letting Meyer build our house.
We are having our house built by Meyer.

If the **Ich** in

Ich habe mir das Frühstück aufs Zimmer bringen lassen

is replaced by **er,** two different sentences are possible, both of which correspond to the ambiguous English sentence

He had his breakfast brought up to his room.
Er hat ihm das Frühstück aufs Zimmer bringen lassen.
Er hat sich das Frühstück aufs Zimmer bringen lassen.

In the first sentence, **er** and **ihm** must be two different people (Jack had Joe's breakfast taken to Joe's room); in the second sentence, **er** and **sich** must be the same person (He had his own breakfast brought to his own room).

Second-Prong Infinitives with **zu**

SCHEINEN

The verb **scheinen,** when meaning *to seem,* is used, like **brauchen,** with a second-prong infinitive. It behaves like a subjective modal and occurs only in the present and in the past.

Er scheint zu schlafen.
Er schien nicht gut geschlafen zu haben.

HABEN

The verb **haben** must be mentioned in this context because it is frequently followed by an infinitive with **zu** which *looks* like a second-prong infinitive. Actually, these infinitives usually follow **etwas, nichts, viel,** and **wenig** and form one single syntactical unit with these words:

etwas zu tun	etwas zu essen
nichts zu tun	nichts zu essen
viel zu tun	viel zu essen
wenig zu tun	wenig zu essen

Wenn ich nur nicht soviel zu tun hätte!
Gestern hatten wir kaum etwas zu tun.
Hast du etwas zu trinken im Hause?

This same construction is frequently found after verbs like **mitbringen** and **kaufen.**

Kannst du mir etwas zu lesen mitbringen?
Kannst du mir etwas zu lesen kaufen?

SEIN

The verb **sein** can be used with a second-prong infinitive provided that the subject of **sein** is the same as the object of the infinitive. English uses this construction in sentences like

He was easy to find.
Er war leicht zu finden.

The English use of the passive infinitive after *to be* cannot be imitated in German:

He was not to be found.
Er war nicht zu finden.

168 End-Field Infinitives

As can be seen from the following examples, the word order of the elements (objects, time phrases, place phrases, etc.) belonging to an end-field infinitive is the same as that found in the inner field preceding a second-prong infinitive.

Ich brauche   ihn heute nicht   **anzurufen.**

Ich habe versprochen,   ihn heute nicht   **anzurufen.**

All elements in the main clause preceding the infinitive clause take their usual position:

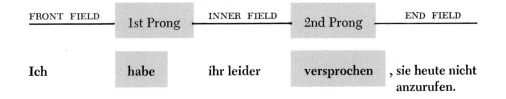

FRONT FIELD	1st Prong	INNER FIELD	2nd Prong	END FIELD
Ich	**habe**	**ihr leider**	**versprochen**	**, sie heute nicht anzurufen.**

As long as only the infinitive with **zu** occupies the end field, it is not separated by a comma.

    Es fing an zu regnen.

In all other cases, a comma is necessary, not only to indicate the pause which separates such infinitive clauses from the preceding part of the sentence, but also to avoid ambiguity.

    Er behauptet schon wieder, in Paris gewesen zu sein.
    Er behauptet, schon wieder in Paris gewesen zu sein.

The Group **anfangen**

The following verbs are frequently used with end-field infinitives:

anfangen	to begin
aufhören	to stop, cease
behaupten	to claim
es langweilig (dumm, etc.) finden	to find boring (stupid, etc.)
hoffen	to hope
vergessen	to forget
versprechen	to promise
versuchen	to try
es wagen	to dare

The Group **befehlen**

In the sentence

    Ich habe ihr gestern versprochen, sie heute anzurufen

the subject of **versprechen** is the same as the subject of the end-field infinitive.

The verbs

befehlen	to give an order to somebody
empfehlen	to make a recommendation to somebody
erlauben	to give permission to somebody
gestatten	to permit (social term)
helfen	to give help to someone in doing something
raten	to give somebody the advice
verbieten	to forbid someone to do something
vorschlagen	to make a suggestion to somebody

all take a personal *dative* object which is the same as the subject of the infinitive clause that follows it.

    Mein Arzt riet mir, einmal an die See zu fahren.
    Darf ich Ihnen vorschlagen, einmal einen Mosel zu versuchen?

The End-Field Infinitive after Predicate Adjectives

The following predicate adjectives are frequently used with end-field infinitives:

bereit	ready	**froh**	glad
erstaunt	astonished	**fähig**	able
glücklich	happy	**schön**	nice
herrlich	wonderful	**nett**	nice

Sie wissen doch, daß ich immer bereit gewesen bin, Ihrem Mann zu helfen.
Warum sind Sie denn so erstaunt, mich hier zu sehen?
Inge war froh, ihren Mann endlich wiedersehen zu dürfen.

Replacement of Prepositional Objects

Verbs which take a prepositional object frequently replace this complement with a **da**-compound which anticipates an infinitive phrase in the end field. (See **132.**)

Ich denke ja gar nicht daran,
Du weißt doch, daß ich gar nicht daran denke,
Ich habe ja nie daran gedacht,
Du weißt doch, daß ich nie daran gedacht habe, ⎫
⎬ **den Meyer zu heiraten.**
⎭

um . . . zu, ohne . . . zu, statt . . . zu

We have already used infinitives with **um . . . zu** in the end-field position. The same construction is possible with **ohne . . . zu** and **statt (anstatt) . . . zu.** All of these infinitives appear most frequently in either end-field or front-field position.

Er fuhr nach Afrika, um dort einen Roman zu schreiben.
Er fuhr nach München, ohne seine Frau mitzunehmen.
Er fuhr nach Afrika, statt zu Hause zu bleiben.

English uses an infinitive as the equivalent of the **um . . . zu** forms (*in order to write a novel*), but for the **ohne . . . zu** and **statt . . . zu** forms, English must use the gerund (*without taking his wife along; instead of staying at home*).

In the above examples, the subject of the infinitive clause is the same as the subject of the main clause. If there is a different subject, the infinitive constructions must be replaced by dependent clauses:

um . . . zu	damit
ohne . . . zu	ohne daß
statt . . . zu	statt daß

Wir bleiben zu Hause, um endlich einmal arbeiten zu können.

Wir bleiben zu Hause, damit mein Mann endlich einmal arbeiten kann.

Er fuhr nach Kairo, ohne seiner Frau etwas davon zu sagen.

Er fuhr nach Kairo, ohne daß seine Frau etwas davon wußte.

Statt den Meyer einmal nach Berlin zu schicken, schicken sie mich schon
wieder.

Statt daß sie den Meyer einmal nach Berlin schicken, muß ich schon wieder
fahren.

169   hin and her

Hin and **her** are both directional adverbs denoting motion. **Hin** indicates
motion away from the speaker or the speaker's position, **her** refers to
motion toward the speaker.

hin and her as Verbal Complements

Hin and **her** can both be used by themselves as complements of certain
verbs denoting various methods of traveling or change of location.

Thus a person told to visit his father immediately might say:

Ich fahre (gehe, reise) sofort hin.

or he might say:

Ich werde sofort hinfahren.
Ich bin sofort hingefahren.
Ich brauche nicht sofort hinzufahren.
Ich weiß nicht, ob ich sofort hinfahren kann.

The father might say:

Mein Sohn ist sofort hergekommen.
Kannst du sofort herkommen?

hin and her with Adverbs of Place and of Time

Since **hin** implies no specific goal and since **her** implies no specific point
of origin, they are frequently found after **da, dort, hier,** and after prepositional phrases expressing goal or origin.

Wer hat dich denn hierhergebracht?
Du willst sofort zum Flughafen? Wer bringt dich denn dahin?
Im nächsten Dorf gibt es ein Hotel? Wie weit ist es denn bis dahin?—Zehn
Kilometer. Wir kommen gerade daher. (dorther, von dorther)

Her may also be used with a temporal meaning.

> Das ist ein alter Freund von mir. Den kenne ich noch *von der Schule her*. Den kenne ich noch *von früher her*.

> Gestern abend waren wir im Theater. *Vor*her haben wir im Regina gegessen, und *nach*her waren wir bei Schmidts.

Hin may be used as a predicate adjective meaning *gone* or *beyond repair*.

> Alles ist hin.

Vorhin is an adverb of time meaning *just a little while ago*.

> Vorhin hat Rosemarie angerufen.

hin and her Following wo

In many cases, the use of **her** and **hin** stems from the "splitting" of **wohin** and **woher**.

> Wohin *gehst* du denn?
> Wo gehst du denn *hin?*
> Wo willst du denn *hin?*
> Wo ist er denn *hin*gegangen?
> Wo *du* hingehst, da will ich *auch* hin.
> Woher *kom*men Sie denn?
> Wo kommen *Sie* denn her?
> Wo kann *der* denn hergekommen sein?
> Wo hast du denn den neuen *Man*tel her?

The unseparated **wohin** and **woher** are today slightly literary in character. They *may* be used in conversation, but the separated forms are heard much more frequently.

hin and her Preceding Another Verbal Prefix

Certain English compound verbs have developed special meanings which are apt to trap a foreigner. It is, for instance, a surprise to a German-speaking person to find out that *he threw in the towel* cannot always be replaced by *he threw the towel in*.

In German, the verbal prefixes **ein-, unter-, auf-,** and **aus-**, if used without **hin-** or **her-**, are apt to develop nonliteral meanings. To express a strictly *spatial* meaning **hinein-** or **herein-, hinunter-** or **herunter-, hinauf-** or **herauf-, hinaus-** or **heraus-** must be used.

For example, **untergehen** may mean not only *to sink*, but also *to come to* *an end, to vanish, to perish.* Note the difference between

Die Inkakultur ging unter.	The Inca civilization vanished.

and

Er ist schon hinuntergegangen.	He has already gone down.

Compare also:

Das Licht ging aus.	The light went out.
Wir sind ausgegangen.	We went out.
Wir sind hinausgegangen.	We went out (of a room).

There are no definite rules governing the use of **hin-** and **her-** in these cases, but in general it can be said that verbs with **hin** and **her** in the complement have a strictly spatial meaning, whereas verbs with the simple complements **ein-**, **unter-**, **auf-**, and **aus-** tend to have figurative meanings:

Kommst du mit dem Geld aus?
Can you get along with the money you have?

Er kam heraus.
He came out (of a room).

Ich konnte mit meinem VW den Mercedes nicht einholen.
With my VW I could not catch up with the Mercedes.

Hast du die Zeitung schon hereingeholt?
Have you brought the paper in yet?

Die Sonne ging auf.
The sun rose.

Wollen Sie bitte in den zweiten Stock hinaufgehen?
Would you please go up to the third floor?

Wir haben Sie im Hotel Zeppelin untergebracht.
We've put you up at the Hotel Zeppelin.

Ihre Koffer habe ich schon hinunterbringen lassen.
I've already had your suitcases brought down.

hin and **her** in "Prepositional Brackets"

The sentence

Wir fuhren durch den Panamakanal

expresses the idea

We went through the Panama Canal.

In order to strengthen the feeling of spatial motion, the preposition **durch** can be reinforced by adding the verbal complement **hindurch**.

Wir fuhren *durch* den Panamakanal *hindurch*.

This **durch . . . hindurch** acts as a prepositional bracket enclosing the noun. Other frequently used brackets are:

> **Er kam** *aus* **dem Haus** *heraus.*
> **Er ging** *in* **das Haus** *hinein.*
> **Er stieg** *auf* **den Turm** [tower] *hinauf.*

Frequently **her,** without a preposition, forms the second bracket; it then expresses continuous motion.

> **Er lief hinter mir her.**
> **Er lief neben mir her.**
> **Er lief vor mir her.**

This tendency to "bracket" is so strong in German that it is found even in such syntactical units as **von Berlin aus,** *from Berlin;* **von da an,** *from then on;* **von mir aus,** *as far as I'm concerned.*

170 Comparison of Adjectives and Adverbs

Forms of the Comparative and the Superlative

Both German adjectives and adverbs form their comparative and superlative forms by adding **-er** and **-(e)st** to the stem, parallel to the English pattern in *fast, fast-er, fast-est:*

> **schnell, schneller, schnellst-**

The English patterns *interesting, more interesting, most interesting,* and *quickly, more quickly, most quickly* are not possible in German:

    interessant, interessanter, interessantest-

The -e- in the superlative forms is added whenever the -st- ending alone would be hard to pronounce—for example, **weitest-, ältest-, kürzest-.** An exception is the superlative form of **groß:**

    groß, größer, größt-

Many monosyllabic adjectives add an umlaut in both the comparative and superlative:

alt, älter, ältest-	old
arm, ärmer, ärmst-	poor
hart, härter, härtest-	hard
jung, jünger, jüngst-	young
kalt, kälter, kältest-	cold
kurz, kürzer, kürzest-	short
lang, länger, längst-	long
oft, öfter, öftest-	often
schwarz, schwärzer, schwärzest-	black
stark, stärker, stärkst-	strong

Adjectives ending in **-el** and **-er** lose the **-e-** in the comparative:

    dunkel, dunkler, dunkelst-
    teuer, teurer, teuerst-

The adjective **hoch** loses the **-c-** in the comparative:

    hoch, höher, höchst-,

and the adjective **nah** adds a **-c-** in the superlative:

    nah, näher, nächst-;

gut and **viel** have irregular forms:

    gut, besser, best-
    viel, mehr, meist-,

and the adverb **gern,** which has no comparative and superlative forms of its own, substitutes the forms of the adjective **lieb:**

    gern, lieber, liebst-.

Superlatives cannot be used without an ending; therefore the superlative forms above are followed by hyphens.

Use of Comparison

In comparisons implying equality, **so . . . wie** is used:

> **Er ist so alt wie ich.**
> **Er ist nicht so alt wie ich.**
> **Er ist so schnell gekommen, wie er nur kommen konnte.**

If the comparison expresses inequality, the comparative form of the adjective is used, followed by **als**:

> **Er ist älter als ich.**
> **Er kann nicht älter sein als ich.**
> **Er ist älter, als ich dachte.**

As *attributive adjectives,* comparative and superlative forms are treated like any other adjective; that is, they add normal adjective endings to the **-er** and **-st** suffixes:

> **Einen interessanteren Roman habe ich nie gelesen.**
> **Ein interessanteres Buch habe ich nie gelesen.**
> **Heute ist der längste Tag des Jahres.**

As *adverbs,* comparative forms do not take an ending, and superlative forms always use the pattern **am** (adjective) **-sten.**

> **Mit deinem Mercedes kommen wir bestimmt schneller nach München als mit meinem VW-Bus.**
>
> **Können Sie mir sagen, wie ich am schnellsten zum Flugplatz komme?**
>
> **Da nehmen Sie am besten ein Taxi.**

As *predicate adjectives,* comparative forms do not take an ending. Superlatives use attributive forms preceded by an article if a noun can be supplied; otherwise they follow the **am** (adjective) **-sten** pattern.

> **Meyers finde ich ja ganz nett, aber Schmidts sind doch netter.**
>
> **Von seinen drei Töchtern ist Ingrid zwar die intelligenteste, aber nicht die schönste (Tochter).**
>
> **Ich reise ja sehr gerne, aber zu Hause ist es doch am schönsten.**

Some Special Forms

1. A few comparatives are used with reference to their opposites. For example,

> **Wir haben längere Zeit in Berlin gewohnt**

means: we did not live there a long time, but longer than a short time. Similarly, **eine ältere Dame** (an elderly lady) does not mean that the lady is old, but that she is no longer young.

2. To express a high degree of a certain quality, German can use **höchst** as the equivalent of English *most*. Observe the degrees:

Das war ganz interessant.	(quite *interesting*)
Das war interessant.	(*interesting*)
Das war sehr interessant.	(*very* interesting)
Das war aber höchst interessant.	(*most* interesting)

3. Where English repeats the comparative to indicate an increase in degree, German uses **immer** with the comparative:

It was getting warmer and warmer.
Es wurde immer wärmer.

171   Nouns Derived from Adjectives

German, like English, has a number of suffixes which can be used to derive nouns from adjectives.

The Suffix -e

A number of adjectives may be changed into feminine nouns by adding the suffix -e and by umlauting when possible. These nouns correspond in meaning to English nouns in *-th* (*strong, strength; long, length*), *-ness* (*weak, weakness; great, greatness*), or *-ty* (*brief, brevity*).

breit	die Breite	breadth
frisch	die Frische	freshness
früh	die Frühe	morning
groß	die Größe	greatness; size
gut	die Güte	goodness, good quality
hart	die Härte	hardness
heiß	die Hitze	heat
hoch	die Höhe	height
kalt	die Kälte	cold(ness) *
kurz	die Kürze	shortness, brevity
lang	die Länge	length
nah	die Nähe	nearness, proximity
rot	die Röte	redness
schwach	die Schwäche	weakness
stark	die Stärke	strength
still	die Stille	peacefulness, calm, quiet
warm	die Wärme	warmth

* But *cold* in the medical sense: **die Erkältung.**

The Suffixes **-heit, -keit, -igkeit**

Many feminine abstract nouns corresponding to English derivatives in
-th, -ity, and *-ness* can be formed by adding one of these three suffixes;
they form their plurals in **-en.** Feel free to use the nouns listed, but do
not try to invent your own: they may not exist. Of high frequency are
the formations in **-keit** added to derivatives in **-bar, -ig,** and **-lich,** and
formations in **-igkeit** added to **-los.**

	dunkel	die Dunkelheit	darkness
	fähig	die Fähigkeit	ability, capability
	frei	die Freiheit	freedom
	ganz	die Ganzheit	wholeness
	gesund	die Gesundheit	health
	hell	die Helligkeit	brightness
	klar	die Klarheit	clarity
	krank	die Krankheit	sickness
	lebendig	die Lebendigkeit	liveliness
	leicht	die Leichtigkeit	ease, facility
	möglich	die Möglichkeit	possibility
	müde	die Müdigkeit	tiredness
	neu	die Neuheit	newness, novelty
		die Neuigkeit	news
	richtig	die Richtigkeit	correctness
	schlecht	die Schlechtigkeit	badness, meanness
	schön	die Schönheit	beauty
	sicher	die Sicherheit	security
	verrückt	die Verrücktheit	craziness
	vergangen	die Vergangenheit	past
	wahr	die Wahrheit	truth
	wahrscheinlich	die Wahrscheinlichkeit	probability
	wichtig	die Wichtigkeit	importance
	wirklich	die Wirklichkeit	reality
	zufrieden	die Zufriedenheit	contentment
	unfähig	die Unfähigkeit	inability
	unzufrieden	die Unzufriedenheit	discontent
	unsicher	die Unsicherheit	insecurity
die Angst, ⸚e (fear)	ängstlich	die Ängstlichkeit	timidity
die Ehre	ehrlich	die Ehrlichkeit	honesty
der Freund, –e	freundlich	die Freundlichkeit	friendliness
das Gesetz, –e	gesetzlich	die Gesetzlichkeit	lawfulness, legality

der Herr, –en	herrlich (magnificent, wonderful)	die Herrlichkeit	glory
das Herz, –en	herzlich	die Herzlichkeit	cordiality
der Hof, ⸚e	höflich	die Höflichkeit	politeness
der Mann, ⸚er	männlich (male, masculine)	die Männlichkeit	masculinity
der Mensch, –en	menschlich	die Menschlichkeit die Menschheit	humaneness mankind, humanity
die Natur	natürlich	die Natürlichkeit	naturalness
die Sache, –n (thing, fact, cause)	sachlich (objective)	die Sachlichkeit	objectivity, matter-of-factness
hassen (to hate)	häßlich (ugly)	die Häßlichkeit	ugliness
lieben	lieblich (lovely)	die Lieblichkeit	loveliness
sterben	sterblich unsterblich	die Sterblichkeit die Unsterblichkeit	mortality immortality
vergessen	vergeßlich (forgetful)	die Vergeßlichkeit	forgetfulness
froh (glad)	fröhlich (gay)	die Fröhlichkeit	gaiety
der Gedanke, –n	gedankenlos	die Gedankenlosigkeit	thoughtlessness
die Hilfe	hilflos	die Hilflosigkeit	helplessness
die Hoffnung	hoffnungslos	die Hoffnungslosigkeit	hopelessness
der Laut, –e (sound)	lautlos	die Lautlosigkeit	soundlessness
die Ruhe	ruhelos	die Ruhelosigkeit	restlessness
der Schlaf	schlaflos	die Schlaflosigkeit	sleeplessness, insomnia
der Dank	dankbar	die Dankbarkeit	gratitude
halten (to last, to hold up)	haltbar (durable)	die Haltbarkeit	durability
der Fehler, – (mistake)	fehlbar (fallible)		
	unfehlbar (infallible)	die Unfehlbarkeit	infallibility
sehen die Sicht (sight)	sichtbar (visible)		
	unsichtbar (invisible)	die Unsichtbarkeit	invisibility

teilen	teilbar	die Teilbarkeit	divisibility
(to divide)	(divisible)		
	unteilbar	die Unteilbarkeit	indivisibility
	(indivisible)		

Note the following special cases:

die Kindheit	childhood
die Gottheit	deity
die Flüssigkeit	liquid
die Seltenheit	rarity
die Einheit	unit, unity
die Einigkeit	accord, being of one mind, unity
einig	in agreement, in accord
vereinigt	united
die Vereinigten Staaten	the United States
die Wiedervereinigung	the reunification
einsam	lonely
die Einsamkeit	loneliness, solitude
einzeln	single (apart from the rest)
die Einzelheit	detail
einzig	single, unique, sole
einfach	simple
die Einfachheit	simplicity

172   The Rhetorical **nicht**

If a speaker asks for a positive confirmation of a statement he makes, he adds *don't you?, aren't you?, haven't you?* etc., in English and **nicht?** or **nicht wahr?** in German.

> **Du warst doch gestern abend mit Inge im Kino, nicht?**
> You and Inge were at the movies last night, weren't you?

This rhetorical **nicht** can be moved into the inner field (between items of news value and items of no news value) if the statement is transformed into a rhetorical question. The normal question

> **Warst du gestern abend mit Inge im Kino?**

thus becomes the rhetorical

> **Warst du nicht gestern abend mit Inge im *Kino*?**

This rhetorical **nicht** appears only in yes-or-no questions. It is never stressed; it is always followed by the stress point of the sentence; and if followed by **ein,** it cannot be replaced by **kein.** An affirmative answer to such rhetorical questions can be either **Ja** or **Doch.** However, even though the speaker always expects a confirmation, the answer can, of course, also be **Nein.**

> **Haben Sie nicht einen Bruder?**   You have a brother, don't you?
> Answer: *Ja, Doch,* or *Nein.*

> *H*a**ben Sie keinen Bruder?**   Don't you *have* a brother?
> Answer: *Doch* or *Nein,* but never *Ja.*

> **Haben Sie einen Bruder?**   Do you have a brother?
> Answer: *Ja* or *Nein,* but never *Doch.*

Further examples:

> **Warum hast du denn den *Mey*er nicht besucht?**
> (Real question; stress point precedes *nicht.*)

> **Hast du den Meyer letzte Woche *nicht* besucht?**
> (Real question; *nicht* is stressed.)

> **Hast du nicht letzte Woche den *Mey*er besucht?**
> (Rhetorical question; stress point follows unstressed *nicht.*)

173   Numbers over 100—Decimals—Ordinal Numbers—
         Fractions

100	**hundert** (**einhundert**)
101	**hunderteins**
102	**hundertzwei**
110	**hundertzehn**
121	**hunderteinundzwanzig**
200	**zweihundert**
600	**sechshundert**
1.000	**tausend** (**eintausend**)
7.625	**siebentausendsechshundertfünfundzwanzig**
1.000.000	**eine Million**
2.000.000	**zwei Millionen**
1.000.000.000	**eine Milliarde** (one billion)

Note that German uses periods where English uses commas: 2.325.641. Conversely, in *decimal numbers,* German uses commas where English uses periods.

0,3	**null komma drei**
12,17	**zwölf komma siebzehn**
6,5342	**sechs komma fünf drei vier zwei**

German *ordinal numbers* are attributive adjectives:

> **der erste**
> **der zweite**

der *dritte*
der vierte
der fünfte
der sechste
der siebte
etc.
der neunzehnte
der zwanzig*ste*
die einundzwanzig*ste*
der dreißig*ste*
etc.

To make a figure indicate an ordinal number, German uses a period.

der 4. Juli
the Fourth of July

NOTE:

Heinrich I. (Heinrich der Erste)
Friedrich Wilhelm IV. (Friedrich Wilhelm der Vierte)
Er war ein Sohn Friedrichs II. (Friedrichs des Zweiten)

Series are expressed as follows:

1. erstens
2. zweitens
3. drittens
4. viertens
5. fünftens
6. sechstens
7. siebtens
etc.
„Erstens bin ich zu alt, und zweitens bin ich zu müde."

Fractions:

die Hälfte, –n
das Drittel, –
das Viertel, –
das Fünftel, –
das Sechstel, –
das Siebtel, –
etc.

halb can be inflected:

Ich hätte gerne ein halbes Pfund Butter.

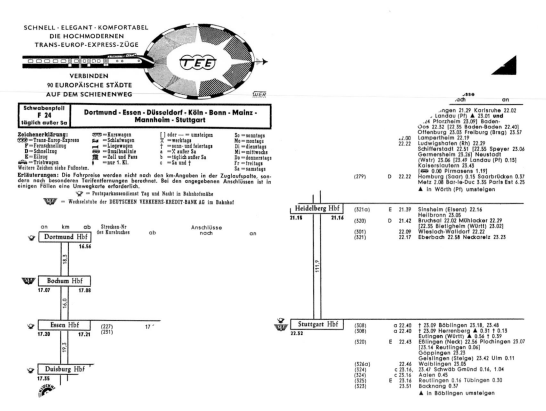

All other fractions are uninflected:

> Ich hätte gerne ein viertel Pfund Butter.

½	ein halb
⅓	ein drittel
¾	drei viertel
⅞	sieben achtel

174 Time

In *colloquial* German, the following terms are used to tell time.

8.00 Uhr	acht Uhr
8.05 Uhr	fünf nach acht
8.10 Uhr	zehn nach acht
8.15 Uhr	viertel nach acht; viertel neun
8.20 Uhr	zwanzig nach acht
8.25 Uhr	fünf vor halb neun
8.30 Uhr	halb neun
8.35 Uhr	fünf nach halb neun

8.40 Uhr	zehn nach halb neun
8.45 Uhr	dreiviertel neun, viertel vor neun
8.50 Uhr	zehn vor neun
8.55 Uhr	fünf vor neun

In a railway station or an airport, the following pattern is used:

0.10 Uhr	null Uhr zehn (12:10 A.M.)
8.05 Uhr	acht Uhr fünf (8:05 A.M.)
20.05 Uhr	zwanzig Uhr fünf (8:05 P.M.)
24.00 Uhr	vierundzwanzig Uhr (midnight)

EXERCISES

A. Express in German. All German sentences must contain a form of **lassen.**

1. That leaves me cold.
2. Why didn't you leave your books at home?
3. I don't want to let him take me home. (Use reflexive pronoun plus *von ihm.*)
4. He has his letters written by his wife. (Use reflexive pronoun plus *von seiner Frau.*)
5. You shouldn't let him go to Africa.
6. I must get myself a haircut.
7. Why don't you have your hair cut?
8. He went downtown to get a haircut.
9. She has left her coat here again.
10. You should leave her in peace.
11. We are having a house built in Cologne. (Use reflexive pronoun.)
12. We want to have Overbeck build us a house. (Use reflexive pronoun plus *von Overbeck.*)
13. I wish we had had Overbeck build us a house. (Use reflexive pronoun plus *von Overbeck.*)

SEE LAB
EXERCISES
11.1–11.4

(pp. 633-634)

B. Restate the following sentences in the perfect.

1. Ich blieb oft vor Alis Haus stehen.
2. Er riet mir, an die See zu fahren.
3. Wir ließen gestern abend den Arzt kommen.
4. Er braucht *doch* nicht nach Berlin zu fahren.
5. Wir dachten damals daran, nach Köln zu ziehen.
6. Um sechs Uhr gingen wir essen.
7. Der Müller war einfach nicht zu verstehen.
8. Gegen Abend fing es dann an zu regnen.
9. Er lief aus dem Haus, ohne ein Wort zu sagen.

SEE LAB
EXERCISES
11.5–11.11

(p. 634)

10. Er läßt sich immer von mir das Essen bezahlen.
11. Er läßt mich einfach nicht in Ruhe.
12. Hans blieb bis um zehn Uhr im Bett liegen.
13. Ich lernte Ingelheim kurz nach dem Krieg kennen.
14. Wir waren wirklich sehr erstaunt, ihn wiederzusehen.
15. Ich dachte nie daran, nach Casablanca zu fahren.

C. Transform the following pairs of sentences into sentences with **ohne . . . zu** or **statt . . . zu.** Note that the negation disappears in the infinitive phrase.

> **Er fuhr nach Afrika. Er nahm seine Frau nicht mit.—ohne**
> **Er fuhr nach Afrika, ohne seine Frau mitzunehmen.**

SEE LAB
EXERCISE
11.12

(p. 634)

1. Er fuhr nach Afrika. Er nahm seine Frau nicht mit.—ohne
2. Er fuhr nach Afrika. Er blieb nicht zu Hause.—statt
3. Er schrieb ihr einen Brief. Er rief sie nicht an.—statt
4. Er war in Berlin. Er hat mich nicht besucht.—ohne
5. Er kaufte sich einen Wagen. Er hatte nicht das Geld dafür.—ohne
6. Er gab den Wagen seinem Sohn. Er hat ihn nicht verkauft.—statt
7. Er war eine Woche in München. Er ist nicht ins Theater gegangen.—ohne
8. Er fuhr schon am Samstag weg. Er blieb nicht bis Sonntag.—statt
9. Er hat vierzehn Tage gearbeitet. Er konnte sich nicht *ein*mal ausschlafen.—ohne

D. Express in German:

SEE LAB
EXERCISES
11.13, 11.14

(p. 634)

1. Where is your coat?—Oh, I left it (hanging) at the Meyers.
2. Perhaps you should try once more to call him.
3. This chair you must leave (standing) in the living room.
4. Now the apartment is in order again at last.—No, you have forgotten to put the chairs back into the living room.
5. He finally had to promise his wife not to go to Africa again.
6. He suggested that my wife should go to the North Sea this year.
7. He suggested that I should send my wife to the North Sea this year.
8. He said that he had heard a woman scream.
9. I'd like to know why she has never learned to drive.
10. You ought to stay home tonight instead of going to the movies.
11. You shouldn't have left the car (standing) in front of the house.

E. Change to comparatives:

> **Ich bin nicht so alt wie er. Er ist älter als ich.**

1. Unser Haus ist nicht so groß wie eures.
2. Bei uns ist es nicht so kalt wie bei euch.
3. Glas ist nicht so hart wie ein Diamant.
4. Der Weg war nicht so lang wie ich dachte. (Use *kurz*.)
5. Ich gehe nicht so oft ins Theater wie du.
6. Amerikanisches Bier ist nicht so stark wie deutsches Bier.
7. Von Köln bis Bonn ist es nicht so weit wie von Frankfurt bis Bonn.
8. Ich kann nicht so viel essen wie du.
9. Bier trinke ich nicht so gerne wie Wein.
10. Ich finde ihn nicht so interessant wie seine Frau.

F. Change the adjectives to superlatives:

1. In Köln hat es mir gut gefallen.
2. Hans hat viel getrunken.
3. München ist eine schöne Stadt.
4. In München gibt es gutes Bier.
5. Im Dezember sind die Tage kurz.
6. Im Juni sind die Tage lang.
7. Der 21. Juni ist ein langer Tag.
8. Giganto ist ein starker Mann.
9. Ich wäre jetzt gern in Deutschland.
10. In Alaska ist das Obst teuer.

G. Read aloud:

21 32 43 54 65 76 87 98 109 120
213 324 435 546 657 768 801
1.003 1.011 1.021 1.248 1.349 1.492
14.395 128.473 847.666 3.492.716
0,3 7,43 421,7 3.746,4519
DM 0,25 DM 7,50 DM 300,00 DM 16.500,00 DM 1.000.000.000
$\frac{2}{3}$ $\frac{3}{4}$ $\frac{7}{8}$ $\frac{15}{16}$ $\frac{19}{20}$

H. Imagine that you have a cousin, Hildegard, who lives in Munich and knows no English. You want to visit her during your stay in Germany, so you decide to write her a letter while on the train to Koblenz. For lack of anything profound to say (owing to your lack of that kind of German), you tell her about your adventures at the Frankfurt railroad station.

The envelope, incidentally, would be addressed as follows.

Fräulein
Hildegard Pfeilguth

8   München 13
Tengstraße 40

After duly addressing her as "Liebe Hildegard!" you tell her that you arrived in Frankfurt after a good flight. Because you wanted to go to Koblenz on the same day, you took a taxi to the station. Then you describe what happened to you until the Hellas-Express finally started moving.

You sign off by writing,

Viele herzliche Grüße

Dein John

VOCABULARY

die Ahnung, –en idea; premonition, hunch
die Alpen the Alps
ändern to change
die Armee', –n army
aufgehen to rise (sun, moon); to open
aufhören to stop
auskommen to get along
aussprechen to pronounce, utter
bedeuten to mean, signify
beenden to conclude, finish
bereit ready
der Beruf, –e profession
  Was sind Sie von Beruf? What is your profession?
beschließen to decide, determine
besonder– special
bestehen aus to consist of
beweisen to prove
die Bibliothek, –en library
blau blue
die Bühne, –n stage
der Chef, –s boss
das Dach, –̈er roof
damit' (conjunction) so that
deshalb for that reason, therefore
Deutsch können (here used in the sense of "to know," "to have a mastery of," as a language. Thus: Er

kann Deutsch, Er kann Französisch, etc.)
der Dezember December
der Dollar, –s dollar
  zwanzig Dollar twenty dollars
das Drittel, – third (fraction)
drucken to print
das Ei, –er egg
einholen to catch up with
der Einwohner, – inhabitant
einzig (adjective) only, sole
die Erfindung, –en invention
der Erfolg, –e success
erhalten to receive, sustain
erlauben to allow, permit
fähig capable
der Februar February
das Feld, –er field
fernsehen to watch TV
  der Fernseher TV set
  das Fernsehen television
die Flut, –en flood
furchtbar frightful, terrible
gefallen to please
  das gefällt mir I like it (that pleases me)
  der Gefallen, – favor
das Gespräch, –e conversation
gestatten to permit, allow
es gibt there is (are) available
gnädige Frau formal way of

addressing a married woman
die Hälfte, –n half
der Händler, – dealer
der Handschuh, –e glove
die Handtasche, –n handbag
hart hard
der Herzog, –̈e duke
die Höhe, –n height
  in die Höhe upward
die Jugend (no pl.) youth (the early years of life; young people collectively)
die Karte, –n map, ticket
  die Fahrkarte, –n (train) ticket
  die Rückfahrkarte, –n round-trip ticket
  der Flugschein, –e plane ticket
  die Landkarte, –n map
die Klasse, –n class
klettern to climb
das Komma, –s comma
langweilig dull, boring
lochen to punch (ticket)
die Lokomoti've, –n locomotive
der Markt, –̈e market(place)
die Milliarde, –n billion
die Million, –en million
der Mittwoch, –e Wednesday
die Möbel (pl.) furniture

nachher afterwards
neulich recently
der Norden the north
  nördlich northern
  der Osten the east
    östlich eastern
  der Süden the south
    südlich southern
  der Westen the west
    westlich western
die Nordsee (*no pl.*) North
  Sea
nutzlos useless
öffentlich public
das Paket, –e package
die Partei, –en party
Polen Poland
  polnisch Polish
Prozent percent
  zwei Prozent two percent
das Rad, ̈-er wheel
reservieren to reserve
der Schalter, – (ticket)
  window
der Schauspieler, – actor
schließlich finally, after all
der Schuß, die Schüsse shot

das Semester, – semester
sobald (*conjunction*) as
  soon as
sogar even
der Spiegel, – mirror
die Stellung, –en position;
  job
der Stock, ̈-e stick; floor (of
  a building)
  im ersten (**zweiten,** etc.)
  Stock on the first
  (second, etc.) floor
das Studium, die Studien
  studies; course of study
der Tabak, –e tobacco
der Teil, –e part
das Testament, –e last will
der Tod, –e death
todschick elegant, "great"
der Traum, ̈-e dream
überhaupt anyway
überzeugen to convince
unbedingt by all means
unterbringen to put up,
  lodge
untergehen to sink, perish; to
  set (sun, moon)

unterkommen to find a place
  to stay
der Verkehr traffic
verlangen demand
das Vermögen, – wealth,
  fortune, estate
der Versuch, –e try, attempt;
  experiment
der Vetter, –n cousin (male)
völlig completely
vorhin a while ago
der Vorschlag, ̈-e suggestion,
  proposal
  vorschlagen to propose,
  suggest
wagen to dare
wandern to wander, migrate,
  hike
  auswandern to emigrate
  einwandern to immigrate
die Wiese, –n meadow
wild wild
der Zaun, ̈-e fence
die Zukunft (*no pl.*) future
der Zwerg, –e dwarf

IRREGULAR VERBS

beschließen to decide, determine
  beschloß, hat beschlossen,
  er beschließt
bestehen aus to consist of
  bestand aus, hat aus . . .
    bestanden, es besteht aus

beweisen to prove
  bewies, hat bewiesen, er
  beweist
erhalten to receive; sustain
  erhielt, hat erhalten, er
  erhält

gefallen to please
  gefiel, hat gefallen, er
  gefällt
vorschlagen to propose,
  suggest
  schlug vor, hat vorge-
  schlagen, er schlägt vor

UNIT 12: Reflexive Verbs—Imperatives

[1] Unstressed Reflexive Objects

Ich will mir ein *Haus* bauen.

Du willst dir ein *Haus* bauen?

Er will sich ein *Haus* bauen.

Sie will sich ein *Haus* bauen.

Wir wollen uns ein *Haus* bauen.

So, ihr wollt euch ein *Haus* bauen?

Meyers wollen sich ein *Haus* bauen.

Sie wollen sich ein *Haus* bauen, Herr Meyer?

Ich habe mich schon ge*ba*det.

Hast du dich schon ge*ba*det?

Er hat sich schon ge*ba*det.

Sie hat sich schon ge*ba*det.

Wir haben uns schon ge*ba*det.

Habt ihr euch schon ge*ba*det?

Die Kinder haben sich schon ge*ba*det.

SEE ANALYSIS **139, 175**

(pp. 384, 546-547)

Lieber Hans, ich wünsche dir und deiner Frau viel Glück. Ich weiß, so eine Frau hast du dir immer gewünscht.

Er hat mich noch nicht gefragt, ob ich ihn heiraten will, und ich frage mich oft, ob er der richtige Mann für mich ist.

Ich hole mir ein Glas Wasser. Darf ich dir auch eins holen?

Als Ingelheim heiratete, baute ihm sein Vater ein kleines Haus. Aber mit seinem letzten Roman hat er soviel Geld verdient, daß er sich ein neues, großes Haus bauen konnte.

VARIATIONS

Using the phrases

> **sich** (accusative) **im Spiegel sehen**
> to look at oneself in the mirror

> **sich** (dative) **einen Bart wachsen lassen**
> to grow a beard

form sentences of your own, beginning with simple sentences like

> **Ich sehe mich im Spiegel.**
> **Ich lasse mir einen Bart wachsen.**

(*Facing*) **Schuhputzer in Berlin**

517

and advancing to more complicated structures like

Du solltest dich mal im Spiegel sehen.

Ich wollte, er hätte sich keinen Bart wachsen lassen.

[2] Stressed Reflexive Objects

SEE
ANALYSIS
139, 175

(pp. 384,
546-547)

Erkenne dich *selbst*. (Know thyself.)

Ich habe Angst vor dem Leben; vielleicht weil ich Angst vor mir *sel*ber habe.

Den Meyer habe ich nicht eingeladen; der hat sich *sel*ber eingeladen.

Du solltest auch einmal an dich (selbst) denken.

Ich muß endlich auch einmal an mich (selber) denken.

Das schenke ich nicht meiner Frau; das schenke ich mir *sel*ber.

Professor Schnarf hat nur ein Thema: sich *selbst*.

VARIATIONS

In the following sentences, change the objects to stressed reflexive objects; use
selbst or **selber** in all cases.

Er hat Angst vor mir.

Wir helfen euch.

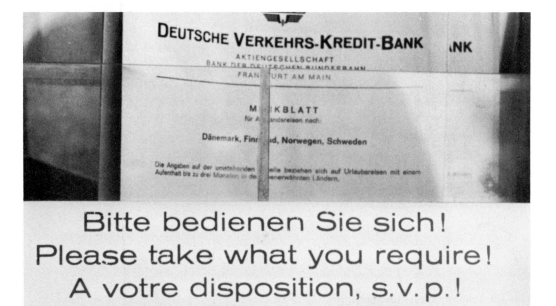

Du mußt ihm helfen.

Er denkt immer nur an mich.

Ich möchte lieber nicht von ihm reden.

Das habe ich für meine Frau gekauft.

Ich kann dich nicht mehr verstehen.

[3] selbst and selber Emphasizing a Noun or Pronoun

Das weiß ich *selbst*.

Ihrer Frau geht es also wieder gut—und wie geht es Ihnen *selbst?*

Ich wollte eigentlich meine Sekretärin nach Berlin schicken; aber ich fahre doch besser *sel*ber hin.

Bei diesem Brief kann ich dir nicht helfen; den mußt du *sel*ber schreiben.

Ich habe nicht mit Meyers Frau gesprochen; ich habe mit ihm *selbst* gesprochen.

Meine Frau hat nicht mit ihm gesprochen; ich habe *selbst* mit ihm gesprochen.

Das kann *ich* ihm nicht sagen; das müssen Sie ihm *selbst* sagen.

Das können Sie doch nicht seiner Sekretärin sagen; das müssen Sie ihm *selbst* sagen.

SEE ANALYSIS 175 (pp. 546-547)

VARIATIONS

Insert **selbst** or **selber** in the appropriate place in the second clause of each sentence.

Das kann ich erst glauben, wenn ich es gesehen habe.

Seine Bücher kenne ich schon lange, aber ihn habe ich noch nicht kennengelernt.

Nein, das hat mir nicht seine Sekretärin gesagt, das habe ich von ihm gehört.

Seine Frau ist ja ganz nett, aber mit Meyer will ich nichts zu tun haben.

[4] Special Cases of selbst and selber

*Da*bei brauchst du mir nicht zu helfen; das kann ich *sel*ber machen.

Was, du mußt den Kleinen immer noch *füt*tern? Kann der sich denn noch nicht *sel*ber füttern?

Muß *ich* denn jeden Morgen zuerst aufstehen? Kannst du dir das Frühstück nicht mal *sel*ber machen?

Diesen Brief kann Johannes nicht *sel*ber geschrieben haben; soviel Englisch *kann* der gar nicht.

SEE ANALYSIS 175 (pp. 546-547)

VARIATIONS

To each of the following sentences, add another one containing **selber** in the meaning of *without help.*

> **Du brauchst doch die Kinder nicht zu baden.**
> **Die können sich doch selber baden.**

Danke, du brauchst mir den Koffer nicht zu tragen.
Du brauchst doch den Kaffee nicht zu kochen.
Warum soll *ich* denn deiner Frau schreiben?
Dein Vater braucht uns kein Auto zu kaufen.
Wer hat euch denn die Reise bezahlt?

Sie *selbst hat* kein Geld; aber ihre *Mut*ter hat *viel* Geld.
Er *selbst* ist ja ganz *nett;* aber mit seiner *Mut*ter könnte ich nicht *le*ben.
*An*dere hat er ge*ret*tet, aber sich *selbst kann* er nicht retten.
Uns schickt Vater jeden Sonntag in die *Kirch*e, aber er *sel*ber bleibt zu *Haus*e und liest die
Zeitung.

VARIATIONS

To each of the following sentences add a contrasting statement containing **selbst**:

> **Ihre *Mut*ter hat *viel* Geld; aber sie *selbst* hat *kein* Geld.**

Mein *Mann* ist schon *oft* in Paris gewesen.   Für *uns* hat er etwas ge*kauft.*
Uns schickt Vater jeden Sommer an die *Nord*see.   *Mir* hat mein Vater ver*bot*en zu
Ihre *Schwe*stern haben alle ge*hei*ratet.   rauchen.

Ich habe *sel*ber kein Geld.
Ich habe *auch* kein Geld.

Ich kann dir nicht helfen; ich habe *sel*ber viel zu tun.
Ich kann gut verstehen, daß dir sein neuer Roman nicht gefällt. Er gefällt mir *sel*ber nicht.

VARIATIONS

To each of the following sentences add a statement containing **selber** meaning **auch.**

Wir können euch kein Geld schicken. Wir haben _____.
Ich weiß, daß dir unsere neue Wohnung nicht gefällt. Sie gefällt _____.
Ich bin gar nicht erstaunt, daß Sie meinen Mann nicht verstehen. Ich kann _____

_____.

Er hat immer gelacht, wenn ich Detektivromane gelesen habe; und jetzt _____

_____.

[5] selbst, sogar, auch meaning *even*

Selbst (sogar, auch) *das* ist ihm zu viel.

SEE ANALYSIS 176 (p. 548)

Selbst (sogar, auch) Herrn Dr. Müller, der sonst immer da ist, konnte ich diesmal nicht sprechen; der war auch in Berlin.

In Berlin sprechen selbst (sogar, auch) kleine Kinder Deutsch.

Selbst (sogar, auch) von seiner Frau läßt er sich nichts sagen.

Gegen Ende des Krieges mußten in Deutschland selbst (sogar, auch) Sechzehnjährige Soldat werden.

In San Franzisko kann es selbst (sogar, auch) im Juni so kalt sein, daß man abends einen Mantel tragen muß.

VARIATIONS

Restate the following sentences, starting with **selbst**.

> **Seiner Frau hat er auch nichts davon gesagt.**
> **Selbst (sogar, auch) seiner Frau hat er nichts davon gesagt.**

In Rom hat es heute *auch* geschneit.

Mein Vater raucht *auch* nicht mehr.

Tante Amalie will *auch* nicht mehr ins Museum.

Amanda ist *auch* nicht sitzengeblieben.

So viel Geld haben auch die Amerikaner nicht.

[6] Reciprocal Pronouns

Note the use of **sich, einander** and **gegenseitig**.

Hat er sie zuerst geküßt oder hat sie ihn zuerst geküßt?—Das weiß ich nicht. Aber es ist sicher, daß sie sich geküßt haben.

SEE ANALYSIS 177 (p. 548)

„Sie fühlten sich zueinander hingezogen. Sie schauten sich in die Augen; ihre Lippen trafen sich, und ihre Herzen hatten einander gefunden." (Ingelheim)

So, ihr wollt beide ein Wochenendhaus bauen? Wenn ihr euch gegenseitig helft, dann ist das gar nicht so schwer.

Im Sommer hat er ihr das erste Mal geschrieben, und seitdem schreiben sie sich jede Woche zweimal, und mindestens einmal im Monat rufen sie sich an.

Heute abend gehe ich mit ihr ins Theater.—Wo triffst du sie denn?—Wir treffen uns am Bahnhof.

Leider sehe ich sie nicht mehr so oft wie früher; aber wenn wir uns sehen, haben wir uns immer viel zu erzählen.

[7] Reflexive Verbs

SEE
ANALYSIS
178-180

(pp. 548-552)

sich verlieben in: verliebt sein in
to fall in love with: to be in love with

Er ist verliebt.

In wen hat er sich denn diesmal verliebt?

Er soll sich in seine Lehrerin verliebt haben.

Er soll in seine Lehrerin verliebt sein.

Mit einem verliebten jungen Mann ist nichts Vernünftiges anzufangen.

sich verloben mit: verlobt sein mit
to become engaged to: to be engaged to

Die Verlobung ihrer Tochter Emma mit

Herrn Generaldirektor Dr. Anton Meyer

zeigen an

Dr. med. Erich Bertram und Frau Luise, geb. Krämer

Ich höre, die Emma soll sich verlobt haben.

Ich dachte, sie wäre schon lange verlobt. Wer ist denn ihr Verlobter?

Darf ich Ihnen meine Verlobte vorstellen, gnädige Frau?

Ich gratuliere dir zu deiner Verlobung. Deine Emma ist wirklich ein nettes Mädchen.

heiraten: sich verheiraten: verheiratet sein mit
to marry: to get married: to be married to

Ich höre, Sie haben sich verlobt. Wann wollen Sie denn heiraten?

Die jüngste Tochter soll sich auch schon verheiratet haben.

Mit wem ist sie denn verheiratet?

Wann heiratest *du* denn, Monika?—Ich muß erst jemanden *finden*, der mich heiraten will.

Sie soll schon dreimal verheiratet gewesen sein.

Ich brauche eine neue Sekretärin; eine verheiratete wäre mir lieber als eine unverheiratete.

sich scheiden lassen von: geschieden sein
to get a divorce from: to be divorced

Kurz nach dem Krieg ließ sich seine erste Frau von ihm scheiden.

Eine geschiedene Frau hat oft ein schweres Leben.

Anton und Emma waren einmal verheiratet; jetzt sind sie geschieden.

Warum haben sie sich denn scheiden lassen?—Weil er sich in seine Sekretärin verliebt hat.

sich umziehen: umgezogen sein
to change (clothes): to have changed (clothes)
Ich muß mich noch umziehen, bevor wir ins Theater gehen.
Ich dachte, du hättest dich schon umgezogen.
Ich brauche mich nicht umzuziehen, ich bin schon umgezogen.

But note: **umziehen, zog um, ist umgezogen** *to move*
Ich höre, Sie sind umgezogen.—Ja, wir wohnen jetzt in der Ingelheimer Straße.

sich anziehen: angezogen sein
to get dressed: to be dressed
Hast du den Kleinen schon angezogen?
Der kann sich jetzt schon selbst anziehen; den brauche ich nicht mehr anzuziehen.
Er ist schon angezogen; er hat sich selber angezogen.

sich ausziehen: ausgezogen sein
to get undressed: to be undressed
Als er nach Hause kam, zog er sich schnell aus und legte sich ins Bett.
Heute abend bin ich zu müde, um noch ins Kino zu gehen. Ich bin schon ausgezogen und
    möchte mich nicht noch einmal anziehen.

sich ausruhen: ausgeruht sein
to take a rest: to be rested
Du hast in der letzten Zeit viel zu viel gearbeitet; du solltest dich endlich einmal ausruhen.
Ich habe heute morgen bis zehn geschlafen und bin ganz ausgeruht.
Nach vier Wochen an der Riviera sollte er sich eigentlich gut ausgeruht haben.

sich ausschlafen: ausgeschlafen sein
to get enough sleep: to have had enough sleep
Nächsten Sonntag kann ich mich endlich einmal ausschlafen.
Warum stehst du denn heute so früh auf?—Ich konnte nicht mehr schlafen. Ich bin aus-
    geschlafen.

sich erholen: erholt sein
to get a rest (to recover one's strength): to be recovered
Du bist so überarbeitet. Du solltest einmal irgendwohin fahren und dich ein bißchen er-
    holen.
Ich war vier Wochen an der See und habe mich gut erholt.
Als er aus dem Schwarzwald zurückkam, war er gut erholt.
Er kam gut erholt aus dem Schwarzwald zurück.

sich rasieren: rasiert sein
to shave: to have shaved, to be shaved
Natürlich mußt du dich noch einmal rasieren, bevor wir zu Erdmanns gehen.

Aber ich habe mich doch heute schon einmal rasiert.

Du siehst aber so unrasiert aus.

Wenn du nicht rasiert bist, kannst du in diesem Hotel unmöglich ins Frühstückszimmer gehen.

sich aufregen über: aufgeregt sein
to get excited (upset) about: to be excited (upset)

Frau Meyer hat über tausend Mark im Kasino verloren, und Meyer hat sich furchtbar darüber aufgeregt.

Warum ist Meyer denn so aufgeregt?—Weil seine Frau schon wieder tausend Mark verloren hat.

Meyer soll furchtbar aufgeregt gewesen sein.

Meyer soll sich furchtbar aufgeregt haben.

sich beruhigen: beruhigt sein
to calm down: to be calmed down

Natürlich ist Meyer sehr aufgeregt, aber wie ich ihn kenne, wird er sich auch wieder beruhigen.

Seine Frau hat ihm versprochen, nie wieder ins Kasino zu gehen.—Na ja, dann kann er ja beruhigt sein.

sich entschließen zu: entschlossen sein zu
to make up one's mind to: to have made up one's mind, to be determined

Lieber Johannes, ich habe mich dazu entschlossen, mich von dir scheiden zu lassen.

Ich bin fest entschlossen, mich von dir scheiden zu lassen.

sich erkälten: erkältet sein
to catch a cold: to have a cold

Bei Niedermeyers gestern abend war es so kalt, daß ich mich erkältet habe.

Hannelore ist auch erkältet. War die auch bei Niedermeyers?

sich gewöhnen an: gewöhnt sein an
to get accustomed (used) to: to be accustomed (used) to

An das Klima hier in Kairo kann ich mich einfach nicht gewöhnen.

An das Klima habe ich mich immer noch nicht gewöhnt.

An das Klima bin ich jetzt ganz gewöhnt.

Ich habe mich so an dich gewöhnt.

Ich bin so an sie gewöhnt, daß ich ihren amerikanischen Akzent gar nicht mehr höre.

sich überzeugen von: überzeugt sein von
to become convinced of: to be convinced of

Ich habe ihm lange nicht geglaubt, aber jetzt habe ich mich davon überzeugen müssen, daß er recht hat.

Ich bin fest davon überzeugt, daß er recht hat.

sich verändern: verändert sein
to change: to have changed, to be changed
Ich habe ihn fast nicht erkannt, so sehr hat er sich verändert.
Er soll sich sehr verändert haben.
Seit dem Tod seiner Frau ist er ganz verändert.

sich vorbereiten auf: vorbereitet sein auf
to prepare for: to be prepared for
Er macht morgen sein Examen.—Hat er sich auch gut darauf vorbereitet?
Ist er auch gut darauf vorbereitet?

sich öffnen: geöffnet sein
to open: to be open
„Die Natur ist ein Buch mit sieben Siegeln [seals], das sich nur dem öffnet, der darin zu
   lesen versteht."
Es ist nur dem geöffnet, der es versteht, darin zu lesen.

sich schließen: geschlossen sein
to close: to be closed
Und hinter ihm schloß sich das Tor.
Das Tor war noch geschlossen, als wir ankamen.

entschuldigen: sich entschuldigen: entschuldigt sein; verzeihen
to excuse oneself: to be excused; to pardon
Ich glaube, Sie sitzen auf meinem Platz.
   I think you're sitting in my seat.
Oh, entschuldigen Sie, Sie haben recht.
   Excuse me, you're right.
Oh, Entschuldigung, Sie haben recht.
   Excuse me, you're right.
Oh, ich bitte um Entschuldigung.
   Excuse me.
Oh, ich bitte um Verzeihung.
   I'm sorry. *or:* I beg your pardon (for example, for stepping on your foot).
Oh, Verzeihung.
   I beg your pardon.
Oh, verzeihen Sie.
   I beg your pardon.

Entschuldigen Sie mich einen Augenblick; ich muß mal eben telephonieren.
Entschuldigen Sie, gnädige Frau, daß ich so spät komme.—Sie brauchen sich gar nicht zu
   entschuldigen, bei dem Regen ist das ja kein Wunder.
Sie kommen allein, Edgar?—Meine Frau läßt sich entschuldigen; sie hat sich erkältet und
   wollte lieber zu Hause bleiben.

Ich kann ja vieles verstehen; aber daß du mich am Frühstückstisch mit Gisela anredest, das ist nicht zu entschuldigen.

Natürlich weiß ich, daß Johannes dich nicht hätte mit Gisela anreden sollen, und ich will ihn ja auch gar nicht entschuldigen. Aber warum du sofort zu deiner Mutter gefahren bist, das kann ich nicht verstehen.

Meyer kommt nicht; er ist entschuldigt, er mußte nach Berlin.

VARIATIONS

Change the following actions into states:

> Sie hat sich in ihren Lehrer verliebt.
>
> Sie hat sich mit ihm verlobt.
>
> Sie soll ihn geheiratet haben.
>
> Sie hat sich scheiden lassen.
>
> Hast du dich schon angezogen?
>
> Meyer soll sich furchtbar darüber aufgeregt haben.
>
> Ich hoffe, du hast dich gut ausgeruht.
>
> Heute habe ich mich endlich einmal ausgeschlafen.
>
> Habt ihr euch schon gebadet, Kinder?
>
> Hast du dich jetzt endlich beruhigt?
>
> Der Bürgermeister soll sich gestern abend schon wieder betrunken haben.
>
> Wir haben uns fest entschlossen, das Haus zu kaufen.
>
> Hast du dich erkältet?

Change the following states into action; use the perfect:

> An das Klima bin ich schon gewöhnt.
>
> Ist er schon wieder nicht rasiert?
>
> Mein Mann ist wirklich überarbeitet.
>
> Ich bin davon überzeugt, daß sie gut küssen kann.
>
> Wir müssen in einer halben Stunde im Theater sein. Bist du schon umgezogen?
>
> Wir waren einfach nicht vorbereitet auf den Krieg.

[8] sich setzen, sich stellen, sich legen

SEE
ANALYSIS
181

(pp. 552-553)

sitzen—setzen—sich setzen

Wer sitzt denn da bei euch am Tisch?—Den kenne ich auch nicht. Der hat sich einfach an unseren Tisch gesetzt.

Nein, unter *die*sen Brief setze ich meinen Namen *nicht*.

Ich wollte mich gerade in die erste Reihe setzen, als ich sah, daß Frau Meier da saß; und da habe ich mich in die letzte Reihe gesetzt.

stehen—stellen—sich stellen

Wer steht denn da bei Frau Schmidt? Ist das nicht Dr. Gerhardt?

Wo ist denn mein Shakespeare? Der hat doch immer hier neben dem Milton gestanden.—
Den habe ich gestern abend gebraucht.—Wenn du damit fertig bist, dann stelle ihn doch
bitte wieder neben den Milton.

Diese amerikanischen Cocktailparties machen mich wirklich müde. Ich habe stundenlang
stehen müssen und war froh, als ich mich endlich setzen konnte.

Bitte, gnädige Frau, wie wäre es, wenn Sie sich hier auf diesen Stuhl setzten? Und Sie
stellen sich links neben Ihre Frau, Herr Doktor. Und der Kleine kann rechts von Ihrer
Frau stehen.—So, und jetzt bitte recht freundlich!

Nein, den Meyer schicke ich nicht nach Italien, und wenn er sich auf den Kopf stellt.

In der Zeitung steht, daß Ingelheim spurlos verschwunden ist.—Auf welcher Seite steht das
denn?

liegen—legen—sich legen

Ich hatte mich gerade ins Bett gelegt, als Erich anrief. „Liegst du etwa schon im Bett?“
sagte er.

Ich lag noch nicht lange im Bett, als Erich anrief. „Hast du dich etwa schon ins Bett gelegt?“ sagte er.

Wo hast du denn mein Buch hingelegt?—Ich habe es auf deinen Schreibtisch gelegt. Liegt
es denn nicht mehr dort?

Köln liegt am Rhein. Wolframs-Eschenbach liegt in der Nähe von Nürnberg.

VARIATIONS

Ich habe den Wein auf den Tisch _____.

Der Wein _____ auf dem Tisch.

Ich habe die Kleine schon in ihren Stuhl _____.

Die Kleine _____ schon in ihrem Stuhl.

Ich habe den Kleinen schon ins Bett _____.

Der Kleine _____ schon im Bett.

Ich liege schon im Bett. Ich habe _____.

Wir sitzen in der ersten Reihe. Wir haben _____.

Ich stand neben ihr am Fenster. Ich hatte _____.

Warum hast du dich noch nicht ins Bett _____?

Warum _____ du noch nicht im Bett?

Warum hast du dich denn in die letzte Reihe _____?

Warum _____ Reihe?

Ihre Frau hält den Kleinen auf den Knien, und Sie, Herr Doktor, _____ sich hinter _____ Frau.

Ihre Frau hält den Kleinen auf den Knien, und Sie, Herr Doktor, _____ hinter _____ Frau.

[9] Imperative, **du**-Form

SEE
ANALYSIS
182–185

(pp. 553-559)

Ruf mich bitte *nicht* vor *acht* an!

Bitte ruf mich *nicht* vor *acht* an!

Aber bitte ruf mich *nicht* vor *acht* an!

Aber ruf mich bitte *nicht* vor *acht* an!

Ruf mich aber bitte *nicht* vor *acht* an!

Aber ruf mich *nicht* vor *acht* an, bitte!

Ruf sie doch noch einmal *an*. Vielleicht ist sie jetzt zu *Hause*.

Bitte ruf sie doch noch einmal *an*!

Ruf sie doch noch mal *an*, bitte!

Bitte bring mir doch etwas zu *le*sen mit!

Bring mir doch bitte etwas zu *le*sen mit!

Bring mir doch etwas zu *le*sen mit, *bit*te!

Fahr doch mit uns in den *Schwarz*wald!

Sei mir nicht böse, aber ich muß jetzt wirklich nach Hause.

Sei doch nicht so nervös!

Bitte sei doch so gut und fahr mich mal eben in die Stadt.

Rede doch nicht so dumm, Anton; du verstehst ja doch nichts davon.

Tu nicht so, als ob du mich nicht gehört hättest.

Entschuldige bitte; ich wußte nicht, daß du schlafen wolltest.

Das Essen ist in zehn Minuten fertig; werde doch nicht immer gleich so ungeduldig.

Sei so gut, Klaus, und trag mir mal meinen Mantel.

Was heißt eigentlich *gadget* auf Deutsch? Finde mir doch mal eine gute Übersetzung.

Fritzchen, gib dem Onkel die Hand und sag schön „guten Tag"!

Fritzchen, nimm die Finger aus dem Mund!

Lauf doch nicht so schnell, Hans, ich kann ja gar nicht mitkommen.

Fürchte dich nicht; denn ich bin bei dir.

Mensch, ärgere dich nicht!

Zieh dich an!

Schlaf dich doch mal aus!

Erkälte dich nicht!

Reg dich doch nicht so darüber auf!

Steh *du* doch mal zuerst auf.

Rede *du* mal mit Meyer, du kennst ihn doch besser als ich.

Bleib *du* doch wenigstens vernünftig.

Arbeite *du* mal acht Stunden im Büro; dann kannst du verstehen, daß ich abends hunde-
müde bin.

Heirate *du* ihn doch, wenn er dir so gut gefällt.

VARIATIONS

Change the following sentences into **du**-form imperatives; use **doch, doch mal,**
or **mal** where appropriate:

Ich bringe dir ein Glas Wasser.

Ich gehe in den Garten.

Ich besuche euch in München.

Ich gebe dir das Buch morgen.

Laufe ich dir zu schnell?

Ich nehme mir eine Taxe.

Ich sehe mal nach, ob Meyer schon da ist.

Ich fahre nach Italien.

Ich bin dir nicht böse.

Ich lasse mir die Haare schneiden.

[10] Imperative, ihr-Form

SEE
ANALYSIS
183
(pp. 554-555)

Kinder, vergeßt nicht, euch die Hände zu waschen.

Bitte vergeßt nicht, euch die Hände zu waschen.

Vergeßt bitte nicht, euch die Hände zu waschen.

Es war schön, daß ihr kommen konntet; besucht uns bald mal wieder.

Und schreibt uns eine Karte, wenn ihr nach Hause kommt.

Wascht euch die Hände, Kinder.

Seid mir nicht böse. Aber ich muß jetzt wirklich nach Hause.

Fahrt doch mit uns in den Schwarzwald!

Also auf Wiedersehen. Und ruft uns an, wenn ihr nach Hause kommt.

Während der Woche haben wir nicht viel Zeit. Aber besucht uns doch mal an einem Sonntag!

Geht ihr ruhig ins Theater. Ich muß noch arbeiten.

Warum ich sonntags immer zu Hause bleibe? Arbeitet *ihr* einmal jeden Tag zehn Stunden, dann wißt ihr warum.

Bleibt *ihr* doch wenigstens vernünftig!

VARIATIONS

Change to **ihr**-form imperatives:

> Wir kommen bald wieder.
>
> Wir gehen heute abend ins Theater.
>
> Wir holen euch am Bahnhof ab.
>
> Wir rufen euch morgen an.
>
> Wir geben doch nicht so viel Geld aus.
>
> Wir trinken doch nicht so viel Kaffee.
>
> Wir sind euch nicht böse.
>
> Wir bringen euch ein paar Blumen mit.
>
> Wir lassen uns das Frühstück aufs Zimmer bringen.
>
> Wir bleiben noch ein bißchen hier.

[11] Imperative, wir-Form

SEE
ANALYSIS
183
(pp. 554-555)

Wo sollen wir denn essen, Rosemarie?—Gehen wir doch mal ins Regina, Klaus, da waren wir schon so lange nicht mehr.

Müssen wir denn heute schon wieder zu Müllers?—Natürlich müssen wir.—Also schön, fahren wir wieder zu Müllers.

Was, schon wieder Fisch, Maria?—Aber Karl, Fisch ist doch jetzt so billig.—Also gut, essen wir wieder Fisch.

Wir brauchen doch nicht jedes Jahr in die Schweiz zu fahren. Gehen wir doch mal nach
   Italien.
Mußt du denn jeden Tag davon reden? Reden wir doch mal von was anderem.
Der Wein ist mir aber zu sauer.—Versuchen wir doch mal einen anderen.

VARIATIONS

Change to the **wir**-form, starting with **Schön, ...**

> **Ich möchte nach München fahren.**
> **Schön, fahren wir doch nach München.**

Ich möchte zu Hause bleiben. ·
Ich möchte heute im Hotel Berlin essen.
Ich möchte heute schwimmen gehen.
Ich möchte Mutter ein Buch schenken.
Ich möchte mich mit dir photographieren lassen.

[12] Imperative, **Sie**-Form

Herr Ober, bringen Sie mir noch ein Glas Wein, bitte.   **SEE
ANALYSIS
183**
(pp. 554-555)
Bitte bringen Sie mir noch ein Glas Wein.
Bringen Sie mir bitte noch ein Glas Wein.
Sehen Sie doch mal, ob Meyer noch dieselbe Adresse hat.
Vergessen Sie bitte nicht, den Brief mit Luftpost zu schicken.
Bitte, Fräulein, geben Sie mir Zimmer 641.
Seien Sie herzlich gegrüßt von Ihrem Hans Meyer.
Seien Sie vorsichtig, Herr Professor, und überarbeiten Sie sich nicht.
Vor allem, trinken Sie abends keinen Kaffee mehr und rauchen Sie nicht mehr so viel.
Bitte glauben Sie mir, ich habe alles getan, was ich tun konnte.
Entschuldigen Sie bitte, gnädige Frau; Ihr Ferngespräch nach Hamburg ist da.
Nehmen Sie ihr doch ein paar Blumen mit.
Es gibt keine bessere Kamera. Fragen Sie Ihren Fotohändler.
Informieren Sie sich in unserem großen Photo-Katalog.
Lassen Sie sich unser neuestes Modell zeigen.
Wenn Ihnen die starken Zigaretten zu stark und die leichten zu leicht sind, so rauchen Sie
   PRIVAT, die Zigarette des Mannes von Format.*

* **Ein Mann von Format** a man of distinction

„Und natürlich Martini ‚on the rocks'."

Freude am Leben! Wundervolle Urlaubstage, in farbigen Kodakbildern! Und natürlich MARTINI† „on the rocks". Machen Sie Ihren Gästen eine Freude, mit MARTINI, Schluck für Schluck.

[13] Impersonal Imperative

SEE ANALYSIS 183
(pp. 554-555)

Alles aussteigen.

Einsteigen bitte.

Bitte einsteigen.

Nicht öffnen, bevor der Zug hält.

Langsam fahren.

Nicht rauchen.

Bitte anschnallen.

Nicht mit dem Fahrer sprechen.

Eintreten ohne zu klingeln.

Nicht stören.

Bitte an der Kasse zahlen.

Nach rechts einordnen.

† This does not mean what you think it means. It means vermouth (distilled by Martini) on the rocks.

Impersonal imperatives

AUS EINEM KOCHBUCH, EIN REZEPT FÜR „CORDON BLEU":

PRO KOPF	PER PERSON
ein Kalbsschnitzel	one veal cutlet
eine Scheibe roher Schinken	one slice of smoked ham
eine halbe Scheibe Emmentaler Käse	one-half slice of Swiss cheese
Tomaten-Ketchup	ketchup
Salz	salt
Bratfett	shortening
zum Panieren: 1 Ei	for breading: one egg
Semmelbrösel	bread crumbs

Die Schnitzel, die nicht zu dünn sein dürfen, an der Seite flach zu einer Tasche auf-
schneiden (oder den Fleischer darum bitten, der es besser kann). Die Fleischtasche mit
Ketchup ausstreichen und mit einer halben Käsescheibe füllen, die in eine Schinken-
scheibe gewickelt ist. Die Schnitzel mit Rouladenspießen zustecken, panieren, in heißem
Fett goldbraun braten und mit Zitronenachteln servieren.

[Cut a pocket in the side of each of the cutlets, which must not be too thin (or ask the
butcher to do this—he can do it better). Spread ketchup inside the pocket, and fill with
half a slice of cheese which is wrapped in a slice of smoked ham. Close the cutlet with
small skewers, dip in beaten egg, roll in bread crumbs, and fry in hot shortening until
golden brown. Serve with wedges (eighths) of lemon.]

READING

Ein Wort über deutsche Hotels

Wie überall in der Welt gibt es in Deutschland teure und billige
Hotels, große und kleine, gute und weniger gute. In den Großstädten
gibt es internationale Hotels, in denen man so komfortabel wohnen
kann wie in internationalen Hotels der ganzen Welt. Im Berlin
Hilton oder im Hotel Berlin, im Frankfurter Hof oder im Hotel 5
Intercontinental in Frankfurt, im Hotel Vier Jahreszeiten in Hamburg und im Hotel Vier Jahreszeiten in München brauchen Sie kein
Deutsch zu können, um sich Ihr Frühstück aufs Zimmer bringen zu
lassen oder um einen Luftpostbrief nach Chicago aufzugeben. Wenn
Sie aber in einem kleineren Hotel wohnen wollen oder in einer 10
Pension, oder wenn Sie in einer Kleinstadt oder auf dem Land in
einem Dorfgasthof ein Zimmer haben wollen, dann ist das schon
etwas anderes. Sie können dann natürlich mit den Händen reden,
aber besser ist es doch, wenn Sie Deutsch sprechen. Doch dazu
brauchen Sie ein bißchen Hotel-Jargon.   15

die Jahreszeit, –en
season

einen Brief aufgeben
to mail a letter

die Pension, –en
tourist home
der Gasthof, ∸e inn

der Jargon'
pronounced as in
French

HOTEL BERLIN

1 Berlin 30 · Kurfürstenstraße 62
Telefon: (03 11) 13 02 91 · Telex: 01 84 332

Zimmerzahl
Number of rooms - Nombre de chambres   264

Anzahl der Betten
Number of beds - Nombre de lits   300

Entfernung vom Bahnhof
Distance from Station - Distance de la gare   5 min.

Entfernung vom Flughafen
Distance from Airport - Distance de l'aéroport   10 min.

Parkplatz für 150 Wagen
Parking lot for 150 cars - Stationnement pour 150 voitures

Alle Zimmer mit Telefon, WC, Bad oder Dusche
Every room with telephon, W.C., private bath or shower
Chaque pièce avec téléphone, W.C., bain ou douche

Einzelzimmer mit Bad oder Dusche
Single room with bath or shower   DM 23,—
Chambre à un lit et salle de bain ou douche

Doppelzimmer mit Bad
Double room with bath   DM 38,—
Chambre à 2 lits avec bain

Service 15 %

Ausgezeichnetes Restaurant - very fine cuisine - Restaurant
francais - Cocktail-Bar - exklusives Grill-Restaurant mit
Grillbar - Gesellschaftsräume -
Conference rooms - Ball rooms - Salle de conférence - Salles

Frühstück - Breakfast - Petit déjeuner   DM 3,50

Mittagessen   ab
Lunch   from   DM 6,—
Déjeuner   à partir de

Abendessen   ab
Dinner   from   DM 8,—
Diner   à partir de

Service 10 %

GASTLICHE EMPFEHLUNGEN FÜR IHRE REISEN:
- „Park-Hotel", 6 Frankfurt/Main, Wiesenhüttenplatz 36—38,
  Tel.: (06 11) 23 01 51, Telex: 04-12 808
- „Park-Hotel", 75 Karlsruhe, Ettlinger Straße 23,
  Tel.: (07 21) 6 04 61, Telex: 07-825 443
- „Schwarzwaldhotel", 75 Karlsruhe, Am Rüppurrer Schloß 1,
  Tel.: (07 21) 3 48 61
- „Conti-Hansa-Hotel", 23 Kiel, Am Schloßgarten,
  Tel.: (04 31) 4 09 01, Telex: 02-92 813
Für Reservierungen in unseren Hotels stehen Ihnen unsere
Fernschreiber kostenlos zur Verfügung.

Wir wollen annehmen, daß Sie in Koblenz übernachten wollen, denn
dorthin haben wir Sie ja mit dem Hellas-Express geschickt. In
Koblenz gibt es etwa 30 Hotels und 25 Gasthöfe und Pensionen. Es
ist nicht immer ganz einfach, den Unterschied zwischen einem Hotel
und einem Gasthof zu sehen. Hotels sind größer als Gasthöfe, und ₅
Gasthöfe sind kleiner als Hotels. (Aber das ist natürlich keine Definition.) Das größte Hotel in Koblenz hat 120 Betten, der kleinste
Gasthof hat 5 oder 6 Betten. Eine Pension ist etwas, was es in

Zwei Gasthöfe und eine Pension

Amerika nicht gibt. Die meisten Pensionen sind Privathäuser, in denen man, ganz ähnlich wie in Gasthöfen, übernachten kann und in denen man Frühstück bekommt. Zum Gasthof gehört noch eine Gaststätte, ein Restaurant (oft ähnlich wie in England die *neighborhood pubs*), wo man abends hingeht, um ein Glas Wein oder 5 ein Bier zu trinken. Die „Gaststätten" heißen in vielen Gegenden Deutschlands „Wirtschaften" oder „Wirtshäuser". Auf dem Land haben solche Gasthäuser oft Namen wie „Zum Löwen", „Zum Ochsen", „Zum Goldenen Lamm", „Zum Deutschen Kaiser".

der Löwe, –n lion
der Ochse, –n ox
das Lamm, ¨er lamb

Außer den Hotels, Gasthöfen und Pensionen gibt es in Koblenz auch 10 eine Jugendherberge mit 540 Betten und einen Campingplatz für etwa 1000 Personen, aber da Sie Ihre erste Nacht in Deutschland weder in einer Jugendherberge noch auf einem Campingplatz verbringen wollen, so gehen Sie in eines der besseren Hotels. In Ihrem Hotelführer haben Sie eins gefunden: Zimmerpreis DM 15,00–18,00, 15 Frühstück DM 3,00, Halbpension DM 18,50–21,50, Vollpension DM 24,00–30,00, und dann heißt es unter „Comfort": *Flw B PB Z G P L T*. Das alles verstehen Sie natürlich erst, wenn Sie unten auf der Seite lesen: T—Zimmertelephon, L—Lift (das normale deutsche Wort für *Lift* ist *Aufzug*), P—Parkplatz, G—Garage (das interessiert 20 Sie nicht, denn Sie sind ja nicht mit Ihrem eigenen Wagen gekommen), Z—Zentralheizung, PB—Privatbad (von den dreißig Hotels haben nur siebzehn Zimmer mit Bad, und von den Gasthöfen nur drei), B—Bad (das heißt, es gibt ein oder mehrere Bäder, aber diese Bäder gehören nicht zum Zimmer, und man bezahlt zwei 25 oder drei Mark extra dafür), Flw—ganzjährig fließendes warmes Wasser. Vollpension heißt, daß man alle Mahlzeiten im Hotel ißt, bei Halbpension ißt man nur eine Mahlzeit im Hause (entweder Mittag- oder Abendessen). Frühstück ist in allen deutschen Hotels obligatorisch; d.h., man muß dafür bezahlen, ob man frühstückt oder 30 nicht. Zum Standard-Frühstück in Deutschland gehören Brötchen, Butter, Marmelade und Kaffee oder Tee.

die Jugendherberge, –n youth hostel

der Aufzug, ¨e elevator

d.h. = das heißt
das Brötchen, – (hard) roll
Marmelade, any kind of jam

So, jetzt haben Sie Ihren Reiseführer lange genug studiert; Sie geben dem Gepäckträger, der Ihre Koffer vor den Bahnhof getragen hat, eine Mark Trinkgeld und nehmen ein Taxi zum Hotel. Der Mann, 35 der Ihnen am Hotel mit Ihrem Gepäck hilft, ist aber kein Gepäckträger, sondern ein Hausdiener. Er bringt Ihre Koffer zum Empfang, und der Mann, der Sie dort empfängt, ist der Portier (oder in manchen größeren Hotels der Empfangschef).

der Gepäckträger, – porter
das Trinkgeld, –er tip
der Hausdiener, – bellhop
der Portier, –s desk clerk
der Empfangschef, –s head clerk

Es folgt ein imaginäres Gespräch zwischen Ihnen und dem Portier. 40

„Ich habe für heute nacht ein Zimmer bestellt."
„Auf welchen Namen, bitte?"

„Ray, aus New York."

„Einen Augenblick, bitte,—und würden Sie inzwischen schon das Anmeldeformular ausfüllen?"

„Sie wollten ein Zimmer mit Bad, Mr. Ray? Leider habe ich nur ein Zimmer mit Dusche, wenn Sie nichts dagegen haben?"

„Das ist mir schon recht. Wie teuer ist denn das Zimmer?"

„18 Mark, plus 15% Bedienung."

„Gut. Und gibt es ein Telefon auf dem Zimmer? Ich muß nämlich noch ein paar Ferngespräche führen."

„Aber sicher. Rufen Sie nur die Zentrale an; die Telefonistin verbindet Sie dann. So, hier ist Ihr Schlüssel,—Zimmer 318. Der Aufzug ist hier drüben links, bitte. Das Gepäck lasse ich Ihnen nach oben bringen."

Es gibt keinen Liftboy, sondern es ist ein Aufzug mit Selbstbedienung. Im dritten Stock gehen Sie einen langen Korridor hinunter und suchen Zimmer 318. Nach Zimmer 315 kommt eine Tür mit „H", dann eine mit „D" und dann kommt erst 316. (Statt H und D finden Sie vielleicht auch nur eine Tür mit 00). Zimmer 318 ist ganz nett, vielleicht ein bißchen altmodisch, aber doch komfortabel. Am interessantesten finden Sie das Federbett, aber wir müssen Sie warnen: Solche Federbetten sind für die meisten Amerikaner erstens zu warm und zweitens zu kurz; wenn man unter einem Federbett schläft, hat man entweder kalte Füße oder kalte Schultern. Sie klingeln also dem Zimmermädchen und bitten sie, Ihnen statt des Federbettes eine Wolldecke zu bringen. Dann wollen Sie telefonieren; zuerst Köln, und dann Ihre Freundin Barbara, die in Augustdorf bei Detmold wohnt.

Ferngespräche

Sie nehmen also den Hörer ab, und dann hören Sie die Stimme der Telefonistin: „Zentrale."

„Ja, Fräulein, ich hätte gerne Köln, 20 37 88 (zwo-null, drei-sieben, acht-acht)."

Am Telephon sagt man immer „zwo" statt „zwei."

„Köln, 20 37 88—bitte legen Sie wieder auf; ich rufe Sie zurück." Nach zwei Minuten klingelt das Telefon.

„Die Nummer ist leider besetzt. Soll ich es in ein paar Minuten noch einmal versuchen?"

„Ja, bitte."

Fünf Minuten später klingelt es wieder.

„Ihr Gespräch nach Köln. Einen Augenblick, bitte; ich verbinde."

Dann hören Sie am anderen Ende eine Frauenstimme: „Hier bei Doktor Fischer", und weil die Stimme „bei Doktor Fischer" sagt, wissen Sie, daß das das Dienstmädchen sein muß. Sie sagen also:

---

anmelden to register; **das Formular, –e** form
ausfüllen to fill out

5 **die Dusche, –n** shower

bedienen to wait on, serve; **die Bedienung** service charge
ein Ferngespräch führen to make a long-distance call
die Zentrale, –n switchboard

20 **die Feder, –n** feather
warnen to warn

25 **die Wolle** wool

(den Hörer) auflegen to put down the receiver

das Dienstmädchen, – maid

„Kann ich bitte Herrn Doktor Fischer sprechen?"
„Darf ich Sie um Ihren Namen bitten?"
„John Ray,—aus New York."
„Einen Augenblick, bitte, Herr Reh."

Ihr Gespräch mit Herrn Fischer ist natürlich Ihre Privatsache, und 5
wir wollen es hier nicht abdrucken. Aber nachdem das Gespräch **abdrucken** to print
zu Ende ist, sprechen Sie wieder mit der Telefonistin, denn Sie
wollen ja Ihre Freundin Barbara auch noch anrufen.

„Sagen Sie, Fräulein, kennen Sie dieses Augustdorf bei Detmold?"
„Nein, nie davon gehört; das muß irgendein Dorf sein."   10
„Ich hatte den Namen auch noch nie gehört, aber so klein kann es
nicht sein, denn die Telefonnummer ist eine Meile lang."   **die Meile, –n** mile
„Was ist denn die Nummer?"
„05237258."
„Nein, nein", lacht die Telefonistin. (Lacht sie über Ihren ameri- 15
kanischen Akzent oder darüber, daß Sie über deutsche Telefon-
nummern nicht Bescheid wissen?) „Da haben Sie die Vorwahl-   **Bescheid wissen** to
nummer mit dazu genommen. Augustdorf ist bestimmt ein Dorf,   know, be informed
                                                               die Vorwahlnummer,
denn die Nummer ist 258. Die Vorwahl ist 05237. Ihre Kölner   **–n** area code
Nummer ist mit der Vorwahlnummer noch länger. Köln hat die 20
Vorwahl 0221;—das heißt, die Nummer, die ich vorhin gewählt habe,
war 0221203788."
„Das wußte ich nicht—unsere amerikanischen Vorwahlnummern
haben nur drei Zahlen. Aber versuchen Sie doch jetzt mal Augustdorf."   25
„Gut,—und bleiben Sie doch bitte gleich am Apparat."   **am Apparat** on the
                                                               line
Aber Sie haben kein Glück. Die Nummer ist zwar nicht besetzt,
aber es antwortet auch niemand. „Da meldet sich leider niemand", **sich melden** to an-
sagt die Telefonistin.   swer (the phone)
„Soll ich es später noch mal versuchen?"
„Nein danke. Ich möchte mir jetzt erst einmal ein bißchen die Stadt 30
ansehen."
„Dann können Sie es ja von der Post aus noch mal versuchen."
„Gute Idee. Ich will sowieso noch einen Brief aufgeben. Vielen
Dank, Fräulein."   35

Ein Mann kommt nach San Franzisko (Fortsetzung)

VIII

März 1953

Der Pfarrer hatte einen Brief geschrieben, und Kerner wußte plötz-
lich, warum er nicht in den Westen gegangen war. Irgendwo in   **das Unterbewußtsein**
seinem Unterbewußtsein mußte er gewußt haben, daß er in Thü-   the subconscious

ringen doch etwas über Barbara erfahren würde. Nicht, daß er von
Barbara selbst gehört hätte, so viel Glück hatte er nicht; aber der
Pfarrer hatte das Stück Papier gefunden, auf das Paul Suhl Namen
und Addresse seines Vetters in Frankfurt geschrieben hatte. Darüber
stand in der zitternden Handschrift des alten Pfarrers: „Barbara 5
Kerner, zu erreichen bei". Lange betrachtete Kerner das Stückchen
Papier, das jemand wahrscheinlich aus einem Taschenkalender ge-
rissen hatte. Er sah nur den Namen und die Adresse; Pauls I.D.
Nummer beachtete er nicht. Und er überlegte sich, daß Barbara im
August siebzehn Jahre alt werden würde.   10

Der Pfarrer schlug vor, daß Kerner zunächst einmal an die Adresse
in Frankfurt schreiben sollte. Wenn Barbara dort noch zu erreichen
wäre, dann könnte er sie ja zu sich kommen lassen. Aber daran
dachte Kerner nicht. Da er politisch unverdächtig war,—er war   **unverdächtig** not
weder für noch gegen das Regime und dachte nur manchmal, daß 15 under suspicion, not
es in Deutschland jetzt zwei „ideale Staaten" gäbe—, fiel es ihm   suspect; **verdächtig**
nicht schwer, eine Reisegenehmigung nach Ost-Berlin zu bekommen.   suspect
Er hatte gesagt, daß er dort seinen Schwager besuchen wolle. Und   **es fällt mir schwer** it
so fuhr er an einem Freitagmorgen im April 1953 mit dem Fahrrad   is hard for me
zum letzten Mal zu Fritz Müller VEB. Es war Frühling in der Luft, 20 **die Genehmigung, –en**
während er seinen letzten Sarg machte. Auf der Fahrt nach Hause   permission, permit
regnete es, und am nächsten Vormittag stieg er in einen Personenzug
der Deutschen Reichsbahn,* die im Westen jetzt Deutsche Bundes-
bahn* hieß. Zwischen Leipzig und Berlin kontrollierte ein humorloser **kontrollieren** to check
Polizist seine Papiere, aber die waren in Ordnung. Er hatte keinen 25
Koffer mitgenommen, denn wer damals mit einem Koffer nach Berlin
fuhr, war sofort verdächtig. Am Abend kam er an, es regnete immer
noch, aber statt zu seinem Schwager zu gehen (er hatte tatsächlich
einen Schwager in Ost-Berlin), setzte er sich in die S-Bahn und fuhr **S-Bahn = Stadtbahn**
kurz hinter dem Bahnhof Friedrichstraße über die Grenze zwischen 30 city railroad
Ost- und West-Berlin.

Auch im Westen regnete es, aber die Neonlichter ließen den Regen
in allen Farben schillern. Im Flüchtlingslager allerdings war der   **schillern** to shimmer,
Regen wieder grau, doch das störte Kerner nicht. Er wußte jetzt,   sparkle
was er wollte; und als man ihn ein paar Wochen später von Berlin 35 **das Flüchtlingslager, –**
nach Frankfurt flog, träumte er davon, daß er mit Barbara in eine refugee camp
kleine Wohnung ziehen wollte und daß er wieder Lehrer werden
und an einem Gymnasium in Frankfurt unterrichten würde. Eines
Tages würde Barbara dann heiraten,—und er dachte über seine
Rolle als zukünftiger Großvater nach. Als sie über Thüringen flogen, 40
dachte er an den Pfarrer da unten in einem der kleinen Täler und

---

* The East-German railroad has retained the old name "Imperial Railways,"
whereas the West-German term is "Federal Railways."

überlegte sich, ob der wohl für den „idealen Staat (Ost)" oder für
den „idealen Staat (West)" wäre. Dann dachte er daran, daß er
Barbara seit fast zehn Jahren nicht gesehen hatte, und er hatte
plötzlich Angst vor seiner erwachsenen Tochter.

IX

Frankfurt, April 1953

Care-Pakete, Lebensmittelkarten und Schwarzer Markt sind ver- 5
gessen; man kann mit gutem Geld kaufen, was man will. Während
man vor der Währungsreform mit amerikanischen Zigaretten alles   **die Währungsreform**
und ohne amerikanische Zigaretten nichts kaufen konnte, bekommt   currency reform
man jetzt in jedem Geschäft jede Menge Zigaretten,—zehn oder
zwölf Stück für eine Deutsche Mark. Man fährt jetzt mit dem 10
Motorrad zur Arbeit; und wer es sich leisten kann, fährt einen Volkswagen. Der Mercedes wird zum Standessymbol. In der Universität   **das Standessymbol, –e**
sitzen keine Soldaten mehr, sondern neunzehn- oder zwanzigjährige status symbol
Studenten, für die der Krieg anfängt, Geschichte zu werden. Ins
Theater oder ins Konzert geht man im dunklen Anzug, und in der 15
Pause trinkt man Coca-Cola oder Sekt. Das Leben ist wieder   **der Sekt** champagne
„normal" geworden; was HICOG war, wissen nur noch wenige, man
lebt jetzt in der Bundesrepublik Deutschland. Der Hunger ist vergessen, und gäbe es nicht noch so viele Ruinen zwischen den neuge-
bauten modernen Häusern, so hätte man wahrscheinlich auch die 20
Bomben längst vergessen. Daß die amerikanischen Soldaten, die man
überall in der Stadt sieht, vor acht Jahren als Feinde ins Land
kamen, daran denkt man auch nicht mehr oft.

Das Haus in der Bettinastraße ist auch wieder aufgebaut. Vier
Stockwerke hoch, moderne Komfortwohnungen, drei Zimmer mit 25 **das Stockwerk, –e**
Bad und Küche. Daß hier einmal das Wasser an den Wänden her-   story
untergelaufen ist, kann man sich nicht mehr vorstellen. Im Erdge- **sich vorstellen**
schoß wohnt ein Arzt, im ersten Stock ein Pfarrer, im zweiten ein imagine
Geschäftsmann und darüber ein Schauspieler. Im ganzen Haus
wohnt nicht ein Frankfurter; alle sind erst nach dem Krieg in die 30
Stadt gezogen.

Als Oswald Kerner gegen drei Uhr nachmittags an der Tür des
Arztes klingelte, machte ihm die Sprechstundenhilfe auf. Als er ver- **die Sprechstunden-**
suchte, ihr zu erklären, daß er nicht krank sei, sondern den Arzt in **hilfe, –n** receptionist
einer persönlichen Sache sprechen möchte, meinte sie nur, der Herr 35 in a doctor's office
Doktor hätte jetzt für private Dinge keine Zeit, und ließ ihn einfach
vor der Tür stehen. Im ersten Stock war niemand zu Hause, und die
Frau des Geschäftsmannes im zweiten Stock öffnete die Tür nur
ein bißchen, sagte: „Ich kaufe nichts", und machte die Tür wieder
zu. Aber die Frau des Schauspielers, klein, rundlich, mit einem 40 **rundlich** plump

freundlichen Mondgesicht, vielleicht Mitte dreißig, ließ ihn nicht vor der Tür stehen. Er hatte kaum angefangen, ihr zu erklären, was er wollte, als sie ihn bat, er möchte doch hereinkommen. Sie sei nämlich auch Breslauerin, und da müßte man sich doch einmal über alte Zeiten unterhalten. Außerdem könne ihr Mann ihm bestimmt 5 helfen; der kenne nämlich so viele Leute hier in der Nachbarschaft, und irgend jemand müsse sich doch an diesen Herrn Suhl erinnern können.

Mitte dreißig in her mid-thirties

die Nachbarschaft neighborhood

Kerner nickte nur müde und resigniert. Als er unten vor der Haustür die Namen an den Briefkästen studiert hatte und den 10 Namen, der allein ihm wichtig war, nicht finden konnte, da war die Welt, von der er geträumt hatte, ganz plötzlich zusammengebrochen, und er wußte auf einmal, daß er Barbara nicht finden würde. Dr. med. H. Jagow. Pfr. Gerhard Maschke. Die Namen interessierten ihn nicht. Joseph Schmidhuber, das war der Ge- 15 schäftsmann im zweiten Stock, und der Schauspieler hieß Jürgen Cramer. Kerner hatte keinen der Namen behalten; er wußte nur, daß kein Ernst Suhl hier einen Briefkasten hatte. Zuerst hatte er gleich weitergehen wollen, und als er dann doch beschloß, sich im Haus zu erkundigen, ob vielleicht jemand wüßte, was aus einem gewissen 20 Herrn Suhl geworden war, da tat er es ohne Hoffnung auf Erfolg. „Ich hätte es mir doch denken können", dachte er, als er jetzt bei Cramers im Wohnzimmer saß und einen Cognac trank.

der Kasten, ∸ box

zusammenbrechen to collapse

Pfr. = Pfarrer

die Hoffnung hope

„Aber Herr Kerner, geben Sie doch nicht so schnell auf", meinte Herr Cramer. „Dieser Suhl kann doch nicht einfach aus der Welt ver- 25 schwunden sein, der muß doch zu finden sein.—Warten Sie, ich rufe einmal nebenan bei Schreiners an, die haben schon im Krieg hier gewohnt. Vielleicht wissen die etwas." Cramer griff zum Telefon, wählte, Frau Schreiner meldete sich. „Stimmt", hörte Kerner ihn sagen, „der muß es gewesen sein, ja, ja, das Mädchen war damals 30 zehn oder elf.—Ausgewandert? Nach Amerika? Da muß doch wohl über das Konsulat etwas zu erfahren sein.—Vielen Dank für die Auskunft, Frau Schreiner, Wiederhören."

sich melden to answer (the telephone)

„Sehen Sie", sagte Kerner, „ich wußte es ja", aber er ließ sich von Cramer doch dazu überreden, zunächst auf die Polizei und dann 35 zum Konsulat zu gehen. Suhl hatte sich, seine Frau und seine adoptierte Tochter Barbara am 3. Mai 1949 polizeilich abgemeldet, ohne eine Adresse in Amerika zu hinterlassen. Auf dem Konsulat versprach man ihm, sich um die Sache zu kümmern, aber erst Monate später erhielt er einen Brief, in dem ihm mitgeteilt wurde, 40 die gegenwärtige Adresse des Herrn Ernst Suhl sei leider nicht festzustellen. Von Paul Suhls Rolle in der ganzen Sache hatte er keine Ahnung.

sich polizeilich abmelden to cancel one's registration with the police
hinterlassen to leave behind
ihm mitgeteilt wurde he was informed

In der Innenstadt, ganz in der Nähe des Doms, hatte er ein Zimmer gefunden. Ab und zu besuchte er den Schauspieler Cramer, der immer wieder versuchte, ihn dazu zu überreden, wieder Lehrer zu werden. Aber Oswald Kerner wollte nicht mehr; „Erstens", meinte er, „bin ich seit vierzehn Jahren in keiner Schule mehr gewesen, und 5 zweitens weigere ich mich, den Kindern Dinge zu sagen, an die ich selbst nicht mehr glaube."

Fünf kurze Jahre hatte er unterrichtet, von 1935 bis 1940; dann war er fünf Jahre lang Soldat gewesen und hatte ganz Europa gesehen. Die sieben Jahre, die er als Kriegsgefangener in Rußland verbracht 10 hatte, waren in seiner Erinnerung zu einer Unendlichkeit geworden: endlose Arbeit, endloser Hunger, endloses Heimweh. Nur der jähr- **das Heimweh** home-liche Wechsel zwischen Sommerhitze und Winterkälte hatte dem sickness Leben einen Rhythmus gegeben. Als er dann nach der hoffnungs-vollen Rückfahrt nach Deutschland der Wirklichkeit gegenüber- 15 stand, war das, was während der sieben langen Jahre für ihn das einzig Wirkliche gewesen war, zu etwas Unwirklichem geworden: seine Frau war tot, seine Tochter verschwunden. Und so hatte er vierzehn Monate lang Särge gemacht, als Hilfsarbeiter bei der **der Hilfsarbeiter, –** Firma Fritz Müller VEB, bis er noch einmal eine hoffnungsvolle 20 unskilled laborer Reise machte, nur um auch dieses Mal zu erfahren, daß Träume und Wirklichkeit nicht dasselbe sind.

So wurde Oswald Kerner wieder Hilfsarbeiter. Durch den Schau- **der Schreiner** spieler bekam er eine Stellung als Schreiner beim Theater in Frank- carpenter **der Kerker, –** dun-furt. Statt Särge zu machen, baute er jetzt Träume, den Kerker für 25 geon *Fidelio,*° die Hölle für *Don Giovanni,*† den Serail für die *Ent-* **die Hölle** hell *führung*‡ und einen fahrbaren Schwan für *Lohengrin.*§ Und abends **der Serail** seraglio, stand er hinter den Kulissen, um dafür zu sorgen, daß der Schwan harem **einen fahrbaren** auch richtig fuhr. **Schwan** a mobile (i.e., on wheels) swan **die Kulisse, –n** wings, drop **sorgen für** to see to it

X

Frankfurt, Juni 1958

Ein warmer Frühsommerabend; während der Pause konnte man auf 30 der Opernterrasse eine Zigarette rauchen. Es gab Glucks *Orpheus,* mit deutschem Text und dem von Gluck angehängten Happy End.‖ „Ich finde das ganz richtig", meinte Barbara. „Jede Liebesgeschichte sollte ein Happy End haben." Paul lachte. „Du bist ja erst drei

° opera by Beethoven
† opera by Mozart
‡ *The Abduction from the Seraglio,* opera by Mozart
§ opera by Wagner
‖ In Gluck's opera, after the second death of Eurydice, with which the Greek myth ends, Amor (Cupid) prevents Orpheus from committing suicide, and Orpheus and Eurydice are happily reunited.

Wochen verheiratet. Warte nur ein paar Jahre, dann tut es dir
bestimmt leid, daß du mich alten Mann geheiratet hast." „Du armer
alter Mann! Komm, ich helfe dir auf deinen Platz zurück." Immer
noch lachend ließ er sich von ihr sanft über die Terrasse schieben.

Während des letzten Aktes stand Oswald Kerner wie immer in den 5
Kulissen. „Hoffentlich fällt die Sonne nicht herunter", sagte er zu
einem Kollegen. Die Sonne war das Glanzstück der Aufführung; in
ihr wurde Amor aus dem Theaterhimmel herabgelassen, um Orpheus
nach dem zweiten Tod der Eurydike vor dem Selbstmord zu bewahren. Kerner hatte immer Angst, daß Amor eines Tages mit der 10
Sonne auf die Bühne fallen könnte; aber er vergaß seine Angst
jedesmal, wenn kurz vorher Orpheus seine letzte Arie sang. „Ach,
ich habe sie verloren", heißt es da im deutschen Text, „all mein
Glück ist nun dahin." Es war Kerners Lieblingsstelle in der ganzen
Oper, und manchmal dachte er dabei an die Frau und die Tochter, 15
die er vor Jahren einmal gehabt hatte. Hier müßte die Geschichte
des Orpheus eigentlich aufhören, dachte Kerner und fand, daß das
glückliche Ende falsch wäre, selbst in einer Oper.

„Würdest du wegen mir auch in die Unterwelt steigen?" flüsterte
Barbara. „Aber sicher", flüsterte Paul zurück, „nur könnte ich nicht 20
so gut singen." Barbara schob ihre Hand in Pauls Hand. „Vorher
gehen wir aber noch oft Erdbeeren essen", sagte sie.

Noch während des Beifalls verließ Kerner das Theater. Er wollte
noch in Sachsenhausen ein Glas Apfelwein trinken. Über dem Main
hing ein romantischer Vollmond; darunter stand, wie eine Kulisse, 25
das Sachsenhäuser Ufer mit der Dreikönigskirche. Auf dem Eisernen
Steg blieb Kerner lange stehen und starrte aufs Wasser. „Komisch",
dachte er, „wenn der Pfarrer damals nicht den Zettel gefunden
hätte, wäre ich wahrscheinlich heute noch in Thüringen und machte
Särge." 30

„Wenn du damals nicht von mir weggelaufen wärst, hätte ich dich
sicher nie nach Frankfurt gebracht", sagte Paul. Sie hatten beschlossen, zu Fuß in ihr kleines Hotel bei der Universität zurück-
zugehen, und auf dem Weg dorthin waren sie in die Nähe der
Bettinastraße gekommen. Obwohl die ganze Straße sich so sehr 35
verändert hatte, erkannte sie das Haus wieder. Sie fing an zu erzählen, unterbrach sich immer wieder mit „Weißt du noch?—Erinnerst du dich?" Dann sprachen sie über Barbaras Auswanderung
mit Ernst und seiner Frau. Sie hatten zuerst bei Pauls Eltern in St.
Louis gewohnt, dann hatte Ernst eine Stellung in New York ge- 40
funden, während Paul nach seiner Rückkehr aus Deutschland in
Chicago arbeitete. Sieben Jahre hatten sie einander nicht gesehen.

der Kolle′ge col-
league
das Glanzstück, –e
showpiece
**wurde . . . herab-
gelassen** was lowered
der Selbstmord, –e
suicide
bewahren to save,
protect
dahin (here) gone

der Beifall (*no pl.*)
applause
der Apfelwein hard
apple cider
das Ufer, – bank,
shore
der Eiserne Steg
(name of a bridge)

die Rückkehr return

Paul und Ernst schrieben sich manchmal Briefe, und Paul wußte,
daß Barbara 1954 aufs College gegangen war. Trotzdem war er überrascht, als Ernst ihm ein Bild von Barbara schickte,—dieses Bild
trug dazu bei, daß er beschloß, im Sommer 1956 seine Ferien mit
Ernst zu verbringen und daß er sich ein halbes Jahr später von 5
seiner Firma nach New York schicken ließ.

beitragen zu to con-
tribute to

Während Barbara und Paul im Hotel noch ein Glas Wein tranken,
saß Oswald Kerner in Sachsenhausen an seinem Stammtisch, trank
Apfelwein und unterhielt sich mit ein paar Bekannten. Er war jetzt
einundfünfzig Jahre alt, sah aber älter aus; er war nicht mehr so 10
zynisch wie vor fünf Jahren, aber die Katastrophen in seinem Leben
hatte er nie überwinden können. Daß er einmal Lehrer gewesen
war, das hatte er fast vergessen. Es ging ihm nicht schlecht, und er
war ganz zufrieden damit, daß er für den Rest seines Lebens Opern-
kulissen machen würde. 15

der Stammtisch, –e
table reserved for reg-
ular guests at a tavern
die Katastro′phe
catastrophe
überwinden to over-
come, get over

(Schluß folgt)

Frankfurt. Blick von Sachsenhausen zum Eisernen Steg und Dom

175 Reflexive and Emphatic Pronouns

The English pronouns *myself, himself, oneself,* etc., can be used in three different ways:

1. as unstressed reflexive objects:

   I almost *killed* myself.

2. as stressed reflexive objects:

   I must also think of my*self.*

3. as emphatic pronouns repeating a preceding noun or pronoun (subject or object):

   I saw Meyer my*self.*
   I saw Meyer him*self.*

Unstressed Reflexive Objects

While English uses the compounds *my-self, him-self, one-self,* etc., German uses the reflexive **sich** for all third-person forms and the normal personal pronouns **mir, mich, dir, dich, uns,** and **euch** for first- and second-person forms. (See **139.**)

Er hat sich ver*giftet.*	He *poisoned* himself.
Sie hat sich ver*giftet.*	She *poisoned* herself.
Sie haben sich ver*giftet.*	They *poisoned* themselves.
Ich hole mir eine Zeitung.	I'm getting myself a *newspaper.*
Du holst dir eine Zeitung.	You're getting yourself a *newspaper.*
Wir holen uns eine Zeitung.	We're getting ourselves a *newspaper.*
Ihr holt euch eine Zeitung.	You're getting yourselves a *newspaper.*

Stressed Reflexive Objects

In such English sentences as

   I must also think of my*self,*

the reflexive is the stress point of the sentence. German can either stress the reflexive pronoun

   Ich muß auch mal an *mich* denken,

or add an undeclinable **selbst** or **selber** which carries the main syntactical stress:

   Ich muß auch mal an mich *selbst* denken.

Emphatic Pronouns

The English reflexive pronouns *myself, yourself, himself*, etc., sometimes merely repeat, for emphasis, a preceding noun or pronoun. When so used, they again carry the main syntactical stress, but nevertheless they are not independent syntactical units.

> He said it him*self*.
> They did it them*selves*.

German cannot repeat a preceding noun or pronoun. Instead, German uses the strongly stressed particles **selbst** or **selber** to emphasize these nouns or pronouns. **Selbst** and **selber** are interchangeable. They always follow the word to be emphasized, either immediately or at the end of the inner field.

Das weiß ich *selbst.*	I know that my*self*.
So! Ihrer Frau geht's gut.	So your wife is fine.
Und wie geht's Ihnen *selbst?*	And how are you your*self?*
Ich fahre morgen *selbst* **nach Berlin.**	I am going to Berlin my*self* tomorrow.
Das war der Direktor *selber.*	That was the boss him*self*.

NOTE:

1. When emphasizing the subject at the end of the inner field, **selber** frequently assumes the meaning "without help" or "others don't have to."

Ich kann mir die Haare auch *selber* **schneiden.**	I can cut my *own* hair.
Du könntest dir das Frühstück auch einmal *selber* **machen.**	You really could get your *own* breakfast, for a change.
Die Kinder können sich *selber* **waschen.**	The children can wash up *without* help.
Das kann ich doch *selber* **machen.**	I can do that *myself*.

2. If **selbst** (or **selber**) appears in the front field, contrast intonation is used, and a contrast with others, of whom the opposite statement is true, is implied.

> **Sie** *selbst hat* **kein Geld; aber ihre** *Mutter* **hat** *viel* **Geld.**
> **Er** *selber* **bleibt zu** *Hause: uns* **schickt er in die** *Kirche.*
> **Sich** *selbst kann* **er nicht retten;** *andere* **hat er ge***rettet*.

3. If **selbst** (or **selber**) appears in the inner field, it may also be a substitute for **auch** and express the notion "just like others."

> **Ich bin** *selber* **arm, so arm wie du.**
> **Ich bin** *selbst* **nicht glücklich, ich bin so unglücklich wie ihr.**

176 selbst, sogar, and auch meaning *even*

Selbst, sogar, and auch, without stress, may form a syntactical unit with
an immediately following stressed word. If so used, they mean *even,*

>   Selbst (sogar, auch) *das* ist ihm zu viel.
>   Er *will* einfach nicht, und solange jemand nicht *will*, kann ihm selbst
>   (sogar, auch) *Gott* nicht helfen.

Compare:

>   Der brave Mann denkt an sich *selbst* zuletzt. (Schiller)
>   A brave man thinks of himself last.

>   Der brave Mann denkt an *sich*, selbst zu*letzt*.
>   A brave man thinks of himself, even at the very end.

177 Reciprocal Pronouns

Normally, the reflexive plural pronouns can also be used as reciprocal
pronouns, and it is not necessary to make a distinction. No one will
misunderstand: **Sie küßten sich.** This can only mean *They kissed each
other,* not *They kissed themselves.*

If it is desirable to express reciprocity, **einander** and **gegenseitig** can be
used. **Einander** is literary and replaces the reflexive; **gegenseitig** follows
the reflexive.

>   Es waren zwei Königskinder, die hatten einander so lieb.*
>   Wenn ihr euch nicht gegenseitig helft, dann werdet ihr nie fertig.

178 Reflexive Verbs

Many German verbs can be used with either a reflexive or a non-
reflexive pronoun object:

REFLEXIVE:	**Ich habe mich gebadet.**	I took a bath.
	Ich habe mich ins Bett gelegt.	I went to bed.
	Er hat sich erschossen.	He shot (and killed) himself.
NONREFLEXIVE:	**Ich habe ihn gebadet.**	I gave him a bath.
	Ich habe ihn ins Bett gelegt.	I put him to bed.
	Er hat ihn erschossen.	He shot (and killed) him.

Neither the syntactical structure of the sentence nor the meaning of the
verb **erschießen** is changed, when **er erschoß sich** is changed to **er
erschoß ihn.** In both cases, the verb is **jemanden erschießen,** *to shoot
somebody;* and sometimes, this "somebody" is the subject itself. A genuine reflexive verb is a verb with a reflexive pronoun which is either not

---

* First line of a folk song: There were (once upon a time) two king's children (a prince and
a princess); they loved each other very much.

replaceable at all or not replaceable without a change of meaning. Take, for instance, English *to enjoy oneself*. It is possible to say

> Good-bye, Mrs. Smith. I had a wonderful time. I really enjoyed myself; and your steaks were delicious.

But I cannot say

> Good-bye Mrs. Smith. I had a wonderful time. I really enjoyed myself and your steaks.

The two sentences *I enjoyed myself* and *I enjoyed it (the steak)* are not parallel. In *I enjoyed it, to enjoy* is a normal transitive verb, meaning "to derive pleasure from"; and the *it* is a real object. But in *I enjoyed myself, to enjoy oneself* means "to have a good time" and the *myself* is not an object, but an irreplaceable part of the verbal pattern *to enjoy oneself*.

From a linguistic point of view, the *to enjoy onself* used in the sentence *I really enjoyed myself last night* is a genuine reflexive verb. English has only a few such verbs. German has hundreds. Compare:

TRANSITIVE:	**Sie konnte die Hand nicht bewegen.**	She could not move her hand.
REFLEXIVE:	**Die Erde bewegt sich um die Sonne.**	The earth moves around the sun.
TRANSITIVE:	**Hast du die Eier schon umgedreht?**	Have you turned the eggs over?
REFLEXIVE:	**Du darfst dich jetzt nicht umdrehen.**	You must not turn around now.

Very often, the reflexive verb is distinguished from the transitive verb by a prefix:

lieben (transitive), *to love*	**Ich liebe meine Frau.**
sich verlieben in (reflexive), *to fall in love with*	**Ich habe mich in Inge verliebt.**

179 The Forms of the Reflexive Verb

ACTIONAL INFINITIVE:	**sich erkälten**	to catch a cold
	sich erkältet haben	to have caught a cold
ACTIONAL PRESENT:	**ich erkälte mich**	I am catching a cold
	du erkältest dich	you are catching a cold
	er erkältet sich	he is catching a cold
	wir erkälten uns	we are catching a cold
	ihr erkältet euch	you are catching a cold
	sie erkälten sich	they are catching a cold
ACTIONAL IMPERATIVE:	**erkälte dich nicht**	don't catch a cold
	erkältet euch nicht	don't catch a cold
	erkälten Sie sich nicht	don't catch a cold
ACTIONAL PAST:	**ich erkältete mich**	I caught a cold

ACTIONAL PERFECT:	**ich habe mich erkältet**	I have caught a cold
STATAL PRESENT: (see below)	**ich bin erkältet**	I have a cold (I am under the weather with a cold)
STATAL PAST:	**ich war erkältet**	I had a cold
STATAL PERFECT:	**ich bin erkältet gewesen**	I've had a cold
STATAL INFINITIVE:	**erkältet sein**	to have a cold

The terms "actional" and "statal" used in this table need an explanation. You are familiar with the fact that intransitive verbs which denote a change in the condition or location of the subject form their compound tenses with **sein**:

Die Preise sind gestiegen.	The prices went up. (or: are up)
Die Preise sind gefallen.	The prices came down. (or: are down)

Forms like **sind gefallen** denote *both* the past event *and* the new present state created by this past event. The difference between action or event (compare English *has gone*) and state (compare English *is gone*) cannot be expressed in German with such intransitive verbs.

However, in the case of reflexive verbs denoting a transition from one state of affairs to another, the difference between event (or action) and state must be expressed. Thus, **sich verlieben**, meaning *to fall in love*, forces the speaker to distinguish between

THE PAST EVENT (OR ACTION):	**Er verliebte sich in Erika.** He fell in love with Erika.
	Er hat sich in Erika verliebt. He fell in love with Erika.
	Er hatte sich in Erika verliebt. He had fallen in love with Erika.
AND THE STATE CREATED BY THIS EVENT:	**Er ist in Erika verliebt.** He is in love with Erika.
	Er war in Erika verliebt. He was in love with Erika.

One can only say:

    Er ist seit drei Wochen in Erika verliebt

and

    Er hat sich vor drei Wochen in Erika verliebt,

but not

    [**Er hat sich seit drei Wochen in Erika verliebt**]

or

    [**Er ist vor drei Wochen in Erika verliebt.**]

180 Reflexives Which Denote Transition to a New State

As stated above, such reflexives distinguish between a past event and
the state reached by this event. Some of these reflexives can also be used
as transitive verbs.

sich anziehen	to get dressed
angezogen sein	to be dressed
sich aufregen über	to get excited (upset) about
aufgeregt sein	to be excited (upset)
sich ausruhen	to take a rest
ausgeruht sein	to have taken a rest, to be rested
sich ausschlafen	to get enough sleep
ausgeschlafen sein	to have had enough sleep
sich ausziehen	to get undressed
ausgezogen sein	to be undressed
sich baden	to take a bath
gebadet sein	to have taken a bath, to be bathed
sich beruhigen	to calm down
beruhigt sein	to have calmed down
sich betrinken	to get drunk
betrunken sein	to be drunk
sich entschließen zu	to make up one's mind
entschlossen sein zu	to be determined
sich entschuldigen	to excuse oneself
entschuldigt sein	to be excused
sich erholen	to get a rest (to recover one's strength)
erholt sein	to be well rested (recovered)
sich erkälten	to catch a cold
erkältet sein	to have a cold
sich gewöhnen an	to get accustomed to
gewöhnt sein an	to be accustomed to
sich öffnen	to open (intransitive)
geöffnet sein	to be open
sich rasieren	to shave
rasiert sein	to have shaved, be shaved
sich scheiden lassen	to get a divorce
geschieden sein	to be divorced
sich schließen	to close (intransitive)
geschlossen sein	to be closed
sich überarbeiten	to overwork
überarbeitet sein	to be overworked

sich überzeugen von	to become convinced of
überzeugt sein von	to be convinced of
sich umziehen	to change (clothes)
umgezogen sein	to have changed
sich verändern	to change
verändert sein	to have changed
heiraten	to marry
sich verheiraten	to get married
verheiratet sein mit	to be married to
sich verlieben in	to fall in love with
verliebt sein in	to be in love with
sich verloben mit	to become engaged to
verlobt sein mit	to be engaged to
sich vorbereiten auf	to prepare for
vorbereitet sein auf	to be prepared for

NOTE: Reflexives like **sich öffnen,** which denote transition into a new state without reference to any agent, frequently correspond to English intransitive verbs.

Die Tür öffnete sich.	The door opened. (process)
Die Tür ist geöffnet.	The door is open. (state)

181 sich legen, sich setzen, sich stellen

The verbs **sitzen, stehen,** and **liegen** describe a state, not an event. They are intransitive—that is, they cannot take an accusative object—and they are strong verbs.

> sitzen, saß, hat gesessen, er sitzt
> stehen, stand, hat gestanden, er steht
> liegt, lag, hat gelegen, er liegt
> Anton und Emma saßen auf der Bank vor dem Haus.
> Das Haus stand am Rhein.
> Auf dem Tisch lag ein Buch.

The weak reflexive verbs **sich setzen, sich stellen,** and **sich legen** describe the action leading to the state of **sitzen, stehen,** and **liegen.**

Er hat sich auf die Bank gesetzt;	jetzt sitzt er auf der Bank.
Er hat sich vor die Haustür gestellt;	jetzt steht er vor der Tür.
Er hat sich ins Bett gelegt;	jetzt liegt er im Bett.

When the weak verbs **setzen, stellen,** and **legen** are used with a non-reflexive accusative object, they also describe an action, again leading to the state of **sitzen, stehen,** and **liegen.**

Sie hat das Kind auf die Bank gesetzt.	Das Kind sitzt auf der Bank.
Er hat die Flasche auf den Tisch gestellt.	Die Flasche steht auf dem Tisch.
Er hat das Buch auf den Tisch gelegt.	Das Buch liegt auf dem Tisch.

NOTE: If a prepositional phrase is used with these verbs, (**sich**) **setzen**, (**sich**) **stellen**, (**sich**) **legen** require the accusative (**auf die Bank**) and **sitzen**, **stehen**, **liegen** require the dative (**auf der Bank**).

182 The Forms of the Imperative

The imperative is that form of a verb which is used for the expression of a command or a request. The following forms occur:

Weak Verbs

du-form:	sag(e)	rede	antworte	entschuldige
ihr-form:	sagt	redet	antwortet	entschuldigt
wir-form:	sagen wir	reden wir	antworten wir	entschuldigen wir
Sie-form:	sagen Sie	reden Sie	antworten Sie	entschuldigen Sie

Impersonal form: identical with infinitive

The **Sie**-form was introduced in Unit 3. Of the personal forms, only the **du**-form is not identical with the corresponding forms of the present indicative. The impersonal form is the infinitive used with imperative force.

In principle, the ending **-e** of the **du**-form is optional. However, verbs whose stems end in **-d** (**reden**) or **-t** (**antworten**), or in the suffix **-ig** (**entschuldigen**) are not usually used without the **-e** ending.

Strong Verbs

du-form:	geh(e)	frag(e)	finde	gib	lauf
ihr-form:	geht	fragt	findet	gebt	lauft
wir-form:	gehen wir	fragen wir	finden wir	geben wir	laufen wir
Sie-form:	gehen Sie	fragen Sie	finden Sie	geben Sie	laufen Sie

Impersonal form: identical with infinitive

du-form:	nimm	sieh	sei	fahre	werde
ihr-form:	nehmt	seht	seid	fahrt	werdet
wir-form:	nehmen wir	sehen wir	seien wir	fahren wir	werden wir
Sie-form:	nehmen Sie	sehen Sie	seien Sie	fahren Sie	werden Sie

Impersonal form: identical with infinitive

Again, only the **du**-form is not identical with the present indicative. The change of vowel from **a** to **ä** (**ich fahre, du fährst**), from **au** to **äu** (**ich laufe, du läufst**), and from **o** to **ö** (**stoßen, du stößt**) does not occur in the imperative. However, the change from **e** to **ie** or **i** (**ich gebe, du gibst; ich sehe, du siehst**) must be observed. These changed-vowel forms never show the ending **-e** in the **du**-form. The **du**-form **werde** is irregular, as are the forms of **sein**. In principle, the ending **-e** of the **du**-form is again optional.

183   The Use of the Various Forms of the Imperative

The Use of the **du**-Form

The **du**-form is used when the persons involved say **du** to each other. It is also used in advertisements.

> Bring mir bitte Zigaretten mit,
> Bring mir doch bitte Zigaretten mit, } wenn du in die Stadt fährst!
> Bitte bring mir Zigaretten mit,
>
> Mach mal Pause, trink Coca-Cola!

This form can be used together with a **du** immediately following the imperative. This **du** always establishes a contrast between the person addressed and someone else.

> Bleib *du* ruhig *lie*gen. Ich frühstücke im *Flug*hafen. (husband to wife)
>
> Steh *du* doch mal zuerst auf! (wife to husband; she usually gets up first)
>
> Rede *du* mal mit Meyer! (wife to husband; she has talked with Meyer already)
>
> Bleib *du* doch wenigstens vernünftig! (husband to wife; her friends are unreasonable)

This pattern is sometimes expressed in English by "Why don't *you* . . ."

The **ihr**-Form

Like the **du**-form, the **ihr**-form is used between persons who say **du** to each other.

> Kinder, vergeßt nicht,
> Kinder, bitte vergeßt nicht, } daß ihr um zehn zu Hause sein sollt.
> Kinder, vergeßt bitte nicht,

The use of **ihr** is parallel to the use of **du** with the **du**-form.

> *Geht* ihr schon! *Ich* komme *spä*ter.
> Geht *ihr* ruhig ins *The*ater! *Ich* möchte noch *ar*beiten.
> Versucht *ihr* doch mal, mit Meyer zu reden. *Mir glaubt* er nicht.

The wir-Form

The **wir**-form can only be used if the speaker includes himself among the persons addressed:

> Wo wollen wir denn essen? Im Regina? Gut, fahren wir ins Regina!
>
> Dir *gefällt* das Programm? *Schön! Bleib*en wir also!

The Sie-Form

The **Sie**-form is used (with or without **bitte**) between persons who say **Sie** to each other.

> (Bitte) bringen Sie mir noch ein Glas Wein.

In advertising it is used without **bitte**.

> Versuchen Sie SUNIL. Sie werden bestimmt zufrieden sein.

The Impersonal Form

The impersonal form is the infinitive used to express a request. It is used to give instructions to the public. It therefore appears on traffic signs, at airports, in planes, in railroad stations, etc. It is also used in advertising and in modern cookbooks, without exclamation marks.

> Alles aussteigen.
> Bitte aussteigen.
> Aussteigen bitte.
> Nicht öffnen, bevor der Zug hält.
> Langsam fahren.
> Nicht rauchen.
> Bitte anschnallen.
> Nicht benutzen, während der Zug hält.

Bitte nicht stören!
Do not disturb please!
Ne pas déranger s.v.p.!

184   The Intonation of Imperatives

The imperative as a command is distinguished from the imperative as a polite request by level of intonation.

The imperative expressing a command follows the usual 2-3-1 assertion pattern; that is, the intonation curve goes up to level 3 and then sinks to level 1:

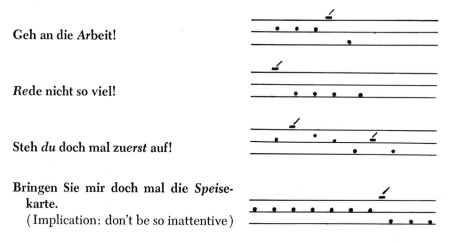

Geh an die *Arbeit!*

Rede nicht so viel!

Steh *du* doch mal zu*erst* auf!

Bringen Sie mir doch mal die *Speise-*
 karte.
 (Implication: don't be so inattentive)

In a polite request using imperative forms, the unstressed syllables preceding the stress-point are usually arranged in a downward trend toward level 1, and then the first stressed syllable is raised only to level 2, not to level 3:

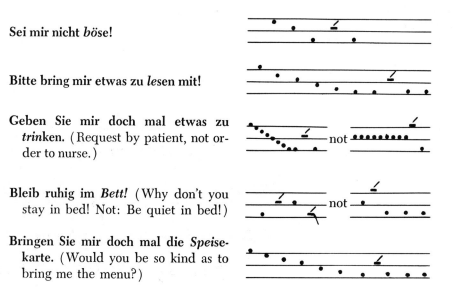

Sei mir nicht *böse!*

Bitte bring mir etwas zu *lesen* mit!

Geben Sie mir doch mal etwas zu
 trinken. (Request by patient, not order to nurse.)

Bleib ruhig im *Bett!* (Why don't you
 stay in bed! Not: Be quiet in bed!)

Bringen Sie mir doch mal die *Speise-*
 karte. (Would you be so kind as to
 bring me the menu?)

Einfahrt freihalten

Parken im Hof verboten

Be-u. Entladen v. 19-16 h
erlaubt.

GEPÄCKBAHNSTEIG
NICHT AUSSTEIGEN

How to express commands and requests is not so much a question of grammatical correctness as of correct social behavior. Nobody likes to be ordered around, and nobody wants to gain the reputation of being "bossy." You are therefore advised to express requests either by questions or by those forms of the imperative which are marked by intonation as requests.

185   The Syntax of the Imperative

The personal forms of the imperative begin the sentence and can be preceded only by **bitte.**

> **Bring mir etwas zu lesen mit!**
> **Bitte bring mir etwas zu lesen mit!**
> **Bring mir bitte etwas zu lesen mit!**
> **Bring mir etwas zu lesen mit, bitte!**

Since the impersonal imperatives are infinitives, they stand at the end of the imperative phrase:

> **Langsam fahren!**
> **Hinten einsteigen!**
> **Bitte die Türen schließen!**
> **Bitte von der Bahnsteigkante zurücktreten!**

When imperatives are negated, **nicht** stands, as usual, at the end of the inner field. Since the impersonal imperative is an infinitive, it must always follow the **nicht.** Thus the sentence

> **Man darf nicht mit dem Fahrer sprechen**

becomes the impersonal imperative

> **Nicht mit dem Fahrer sprechen!**

> **Bitte fahr morgen nicht nach Berlin!**
> **Sei doch nicht so ungeduldig!**
> **Warte heute nicht auf mich!**
> **Vergiß mich nicht!**
> **Bitte ruf mich morgen nicht an!**
> **Nicht hinauslehnen.**

Any imperative constitutes direct discourse. In order to report, by indirect discourse, that a request was made or a command given, **sollen** is used:

<u>IMPERATIVE:</u>

Fahren Sie doch einmal an die See.

<u>INDIRECT DISCOURSE:</u>

Der Arzt meinte, ich solle (sollte) doch einmal an die See fahren.
Der Arzt meinte, er solle (sollte) doch einmal an die See fahren.
Der Arzt meinte, wir sollten doch einmal an die See fahren.

186 doch einmal, doch mal

When **einmal** or the shorter **mal** is used in assertions and requests, they may mean *once, for once,* or *for a change:*

Ich will dieses Jahr nicht an die See. Ich möchte mal in die Berge fahren.
I don't want to go to the beach this year. I'd like to go to the mountains for a change.

Steh *du* doch mal zuerst auf.
Why don't you get up first for a change?

Very often, however, the short **mal** loses its literal meaning and expresses simply a note of casualness.

Ich geh' mal in die Stadt.
Ich muß mal telefonieren.

In requests, this casual **mal** is usually preceded by an unstressed **doch.**

Mach uns doch mal eine Tasse Kaffee.
How about fixing us a cup of coffee?

Noch (ein)mal and **doch noch (ein)mal** always mean *once more* or *again.*

Ruf sie doch noch mal an.
Call her up again.

187 eben and gerade

If **eben** is used with a full lexical meaning, it means either *flat, even,* or *just (a while ago):*

ebenes (flaches) Land	flat land
die Ebene, -n	the plain
die Norddeutsche Tiefebene	the North German Plain
er ist eben gekommen	he just came

Eben can also be used as a sentence adverb meaning "it won't take long; I hope you won't mind the interruption." In this function, it minimizes the significance of the action, and for this reason is frequently used in connection with the casual **mal**. As a sentence adverb, **eben** is never stressed.

> **Ich muß mal eben in die Stadt.**
> I've got to run downtown for a minute. (Nothing important; I'll be right back.)

> **Entschuldigst du mich einen Augenblick? Ich muß mal eben telefonieren.**
> Will you excuse me for a minute? I just want to make a quick phone call.

If **gerade** is used with full lexical meaning, it means *straight:*

> **eine gerade Linie**   a straight line

In connection with numbers, one speaks of **gerade Zahlen** and **ungerade Zahlen** (even and odd numbers). It can also mean *just then* or *just now* (see **eben** above):

> **er ist gerade gekommen**   he just came
> **Ich war gerade (eben) nach Hause gekommen, als das Telefon klingelte.**

188   ruhig

German **ruhig** can be used either as an adjective or as a sentence adverb. As an adjective, it means *calm, quiet.*

> **Sei ruhig.**   Be quiet.
> **Nun sei mal ganz ruhig, Gerda, und versuche, uns zu erzählen, was passiert ist.**

If used as a sentence adverb, **ruhig** denotes that the speaker will remain "quiet" and has no objections.

> **Bleib du ruhig im Bett; ich frühstücke im Flughafen.**
> Don't bother to get up for me; I'll have breakfast at the airport.

> **Ihr könnt ruhig laut sein, Kinder, ich will jetzt *doch* nicht schlafen.**
> I won't mind your being loud; I don't want to sleep now anyway.

EXERCISES

A. In the following sentences, insert **selbst** or **selber** in as many places as possible and translate the resulting sentences into English. The number of possibilities is indicated in parentheses.

SEE LAB
EXERCISE
12.1

(p. 634)

1. Erika fährt nicht. (4)
2. Ich wollte, ich könnte einmal mit Meyer reden. (2)
3. Warum denkst du eigentlich nie an dich? (1)
4. Meyer geht jeden Sonntag in die Kirche. (3)
5. Ich habe Angst gehabt. (3)
6. Mit Erika könnte ich, wenn nötig, ins Museum gehen. (5)

B. Restate the following sentences by using the subject indicated in parentheses. Be sure to distinguish between dative and accusative reflexives.

1. Natürlich haben sie sich schon einmal geküßt. (wir)
2. Kann er sich schon selber anziehen? (du)
3. Und dann sah er sich im Spiegel. (ich)
4. Ich muß mir morgen eine Wohnung suchen. (wir) (ihr)
5. Das können sie sich nicht kaufen. (ich) (du) (er) (Erika)
6. Sie trafen sich am Bahnhof. (wir)
7. Du mußt auch einmal an dich selbst denken. (Sie)
8. Kannst du dir das Frühstück nicht einmal selber machen? (er)
9. Sie hat sich in ihn verliebt. (er)
10. Hat er sich schon umgezogen? (du)
11. Hast du dich endlich beruhigt? (ihr)
12. Ich habe mich endlich einmal ausgeschlafen. (wir) (er)
13. Ich hoffe, du hast dich nicht erkältet. (Sie) (sie)
14. Haben sie sich scheiden lassen? (er) (du)
15. Hat er sich schon rasiert? (du)
16. Warum setzen Sie sich denn nicht? (wir)
17. Hat sie sich schon wieder so einen komischen Hut gekauft? (du)

SEE LAB
EXERCISE
12.2

(p. 634)

C. Restate the following sentences containing a statal present by using the corresponding perfect of the reflexive.

1. Ich bin gut ausgeruht.
2. Er ist schon rasiert.
3. Er ist seit einer Woche mit meiner Schwester verlobt.
4. Er ist in Rosemarie verliebt.
5. Ich bin schwer erkältet.
6. Bist du schon angezogen?
7. Sind die Kinder schon gebadet?
8. Er ist sehr gut vorbereitet.
9. Ist sie jetzt beruhigt?
10. Ich bin jetzt so an dieses Haus gewöhnt.

D. Restate the following sentences by replacing the reflexives by a statal present.

1. Mit wem hat er sich denn verlobt?
2. Warum hat er sich denn so aufgeregt?
3. Hat Hans sich vorbereitet?
4. Hast du dich schon wieder erkältet?
5. Ich habe mich entschlossen, das Haus zu kaufen.
6. Ich habe mich noch nicht umgezogen.
7. Weißt du schon, daß Meyers sich haben scheiden lassen?
8. Jetzt habe ich mich endlich einmal ausgeschlafen.

SEE LAB
EXERCISE
12.3, 12.4

(pp. 634-635)

9. Ich habe mich einfach überarbeitet.
10. Haben Sie sich jetzt endlich davon überzeugt?

E. In the following sentences, fill in the blanks by using the correct form of **setzen, sitzen; stellen, stehen; legen, liegen.**

SEE LAB
EXERCISE
12.5, 12.6

(p. 635)

1. Als ich nach Hause kam, _____ meine Frau schon im Bett.
2. Als ich nach Hause kam, hatte meine Frau sich schon ins Bett _____.
3. Hast du die Schuhe schon vor die Tür _____?
4. Meine Frau geht nur dann ins Theater, wenn sie in der ersten Reihe _____ kann.
5. Ich hatte einen guten Platz. Aber dann _____ sich der dicke Meyer vor mich, und ich konnte nichts mehr sehen.
6. Gestern im Theater habe ich neben Rosemarie _____.
7. Heute möchte ich eigentlich gern im Garten _____.
8. Ich habe deinen Mantel aufs Bett _____.
9. Der Zug war so voll, daß ich keinen Sitzplatz finden konnte, und ich mußte von Köln bis nach Frankfurt _____.
10. Wir haben den Tisch jetzt an die Wand _____.

F. In the following sentences, replace the transitives **setzen, stellen, legen** or the reflexives **sich setzen, sich stellen, sich legen** with the intransitives **sitzen, stehen, liegen,** or vice versa. Observe the difference in tense and, in some cases, the change of subject; remember also that you have to change case in the prepositional phrase.

> **Sie liegt schon im Bett.**
> **Sie hat sich schon ins Bett gelegt.**

1. Er hat sich neben sie gesetzt.
2. Wir saßen in der ersten Reihe.
3. Sie sitzen alle im Garten.
4. Warum hast du dich denn noch nicht ins Bett gelegt?
5. Er muß sich schon ins Bett gelegt haben.
6. Sie hatte sich direkt neben den Zollausgang gestellt.
7. Er stand am Fenster.
8. Er hat das Buch auf den Nachttisch gelegt.
9. Ich habe meine Schuhe vor die Tür gestellt.
10. Er saß schon am Frühstückstisch.
11. Vor ihm stand eine Tasse Kaffee. (New subject: Ingrid)
12. Er legte die Bibel vor sich auf den Tisch.
13. Wo hast du denn meinen Hut hingelegt?
14. Wo sitzt denn deine Frau? (Start new question with *Wo*)
15. Wo steht denn mein Wagen? (Start question with *Wohin?*; new subject: *du*)

G. Express in German by using a reflexive verb.

SEE LAB
EXERCISE
12.7

(p. 635)

1. Why don't you go to bed?
2. Did you shave this morning?
3. They got engaged.
4. They got a divorce.
5. They got drunk.
6. Can't Fritzchen take a bath by himself now?
7. You ought to change before Tante Amalie comes.
8. I broke my arm and I can't undress my*self*.
9. Have you had enough sleep?
10. Did you have a good rest?
11. He always gets so excited.
12. Did she finally calm down?
13. I've decided to go to Italy this summer.
14. I think I've caught a cold.
15. I just can't get used to it.
16. He told me that I had changed, but he himself had changed, too.
17. Had he prepared himself well?

H. By placing **bitte** in the front field, inner field, and end field, repeat the following sentences three times.

1. Sei doch nicht so aufgeregt!
2. Laß mich in Ruhe!
3. Sprechen Sie etwas lauter!
4. Ruf mich nicht vor acht an!
5. Komm nicht wieder erst um zwei nach Hause!

I. Change the following sentences to imperative sentences, using **doch mal** in the inner field.

1. Könntest du uns eine Tasse Kaffee machen?
2. Würdest du mir etwas zu lesen mitbringen?
3. Könnten Sie uns an einem Sonntag besuchen?
4. Haben Sie Meyers Telefonnummer? (Use *geben*)
5. Haben Sie schon nachgesehen, wo Meyer jetzt wohnt?
6. Wie wäre es denn, wenn *du* das Auto in die Garage führest?
7. Muß *ich* denn immer das Licht ausmachen?
8. Ich rate Ihnen, an die See zu fahren, gnädige Frau.

J. Change the following complaints into imperatives. Use **doch bitte** in the inner field.

1. Du rauchst zuviel.
2. Du gibst zuviel Geld aus.
3. Du bist immer so unfreundlich.

4. Können Sie mir kein Zimmer mit Bad geben?
5. Kannst du nicht mal vernünftig sein?
6. Mußt du dich denn immer so aufregen?
7. Warum schreibt ihr uns nicht, wie es euch geht?

K. Change the following imperatives to the **du**-form. Use **du** and **ihr** only when **Sie** is italicized.

1. Seien Sie doch nicht so aufgeregt!
2. Stehen Sie doch morgen etwas früher auf!
3. Bringen Sie mir ruhig noch eine Tasse Kaffee!
4. Gehen *Sie* doch mal mit Tante Amalie ins Museum!
5. Sprechen Sie ruhig lauter!
6. Gute Nacht, schlafen Sie gut.
7. Ich weiß, dies ist kein schönes Zimmer. Aber finden Sie hier mal ein besseres!
8. Denken Sie mal, wen ich gestern getroffen habe!
9. Fahren Sie doch mal eben zur Post.
10. Verbieten Sie ihm doch einfach, daß er Sie zu Hause anruft.
11. Schlagen *Sie* mir mal etwas vor.
12. Bringen Sie die Bücher bitte in die Bibliothek zurück.
13. Nehmen Sie uns doch bitte mit.
14. Schreien Sie doch nicht so laut!
15. Schwimmen *Sie* doch mal über den Rhein!
16. Bleiben Sie doch ruhig noch ein paar Tage.
17. Fahren Sie doch *mit* an die Nordsee.
18. Also, fangen wir an!
19. Gehen wir doch nach Hause!
20. *Sprechen* Sie doch mal mit ihm.
21. Sprechen *Sie* doch mal mit ihm.
22. Laden Sie ihn doch mal ein.
23. Fallen Sie nicht.
24. Fliegen Sie doch das nächste Mal mit der Lufthansa.
25. Lernen Sie ihn erst mal etwas besser kennen, dann können Sie ihn auch verstehen.
26. Laufen Sie doch nicht so schnell!
27. Schreiben Sie mir bitte.
28. Stehen Sie doch bitte mal auf.
29. Vergessen Sie nicht, mich anzurufen.
30. Versprechen Sie mir, daß Sie bald wiederkommen.
31. Tun Sie doch nicht so, als ob Sie alles wüßten.
32. Reden Sie nicht so viel.
33. Wünschen Sie mir Glück; ich brauche es.
34. Holen Sie mich bitte am Bahnhof ab.
35. Nun erzählen Sie mir mal, wie es war.
36. Bitte lachen Sie nicht darüber!

L. Change the following imperatives to indirect discourse, starting with **Er sagte,** . . . Use both forms of the subjunctive where possible.

SEE LAB
EXERCISE
12.8

(p. 635)

1. Fahren Sie doch mal an die See.
2. Sei nicht so unfreundlich.
3. Schicken Sie mir den Brief nach.
4. Geht doch mit ins Theater.
5. Seid vorsichtig, und macht dem Wolf nicht die Tür auf.
6. Ruf mich doch bitte morgen an.
7. Reg dich nicht so auf.
8. Schlaft euch endlich einmal aus.
9. Wünschen Sie mir Glück; ich brauche es.
10. Werde doch endlich einmal vernünftig.

M. Composition.

After you have spent your first night in a German hotel, you decide to write to your cousin Hildegard again. This time, describe what happened to you after your arrival in Koblenz; how you took a taxi to your hotel, and how surprised you were at the difference between this German hotel and American hotels. Tell her what an American motel is like; are there any motels in Germany at all? Then tell her that you have tried to call your friend Barbara, but haven't been able to reach her yet. You will try again and you hope that you'll be able to visit her. Ask Hildegard to write to you in Augustdorf and to let you know whether it is all right with her if you come to Munich in about two weeks.

Restrict yourself to the vocabulary and to the patterns you know. The reading selections of Units 10–12 should provide you with all you need; review them before you start writing.

VOCABULARY

ab und zu off and on
ähnlich similar
altmodisch old-fashioned
anreden mit to address by
sich anschnallen to fasten seat belts
   die Schnalle, –n buckle
anzeigen to announce
sich anziehen to get dressed
   der Anzug, ⸚e suit
sich ärgern über to be angry, mad at
die Aufführung, –en performance

sich aufregen über to get excited about
der Aufzug, ⸚e elevator
der Augenblick, –e moment, instant
die Auskunft, ⸚e information
sich ausruhen to rest; to get a rest
sich ausschlafen to get enough sleep
aussteigen to get out (of a vehicle)
sich ausziehen to undress
der Bart, ⸚e beard

beachten note, notice
bedienen to serve
   die Bedienung service
behalten to retain, remember, keep
benutzen to use
(sich) beruhigen to calm down
   beruhigt sein to be calmed down
betrachten to look at, observe
sich betrinken to get drunk
   betrunken sein to be drunk

billig inexpensive; cheap
der Bürger, – citizen
   der Bügermeister, – mayor
die Decke, –n ceiling; blanket
einander each other
sich einordnen (traffic) to get into the correct lane; to merge
empfangen to receive
   der Empfang, ⸚e reception
sich entschließen zu to make up one's mind to
   entschlossen sein zu to be determined
(sich) entschuldigen to excuse (oneself)
   entschuldigt sein to be excused
sich erholen to get a rest (to recover one's strength)
   erholt sein to be well rested (recovered)
sich erinnern an to remember
   die Erinnerung, –n memory
sich erkälten to catch a cold
   erkältet sein to have a cold
sich erkundigen to inquire
das Fahrrad, ⸚er bicycle
   das Motorrad, ⸚er motorcycle
falsch false, wrong
farbig in color, colored
der Feind, –e enemy
die Ferien (*pl.*) vacation
feststellen to determine; find out; conclude
flüstern whisper
der Führer, – guide; leader
sich fürchten vor to be afraid of
die Geduld (*no pl.*) patience
   geduldig patient
gegenseitig each other, mutual
die Gegenwart present (time); presence
   gegenwärtig present
das Gepäck (*no pl.*) baggage
das Geschäft, –e business, store

gewiß certain
sich gewöhnen an to get used to
   gewöhnt sein an to be used to
die Grenze, –n border
die Großstadt, ⸚e large city; metropolis
   die Kleinstadt, ⸚e small town
die Handschrift handwriting
die Hitze (*no pl.*) heat
inzwischen meanwhile, in the meantime
die Kälte (*no pl.*) cold
die Kasse, –n cash register, cash box
das Klima climate
das Knie, – knee
komisch funny, odd; comical
das Konzert', –e concert
sich kümmern um to take care of; to be concerned with
das Land country
   auf dem Land in the country
legen to lay
   liegen to lie
   sich legen to lie down
sich leisten to afford
die Lippe, –n lip
die Luft, ⸚e air
   die Luftpost air mail
die Menge, –n quantity, mass, crowd
   jede Menge any amount
nachsehen to look up; to investigate
nebenan next door
nervös' nervous
nicken to nod
(sich) öffnen to open
   geöffnet sein to be open
die Person', –en person
   persönlich personal
   der Personenzug local train
sich rasieren to shave
reißen to tear
retten to save

sanft soft
schauen look, gaze
sich scheiden lassen von to get a divorce from
   geschieden sein to be divorced
(sich) schließen to close
   geschlossen sein to be closed
schlucken to swallow
   der Schluck sip
schneien to snow
   der Schnee (*no pl.*) snow
die Schulter, –n shoulder
der Schwager, ⸚ brother-in-law
der Schwarzwald Black Forest
selbst, selber (*indeclinable*) self (see **175**); even (see **176**)
setzen to set
   sitzen to sit
   sich setzen to sit down
sowieso anyhow, anyway
starren to stare
stellen to place
   sich stellen to place oneself (to stand)
   die Stelle, –n place
stören to disturb
das Tal, ⸚er valley
das Thema, die Themen topic; subject; theme
das Tor, –e gate
träumen to dream
treffen to hit; to meet
sich überlegen to think about, meditate, consider
überraschen to surprise
überreden to persuade
(sich) überzeugen von to convince (oneself) of
   überzeugt sein von to be convinced of
sich umziehen to change (clothes)
unendlich infinite
(sich) unterbrechen to interrupt (oneself)
sich unterhalten to converse, have a conversation

unterrich'ten to teach, instruct
der Urlaub furlough; vacation
sich verändern to change
verändert sein to be
changed, different
verbinden to connect
sich verheiraten to get married
sich verlieben in to fall in
love with

verliebt sein in to be in
love with
sich verloben mit to get engaged to
verlobt sein mit to be engaged to
der Verlobte, –n fiancé
die Verzeihung pardon
verzeihen to pardon, ex-
cuse
voll full
vor allem above all

sich vorbereiten auf to prepare for
die Vorsicht (*no pl.*) caution
vorsichtig careful; cautious
vorstellen introduce (socially)
wachsen to grow
erwachsen (*adj.*) grown
up, adult
der Wechsel, – change
sich weigern to refuse
das Wunder, – miracle, wonder
die Zahl, –en number

IRREGULAR VERBS

behalten to retain, keep; to
remember
behielt, hat behalten, er
behält
empfangen to receive
empfing, hat empfangen, er
empfängt
reißen to tear
riß, hat gerissen, er reißt
schließen to close

schloß, hat geschlossen, er
schließt
treffen to hit; to meet
traf, hat getroffen, er trifft
sich umziehen to change
clothes
zog sich um, hat sich um-
gezogen, er zieht sich
um
sich unterhalten to converse,

have a conversation
unterhielt sich, hat sich unterhalten, er unterhält
sich
verzeihen to pardon, excuse
verzieh, hat verziehen, er
verzeiht
wachsen to grow
wuchs, ist gewachsen, er
wächst

UNIT 13: The Passive—es in the Front Field—
Pre-Noun Inserts

[1] Reflexives Denoting a (Mental) State

langweilen—sich langweilen—gelangweilt sein

SEE
ANALYSIS
189
(p. 595)

Meine Damen und Herren, ich hoffe, ich langweile Sie nicht, aber der Oedipuskomplex ist wirklich ein sehr wichtiges Problem.

Meine Damen und Herren, ich sehe, Sie sind gelangweilt. Sie scheinen nicht zu verstehen, daß der Oedipuskomplex ein sehr wichtiges Problem ist.

Der Professor von Schnarppe und seine „wichtigen Probleme"! Ich habe mich noch nie so gelangweilt.

sich bemühen um—bemüht sein

Gnädige Frau, wir haben uns sehr bemüht, ein Zimmer für Sie zu finden, aber wir haben nichts finden können.

Er behauptet, daß er mich liebt, und er ist sehr bemüht (er bemüht sich sehr), Mama davon zu überzeugen.

sich interessieren für—interessiert sein an (plus dative)

Interessieren Sie sich nicht für moderne Tänze?

An einem Chronometer bin ich nicht interessiert.

ärgern, sich ärgern über

Der Meyer ist wirklich ein Dummkopf. Ich habe mich gestern abend furchtbar über ihn geärgert.

Es ärgert mich, daß Meyer immer zu spät kommt.

Ich ärgere mich auch immer darüber, daß er so spät kommt.

erinnern an—sich erinnern an

Ich bin Renate Pfeiffer, Herr Professor. Sie erinnern sich sicher nicht mehr an mich, aber ich war vor zwanzig Jahren in Ihrem Faust-Seminar.

Oh doch, ich erinnere mich sehr gut an Sie, Fräulein Wilke. Sie kamen immer zehn Minuten zu spät.

(Facing) **Zwei alte Frankfurter in Sachsenhausen**

*Da*ran kann ich mich aber nicht mehr erinnern, Herr Professor.

Du mußt mich morgen unbedingt daran erinnern, daß ich den Mehrens anrufen muß.

Ihre Frau hat gerade angerufen; sie wollte Sie daran erinnern, daß Sie heute abend Gäste haben.—Oh, das erinnert mich, ich muß noch Zigarren kaufen; Dr. Mertens raucht keine Zigaretten.

Deine neue Sekretärin erinnert mich an Tante Amalie; die hat auch immer so komische Hüte getragen.

Sie kennen doch den Pfeiffer. Ist seine Frau nicht eine geborene [née] Schmidt?—Nein, wenn ich mich recht erinnere, hieß sie früher Wilke.

sich freuen auf

Du kommst doch auch nächsten Samstag zu unserer Party?—Ja, ich freue mich schon darauf.

Also, lieber Herr Raschke, wir erwarten Sie am Freitag gegen vier; wir freuen uns sehr auf Ihren Besuch.

sich freuen über

Und vielen Dank für die Blumen; ich habe mich sehr darüber gefreut.

Über die elektrische Eisenbahn hat Fritzchen sich ganz besonders gefreut.

Vater hat sich sehr darüber gefreut, daß du seinen Geburtstag nicht vergessen hast.

fürchten—sich fürchten vor

Ich fürchte, Herr Meyer ist schon nach Hause gegangen.

Ich habe mich wirklich davor gefürchtet, mit ihm in einem Büro sitzen zu müssen. Aber jetzt sind wir gute Freunde.

Wirklich? Ich habe mich nie vor ihm gefürchtet.

sich wundern über

Ich habe mich doch gestern abend über den Fritz gewundert. Daß der gar nichts getrunken hat! Früher hat er immer zu viel getrunken.

Was, sogar Professor von Schnarppe läßt sich jetzt analysieren?—Na und? *Ich* wundere mich über *gar* nichts mehr.

sich verlassen auf

Wenn du den Nolte nach Berlin geschickt hast, kannst du beruhigt sein. Auf den kann man sich verlassen.

Kann ich mich darauf verlassen, daß du um fünf zu Hause bist?

sich beschäftigen mit—beschäftigt sein mit

Meyer kennt nur eine Beschäftigung: Geld verdienen. Augenblicklich ist er damit beschäftigt (beschäftigt er sich damit), das Land, das er letztes Jahr billig gekauft hat, teuer zu verkaufen.

Herr Dr. Müller ist jetzt leider nicht zu sprechen; er ist beschäftigt.

Womit ist er denn beschäftigt?

VARIATIONS

Complete the following sentences:

1. **sich ärgern**

Hast du _____ heute wieder _____ müssen im Büro?

Über _____ hast du _____ denn heute _____?

Ja, heute habe ich _____ über Meyer geärgert.

Ich glaube, du bist nicht glücklich, wenn du dich nicht _____ kannst.

2. **sich freuen**

Ich habe mich sehr _____ gefreut, daß sie gekommen ist.

Ich freue mich sehr _____, daß sie morgen kommt.

Über die elektrische Eisenbahn hat Fritzchen sich sehr _____.

Worauf hast du _____ denn am meisten gefreut? _____ dich, Liebling.

3. **sich interessieren**

Interessieren _____ _____ eigentlich für Wagner?

Wären Sie vielleicht _____ einer Opernkarte interessiert?

Nein, ich interessiere mich nicht _____ die Oper.

Inge soll sich früher einmal für Meyer _____ haben.

_____ interessierst du dich denn eigentlich? Für gar nichts?

4. **sich erinnern**

Erinnerst du dich noch _____ Professor von Schnarppe?

Nein, an _____ kann ich _____ nicht mehr erinnern.

Bitte, _____ mich doch daran, daß ich morgen zum Arzt muß.

Ich hab's vergessen; du hättest mich _____ _____ sollen.

Der Flamingo da drüben _____ _____ an Frau von Schnarppe.

[2] Reflexives Denoting Physical Motion

sich bewegen

SEE ANALYSIS 189 (p. 595)

Der Mond bewegt sich um die Erde, und die Erde bewegt sich um die Sonne.

Ich war so müde, ich konnte mich kaum bewegen.

Du solltest nicht so viel sitzen; du brauchst mehr Bewegung.

Es wäre gut, wenn du dich etwas mehr bewegtest.

sich eilen—sich beeilen

Ich brauche mindestens zehn Minuten, um mich umzuziehen.—Kannst du dich nicht mal ein bißchen eilen (beeilen)?

Eilt euch, Kinder, der Vater wartet schon.

Wenn du noch auf die Bank willst, mußt du dich aber beeilen.

sich verfahren—sich verlaufen

Natürlich brauchen wir eine Straßenkarte, sonst verfahren wir uns wieder.

Fritz hatte keine Karte im Wagen, und da hat er sich natürlich verfahren.

In München kann man sich leicht verlaufen.—Wieso denn? Ich habe mich in München noch nie verlaufen.

sich umdrehen

Sie hat sich nach mir umgedreht.

VARIATIONS

Complete the following sentences:

1. sich verfahren

Wo bleibt er denn? Ob er sich schon wieder _____ hat?

Ich brauche keine Straßenkarte; ich _____ mich nie.

Mit dieser Karte kann man _____ nicht _____.

Er soll sich gestern abend schon wieder _____ _____.

2. sich umdrehen

_____ dich nicht um; da hinten kommt Frau Meyer.

Als er mich sah, hat er sich sofort _____.

Aber Anton, du brauchst dich doch nicht immer _____, wenn ein hübsches Mädchen vorbeigeht.

[3] Dative Reflexives

SEE
ANALYSIS
189
(p. 595)

Ich stelle mich vor—ich stelle mir vor

Darf ich mich vorstellen? Ich bin Dr. Ingelheim.

Gnädige Frau, darf ich Ihnen Herrn Dr. Ingelheim vorstellen?

Ich habe mich Ihnen noch nicht vorgestellt, gnädige Frau; ich bin Dr. Ingelheim.

Darf ich vorstellen? Herr Doktor Ingelheim—Fräulein Wedemeyer.

Ich kann mir nicht vorstellen, daß Ingelheim ein guter Soldat gewesen ist.

Ein Leh-aut-mann? Was ist denn das? Darunter kann ich mir nichts vorstellen.

Ich hatte mir das alles viel leichter vorgestellt.

sich etwas einbilden—eingebildet sein

Das stimmt doch gar nicht; das bildest du dir nur ein.

Und er hat sich eingebildet, ich wollte ihn heiraten.

Den Erich heirate ich nicht; der ist mir viel zu eingebildet.

sich etwas denken

Du kannst dir gar nicht denken, wie ich mich darauf freue, Dich endlich wiederzusehen.

Ich habe mir gar nichts dabei gedacht, als ich sie fragte, wie es ihrem Mann ginge. Wie konnte ich denn wissen, daß sie geschieden ist?

sich etwas überlegen

Ich überlege mir oft, ob es nicht besser wäre, wenn wir nach Heidelberg zögen.

Wir wollen unser Landhaus verkaufen und in die Stadt ziehen.—Habt ihr euch das auch gut überlegt?—Hast du dir das gut überlegt, Maria?

Wie wäre es, wenn Sie auch in die Stadt zögen?—Das muß ich mir erst noch überlegen.

sich etwas ansehen—sich etwas anschauen

Ich wollte mir den Hitchcock Film eigentlich gar nicht ansehen; aber du kennst ja Tante Amalie. Sie interessiert sich nur noch für Hitchcock und Picasso.

Schau dir das an! Da kommt Edith Maschke mit ihrem neuen Freund.—Die hat sich ja ganz verändert! Seit wann ist sie denn blond?—Sie hat sich die Haare färben lassen.

Wenn ihr nach Frankfurt kommt, müßt ihr euch unbedingt das Goethe-Haus ansehen.

VARIATIONS

Complete the following sentences:

Vater freut sich _____ Weihnachten.

Das kann ich _____ nicht vorstellen.

Ich habe _____ noch nicht vorgestellt; ich bin Hans Ingelheim.

Ich kann _____ gar nicht denken, was er _____ dabei gedacht hat.

Das solltest du _____ gut überlegen.

Er soll _____ eingebildet haben, ich wollte _____ heiraten.

Was kann er _____ nur dabei gedacht _____?

Habt ihr _____ schon überlegt, welchen Film _____ euch anschauen wollt?

Hast du	dir schon	die Zähne	geputzt?
Ich muß	mir noch	die Schuhe	putzen.
Du solltest	dir *auch*	die Haare	färben lassen.
Darf ich	mir mal	die Hände	waschen?
Wann läßt du	dir endlich mal	die Haare	schneiden?
Wo kann ich	mir hier	die Haare	schneiden lassen?
Erika hat	sich	den Arm	gebrochen.
Fritz läßt	sich tatsächlich	einen Bart	wachsen.
Ich lasse	mir *auch*	einen Bart	wachsen.
Fritzchen, putz	dir mal	die Nase!	

| Warum ziehst du | dir nicht | einen Mantel | an? |
| Du solltest | dir auch | einen Hut | aufsetzen. |

Form your own variations for the above sentences.

[4] Impersonal Reflexives

SEE
ANALYSIS
189

Es stellte sich heraus, daß Erich das Geld gestohlen hatte.

Es erwies sich, daß das Problem *so* nicht zu lösen war.

Es zeigte sich, daß auch die Elektronen sich um ihre Achse drehen.

Worum handelt es sich denn eigentlich?

Es handelt sich um ein wichtiges Problem.

Mein Vater hat mit Diamanten gehandelt.

Wovon handelt dieser Roman denn?

Ich hatte keine Zeit, darüber nachzudenken; ich mußte sofort handeln.

[5] The Active Voice of Transitive and Intransitive Verbs; Actional and Statal Forms of the Passive

This is a presentation of basic forms. Study these examples *after* you have read
190–192.

SEE
ANALYSIS
190–192

PRESENT

INTRANSITIVE	Kochen die Kartoffeln schon?
TRANSITIVE	Mutter kocht jeden Tag Kartoffeln.
ACTIONAL PASSIVE	Bei uns werden jeden Tag Kartoffeln gekocht.
STATAL PASSIVE	Sind die Kartoffeln schon gekocht?

PAST

INTRANSITIVE	Als ich nach Hause kam, standen die Kartoffeln schon auf dem Herd und kochten.
TRANSITIVE	Mutter kochte damals jeden Tag fünf Pfund Kartoffeln.
ACTIONAL PASSIVE	Bei uns wurden früher jeden Tag fünf Pfund Kartoffeln gekocht.
STATAL PASSIVE	Als ich nach Hause kam, waren die Kartoffeln schon gekocht. Wenn die Kartoffeln schon gekocht gewesen wären, hätten wir sofort essen können.

PERFECT

INTRANSITIVE	Die Kartoffeln haben noch gar nicht gekocht.
TRANSITIVE	Hast du auch genug Kartoffeln gekocht?
ACTIONAL PASSIVE	Bei uns sind noch nie soviel Kartoffeln gekocht worden wie in den letzten Tagen.

INFINITIVES

ACTIVE VOICE, PRESENT

Ingelheim will *Die Frau mit dem Flamingo* an den Exotica-Verlag verkaufen.

> Ingelheim wants to sell *Die Frau mit dem Flamingo* to the Exotica pub-
> lishing house.

ACTIVE VOICE, PAST

Ingelheim soll *Die Frau mit dem Flamingo* an den Exotica-Verlag verkauft
haben.

> Ingelheim is reported to have sold *Die Frau mit dem Flamingo* to the
> Exotica publishing house.

ACTIONAL PASSIVE, PRESENT

In Kanada darf *Die Frau mit dem Flamingo* nicht verkauft werden.

> In Canada, *Die Frau mit dem Flamingo* cannot be sold.

ACTIONAL PASSIVE, PAST

Im letzten Jahr sollen über 100.000 Exemplare verkauft worden sein.

> More than 100,000 copies are supposed to have been sold last year (are
> reported to have been sold).

STATAL PASSIVE, PRESENT

Die ganze erste Auflage soll schon verkauft sein.

> We hear that the entire first printing has already been sold (is said to have
> been sold).

STATAL PASSIVE, PAST

Haben Sie gehört, die ganze erste Auflage soll schon nach vier Wochen verkauft
  gewesen sein.

> Have you heard that the entire first printing was sold out (is said to have
> been sold) after four weeks?

[6] Distinction between Actional and Statal Passive Forms

SEE
ANALYSIS
191–192

(pp. 599-601)

Bei uns werden alle Briefe mit der Maschine geschrieben.

Diese Briefe sind mit der Maschine geschrieben.

Wann ist das Pulver denn erfunden worden?

Das weiß ich nicht. Als ich geboren wurde, war es schon erfunden.

Dieses Zimmer ist aber kalt. Ist das Zimmer nicht geheizt, oder kann es nicht geheizt
  werden?

Es sollte eigentlich verboten werden, daß kleine Kinder in einer Fabrik arbeiten.

Aber das ist doch schon seit Jahren verboten.

Die Trans-Pacific-Eisenbahn
wurde nicht an einem Tag gebaut

**Auch die
Frankfurter Stadtbahn
braucht ihre Bauzeit**

Ich höre, das Haus neben der Kirche soll verkauft werden.
Es ist schon verkauft.

Die Kleine ist gut erzogen!
Wer hat sie denn erzogen?
Sie ist in einer Privatschule erzogen worden.

Ich bin noch nie von einem Menschen so enttäuscht worden wie von Ingelheim.
Ich bin noch nie so enttäuscht gewesen.
Nein, wirklich! Ingelheims neuer Roman hat mich enttäuscht.

VARIATIONS

Change the following statal passive sentences to the actional passive.

> Der Brief war mit der Maschine geschrieben.
> Das Haus ist schon verkauft.
> Ist die Stadt wiederaufgebaut?
> Das müßte verboten sein.
> Ist meine Schreibmaschine schon repariert?

[7] "Transformations" from Active Voice to Actional Passive

Wer hat denn den Bunsenbrenner erfunden?
Der Bunsenbrenner ist von Bunsen erfunden worden.
Bunsen soll den Bunsenbrenner erfunden haben.
Der Bunsenbrenner soll von Bunsen erfunden worden sein.

SEE ANALYSIS 193 (pp. 601-602)

Wer hat Amerika entdeckt?
Amerika ist von Kolumbus entdeckt worden.
Schon die Wikinger sollen Amerika entdeckt haben.
Amerika soll schon von den Wikingern entdeckt worden sein.

Können Sie diese Schreibmaschine reparieren?
Wir reparieren alle Maschinen.
Die Maschine muß repariert werden.
Wo ist denn meine Schreibmaschine?—Sie wird gerade repariert.
Wer hat diese Maschine denn repariert?
Von wem ist die Maschine denn repariert worden?
Meyer soll sie repariert haben.
Sie soll von Meyer repariert worden sein.
Was! Diese Maschine soll repariert sein? Sie funktioniert ja immer noch nicht.

Die Polizei sucht ihn.
Die Polizei soll ihn suchen.
Er wird von der Polizei gesucht.
Er soll von der Polizei gesucht werden.
Die Polizei suchte ihn überall.
Er wurde von der Polizei gesucht.
Hat ihn die Polizei nie gefunden?
Ist er nie gefunden worden?
Doch! Die Polizei soll ihn gestern gefunden haben.
Doch! Er soll gestern gefunden worden sein.

Eine einzige Atombombe zerstört eine ganze Stadt.
Eine einzige Atombombe kann eine ganze Stadt zerstören.
Durch eine einzige Atombombe wird eine ganze Stadt zerstört.
Durch eine einzige Atombombe kann eine ganze Stadt zerstört werden.

Eine einzige Bombe hat das Haus zerstört.
Das Haus ist durch eine einzige Bombe zerstört worden.
Das Haus soll durch eine einzige Bombe zerstört worden sein.
Eine einzige Bombe soll das ganze Haus zerstört haben.

Warum schreibst du denn den Brief nicht mit der Maschine?
Bei uns werden alle Briefe mit der Maschine geschrieben.
Bei uns müssen alle Briefe mit der Maschine geschrieben werden.
Kannst du diese Briefe nicht auch mit der Maschine schreiben?

VARIATIONS

Transform the following sentences to the statal and the actional passive. Leave out the agent.

> Man hat die ganze Stadt zerstört.
> Dr. Müller schreibt alle seine Briefe mit der Maschine.
> Er hat das Haus verkauft.
> Er soll das Haus schon verkauft haben.
> Wir haben ihn gerettet.

[8] Dative Objects

Wir konnten ihm nicht helfen.
Dem Manne kann geholfen werden. (Schiller, *Die Räuber*)
Ihm ist nicht zu helfen.
Man half ihm sofort.

Ihm wurde sofort geholfen.

Jemand hat mir gesagt, ich sollte um drei Uhr hier sein.

Mir wurde gesagt, ich sollte um drei Uhr hier sein.

Es wurde mir gesagt, ich sollte um drei Uhr hier sein.

Davon ist mir nie etwas gesagt worden.

Jemand muß es ihm gesagt haben.

[9] Passive Forms to Express Activity as Such

Mutter kocht jeden Tag für fünf Personen.

Bei uns wird jeden Tag für fünf Personen gekocht.

Damals kochte Mutter jeden Tag für fünf Personen.

Damals wurde bei uns jeden Tag für fünf Personen gekocht.

Mutter hat oft für fünf Personen gekocht.

Bei uns ist schon immer für fünf Personen gekocht worden.

Ich wollte, Mutter kochte nicht jeden Tag für fünf Personen.

Ich wollte, bei uns würde nicht jeden Tag für fünf Personen gekocht.

Ich wollte, Sie hätten heute nicht für hundert Personen gekocht.

Ich wollte, heute wäre nicht für hundert Personen gekocht worden.

Mutter soll damals den ganzen Sommer für zwanzig Personen gekocht haben.

Bei Meyer soll während der Ernte sogar für vierzig Personen gekocht worden sein.

SEE ANALYSIS 195 (pp. 602-603)

Wir waschen nur mit Persil.

Bei uns wird nur mit Persil gewaschen, denn Persil bleibt Persil.

Hier wird gearbeitet.

Jeden Samstag abend wird dort getanzt.

In meinem Elternhaus ist viel musiziert worden.

In seinem Elternhaus soll viel musiziert worden sein.

In Kalifornien wird fast nur mit Gas geheizt.

Bei euch im Büro wird viel zu viel geredet.

In Deutschland wird heute viel gereist.

Wann wird denn hier morgens gefrühstückt?

In diesem Hotel wird nur vom 15. September bis zum 1. Mai geheizt.

Hier darf nicht getanzt werden.

Ingelheim ist mir zu sentimental; in seinen Romanen wird auf jeder dritten Seite geweint.

Es wird höflich um Ruhe gebeten.

Es wird gebeten, nicht zu rauchen.

VARIATIONS

Change to actional passive, expressing "activity as such."

> Wir arbeiten hier schwer.
> Man hat hier noch nie getanzt.
> Und um eins essen wir hier zu Mittag.
> In unserer Familie lachen wir viel.
> Ihr trinkt hier aber wirklich viel.

[10] Syntactical Variations

SEE
ANALYSIS
190-198
(pp. 598-605)

zeigen

Der neue schwedische Film wird jetzt auch in Deutschland gezeigt.
Könnte man ihn nicht auch in den Vereinigten Staaten zeigen?
Während der internationalen Filmfestspiele in Berlin wurde auch der neue schwedische Film gezeigt.
Der Film soll sehr gut sein, aber in Amerika ist er noch nicht gezeigt worden.
Es wäre besser, wenn dieser Film auch in Berlin nicht gezeigt worden wäre.
Es tut mir leid, daß der Film gezeigt wird. Ich wollte, er würde nicht gezeigt.

When is it supposed to be shown here?   _____
It can never be shown here.   _____

essen

In den Vereinigten Staaten wird mehr Fleisch gegessen als in Deutschland.
Wo ist denn die Salami, die du letzte Woche gekauft hast?—Die ist schon längst gegessen.
Wann wird denn heute abend gegessen?

Die Amerikaner haben schon immer mehr Fleisch gegessen als die Deutschen.
In Amerika _____ als in Deutschland.

einladen

So, ihr seid schon wieder bei Schultes eingeladen?
So, Schultes haben euch schon wieder eingeladen?
Ich werde leider nie eingeladen.
Mich haben sie noch nie eingeladen.
Warum warst du denn gestern abend nicht bei Schultes?
Ich war nicht eingeladen.

Ich wollte, ich würde auch einmal eingeladen.
Ich wollte, ich wäre damals auch eingeladen gewesen.

Den Eugen Wilke treffe ich wahrscheinlich heute bei Schultes. Er soll auch eingeladen sein.

Karola Kirchhoff soll eingeladen worden sein, in Stuttgart die Desdemona zu spielen.

Natürlich freue ich mich darüber, daß ich eingeladen bin, hier in Stuttgart die Desdemona zu spielen. Aber ich bin nicht überrascht. Ich wäre sehr enttäuscht gewesen, wenn ich nicht eingeladen worden wäre.

I wish they would invite us.	Ich wollte, _____.
I wish we were invited.	Ich wollte, _____.
I wish Ingrid had invited us.	Ich wollte, _____.
I wish we had been invited by Ingrid.	Ich wollte, _____.
I wish we had been invited.	Ich wollte, _____.

enttäuschen

Ingelheims neuer Roman hat mich sehr enttäuscht.

Ingelheims letzter Roman war eine große Enttäuschung.

Ingelheims erster Roman wurde mit Recht überall gelobt; aber von seinem letzten Roman war ich sehr enttäuscht.

Auf das Essen im „Löwen" kann man sich immer verlassen; *ich* bin jedenfalls noch *nie* enttäuscht worden.

I am terribly disappointed.	Ich _____.
I was terribly disappointed.	Ich _____.
I have never been so disappointed.	Ich _____.

denken

Aber Herr Leutnant, ich dachte. . .—Hier wird nicht gedacht; hier wird nur getan, was befohlen ist. Gedacht wird hier nur vom General aufwärts.

reden

Meine Herren, Sie wissen, ich bin hier neu; aber eines habe ich schon festgestellt. Hier wird zu viel geredet, zu viel geraucht, zu viel Kaffee getrunken und zu wenig gearbeitet.

Auf dem Weg nach Hause redeten wir kaum ein Wort miteinander.

Auf dem Weg nach Hause wurde kaum geredet.

Auf dem Weg nach Hause wurde kaum ein Wort geredet.

Über seine Reise nach Kairo ist schon so viel geredet worden, daß es langsam langweilig wird. Ich finde, darüber ist jetzt genug geredet.

Express in the actional passive:

Wir haben genug geredet; jetzt müssen wir etwas tun.

entdecken

Kolumbus entdeckte Amerika, weil er einen Weg nach Indien suchte.

Amerika war zwar schon von den Wikingern entdeckt worden, aber als Kolumbus Amerika entdeckte, waren die Fahrten der Wikinger längst vergessen.

Amerika wurde, wie Sie wissen, 1492 von Kolumbus entdeckt.

In einem deutschen Lied heißt es von den Indianern: Sie schrien laut „Wir sind entdeckt.“

If America had not been discovered by Columbus, it would have been discovered by somebody else. Wenn Amerika nicht ————————————————————————————————.

retten

Das Schiff sank so schnell, daß sich nur wenige retten konnten.

Nur wenige konnten gerettet werden.

Gottseidank sind die meisten gerettet worden.

Gottseidank, daß sie alle gerettet sind.

I hope they can all be saved.	Ich hoffe, ————————————————.
I hope they could all be saved.	Ich hoffe, ————————————————.
I wish they could all have been saved.	Ich wünschte, ——————————————.
Unfortunately, they could not all be saved.	Leider ———————————————————.

lösen

Es wurde zwar schon im Altertum angenommen, daß sich die Materie aus gewissen „Elementen“ zusammensetzt, aber das Problem, aus welchen Elementen die Materie tatsächlich zusammengesetzt ist, konnte viele Jahrhunderte lang nicht gelöst werden.

Man konnte das Problem lange nicht lösen.

Das Problem war einfach nicht zu lösen.

Man glaubte, das Problem wäre nicht zu lösen.

Das Problem ließ sich lange nicht lösen.

Das Problem ist erst vor wenigen Jahren gelöst worden.

Das Problem konnte erst vor wenigen Jahren gelöst werden.

Ohne die Entdeckung des Radiums hätte das Problem nie gelöst werden können.

Im Mittelalter war das Problem noch nicht gelöst.

Erst die moderne Wissenschaft hat das Problem gelöst.

Heute ist das Problem gelöst.

ändern   *to change something, to enforce change*
sich ändern   *to become different, to change in nature or character*
sich verändern   *to change in physical appearance or behavior*

Glücklich ist, wer vergißt, was doch nicht zu ändern ist. (Johann Strauss, *Die Fledermaus*)
Ich habe meine Meinung geändert.
Der Mantel ist mir viel zu groß; den muß ich ändern lassen.

Haben Sie meinen Mantel schon geändert?

Ja, der Mantel ist schon geändert.

Während der Inflation wurden die Preise jeden Tag geändert.

Gestern sind sie auch wieder geändert worden.

Die Preise ändern sich jeden Tag.

Bei uns gibt es nichts Neues; bei uns ändert sich nie etwas.

Der Marktplatz ist noch immer der alte, und nichts scheint sich hier geändert zu haben.
   Aber die Menschen, die hier wohnen, die haben sich sehr geändert.

Morgen soll sich das Wetter endlich ändern.

Nein, meine Herren, so geht das nicht; das muß anders werden.—Das läßt sich aber leider
   nicht ändern.

Es bleibt, wie es ist, daran läßt sich nichts ändern.

Du hast dich aber verändert, Otto.

Gnädige Frau, Sie haben sich gar nicht verändert.

Die Maria hat sich aber verändert; die muß ja mindestens fünfundzwanzig Pfund abge-
   nommen haben.—Ja, verändert hat sie sich, aber geändert hat sie sich nicht; es ist immer
   noch dieselbe alte Maria.

Of course I've changed; I'm ten years older.	Natürlich _____.
Karl has really changed; he doesn't drink any more.	Karl hat _____ _____.
I thought you had had your coat altered.	Ich dachte, _____.

[11] The Impersonal es

Be prepared to produce these and similar sentences orally.

SEE
ANALYSIS
199
(pp. 605-608)

Niemand war zu Hause.
Es war niemand zu Hause.

Jemand hat heute nachmittag nach Ihnen gefragt.
Es hat heute nachmittag jemand nach Ihnen gefragt.

Leider meldete sich niemand.
Es meldete sich leider niemand.

Jetzt werden wieder Häuser gebaut.
Es werden jetzt wieder Häuser gebaut.

Viele Leute waren nicht *da*.
Es waren nicht viele *Leu*te da.

Ach Emma, du bist's!
Wer ist denn da?—Ich bin's, Emma.
Meyer kann es nicht gewesen sein.

Wer war denn der ältere Herr gestern abend?—Das war mein Vater.
Wer ist denn das auf diesem Bild hier?—Das sind meine Eltern.

Um was für Probleme handelt es sich denn diesmal?—
Es sind immer noch dieselben alten Probleme.

Es war ein Tag wie heute.
Das waren schöne Tage damals in München.

Das sind ja alles deutsche Bücher; die kann ich doch nicht lesen.
Es sind Bücher, die ich aus Deutschland mitgebracht habe.

Es regnet schon seit Tagen.
Hier regnet es schon seit Tagen.

Es hat schon wieder gehagelt.
Hier hat es heute schon wieder gehagelt.

Es hat die ganze Nacht geschneit.
Heute morgen hat es ein bißchen geschneit.

Es hat stundenlang gedonnert und geblitzt, aber geregnet hat es nicht.

Wie geht es denn deinem Vater?—Danke, es geht ihm gut.
Dem Anton geht's immer gut.
Mir geht es heute gar nicht gut; mir geht's schlecht.
Guten Tag, Herr Müller. Ich habe Sie lange nicht gesehen; wie geht's Ihnen denn?

Vor hundert Jahren gab es noch keine Flugzeuge.
Da oben ist ein Flugzeug.

Es gibt jeden Tag Schweinebraten.
Das ist doch kein Schweinebraten, das ist Kalbsbraten.

Wieviele Hotels gibt es denn hier?
Heute gibt es nicht mehr viele Familien mit neun Kindern.
Was gibt's denn zum Mittagessen?

[12] The Impersonal **es** Anticipating a Subject Clause

SEE
ANALYSIS
199
(pp. 605-608)

Es ist nicht gestattet, während der Fahrt mit dem Wagenführer zu sprechen.
Natürlich ist es nicht gestattet, während der Fahrt mit dem Wagenführer zu sprechen.

Es ist leider nicht erlaubt, vor dem Rathaus zu parken.
Leider ist es nicht erlaubt, vor dem Rathaus zu parken.

Es ist verboten, die Türen während der Fahrt zu öffnen.
Ist es verboten, die Türen während der Fahrt zu öffnen?

Ist es erlaubt, hier zu rauchen?—Nein, dies ist ein Nichtraucher!

Es wurde berichtet, daß Ingelheim spurlos verschwunden wäre.
Heute wird aus Kairo berichtet, daß die erste Meldung auf einem Irrtum beruhte.

Es wurde behauptet, er hätte sein ganzes Geld verloren.
Von seinen Freunden wurde behauptet, er hätte sein ganzes Geld verloren.

Es muß leider angenommen werden, daß er nicht mehr am Leben ist.
Leider muß angenommen werden, daß er nicht mehr am Leben ist.

Es wurde vorgeschlagen, eine neue Brücke über den Rhein zu bauen.
Von allen Seiten wurde vorgeschlagen, eine neue Brücke über den Rhein zu bauen.

Es wird oft behauptet, daß Männer besser Auto fahren können als Frauen.
Früher wurde oft behauptet, daß Männer besser Auto fahren könnten als Frauen.

Es wurde beschlossen, endlich eine neue Klinik zu bauen.
Gestern abend wurde beschlossen, endlich eine neue Klinik zu bauen.

Leider konnte nicht festgestellt werden, wer der Dieb ist.
Es konnte nicht festgestellt werden, wer der Dieb ist.
Wer der Dieb ist, konnte bis jetzt nicht festgestellt werden.

Invent anticipating clauses with **es** for the following subject clauses.

_____ das Kind in eine Privatschule zu schicken.
_____ Ingelheim hätte sich scheiden lassen.
_____ daß er nicht gerettet worden ist.
_____ ohne Visum nach Deutschland zu fahren?
_____ hier ein Bürohaus zu bauen.

[13] Pre-Noun Inserts

Mein Chef, der gottseidank nicht sehr intelligent ist, weiß gar nicht, daß es in Berlin auch
  billigere Hotels gibt.
Mein (gottseidank nicht sehr intelligenter) Chef weiß gar nicht, daß es in Berlin auch billigere Hotels gibt.

SEE
ANALYSIS
201
(pp. 609-612)

Der Winter, der selbst für Norwegen ungewöhnlich kalt war, wollte gar kein Ende nehmen.
Der (selbst für Norwegen ungewöhnlich kalte) Winter wollte gar kein Ende nehmen.

Dieser Roman, der nach der Meinung mancher Kritiker viel zu lang war, erhielt den Nobelpreis.
Dieser (nach der Meinung mancher Kritiker viel zu lange) Roman erhielt den Nobelpreis.

Die Fluggäste, die soeben mit Lufthansa Flug Nummer 401 aus Frankfurt angekommen sind, werden gebeten, den Warteraum nicht zu verlassen.

Die (soeben mit Lufthansa Flug Nummer 401 aus Frankfurt angekommenen) Fluggäste werden gebeten, den Warteraum nicht zu verlassen.

Die Schifahrer werden natürlich über den Schnee, der während der letzten vierundzwanzig Stunden gefallen ist, hoch erfreut sein.

Die Schifahrer werden natürlich über den (während der letzten vierundzwanzig Stunden gefallenen) Schnee hoch erfreut sein.

Karthago, das von den Römern zerstört wurde, ist nicht wiederaufgebaut worden.

Das (von den Römern zerstörte) Karthago ist nicht wiederaufgebaut worden.

Heute ist es jedem klar, daß mit der Atombombe, die über Hiroshima abgeworfen wurde, eine neue Epoche begonnen hat.

Heute ist es jedem klar, daß mit der (über Hiroshima abgeworfenen) Atombombe eine neue Epoche begonnen hat.

Aloys Hinterkofer, der seit Wochen von der Polizei gesucht wird, soll gestern in der Regina-Bar gesehen worden sein.

Der (seit Wochen von der Polizei gesuchte) Aloys Hinterkofer soll gestern in der Regina-Bar gesehen worden sein.

Die Züge, die im Sommer von München nach Italien fahren, sind meistens überfüllt.

Die (im Sommer von München nach Italien fahrenden) Züge sind meistens überfüllt.

Dieser junge Mann hat ein Buch geschrieben, das selbst die Kritiker überraschte.

Dieser junge Mann hat ein (selbst die Kritiker überraschendes) Buch geschrieben.

Alle Studenten, die sich für das Projekt interessierten, das Professor Behrens vorgeschlagen hatte, wurden gebeten, sich am nächsten Tag auf dem Sekretariat zu melden.

Alle (an dem von Professor Behrens vorgeschlagenen Projekt interessierten) Studenten wurden gebeten, sich am nächsten Tag auf dem Sekretariat zu melden.

Keiner von uns konnte sich an das kalte Klima in der Arktis gewöhnen. Uns war es immer zu kalt, während die (an das kalte Klima gewöhnten) Eskimos sich nichts dabei dachten.

If you can figure out the next sentence, you have really mastered the last few lessons:

Meine Damen und Herren, es handelt sich hier um ein (von der Wissenschaft bis heute noch kaum beachtetes und, soweit ich das aufgrund meiner Untersuchungen beurteilen kann, immer wichtiger werdendes) mathematisches Problem.

Ein Mann kommt nach San Franzisko (Schluß)

XI

Frankfurt, Dezember 1960

„Was ich nicht verstehen kann, Herr Kerner, ist, daß Sie damals nicht weitergesucht haben. Als Sie vom Konsulat diesen negativen Brief bekamen, hätten Sie einfach wieder hingehen sollen. Irgendwo hätten die Ihre Tochter schon gefunden."

„Das sagen Sie so, Herr Müller, aber Sie dürfen nicht vergessen, daß ₅ ich gerade aus dem Osten gekommen war. Und außerdem hatte ich zum zweiten Mal alles verloren. Nein, ich habe damals einfach aufgegeben; es hatte ja doch alles keinen Sinn mehr. Ich habe auch nie wieder davon gesprochen. Heute war eigentlich das erste Mal, daß ich die ganze Geschichte wieder erzählt habe. Komisch, wie man sich ₁₀ plötzlich wieder an Dinge erinnern kann, an die man seit Jahren nicht mehr gedacht hat."

Es war wieder ein Samstagabend, und Kerner saß mit seinen Bekannten an seinem Sachsenhäuser Stammtisch beim Apfelwein. Irgend jemand hatte angefangen, vom Krieg zu sprechen; Müller ₁₅ hatte davon erzählt, daß seine Frau bei dem Luftangriff auf Dresden umgekommen war,—und das hatte ganz unerwartet bei Kerner viele Erinnerungen wachgerufen. Er hatte von den paar Jahren vor dem Krieg erzählt, als er in Breslau Lehrer gewesen war, von seinen Erlebnissen in ganz Europa während des Krieges, von seiner Ver- ₂₀ wundung vor Stalingrad und von seiner Gefangennahme in Pommern. Über die Jahre der Gefangenschaft wußte er nicht viel zu sagen, aber an die beiden Fahrten, die mit Hoffnung begonnen und mit Enttäuschung geendet hatten, nach Thüringen und nach Frankfurt, wußte er sich genau zu erinnern. ₂₅

„Ich kenne den Kerner ja schon seit Jahren", meinte Müller, „aber so viel wie heute habe ich ihn noch nie reden hören."

Kerner hatte seine Brieftasche aus der Jacke gezogen. „Ja, sehen Sie, ich hatte ja nur die Adresse hier",—er zeigte den anderen Paul Suhls Zettel, „da ist heute bestimmt nichts mehr mit zu machen. Und ₃₀ selbst wenn ich die Barbara finden könnte,—das Kind hat doch schon längst vergessen, daß ich einmal ihr Vater war. ,Das Kind' sage ich, dabei ist sie vierundzwanzig Jahre alt und ist wahrscheinlich verheiratet. Vielleicht bin ich sogar schon Großvater, ohne es zu

der Angriff, –e attack, raid

wachrufen to awaken

die Brieftasche, –n billfold
die Jacke, –n jacket
der Zettel, – slip of paper

dabei at that, actually

wissen." Der Gedanke schien seine gute Laune gestört zu haben. **die Laune** mood,
„Reden wir nicht mehr davon; das macht einen ja direkt melan- humor
cholisch."

„Darf ich Sie doch noch etwas fragen, Herr Kerner?" Der jüngere
Mann, der Kerner gegenüber an dem großen runden Tisch saß, hatte 5
sich gerade Pauls Zettel sehr intensiv angesehen. „Wissen Sie, was
das für eine komische Zahl ist hier unten?"

„Ach, diese Zahl", sagte Kerner. „Ich habe mir damals oft überlegt,
was das sein könnte; aber die steht wahrscheinlich nur aus Zufall da."

„Das glaube ich nicht. Ich habe doch jahrelang bei den Amerikanern 10
gearbeitet, und ich weiß, daß die Soldaten alle so eine lange Nummer
haben."

„Na ja, und?"

„Das könnte doch sehr gut die Nummer von dem Soldaten sein,
der die Adresse geschrieben hat,—ist doch die gleiche Handschrift. 15
Wissen Sie was, Herr Kerner, lassen Sie mich die Nummer ab- **abschreiben** to copy
schreiben. Ich habe einen Bekannten auf dem amerikanischen Konsulat, den werde ich fragen, ob man damit etwas machen kann."

„Von mir aus." Kerner zuckte die Achseln. „Da wird doch nichts **die Achseln zucken**
draus." 20 to shrug one's
shoulders
da wird nichts draus
Kerner sagte nichts mehr. Dann stand er abrupt auf: es sei spät und nothing will come of it
er müsse nach Hause, die anderen möchten ihn entschuldigen, aber
es ginge ihm schon den ganzen Tag nicht gut. Er bezahlte und ging.
Es ärgerte ihn, daß seine Bekannten ihm wieder Hoffnung gemacht **es ärgerte ihn** it made
hatten,—Hoffnung auf etwas, woran er seit Jahren kaum mehr ge- 25 him mad
dacht hatte. Aber noch mehr ärgerte er sich darüber, daß er überhaupt geredet hatte. Warum hatte er diesen Leuten seine Ge-
schichte erzählt, verdammt noch mal. Er hätte ja auch den Mund **verdammt noch mal**
halten können. dammit

Er beschloß, nicht mehr samstagabends nach Sachsenhausen zu 30
gehen.

Aber wenn der Herr Kerner nicht mehr an seinem Stammtisch erschien, so mußte eben der Stammtisch zu Herrn Kerner kommen.
Wochen später standen eines Abends Herr Müller und der Mann,
der die I.D. Nummer abgeschrieben hatte, aufgeregt vor Kerners 35
Tür. Neuigkeiten hatten die beiden, und Oswald Kerner war so
überrascht, daß er zunächst kein Wort herausbringen konnte. Danach kämpfte Kerner drei Tage lang mit sich selbst,—„Soll ich oder
soll ich nicht?"—und schließlich setzte er sich an einem Sonntag-
vormittag hin und schrieb einen Brief. 40

XII

Frankfurt, 21. April 1961

Sehr geehrter Herr Suhl!

Durch Zufall bin ich in den Besitz Ihrer Adresse gelangt und schreibe Ihnen in der Hoffnung, daß Sie mir vielleicht etwas über meine Tochter Barbara Kerner mitteilen können.

> **der Besitz** possession; **in den Besitz gelangen** to acquire

Meine Frau und meine Tochter waren kurz vor Ende des Krieges aus Breslau in den Thüringer Wald geflüchtet. Nach dem Tod 5 meiner Frau sollen amerikanische Soldaten, als die Russen nach Thüringen kamen, meine Tochter mit nach Frankfurt genommen haben.

> **flüchten** to flee

Als ich nach sieben Jahren russischer Gefangenschaft selbst nach Thüringen kam, war der einzige Hinweis auf das weitere Schicksal 10 meiner Tochter ein Zettel mit der Adresse eines Herrn Ernst Suhl in Frankfurt. Da der Pfarrer, in dessen Papieren der Zettel gefunden worden war, nicht mehr lebte, konnte ich nichts weiteres erfahren. Vor allem wurde mir nicht klar, daß die Zahl, die außer der Adresse noch auf dem Zettel stand, die I.D. Nummer eines amerikanischen 15 Soldaten war.

> **der Hinweis, –e** indication, clue, hint
> **das Schicksal** fate

Als es mir 1953 gelang, nach dem Westen zu kommen, mußte ich leider erfahren, daß meine Tochter von Herrn und Frau Suhl adoptiert worden war und mit ihren Adoptiveltern nach Amerika ausgewandert war. Aber es gelang mir nicht, die Adresse meiner 20 Tochter in den Staaten festzustellen. Seitdem lebe ich in Frankfurt, wo ich bei den Städtischen Bühnen als Bühnenarbeiter beschäftigt bin.

> **feststellen** to ascertain

Die Hoffnung, meine Tochter wiederzufinden, hatte ich längst aufgegeben, als ein Bekannter, dem ich den Zettel mit Herrn Ernst 25 Suhls Adresse zeigte, in der langen Zahl eine amerikanische Soldatennummer erkannte. Durch einen Herrn auf dem amerikanischen Generalkonsulat hat mein Bekannter dann Ihre Adresse in St. Louis finden können.

Ich habe lange gezögert, bevor ich mich endlich doch entschloß, 30 Ihnen zu schreiben. Für meine Tochter sind Herr und Frau Suhl seit vielen Jahren die „richtigen" Eltern, und ich dachte zuerst, daß ich Barbara bei dem Glauben lassen sollte, daß ihr Vater, den sie kaum gekannt hat, irgendwo im Osten umgekommen ist. Ich weiß nicht, was mich zwingt, Ihnen doch zu schreiben. Zweimal bin ich 35 enttäuscht worden, als ich Barbara schon handgreiflich vor mir sah; und so treibt es mich, einen dritten Versuch zu machen. Als ich

> **handgreiflich** within reach
> **treiben, trieb, getrieben** to drive

Barbara das letzte Mal sah, war sie acht Jahre alt; im kommenden
August wird sie fünfundzwanzig.

Verzeihen Sie einem alten Mann, daß er Sie belästigt. Vielleicht   **belästigen** to bother
wissen Sie gar nicht, was aus meiner Tochter geworden ist. Sollten
Sie aber doch etwas von ihr wissen, dann wäre ich Ihnen dankbar, 5
wenn Sie mich wissen lassen wollten, wo und wie sie lebt.

Ihr

Oswald Kerner

XIII

San Francisco, den 8. Mai 1961

Mein lieber Vater,

Wie seltsam das klingt,—„Mein lieber Vater". Aber du bist ja mein
Vater, und ich bin Deine Tochter, auch wenn ich seit vielen Jahren
geglaubt habe, Du wärst tot.

Verzeih mir, daß ich so anfange. Wie beginnt man einen solchen 10
Brief? Sollte ich schreiben, „Lieber Vater, ich habe mich sehr ge-
freut, endlich von Dir zu hören"? Nein, gefreut habe ich mich nicht.
—Aber das ist auch falsch. Natürlich habe ich mich gefreut. Aber als
Pauls Eltern uns Deinen Brief von St. Louis aus nachgeschickt
haben, konnte ich zuerst gar nicht begreifen, was geschehen war. 15
Dann habe ich geweint, bis Ernst (das ist mein Vater,—mein
Adoptivvater) sagte, „Aber Kindchen, jetzt hast du eben zwei Väter,
—und es gibt nicht viele Menschen, die das von sich behaupten
können."

Verstehst Du, wie schwer das alles für mich ist? Ich muß mich erst 20
daran gewöhnen, daß ich wirklich zwei Väter habe. Ich kann mich
ja kaum an Dich erinnern. Ich weiß noch, wie Du im Krieg einmal
auf Urlaub gekommen bist; ich saß in der Küche, als plötzlich die
Tür aufging und ein großer fremder Mann in Uniform hereinkam,
und ich hatte Angst vor Dir, und Mutti sagte immer wieder, Bär- 25
belchen, kennst du denn deinen Vater nicht mehr? Seltsam, daß mir
diese Szene in Erinnerung geblieben ist. Ich muß noch sehr klein
gewesen sein, vielleicht vier oder fünf.—Doch ich glaube, daß ich
mich an vieles werde erinnern können, nur brauche ich Zeit. Es ist
ja so viel passiert in den letzten fünfzehn Jahren.   30

Kurz nachdem Mutti gestorben ist, habe ich Paul kennengelernt. Er   **das Mitleid** pity,
hatte wohl Mitleid mit mir; er hat mir erzählt, daß ich ein ver-   sympathy
ängstigtes, scheues kleines Mädchen gewesen wäre, und daß die   **verängstigt** timid,
anderen Kinder nicht mit mir spielen wollten. Paul war damals   scared
                                                                     scheu shy

einundzwanzig und hat mich dann mit nach Frankfurt genommen,
zu seinem Vetter, obwohl er das eigentlich gar nicht hätte tun
dürfen. Paul und Ernst haben damals alles versucht, Dich zu finden,
aber Du warst und bliebst verschwunden, und als Irene und Ernst
nach Amerika auswandern wollten, haben sie mich adoptiert. Wir 5
haben dann lange in New York gewohnt. Paul habe ich erst sieben
Jahre später wiedergesehen, als ich schon auf dem College war, und
dann habe ich mich in ihn verliebt, und 1958 haben wir geheiratet.
Im September 1959 sind unsere Kinder geboren, Paul Jr. und Bar-
bara. Du bist also der Großvater von Zwillingen. Seit 1959 wohnen 10 **der Zwilling, –e** twin
wir hier in San Francisco, und seit einem halben Jahr wohnen Irene
und Ernst ganz hier in der Nähe.

Jetzt habe ich plötzlich das Gefühl, daß ich Dir noch Seiten und
Seiten schreiben könnte, aber das tue ich lieber das nächste Mal.
Dieser Brief soll jetzt schnell auf die Post. 15

Plötzlich habe ich auch tausend Fragen. Wo warst Du am Ende des
Krieges? Wie hast Du gewußt, daß ich in Thüringen war? Warum
hat man Dir auf dem Konsulat nicht gesagt, was die Nummer auf
dem Zettel bedeutete? Was hast Du in den zwei Jahren in Thüringen
gemacht? Hast Du wieder unterrichtet? Und warum bist Du in 20
Frankfurt nicht wieder Lehrer geworden? Weißt Du, daß wir auf **die Hochzeit, –en**
unserer Hochzeitsreise auch in Frankfurt waren, und wir waren auch wedding
zwei oder drei Mal im Theater. Wer weiß, vielleicht haben wir einander sogar gesehen.

Lieber Vater, sei mir nicht böse, daß ich so unzusammenhängend 25
schreibe. Ich bin immer noch verwirrt und kann nicht recht glauben, **verwirrt** confused
daß das alles wahr ist. Für Dich wird mein Brief sicher auch ein
Schock sein. Wir müssen uns eben langsam an den Gedanken gewöhnen, daß wir für einander nun wieder existieren. Ernst sagt
immer, Kinder, das wird sich schon finden; und ich weiß, daß er 30
recht hat.

Herzlich,

Deine Barbara

P.S. Ich lege ein Bild von den Kindern bei. Von Paul und mir habe
ich im Moment kein gutes.

XIV

San Franzisko, November 1962

Die Lufthansa-Maschine aus Frankfurt ist gerade angekommen. Die
Fluggäste drängen zum Ausgang; alle wollen so schnell wie möglich 35 **drängen** to push
durch den Zoll kommen. Die meisten werden draußen erwartet, von

ihren Eltern, oder ihren Kindern. Ein paar Geschäftsleute sind unter den Fluggästen, die von ihren Frauen abgeholt werden; andere haben in Deutschland Verwandte besucht; auch ein paar typische Touristen sind dabei.

die Geschäftsleute (*pl.*) businessmen; **der Geschäftsmann** (*sing.*)

Oswald Kerner wartet, bis alle anderen das Flugzeug verlassen 5 haben. Er hat Angst,—Angst vor dem neuen Land, Angst vor der fremden Sprache. Er fürchtet sich vor den Menschen, die da draußen auf ihn warten, er fürchtet sich vor allem vor der jungen Frau, die seine Tochter ist, und als er jetzt zum Zoll geht, merkt er auf einmal, daß ihm die Hände zittern. Ganz grau ist er geworden, und er denkt 10 wieder, wie so oft in diesen letzten Monaten, daß er hätte in Deutschland bleiben sollen, daß es ein Fehler gewesen war, den ersten Brief an Paul zu schreiben. War er denn nicht zufrieden gewesen mit seinem Leben? Warum hatte er sich in das Leben dieser Menschen drängen müssen, auch wenn einer dieser Menschen seine 15 eigene Tochter war?

Bei der Paßkontrolle sprach ein Beamter auf ihn ein, und er verstand kein Wort. Als sein Koffer kontrolliert wurde, dachte er, jetzt schicken sie dich bestimmt wieder zurück,—und plötzlich fiel ihm der Polizist ein, der damals im Zug seine Papiere kontrolliert hatte, 20 als er von Thüringen nach Berlin fuhr. Aber der amerikanische Beamte war sehr freundlich und mußte mehrere Male "OK, Sir" sagen, bevor Kerner begriff, daß er gehen konnte. Er war der letzte, und als er jetzt auf die Tür zuging, durch die die anderen Fluggäste verschwunden waren, überfiel ihn wieder die Angst. Langsam öff- 25 nete er die Tür. Der Korridor war leer, er sah ängstlich nach links und nach rechts und wußte nicht, in welche Richtung er gehen sollte.

einsprechen auf to talk (intensely) to

überfallen to over-come

Dann kamen plötzlich zwei junge Leute den Korridor herunter-gerannt, ein junger Mann und eine junge Frau. Kerner wußte sofort, das waren Barbara und Paul; aber als sie ihn begrüßten und auf ihn 30 einsprachen, konnte er kein Wort sagen. Er hielt sich an seiner Tasche und an seinem Koffer fest und wollte sich nicht helfen lassen. Dann ließ er es aber doch geschehen, daß sie ihm Tasche und Koffer abnahmen, daß sie ihn zwischen sich nahmen und langsam den Korridor hinunterführten. Dort unten, am Eingang zum Empfangs- 35 gebäude, standen Irene und Ernst mit den beiden Kindern.

Ein paar Minuten später,—die anderen Fluggäste waren längst in die Empfangshalle verschwunden,—kniete Oswald Kerner auf dem Boden, hatte in jedem Arm eines der beiden Kinder, blickte immer wieder von dem kleinen Mädchen zur Mutter und von der Mutter 40 zur Tochter und sagte „Barbara, Barbara." Er lächelte und schien

gar nicht mehr so alt und grau wie vor zehn Minuten. Dann stand
er auf, zog den Zettel aus seiner Brieftasche, gab ihn Paul und sagte:
„Hier, das ist es. Ohne dieses Stück Papier hätte ich euch nie
gefunden."

Wie oft läßt sich ein Körper teilen?

Die Frage, wie oft sich ein Körper teilen läßt, ist schon im Altertum 5
gestellt worden. Was geschieht zum Beispiel, so fragte man, wenn
man ein kleines Körnchen Salz mit immer feineren Messern in immer   **das Körnchen, –** little
kleinere Teile teilt? Auch das kleinste Teilchen wäre ja kein mathe- grain
matischer Punkt. Auch von dem kleinsten Teilchen müßte immer
noch ein gewisser, wenn auch sehr kleiner, Raum ausgefüllt werden; 10
und rein theoretisch müßte sich dieser Raum, und damit der Körper,   **rein** pure(ly)
von dem dieser Raum ausgefüllt ist, weiter teilen lassen.

Nach Demokrit kann ein Körper nicht unendlich oft geteilt werden.
Bei einem letzten Schnitt entstehen zwei Teile, die sich nicht weiter
teilen lassen. Diese kleinsten Teilchen nannte er Atome; und er 15
scheint gelehrt zu haben (seine Lehre ist uns nur durch die   **die Lehre, –n** teach-
Schriften seiner Gegner überliefert), daß es außer diesen Atomen   ing
nur blinde Kräfte, wie z.B. die Gravitation, gibt, aber keinen Geist, **der Gegner, –** oppo-
der „über" der Materie steht.   nent
                                                                      überliefern transmit
                                                                      die Kraft, –̈e force
Aristoteles ging von dem Gegensatz zwischen „Form" und „Stoff" 20   **der Geist, –er** spirit
aus. Nach dieser Lehre, von der auch das Denken des Mittelalters   **die Materie** matter
beherrscht war, ist der Unterschied zwischen dem Element Wasser   **der Stoff, –e** sub-
und dem Element Luft auf den Unterschied zwischen der „Form"   stance, matter
(oder Struktur) des Wassers und der „Form" (oder Struktur) der   **beherrschen** to rule
Luft zurückzuführen. Wird z.B. ein Tropfen Wasser immer weiter 25   **der Tropfen, –** drop
geteilt, so muß schließlich ein Augenblick kommen, wo die für das
Wasser charakteristische Struktur zerstört wird. Das letzte Teilchen
Wasser kann also zwar noch geteilt werden, aber das Resultat wären
nicht zwei noch kleinere Tröpfchen Wasser, sondern vielleicht zwei
Teilchen Luft oder Feuer, von denen jedes die für die Luft oder 30
für das Feuer charakteristische „Form" (oder Struktur) hätte. Nach
dieser Lehre kann die formlose oder strukturlose Materie, die
materia prima, nicht als solche existieren. Alle Körper enthalten   **enthalten** to contain
zwar *materia prima*, aber sie sind das, was sie sind (Luft, Feuer,
Erde, Wasser, Gold), nicht durch die in ihnen steckende Materie, 35   **steckend** existing,
sondern durch die für sie charakteristische Form.   contained

Bei den Versuchen der Alchimisten, Blei in Gold zu verwandeln,   **das Blei** lead
                                                                      verwandeln transform

war die Lehre von dem Gegensatz zwischen *materia prima* und *forma* stets vorausgesetzt. Wir wissen heute, daß die Alchimisten im letzten Grunde recht hatten. Die von ihnen vorausgesetzte Einheit alles Stofflichen ist heute sichergestellt, ja, sogar die Verwandlung eines Metalls in ein anderes, z.B. von Natrium in Magnesium, 5 ist bereits Tatsache geworden.

die vorausgesetzte Einheit the presupposed unity
sicherstellen to secure
das Natrium sodium
das Magnesium magnesium
die Tatsache, –n fact

Aber den Alchimisten fehlte die wissenschaftliche Methode, d.h. eine Methode, die Natur durch gut ausgedachte Experimente dazu zu zwingen, eine ihr gestellte Frage so zu beantworten, daß diese Antwort durch weitere Experimente geprüft und bestätigt werden 10 kann.

prüfen to test
bestätigen to confirm

Vor allem aber fehlte den Alchimisten die Geduld. Sie wollten das Gebäude der Wissenschaft sozusagen mit dem Dach anfangen. Es ist das große Verdienst Robert Boyles (1627–1691), seine Kollegen dazu gebracht zu haben, daß sie sich zunächst einmal mit dem Bau 15 des Fundamentes beschäftigten, d.h. mit der Frage, wieviele Elemente es denn eigentlich gibt. Wir können uns heute kaum noch vorstellen, wieviel Boyle von seiner Zeit verlangte, als er das Spekulieren über die *materia prima* beiseite schob und lehrte: In dem roten Mineral Zinnober stecken tatsächlich die beiden Stoffe Schwefel und 20 Quecksilber. Der Zinnober besteht aus ihnen, so wie etwa ein Haus aus Steinen und aus Holz besteht. Diese Behauptung schien paradox zu sein, denn von den Eigenschaften beider „Elemente" ist ja nichts mehr wahrzunehmen, sobald sie sich „verbunden" haben.

das Verdienst, –e merit
der Bau, –ten building, construction
das Fundament, –e foundation
das Spekulieren speculation
beiseite aside
der Zinnober cinnabar
der Schwefel sulphur
das Quecksilber mercury, quicksilver
die Eigenschaft, –en characteristic
wahrnehmen to observe, perceive, notice

Aber erst als man sich entschloß, dieses Paradox zunächst einmal— 25 obwohl noch ungelöst—zu vergessen, wurde es möglich, durch langsame Arbeit die 92 Elemente zu entdecken, aus denen die materielle Welt besteht. Als mit dieser Entdeckung das wissenschaftliche Fundament gelegt war, konnte die Frage gestellt werden, ob diese 92 Elemente vom Wasserstoff bis zum Uran sich vielleicht doch 30 noch weiter „teilen" lassen.

der Wasserstoff hydrogen

Die Suche nach dem Glück

Wir wollen hier nun endlich die Frage stellen, ob das Suchen nach dem Glück wirklich ein sinnvolles Suchen ist. Das Glück hängt ja nicht nur von materiellen Dingen ab, es hängt vor allem ab von der Empfänglichkeit des Menschen, davon, ob er fähig ist, glücklich 35 zu sein. Diese Glücksfähigkeit aber leidet unter dem Suchen nach Glück: Sie ist am größten, wenn ein geschenktes Gut nicht gesucht war; sie ist am geringsten, wenn dieses Gut leidenschaftlich gewünscht wurde. Das Wünschen selbst, so scheint es, zerstört den Glückswert des Gewünschten, und das Erreichen wird illusorisch, 40

die Empfänglichkeit, –en receptivity

am geringsten least
leidenschaftlich passionate(ly)
der Wert, –e value

weil das Erreichte für den Wünschenden nicht mehr dasselbe Glück ist, das er suchte und das er erwartete. Das wirkliche Glück kommt immer von einer anderen Seite als man es meint; es liegt immer da, wo man es nicht sucht. Es kommt immer als Geschenk und läßt sich dem Leben nicht abzwingen. Denn das Glück liegt in den Werten 5 des Lebens, die zwar immer da sind, die aber nur der findet, der diese Werte selbst sucht und nicht das Glück, das sie versprechen. Das Glück begleitet diese Werte, aber wer nur dem Glück nachläuft und nicht die Werte selbst sucht, dem bleibt das Glück für immer ein Phantom. 10

(nach Nicolai Hartmann, *Ethik*)

ANALYSIS

189 Other Reflexive Verbs of High Frequency

The reflexives introduced in Unit 12 all denote transition from one state to another. Not all reflexives can be classified as "transitional." The following four groups are found very frequently.

Verbs Denoting a Mental State with an Accusative Reflexive Pronoun

sich ärgern über	to be mad, annoyed, angry, peeved
sich erinnern an	to remember
sich freuen auf	to look forward to
sich freuen über	to be glad about
sich fürchten vor	to be afraid of
sich verlassen auf	to rely on
sich wundern über	to be amazed at (about)
sich bemühen um	to be trying hard
bemüht sein um	to be trying hard
sich beschäftigen mit	to occupy oneself with
beschäftigt sein mit	to be occupied with
sich langweilen	to be bored
gelangweilt sein	to be bored
sich interessieren *für*	to be interested in
interessiert sein *an*	to be interested in

Note that some of these verbs have a statal as well as a reflexive form. For all practical purposes, these two forms are synonymous, for all the verbs in this group are "durative verbs."

Durative verbs are verbs denoting action without a built-in end. While the action described by verbs like **sterben** or **ankommen** must by definition come to an end, that of verbs like **lieben** or **wohnen** can, at least theoretically, go on indefinitely. Verbs like **sterben** and **ankommen** are called perfective verbs.

The reflexives introduced in Unit 12 are all perfective. Thus the activity of **sich verlieben** (*falling in love*) cannot go on indefinitely, but must end in the state of **verliebt sein** (*being in love*). On the other hand, there is very little difference between **sich beschäftigen** (*to occupy oneself*) and **beschäftigt sein** (*to be occupied, to be busy*). The reflexive itself (**sich beschäftigen**) denotes a continuous action, and the state (**beschäftigt sein**) does not follow upon the completion of the action, but is simultaneous with it.

NOTE: **sich wundern über** cannot be used as the equivalent of English *to wonder:*

Beware!	[Ich wundere, wo er ist.]
Americanism!	
Correct:	**Ich möchte wissen, wo er ist.**
Correct:	**Darüber wundere ich mich gar nicht.**
	(I am not at all surprised at that.)

Verbs Denoting Physical Motion with an Accusative Reflexive Pronoun

sich bewegen	to move
sich eilen or sich beeilen	to hurry
sich verlaufen	to lose one's way (walking)
sich verfahren	to lose one's way (driving)
sich umdrehen	to turn around

Verbs with a Dative Reflexive Pronoun

A small number of German reflexives are used with a dative pronoun.

    sich etwas anschauen, sich etwas ansehen   to (take a) look at something
        Hast du dir den Film schon angesehen?

    sich etwas überlegen   to think (meditate) about something
        Willst du mit uns nach Italien fahren?
        Das muß ich mir überlegen.
        I must think about that.

    sich etwas denken (bei)   to think, to imagine, to have thoughts about
      something

Ich kann mir nicht denken, daß sie ihn heiraten will.
I can't imagine that she is going to marry him.

Was hast du dir denn dabei gedacht?
What in the world did you think you were doing (or saying)?

sich etwas einbilden to imagine something falsely

Das stimmt doch gar nicht; das bildest du dir nur ein.
That's not so at all; you're just imagining it.

Und er hat sich eingebildet, ich wollte ihn heiraten.
And he imagined that I was going to marry him.

NOTE: **eingebildet sein** means *to be conceited.*

sich etwas vorstellen to imagine, to form a mental picture of something

Ich kann mir nicht vorstellen, daß Ingelheim Lehrer geworden ist.
I can't imagine that Ingelheim has become a teacher.

Was sagst du? Heinrich ist ein Leh-aut-mann? Was ist denn das?
Darunter kann ich mir nichts vorstellen.
That doesn't mean a thing to me.
The word does not suggest a picture to me.

NOTE: **vorstellen** can also be used with the accusative; it then means *to introduce:*

Darf ich mich vorstellen? Ich bin Dr. Ingelheim.
Gnädige Frau, darf ich Ihnen Herrn Dr. Ingelheim vorstellen?
Darf ich vorstellen? Herr Dr. Ingelheim—Fräulein Wedemeyer.

To this group belong a number of verbs which call for a dative reflexive where English uses a possessive pronoun. A German would say: "She washed herself the hands" instead of "She washed her hands." Some of these verbs have already been used.

sich die Zähne putzen	to brush one's teeth
sich die Schuhe putzen	to polish one's shoes
sich die Haare färben	to dye one's hair
sich die Hände waschen	to wash one's hands
sich die Haare schneiden lassen	to have one's hair cut
sich den Arm brechen	to break one's arm
sich einen Bart wachsen lassen	to grow a beard
sich die Haare kämmen	to comb one's hair
sich die Nase putzen	to blow one's nose
sich den Mantel anziehen	to put on one's coat
sich den Hut aufsetzen	to put on one's hat

Impersonal Reflexive Verbs

Es zeigte sich, daß . . . It became apparent that . . .
Es stellte sich heraus, daß . . . It turned out that . . .
Es erwies sich, daß . . . It was proved that . . .

Es handelte sich um It was a matter of, we were dealing with
Es handelt sich um Geld. It is a matter of money.
Es handelt sich hier um eine wichtige Sache.
We are dealing here with an important problem.

But note:

Er handelt *mit* Bananen.
He sells bananas; he is in the banana business.
Sein neuer Roman handelt *von* den Kämpfen in der Normandie.
His new novel deals with the battles in Normandy.
Wir haben lange genug geredet. Jetzt müssen wir handeln.
We've talked long enough; now we must act.

190 Active Voice and Passive Voice

Compare these two groups of sentences:

We feed him once a day.   He is fed once a day.
We fed him once a day.   He was fed once a day.
We have always fed him once a day.   He has always been fed once a day.
We ought to feed him once a day.   He ought to be fed once a day.
We ought to have fed him once a day.   He ought to have been fed once a day.

The comparison shows that the forms of the transitive verb *to feed* (*a dog*)—that is, of a verb that can take a direct object—fall into two groups, called the "active voice" and the "passive voice":

	ACTIVE VOICE	PASSIVE VOICE
PRESENT	he feeds	he is fed
PAST	he fed	he was fed
PRESENT PERFECT	he has fed	he has been fed
PRESENT INFINITIVE	to feed	to be fed
PAST INFINITIVE	to have fed	to have been fed

It is easy to see why the terms "active" and "passive" were chosen to identify these forms. In sentences like *We feed our dog,* the grammatical subject acting upon the object is an "active agent," whereas in *Our dog is fed once a day,* the grammatical subject plays the role of a "passive patient" who "suffers" the agent's activity.

191 Action and State

The phrase *was fed* in the two sentences

The dog was fed well

and

The dog was well fed

refers to two fundamentally different situations; for *was fed well* expresses the repeated action of feeding the dog, whereas *was well fed* refers to the state resulting from this action. However, though the difference between state and action is expressed in this particular case by word order, English has not developed a system which forces the speaker to differentiate at all times between an action and the state resulting from this action. Thus the sentence

The house was built on a hill

can refer both to the action of building the house "from scratch" and to the accomplished fact that the house had been built and was sitting on a hill.

In contrast to English, German forces the speaker to select his passive-voice forms in such a way that they refer either to an action or to the state resulting from this action. An ambiguous form comparable to English *was built* simply does not exist. Actions are expressed by the "actional passive"—a form of **werden** plus a participle—and the resulting state is expressed by the "statal passive"—a form of **sein** plus a participle.

ACTION	STATE
Das Haus wird morgen verkauft.	
Das Haus ist gestern verkauft worden.	Das Haus ist schon verkauft.
Ich werde von der Direktion gezwungen, alle Arbeiter über fünfzig zu entlassen.	Ich bin gezwungen, alle Arbeiter über fünfzig zu entlassen.
I am being forced by the management to dismiss all workers over fifty.	I am forced to dismiss all workers over fifty.

The forms of the actional passive and those of the statal passive are never interchangeable. Occasionally the difference between the statal passive and the actional passive is quite dramatic. Thus the statal forms of **erschießen**, *to shoot and kill*, and of **erschlagen**, *to slay*, have developed a metaphorical meaning:

Ich bin erschossen, ich bin erschlagen.
I am shot, I am pooped, I am dead tired.

The actional forms

Ich bin erschossen worden.	I have been shot dead.
Ich bin erschlagen worden.	I have been slain.

could only be used at the Pearly Gates.

In the case of some verbs, the actional passive and the statal passive occur with equal frequency. Thus it makes linguistic sense to say *either*

Die Stadt war zerstört	The city was (already) destroyed (as the result of previous bombings)

or

Die Stadt wurde zerstört.	The city was destroyed (during the war by bombing).
Die Stadt ist zerstört worden.	

However, in cases like **Das Haus war nicht versichert,** *The house was not insured,* the speaker is usually more interested in the state; and therefore the actional passive

Das Haus wurde versichert	The house was (going through the act of being) insured

hardly ever occurs.

192   The Forms of the Statal and Actional Passive

	STATAL PASSIVE	ACTIONAL PASSIVE
PRESENT	ist enttäuscht	wird enttäuscht
PAST	war enttäuscht	wurde enttäuscht
PERFECT	ist enttäuscht gewesen	ist enttäuscht worden
FUTURE	wird enttäuscht sein	wird enttäuscht werden
INFINITIVE	enttäuscht sein	enttäuscht werden
	enttäuscht gewesen sein	enttäuscht worden sein

NOTE: The participle of **werden,** when used as an auxiliary, is **worden,** not **geworden.**

193   Choice between Active and Passive Voice

In order to describe the difference between *His father punished him* and *He was punished by his father,* it is sometimes stated that the direct object (*him*) of an active verb becomes the grammatical subject (*he*) of the passive verb. This is true. However, it is necessary to point out two things.

First, the German passive is used only if there is a situation in which an "active agent" somehow focuses his action or attention on an object. German is much more rigid in this respect than English. It is perfectly acceptable English to say

Ingelheim was killed in an accident,

although this statement does not mean that some "active agent" killed him. German, on the other hand, because there is no "active agent" involved, cannot use a passive and will use the intransitive verb **verunglücken,** *to die in an accident,* instead:

Ingelheim ist gestern verunglückt.

Second, if the sentence *My sister has adopted a child,* which does contain both an agent and a patient being acted upon, is transformed into the statement *A child was adopted by my sister,* this indicates a change in the speaker's focus of attention.

When I say *My sister adopted a child, my sister* is not only the grammatical subject, but also the focus of my attention. I am making a statement about my sister, not a statement about a child. Conversely, the attention of a nurse in a home for orphans is focused on the children under her care. She might, therefore, say, *Last week we got six babies; three have already been adopted. One was adopted by my sister.*

Nobody ever mentally forms an active sentence and then transforms it into a passive sentence. Such transformations are only classroom exercises. Nevertheless, the term "transformation" is not useless, as long as one realizes that one does not transform an active sentence into a passive sentence, but rather shifts the focus of attention from the "agent" to the "patient."

194   Dative Objects

The event reported by the English sentence *They gave him a pill* can also be reported by saying *He was given a pill*. The indirect object *him* of the active clause has been "transformed" into the grammatical subject *He* of the passive clause.

In German, no dative object can be transformed into a nominative subject. Not ever! **Nie!**

> *Americanism!*   [Ich wurde sofort geholfen.]
> CORRECT: **Der Arzt half mir sofort.**

However, to shift the focus from the doctor to myself, the active sentence **Der Arzt half mir sofort** can be changed into **Mir wurde sofort geholfen.** The result is a sentence without a subject; **wurde geholfen** is an impersonal form not depending on **mir.**

If the speaker wants to place this **mir** in the inner field, he cannot leave the front field empty; for that would change the statement into the question
> **Wurde mir sofort geholfen?**

The declarative force of **mir wurde sofort geholfen** can be maintained in such a case by putting the meaningless "filler" **es** into the front field:
> **Es wurde mir sofort geholfen.**

This **es** has only one function: it preserves verb-second position. It disappears as soon as the front field is occupied:
> **Natürlich wurde mir sofort geholfen.**

195   Use of the Actional Passive to Express Activity as Such

German verbs like **arbeiten, tanzen, schießen, warten** do not normally govern an accusative object and can therefore not be used to describe situations in which an agent acts upon a patient. One would not expect them, therefore, to appear in passive sentences. But they do!

The question *What is going on here?* is frequently answered in German by a form of the actional passive.

QUESTION   **Was ist denn hier los?**
ANSWER   **Hier wird gearbeitet.**
                 Hier wird getanzt.

Note that such short sentences do not contain a grammatical subject. The form **wird gearbeitet**, structurally not possible in English, denotes the activity of **arbeiten** as such. **Hier wird gearbeitet** means "The activity of working is going on here."

Further examples:

> **In meinem Elternhaus wurde viel musiziert.**
> **Bei uns wird auch sonntags gearbeitet.**
> **Seit heute morgen wird zurückgeschossen.**
> (Hitler, on September 1, 1939)

The use of this important actional passive is becoming more and more popular in German. You will find such sentences as **Der Kommandeur besichtigte sein Regiment, und dann wurde wieder gewartet, gefroren und geflucht** (Bergengruen). *The commanding officer inspected his regiment and then again there was waiting, shivering, and cursing (we waited, shivered, and cursed).*

196 The Use of **von, durch,** and **mit** in Passive Sentences

A large percentage of German passive sentences contain only the "passive patient" (the grammatical subject) and no active agent.

If a *personal* agent is mentioned, **von** is used:

> **Jerusalem wurde von den Römern zerstört.**
> Jerusalem was destroyed by the Romans.

Mit is used for the instrument "handled" by a personal agent:

> **Abel wurde von Kain mit einem Stein erschlagen.**
> Abel was slain by Cain with a rock.
> **Das ganze Zimmer war mit Blumen geschmückt.**
> The whole room was decorated with flowers.

Abstract causes, impersonal causes, and impersonal means of destruction are introduced by **durch:**

> **Sie wurden durch ein neues Gesetz gezwungen, das Land zu verlassen.**
> They were forced by a new law to leave the country.

Lissabon wurde durch ein Erdbeben zerstört.
Lisbon was destroyed by an earthquake.

Dresden wurde durch Bomben zerstört.
Dresden was destroyed by bombs.

197 Examples Illustrating the Difference between Action and State

The difference between action and state was introduced in **179** in connection with the reflexives. It was pointed out that **Fritzchen ist schon gebadet** denotes the state resulting from **Fritzchen hat sich gebadet.** We now have to point out that **ist gebadet** may also be the state resulting from the actional passive **Er ist gerade gebadet worden.** Of course, **Fritzchen ist schon gebadet** can also denote the state resulting from an active statement such as **Ich habe Fritzchen schon gebadet.**

	EVENT	STATE
ACTIVE VOICE	**Die Polizei hat ihn gerettet.** (Perfect)	
ACTIONAL PASSIVE	**Er ist gerettet worden.** (Perfect)	**Er ist gerettet.** (Present)
REFLEXIVE	**Er hat sich gerettet.** (Perfect)	
ACTIVE VOICE	**Sein Vater hatte ihn gut vorbereitet.** (Pluperfect)	
ACTIONAL PASSIVE	**Er war gut vorbereitet worden.** (Pluperfect)	**Er war gut vorbereitet.** (Past)
REFLEXIVE	**Er hatte sich gut vorbereitet.** (Pluperfect)	
ACTIVE VOICE	**Wir haben das Problem gelöst.** (Perfect)	
ACTIONAL PASSIVE	**Das Problem ist gelöst worden.** (Perfect)	**Das Problem ist gelöst.** (Present)
REFLEXIVE	**Das Problem hat sich gelöst.** (Perfect)	

198 sich . . . lassen

In **167** we introduced sentences like

Wir ließen ihn das Essen bezahlen.
We let him pay (for) the dinner.

Such sentences are structurally very similar to their English equivalents.

This similarity disappears if the subject of the infinitive (**ihn**) is left out:

Wir ließen das Essen bezahlen.
We had (somebody) pay for the dinner.
We arranged to have the dinner paid for.

The situation gets worse if, instead of the subject of the infinitive (**ihn**), there is a dative object of the infinitive:

Ich ließ mir das Essen bezahlen.
I had (somebody) pay for my dinner.
I let somebody else foot the bill for my dinner.

From an English point of view, the dependent infinitive may have a passive meaning. This is particularly true if the object is reflexive:

DATIVE REFLEXIVES

Ich lasse mir einen Mantel machen.
I'm having a coat made.
I cause somebody to make me a coat.

ACCUSATIVE REFLEXIVES

Warum läßt du dich nie mehr sehen?
Why don't you let yourself be seen any more?
Why don't we ever see you any more?

Das Problem ließ sich lange nicht lösen.
The problem couldn't be solved for a long time.

Wie oft läßt sich ein Körper teilen?
How often can a body be divided?

So schnell lasse ich mich nicht überzeugen.
I won't let myself be convinced that fast.

Note the following idiomatic use of **sich lassen**:

Der **Wein läßt sich trinken.**
This wine is worth drinking.

Das **Buch läßt sich lesen.**
This book is quite readable.

Das **läßt sich hören.**
That sounds interesting; that's a good suggestion.

199 The Impersonal **es** in the Front Field

Before discussing the impersonal **es** in the front field, it is necessary to recall that an **es** in the front field cannot be a normal accusative object. For if the **es** in the sentence

Ich weiß es nicht

is shifted into the front field, it becomes **das:**

> **Das weiß ich nicht.**

Compare English *I don't know it* and *That I don't know.*

The impersonal **es** in the front field has one of three functions: It can (a) be a meaningless "filler" to preserve verb-second position; it can (b) be the grammatical subject of impersonal verbs; and it can (c) be used to anticipate a following dependent clause.

The Use of **es** as a Filler

In a short sentence like

> **Niemand war zu Hause**

the inner field is empty. Both **war,** the first prong, and **zu Hause,** the second prong, are position-fixed. If the speaker, in order to put greater news value on **niemand,** decides to put **niemand** in the inner field, he must put something else in the front field; otherwise he would come up with the question

> **War niemand zu Hause?**

Verb-second position, in these cases, can be preserved by filling the front field with a meaningless **es:**

> **Es war niemand zu Hause.**
> **Es hat niemand angerufen.**

This use of **es** as a filler is rather frequent in connection with the passive voice:

> **Es werden wieder Häuser gebaut.**
> **Es wird wieder gearbeitet.**

In all these cases, **es** disappears when the front field is occupied by another unit:

> **Gestern war niemand zu Hause.**
> **Gestern hat niemand angerufen.**
> **Hier werden wieder Häuser gebaut.**
> **Hier wird wieder gearbeitet.**

NOTE:

1. The **es** used in identification sentences was discussed in **73.** This **es** is not a meaningless filler that disappears when the front field is filled; it can appear either in the front field or as the second prong.

> **Es war nicht mein Bruder.**
> **Mein Bruder war es nicht.**

In short sentences like **Ich bin's, du bist's, wir sind's,** etc., the **es** means "the thing to be identified." **Ich bin's** corresponds to *it's me,* which cannot be expressed by [**Es bin ich**] or [**Es ist ich**].

2. **Es** as a filler is also used in the standard introduction of German fairy tales and folksongs. **Es war einmal ein König** corresponds to *Once upon a time there was a king.* Since the entire news value is concentrated in **ein König,** the subject cannot stand in the front field.

> **Es war einmal eine alte Geiß.**
> **Es war ein König in Thule.**
> **Es waren zwei Königskinder.**
> **Es steht ein Baum im Odenwald.**

es as the Grammatical Subject of Impersonal Verbs

The verbs most frequently used with the impersonal subject **es** are:

> **Es regnet, es schneit, es donnert, es hagelt**
> **Es geht mir (ihm, ihr, etc.) gut**
> **Es geht mir (ihm) schlecht**
> **Es ist mir zu warm (zu kalt, zu heiß)**
> **Es ist zehn Uhr (schon spät, noch früh)**
> **Es gelingt mir**

In all these cases, the **es** must appear in the inner field if the front field is occupied by some other unit:

Es hat gestern geregnet.	**Gestern hat es geregnet.**
Es schneit schon wieder.	**Schneit es schon wieder?**
Es ist mir hier zu warm.	**Hier ist es mir zu warm.**
Es geht ihm leider nicht gut.	**Leider geht es ihm nicht gut?**
Es ist doch schon zehn!	**Was? Zehn Uhr ist es schon!**
Es ist mir gelungen.	*Mir* **ist es** *nicht* **gelungen.**

Also, the idiom **es gibt** belongs to this group of "impersonal verbs." **Es gibt,** translatable by either *there is* or *there are,* and roughly meaning "the situation provides," governs the accusative. In connection with a food term, it expresses what will be served. In other cases, it expresses that certain things exist as a permanent part of the environment or of nature.

> **Heute mittag gibt es Kartoffelsuppe.**
> **In Afrika gibt es noch immer wilde Elefanten.**
> **Gibt es hier ein Hotel?**

Unlike the English *there is,* **es gibt** can never be used to point at a specific thing or person:

| *Americanism!* | [Da oben gibt es ein Flugzeug.] |
| CORRECT: | **Da oben ist ein Flugzeug.** |

The Anticipating **es**

The use of **es** to anticipate a following dependent clause is comparable to the use of English *it* in

> I have *it* on good authority that Smith will be our next boss.
> *It* simply is not true that she has gone to college.

where the *it*, which cannot be left out, anticipates the following *that*-clause.

The German anticipatory **es** refers forward to a dependent (subject) clause, and **es** is the grammatical subject of the main clause.

> **Es ist möglich, daß Ingelheim noch lebt.**
> **Es ist nicht wahrscheinlich, daß Ingelheim noch lebt.**
> **Es ist nicht leicht, mit einer Frau wie Ilse verheiratet zu sein.**
> **Es tut ihm leid, daß ich gestern nicht kommen konnte.**
> **Es wird berichtet, daß Ingelheim spurlos verschwunden ist.**
> **Es freut mich, daß Sie kommen konnten.**

As long as this anticipatory **es** precedes the clause it anticipates, it does not disappear when the front field is occupied by some other unit:

> **Natürlich ist es auch möglich, daß Ingelheim noch lebt.**
> **Wahrscheinlich ist es allerdings nicht, daß Ingelheim noch lebt.**
> **Natürlich tut es mir leid, daß ich gestern nicht kommen konnte.**

Only the actional passive in such phrases as **Es wird berichtet, daß** . . . becomes **Gestern wurde berichtet, daß** . . .

If the dependent clause precedes the main clause, the anticipatory **es** disappears, because there is nothing left to anticipate.

> **Daß Ingelheim noch lebt, ist ganz unwahrscheinlich.**

200 **jetzt** and **nun**

Though both **jetzt** and **nun** are frequently equivalent to English *now*, they are not always interchangeable. **Jetzt** is an adverb of time without any implications.

> **Es ist jetzt zwölf Uhr fünfzehn.**
> **Meyer wohnt jetzt in München.**

Nun, on the other hand, always implies a reference to something which precedes; it therefore contains the idea that one state of affairs is superseded by another:

Und nun wohnt er in München.
(He used to live elsewhere.)

Und nun ist er schon drei Jahre tot.
(He used to be so full of life.)

Bist du nun zufrieden?
(I know you were dissatisfied before.)

Und nun hören Sie zum Abschluß unserer Sendung „Eine kleine Nacht-musik" von Wolfgang Amadeus Mozart.
And now we conclude our broadcast with Mozart's "Eine kleine Nacht-musik."

Because of the connotation "this is something new," **nun mal** (**nun ein-mal**) has the flavor "you might as well get used to it."

Das *ist* nun einmal so.
That's the way it is.

Ich *bin* nun mal nicht so intelligent wie du.
You might as well accept the fact that I'm not as intelligent as you are.

Na und? Ich bin nun mal kein Genie.
So what? I'm not a genius, and that's that.

201 Pre-Noun Inserts

Syntactical units like *a child* can be separated by adjectives, which are placed between the article and the noun. We shall call such inserted adjectives "pre-noun inserts." For the sake of clarity and illustration, pre-noun inserts are placed within parentheses in this section.

In English, one can speak of *a (healthy) child* or even of *a (healthy but somewhat retarded) child*. However, one cannot speak of

a (by a series of unfortunate childhood experiences somewhat retarded, but otherwise quite healthy) child.

English speakers don't have that long a syntactical breath. In German, pre-noun inserts of considerable length are a standard characteristic of expository prose and academic lectures:

Man sollte dieses (**durch eine Reihe von unglücklichen Kindheitserlebnissen leider etwas zurückgebliebene, aber sonst ganz gesunde**) *Mädchen nicht der Gefahr aussetzen, von* (**gleichaltrigen, nicht zurückgebliebenen**) *Kindern unfreundlich behandelt zu werden.*

One should not expose this girl, (who, though quite healthy, is unfortunately retarded by a number of unhappy childhood experiences,) *to the danger of being treated in an unfriendly way by children* (of the same age who are not retarded).

Both in English and in German, pre-noun adjective inserts can be viewed as "shorthand" versions of dependent clauses, usually relative clauses. Thus

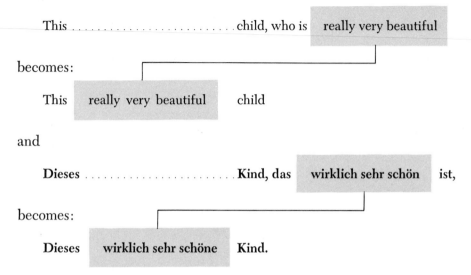

becomes:

and

becomes:

The example shows that

1. When a German dependent clause is transformed into a pre-noun insert, it drops its subject and the inflected verb belonging to it.

2. Since this transformation changes a predicate adjective or a participle into an attributive adjective, the adjective acquires an ending.

As far as German is concerned, pre-noun inserts, with the exception of (5) below, consist of an inner field plus a second prong. The usual word order is preserved. Pre-noun inserts can originate in the following ways:

1. The second prong is a predicate adjective:

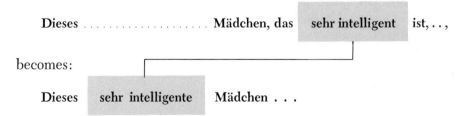

becomes:

2. The second prong is the participle of an intransitive verb like **ankommen, fallen, sterben,** or **zurückbleiben,** which forms its compound tenses with **sein:**

Dieses ············· Kind, das   leider etwas zurückgeblieben   ist,

becomes:

Dieses   leider etwas zurückgebliebene   Kind . . .

3. The second prong is the participle used to form the actional or statal passive:

Diese Stadt, die   während des letzten Krieges zerstört   wurde (Actional Passive)

becomes:

Diese   während des letzten Krieges zerstörte   Stadt . . .

Diese Stadt, die   noch nicht wiederaufgebaut   ist (Statal Passive)

becomes:

Diese   noch nicht wiederaufgebaute   Stadt . . .

Diese (während des letzten Krieges zerstörte) und (noch nicht wiederaufgebaute)
Stadt war einmal ein wichtiges Kulturzentrum.

4. The second prong is the participle belonging to a reflexive verb:

Der Gast, der sich   betrunken   hat (event)

The guest who got drunk

and

Der Gast, der   betrunken   ist (state)

The guest who is drunk

become:

Der   betrunkene   Gast

5. As long as it makes sense, any present and past form of the *active* voice may be changed into a **-d** adjective. This **-d** adjective, preceded by its inner field, can then be used as a pre-noun insert.

Das Kind, das   laut schrie

becomes:

Das   laut schreiende   Kind

Die allgemeine Frage, die (hinter diesem speziellen Problem steckt), . . .
The general question which stands behind this special problem . . .
   Die (hinter diesem Problem steckende) allgemeine Frage . . .

Die Bevölkerung Chinas, die (immer schneller wächst), . . .
The population of China, which is growing faster and faster . . .
   Die (immer schneller wachsende) Bevölkerung Chinas . . .

Der Weg, der (vom Dorf aus in den Wald) führt, . . .
The path which leads from the village to the forest . . .
   Der (vom Dorf aus in den Wald führende) Weg . . .

Die Konsequenzen, die (sich daraus ergeben), . . .
The consequences which result from this . . .
   Die (sich daraus ergebenden) Konsequenzen . . .

Die Studenten, die (in München wohnen), . . .
The students who live in Munich . . .
   Die (in München wohnenden) Studenten . . .

Die Studenten, die (ihr akademisches Recht verlangen), . . .
The students who demand their academic rights . . .
   Die (ihr akademisches Recht verlangenden) Studenten . . .

Auch dieses Buch, das (die Ergebnisse unserer Untersuchungen zusammenfaßt), wird in wenigen Jahren überholt sein.
This book, too, which summarizes the results of our investigations, will be outdated in a few years.
   Auch dieses (die Ergebnisse unserer Untersuchungen zusammenfassende) Buch wird in wenigen Jahren überholt sein .

EXERCISES

A. Express the following sentences in German. These sentences all contain reflexives introduced in Units 12 and 13. Do not use statal forms.

1. Are you still interested in her?
2. Think of yourself for a change.
3. I was really mad at him last night.
4. She fell in love with her teacher.
5. We have never been so bored.
6. I've bought myself a new coat.
7. They want to get a divorce.
8. May I introduce myself?
9. Just imagine: after twenty years he still remembered me.
10. I know she has nothing against you; you just imagine that.
11. I am looking forward to seeing her again.
12. We want to have a look at Meyer's new house.
13. I haven't changed yet, and I still have to shave.
14. Hurry up!
15. Don't get so excited.
16. Has she calmed down again?
17. I simply can't get used to his Russian accent.
18. Did you lose your way again? (Hiking) (Driving)
19. It turned out that Erich wasn't the thief at all.
20. We are dealing with people, gentlemen, and not with machines.

SEE LAB EXERCISE 13.1 (p. 635)

B. Change the following short sentences from the active voice to the actional passive. Do not change the tense. Omit the subject of the active sentence.

> **Man brachte ihn zurück.**
> **Er wurde zurückgebracht.**

1. Man führte uns durch den Garten.
2. Man trennte die Kinder von ihren Eltern.
3. Um acht Uhr schloß man das Tor.
4. Mich nimmt man nie mit.
5. Man suchte ihn, aber man fand ihn nicht.
6. Man schickte ihn nach Hause.
7. Man hielt ihn für einen Spion und erschoß ihn.
8. Man brachte uns im „Löwen" unter.
9. Man hat uns wieder im „Löwen" untergebracht.
10. Man hat ihn schon wieder gebeten, eine Rede zu halten.
11. Das Baden hat man hier leider verboten.

SEE LAB EXERCISES 13.2, 13.3 (p. 635)

12. Man hat ihn überall gehaßt.
13. Man hat ihn in London gesehen.
14. Man hatte uns gar nicht erwartet.
15. Hier kann man uns nicht beobachten.
16. Den Dieb hat man nie gefunden.
17. Nichts hatte man vergessen.
18. Man hat ihn gestern der Königin vorgestellt.
19. Man konnte ihn leider nicht erreichen.
20. Warum hat man ihn denn nicht eingeladen?
21. Man erwartet mich zum Frühstück.
22. Man soll ihn schon gestern erwartet haben.
23. Man soll ihn in London gesehen haben.
24. Man wird mich wohl an die Westfront schicken.
25. Man wird ihn wahrscheinlich nicht eingeladen haben.

C. In the following sentences, change the present actional passive forms into
   (a) Present statal passive forms and
   (b) Perfect actional passive forms.

> **Die Stadt wird zerstört.**
> **(a) Die Stadt ist zerstört.**
> **(b) Die Stadt ist zerstört worden.**

1. Die Brücke wird schon gebaut.
2. Die Schweine werden gefüttert.
3. Der Brief wird schon geschrieben.
4. Es wird beschlossen.
5. Es wird gefunden.
6. Die Tür wird geschlossen.
7. Die Erfahrungen werden gewonnen.
8. Hier soll das Baden verboten werden.
9. Das Problem muß bis morgen gelöst werden.
10. In diesem Buch sollen die Kämpfe in der Normandie beschrieben werden.

D. Change the following active sentences into actional passive sentences. Omit the subject of the
   active sentence.

> **Wir zeigen den Film jetzt auch in Deutschland.**
> **Der Film wird jetzt auch in Deutschland gezeigt.**

1. In den Vereinigten Staaten trinkt man mehr Bier als in Deutschland.
2. Mich lädt nie jemand ein.

3. In unserem Elternhaus haben wir viel musiziert.
4. Kolumbus hat Amerika 1492 entdeckt.
5. Sie konnten nur wenige retten.
6. Wann hat Ihr Vater denn dieses Haus gebaut?
7. Darüber haben wir jetzt genug geredet.
8. Von seinem ersten Roman sprach man damals überall.
9. Wir haben das noch nie versucht.
10. Man bewundert ihn immer noch.

E. In the following sentences, supply **von, mit,** or **durch.**

1. Die Stadt wurde _____ ein Erdbeben völlig zerstört.
2. Die Stadt wurde _____ einen Bombenangriff völlig zerstört.
3. Die Stadt wurde _____ den Russen zerstört.
4. Er ist _____ einem Stein erschlagen worden.
5. Er ist _____ seinem Bruder erschlagen worden.
6. Der Brief ist mir _____ meinem Vater nachgeschickt worden.
7. Er hat den Brief zwar unterschrieben, aber der Brief ist nicht _____ ihm selbst geschrieben worden.
8. Er hat alle seine Briefe _____ der Schreibmaschine geschrieben.
9. Ich wurde _____ meinem Chef nach Afrika geschickt.
10. Amerika ist _____ Kolumbus _____ Zufall entdeckt worden.

F. In the following sentences, supply either a form of **werden** or a form of **sein.**

1. Daß die Erde sich um die Sonne bewegt, _____ schon lange bewiesen.
2. Die Stadt _____ im Jahre 1944 zerstört.
3. Im Jahre 1950 _____ die Stadt noch nicht wieder aufgebaut.
4. Der weiße Mercedes _____ schon verkauft.
5. Das Haus neben der Kirche soll nächste Woche verkauft _____.
6. Der Film hat mir gar nicht gefallen. Ich _____ wirklich enttäuscht.
7. Das Haus soll schon verkauft _____.
8. Ich wußte gar nicht, daß du morgen auch bei Meyers eingeladen _____.
9. Frau Meyer hat etwas gegen meine Frau; von denen _____ wir bestimmt nie eingeladen.
10. Kommst du auch, Emma? Oder _____ du nicht eingeladen?

G. Change the following relative clauses into pre-noun inserts.

1. Der Zug, der soeben aus München angekommen ist, fährt in zehn Minuten weiter.
2. Für einen jungen Menschen, der in einem Dorf in den bayerischen Alpen großgeworden ist, ist es nicht leicht, sich an die Großstadt zu gewöhnen.
3. Hans ist jetzt Arzt, aber sein Bruder, der viel intelligenter ist, hat nie seinen Doktor gemacht.
4. Ingrids Vater war ein Architekt, der auch in Amerika bekannt war.

5. Die Städte, die während des Krieges zerstört wurden, sind heute fast alle wieder aufgebaut.
6. Die Douglas-Maschinen, die in Amerika gebaut werden, sieht man heute auf allen deutschen Flughäfen.
7. Der Juwelendieb, der seit Wochen von der Polizei gesucht wird, soll gestern in München gesehen worden sein.
8. Der Preis, der für diesen Rembrandt bezahlt worden ist, ist nach meiner Meinung viel zu hoch.
9. Seine Mutter, die noch immer in Berlin wohnte, hatte er seit Jahren nicht gesehen.
10. Er sah sie mit einem Blick an, der viel sagte.

VOCABULARY

abhängen von to depend upon
abnehmen to take away; to lose weight
  zunehmen to gain weight
eine Bombe abwerfen to drop a bomb
die Achse, –n axle; axis
das Altertum antiquity
sich ändern to change
sich etwas anschauen, sich etwas ansehen to look at something
auf (die Tür) zu toward (the door)
aufgeregt excited
die Auflage, –n printing
aufsetzen to put on (hat)
aufwärts up, upward
augenblicklich momentarily; instantly
begreifen to comprehend
sich bemühen um, bemüht sein um to be concerned about, with
berichten to report
beruhen auf to be based on
sich beschäftigen mit to occupy oneself with
  beschäftigt sein to be occupied, employed

die Beschäftigung, –en occupation
beurteilen to judge, to make a judgment
sich bewegen to move
  die Bewegung, –en movement; motion; exercise
blitzen to lighten, flash
  der Blitz, –e lightning
die Bombe, –n bomb
braten to roast, fry
  der Braten, – roast
  der Schweinebraten pork roast
  der Kalbsbraten veal roast
brennen to burn
sich etwas denken to imagine
  Was hast du dir denn dabei gedacht? What in the world did you think you were doing?
  Ich habe mir gar nichts dabei gedacht I didn't think a thing of it
donnern to thunder
  der Donner (*no pl.*) thunder
sich drehen um to turn (around something), to revolve; to concern, to be a matter of

sich umdrehen to turn around
sich eilen, sich beeilen to hurry
sich etwas einbilden to imagine something
  eingebildet sein to be conceited
einfallen to occur (to one's mind)
  es fällt mir ein I remember
das Element', –e element
entdecken to discover
entstehen to originate, come into being
enttäuschen to disappoint
erfinden to invent
erfreut sein to be pleased, glad
erinnern an to remind of
  sich erinnern an to remember
die Ernte, –n harvest
sich erweisen to turn out, show
erziehen to educate, raise
das Exemplar', –e copy (of a book, etc.)
die Fabrik', –en factory
färben to color; dye
das Filmfestspiel, –e film festival

eine Frage stellen to ask a question
  eine Frage beantworten to answer a question
sich freuen auf to look forward to
sich freuen über to be happy (glad) about
funktionieren to function, work
das Gas, –e gas
geboren werden to be born
der Gegensatz, ¨e contrast
gegenüber (*with dative*) opposite
gelingen to succeed
  es gelingt mir I succeed
gewöhnlich usual
der Grund, ¨e reason, ground
  aufgrund (*prep. with gen.*) on the basis of
hageln to hail
handeln to act
  sich handeln um to be a matter of
  handeln mit to deal with (objects)
  handeln von to deal with (subject matter)
sich herausstellen to turn out, to become apparent
der Herd, –e stove
hinten (*adverb*) in the back
höflich polite
das Holz, ¨er wood
Indien India
  der Inder, – (East) Indian
  der Indianer, – (American) Indian
sich interessieren für, interessiert sein an to be interested in

der Irrtum, ¨er error
das Jahrhundert, –e century
jedenfalls at any rate
kämmen to comb
die Kartoffel, –n potato
klingen to sound
der Körper, – body
langweilen to bore
  sich langweilen, gelangweilt sein to be bored
  langweilig boring
leer empty
leiden to suffer
das Lied, –er song
loben to praise
los loose
  was ist los? what's the matter? what's going on?
lösen to solve, dissolve
die Mate′rie matter
sich melden to report (to somebody); to answer (the phone)
das Messer, – knife
mitteilen to report (something)
das Mittelalter Middle Ages
musizieren to make music
die Neuigkeit, –en news
das Pulver, – powder; gunpowder
putzen to clean
der Raum, ¨e room; space
mit Recht rightfully
reisen to travel
reparieren to repair
die Richtung, –en direction
rund round
das Salz, –e salt
schießen to shoot
sinken to sink
der Sinn, –e sense

soeben just, just now
die Sprache, –n language
stimmen to be correct
  das stimmt nicht that's wrong
die Suche, –n search
der Tanz, ¨e dance
überfüllt overflowing
umkommen to perish
sich verbinden to unite, compound
die Vereinigten Staaten the United States
sich verfahren to lose one's way (driving)
der Verlag, –e publishing house, publisher
sich verlassen auf to depend or rely upon
sich verlaufen to lose one's way (walking)
die Verwandlung, –en change, metamorphosis
das Visum, die Visen visa
vorbeigehen to pass
sich vorstellen (*dat*) to imagine
  sich vorstellen (*acc.*) to introduce (oneself)
Weihnachten Christmas
wiederaufbauen to reconstruct
die Wissenschaft, –en science
  wissenschaftlich scientific
sich wundern über to be amazed at
der Zahn, ¨e tooth
sich zeigen (*impersonal*) to turn out, show
zögern to hesitate
sich zusammensetzen aus to be composed of

IRREGULAR VERBS

begreifen to comprehend
  begriff, hat begriffen, er
    begreift
braten to roast, fry
  briet, hat gebraten, er brät
brennen to burn
  brannte, hat gebrannt, er
    brennt
entstehen to originate
  entstand, ist entstanden, er
    entsteht
erfinden to invent
  erfand, hat erfunden, er er-
    findet

sich erweisen to turn out,
  show
  erwies sich, hat sich er-
    wiesen, es erweist sich
erziehen to educate, to raise
  erzog, hat erzogen, er er-
    zieht
gelingen to succeed
  es gelang, es ist mir ge-
    lungen, es gelingt
klingen to sound
  klang, hat geklungen, es
    klingt
leiden to suffer
  litt, hat gelitten, er leidet

schießen to shoot
  schoß, hat geschossen, er
    schießt
sinken to sink
  sank, ist gesunken, er sinkt
sich verbinden to unite, compound
  verband sich, hat sich ver-
    bunden, er verbindet
    sich
sich verlassen auf to depend
  (rely) upon
  verließ sich auf, hat sich
    verlassen auf, er verläßt
    sich auf

LABORATORY EXERCISES

GRAMMATICAL TABLES

PRINCIPAL PARTS OF STRONG AND IRREGULAR VERBS

VOCABULARY: German-English; English-German

INDEX

LABORATORY EXERCISES

The Lab Exercises are an integral part of each lesson. Their use is not restricted to the language laboratory; your instructor may use these exercises for additional drill in class. Only the instructions and one or two examples will be printed for each lab exercise. In addition to exercises in which you will be asked to do something with the sentences you hear, there will be exercises that require you simply to "listen and repeat." In these "listen-and-repeat" exercises you will hear the pattern sentences of each lesson. As it is very important that you learn to comprehend spoken German, you should listen to and repeat these sentences as often as possible, first with your book open and then with your book closed. Imitate carefully the pronunciation and intonation of the speakers. You should be aware of each sentence as a unit of sound and meaning, but at the same time, as you hear each sentence, we want you to understand it as an organized linguistic structure. The following English examples show what we have in mind. If you hear

or
> She's kind of nice
> He should have come

and you write these sentences down as

and
> She's kinda nice
> He should of come

you prove that you have understood the total meaning of these two sentences, but have not comprehended them linguistically. While, in *He should of come,* the verb *have* is actually pronounced very much like *of,* you certainly would not write *I'd like to of something to eat.* Unless you achieve structural understanding even of the short sentences presented in the first lessons, you will never learn how to participate in a conversation and you certainly will never learn to understand a lecture or a radio broadcast in German, while "it is coming at you."

Classroom time is not sufficient to achieve listening comprehension. Since you don't have as much time as German children to acquire this skill, we urge you to listen faithfully to all tapes, whether they are "listen-and-repeat" exercises or active exercises.

In Unit 1, the Patterns will be spoken very carefully and rather slowly, but as time goes on, you will hear them at the natural speed of a native speaker.

LAB EXERCISES—UNIT 1

1.1 Listen and repeat (Patterns, groups 1–4). After each sentence there will be a pause for you to repeat the sentence. You will then hear the sentence again.

1.2 Listen and repeat (Patterns, groups 5–6).

1.3 Dictation.

1.4 Listen and repeat (Patterns, groups 7–8).

1.5 Now you will hear a verb form preceded by a subject—for instance, **ich bin.** You will then hear a new subject—for instance, **er.** In the pause, provide the correct verb form for the new subject. You will then hear the new form—for instance, **er ist.**

> You hear: **ich bin; wir**
> You say: **wir sind**

1.6 Dictation.

1.7 In the first pause after each of the following sentences, repeat the sentence you have just heard. You will then hear the sentence again. In the second pause, switch word order by starting your own sentence with the last unit of the sentence you hear. You will then hear the sentence with the new word order.

> You hear: **Wir arbeiten heute.**
> You say: **Wir arbeiten heute.**
> You hear again: **Wir arbeiten heute.**
> You say: **Heute arbeiten wir.**
> You hear: **Heute arbeiten wir.**

1.8 You will now hear yes-or-no questions. In the pauses, give *affirmative* answers. After the pause, you will hear the answers that were expected of you. In the answers, substitute pronouns for personal names.

> You hear: **Ist Herr Lenz in Köln?**
> You say: **Ja, er ist in Köln.**

1.9 Now we want to find out whether you can form that yes-or-no question to which the statement you hear is the answer. For instance, the statement **Ja, er hat Geld** is the answer to the question **Hat er Geld?**, and it is this question which you are to form.

> You hear: **Ja, er hat Geld.**
> You say: **Hat er Geld?**
> You then hear: **Hat er Geld?—Ja, er hat Geld.**

1.10 You will hear short assertions. Change each assertion to a question by changing intonation. Do not change word order.

> You hear: **Meyer ist intelligent.**
> You say: **Meyer ist intelligent?**

1.11 Listen and repeat (Conversation). You will hear the various groups of sentences in the Conversation section of Unit 1. At first, the whole section will be spoken in its entirety, but rather slowly. Thereafter, each sentence will be spoken separately. Repeat each sentence. You will then hear the whole section again, but at normal speed.

LAB EXERCISES—UNIT 2

2.1 Since it is very important for you to be able to use the German pronouns automatically and without having to think about them, you will hear all the pattern sentences of group 1. After hearing the first half of the sentence, repeat that first half and then complete it. Do not consult the text. You will then hear the complete pattern.

> You hear: **Du brauchst mich.**
> You say: **Du brauchst mich, und ich brauche dich.**

2.2 Listen and repeat (Patterns, groups 2–3).

2.3 Listen and repeat (Patterns, groups 4–6).

2.4 Dictation.

2.5 Listen and repeat (Patterns, group 7).

2.6 The sentences you will now hear all contain a compound verb and therefore, at the end of the sentence, a second prong. After hearing the sentence, repeat it by exchanging the unit in the front field with the first unit in the inner field. You will then hear the sentence as you were expected to say it.

> You hear: **Jetzt mache ich das Licht an.**
> You say: **Ich mache jetzt das Licht an.**

2.7 This exercise follows the same pattern as Lab Exercise **2.1**. We want to make sure that you can use the pronouns automatically.

> You hear: **Ich** brauche <u>dich</u>.
> You say: **Ich** brauche <u>dich</u>, und du brauchst <u>mich</u>.

2.8 Dictation.

2.9 You will now hear the Conversation section. At first it will be spoken in its entirety, but rather slowly. Thereafter, each sentence will be spoken separately and slowly. Repeat each sentence during the pause that follows. You will then hear each sentence again, this time at normal speed. Repeat again in the pause that follows. Finally, you will hear the entire conversation at normal speed.

2.10 On this tape you will hear the Reading section.

LAB EXERCISES—UNIT 3

3.1 Listen and repeat (Patterns, groups 1–5).

3.2 Listen and repeat (Patterns, group 6).

3.3 You will now hear questions. Starting with **nein,** give a negative answer to each question. In your answer put the main syntactical stress on the first prong.

> You hear: **Hast du einen <u>Hund</u>?**
> You say: **Nein, ich <u>habe</u> keinen Hund.**

3.4 You will now hear affirmative sentences. Negate these sentences by using **nicht** without shifting the position of any of the syntactical units. Put the main syntactical stress on **nicht.**

> You hear: **Erikas Vater ist ge<u>sund</u>.**
> You say: **Erikas Vater ist <u>nicht</u> gesund.**

3.5 Listen and repeat (Patterns, group 7).

3.6 Listen and repeat (Patterns, group 8).

3.7 Listen and repeat (Patterns, groups 9–14).

3.8 You will again hear affirmative sentences. Negate them by using either **kein** or **nicht.**

> You hear: **Er scheint Geld zu haben.**
> You say: **Er scheint kein Geld zu haben.**
>
> or
>
> You hear: **Er scheint gesund zu sein.**
> You say: **Er scheint nicht gesund zu sein.**

3.9 Listen and repeat (Patterns, groups 15–17).

3.10 You will hear affirmative sentences with only one strongly stressed syllable. By shifting this strongly stressed syllable into the front field and using a stressed **nicht** for negation, pronounce these sentences with contrast intonation.

> You hear: **Sie hat <u>Geld</u>.**
> You say: **<u>Geld</u> hat sie <u>nicht</u>.**

3.11 You will now hear negative statements with contrast intonation. In each case the subject follows the inflected verb. Repeat the negative statement, but start your sentence with the subject.

> You hear: **Ein <u>Dummkopf</u> ist Meyer <u>nicht</u>.**
> You say: **Meyer ist kein <u>Dummkopf</u>.**

3.12 Listen and repeat (Patterns, group 18).

3.13 Listen and repeat (rapid reading).

3.14 Listen and repeat (Conversations I and II).

3.15 Listen (Reading).
You will hear the Reading section twice. The first time, listen with your book open; the second time, keep your book closed.

3.16 Dictation.

LAB EXERCISES—UNIT 4

4.1 You will hear the first group of the Patterns. After the first half of each sentence, there will be a pause for you to supply the second half. You will then hear the correct entire sentence.

> You hear: **Heute helfe ich dir,**
> You say: **und morgen hilfst du mir.**
> You hear: **Heute helfe ich dir, und morgen hilfst du mir.**

4.2 Listen and repeat (Patterns, groups 2–4).

4.3 Listen and repeat (Patterns, groups 5–6).

4.4 Restate the following assertions and questions by using the verb **gehören**.

> You hear: **Das ist dein Wagen.**
> You say: **Er gehört dir.**

4.5 Listen and repeat (Patterns, group 8).

4.6 Listen and repeat (Patterns, groups 10–11).

4.7 Listen and repeat (Patterns, groups 12–13).

4.8 You will hear short sentences in the present tense. Repeat these sentences in the present tense. Then you will hear the same sentences once more; repeat them again, but this time in the perfect tense.

> You hear: **Ich lese.**
> You say: **Ich lese.**
> You hear: **Ich lese.**
> You say: **Ich habe gelesen.**

4.9 Listen and repeat (Patterns, group 14).

4.10 Each of the following German sentences will be read three times. Printed below are pairs of English sentences. After hearing a German sentence, mark by a check that English sentence in each pair which, in your opinion, corresponds most closely in meaning to the German sentence you heard.

> You hear: **Wir haben hier lange kein Fleisch kaufen können.**
> You check one sentence of this pair:
> a. Yes, we can again buy meat here.
> b. We still can buy no meat here.

1a. He went to the States for one year.
1b. He left for the States a year ago.

2a. Fritz is now able to work again.

2b. For quite some time now, Fritz has not been able to work.

3a. Fritz has been an invalid for years.

3b. For a number of years, Fritz was unable to work.

4a. Two years ago, Fritz was no longer living in Berlin.

4b. During these last two years, Fritz has not once been in Berlin.

5a. Erika was married for six years.

5b. Erika married six years ago.

6a. Three years ago, I was told to stop eating meat.

6b. Thank goodness, I can eat meat again! For three years, I was not allowed to eat any meat.

7a. Erika was a good girl. She never smoked.

7b. Erika is a good girl. Up to now, she has never smoked.

8a. I now believe in God.

8b. I have been an atheist for a long time.

9a. I have been an atheist for a long time.

9b. For a long time I did not believe in God.

10a. I no longer hope that my husband will return.

10b. I still hope my husband will return some day.

4.11 Dictation.

4.12 Listen and repeat (Conversation and Reading).

LAB EXERCISES—UNIT 5

5.1 Listen and repeat (Patterns, group 2). After hearing and repeating each sentence, you will hear, in German, the new subject indicated in your text. Repeat the sentence again, but this time with the new subject.

> You hear: **Leider glaubte sie mir nicht.**
> You say: **Leider glaubte sie mir nicht.**
>
> You hear: **du**
> You say: **Leider glaubtest du mir nicht.**

5.2 Listen and repeat (Patterns, groups 3–5).

5.3 The next sentences you will hear are in the present tense. Change these sentences to the perfect tense.

> You hear: **Hans arbeitet heute in Bonn.**
> You say: **Hans hat heute in Bonn gearbeitet.**

5.4 You will again hear sentences in the present tense. This time change to the past tense and add **damals**.

> You hear: **Es regnet sehr oft.**
> You say: **Es regnete damals sehr oft.**

5.5 Listen and repeat (Patterns, group 6). After hearing and repeating each sentence, you will hear, in German, the new subject indicated in your text. Repeat the sentence again with the new subject.

> You hear: **Er fuhr jeden Morgen um sieben Uhr ab.**
> You say: **Er fuhr jeden Morgen um sieben Uhr ab.**
> You hear: **Wir**
> You say: **Wir fuhren jeden Morgen um sieben Uhr ab.**

5.6 Listen and repeat (Patterns, group 7).

5.7 You will again hear sentences in the present tense. Change to the past tense and add **damals.**

> You hear: **Sie bleiben zu Hause.**
> You say: **Sie blieben damals zu Hause.**

5.8 Listen and repeat (Patterns, groups 8–9).

5.9 Repeat the following statements by starting them with **Ich weiß, daß** . . .

> You hear: **Er bleibt heute abend zu Hause.**
> You say: **Ich weiß, daß er heute abend zu Hause bleibt.**

5.10 Listen and repeat (Patterns, group 10).

5.11 You will hear pairs of short sentences. Combine these pairs into open conditions, always beginning with **wenn.**

> You hear: **Er kommt. Er ist um vier Uhr hier.**
> You say: **Wenn er kommt, ist er um vier Uhr hier.**

5.12 You will hear short sentences like **Ich gehe ins Kino.** Transform these into open conditions by inserting **nur** before the second prong—**Ich gehe nur ins Kino**—and adding **wenn du auch ins Kino gehst.**

> You hear: **Ich fahre nach Köln.**
> You say: **Ich fahre nur nach Köln, wenn du auch nach Köln fährst.**

5.13 Listen and repeat (rapid reading practice: Patterns, group 12).

5.14 Conversation I and II; Reading.

LAB EXERCISES—UNIT 6

6.1 Listen and repeat (Patterns, group 1).

6.2 Change the following sentences to the future tense. Leave out the time expressions.

> You hear: **Ich fahre morgen nach Berlin.**
> You say: **Ich werde nach Berlin fahren.**

6.3 Listen and repeat (Patterns, groups 2–4).

6.4 You will hear short sentences in the indicative. Restate these sentences as wishes, starting with **Ich wollte.** Use only the present subjunctive.

> You hear: **Er ist hier.**
> You say: **Ich wollte, er wäre hier.**

6.5 You will hear wishes contrary to fact in the present time. Repeat the sentences and add a statement about the actual facts in the present indicative, starting with **aber**. Change affirmative to negative, and negative to affirmative statements.

> You hear: **Ich wollte, du wärst hier.**
> You say: **Ich wollte, du wärst hier, aber du <u>bist</u> nicht hier.**

6.6 Listen and repeat (Patterns, groups 5–7).

6.7 You will hear short sentences in the indicative. Change these sentences to *if*-clauses in the subjunctive and add **nur** wherever appropriate. Change negative statements to affirmative statements and vice versa.

> You hear: **Er ist nicht hier.**
> You say: **Wenn er nur hier wäre.**

6.8 You will hear pairs of sentences. Combine these pairs into irreal conditions. Use **würde**-forms when appropriate.

> You hear: **Hans ist nicht hier. Wir können nicht ins Kino gehen.**
> You say: **Wenn Hans hier wäre, könnten wir ins Kino gehen.**

6.9 You will hear sentences with double infinitives. Restate these sentences in the past tense.

> You hear: **Er hat zu Hause bleiben müssen.**
> You say: **Er musste zu Hause bleiben.**

6.10 The sentences you will hear all contain a modal in the present or past tense. Change these sentences to the perfect.

> You hear: **Er muss zu Hause bleiben.**
> You say: **Er hat zu Hause bleiben müssen.**

6.11 Listen and repeat (Patterns, groups 8–10).

6.12 Listen and repeat (Patterns, groups 11–12).

6.13 You will hear statements in indirect discourse. Change these to direct discourse in the present indicative.

> You hear: **Er sagte, daß er hier wäre.**
> You say: **Ich bin hier.**

6.14 Listen and repeat (Patterns, groups 13–15).

6.15 Change the following statements to indirect discourse, starting with **Er sagte, ...** You will then hear all the sentences again. Change them again to indirect discourse, but this time starting with **Er sagte, daß . . .**

> You hear: **Ich komme nicht.**
> You say: **Er sagte, er käme nicht.**
> You hear: **Ich komme nicht.**
> You say: **Er sagte, dass er nicht käme.**

6.16 You will hear statements in indirect discourse in past time. Change these to direct discourse in either the past or the perfect.

        You hear: **Er sagte, er wäre erst gestern gekommen.**
        You say: **Ich bin erst gestern gekommen.**

6.17 Conversation and Reading.

LAB EXERCISES—UNIT 7

7.1 Listen and repeat (Patterns, group 1).

7.2 Dictation.

7.3 You will hear sentences containing an adverbial phrase of place. Formulate questions asking for these locations, using either **wo** or **wohin.**

        You hear: **Er wohnt seit Jahren an der Riviera.**
        You ask: **Wo wohnt er?**
        Then you hear: **Wo wohnt er?—An der Riviera.**

or

        You hear: **Mein Hund läuft immer unter den Tisch.**
        You ask: **Wo läuft er hin? or: Wohin läuft er?**
        Then you hear: **Wo läuft er hin?—Unter den Tisch.**

7.4 You will hear sentences with an adverbial phrase of place, followed by a **wo** question. Answer this question; be sure to change the adverbial phrase from accusative to dative.

        You hear: **Sie ist ins Haus gegangen.—Wo ist sie jetzt?**
        You say: **Sie ist im Haus.**
        Then you hear: **Sie ist im Haus.**

7.5 Dictation.

7.6 Complete the problems.

        You hear: **Sechs und acht**
        You say: **Sechs und acht ist vierzehn.**

7.7 Listen and repeat (Patterns, groups 2–5).

7.8 You will hear sentences with **gehören.** Change each sentence in one of the three ways indicated in the examples.

        You hear: **Das Buch gehört meinem Vater.**
        You say: **Das ist das Buch meines Vaters.**

or

        You hear: **Das Buch gehört Karl.**
        You say: **Das ist Karls Buch.**

or

        You hear: **Das Buch gehört ihm.**
        You say: **Das ist sein Buch.**

7.9 Listen and repeat (Patterns, group 6).

7.10 You will hear sentences containing **ein**-words followed by a noun. Restate the sentences, leaving out these nouns.

        You hear: **Wir haben schon ein Auto.**
        You say: **Wir haben schon eins.**

7.11 Listen and repeat (Patterns, group 7).

7.12 Conversation.

7.13 Reading.

LAB EXERCISES—UNIT 8

8.1 Listen and repeat (Patterns, groups 1 and 2).

8.2 Listen and repeat (Patterns, group 3).

8.3 You will hear ten questions starting with **wann**. Change to indirect questions introduced by **Ich weiss nicht, ...**

> You hear: Wann hat Inge ihren Mann denn abgeholt?
> You say: Ich weiss nicht, wann Inge ihren Mann abgeholt hat.

8.4 Listen and repeat (Patterns, group 4).

8.5 You will hear yes-or-no questions. Change to indirect questions introduced by **Ich möchte wissen, ob . . . .**

> You hear: War sie denn schon im Haus?
> You say: Ich möchte wissen, ob sie schon im Haus war.

8.6 Listen and repeat (Patterns, group 5).

8.7 You will hear pairs of sentences. Restate these, using the second one as the introductory statement to an **als ob** clause. Note that some sentences will have to start with **er tut**, and others with **er tat**.

> You hear: Er schläft nicht; er tut nur so.
> You say: Er tut, als ob er schliefe.

8.8 Listen and repeat (Patterns, groups 6 and 7).

8.9 You will hear pairs of sentences. Change the first sentence of each pair to a dependent clause starting with **als**.

> You hear: Ingelheim kam ins Hotel. Ein Brief wartete auf ihn.
> You say: Als Ingelheim ins Hotel kam, wartete ein Brief auf ihn.

8.10 Listen and repeat (Patterns, group 8).

8.11 You will hear pairs of sentences. Change these either to open conditions or to irreal conditions.

> You hear: Vielleicht regnet es morgen. Dann bleiben wir zu Hause.
> You say: Wenn es morgen regnet, bleiben wir zu Hause.
>
> or
>
> You hear: Ich habe leider kein Geld; sonst könnte ich mir einen Mantel kaufen.
> You say: Wenn ich Geld hätte, könnte ich mir einen Mantel kaufen.

8.12 You will hear pairs of sentences. Restate these by starting with **Jedesmal**.

> You hear: Tante Amalie kam oft zu uns, und ich mußte jedesmal mit ihr ins Museum gehen.
> You say: Jedesmal, wenn Tante Amalie zu uns kam, mußte ich mit ihr ins Museum gehen.

8.13 Dictation.

8.14 Listen and repeat (Patterns, group 9).

8.15 Negate the sentences you next hear by using **gar nicht, gar kein,** or **gar nichts.**

> You hear: **Ich habe gestern gut geschlafen.**
> You say: **Ich habe gestern gar nicht gut geschlafen.**

8.16 Listen and repeat (Patterns, groups 10 and 11).

8.17 You will hear sentences containing a prepositional phrase. Restate these sentences by substituting a **da**-compound for the prepositional phrase.

> You hear: **Er hat viel Geld für das Haus bezahlt.**
> You say: **Er hat viel Geld dafür bezahlt.**

8.18 Listen and repeat (Patterns, group 12).

8.19 Listen and repeat (Patterns, groups 13 and 14).

8.20 This exercise is designed to help you realize that the question **auf wen?** elicits an answer concerning a person, whereas the question **worauf?** calls for an answer about a thing.

> You hear: **Ich warte schon seit drei Stunden.**
> You ask: **Auf wen denn?**
> You hear: **Auf wen denn? Auf Heidi.**
> Then you ask: **Worauf denn?**
> And you hear: **Worauf denn? Auf die Post.**

8.21 You will hear sentences containing prepositional objects. Restate these sentences, changing the prepositional object to a **da**-compound.

> You hear: **Wir hoffen auf Regen.**
> You say: **Wir hoffen darauf.**

8.22 Listen and repeat (Patterns, group 15).

8.23 Prepare for this exercise by repeating exercise R.

> You hear: **Ich glaube nicht daran, daß er Hepatitis hat.**
> You say: **Daran, daß er Hepatitis hat, glaube ich nicht.**
> And you say: **Daß er Hepatitis hat, daran glaube ich nicht.**

8.24 Conversation and Reading.

LAB EXERCISES—UNIT 9

9.1   Listen and repeat (Patterns, group 1).

9.2   Listen and repeat (Patterns, group 2).

9.3 You will hear arithmetic problems. Repeat each problem and provide the answer.

> You hear: **drei mal sieben**
> You say: **drei mal sieben ist einundzwanzig.**

or

> You hear: **zwanzig durch fünf**
> You say: **zwanzig durch fünf ist vier.**

9.4 Dictation.

9.5 Listen and repeat (Patterns, groups 4–11).

9.6 Listen and repeat (Patterns, group 12).

9.7 Change the following sentences in two ways: (a) change the modal to the perfect, and (b) change the present infinitive to a past infinitive.

> You hear: **Er kann um sechs noch nicht hier sein.**
> You say first: **Er hat um sechs noch nicht hier sein können.**
> And then: **Er kann um sechs noch nicht hier gewesen sein.**

9.8 Dictation.

9.9 Change from the present indicative to the present subjunctive, and add **eigentlich.**

> You hear: **Er kann schon hier sein.**
> You say: **Er könnte eigentlich schon hier sein.**

9.10 Change from the past indicative to the past subjunctive, and add **eigentlich.**

> You hear: **Er musste gestern arbeiten.**
> You say: **Er hätte gestern eigentlich arbeiten müssen.**

9.11 Dictation.

9.12 Listen and repeat (Patterns, group 13).

9.13 Change the following sentences to the first person.

> You hear: **Er will sich ein Haus bauen.**
> You say: **Ich will mir ein Haus bauen.**
> Or you hear: **Er hat sich schon gebadet.**
> And you say: **Ich habe mich schon gebadet.**

9.14 Listen and repeat (Patterns, group 14).

9.15 Change the following statements to wishes contrary to fact, using either **doch nur** or **doch nur nicht.**

> You hear: **Er ist gekommen.**
> You say: **Wäre er doch nur nicht gekommen.**

9.16 Conversation and Reading.

LAB EXERCISES—UNIT 10

10.1 Listen and repeat (Patterns, groups 1–5).

10.2 You will hear short sentences containing a noun in the singular, preceded by an adjective. Restate the sentences and change adjectives and nouns to the plural.

> You hear: **Wer wohnt denn in diesem alten Haus?**
> You say: **Wer wohnt denn in diesen alten Häusern?**

10.3 Dictation.

10.4 The following sentences contain an adjective and a noun in the plural. Restate the sentences in the singular.

> You hear: **Was soll ich denn mit diesen alten Büchern?**
> You say: **Was soll ich denn mit diesem alten Buch?**

10.5 Listen and repeat (Patterns, groups 6–9).

10.6 Now you will hear sentences with **ein**-words. Change from singular to plural.

> You hear: **Da drüben steht ein modernes Bürohaus.**
> You say: **Da drüben stehen moderne Bürohäuser.**

10.7 The following sentences contain plural nouns. Change to the singular by using the appropriate form of an **ein**-word.

> You hear: **Nur reiche Ausländer können so etwas kaufen.**
> You say: **Nur ein reicher Ausländer kann so etwas kaufen.**

10.8 Listen and repeat (Patterns, groups 10–12).

10.9 Dictation.

10.10 Listen and repeat (Patterns, groups 13–15).

10.11 Listen and repeat (Patterns, groups 16–17).

10.12 You will now hear short sentences containing a noun. After each sentence, you will hear an adjective without an ending. Repeat the sentence and insert the adjective with the proper ending.

> You hear: **Zu Hause wartete ein Brief auf mich.—lang**
> You say: **Zu Hause wartete ein langer Brief auf mich.**

10.13 Reading.

LAB EXERCISES—UNIT 11

11.1 Listen and repeat (Patterns, groups 1–4).

11.2 Dictation.

11.3 In the pauses, change the following sentences to the perfect. You will then hear the correct transformations.

    You hear: **In Zürich lernten wir viele Amerikaner kennen.**
    You say: **In Zürich haben wir viele Amerikaner kennengelernt.**

11.4 Listen and repeat (Patterns, group 5).

11.5 Listen and repeat (Patterns, group 6).

11.6 You will hear sentences in the past indicative. In the pauses, restate the sentences in the past subjunctive, starting with **Er sagte.**

    You hear: **Von der Stadt war nichts zu sehen.**
    You say: **Er sagte, von der Stadt wäre nichts zu sehen gewesen.**

11.7 Listen and repeat (Patterns, groups 7 and 8).

11.8 You will hear sentences with an infinitive with **zu** in the end field. Change these sentences to the perfect.

    You hear: **Es fing an zu regnen.**
    You say: **Es hat angefangen zu regnen.**

11.9 Listen and repeat (Patterns, groups 9 and 10).

11.10 Restate the following pairs of sentences, starting with the second one, which contains a **da**-compound, and transform the first one into an infinitive phrase.

    You hear: **Ich soll mit ihm ins Theater gehen.**
                   Er hat mich dazu eingeladen.
    You say: **Er hat mich dazu eingeladen, mit ihm ins Theater zu gehen.**

11.11 Change the following sentences from the perfect to the past tense.

    You hear: **Er ist abgefahren.**
    You say: **Er fuhr ab.**

11.12 Dictation.

11.13 Listen and repeat (Patterns, group 12).

11.14 Listen and repeat (Patterns, groups 13 and 14).

11.15 Reading.

LAB EXERCISES—UNIT 12

12.1 Listen and repeat (Patterns, groups 1–5, with variations).

12.2 Listen and repeat (Patterns, groups 6–7, with variations).

12.3 You will hear assertions or questions with reflexives. Restate these sentences by using the subject indicated.

    You hear: **Hat er sich schon die Hände gewaschen?—Du**
    You say: **Hast du dir schon die Hände gewaschen?**

12.4 You will hear sentences in the perfect tense. Restate these sentences in the statal present.

> You hear: **Ich habe mich verliebt.**
> You say: **Ich bin verliebt.**

12.5 You will hear sentences in the statal present. Restate these sentences in the perfect, using reflexives.

> You hear: **Ich bin schon daran gewöhnt.**
> You say: **Ich habe mich schon daran gewöhnt.**

12.6 You will hear sentences containing **sitzen, stehen, liegen.** Restate these sentences using the perfect or pluperfect of **sich setzen, sich stellen, sich legen.**

> You hear: **Sie liegt schon im Bett.**
> You say: **Sie hat sich schon ins Bett gelegt.**

12.7 Listen and repeat (Patterns, groups 8–12, with variations).

12.8 Replace the following assertions by imperatives.

> You hear: **Du sollst vorsichtig sein.**
> You say: **Sei vorsichtig.**

12.9 Reading.

LAB EXERCISES—UNIT 13

13.1 Listen and repeat (Patterns, groups 1–4, with variations).

13.2 Listen and repeat (Patterns, groups 5–12, with variations).

13.3 Dictation.

13.4 Reading.

GRAMMATICAL TABLES

Personal Pronouns
Relative and Demonstrative Pronouns
der-Words
ein-Words
Interrogatives
Nouns
Prepositions
Declension of Adjectives
The Cardinal Numerals
The Ordinal Numerals
The Fractional Numerals
Irregular Verbs
The Modals
Regular Verbs
Active, Actional Passive, Statal Passive
Reflexive Verbs
Fraktur

GRAMMATICAL TABLES

Personal Pronouns

SINGULAR

	1ST PERS.	2ND PERS.	3RD PERS. MASC.	3RD PERS. FEM.	3RD PERS. NEUT.	2ND PERS. POLITE	3RD PERS. REFLEX.
NOM.	ich	du	er	sie	es	Sie	
GEN.							
DAT.	mir	dir	ihm	ihr	ihm	Ihnen	sich
ACC.	mich	dich	ihn	sie	es	Sie	sich

PLURAL

	1ST PERS.	2ND PERS.	3RD PERS. ALL GENDERS	2ND PERS. POLITE	3RD PERS. REFLEX.
NOM.	wir	ihr	sie	Sie	
GEN.					
DAT.	uns	euch	ihnen	Ihnen	sich
ACC.	uns	euch	sie	Sie	sich

Relative and Demonstrative Pronouns

SINGULAR

	MASC.	FEM.	NEUT.
NOM.	der	die	das
GEN.	dessen	deren	dessen
DAT.	dem	der	dem
ACC.	den	die	das

PLURAL

	ALL GENDERS
NOM.	die
GEN.	deren (*demonstrative:* derer)
DAT.	denen
ACC.	die

NOTE: The demonstrative pronouns, if referring to a noun in the preceding sentence, are used as a front-field substitute for the third person personal pronouns:

Wann haben Sie Dr. Meyer getroffen?
Den habe ich in Berlin getroffen.

638

der-Words

SINGULAR

	MASC.	FEM.	NEUT.	MASC.	FEM.	NEUT.	MASC.	FEM.	NEUT.
NOM.	der	die	das	dieser	diese	dieses	jeder	jede	jedes
GEN.	des	der	des	dieses	dieser	dieses	jedes	jeder	jedes
DAT.	dem	der	dem	diesem	dieser	diesem	jedem	jeder	jedem
ACC.	den	die	das	diesen	diese	dieses	jeden	jede	jedes

PLURAL

	ALL GENDERS	ALL GENDERS	ALL GENDERS
NOM.	die	diese	alle
GEN.	der	dieser	aller
DAT.	den	diesen	allen
ACC.	die	diese	alle

SINGULAR

	MASC.	FEM.	NEUT.
NOM.	jeder Mann	jede Frau	jedes Kind
GEN.	jedes Mannes	jeder Frau	jedes Kindes
DAT.	jedem Mann	jeder Frau	jedem Kind
ACC.	jeden Mann	jede Frau	jedes Kind

PLURAL

	ALL GENDERS
NOM.	alle Menschen
GEN.	aller Menschen
DAT.	allen Menschen
ACC.	alle Menschen

Jener, mancher, solcher, and **welcher** are also **der**-words

ein-Words

SINGULAR

	MASC.	FEM.	NEUT.	MASC.	FEM.	NEUT.	MASC.	FEM.	NEUT.
NOM.	ein	eine	ein	kein	keine	kein	sein	seine	sein
GEN.	eines	einer	eines	keines	keiner	keines	seines	seiner	seines
DAT.	einem	einer	einem	keinem	keiner	keinem	seinem	seiner	seinem
ACC.	einen	eine	ein	keinen	keine	kein	seinen	seine	sein

PLURAL

	ALL GENDERS	ALL GENDERS	ALL GENDERS
NOM.	(no plural)	keine	seine
GEN.		keiner	seiner
DAT.		keinen	seinen
ACC.		keine	seine

The possessive pronouns (possessive adjectives) **mein, dein, sein, ihr** (*her*), **unser, euer, ihr** (*their*), and **Ihr** (*your*) are all **ein**-words.

SINGULAR

	MASC.	FEM.	NEUT.
NOM.	unser Sohn	unsere Tochter	unser Kind
GEN.	unseres Sohnes	unserer Tochter	unseres Kindes
DAT.	unserem Sohn	unserer Tochter	unserem Kind
ACC.	unseren Sohn	unsere Tochter	unser Kind

PLURAL

	ALL GENDERS
NOM.	unsere Söhne (Töchter, Kinder)
GEN.	unserer Söhne (Töchter, Kinder)
DAT.	unseren Söhnen (Töchtern, Kindern)
ACC.	unsere Söhne (Töchter, Kinder)

	NEUT. SING.	PL. ALL GENDERS
u	welches Kind	welche Leute
er Frau	welchem Kind	welchen Leuten
he Frau	welches Kind	welche Leute

things; **welcher, welche, welches**
ly be used together with a following
derstood).

	FEM. SING.	NEUT. SING.
	was für eine Maschine	was für ein Gesicht
n	was für einer Maschine	was für einem Gesicht
en	was für eine Maschine	was für ein Gesicht

ITHOUT ARTICLE	PLURAL NOUN WITHOUT ARTICLE
sch (ist das?)	was für Leute (sind das?)
	(bei) was für Leuten (wohnt er?)
Fleisch (haben Sie?)	was für Leute (haben Sie hier?)

ns "what kind of." It precedes either a singular noun with
gular or plural noun without article. The case of **ein** or of the
not depend on **für** but on the syntactical function of the
t.

REGULAR NOUNS

Regular monosyllabic masculine and n̶ singular and an optional **-e** in the dative of all genders add **-n** or **-en** to the nominativ̶ plural already ends in **-n.**

NOM.	der Mann	der Wagen	die Frau	
GEN.	des Mannes	des Wagens	der Frau	
DAT.	dem Mann(e)	dem Wagen	der Frau	
ACC.	den Mann	den Wagen	die Frau	d̶
NOM.	die Männer	die Wagen	die Frauen	di̶
GEN.	der Männer	der Wagen	der Frauen	der̶
DAT.	den Männern	den Wagen	den Frauen	den B̶
ACC.	die Männer	die Wagen	die Frauen	die Brü̶

NOUNS IRREGULAR IN THE SINGULAR

NOM.	der Mensch	der Herr	das Herz	der B̶
GEN.	des Menschen	des Herrn	des Herzens	des Bau̶
DAT.	dem Menschen	dem Herrn	dem Herzen	dem Bau̶
ACC.	den Menschen	den Herrn	das Herz	den Bauer̶

NOTE: Since there are no reliable rules for the formation of plurals, all p̶ must be learned together with the singular.

	SING.	SING.	MASC. SING.
NOM.	wer	was	welcher Mann
GEN.	wessen		
DAT.	wem	was	welchem Mann
ACC.	wen	was	welchen Mann

Wer asks for persons; **was** asks for
means "which particular" and can on
noun (which may, however, be un

	MASC. SING.
NOM.	was für ein Wagen
GEN.	
DAT.	was für einem Wage
ACC.	was für einen Wag

	SING. NOUN w
NOM.	was für Fle
GEN.	
DAT.	
ACC.	was für

Was für mea
ein or a sing
noun does
whole uni

...s add **-es** or **-s** in the genitive
...r. In the dative plural, nouns
...al form, unless the nominative

die Brücke	das Kind	das Auge
der Brücke	des Kindes	des Auges
der Brücke	dem Kind(e)	dem Auge
die Brücke	das Kind	das Auge
...e Brücken	die Kinder	die Augen
...Brücken	der Kinder	der Augen
...rücken	den Kindern	den Augen
...cken	die Kinder	die Augen

...auer	der Friede
...ern	des Friedens
...ern	dem Frieden
	den Frieden

...lurals

Prepositions

PREPOSITIONS WITH THE GENITIVE

trotz	trotz des schlechten Wetters
während	während des letzten Krieges
wegen	wegen des schlechten Wetters

NOTE: **trotz** and **wegen** are also used with the dative.

PREPOSITIONS WITH THE DATIVE

aus	aus dem Bahnhof
außer	außer meiner Freundin
bei	bei meiner Tante
mit	mit meinem Freund
nach	nach einer Stunde
seit	seit einem Jahr
von	von meinem Vater
zu	zum Bahnhof

PREPOSITIONS WITH THE ACCUSATIVE

durch	durch die Stadt
für	für mich
gegen	gegen mich
ohne	ohne mich
um	um diese Zeit

NOTE: **bis** (*until*) is followed by the accusative in such time expressions as **bis nächste Woche, bis nächsten Sonntag.** Usually, **bis** is an adverb meaning *up to* or *as far as* followed by prepositions like **an, in, nach, über, zu,** which then govern the case of the noun.

bis an das Ende der Welt
bis tief in die Nacht
bis nach München
bis über die Ohren verliebt
bis zu diesem Tage

PREPOSITIONS WITH EITHER ACCUSATIVE OR DATIVE

an	neben	unter
auf	in	vor
hinter	über	zwischen

Declension of Adjectives

Adjectives Preceded by der-Words

SINGULAR

	MASC.	FEM.	NEUT.
NOM.	der junge Mann	jede schöne Frau	dieses kleine Haus
GEN.	des jungen Mannes	jeder schönen Frau	dieses kleinen Hauses
DAT.	dem jungen Mann	jeder schönen Frau	diesem kleinen Haus
ACC.	den jungen Mann	jede schöne Frau	dieses kleine Haus

PLURAL

NOM.	die jungen Männer	alle schönen Frauen	diese kleinen Häuser
GEN.	der jungen Männer	aller schönen Frauen	dieser kleinen Häuser
DAT.	den jungen Männern	allen schönen Frauen	diesen kleinen Häusern
ACC.	die jungen Männer	alle schönen Frauen	diese kleinen Häuser

Adjectives Preceded by ein-Words

SINGULAR

	MASC.	FEM.	NEUT.
NOM.	ein junger Mann	keine schöne Frau	sein kleines Haus
GEN.	eines jungen Mannes	keiner schönen Frau	seines kleinen Hauses
DAT.	einem jungen Mann	keiner schönen Frau	seinem kleinen Haus
ACC.	einen jungen Mann	keine schöne Frau	sein kleines Haus

PLURAL

NOM.	junge Männer	keine schönen Frauen	seine kleinen Häuser
GEN.	junger Männer	keiner schönen Frauen	seiner kleinen Häuser
DAT.	jungen Männern	keinen schönen Frauen	seinen kleinen Häusern
ACC.	junge Männer	keine schönen Frauen	seine kleinen Häuser

Adjectives Not Preceded by der- or ein-Words

SINGULAR

	MASC.	FEM.	NEUT.
NOM.	guter Wein	frische Butter	warmes Wasser
GEN.	(guten Weines)	frischer Butter	(warmen Wassers)
DAT.	gutem Wein	frischer Butter	warmem Wasser
ACC.	guten Wein	frische Butter	warmes Wasser

Declension of Adjectives (cont.)

Adjectives Not Preceded by *der-* or *ein*-Words *(cont.)*

PLURAL

	ALL GENDERS
NOM.	intelligente Kinder
GEN.	intelligenter Kinder
DAT.	intelligenten Kindern
ACC.	intelligente Kinder

Adjectives Used as Nouns

SINGULAR

	MASC.	FEM.	NEUT.
NOM.	jeder Deutsche	jede Deutsche	alles Schöne
GEN.	jedes Deutschen	jeder Deutschen	alles Schönen
DAT.	jedem Deutschen	jeder Deutschen	allem Schönen
ACC.	jeden Deutschen	jede Deutsche	alles Schöne
NOM.	ein Deutscher	eine Deutsche	etwas Schönes
GEN.	eines Deutschen	einer Deutschen	
DAT.	einem Deutschen	einer Deutschen	etwas Schönem
ACC.	einen Deutschen	eine Deutsche	etwas Schönes

PLURAL

	ALL GENDERS
NOM.	die Deutschen
GEN.	der Deutschen
DAT.	den Deutschen
ACC.	die Deutschen
NOM.	Reiche und Arme
GEN.	Reicher und Armer
DAT.	Reichen und Armen
ACC.	Reiche und Arme

Declension of Adjectives (cont.)

Participles Used as Nouns

SINGULAR

	MASC.	FEM.	NEUT.
NOM.	der Gefangene	die Geliebte	alles Verlorene
GEN.	des Gefangenen	der Geliebten	
DAT.	dem Gefangenen	der Geliebten	allem Verlorenen
ACC.	den Gefangenen	die Geliebte	alles Verlorene
NOM.	ein Gefangener	meine Geliebte	
GEN.	eines Gefangenen	meiner Geliebten	
DAT.	einem Gefangenen	meiner Geliebten	
ACC.	einen Gefangenen	meine Geliebte	

PLURAL

	ALL GENDERS
NOM.	die Gefangenen
GEN.	der Gefangenen
DAT.	den Gefangenen
ACC.	die Gefangenen

The Cardinal Numerals

1 eins	6 sechs	11 elf	16 sechzehn
2 zwei	7 sieben	12 zwölf	17 siebzehn
3 drei	8 acht	13 dreizehn	18 achtzehn
4 vier	9 neun	14 vierzehn	19 neunzehn
5 fünf	10 zehn	15 fünfzehn	20 zwanzig

21 einundzwanzig	40 vierzig	100 hundert
22 zweiundzwanzig	50 fünfzig	101 hunderteins
23 dreiundzwanzig	60 sechzig	102 hundertzwei
24 vierundzwanzig	70 siebzig	111 hundertelf
25 fünfundzwanzig	80 achtzig	121 hunderteinundzwanzig
30 dreißig	90 neunzig	135 hundertfünfunddreißig

199 hundertneunundneunzig	1001 tausendeins
200 zweihundert	1009 tausendneun
201 zweihunderteins	2000 zweitausend
267 zweihundertsiebenundsechzig	6843 sechstausendachthundertdreiundvierzig
300 dreihundert	100,000 hunderttausend
1000 tausend	1,000,000 eine Million

0 Null
0,345 Null Komma drei vier fünf

The Ordinal Numerals

All ordinal numerals are adjectives. Since uninflected forms do not occur, either the proper strong or the proper weak ending must be added to the forms of the following table:

1. erst-	8. acht-	20. zwanzigst-
2. zweit-	9. neunt-	23. dreiundzwanzigst-
3. dritt-	10. zehnt-	98. achtundneunzigst-
4. viert-	11. elft-	100. hundertst-
5. fünft-	12. zwölft-	101. hunderterst-
6. sechst-	13. dreizehnt-	102. hundertzweit-
7. siebt-	19. neunzehnt-	1000. tausendst-

The Fractional Numerals

The denominators of fractions are neuter nouns of the type **das Viertel, die Viertel.** They are declined like regular nouns. An exception is **die Hälfte, die Hälften.** When the fractionals ending in **-el** are used as adjectives, they are indeclinable. The adjective **halb,** however, is declined like any other attributive adjective.

SINGULAR

NOM.	die Hälfte	ein Drittel	eine Viertelstunde	eine halbe Stunde
GEN.	der Hälfte	eines Drittels	einer Viertelstunde	einer halben Stunde
DAT.	der Hälfte	einem Drittel	einer Viertelstunde	einer halben Stunde
ACC.	die Hälfte	ein Drittel	eine Viertelstunde	eine halbe Stunde

PLURAL

NOM.	die Hälften	zwei Drittel	zwei Viertelstunden	zwei halbe Stunden
GEN.	der Hälften			
DAT.	den Hälften	zwei Dritteln	zwei Viertelstunden	zwei halben Stunden
ACC.	die Hälften	zwei Drittel	zwei Viertelstunden	zwei halbe Stunden

$\frac{1}{3}$ ein Drittel	$\frac{3}{7}$ drei Siebtel	$\frac{9}{30}$ neun Dreißigstel
$\frac{3}{4}$ drei Viertel	$\frac{7}{10}$ sieben Zehntel	$\frac{11}{100}$ elf Hundertstel
$\frac{4}{5}$ vier Fünftel	$\frac{2}{20}$ zwei Zwanzigstel	$\frac{3}{1000}$ drei Tausendstel

Irregular Verbs

<u>INFINITIVE</u>

sein	haben	werden	wissen

<u>PAST INFINITIVE</u>

gewesen sein	gehabt haben	geworden sein	gewußt haben

<u>PARTICIPLE</u>

gewesen	gehabt	geworden	gewußt

<u>PRINCIPAL PARTS</u>

sein, war, ist gewesen, ist
haben, hatte, hat gehabt, hat
werden, wurde, ist geworden, wird
wissen, wußte, hat gewußt, weiß

<u>PRESENT INDICATIVE</u>

ich	bin	habe	werde	weiß
du	bist	hast	wirst	weißt
er	ist	hat	wird	weiß
wir	sind	haben	werden	wissen
ihr	seid	habt	werdet	wißt
sie	sind	haben	werden	wissen

<u>PRESENT SUBJUNCTIVE</u>

ich	wäre	hätte	würde	wüßte
du	wär(e)st	hättest	würdest	wüßtest
er	wäre	hätte	würde	wüßte
wir	wären	hätten	würden	wüßten
ihr	wär(e)t	hättet	würdet	wüßtet
sie	wären	hätten	würden	wüßten

<u>PRESENT INDIRECT-DISCOURSE SUBJUNCTIVE</u>

ich	sei			wisse
du	sei(e)st			wissest
er	sei	habe	werde	wisse
wir	seien			
ihr	seiet			
sie	seien			

Irregular Verbs (cont.)

PAST INDICATIVE

ich	war	hatte	wurde	wußte
du	warst	hattest	wurdest	wußtest
er	war	hatte	wurde	wußte
wir	waren	hatten	wurden	wußten
ihr	wart	hattet	wurdet	wußtet
sie	waren	hatten	wurden	wußten

PAST SUBJUNCTIVE

ich	wäre gewesen	hätte gehabt	wäre geworden	hätte gewußt
du	wär(e)st gewesen	hättest gehabt	wär(e)st geworden	hättest gewußt
er	wäre gewesen	hätte gehabt	wäre geworden	hätte gewußt
wir	wären gewesen	hätten gehabt	wären geworden	hätten gewußt
ihr	wär(e)t gewesen	hättet gehabt	wär(e)t geworden	hättet gewußt
sie	wären gewesen	hätten gehabt	wären geworden	hätten gewußt

PAST INDIRECT-DISCOURSE SUBJUNCTIVE

ich	sei gewesen		sei geworden	
du	sei(e)st gewesen		sei(e)st geworden	
er	sei gewesen	habe gehabt	sei geworden	habe gewußt
wir	seien gewesen		seien geworden	
ihr	seiet gewesen		seiet geworden	
sie	seien gewesen		seien geworden	

PERFECT

ich	bin gewesen	habe gehabt	bin geworden	habe gewußt
du	bist gewesen	hast gehabt	bist geworden	hast gewußt
er	ist gewesen	hat gehabt	ist geworden	hat gewußt
wir	sind gewesen	haben gehabt	sind geworden	haben gewußt
ihr	seid gewesen	habt gehabt	seid geworden	habt gewußt
sie	sind gewesen	haben gehabt	sind geworden	haben gewußt

PAST PERFECT

ich	war gewesen	hatte gehabt	war geworden	hatte gewußt
du	warst gewesen	hattest gehabt	warst geworden	hattest gewußt
er	war gewesen	hatte gehabt	war geworden	hatte gewußt
wir	waren gewesen	hatten gehabt	waren geworden	hatten gewußt
ihr	wart gewesen	hattet gehabt	wart geworden	hattet gewußt
sie	waren gewesen	hatten gehabt	waren geworden	hatten gewußt

Irregular Verbs (cont.)

ich	werde sein	werde haben	werde werden	werde wissen
du	wirst sein	wirst haben	wirst werden	wirst wissen
er	wird sein	wird haben	wird werden	wird wissen
wir	werden sein	werden haben	werden werden	werden wissen
ihr	werdet sein	werdet haben	werdet werden	werdet wissen
sie	werden sein	werden haben	werden werden	werden wissen

FUTURE SUBJUNCTIVE (CONDITIONAL)

ich	würde sein	würde haben	würde werden	würde wissen
du	würdest sein	würdest haben	würdest werden	würdest wissen
er	würde sein	würde haben	würde werden	würde wissen
wir	würden sein	würden haben	würden werden	würden wissen
ihr	würdet sein	würdet haben	würdet werden	würdet wissen
sie	würden sein	würden haben	würden werden	würden wissen

FUTURE INDIRECT-DISCOURSE SUBJUNCTIVE

ich				
du				
er	werde sein	werde haben	werde werden	werde wissen
wir				
ihr				
sie				

IMPERATIVES

sei (du)	habe (du)	werde (du)	(wisse)
seien wir	haben wir	werden wir	
seid (ihr)	habt (ihr)	werdet (ihr)	(wißt)
seien Sie	haben Sie	werden Sie	

The Modals

	dürfen	können	mögen		müssen	sollen	wollen

PRESENT INDICATIVE

ich	darf	kann	möchte	(mag)	muß	soll	will
du	darfst	kannst	möchtest	(magst)	mußt	sollst	willst
er	darf	kann	möchte	(mag)	muß	soll	will
wir	dürfen	können	möchten	(mögen)	müssen	sollen	wollen
ihr	dürft	könnt	möchtet	(mögt)	müßt	sollt	wollt
sie	dürfen	können	möchten	(mögen)	müssen	sollen	wollen

PRESENT SUBJUNCTIVE

ich	dürfte	könnte	möchte		müßte	sollte	wollte
du	dürftest	könntest	möchtest		müßtest	solltest	wolltest
er	dürfte	könnte	möchte		müßte	sollte	wollte
wir	dürften	könnten	möchten		müßten	sollten	wollten
ihr	dürftet	könntet	möchtet		müßtet	solltet	wolltet
sie	dürften	könnten	möchten		müßten	sollten	wollten

PRESENT INDIRECT-DISCOURSE SUBJUNCTIVE

ich	dürfe	könne		(möge)	müsse	solle	wolle
du							
er	dürfe	könne		(möge)	müsse	solle	wolle
wir							
ihr							
sie							

PAST INDICATIVE

ich	durfte	konnte	(*usually*	(mochte)	mußte	sollte	wollte
du	durftest	konntest	*replaced*	(mochtest)	mußtest	solltest	wolltest
er	durfte	konnte	*by* wollen)	(mochte)	mußte	sollte	wollte
wir	durften	konnten		(mochten)	mußten	sollten	wollten
ihr	durftet	konntet		(mochtet)	mußtet	solltet	wolltet
sie	durften	konnten		(mochten)	mußten	sollten	wollten

The Modals (cont.)

ich hätte
du hättest
er hätte

wir hätten
ihr hättet
sie hätten

plus dependent infinitive plus dürfen, können, mögen, müssen, sollen, wollen

or plus gedurft, gekonnt, (gemocht), gemusst, gewollt

ich
du
er habe
wir
ihr
sie

plus dependent infinitive plus dürfen, können, (mögen), müssen, sollen, wollen, *or plus* gedurft, gekonnt, (gemocht), gemußt, gesollt, gewollt

ich habe
du hast
er hat

wir haben
ihr habt
sie haben

plus dependent infinitive plus dürfen, können, (mögen), müssen, sollen, wollen

or

plus gedurft, gekonnt, (gemocht), gemußt, gesollt, gewollt

The forms under **mögen** without a parenthesis are used more frequently than the other forms of **mögen.** They express a momentary wish. The form **möchte** functions both as a present indicative (**Die Dame möchte heute keinen Kaffee**) and as a subjunctive (**Sie sagte, sie möchte heute keinen Kaffee**). The past of **Die Dame möchte heute keinen Kaffee** is **Die Dame wollte gestern keinen Kaffee.**

The forms in parentheses either express a permanent like or dislike (**Möchten Sie ein Täßchen Tee, gnädige Frau?—Tee mag ich nicht, Herr Ober.**), *or* they are used with a subjective meaning (**Sie mag achtzehn sein.**) Do not use these forms before Unit 9.

Regular Verbs

Summary of the Active Voice

(**Bleiben** and intransitive verbs denoting a change in the state or position of the subject form their compound tenses with **sein**.)

PRESENT INFINITIVE

wohnen	bleiben	verschwinden	fallen

PAST INFINITIVE

gewohnt haben	geblieben sein	verschwunden sein	gefallen sein

PARTICIPLE

gewohnt	geblieben	verschwunden	gefallen

PRINCIPAL PARTS

wohnen, wohnte, hat gewohnt, er wohnt
bleiben, blieb, ist geblieben, er bleibt
verschwinden, verschwand, ist verschwunden, er verschwindet
fallen, fiel, ist gefallen, er fällt

PRESENT INDICATIVE

ich	wohne	bleibe	verschwinde	falle
du	wohnst	bleibst	verschwindest	fällst
er	wohnt	bleibt	verschwindet	fällt
wir	wohnen	bleiben	verschwinden	fallen
ihr	wohnt	bleibt	verschwindet	fallt
sie	wohnen	bleiben	verschwinden	fallen

PRESENT SUBJUNCTIVE

ich	wohnte	bliebe	verschwände	fiele
du	wohntest	blieb(e)st	verschwändest	fiel(e)st
er	wohnte	bliebe	verschwände	fiele
wir	wohnten	blieben	verschwänden	fielen
ihr	wohntet	blieb(e)t	verschwändet	fiel(e)t
sie	wohnten	blieben	verschwänden	fielen

PRESENT INDIRECT-DISCOURSE SUBJUNCTIVE

ich				
du				
er	wohne	bleibe	verschwinde	falle
wir				
ihr				
sie				

Regular Verbs (cont.)

PAST INDICATIVE

ich	wohnte	blieb		verschwand	fiel
du	wohntest	bliebst		verschwand(e)st	fielst
er	wohnte	blieb		verschwand	fiel
wir	wohnten	blieben		verschwanden	fielen
ihr	wohntet	bliebt		verschwandet	fielt
sie	wohnten	blieben		verschwanden	fielen

PAST SUBJUNCTIVE

ich	hätte	gewohnt	wäre	geblieben	verschwunden	gefallen
du	hättest	gewohnt	wär(e)st	geblieben	verschwunden	gefallen
er	hätte	gewohnt	wäre	geblieben	verschwunden	gefallen
wir	hätten	gewohnt	wären	geblieben	verschwunden	gefallen
ihr	hättet	gewohnt	wär(e)t	geblieben	verschwunden	gefallen
sie	hätten	gewohnt	wären	geblieben	verschwunden	gefallen

PAST INDIRECT-DISCOURSE SUBJUNCTIVE

ich			sei	
du			sei(e)st	
er	habe	gewohnt	sei	geblieben, verschwunden, gefallen
wir			seien	
ihr			seiet	
sie			seien	

PERFECT

ich	habe	gewohnt	bin	
du	hast	gewohnt	bist	
er	hat	gewohnt	ist	geblieben, verschwunden, gefallen
wir	haben	gewohnt	sind	
ihr	habt	gewohnt	seid	
sie	haben	gewohnt	sind	

PAST PERFECT

ich	hatte	gewohnt	war	
du	hattest	gewohnt	warst	
er	hatte	gewohnt	war	geblieben, verschwunden, gefallen
wir	hatten	gewohnt	waren	
ihr	hattet	gewohnt	wart	
sie	hatten	gewohnt	waren	

Regular Verbs (cont.)

FUTURE INDICATIVE

ich	werde
du	wirst
er	wird
wir	werden
ihr	werdet
sie	werden

wohnen, bleiben, verschwinden, fallen

FUTURE SUBJUNCTIVE

ich	würde
du	würdest
er	würde
wir	würden
ihr	würdet
sie	würden

wohnen, bleiben, verschwinden, fallen

FUTURE INDIRECT-DISCOURSE SUBJUNCTIVE

ich	
du	
er	werde
wir	
ihr	
sie	

wohnen, bleiben, verschwinden, fallen

IMPERATIVE

wohne (du)	bleibe (du)	verschwinde (du)	falle (du)
wohnen wir	bleiben (wir)	verschwinden wir	fallen wir
wohnt (ihr)	bleibt (ihr)	verschwindet (ihr)	fallt (ihr)
wohnen Sie	bleiben Sie	verschwinden Sie	fallen Sie

NOTE: In some cases, intransitive verbs expressing a change can denote either the event or the state attained. Thus **Ihr seid gestern abend aber früh verschwunden** (*You certainly disappeared early last night*) denotes an event; but **Er ist seit drei Wochen verschwunden** denotes a state reached by **verschwunden** and can then be interpreted as a present tense consisting of **ist** plus the predicative adjective **verschwunden.**

Active, Actional Passive, Statal Passive

(Only transitive verbs, i.e. verbs that are used with an accusative object, can be used as in this table. They have active forms, actional passive forms, and statal passive forms. Not many of these verbs occur in all the forms which are theoretically possible; but **enttäuschen** and **verlassen** have a complete set of forms.)

	ACTIVE		ACTIONAL PASSIVE		

PRESENT INFINITIVES

	ACTIVE	ACTIONAL PASSIVE
	enttäuschen	enttäuscht werden
	verlassen	verlassen werden

PAST INFINITIVES

	ACTIVE	ACTIONAL PASSIVE
	enttäuscht haben	enttäuscht worden sein
	verlassen haben	verlassen worden sein

PARTICIPLE

enttäuscht
verlassen

PRINCIPAL PARTS:

enttäuschen, enttäuschte, hat entäuscht, enttäuscht
verlassen, verließ, hat verlassen, verläßt

PRESENT INDICATIVE

ich	enttäusche	(verlasse)	werde	enttäuscht	(verlassen)
du	enttäuschst	(verläßt)	wirst	enttäuscht	(verlassen)
er	enttäuscht	(verläßt)	wird	enttäuscht	(verlassen)
wir	enttäuschen	(verlassen)	werden	enttäuscht	(verlassen)
ihr	enttäuscht	(verlaßt)	werdet	enttäuscht	(verlassen)
sie	enttäuschen	(verlassen)	werden	enttäuscht	(verlassen)

PRESENT SUBJUNCTIVE

ich	enttäuschte	(verließe)	würde	enttäuscht	(verlassen)
du	enttäuschtest	(verließest)	würdest	enttäuscht	(verlassen)
er	enttäuschte	(verließe)	würde	enttäuscht	(verlassen)
wir	enttäuschten	(verließen)	würden	enttäuscht	(verlassen)
ihr	enttäuschtet	(verließet)	würdet	enttäuscht	(verlassen)
sie	enttäuschten	(verließen)	würden	enttäuscht	(verlassen)

Active, Actional Passive, Statal Passive (cont.)

STATAL PASSIVE

<u>PRESENT INFINITIVES</u>

enttäuscht sein
verlassen sein

<u>PAST INFINITIVES</u>

enttäuscht gewesen sein
verlassen gewesen sein

<u>PRESENT INDICATIVE</u>

ich	bin	enttäuscht	(verlassen)
du	bist	enttäuscht	(verlassen)
er	ist	enttäuscht	(verlassen)
wir	sind	enttäuscht	(verlassen)
ihr	seid	enttäuscht	(verlassen)
sie	sind	enttäuscht	(verlassen)

<u>PRESENT SUBJUNCTIVE</u>

ich	wäre	enttäuscht	(verlassen)
du	wär(e)st	enttäuscht	(verlassen)
er	wäre	enttäuscht	(verlassen)
wir	wären	enttäuscht	(verlassen)
ihr	wär(e)t	enttäuscht	(verlassen)
sie	wären	enttäuscht	(verlassen)

Active, Actional Passive, Statal Passive (cont.)

	ACTIVE			ACTIONAL PASSIVE			

PRESENT INDIRECT-DISCOURSE SUBJUNCTIVE

ich						
du						
er	enttäusche	(verlasse)		werde	enttäuscht	(verlassen)
wir						
ihr						
sie						

PAST INDICATIVE

ich	enttäuschte	(verließ)		wurde	enttäuscht	(verlassen)
du	enttäuschtest	(verließt)		wurdest	enttäuscht	(verlassen)
er	enttäuschte	(verließ)		wurde	enttäuscht	(verlassen)
wir	enttäuschten	(verließen)		wurden	enttäuscht	(verlassen)
ihr	enttäuschtet	(verließt)		wurdet	enttäuscht	(verlassen)
sie	enttäuschten	(verließen)		wurden	enttäuscht	(verlassen)

PAST SUBJUNCTIVE

ich	hätte	enttäuscht	(verlassen)	wäre	enttäuscht	(verlassen)	worder
du	hättest	enttäuscht	(verlassen)	wär(e)st	enttäuscht	(verlassen)	worder
er	hätte	enttäuscht	(verlassen)	wäre	enttäuscht	(verlassen)	worder
wir	hätten	enttäuscht	(verlassen)	wären	enttäuscht	(verlassen)	worder
ihr	hättet	enttäuscht	(verlassen)	wär(e)t	enttäuscht	(verlassen)	worder
sie	hätten	enttäuscht	(verlassen)	wären	enttäuscht	(verlassen)	worder

PAST INDIRECT-DISCOURSE SUBJUNCTIVE

ich				sei	enttäuscht	(verlassen)	worder
du				sei(e)st	enttäuscht	(verlassen)	worder
er	habe	enttäuscht	(verlassen)	sei	enttäuscht	(verlassen)	worder
wir				seien	enttäuscht	(verlassen)	worder
ihr				seiet	enttäuscht	(verlassen)	worder
sie				seien	enttäuscht	(verlassen)	worder

PERFECT

ich	habe	enttäuscht	(verlassen)	bin	enttäuscht	(verlassen)	worder
du	hast	enttäuscht	(verlassen)	bist	enttäuscht	(verlassen)	worder
er	hat	enttäuscht	(verlassen)	ist	enttäuscht	(verlassen)	worder
wir	haben	enttäuscht	(verlassen)	sind	enttäuscht	(verlassen)	worder
ihr	habt	enttäuscht	(verlassen)	seid	enttäuscht	(verlassen)	worder
sie	haben	enttäuscht	(verlassen)	sind	enttäuscht	(verlassen)	worder

Active, Actional Passive, Statal Passive (cont.)

STATAL PASSIVE

PRESENT INDIRECT-DISCOURSE SUBJUNCTIVE

ich	sei	enttäuscht	(verlassen)
du	sei(e)st	enttäuscht	(verlassen)
er	sei	enttäuscht	(verlassen)
wir	seien	enttäuscht	(verlassen)
ihr	seiet	enttäuscht	(verlassen)
sie	seien	enttäuscht	(verlassen)

PAST INDICATIVE

ich	war	enttäuscht	(verlassen)
du	warst	enttäuscht	(verlassen)
er	war	enttäuscht	(verlassen)
wir	waren	enttäuscht	(verlassen)
ihr	wart	enttäuscht	(verlassen)
sie	waren	enttäuscht	(verlassen)

PAST SUBJUNCTIVE

ich	wäre	enttäuscht	(verlassen)	gewesen
du	wär(e)st	enttäuscht	(verlassen)	gewesen
er	wäre	enttäuscht	(verlassen)	gewesen
wir	wären	enttäuscht	(verlassen)	gewesen
ihr	wär(e)t	enttäuscht	(verlassen)	gewesen
sie	wären	enttäuscht	(verlassen)	gewesen

PAST INDIRECT-DISCOURSE SUBJUNCTIVE

ich	sei	enttäuscht	(verlassen)	gewesen
du	sei(e)st	enttäuscht	(verlassen)	gewesen
er	sei	enttäuscht	(verlassen)	gewesen
wir	seien	enttäuscht	(verlassen)	gewesen
ihr	seiet	enttäuscht	(verlassen)	gewesen
sie	seien	enttäuscht	(verlassen)	gewesen

PERFECT

ich	bin	enttäuscht	(verlassen)	gewesen
du	bist	enttäuscht	(verlassen)	gewesen
er	ist	enttäuscht	(verlassen)	gewesen
wir	sind	enttäuscht	(verlassen)	gewesen
ihr	seid	enttäuscht	(verlassen)	gewesen
sie	sind	enttäuscht	(verlassen)	gewesen

Active, Actional Passive, Statal Passive (cont.)

ACTIVE				ACTIONAL PASSIVE			

PAST PERFECT

ich	hatte	enttäuscht	(verlassen)	war	enttäuscht	(verlassen)	worden
du	hattest	enttäuscht	(verlassen)	warst	enttäuscht	(verlassen)	worden
er	hatte	enttäuscht	(verlassen)	war	enttäuscht	(verlassen)	worden
wir	hatten	enttäuscht	(verlassen)	waren	enttäuscht	(verlassen)	worden
ihr	hattet	enttäuscht	(verlassen)	wart	enttäuscht	(verlassen)	worden
sie	hatten	enttäuscht	(verlassen)	waren	enttäuscht	(verlassen)	worden

FUTURE INDICATIVE

ich	werde	enttäuschen	(verlassen)	werde	enttäuscht	(verlassen)	werden
du	wirst	enttäuschen	(verlassen)	wirst	enttäuscht	(verlassen)	werden
er	wird	enttäuschen	(verlassen)	wird	enttäuscht	(verlassen)	werden
wir	werden	enttäuschen	(verlassen)	werden	enttäuscht	(verlassen)	werden
ihr	werdet	enttäuschen	(verlassen)	werdet	enttäuscht	(verlassen)	werden
sie	werden	enttäuschen	(verlassen)	werden	enttäuscht	(verlassen)	werden

FUTURE SUBJUNCTIVE

ich	würde	enttäuschen	(verlassen)	würde	enttäuscht	(verlassen)	werden
du	würdest	enttäuschen	(verlassen)	würdest	enttäuscht	(verlassen)	werden
er	würde	enttäuschen	(verlassen)	würde	enttäuscht	(verlassen)	werden
wir	würden	enttäuschen	(verlassen)	würden	enttäuscht	(verlassen)	werden
ihr	würdet	enttäuschen	(verlassen)	würdet	enttäuscht	(verlassen)	werden
sie	würden	enttäuschen	(verlassen)	würden	enttäuscht	(verlassen)	werden

FUTURE INDIRECT-DISCOURSE SUBJUNCTIVE

ich							
du							
er	werde	enttäuschen	(verlassen)	werde	enttäuscht	(verlassen)	werden
wir							
ihr							
sie							

IMPERATIVE

enttäusche (du)	verlasse (du)
enttäuschen wir	verlassen wir
enttäuscht (ihr)	verlasst (ihr)
enttäuschen Sie	verlassen Sie

Active, Actional Passive, Statal Passive (cont.)

STATAL PASSIVE

PAST PERFECT

ich	war	enttäuscht	(verlassen)	gewesen
du	warst	enttäuscht	(verlassen)	gewesen
er	war	enttäuscht	(verlassen)	gewesen
wir	waren	enttäuscht	(verlassen)	gewesen
ihr	wart	enttäuscht	(verlassen)	gewesen
sie	waren	enttäuscht	(verlassen)	gewesen

FUTURE INDICATIVE

ich	werde	enttäuscht	(verlassen)	sein
du	wirst	enttäuscht	(verlassen)	sein
er	wird	enttäuscht	(verlassen)	sein
wir	werden	enttäuscht	(verlassen)	sein
ihr	werdet	enttäuscht	(verlassen)	sein
sie	werden	enttäuscht	(verlassen)	sein

FUTURE SUBJUNCTIVE

ich	würde	enttäuscht	(verlassen)	sein
du	würdest	enttäuscht	(verlassen)	sein
er	würde	enttäuscht	(verlassen)	sein
wir	würden	enttäuscht	(verlassen)	sein
ihr	würdet	enttäuscht	(verlassen)	sein
sie	würden	enttäuscht	(verlassen)	sein

FUTURE INDIRECT-DISCOURSE SUBJUNCTIVE

ich				
du				
er	werde	enttäuscht	(verlassen)	sein
wir				
ihr				
sie				

Reflexive Verbs

ACTIONAL FORMS			STATAL FORMS		

PRESENT INFINITIVE

sich	verlieben		verliebt	sein	

PAST INFINITIVE

sich	verliebt	haben	verliebt	gewesen	sein

PRESENT INDICATIVE

ich	verliebe	mich	ich	bin	verliebt
du	verliebst	dich	du	bist	verliebt
er	verliebt	sich	er	ist	verliebt
wir	verlieben	uns	wir	sind	verliebt
ihr	verliebt	euch	ihr	seid	verliebt
sie	verlieben	sich	sie	sind	verliebt

PRESENT SUBJUNCTIVE

ich	verliebte	mich	ich	wäre	verliebt
du	verliebtest	dich	du	wär(e)st	verliebt
er	verliebte	sich	er	wäre	verliebt
wir	verliebten	uns	wir	wären	verliebt
ihr	verliebtet	euch	ihr	wär(e)t	verliebt
sie	verliebten	sich	sie	wären	verliebt

PRESENT INDIRECT-DISCOURSE SUBJUNCTIVE

ich			ich	sei	verliebt
du			du	sei(e)st	verliebt
er	verliebe	sich	er	sei	verliebt
wir			wir	seien	verliebt
ihr			ihr	seiet	verliebt
sie			sie	seien	verliebt

PAST INDICATIVE

ich	verliebte	mich	ich	war	verliebt
du	verliebtest	dich	du	warst	verliebt
er	verliebte	sich	er	war	verliebt
wir	verliebten	uns	wir	waren	verliebt
ihr	verliebtet	euch	ihr	wart	verliebt
sie	verliebten	sich	sie	waren	verliebt

Reflexive Verbs (cont.)

PAST SUBJUNCTIVE

ich	hätte	mich	verliebt	ich	wäre	verliebt	gewesen
du	hättest	dich	verliebt	du	wär(e)st	verliebt	gewesen
er	hätte	sich	verliebt	er	wäre	verliebt	gewesen
wir	hätten	uns	verliebt	wir	wären	verliebt	gewesen
ihr	hättet	euch	verliebt	ihr	wär(e)t	verliebt	gewesen
sie	hätten	sich	verliebt	sie	wären	verliebt	gewesen

PAST INDIRECT-DISCOURSE SUBJUNCTIVE

ich				ich	sei	verliebt	gewesen
du				du	sei(e)st	verliebt	gewesen
er	habe	sich	verliebt	er	sei	verliebt	gewesen
wir				wir	seien	verliebt	gewesen
ihr				ihr	seiet	verliebt	gewesen
sie				sie	seien	verliebt	gewesen

PERFECT

ich	habe	mich	verliebt	ich	bin	verliebt	gewesen
du	hast	dich	verliebt	du	bist	verliebt	gewesen
er	hat	sich	verliebt	er	ist	verliebt	gewesen
wir	haben	uns	verliebt	wir	sind	verliebt	gewesen
ihr	habt	euch	verliebt	ihr	seid	verliebt	gewesen
sie	haben	sich	verliebt	sie	sind	verliebt	gewesen

PAST PERFECT

ich	hatte	mich	verliebt	ich	war	verliebt	gewesen
du	hattest	dich	verliebt	du	warst	verliebt	gewesen
er	hatte	sich	verliebt	er	war	verliebt	gewesen
wir	hatten	uns	verliebt	wir	waren	verliebt	gewesen
ihr	hattet	euch	verliebt	ihr	wart	verliebt	gewesen
sie	hatten	sich	verliebt	sie	waren	verliebt	gewesen

FUTURE

ich	werde	mich	verlieben	ich	werde	verliebt	sein
du	wirst	dich	verlieben	du	wirst	verliebt	sein
er	wird	sich	verlieben	er	wird	verliebt	sein
wir	werden	uns	verlieben	wir	werden	verliebt	sein
ihr	werdet	euch	verlieben	ihr	werdet	verliebt	sein
sie	werden	sich	verlieben	sie	werden	verliebt	sein

Reflexive Verbs (cont.)

ich	würde	mich	verlieben	ich	würde	verliebt	sein
du	würdest	dich	verlieben	du	würdest	verliebt	sein
er	würde	sich	verlieben	er	würde	verliebt	sein
wir	würden	uns	verlieben	wir	würden	verliebt	sein
ihr	würdet	euch	verlieben	ihr	würdet	verliebt	sein
sie	würden	sich	verlieben	sie	würden	verliebt	sein

ich				ich			
du				du			
er	werde	sich	verlieben	er	werde	verliebt	sein
wir				wir			
ihr				ihr			
sie				sie			

verliebe (du) dich
verlieben wir uns
verliebt (ihr) euch
verlieben Sie sich

Fraktur

Until not too long ago, German was mostly printed in gothic type, called **Fraktur.** Today, this type is no longer in common use. Since, however, you are apt to encounter the gothic alphabet in the course of your studies, it is advisable to familiarize yourself with it.

ROMAN		FRAKTUR		ROMAN		FRAKTUR		
A	a	𝔄	𝔞	N	n	𝔑	𝔫	
B	b	𝔅	𝔟	O	o	𝔒	𝔬	
C	c	ℭ	𝔠	P	p	𝔓	𝔭	
D	d	𝔇	𝔡	Q	q	𝔔	𝔮	
E	e	𝔈	𝔢	R	r	𝔑	𝔯	
F	f	𝔉	𝔣	S	s	𝔖	𝔰	𝔰
G	g	𝔊	𝔤	T	t	𝔗	𝔱	
H	h	𝔥	𝔥	U	u	𝔘	𝔲	
I	i	𝔍	𝔦	V	v	𝔙	𝔳	
J	j	𝔍	𝔧	W	w	𝔚	𝔴	
K	k	𝔎	𝔨	X	x	𝔛	𝔵	
L	l	𝔏	𝔩	Y	y	𝔜	𝔶	
M	m	𝔐	𝔪	Z	z	ℨ	𝔷	

Set in **Fraktur,** the first three paragraphs on page 79 would look as follows:

Der Mensch, das kann man schon bei Aristoteles lesen, ist ein Tier. Aber dieses Tier, sagt Aristoteles, hat Vernunft.

Und was ist Vernunft? Vernunft ist nicht Intelligenz. Vernunft ist mehr als Intelli=genz.

Wer nur intelligent ist, glaubt: „Alle Menschen sind egoistisch. Ja, sie müssen egoistisch sein. Denn jeder Mensch will glücklich werden. Das heißt aber, der Emil möchte haben, was Fritz hat; und der Fritz möchte sein, was Emil ist. Aber der Emil kann nicht im=mer alles haben, was er möchte; und Fritz kann nicht sein, was Emil ist. Und darum haßt der Fritz den Emil, und der Emil den Fritz. Darum haßt ein Sohn seinen Vater, und darum haßt Nation A Nation B. Der Krieg zwischen Fritz und Emil, zwischen Sohn und Vater und zwischen Nation A und Nation B ist also natürlich. So ist es und so bleibt es. Leider!"

PRINCIPAL PARTS OF STRONG AND IRREGULAR VERBS

NOTE: Many compound verbs, such as **aufmachen** and **ausgehen,** are not included in this table. The principal parts of such verbs will be identical in basic form with those of the corresponding simple verbs (**machen, gehen**).

abhängen von to depend upon
  hing ab von, hat abgehangen von, es hängt ab von
anfangen to begin, start
  fing an, hat angefangen, er fängt an
ankommen to arrive
  kam an, ist angekommen, er kommt an
annehmen to accept; to assume
  nahm an, hat angenommen, er nimmt an
anrufen to call up (on the telephone)
  rief an, hat angerufen, er ruft an
aufstehen to get up, to rise
  stand auf, ist aufgestanden, er steht auf

backen to bake
  backte (also buk), hat gebacken, er bäckt
befehlen to order, command
  befahl, hat befohlen, er befiehlt
beginnen to begin, start
  begann, hat begonnen, er beginnt
begreifen to comprehend
  begriff, hat begriffen, er begreift
behalten to keep, retain; to remember

behielt, hat behalten, er behält
bekommen to get, receive
  bekam, hat bekommen, er bekommt
beschließen to decide, determine
  beschloß, hat beschlossen, er beschließt
beweisen to prove
  bewies, hat bewiesen, er beweist
binden to bind, tie
  band, hat gebunden, er bindet
bitten to ask for, request
  bat, hat gebeten, er bittet
bleiben to stay, remain
  blieb, ist geblieben, er bleibt
braten to roast; to fry
  briet, hat gebraten, er brät
brechen to break
  brach, hat gebrochen, er bricht
brennen to burn
  brannte, hat gebrannt, er brennt
bringen to bring
  brachte, hat gebracht, er bringt

denken to think
  dachte, hat gedacht, er denkt
dürfen to be permitted to
  durfte, hat gedurft, er darf

einladen to invite
  lud ein, hat eingeladen, er lädt ein
empfangen to receive
  empfing, hat empfangen, er empfängt
empfehlen to recommend
  empfahl, hat empfohlen, er empfiehlt
sich **entschließen** to decide, make up one's mind
  entschloß sich, hat sich entschlossen, entschließt sich
entsprechen to correspond to
  entsprach, hat entsprochen, es entspricht
entstehen to originate, come into being
  entstand, ist entstanden, er entsteht
erfahren to find out, learn
  erfuhr, hat erfahren, er erfährt
erfinden to invent
  erfand, hat erfunden, er erfindet
erhalten to receive; to sustain
  erhielt, hat erhalten, er erhält
erkennen to recognize
  erkannte, hat erkannt, er erkennt
erscheinen to appear
  erschien, ist erschienen, er erscheint
erschrecken to be frightened

erschrak, ist erschrocken, er erschrickt

ertrinken to drown
   ertrank, ist ertrunken, er ertrinkt

sich erweisen to turn out, show
   erwies sich, hat sich erwiesen, es erweist sich

erziehen to educate, raise
   erzog, hat erzogen, er erzieht

essen to eat
   aß, hat gegessen, er ißt

fahren to drive, go (by train, boat, plane, car)
   fuhr, ist gefahren, er fährt

fallen to fall
   fiel, ist gefallen, er fällt

finden to find
   fand, hat gefunden, er findet

fliegen to fly
   flog, ist geflogen, er fliegt

fliehen to flee, escape
   floh, ist geflohen, er flieht

fließen to flow
   floß, ist geflossen, er fließt

fressen to eat (said of animals)
   fraß, hat gefressen, er frißt

frieren to freeze; to be cold
   fror, hat gefroren, er friert

geben to give
   gab, hat gegeben, er gibt

gefallen to please
   gefiel, hat gefallen, er gefällt

gefangennehmen to capture, take prisoner
   nahm gefangen, hat gefangengenommen, er nimmt gefangen

gehen to go, walk
   ging, ist gegangen, er geht

gelingen to succeed
   gelang, ist gelungen, es gelingt

geschehen to happen, occur
   geschah, ist geschehen, es geschieht

gewinnen to win

gewann, hat gewonnen, er gewinnt

greifen to grasp
   griff, hat gegriffen, er greift

haben to have
   hatte, hat gehabt, er hat

halten to hold; to stop
   hielt, hat gehalten, er hält

heissen to be called, to mean
   hieß, hat geheißen, er heißt

helfen to help
   half, hat geholfen, er hilft

kennen to know, be acquainted with
   kannte, hat gekannt, er kennt

klingen to sound
   klang, hat geklungen, es klingt

kommen to come
   kam, ist gekommen, er kommt

können to be able to
   konnte, hat gekonnt, er kann

lassen to let; to leave
   ließ, hat gelassen, er läßt

laufen to run
   lief, ist gelaufen, er läuft

leiden to suffer
   litt, hat gelitten, er leidet

lesen to read
   las, hat gelesen, er liest

liegen to lie (flat); to be situated
   lag, hat gelegen, er liegt

lügen to tell a lie
   log, hat gelogen, er lügt

mögen to like
   mochte, hat gemocht, er mag

müssen to have to
   mußte, hat gemußt, er muß

nachdenken to reflect, meditate
   dachte nach, hat nachgedacht, er denkt nach

nehmen to take
   nahm, hat genommen, er nimmt

raten to advise, to guess
   riet, hat geraten, er rät

reißen to tear
   riß, hat gerissen, er reißt

rennen to run
   rannte, ist gerannt, er rennt

rufen to call
   rief, hat gerufen, er ruft

scheinen to seem; to shine
   schien, hat geschienen, er scheint

schieben to push, shove
   schob, hat geschoben, er schiebt

schießen to shoot
   schoß, hat geschossen, er schießt

schilaufen to ski
   lief Schi, ist schigelaufen, er läuft Schi

schlafen to sleep
   schlief, hat geschlafen, er schläft

schlagen to beat; hit
   schlug, hat geschlagen, er schlägt

schließen to close
   schloß, hat geschlossen, er schließt

schneiden to cut
   schnitt, hat geschnitten, er schneidet

schreiben to write
   schrieb, hat geschrieben, er schreibt

schreien to scream, cry
   schrie, hat geschrie(e)n, er schreit

schweigen to be silent, say nothing
   schwieg, hat geschwiegen, er schweigt

schwimmen to swim
   schwamm, ist geschwommen, er schwimmt

sehen to see
   sah, hat gesehen, er sieht

sein to be
   war, ist gewesen, er ist

senden to send; to broadcast
   sandte, hat gesandt, er sendet

singen to sing
   sang, hat gesungen, er singt

sinken to sink

sank, ist gesunken, er sinkt
sitzen to sit
saß, hat gesessen, er sitzt
sollen to be supposed to
sollte, hat gesollt, er soll
spazierengehen to go for a walk
ging spazieren, ist spazierengegangen, er geht spazieren
sprechen to speak, talk
sprach, hat gesprochen, er spricht
springen to jump
sprang, ist gesprungen, er springt
stehen to stand
stand, hat gestanden, er steht
stehenbleiben to stop (walking or moving)
blieb stehen, ist stehengeblieben, er bleibt stehen
stehlen to steal
stahl, hat gestohlen, er stiehlt
steigen to climb
stieg, ist gestiegen, er steigt
sterben to die
starb, ist gestorben, er stirbt
streichen to spread; to stroke; to paint
strich, hat gestrichen, er streicht

tragen to carry
trug, hat getragen, er trägt
treffen to meet; to hit
traf, hat getroffen, er trifft

treten to step
trat, ist getreten, er tritt
trinken to drink
trank, hat getrunken, er trinkt
tun to do
tat, hat getan, er tut

sich unterhalten to converse, have a conversation
unterhielt sich, hat sich unterhalten, er unterhält sich

verbieten to forbid
verbot, hat verboten, er verbietet
verbinden to unite; to compound
verband, hat verbunden, er verbindet
verbringen to spend (time)
verbrachte, hat verbracht, er verbringt
vergessen to forget
vergaß, hat vergessen, er vergißt
verlassen to leave
verließ, hat verlassen, er verläßt
verlieren to lose
verlor, hat verloren, er verliert
verschwinden to disappear
verschwand, ist verschwunden, er verschwindet
versprechen to promise
versprach, hat versprochen, er verspricht

verstehen to understand
verstand, hat verstanden, er versteht
verzeihen to pardon, excuse
verzieh, hat verziehen, er verzeiht
vorschlagen to suggest; to propose
schlug vor, hat vorgeschlagen, er schlägt vor

wachsen to grow
wuchs, ist gewachsen, er wächst
waschen to wash
wusch, hat gewaschen, er wäscht
werden to become
wurde, ist geworden, er wird
werfen to throw
warf, hat geworfen, er wirft
wissen to know
wußte, hat gewußt, er weiß
wollen to want to
wollte, hat gewollt, er will
wiegen to weigh
wog, hat gewogen, er wiegt

ziehen to move (from one place to another)
zog, ist gezogen, er zieht
ziehen to pull
zog, hat gezogen, er zieht
zwingen to force
zwang, hat gezwungen, er zwingt

VOCABULARY: German – English

This vocabulary is intended primarily for quick reference; it is not meant to be a substitute for a dictionary of the German language. The English equivalents given here do not include all the meanings of the corresponding German words that are found in a German dictionary. Most of the translations are limited to the meanings in which the German words are used in this book.

NOUNS

All nouns are preceded by the definite article to show their gender and are followed by an indication of the plural form. Thus the entries

der Mann, ̈er	man
die Blume, –n	flower
das Fenster, –	window

mean that **Mann** is masculine and its plural is **Männer, Blume** is feminine and its plural is **Blumen,** and **Fenster** is neuter and is unchanged in the plural. Nouns for which no plural form is shown are not used in the plural. If two case endings are listed, the first indicates the genetive singular and the second the nominative plural.

ACCENTUATION

An accent mark shows the pronunciation of words with an unusual accentuation in German (e.g. **Schokola'de**). If the stress shifts to another syllable in the plural, the complete plural form is shown with an accent mark indicating the stress (**der Doktor, die Dokto'ren**). Stress is not indicated for words in which the first syllable is an unaccented prefix such as **be-** or **er-** or for compound verbs.

VERBS

The vowel changes of "regular" strong verbs are indicated (e.g. **schreiben, ie, ie**), the vowels given being respectively the stem vowels of the past indicative and the past participle. With verbs that have a change of stem vowel in the present, the third person singular present is also given (e.g. **schlafen, ie, a, er schläft**). "Irregular" strong verbs have their principal parts given in full (e.g. **stehen, stand, gestanden**). For further reference a summary list of strong and irregular verbs used in this text precedes this vocabulary.

Verbs that require the auxiliary **sein** to form the perfect tenses are indicated by (**ist**) [e.g. **bleiben, ie, ie, (ist)** stay].

672

In compound verbs written as one word a dot between the complement and the verb (aus·gehen, nach·denken) indicates that the two parts are separated in the present and past tenses (er geht aus, er denkt nach).

With irregular or strong verbs that have separable prefixes the prefix is not repeated, but the principal parts are given thus: auf·stehen, stand –, –gestanden.

ABBREVIATONS

The following abbreviations are used in the entries:

acc.	= accusative		*gen.*	= genitive
adv.	= adverb		*pers.*	= person, personal
colloq.	= colloquial		*prep.*	= preposition
conj.	= conjunction		*sent. adv.*	= sentence adverb
dat.	= dative		*trans.*	= transitive
demonstr.	= demonstrative			

ab off
ab und zu now and then; off and on
der **Abend, –e** evening
　abends evenings
　gestern abend yesterday evening, last night
　heute abend this evening, tonight
　morgen abend tomorrow evening
das **Abendessen, –** supper
aber but; however
ab·fahren, u, a, (ist), er fährt ab to depart, leave
ab·hängen, i, a, von to depend upon
ab·holen to pick up
das **Abitur'** final examination in secondary school
ab·nehmen, nahm –, –genommen, er nimmt ab to lose weight
(eine Bombe) **ab·werfen, a, o, er wirft ab** to drop (a bomb)
ach oh
　ach so oh, I see
die **Achse, –n** axle, axis
acht eight
achtzehn eighteen
achtzig eighty
adressie'ren to address
　die **Adres'se, –n** address

Ägyp'ten Egypt
ähnlich similar
die **Ahnung, –en** idea; premonition; hunch
alle all, all of us
　alle all gone
allein alone
allerdings' however; admittedly
alles everything
die **Alpen** the Alps
als than; when; as
also therefore; well; in other words
alt old
das **Altertum** antiquity
alt'modisch old-fashioned
der **Amerika'ner, –** American
an on; at
ander- other
　anders different
(sich) **ändern** to change
an·fangen, i, a, er fängt an to begin, start
　der **Anfang, ⸚e** beginning, start
an·gehen, ging –, –gegangen, (ist) to begin, go on
der **Anglist', –en, –en** Anglicist
die **Angst, ⸚e** fear, anxiety
　Angst haben vor to be afraid of

an·kommen, kam –, –gekommen, (ist) to arrive
die **Ankunft** arrival
an·nehmen, nahm –, –genommen, er nimmt an to accept; to assume, take on
an·reden mit to address by
an·rufen, ie, u to call up (on the telephone)
sich etwas **an·schauen** to look at something
an·schnallen to fasten seat belts
　die **Schnalle, –n** buckle
an·sehen, a, e, er sieht an to look at
　sich etwas **an·sehen** to look at something
die **Ansicht, –en** view, opinion
antworten (*plus dat. of pers.*) to answer
　die **Antwort, –en** answer, reply
an·zeigen to announce
sich **an·ziehen, zog –, –gezogen** to get dressed
　angezogen sein to be dressed
der **Anzug, ⸚e** suit
der **Apfel, ⸚** apple
der **April'** April
arbeiten to work
　die **Arbeit, –en** work

sich ärgern über to be angry about, mad at
arm poor
der Arm, –e arm
die Armee', die Arme'en army
der Arzt, ⁔e physician, doctor
der Ast, ⁔e branch
auch also, too
auf on, on top of; up; open
  auf sein to be up, open
  auf (die Tür) zu toward (the door)
die Aufführung, –en performance
auf·geben, a, e, er gibt auf to give up; mail, post (a letter)
auf·gehen, ging –, –gegangen (ist) to rise (sun, moon); to open
aufgrund' (*prep. with gen.*) on the basis of
auf·hören to stop
die Auflage, –n printing
auf·machen to open
die Aufnahme, –n picture, photo
sich auf·regen über to get excited about
  aufgeregt sein über to be excited about
auf·schreiben, ie, ie to write down, note
auf·setzen to put on (a hat)
auf·springen, a, u, (ist) to jump up
auf·stehen, stand –, –gestanden, (ist) to get up, stand up
aufwärts up, upward
der Aufzug, ⁔e elevator
das Auge, –n eye
der Augenblick, –e moment, instant
  augenblicklich momentarily; instantly
der August' August
aus out, out of
aus·geben, a, e, er gibt aus to spend
aus·gehen, ging –, –gegangen, (ist) to go out
aus·kommen, kam –, –gekommen, (ist) to get along
die Auskunft, ⁔e information

aus·lachen to laugh at, make fun of
das Ausland foreign countries
  er lebt im Ausland he lives abroad
sich aus·ruhen to rest; to get a rest
  ausgeruht sein to be rested
(sich) aus·schlafen, ie, a, er schläft (sich) aus to get enough sleep
aus·sehen, a, e, er sieht aus to look, appear
außer besides, except for
  außerdem moreover
aus·sprechen, a, o, er spricht aus to pronounce, utter
aus·steigen, ie, ie, (ist) to get out (of a vehicle)
aus·wandern to emigrate
ausverkauft sold out
sich aus·ziehen, zog –, –gezogen to undress
  ausgezogen sein to be undressed
das Auto, –s car

backen, backte or buk, gebacken to bake
der Bäcker, – baker
baden to bathe
  das Bad, ⁔er bath
die Badewanne, –n bathtub
der Bahnhof, ⁔e railway station
  zum Bahnhof to the station
  im Bahnhof within the station
  auf dem Bahnhof on the platform
bald soon
die Bank, ⁔e bench
die Bank, –en bank
der Bart, ⁔e beard
der Bauch, ⁔e stomach, belly
bauen to build
der Bauer, –n peasant, farmer
der Baum, ⁔e tree
beachten to note, notice
der Beamte, –n, –n civil servant, (government) official
  die Beamtin, –nen official (female)
beantworten (*trans.*) to answer (a letter)

bedeuten to mean, signify
bedienen to serve
  die Bedienung service
beenden to conclude, finish
befehlen, a, o, er befiehlt (*plus dat. of pers.*) to command, order
beginnen, a, o to begin, start
begleiten to accompany
begreifen, begriff, begriffen to comprehend
behalten, ie, a, er behält to keep, retain
behaupten to maintain, claim
bei at, at the home of; near; with
  bei Schmidts at the Schmidts'
  beim Essen while eating
beide both
das Bein, –e leg
das Beispiel, –e example
  zum Beispiel (z.B.) for example
bekannt well-known
  der Bekannte, –n, –n acquaintance
bekommen, bekam, bekommen to get, receive
bellen to bark
bemerken to notice, mention, note, say
sich bemühen um, bemüht sein um to be concerned about, with
benutzen to use
beobachten to observe, watch
bereit ready
der Berg, –e mountain
berichten to report
der Beruf, –e profession
  Was sind Sie von Beruf? What is your profession?
beruhen auf to be based on
(sich) beruhigen to calm down
  beruhigt sein to be calmed down
sich beschäftigen mit to occupy oneself with
  beschäftigt sein to be occupied, employed
  die Beschäftigung, –en occupation

beschließen, beschloß, beschlossen to decide, determine
besetzen to occupy
  besetzt busy (telephone)
besonder- special
  besonders especially
besser better
bestehen aus, bestand, bestanden to consist of
bestellen to order
bestimmt definitely
besuchen to visit
  der **Besuch, –e** visit
betrachten to look at, observe
sich **betrinken, a, u** to get drunk
  betrunken sein to be drunk
das **Bett, –en** bed
beurteilen to judge, make a judgment
bevor (*conj.*) before
sich **bewegen** to move
  die **Bewegung, –en** movement
beweisen, ie, ie to prove
bezahlen to pay
die **Bibliothek', –en** library
das **Bier, –e** beer
das **Bild, –er** picture
billig inexpensive; cheap
binden, a, u to bind, tie
bis until, up until; up to, as far as
  bis gestern until yesterday
  bis Köln as far as Cologne
  bis zum Winter (up) until winter
  bis zum Bahnhof as far as the station
  zwei bis drei two to three
ein bißchen a bit, a little
die **Bitte, –n** request
bitte please
bitten um, bat, gebeten to request, ask for
blau blue
bleiben, ie, ie, (ist) to stay, remain
blicken to look, glance
  der **Blick, –e** look, glance; view
blitzen to lighten
  der **Blitz, –e** lightning

blühen to bloom, blossom, flower
die **Blume, –n** flower
der **Boden, ⸚** ground; floor
die **Bombe, –n** bomb
böse mad, angry at; evil
  (**jemandem**) **böse sein** to be angry (mad) at somebody
braten, ie, a to roast, fry
  der **Braten, –** roast
  der **Kalbsbraten, –** veal roast
  der **Schweinebraten, –** pork roast
brauchen to need
braun brown
die **Braut, ⸚e** bride
  der **Bräutigam, –e** bridegroom
brechen, a, o, er bricht to break
breit broad, wide
brennen, brannte, gebrannt to burn
der **Brief, –e** letter
  die **Brieftaube, –n** carrier pigeon
der **Briefträger, –** mailman
bringen, brachte, gebracht to bring
  ich bringe dich nach Hause I'll take you home
das **Brot, –e** bread
die **Brücke, –n** bridge
der **Bruder, ⸚** brother
der **Brunnen, –** well, fountain
das **Buch, ⸚er** book
der **Buchstabe, –n, –n** letter (of the alphabet)
die **Bühne, –n** stage
die **Bundesregierung** Federal Government (of Germany)
der **Bürger, –** citizen
  der **Bürgermeister, –** mayor
das **Büro', –s** office
der **Bus, –se** bus
die **Butter** butter

das **Café, –s** café
der **Chef, –s** boss

da there; then; under these

circumstances; (*conj.*) since
  da drüben over there
das **Dach, ⸚er** roof
daher therefore; from there, from that place
dahin there, toward that place
damals at that time
die **Dame, –n** lady, woman
damit (*conj.*) so that
dankbar grateful, thankful
danken (*plus pers. dat.*) to thank
  danke thank you, thanks
  danke schön thank you very much
  vielen Dank thank you very much
dann then
darum for that reason
das that (*demonstr.*)
daß that (*conj.*)
dauern to last, take (time)
die **Decke, –n** ceiling; blanket
denken, dachte, gedacht to think
  sich etwas denken to imagine
denn for (*conj.*)
dersel'be the same (see **158**)
deshalb therefore
Deutsch German (language)
  Deutschland Germany
  Deutsch können to know German
der **Dezember** December
der **Dieb, –e** thief
dieser, diese, dieses this
das **Ding, –e** thing
doch (see **36**)
der **Dok'tor, die Dokto'ren** doctor
der **Dollar, –s** dollar
der **Dom, –e** cathedral
donnern to thunder
  der **Donner** (*no pl.*) thunder
der **Donnerstag, –e** Thursday
das **Dorf, ⸚er** village
dort there
draußen (*adv.*) outside
sich **drehen um** to turn (around something), to revolve; to concern, to be a matter of

sich **um·drehen** to turn around

drei three

dreißig thirty

dreizehn thirteen

das **Drittel, –** third

drüben over there

drucken to print

drücken to push, press

dumm stupid, dumb

der **Dummkopf, ⸚e** dumbbell, fool

dunkel dark

durch through

durch·machen to go through, suffer

durstig thirsty

der **Durst** (*no pl.*) thirst

dürfen, durfte, gedurft (see 49 ff.)

eben just

die **Ecke, –n** corner

egoi'stisch egotistic, selfish

die **Ehre, –n** honor

das **Ei, –er** egg

eigen (*adj.*) own

eigentlich actually, really

sich **eilen**, sich **beeilen** to hurry

einander each other

sich **etwas ein·bilden** to imagine something

eingebildet sein to be conceited

eineinhalb one and a half

einfach easy, simple

ein·fallen, fiel –, –gefallen, (ist), es fällt ein to remember, occur (to one's mind)

es fällt mir ein I've just remembered

der **Einfluß, die Einflüsse** influence

ein·holen to catch up with

einige some, several, a few

ein·laden, u, a, er lädt ein to invite

einmal (*colloq.* **mal**) once, at some time

zweimal twice

dreimal three times

viermal four times

etc.

(**noch**) **nicht' einmal** not even

nicht ein'mal not once

noch einmal once more

sich **ein·ordnen** (traffic) to get into the correct lane; to merge

eins one (cardinal number)

ein·schlafen, ie, a, (ist), er schläft ein to fall asleep

ein·steigen, ie, ie, (ist) to enter, board (a plane or train)

ein·wandern to immigrate

der **Einwohner, –** inhabitant

die **Einzelheit, –en** detail

einzig only, sole

die **Eisenbahn, –en** railroad

das **Element', –e** element

elf eleven

die **Eltern** (*no singular*) parents

empfangen, i, a, er empfängt to receive

der **Empfang, ⸚e** reception

empfehlen, a, o, er empfiehlt to recommend

das **Ende, –n** end

zu Ende to an end, to a conclusion

endlich at last, finally

eng narrow

entdecken to discover

entfernt distant

sich **entschließen zu, entschloß, entschlossen** to decide, make up one's mind

entschlossen sein zu to be determined

(sich) **entschuldigen** to excuse oneself

entschuldigt sein to be excused

entsprechen (*plus dat.*)**, a, o** to correspond to

entstehen, entstand, entstanden (ist) to originate, come into being

enttäuschen to disappoint

entweder . . . oder either . . . or

die **Erde, –n** earth

erfahren, u, a, er erfährt to find out, learn; experience

erfinden, a, u to invent

die **Erfindung, –en** invention

der **Erfolg, –e** success; result

erfreut sein to be pleased, glad

erhalten, ie, a, er erhält to receive

sich **erholen** to get a rest

erholt sein to be well rested

erinnern an to remind of

sich **erinnern an** to remember

die **Erinnerung, –en** memory

sich **erkälten** to catch a cold

erkältet sein to have a cold

erkennen (an), erkannte, erkannt to recognize (by)

erklären to explain

sich **erkundigen** to inquire

erlauben to allow, permit

erleben to experience

das **Erlebnis, –se** experience, adventure

die **Ernte, –n** harvest

erreichen to reach, attain, achieve

erscheinen, ie, ie, (ist) to appear

erschrecken, erschrak, erschrocken, (ist), er erschrickt to be frightened

erst first; not until, only

erst dann not until then, only then

erst gestern not until yesterday, only yesterday

zuerst at first, first

erstaunt astonished, amazed

erstens first(ly)

zweitens second(ly)

drittens third(ly)

viertens fourth(ly)

etc.

ertrinken, a, u, (ist) to drown

erwachsen (*adj.*) grown-up, adult

erwarten to expect

sich **erweisen, ie, ie** to turn out, show

erzählen to tell, relate

erziehen, erzog, erzogen to educate, raise

essen, aß, gegessen, er ißt to eat

das Essen, – food, meal

etwa about; by any chance

etwas something; somewhat

Euro'pa Europe

europä'isch European

das Exemplar', –e copy (of a book, etc.)

die Fabrik', –en factory

fähig capable

fahren, u, a, (ist) er fährt to drive, go (by train, boat, plane, car)

fahren lernen to learn to drive

die Fahrkarte, –n (train) ticket

das Fahrrad, ̈er bicycle

fallen, fiel, gefallen, (ist) er fällt to fall, drop

der Fall, ̈e case, fall

auf jeden Fall in any case, at any rate

auf keinen Fall in no case, under no circumstances

falsch false, wrong

die Fami'lie, –n family

die Farbe, –n color

die Lieblingsfarbe, –n favorite color

färben to color; dye

farbig in color, colored

fast almost

der Februar February

der Fehler, – mistake

fein fine

der Feind, –e enemy

das Feld, –er field

das Fenster, – window

die Ferien (no singular) vacation

fern far away, distant

die Ferne distance

fern'·sehen, a, e, er sieht fern to watch TV

das Fernsehen television

der Fernseher, – TV set

fertig ready, complete, finished

fest firm(ly)

fest·stellen to determine; find out; conclude

das Feuer, – fire

das Feuerwerk, –e fireworks

der Film, –e movie, film

das Filmfestspiel, –e film festival

finden, a, u to find

der Finger, – finger

fischen to fish

der Fisch, –e fish

die Flasche, –n bottle

das Fleisch (no pl.) meat

fliegen, o, o, (ist) to fly

der Flieger, – flyer

der Tiefflieger, – strafing plane

fliehen, o, o, (ist) to escape, flee

fließen, o, geflossen, (ist) to flow

der Flug, ̈e flight

der Abflug, ̈e departure

der Fluggast, ̈e passenger

der Flughafen, ̈ airport

der Flugschein, –e plane ticket

das Flugzeug, –e airplane

flüstern to whisper

die Flut, –en flood

folgen (with dat.) to follow

fort away

der Fortschritt, –e progress

fragen to ask

die Frage, –n question

eine Frage stellen to ask a question

eine Frage beantworten to answer a question

Frankreich France

die Frau, –en woman, wife, Mrs.

das Fräulein, – young lady, Miss

frei free, unoccupied

der Freitag, –e Friday

freiwillig voluntary

fremd strange, alien

fressen, a, e, er frißt to eat (said of animals)

die Freude joy, pleasure

sich freuen auf to look forward to

sich freuen über to be happy (glad) about

der Freund, –e friend (male)

die Freundin, –nen friend (female)

frieren, o, o to freeze

frisch fresh

froh glad, gay

früh early

früher earlier; formerly

frühestens at the earliest

der Frühling, –e spring

frühstücken to breakfast, have breakfast

das Frühstück, –e breakfast

fühlen to feel

das Gefühl, –e feeling

führen to lead, guide

der Führer, – leader; guide

füllen to fill

fünf five

fünfzehn fifteen

fünfzig fifty

funktionie'ren to function, work

für for

furchtbar terrible, frightful

fürchten to fear

sich fürchten vor to be afraid of

der Fuß, ̈e foot

der Fußabdruck, ̈e footprint

füttern to feed

ganz whole, entire

ganz gut pretty good, not bad

gar nicht (kein, nichts) not (no . . . , nothing) at all

der Garten, ̈ garden

das Gas, –e gas

der Gast, ̈e guest

das Gebäude, – building

das Hauptgebäude, – main building

geben, a, e, er gibt to give

es gibt there is (are) available

aus·geben, a, e, er gibt aus to spend (money)

geboren born

ich bin geboren I was born

geboren werden to be born

die Geburt, –en birth

der Geburtstag, –e birthday

der **Gedanke,** –ns, –n thought, idea
   auf den Gedanken kommen to hit upon the idea
die **Geduld** (*no pl.*) patience
   geduldig patient
die **Gefahr,** –en danger
   gefährlich dangerous
gefallen, gefiel, gefallen, er gefällt to please
   das gefällt mir I like it (that pleases me)
der **Gefallen,** – favor
gefangen·nehmen, nahm –, –genommen, er nimmt gefangen to capture, take prisoner
gegen against
   gegen sechs Uhr around six o'clock
die **Gegend,** –en area
der **Gegensatz,** ⸚e contrast
gegenseitig each other, mutual
gegenü'ber (*with dat.*) opposite
die **Gegenwart** (*no pl.*) present; presence
   gegenwärtig present
geheim secret
   das **Geheimnis,** –se secret
gehen, ging, gegangen, (ist) to go, walk
gehorchen to obey
gehören (*plus pers. dat.*) to belong to (property)
   gehören zu to belong to (membership)
die **Geiß,** –en goat
der **Geist** intellect, mind, spirit; ghost
das **Geld** money
gelingen, a, u, (ist) to succeed
   es gelingt mir I succeed
das **Gemüse,** – vegetable
genau exact
der **General',** ⸚e general
genug enough
das **Gepäck** (*no pl.*) baggage
gerade just, straight
gern(e) gladly
   ich esse gern(e) I like to eat
   ich möchte gern(e) etwas

essen I'd like to eat something
der **Gesandte,** –n ambassador, envoy
das **Geschäft,** –e business; store
geschehen, a, e, (ist), es geschieht to happen, occur
das **Geschenk,** –e present, gift
die **Geschichte,** –n story, history
das **Gesetz,** –e law
das **Gesicht,** –er face
das **Gespräch,** –e conversation
gestatten to permit, allow
gestern yesterday
   gestern abend last night, yesterday evening
gesund well, healthy
gewinnen, a, o to win
gewiß certain
sich gewöhnen an to get used to
   gewöhnt sein an to be used to
gewöhnlich usual
das **Glas,** ⸚er glass
der **Glaube,** –ns (*no pl.*) belief, faith
   glauben to think, believe
   glauben an (*with acc.*) to believe in
gleich equal, same, like; (*time adv.*) immediately, presently
das **Glück** (*no pl.*) happiness; luck, good luck; fortune
   Glück haben to be lucky
   glücklich happy
glücklicherwei'se fortunately, happily
gnädige Frau formal way of addressing a married woman
der **Gott,** ⸚er god
   Gott God
gottseidank' thank heavens, thank goodness
gratulie'ren to congratulate
grau gray
greifen, griff, gegriffen to grasp, reach out (for something)

die **Grenze,** –n border
groß big, great, tall
   die **Großstadt,** ⸚e large city, metropolis
der **Großvater,** ⸚ grandfather
grün green
der **Grund,** ⸚e reason, ground
   aufgrund' (*with gen.*) on the basis of
grüßen to greet
   der **Gruß,** ⸚e greeting
gut good
das **Gymna'sium, die Gymna'sien** German secondary school, grades 5–13)

das **Haar,** –e hair
haben to have
hageln to hail
halb half
die **Hälfte,** –n half
die **Halle,** –en hall, lobby
halten, ie, a, er hält to hold, stop
   halten für to consider
   halten von to think of
die **Hand,** ⸚e hand
handeln to act
   sich handeln um to be a matter of
   handeln mit to deal with (objects)
   handeln von to deal with (subject matter)
der **Händler,** – dealer
die **Handschrift** handwriting
der **Handschuh,** –e glove
die **Handtasche,** –n handbag
hart hard
hassen to hate
das **Haus,** ⸚er house
   ich gehe nach Hause I go home
   ich bin zu Hause I am at home
heilen to heal
   geheilt healed, well
heiraten to get married, marry
   verheiratet married
   ich bin verheiratet I am married
heiß hot

heißen, ie, ei to be called; to mean
heizen to heat
  die **Heizung** heating system, radiator
  die **Zentral′heizung** central heating
helfen (*plus pers. dat.*), **a, o, er hilft** to help
hell light, bright
das **Hemd, –en** shirt
her toward the speaker (in the sense of *hither*)
  heraus′ out
  herbei′ here
  herein′ in
  her·kommen to come here
sich heraus·stellen to turn out, become apparent
der **Herd, –e** stove
der **Herr, –en** (*gen., dat. and acc. sing.* **Herrn**) gentleman
herrlich magnificent, splendid, marvelous
herum′ around
das **Herz, –ens, –en** (*dat.:* **dem Herzen**) heart
der **Herzog, ⁻e** duke
heute today
  heute abend this evening, tonight
  heute morgen this morning
hier here
die **Hilfe** help
der **Himmel** heaven, sky
  himmlisch heavenly
hin away from the speaker
  hinein′ in
  hin·fahren, u, a, (ist), er fährt hin to go there
hinten (*adv.*) in the back
hinter (*prep.*) behind, beyond, on the other side of
der **Hintergrund, ⁻e** background
hinun′ter down
  den (Rhein) hinunter down the (Rhine)
die **Hitze** (*no pl.*) heat
hoch high
  höchstens at the most
der **Hof, ⁻e** court, yard

der **Hofgarten** the Royal Gardens
hoffen to hope
  hoffentlich I hope (*sent. adv.*)
höflich polite
die **Höhe, –n** height
  in die Höhe upward
holen to get, fetch
das **Holz, ⁻er** wood
hören to hear
  der **Hörer, –** telephone receiver; listener
das **Hotel′, –s** hotel
hübsch pretty
der **Hund, –e** dog
hundert hundred
der **Hunger** hunger
  ich habe Hunger I am hungry
  hungrig hungry
der **Hut, ⁻e** hat

die **Idee′, die Ide′en** idea
immer always
  immer noch, noch immer still
  immer wieder again and again
in in
In′dien India
  der **In′der, –** (East) Indian
  der **India′ner, –** (American) Indian
der **Ingenieur′, –e** engineer
intelligent′ intelligent
  die **Intelligenz′** intelligence, intellect
interessant′ interesting
sich interessie′ren für, interessiert sein an to be interested in
inzwi′schen meanwhile, in the meantime
irgendetwas something, anything
irgendwo somewhere
  irgendwohin somewhere
der **Irrtum, ⁻er** error
Ita′lien Italy
  italie′nisch Italian

ja yes; indeed
das **Jahr, –e** year

das **Jahrhun′dert, –e** century
der **Januar** January
je, jemals ever
jedenfalls at any rate
jeder, jede, jedes each, every
jedoch however
jemand somebody, someone
jetzt now
die **Jugend** (*no pl.*) youth (*collective noun*); time of youth
der **Ju′li** July
jung young
der **Junge, –n** boy
der **Ju′ni** June

der **Kaffee** coffee
kalt cold
  die **Kälte** (*no pl.*) cold
kämmen to comb
kämpfen to fight
  der **Kampf, ⁻e** fight, battle
das **Kapi′tel, –** chapter
die **Karte, –n** map; ticket
  die **Landkarte, –n** map
  die **Fahrkarte, –n** (train) ticket
  die **Rückfahrkarte, –n** round-trip ticket
die **Kartof′fel, –n** potato
die **Kasse, –n** cash register, cash box
der **Kasten, ⁻** chest, box
kaufen to buy
kaum hardly
kein no (not any)
der **Kellner, –** waiter
  der **Oberkellner, –** headwaiter
  "Herr Ober" normal way of addressing a waiter
kennen, kannte, gekannt to know, be acquainted with
kennen·lernen to meet, become acquainted with
das **Kind, –er** child
das **Kino, –s** movie house
die **Kirche, –n** church
  ich gehe in die Kirche I go to church
klar clear
die **Klasse, –n** class
das **Klavier′, –e** piano
das **Kleid, –er** dress

klein little
klettern to climb
das **Klima** climate
klingeln to ring (bell)
klingen, a, u to sound
klopfen to knock
  an·klopfen to knock (at the door)
das **Knie, die Kni'e** knee
kochen to cook, boil
der **Koffer, –** suitcase
komisch funny; odd; comical
das **Komma, –s** comma
kommen, kam, gekommen, (ist) to come
der **König, –e** king
können, konnte, gekonnt, er kann (see 49 ff.)
das **Konzert', –e** concert
der **Kopf, –̈e** head
  die **Kopfschmerzen** (*pl.*) headache
der **Körper, –** body
kosten to cost
krank sick
  die **Krankheit, –en** illness, disease
die **Kreide** chalk
der **Kreis, –e** circle
der **Krieg, –e** war
kriegen (*colloq.*) = **bekommen** to get
die **Küche, –n** kitchen
die **Kugel, –n** ball, globe; bullet
  der **Kugelschreiber, –** ball-point pen
sich **kümmern um** to take care of; to be concerned with
kurz short
die **Kusi'ne, –n** (female) cousin
küssen to kiss

lächeln to smile
  das **Lächeln** smile
lachen to laugh
  das **Lachen** laughter
das **Land, –̈er** country; land
  auf dem Land in the country
landen to land
die **Landkarte, –n** map
lang long
  lange for a long time

jahrelang for years
  fünf Jahre lang for five years
langsam slow
längst, schon längst for a long time, a long time ago
lang'·weilen to bore
  sich **langweilen, gelangweilt sein** to be bored
langweilig boring
der **Lärm** (*no pl.*) noise; din
lassen, ie, a, er läßt to let, leave
  die **Kinder zu Hause lassen** to leave the children at home
die **Later'ne, –n** street light
laufen, ie, au, er läuft to run
laut loud
leben to live, be alive
  das **Leben, –** life
  am Leben sein to be alive
  ums Leben kommen to lose one's life
das **Leder** leather
leer empty
legen to lay, place
  sich **legen** to lie down
lehren to teach
  der **Lehrer, –** teacher
leicht easy; light (in weight)
leiden, litt, gelitten to suffer
leider unfortunately (*sent. adv.*)
leid tun to be sorry
  es tut mir leid I am sorry
  er tut mir leid I am sorry for him
leise soft, without noise
sich **leisten** to afford
lernen to learn
lesen, a, e, er liest to read
letzt– last
  letzten Mai last May
  letzte Woche last week
  letztes Jahr last year
leuchten to shine
die **Leute** (*pl. only*) people
der **Leutnant, –e** lieutenant
das **Licht, –er** light
lieb dear
  lieber rather (*adv.*)
  am liebsten (to like) most of all
  lieb·haben to love

lieben to love
  die **Liebe** love
lieblich lovely
der **Liebling, –e** darling, favorite
das **Lied, –er** song
liegen, a, e to lie (flat); to be situated
link– left
  links to the left
die **Lippe, –n** lip
loben to praise
lochen to punch (a ticket)
  das **Loch, –̈er** hole
die **Lokomoti've, –n** locomotive
los loose
  was ist los what's the matter
lösen to solve, dissolve
die **Luft, –̈e** air
  die **Luftpost** airmail
lügen, o, o to tell a lie

machen to make; to do
  es macht nichts it doesn't matter
  an·machen to turn on
  aus·machen to turn off
das **Mädchen, –** girl
die **Mahlzeit, –en** meal
der **Mai** May
das **Mal** time
  dieses Mal this time
  diesmal this time
  einmal once
  zweimal twice
  noch einmal once more
  manchmal sometimes
  jedesmal every time
  zwei mal zwei two times two
man (*dat.:* **einem** *acc.:* **einen**) one (*pronoun*)
mancher many a (see 152)
  manchmal sometimes
der **Mann, –̈er** man, husband
der **Mantel, –̈** coat, overcoat
die **Mark** mark
  zwei Mark two marks
der **Markt, –̈e** market; market place
die **Maschi'ne, –n** machine; typewriter

die **Mate′rie** (*no pl.*) matter
die **Mathematik′** mathematics
die **Medizin′** medicine; science of medicine
das **Mehl** flour
mehr more
  mehr als more than
  nicht mehr no longer
mehrere several
die **Meile, –n** mile
meinen to mean, be of the opinion, say, have an opinion
die **Meinung, –en** opinion
meist– most
meistens usually, mostly
sich **melden** to report (to somebody); to answer (the phone)
die **Menge, –n** quantity, mass, crowd
  jede Menge any amount
der **Mensch, –en, –en** man, human being
merken to notice
das **Messer, –** knife
das **Meter, –** meter
die **Milch** (*no pl.*) milk
mild mild
die **Milliar′de, –n** billion
die **Million′, –en** million
mindestens at least
die **Minu′te, –n** minute
mit with, along
mit·machen to go along, cooperate
der **Mittag, –e** noon
  der **Nachmittag, –e** afternoon
das **Mittagessen, –** dinner (noon meal, the main meal in Germany)
mit·teilen to inform, let know, report (something)
das **Mittelalter** Middle Ages
Mitternacht midnight
der **Mittwoch, –e** Wednesday
die **Möbel** (*pl.*) furniture
modern′ modern
mögen, mochte, gemocht, er mag (see **137** ff.)
möglich possible

unmöglich impossible; (*sent. adv.*) not possibly
möglicherweise possibly
die **Möglichkeit, –en** possibility
der **Mo′nat, –e** month
der **Mond, –e** moon
der **Montag, –e** Monday
der **Morgen, –** morning
  heute morgen this morning
  morgen tomorrow
  morgen abend tomorrow evening
das **Motorrad, ¨er** motorcycle
müde tired
der **Müller, –** miller
der **Mund** mouth
  mündlich oral
das **Muse′um, die Muse′en** museum
musizie′ren to make music
müssen, mußte, gemußt, er muß (see **49** ff.)
die **Mutter, ¨** mother
  Mutti Mom, Mommy

na well
  na sowas! (expression of astonishment) you don't mean it, what do you think of that
  na und? so what?
nach to, toward; after
der **Nachbar, –n, –n** neighbor
nachdem′ (*conj.*) after
nach·denken über, dachte –, –gedacht to reflect, meditate about
nachher afterwards
der **Nachmittag, –e** afternoon
der **Nachname, –ns, –n** last name
nach·schicken to forward (mail)
nach·sehen, a, e, er sieht nach to look up; to investigate
nächst– next
  nächstes Jahr next year
nächstens in the near future
die **Nacht, ¨e** night
  heute nacht this coming night; last night
  but: **gestern abend** last

night (before going to bed), yesterday evening
nah near, close by
  die **Nähe** proximity, closeness, nearness
nähen to sew
der **Name, –ns, –n** (*dat.:* dem Namen; *acc.:* den Namen) name
  der **Vorname, –ns, –n** first name
  der **Nachname, –ns, –n** last name
nämlich namely; that is to say; you know
die **Nase, –n** nose
die **Natur′** nature
  natür′lich naturally, of course
neben next to, beside
der **Nebel** fog
  neblig foggy
nebenan′ next door
nee (*colloq.*) = **nein** no
nehmen, nahm, genommen, er nimmt to take
nein no
nervös′ nervous
nett nice
neu new
  das ist mir neu that's news to me
  die **Neuigkeit, –en** news
neulich recently
neun nine
neunzehn nineteen
nicht not
  nicht mehr no longer
  noch nicht not yet
nichts nothing
nicken to nod
nie never
niemand nobody, no one
nirgends nowhere
noch still
  noch nicht not yet
  noch einmal once more
der **Norden** the north
  nördlich northern
die **Nordsee** the North Sea
normalerweise normally
Norwegen Norway
der **November** November
null zero
die **Nummer, –n** number
nun now

nur only
nutzlos useless

ob whether, if
oben up (above); upstairs, on top
das **Obst** (*no pl.*) fruit
obwohl although
oder or
öffentlich public
der **Offizier'**, **–e** officer
(sich) **öffnen** to open
  geöffnet sein to be open
  offen (*adj.*) open
oft often
ohne (*with acc.*) without
der **Onkel**, **–** uncle
die **Oper**, **–n** opera; opera house
die **Ordnung** order
  in Ordnung in order, all right, O.K.
der **Osten** the east
  östlich eastern

das **Paar**, **–e** pair, couple
  ein paar a few
das **Paket'**, **–e** package, parcel
das **Papier'**, **–e** paper
die **Partei'**, **–en** party
der **Paß**, die **Pässe** passport; pass
passieren to happen
die **Pause**, **–n** pause, intermission, break
(das) **Persil'** a German detergent
die **Person'**, **–en** person
  persön'lich personal
  der **Perso'nenzug**, **–̈e** local train
der **Pfarrer**, **–** pastor
der **Pfennig**, **–e** pfennig, penny
das **Pfund**, **–e** pound
die **Physik'** (*no pl.*) physics
der **Plan**, **–̈e** plan
die **Platte**, **–n** (phonograph) record, plate, flagstone
der **Platz**, **–̈e** place, plaza, square; seat
  der **Sitzplatz**, **–̈e** seat
  Platz nehmen to sit down, have a seat
plötzlich suddenly

plus plus, and
Polen Poland
  polnisch Polish
die **Polizei'** (*no pl.*) police
  der **Polizist'**, **–en** policeman
die **Post** mail; post office
der **Preis**, **–e** price; prize
prima (*colloq.*) wonderful
das **Problem'**, **–e** problem
der **Profes'sor**, die **Professo'-ren** professor
Prozent' percent
die **Psychologie'** psychology
das **Pulver**, **–** powder; gunpowder
der **Punkt**, **–e** point, period
putzen to clean

das **Rad**, **–̈er** wheel
sich **rasie'ren** to shave
  rasiert sein to be shaved
raten, **ie**, **a**, **er rät** to advise; give counsel; guess
  der **Rat** advice, counsel; council; councilor
  das **Rathaus**, **–̈er** town (city) hall
rauchen to smoke
der **Raum**, **–̈e** room; space
reagie'ren auf to react to
recht right; correct
  rechts to the right
  das ist mir recht that's all right with me
  recht haben to be right
  mit Recht rightfully
rechtzeitig on time
reden to talk, speak
die **Regie'rung**, **–en** government
  die **Bun'desregierung** Federal Government (of Germany)
regnen to rain
  der **Regen** rain
reich rich
die **Reihe**, **–n** row; series
  ich bin an der Reihe it's my turn
reisen to travel
  die **Reise**, **–n** trip
  eine Reise machen to take a trip
reißen, **riß**, **gerissen** to tear

rennen, **rannte**, **gerannt** (**ist**) to run
reparie'ren to repair
reservie'ren to reserve
retten to save
der **Rhein** the Rhine
richtig correct, accurate
die **Richtung**, **–en** direction
der **Ring**, **–e** ring
rollen to roll
der **Roman**, **–e** novel
die **Rose**, **–n** rose
rot red
die **Rückfahrkarte**, **–en** round-trip ticket
rufen, **ie**, **u** to call
ruhig quiet, restful; (*sent. adv.*) it won't bother me, I'll stay calm about it
  unruhig restless
  die **Ruhe** rest; quietness
  in aller Ruhe at leisure
rund round
russisch Russian
Rußland Russia

die **Sache**, **–n** thing, matter
sagen to say
das **Salz**, **–e** salt
der **Samstag**, **–e** Saturday
  samstags on Saturdays
sanft soft
der **Sänger**, **–** singer
sauer sour
schade too bad
der **Schalter**, **–** (ticket) window
der **Schauspieler**, **–** actor
schauen to look, gaze
sich **scheiden lassen von** to get a divorce from
  geschieden sein to be divorced
scheinen, **ie**, **ie** to seem; to shine
  er scheint zu schlafen he seems to be asleep
schenken to give (as a present), present
  das **Geschenk**, **–e** present, gift
schicken to send
schieben, **o**, **o** to push, shove
das **Schiff**, **–e** ship, boat

schi·laufen to ski

der **Schinken**, – ham

schlafen, ie, a, er schläft to sleep

schlagen, u, a, er schlägt to beat, hit

schlank slender, slim

schlecht bad

(sich) **schließen, schloß, geschlossen** to close

   geschlossen sein to be closed

schließlich finally, after all

schlucken to swallow

   der **Schluck** sip

der **Schluß, die Schlüsse** end; conclusion

der **Schlüssel**, – key

die **Schnalle**, –n buckle

schnarchen to snore

der **Schnee** (*no pl.*) snow

schneiden, schnitt, geschnitten to cut

   der **Schnitt**, –e cut

schneien to snow

schnell fast, rapid

die **Schokola′de** chocolate

schon already

schön beautiful, pretty; good, O.K.

der **Schrank**, ⸚e cupboard, wardrobe

schreiben, ie, ie to write

schreien, ie, ie to scream, cry

   der **Schrei**, –e scream

   der **Schriftsteller**, – writer

der **Schuh**, –e shoe

die **Schule**, –n school

   auf der Schule in school

der **Schüler**, – pupil, (Gymnasium) student

die **Schulter**, –n shoulder

der **Schuß, die Schüsse** shot

schwach weak

der **Schwager**, ⸚ brother-in-law

schwarz black

der **Schwarzwald** Black Forest

schweigen, ie, ie to be silent, say nothing

das **Schwein**, –e pig; swine

   das **Schweinefleisch** (*no pl.*) pork

die **Schweiz** Switzerland

schwer hard, heavy, difficult

die **Schwester**, –n sister

schwimmen, a, o, (ist) to swim

   das **Schwimmbecken**, – swimming pool

sechs six

sechzehn sixteen

sechzig sixty

der **See, die Se′en** lake

die **See** (*no pl.*) sea, ocean

sehen, a, e, er sieht to see

sehr very

sein, war, gewesen, (ist), er ist to be

seit since

   seitdem (*conj.*) since; (*adv.*) since then, since that time

   seit langem for a long time

   seit Anfang Mai since the beginning of May

die **Seite**, –n page, side

der **Sekretär′**, –e secretary

selbst, selber –self (see **175**); even (see **176**)

selten rare, seldom

seltsam strange, peculiar

das **Seme′ster**, – semester

senden, sandte, gesandt to send; broadcast

   der **Sender**, – sender; broadcasting station

der **September** September

setzen to set

   sich setzen to sit down

sicher certain, sure; probably

sieben seven

siebzehn seventeen

singen, a, u to sing

sinken, a, u, (ist) to sink

der **Sinn**, –e sense

die **Situation′**, –en situation

sitzen, saß, gesessen to sit

   der **Sitzplatz**, ⸚e seat

so so

   so etwas something like this

sobald′ (*conj.*) as soon as

soe′ben just, just now

sofort′ at once, immediately

sogar′ even

der **Sohn**, ⸚e son

solan′ge (*conj.*) as long as

solcher such (see **153**)

der **Soldat′**, –en, –en soldier

sollen (see **49** ff.)

der **Sommer**, – summer

sondern but

die **Sonne**, –n sun

der **Sonntag**, –e Sunday

   jeden Sonntag every Sunday

   sonntags on Sundays, every Sunday

sonst otherwise

soviel so much, as much; (*conj.*) as far as

sowieso anyhow, anyway

spät late

spätestens at the latest

spazie′ren·fahren, u, a, (ist), er fährt spazieren to go for a ride

spazie′ren·gehen, ging –, –gegangen, (ist) to go for a walk

der **Spiegel**, – mirror

spielen to play

der **Sport** (*no pl.*) sport, sports, athletics

sprechen, a, o, er spricht to speak, talk

die **Sprache**, –n language

springen, a, u, (ist) to jump

   auf′springen to jump up

die **Spur**, –en trace

   spurlos without a trace

der **Staat**, –en state

die **Stadt**, ⸚e town, city

stark strong, heavy

starren to stare

statt (*with gen.*) instead of

   statt . . . zu (kaufen) instead of (buying)

stecken to stick, put

stehen, stand, gestanden to stand

   auf′stehen, (ist) to arise, stand up, get up, rise

stehen·bleiben, ie, ie, (ist) to stop

stehlen, a, o, er stiehlt to steal

steigen, ie, ie, (ist) to climb

   ein′steigen to enter, board (a train or plane)

der **Stein**, –e stone

stellen to place, put (upright)

die **Stelle**, –n place

die **Stellung**, –en position; job

sterben, a, o, (ist), er stirbt to die
still quiet, still
die **Stimme, –n** voice
stimmen to be correct
  das stimmt nicht that's wrong
der **Stock, ⁻e** stick; floor (of a building)
  im ersten (zweiten, etc.) Stock on the first (second, etc.) floor
der **Stolz** (*no pl.*) pride
  stolz proud
stören to disturb
die **Straße, –n** street
die **Straßenbahn, –en** streetcar
streichen, i, i to spread; to stroke; to paint
das **Stück, –e** piece; play
  das **Goldstück, –e** gold coin
der **Student, –en, –en** student (masculine)
  die **Studentin, –nen** student (feminine)
studie′ren to study
  das **Stu′dium, die Stu′dien** studies, course of study
der **Stuhl, ⁻e** chair
die **Stunde, –n** hour
suchen to look for, seek, search
  die **Suche** search
der **Süden** the south
  südlich southern
die **Suppe, –n** soup

der **Tabak, –e** tobacco
der **Tag, –e** day
das **Tal, ⁻er** valley
die **Tante, –n** aunt
tanzen to dance
  der **Tanz, ⁻e** dance
die **Tasche, –n** pocket; bag, handbag; briefcase
die **Tasse, –n** cup
tatsächlich actual(ly), indeed, as a matter of fact
tausend thousand
das **Taxi, –s; die Taxe, –n** taxi
der **Tee** tea
teilen to divide
  geteilt durch divided by
  der **Teil, –e** part

das **Telefon, –e** telephone
telefonie′ren (mit) to talk on the phone (with), to make a phone call (to)
die **Terras′se, –n** terrace
das **Testament′, –e** last will
teuer expensive
das **Thea′ter, –** theater
das **Thema, die Themen** topic; subject; theme
das **Tier, –e** animal
der **Tisch, –e** table
die **Tochter, ⁻** daughter
der **Tod, –e** death
  todschick elegant, "great"
das **Tor, –e** gate
tot dead
tragen, u, a, er trägt to carry; to wear
träumen to dream
  der **Traum, ⁻e** dream
treffen, traf, getroffen, er trifft to meet; to hit
trennen to separate
treten, a, e, (ist) er tritt to step
trinken, a, u to drink
trotz (*prep.*) in spite of
trotzdem (*adv.*) in spite of, despite, nevertheless
tun, tat, getan to do
die **Tür, –en** door

über over
überall everywhere
überfüllt′ overflowing
überhaupt anyway
sich überle′gen to think about, meditate, consider
überra′schen to surprise
überre′den to persuade
überset′zen to translate
  die **Überset′zung, –en** translation
(sich) überzeu′gen to convince (oneself)
  überzeugt sein von to be convinced
übrigens by the way, incidentally
die **Uhr, –en** clock, watch
  sechs Uhr six o'clock
  wieviel Uhr what time
um around; about; at
um . . . zu in order to

um·kommen, kam –, –gekommen, (ist) to perish
um·werfen to knock over
um·ziehen, zog –, –gezogen, (ist) to move
sich um·ziehen to change (clothes)
  umgezogen sein to be changed
unbedingt absolute(ly), by all means
und and
unendlich infinite
ungefähr approximate(ly), about
die **Universität, –en** university
unmöglich impossible
unruhig restless
der **Unsinn** nonsense
unten (*adv.*) down, down below, downstairs
(sich) unterbre′chen, a, o, er unterbricht to interrupt
unter·bringen, brachte –, –gebracht to put up, lodge
unter·gehen, ging –, –gegangen, (ist) to sink, perish; to set (sun, moon)
die **Untergrundbahn, –en** subway
sich unterhal′ten, ie, a, er unterhält sich to converse, have a conversation
unter·kommen, kam –, –gekommen, (ist) to find a place to stay
unterrich′ten to teach, instruct
der **Unterschied, –e** difference
untersu′chen to investigate
der **Urlaub** (*no pl.*) furlough; vacation

die **Vase, –n** vase
der **Vater, ⁻** father
sich verändern to change
  verändert sein to be changed, different
verbieten, o, o to forbid, prohibit

(sich) **verbinden, a, u** to unite; to compound; to connect

verbringen, verbrachte, verbracht to spend (time)

verdienen to earn, deserve

die **Vereinigten Staaten** the United States

sich **verfahren, u, a, er verfährt sich** to lose one's way (driving)

vergessen, vergaß, vergessen er vergißt to forget

vergiften to poison

sich **verheiraten** to get married

verkaufen to sell

der **Verkehr** traffic

der **Verlag, –e** publishing house, publisher

verlangen to demand

verlassen, verließ, verlassen, er verläßt to leave (somebody or something)

sich **verlassen auf** to depend, rely upon

sich **verlaufen, ie, au, er verläuft sich** to lose one's way (walking)

der **Verleger, –** publisher

sich **verlieben in** to fall in love with

verliebt sein in to be in love with

verlieren, o, o to lose

sich **verloben mit** to get engaged to

verlobt sein mit to be engaged to

verlobt engaged

der **Verlobte, –n** fiancé

das **Vermögen, –** wealth, fortune, estate

die **Vernunft** reason (intellect)

vernünftig reasonable

verrückt crazy

verschwinden, a, u, (ist) to disappear

verschwunden (*adj.*) lost

die **Verspätung, –en** delay

Verspätung haben to be late, not on schedule

versprechen, a, o, er verspricht to promise

der **Verstand** (*no pl.*) mind, reason

verstehen, verstand, verstanden to understand

versuchen to try, attempt

der **Versuch, –e** try, attempt; experiment

die **Verwandlung, –en** change, metamorphosis

verwandt related

der **Verwandte, –n, –n** relative

verwunden to injure, wound

verzeihen, ie, ie to pardon, excuse

die **Verzeihung** pardon

der **Vetter, –n** cousin (male)

viel much

viele many

soviel so much, as much

zuviel too much

vielleicht' perhaps

vier four

vierzehn fourteen

vierzig forty

das **Visum, die Visen** visa

das **Volk, ‒er** people

voll full

völlig completely

von from

von (Paris) aus from (Paris)

vor before; in front of; ago

vor einem Jahr a year ago

vor allem above all

vorbei' (*adv.*) gone, past

vorbei'·gehen, ging –, –gegangen, (ist) to pass

sich **vor·bereiten auf** to prepare for

vorbereitet sein auf to be prepared for

vorgestern day before yesterday

vorher (*adv.*) before, earlier

vorhin' a little while ago

der **Vorname, –ns, –n** first name

vorne in front

vor·schlagen, u, a, er schlägt vor to propose, suggest

der **Vorschlag, ‒e** suggestion, proposal

die **Vorsicht** (*no pl.*) caution

vorsichtig careful

sich **vor·stellen** (*dat. reflexive*) to imagine

(sich) **vor·stellen** (*acc. reflexive*) to introduce (oneself)

wachsen, u, a, (ist), er wächst to grow

erwachsen (*adj.*) grownup, adult

wagen to dare

der **Wagen, –** car; wagon

wählen to choose; to dial

wahr true

während during

wahrschein'lich probably

der **Wald, ‒er** woods, forest

die **Wand, ‒e** wall

wandern to wander, migrate, hike

aus·wandern to emigrate

ein·wandern to immigrate

wann when

warm warm

warten auf (*with acc.*) to wait for

warum why

was what

was für what kind of (see 159)

waschen, u, a, er wäscht to wash

das **Wasser** water

der **Wechsel, –** change

weder ... noch neither ... nor

weg away

weg·fahren, u, a, (ist), er fährt weg to drive away, leave

der **Weg, –e** way, path

wegen because of

sich **weigern** to refuse

Weihnachten Christmas

weil (*conj.*) because

der **Wein, –e** wine

weinen to cry, weep

weiß white

weit far

welcher which

die **Welt, –en** world

wenig little

weniger minus, less

wenigstens at least

wenn when, whenever, if

wer who

werden, wurde, geworden (ist), er wird to become
werfen, a, o, er wirft to throw
um·werfen to knock over
der Westen the west
die Westfront Western Front
westlich western
wetten um to bet
das Wetter weather
wichtig important
wie as; like; how
wie gesagt as I said
wieder again (i.e., second or third time); back (to the place of origin)
wiederauf'bauen, ich baue wieder auf to reconstruct
wiederho'len to repeat
wieder·sehen, a, e, er sieht wieder to see again
auf Wiedersehen good-by
auf Wiederhören good-by (telephone)
wiegen, o, o to weigh
Wien Vienna
die Wiese, –n meadow
wieviel how much
wieviel Uhr what time
wild wild
der Winter, – winter
im Winter in the winter
wirklich really
die Wirklichkeit, –en reality
der Wirt, –e innkeeper, landlord
wissen, wußte, gewußt, er weiß to know (as a fact)
wissen Sie you know (sent. adv.)
das Wissen knowledge
die Wissenschaft, –en science
wissenschaftlich scientific
wo where

die Woche, –n week
woher from where
wohin where, where to (direction)
wohl well; probably
wohnen to reside, live
die Wohnung, –en apartment
der Wolf, ̈e wolf
wollen, er will (see 49 ff.)
das Wort, ̈er (also –e) word
die Wunde, –n wound
das Wunder, – miracle, wonder
wunderbar wonderful, marvelous
sich wundern über to be amazed at
der Wunsch, ̈e wish
wünschen to wish
die Wurst, ̈e sausage, cold cuts
das Würstchen, – sausage
wütend mad, angry

zahlen to pay (in a restaurant)
zählen to count
die Zahl, –en number
der Zahn, ̈e tooth
der Zaun, ̈e fence
zehn ten
zeigen to show
sich zeigen (impersonal) to turn out, show
die Zeile, –n line (of print, poetry, verse)
die Zeit, –en time
eine Zeitlang for a while (not: for a long time)
die Zeitung, –en newspaper
zerstören to destroy
ziehen, zog, gezogen to pull; (ist) to move (from one place to another)

er hat gezogen he has pulled
er ist nach (Köln) gezogen he has moved to (Cologne)
die Zigaret'te, –n cigarette
die Zigar're, –n cigar
das Zimmer, – room
zittern to tremble, shake
zögern to hesitate
der Zoll, ̈e customs; duty
zu to; too; at
zuviel too much
zuerst first, at first
der Zufall, ̈e accident, coincidence
durch Zufall by accident
zufällig by coincidence, by chance, accidentally
zufrie'den (adj.) satisfied, content
der Zug, ̈e train
die Zugspitze highest mountain in Germany
zu·hören to listen to
die Zukunft (no pl.) future
zunächst' first, first of all
zu·nehmen, nahm –, –genommen, (ist), er nimmt zu to gain weight
zurück' back
wieder zurück back, back again
zusam'men together
sich zusam'men·setzen aus to be composed of
zwanzig twenty
zwar to be sure
zwei two
der Zwerg, –e dwarf
zwingen, a, u to force
zwischen between
zwölf twelve

VOCABULARY: English–German

able: to be able to können
to accept annehmen
accidentally zufällig
to act (as if) tun (als ob)
afraid: to be afraid (of) Angst
   haben (vor)
after all doch
again wieder
airport der Flughafen
alone allein
along mit
already schon
also auch
although obwohl
always immer
to **answer** antworten
apartment die Wohnung
approximately ungefähr
arm der Arm
to **arrive** ankommen
to **ask** fragen
aunt die Tante
away weg

back zurück
bank die Bank, -en
to bathe, take a bath (sich)
   baden
beautiful schön
because weil
to **become** werden
bed das Bett
to **begin** anfangen
   beginning der Anfang
to **believe** glauben, denken
   to believe in glauben an
to **belong to** gehören
bench die Bank, ⁓e
birthday der Geburtstag
book das Buch
bored: to be bored sich
   langweilen
to **break** brechen
breakfast das Frühstück
brother der Bruder

to **build** bauen
but aber; sondern
to **buy** kaufen

to **call (up)** anrufen
called: to be called heißen
to **calm down** sich beruhigen
car der Wagen
to **catch a cold** sich erkälten
chair der Stuhl
to **change** (sich) ändern,
   (sich) verändern
to **change** (clothes) sich
   umziehen
child das Kind
church die Kirche
city die Stadt
coat der Mantel
coffee der Kaffee
cold kalt
to **come** kommen
correct: to be correct
   stimmen
to **count** zählen
of course natürlich
cup die Tasse

darling Liebling
daughter die Tochter
day der Tag
dead tot
to **deal with** sich handeln um
   (*impersonal*)
dear lieb
to **decide** sich entschließen
to **die** sterben
different(ly) ander-, anders
dinner das Essen, das
   Mittagessen, das
   Abendessen
to **disappear** verschwinden
divorce: to get a divorce sich
   scheiden lassen
to **do** tun
doctor der Arzt, der Doktor

dog der Hund
door die Tür
downtown in die Stadt
to **drink** trinken
to **drive** fahren
drunk: to get drunk sich
   betrinken
dumbell der Dummkopf

each jeder, jede, jedes
early früh
to **eat** essen
end das Ende
engaged: to get engaged sich
   verloben
every jeder, jede, jedes
everything alles
excited: to get excited (about)
   sich aufregen (über)
to **expect** erwarten
expensive teuer
to **experience** erfahren
eye das Auge

far weit
father der Vater
to **feel** fühlen
few wenige
   a few ein paar, einige
to **fight** kämpfen
finally endlich, schließlich
flower die Blume
to **fly** fliegen
footprint der Fußabdruck
for (*conj.*) denn
to **forget** vergessen
free frei
friend der Freund, die
   Freundin

garden der Garten
girl das Mädchen
to **give** geben
to **go** gehen

687

goldpiece das Goldstück
good gut

haircut: to get a haircut sich
  die Haare schneiden
  lassen
to **happen** geschehen,
  passieren
happy glücklich
hat der Hut
to **have** haben
  to **have to** müssen
healthy gesund
to **hear** hören
to **help** helfen
here hier
hole das Loch
home (*adv.*) nach Hause
  at home zu Hause
to **hope** hoffen
hot heiß
hour die Stunde
house das Haus
how wie
human being der Mensch
hungry hungrig
to **hurry up** sich eilen, sich
  beeilen
husband der Mann

if wenn
to **imagine** sich vorstellen,
  sich (etwas) einbilden
immediately sofort
important wichtig
instead of statt . . . zu
intelligent intelligent
to **intend to** wollen
interested: to be interested in
  sich interessieren für
interesting interessant
to **introduce (oneself)** (sich)
  vorstellen
to **invite** einladen

just gerade

key der Schlüssel
to **knock** klopfen
to **know** (a person) kennen
  to **know** (facts) wissen

large groß
last letzt-; zuletzt

at last endlich
late spät
law das Gesetz
to **learn** lernen
least: at least mindestens,
  wenigstens
to **leave** lassen; abfahren
to **let** lassen
letter der Brief
to **lie** liegen
life das Leben
light das Licht
little klein; wenig
to **live** wohnen; leben
living room das Wohnzimmer
long lang; (*adv.*) lange
to **look** aussehen
to **look forward to** sich
  freuen auf
to **lose one's way** sich
  verlaufen, sich verfahren
to **love** lieben
to **fall in love with** sich
  verlieben in

mad: to be mad at sich
  ärgern über
to **make** machen
many viele
married: to be married
  verheiratet sein
to **marry, to get married**
  heiraten
to **meet** kennenlernen
mistake der Fehler
moment der Augenblick
money das Geld
more mehr
mother die Mutter
movie (house) das Kino
much viel

to **need** brauchen
never nie
new neu
newspaper die Zeitung
nice nett
nobody niemand
not nicht
  not until erst
  not yet noch nicht
nothing nichts
novel der Roman
now jetzt

o'clock: at (three) o'clock um
  (drei) Uhr
often oft
old alt
once einmal; früher
only nur; erst
order: in order in Ordnung
in order to um . . . zu
other ander-
overcoat der Mantel

to **pay** bezahlen
people die Leute
perhaps vielleicht
permitted: to be permitted to
  dürfen
to **pick up, meet** abholen
picture das Bild
please bitte
to **prepare (oneself) for** (sich)
  vorbereiten auf
to **promise** versprechen
to **put** setzen; stellen; legen

quite ganz

to **rain** regnen
rather lieber
to **reach** erreichen
to **read** lesen
really wirklich
to **remember** sich erinnern an
to **rest** sich ausruhen
restless unruhig
to **ring** (a telephone) klingeln
reason die Vernunft
  reasonable vernünftig
to **recognize** erkennen
relative der Verwandte
room das Zimmer

shoe der Schuh
school die Schule
to **scream** schreien
to **see** sehen
to **seem** scheinen
to **send** schicken
several mehrere
to **shave** sich rasieren
to **show** zeigen
sick krank
silent: to be silent schweigen
simple einfach
sister die Schwester
to **sit** sitzen
to **sleep** schlafen

to **get enough sleep** (sich) ausschlafen
small klein
to **smoke** rauchen
soldier der Soldat
some einige, ein paar, manche; etwas
somebody jemand
something etwas
somewhere irgendwo, irgendwohin
son der Sohn
to **speak** sprechen
to **stand** stehen
station der Bahnhof
to **stay** bleiben
still noch
stone der Stein
stop halten, stehenbleiben
story die Geschichte
student der Student, die Studentin
to **study** studieren
such solch
suddenly plötzlich
to **suggest** vorschlagen
Sunday der Sonntag
supposed: to be supposed to sollen
swimming pool das Schwimmbecken

to **switch off** ausmachen

table der Tisch
to **take** nehmen
to **talk** reden, sprechen
teacher der Lehrer
to **tell** sagen; erzählen
to **thank** danken
thief der Dieb
to **think (of)** denken (an)
tile die Platte
time die Zeit
   at the time damals
tired müde
today heute
tomorrow morgen
tonight heute abend
too auch
trace die Spur
   without a trace spurlos
train der Zug
to **try** versuchen
to **turn off** (light) ausmachen
to **turn out** sich herausstellen (*impersonal*)

to **understand** verstehen
to **undress** sich ausziehen
unfortunately leider
until bis

to **get used to** sich gewöhnen an

very sehr
to **visit** besuchen

to **wait for** warten auf
wall die Wand
to **want to** wollen
war der Krieg
watch die Uhr
week die Woche
weekend das Wochenende
well gesund; gut
when wann
where wo; wohin
whether ob
why warum
wife die Frau
wine der Wein
winter der Winter
without ohne
woman die Frau
to **work** arbeiten
writer der Schriftsteller

year das Jahr
yesterday gestern
young jung

INDEX